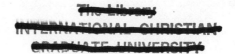

PLATONIC STUDIES

GREGORY VLASTOS

——

PLATONIC
STUDIES

The King's Library

PRINCETON
UNIVERSITY PRESS

To the Memory of

VERNON ABBOTT LADD VLASTOS

(May 27, 1909 – October 17, 1970)

Φιλτάτη συνεργάτις

PREFACE TO THE SECOND PRINTING

THIS new printing contains all of the essays in the first, along with three additional, very short, pieces, written in clarification and support of positions taken there. Two of the new papers and almost all of the additional notes are byproducts of research I have been pursuing in the area in which most of my thinking and teaching has concentrated during the past two years: the philosophy of Socrates. In the course of this work I have had to deal again and again with that perplexing Socratic doctrine I had discussed in the tenth essay in the book, "The Unity of the Virtues in the *Protagoras*" ("*UVP*"). The interpretation offered there was fated to become almost immediately the object of hot controversy. A radically different one by Terry Penner[1] appeared in the very year of the publication of *Platonic Studies* and was adopted (with minor modifications) in two admirable books appearing soon after.[2] Their authors did me the invaluable service of devoting detailed criticism to *UVP*. This new printing gives me the opportunity to respond. I am doing so by way of numerous new notes to *UVP* and a companion piece, the twentieth essay in the present volume, "Socrates on 'the Parts of Virtue'." To the same end I offer, along with this new material, the short paper, "What did Socrates understand by his 'What is F?' question?" This had been written earlier (1976) and circulated among friends but had remained unpublished. A fuller treat-

[1] "The Unity of Virtue," *Philosophical Review* 82 (1973), 35-68.
[2] C. C. W. Taylor, *Plato: Protagoras* (Clarendon Press, Oxford, 1976); T. H. Irwin, *Plato's Moral Theory* (Clarendon Press, Oxford, 1977).

ment of the same topic I reserve for the book I am now writing on the philosophy of Socrates.

The other topics I have researched since the first printing of *Platonic Studies* fall in the area of Plato's social philosophy. This was the theme of my Paul Carus lectures to the American Philosophical Association in 1976. Duly expanded and revised, these will be published in due course. Two essays I have published in the interim give some indication of the direction in which my thought has moved in this area.[3] But neither these, nor anything else I have yet put into print, give adequate indication of the most substantial change my understanding of Plato's social philosophy has undergone in recent years. This was a direct result of further study of Plato's attitude to slavery. Researching afresh in 1975-76 the provisions affecting slaves in the criminal code of Plato's *Laws*, I reached an assessment of the status of the slave in Plato's theory of justice which differs radically from the one adopted by G. R. Morrow in his classical work on this topic[4] and, after him, by many scholars, including myself. My new conclusions on this subject, adumbrated in one of the Carus lectures, do not invalidate the argument of the sixth essay in the present volume, "Does Slavery Exist in Plato's *Republic?*" But they do require a fundamental revision of the interpretation of the moral justification of slavery in Plato's philosophy in the seventh essay, "Slavery in Plato's Thought," which had been written under Morrow's influence forty years ago. This revision cannot be implemented through piecemeal notes to that essay or in brief appendages to it. It calls for systematic exposition and argument which must await the publication of my Carus lectures. I have, therefore, left this essay uncorrected, save for misprints and the like.

Similarly uncorrected is that extensive segment of the book (essays *11, 12, 13,* and *14*) which deals with the ontology of the later period of Plato's philosophy. In this area I have nothing to add for the present, save the short piece I have included as the eighteenth essay, "A Note on 'Pauline Predications' in Plato," which had been written in 1974 to clarify a thesis which runs through essays *10, 11,* and *12* of *Platonic Studies.* Much important work has been published in this area in recent years involving, explicitly or implicitly, objections to views upheld in those essays. Grateful as I have been for critical comment devoted to this part of the book, I venture no replies to it in this

---

[3] "The Theory of Social Justice in Plato's Republic," in *Interpretations of Plato*, edited by Helen F. North, *Mnemosyne*, Suppl. Volume for 1977, 1-40; "The Rights of Persons in Plato's Conception of the Foundations of Justice," in *Morals, Science and Society*, ed. by H. T. Engelhardt and D. Callahan (The Hastings Center, Hastings, New York, 1978, 172-201).

[4] *Plato's Law of Slavery* (Urbana, Illinois, 1939; reprinted by Arno Press, New York, 1976); "Plato and Greek Slavery," *Mind* 48 (1939), 186-201.

new printing of the book nor do I undertake to make any other changes that might be required on this or on other grounds. Except for the correction of misprints and of other mechanical errors, I have left untouched essays *11-14* for the simple reason that I have not yet had the opportunity to do fresh concentrated thinking in their area. To make *ad hoc* corrections without rethinking my position in it as a whole would serve no useful purpose. For the same reason I have made no response to criticism of other essays in the book, except in half a dozen cases where the point at issue seemed simple enough to warrant a brief clarification.

The Preface to the first printing, intensely personal and strongly slanted to the occasion, has been omitted. Otherwise the book is the same, save for the added material, a few new titles in the Bibliography, and correction of misprints. I regret that it has not proved feasible to expand the Bibliography to include more recent publications nor to revise the indices (Index of Greek Words, Index of Names, and Index of Passages) to cover the new material: everything after p. 404 (new essays *18, 19, 20,* and the starred notes to the old material) remains unindexed. I acknowledge gratefully the help given me by several scholars in reporting to me typographical and other errors, most particularly that of Professors Diskin Clay, Alan Code, Howard DeLong, and Gregory Ziegler. What I owe to Alan Code on this score is the least of my debts to him. Discussion with him has saved me from many mistakes and has helped me to understand Plato better. I have never had more helpful comment on my work from a colleague.

GREGORY VLASTOS

April, 1981

ACKNOWLEDGMENTS

═══

I am grateful

To the *Philosophical Review* for permission to reprint:

"Slavery in Plato's Thought," 50 (1941), 289–304.
"Self-Predication In Plato's Later Period," 78 (1969), 74–78.
"Reasons and Causes in the *Phaedo*," 78 (1969), 291–325.
The review of John Gould, *The Development of Plato's Ethics*, 66 (1957), 226–38.
The review of I. M. Crombie, *An Examination of Plato's Philosophical Doctrines*, Vol. II, 75 (1966), 526–30.

To the *Journal of Philosophy* for permission to reprint material contained in:

"The Argument in the *Republic* that Justice Pays," 65 (1968), 665–74.
"Justice and Psychic Harmony in the *Republic*," 66 (1969), 505–21.

To *Isis* for permission to reprint:

"Plato's Supposed Theory of Irregular Atomic Figures," 57 (1967), 204–09.

To *Classical Philology* for permission to reprint:

"Does Slavery Exist in the Republic?" 63 (1968), 291–95.

To *Gnomon* for permission to reprint:

The review of J. H. Krämer, *Arete bei Platon und Aristoteles*, 41 (1963), 641–55.

To the *Philosophical Quarterly* for permission to reprint:

"Plato's 'Third Man' Argument (*Parm.* 132A1-B2): Text and Logic," 19 (1969), 289–301.

To the *Review of Metaphysics* for permission to reprint:

"The Unity of the Virtues in the *Protagoras*," 25 (1972), 415–58.

To the editor, Renford Bambrough, and publishers, Routledge & Kegan Paul Ltd., of *New Essays in Plato and Aristotle* (London, 1965) for permission to reprint

"Degrees of Reality in Plato."

To the American Philosophical Association for permission to reprint from *Proceedings and Addresses of the Amer. Philos. Association*, 39 (1966), 5–19

"A Metaphysical Paradox."

To the editors, Jürgen Mau and E. G. Schmidt, and publishers, Akademie-Verlag, Berlin, of *Isonomia: Studien zur Gleichheitsvorstellung im Griechischen Denken* (Berlin, 1964) for permission to reprint

"*Isonomia Politikē.*"

To *Phronesis* for permission to reprint: "A Note on 'Pauline Predications' in Plato," 19 (1974), 95-101.

ABBREVIATIONS

To the papers included in this volume I shall refer by the abbreviations recorded after their titles as listed in the Table of Contents.

To other works the usual reference will be by author, date of publication, and page. For the title the reader should consult the Bibliography at the end of the volume.

To the *Greek-English Lexicon* by H. G. Liddell and R. Scott, New Edition by H. S. Jones (Oxford, 1925–40), I shall refer by *LSJ*.

To *Lexicon Platonicum* by D. F. Ast (Munich, 1835, reprinted Berlin, 1908), I shall refer by "Ast."

To the titles of Platonic dialogues and Aristotelian treatises I shall refer mainly by the abbreviations used in *LSJ* (listed there under "Authors and Works," *s.v. Aristotle, Plato*).

To the translations (with notes) of Platonic dialogues (by various authors) published by the Société d'Édition "Les Belles Lettres" (Paris, various dates) under the auspices of the Association Guillaume Budé I shall refer to as "the Budé" translation.

To the two-volume translation (with notes) of the Platonic corpus (by L. Robin with the collaboration of M. J. Moreau) published by the Bibliothèque de la Pléiade (Paris, 1950) I shall refer as "the Pléiade" translation.

To *Index Aristotelicus* by H. Bonitz (Berlin, 1870) I shall refer by "Bonitz."

CONTENTS

PLATONIC STUDIES

PART I

———

Morals,
Politics,
Metaphysics

1

The Individual as
an Object of Love in Plato*

(1969; IOLP)

I

"LET φιλεῖν be defined," writes Aristotle in the *Rhetoric*, "as wishing for someone what you believe to be good things—wishing this not for your own sake but for his—and acting so far as you can to bring them about."[1] The same thing is said about φίλος in the essay on friendship in the *Nicomachean Ethics*: "They define a φίλος as one who wishes and acts for the good, or the apparent good, of one's φίλος, for the sake of one's φίλος; or as one who wishes for the existence and life of one's φίλος for that man's sake."[2] In the standard translations of these passages φίλος

* A slightly revised form of an address at the University of Montana on May 5, 1969, at a celebration honoring the retirement of Professor Edwin L. Marvin, who had served the university with distinction as a teacher and founder of its department of philosophy. I have read drafts to other groups and profited from their criticism. My greatest debt is to the members of the Philosophical Discussion Club of Cornell University, and most particularly to Norman Kretzmann and William Nelson, who helped me detect a confusion from which no earlier draft had been free. I must also express thanks to Charles Kahn, Richard Rorty, and Terry Irwin for suggestions and criticisms which enabled me to correct other mistakes.

[1] *Rhet.* 1380B35-1381A1: . . . τὴν φιλίαν καὶ τὸ φιλεῖν ὁρισάμενοι λέγωμεν. ἔστω δὴ τὸ φιλεῖν τὸ βούλεσθαί τινι ἃ οἴεται ἀγαθά, ἐκείνου ἕνεκα ἀλλὰ μὴ αὑτοῦ, καὶ τὸ κατὰ δύναμιν πρακτικὸν εἶναι τούτων.

[2] *N.E.* 1166A2-5: τιθέασι γὰρ φίλον τὸν βουλόμενον καὶ πράττοντα τἀγαθὰ ἢ τὰ φαινόμενα ἐκείνου ἕνεκα, ἢ τὸν βουλόμενον εἶναι καὶ ζῆν τὸν φίλον αὐτοῦ χάριν.

comes through as "friend," φιλεῖν as "friendly feeling," and φιλία as "friendship." This blunts the force of Aristotle's Greek, as should be clear from one of his illustrations: maternal affection is one of his star examples of φιλεῖν and φιλία;[3] would "friendly feeling" do justice to what we normally have in view when we speak of a mother's love for her child? Or again, consider the compounds: φιλάργυρος, φιλότιμος, φιλόνικος, φιλόκαλος, and so forth: twenty-two columns of them in Liddell and Scott. φιλάργυρος is Greek for "miser." A man would need to have something considerably stronger than "friendly feeling" for money to live up (or down) to that name. Much the same would be true in the case of the vast majority of the other compounds. "Money-lover," "honor-lover," etc. would be the best that we could do to approach the natural sense of the Greek words. "Love" is the only English word that is robust and versatile enough to cover φιλεῖν and φιλία.[4] Nor is there any difficulty in seeing why Aristotle should undertake to define "love" in order to elucidate the meaning of "friendship": he thinks of friendship as a special case of inter-personal love.

So what Aristotle is telling us is that to love another person is to wish for that person's good for that person's sake, doing whatever you can to make that wish come true. This is not meant to be a run-of-the-mill definition. Its purpose is not to explain all uses of φιλεῖν but only those

---

[3] The second citation runs on: "as mothers do for their children. . . ." Parental affection is used to illustrate φιλία already in the first chapter of the Essay on φιλία (N.E. VIII.1). Cf. my reference to 1159A27-33 in the third paragraph of this essay.

[4] As is shown, e.g., by the fact that the translator is compelled to use "love" when translating the verb φιλεῖν and that the commentators shift without apology to "love" and "beloved" when they gloss φιλεῖν and φίλον in the Lysis. I say that "love" covers these Greek terms, bearing in mind that its connotation is considerably broader, since it does also the work of ἐρᾶν, which overlaps with φιλεῖν, but differs from it in three respects: (i) it is more intense, more passionate (cf. Plato, Lg. 837A: ὅταν δὲ ἑκάτερον [sc. φίλον] γίγνηται σφοδρόν, 'ἔρωτα' ἐπονομάζομεν); (ii) it is more heavily weighted on the side of desire than of affection (desire, longing, are the primary connotations of ἔρως, fondness that of φιλία); (iii) it is more closely tied to the sexual drive, (though φιλεῖν may also refer to sexual love [LSJ s.v. φιλεῖν, 3]): for non-incestuous familial love one would have to turn to φιλία in lieu of ἔρως (cf. Plato, Symp. 179C: Alcestis had φιλία for her husband, Admetus, and so did his parents; but "because of her ἔρως for him she so surpassed them in φιλία" that she was willing to die in his place, while they were not.)

that answer to what Aristotle takes to be its "focal meaning"[5]—to capture
the kind of love we can have only for persons and could not possibly have
for things, since in their case it would make no sense to speak of wishing
for their own good *for their own sake:* "It would be absurd, no doubt,"
says Aristotle, "to wish good for wine; if one wishes it at all, it is that the
wine may keep, so that we may have it for ourselves."[6] He says this,
knowing quite well that love for persons *could* be just like love for inani-
mates in this crucial respect. This is how Swann loves Odette in *Swann's
Way.* At the height of his infatuation he is so far from wishing for her
good for her own sake, that he is scarcely capable of thinking of her at
all except as an adjunct to his own existence. A chance remark about her
from someone who had seen her in an outfit she had never worn for him
comes as a shock: "It upset him because it made him realize all of a sudden
that Odette had a life which was not wholly his."[7] Aristotle recognizes
two varieties of this kind of love, admitting them as φιλίαι of an incomplete, imperfect kind: "φιλία δι' ἡδονήν, φιλία διὰ τὸ χρήσιμον,"[8]
"pleasure-love," "utility-love," affective bonds with men or women whose
good we want because they serve our need, or interest, or pleasure, and for
no other reason.

But suppose we do wish for someone's good for his own sake. Must
we then forfeit utility and pleasure? Not necessarily, Aristotle would insist,
and not at all when the relation is "complete" or perfect φιλία. In friend-
ships with good and noble men one who is himself good and noble will
find both profit and delight;[9] so he will love his friends for his own sake

[5] A useful term we owe to G. E. L. Owen (1960, p. 169) for what Aristotle
calls πρὸς ἓν λεγόμενον (a phrase applied to the definition of φιλία in the
Eudemian Ethics, 1236A16-B27,) on which see below *JHR,* n.60.

[6] 1155B29-31. The parenthesis which Bywater closes here in the Oxford
text should rather close at the end of the immediately following remark which
explains the point of the example: τῷ δὲ φίλῳ φασὶ δεῖν βούλεσθαι τἀγαθὰ
ἐκείνου ἕνεκα).

[7] "Ce simple croquis bouleversait Swann parce qui'il lui faisait tout d'un
coup apercevoir qu'Odette avait une vie qui n'était pas tout entière a lui, . . ."
A la recherche du temps perdu, Vol. I of the *Pléiade* Edition (Paris, 1954), 240.

[8] N.E. 8. 3-5, 1156A6 ff. These are φιλίαι κατὰ συμβεβηκός, 1156A17-18.
They are called φιλία "by similitude" (καθ' ὁμοιότητα, 1157A31-32; cf. ὁμοίωμα
ἔχει, 1157A1) of the kind which is "truly" (ὡς ἀληθῶς), "primarily" (πρώτως),
and "strictly" or "chiefly" (κυρίως) φιλία (*loc. cit.* A24 and 30-31), the only
kind Aristotle considers "complete" or "perfect" (τελεία) φιλία (1156B34,
1158A11).

[9] This is implied unambiguously in his discussion of what he calls "τελεία
φιλία" in 1156B7ff, "μάλιστα φιλία" in 1157B1-1158A1.

as well as for theirs. This is the only kind of love that gets a high rating in Aristotle's design of life. What then of that mother, in one of his examples, whose children, separated from her, do not know her, while she loves them, wishes for their good and works for it, yet gets nothing from them in return, and expects nothing (1159A27-33)? Though he cites this as evidence (σημεῖον) that "love is thought to consist more in loving than in being loved,"[10] it will not fit his concept of "perfect" φιλία. So what could he have made of it? He does not say. Either he fails to see that his concept of φιλία makes no provision for this and other hard cases or, if he does, the discrepancy does not disturb him. The only love of persons as persons that really interests him is that between the members of a social élite, each of whom can afford disinterested affection for his peers, assured in advance that he will normally have theirs in return, so that "in loving the friend each will love what is good for himself."[11] That Aristotle's notion of "perfect" love should be so limited is disappointing.[12] But this does not spoil it for my purposes in this essay. All I need here is to find a standard against which to measure Plato's concept of love—a standard from his own time and place, so that I would not have to risk gross anachronism by going with Anders Nygren[13] so far afield as the New Testament. This standard Aristotle does supply. That to love a person we must wish for that person's good for that person's sake, not for ours— so much Aristotle understands. Does Plato?

II

I start with the *Lysis*—one of those earlier dialogues where Plato's thought still moves within the ambit of his Socratic heritage.[14] What does Socrates

---

[10] *N.E.* 1159A27-28, [φιλία] δοκεῖ . . . ἐν τῷ φιλεῖν μᾶλλον ἢ ἐν τῷ φιλεῖσθαι εἶναι.

[11] *N.E.* 1157B33, καὶ φιλοῦντες τὸν φίλον τὸ αὑτοῖς ἀγαθὸν φιλοῦσι.

[12] Cf. n. 100, below.

[13] *Eros and Agape* (English translation by P. S. Watson, Harper Torchbook edition, New York, 1969)—a distinguished, influential, and very one-sided book, whose treatment of the "Greek" idea of love fails to reckon with the elementary fact that *philia* is a near-synonym of *agape*, and that, regardless of what their philosophers said, Greeks, being human, were as capable of genuine, non-egoistic, affection as are we. Ignoring *philia* (save for a passing notice of the *Lysis* on p. 180, where Nygren translates the word by "friendship" and uses the dialogue as further evidence "of the egocentric nature of Eros" in Plato, 181, n. 3), he fails to take the slightest cognizance of Aristotle's conception of it.

[14] See Appendix I to this essay, below, pp. 35 ff.

here make of φιλία Consider this exchange:

> And shall we be dear [φίλοι] to anyone, and will anyone love us [φιλήσει], in those respects in which we are unprofitable [ἀνωφελεῖς]?
> Of course not, he said.
> So your father does not love [φιλεῖ] you now, nor do others love anyone so far as he is useless [ἄχρηστος]?
> Evidently not, he said.
> So if you become wise [σοφός], my boy, everyone will love you and all will be your οἰκεῖοι[15]—for you will be useful and good—otherwise no one will love you[16]: Neither your father nor your mother nor your οἰκεῖοι. (210CD)

"Useful" and "profitable" in Plato—as in Greek usage generally—must not be given the narrow sense these adjectives ordinarily have in English. Plato uses them to cover any attribute—physical, economic, aesthetic, intellectual, or moral—that makes the one who has it a valuable asset. It is as broad as "good-producing," with no strings on the kind of good produced; and with Socrates as the speaker we can count on a bias in favor of moral and spiritual good. Socrates then is saying that a person will be loved if, and only if, he produces good. Produces it *for whom?* Jowett translated as though our text had said that A will love B only if B produces good *for A*.[17] If that were right, what Socrates calls "love" would coincide with Aristotle's utility-love: the Socratic lover would look on those he loves simply as sources of benefits to him. But the text does not say this. For all that is said there to the contrary, A might love B because B produces benefits for a third person or for a group or groups of persons or, for that matter, for B himself. So far, then, Socrates

---

[15] Literally *"in* [or *of] the house"*; here "family-relation, kinsman" in the extended sense of "intimate," "near and dear."

[16] Good examples in this citation of the unavoidability of the resort to "love" when translating the verb *philein.*

[17] His rendering for 210C5-8 reads: "And shall we be friends to others, and will any others love us, in matters where we are useless *to them?*—Certainly not.—Then neither does your father love you, nor does anybody love anybody else, in so far as he is useless *to him* ?" The italicized words answer to nothing in the Greek text. Similar mistranslation of the second sentence in the Pléiade translation by Robin (1950), "En consequence, ton père non plus, dans la mesure où tu ne *lui* es bon à rien, n'a donc pas d'amitié pour toi. . . ." (My emphasis). The passage had been correctly translated in the Budé translation by A. Croiset (1956).

has said nothing which could fairly be said to endorse the egocentricity of utility-love. Yet neither has he made a place, even marginally, for what we found at dead center in Aristotle's conception of love: wishing another person's good *for that person's sake*. Nothing of this is said or even hinted at in our passage. There is not a word here to imply that Lysis' father and mother love him when he is "wise" because they see how beneficial it would be *for Lysis* if he were wise, and that they wish this for him just because their loving him *means* wishing for his own good for his own sake. What Socrates says of their love for the boy would have been perfectly true even if they had happened to be arrant egoists who wanted their son to be sensible and well-behaved only because of the trouble this would spare them and the credit it would bring on them. So egoistic love is not excluded though, so far, neither is it implied.

But as we go on reading in the dialogue we find that it is implied, in effect, after all.[18] This happens when Socrates goes on to argue (213E ff.) that if A loves B, he does so because of some benefit *he* needs from B and for the sake of just that benefit: The sick man loves his[19] doctor for the sake of health (ἕνεκα ὑγιείας, 218E); the poor love the affluent and the weak the strong for the sake of aid (τῆς ἐπικουρίας ἕνεκα, 215D); "and everyone who is ignorant has affection and love for the one who has knowledge" (*loc. cit.*) This is straightforward utility-love: the doctor, the rich, the wise are loved by one who needs them for what *he* can get out of them, and no reason is offered why we could love anyone except for what we could get out of him. The egoistic perspective of "love" so conceived becomes unmistakable when Socrates, generalizing, argues that "if one were in want of nothing, one would feel no affection, . . . and he who felt no affection would not love."[20] The lover Socrates has in

---

[18] It must have been an unconscious anticipation of this sequel that led Jowett to mistranslate the earlier passage.

[19] The pronoun is not in the text. But the reflexive reference is definitely implied in the context. Thus Socrates observes at 217A that "no one, while healthy, loves a doctor for the sake of health": so when persons "love a doctor for the sake of health" it must be for the sake of the health *they* have lost and wish, with *their* doctor's aid, to regain. And cf. the next note.

[20] 215BC: ὁ δὲ μή του δεόμενος οὐδέ τι ἀγαπῴη ἂν . . . οὐδ' ἂν φιλοῖ. This is reinforced by the general formula in 218D7-9: When A loves B it is always for the sake of (ἕνεκά του) something, *x*, and because of something (διά τι), *y*, where *x* ranges over goods and *y* over "evils" remedied by the appropriate values of *x*. The "evil" here stands for a remediable deficiency in A which B has power to remedy: ". . . that which desires, desires that of which it is in want. . . . Hence that which is in want loves that of which it is in

view seems positively incapable of loving others for their own sake,[21] else why must he feel no affection for anyone whose good-producing qualities *he* did not happen to need?[22]

---

want . . ." (221D7-E2). This is Socrates' last word on this aspect of the topic (and, therefore, reassures us that the question in 215C3-4, "But tell me, Lysis, in what way [πῇ] have we gone off the track? Are we perchance wholly mistaken?" is not meant to invalidate everything in the preceding paragraph and, in particular, is not meant to impugn the statement that "if one were in want of nothing one would feel no affection.")

This feature of the theory of *philia* in the *Lysis* is conserved and elaborated in what I take to be the Socratic component in the theory of eros expounded in the *Symposium*, i.e., in Socrates' dialogue with Agathon (199C-201C) and in the first part of his dialogue with Diotima (201D-206A): what we learn about love here is that it is caused by a deficiency in the lover and expresses the lover's longing for the good whose possession will relieve the deficiency. (For the shift in perspective at 206B, cf. Marcus in n. 56 below, and paragraph 1 of Section IV of the present essay and n. 58). This notion finds its complement in the thesis, emphasized in both dialogues (more briefly in the *Lysis* [216D-217A], at greater length in the *Smp.* [201B-204C]), that the lover is in a condition intermediate between goodness and evil, or beauty and ugliness, hence *qua* lover neither good nor evil, neither beautiful nor ugly: if he were wholly the former, he would have no need to love.

[21] It might be objected that Socrates cannot mean to endorse this view of love, for it would belie his own profession of love for his fellow-citizens: he says that he loves them (*Ap.* 29D), but does not impute to them either wisdom (just the opposite!) nor any other quality which would elicit utility-love. But what does this prove? Can't a man be better than his theory? And what precisely *is* the "love" which Socrates professes for his fellows? Does it measure up to the Aristotelian definition? I do not think so, but to argue out the point would require an extended discussion which I cannot pursue here. Cf. n. 91 below.

[22] R. A. Gauthier and J. V. Jolif take no account of this passage when they see the *Lysis* as an expression of "l'amour de bienveillance où amour désintéressé" (1970, 671; cf. 726). Since they do not argue for this extraordinary suggestion, one is reduced to surmise as to how it ever occurred to them that this is the message of the *Lysis*. What apparently suggested it to them is the example in 219E2-220B5 (cf. n. 23 below): they quote this passage in full (670-71) and cap the citation with a remark which shows that they are taking the father's love for the wine and his love for the son to stand respectively for "amour de concupiscence" and "amour désintéressé," without a word of explanation or argument to convince us that this is what Plato is illustrating in this passage. What he *says* he is illustrating is concern for an object which is valued not for its own sake, but for the sake of another (πᾶσα ἡ τοιαύτη σπουδὴ οὐκ ἐπὶ τούτοις ἐστὶν ἐσπουδασμένη, ἐπὶ τοῖς ἕνεκά του παρασκευαζομένοις, ἀλλ᾽ ἐπ᾽ ἐκείνῳ οὗ ἕνεκα πάντα τὰ τοιαῦτα παρασκευάζεται, 219E7-220A1). One

Socrates then goes on to argue that just as we love the doctor for the sake of health, so we love health for the sake of something else; hence, short of an infinite regress, there must be a πρῶτον φίλον, οὗ ἕνεκα καὶ τὰ ἄλλα φαμὲν πάντα φίλα εἶναι—a "first [i.e., terminal] object of love, for whose sake, we say, all other objects are loved" (219D), this being the only thing that is "truly" (ὡς ἀληθῶς) or "really" (τῷ ὄντι) loved—or, more precisely that *should be* so loved. There is danger, Socrates warns, that "those other objects, of which we said that they are loved for *its* sake, should deceive us, like so many images[23] of it" (219D2-4). So unless a man we loved actually *was* this πρῶτον φίλον, it would be a mistake to love him "for his own sake," to treat him, in Kant's phrase, as "an end in himself."[24] We would then stand in need of a philosopher, like Socrates, to cure us by his dialectic, to break the illusion, and make us see that what we "really" love is something else.[25] What is it then, this sovereign πρῶτον φίλον? All Socrates seems to be prepared to say is that it is "the good";[26]

---

wonders if they are confusing the difference between instrumental and intrinsic value (which is the immediate point of the example) with that between egoistic and non-egoistic valuation, losing sight of the fact that the former difference would be as valid for the egoist as for anyone else: there is no reason in the world why an egoist should not attach intrinsic value to certain things, desiring them as ends (*his* ends), not as mere means.

[23] Or "phantoms" (εἴδωλα). In the terms of the accompanying example (219D5ff.), the mistake would be to put such a value on wine as to refuse it to one's son when he is in mortal need of it, having drunk hemlock for which the wine is the only available antidote. In the analogy the father's love for the wine stands to love for his son as would love for a particular person to love for the πρῶτον φίλον. It would be hard to think of a stronger way of making the point that in our love for persons we should *not* treat them as "ends in themselves" (cf. the next note).

[24] For an interpretation of this phrase see Vlastos 1962, 48-49, and notes. Aristotle's "wishing another's good for his sake, not for yours," though still far from the Kantian conception of treating persons as "ends in themselves," is the closest any philosopher comes to it in classical antiquity.

[25] Just as "it is not altogether true [οὐδέν τι μᾶλλον οὕτω τό γε ἀληθὲς ἔχη]" that we set great stock by money, since we give it up readily when we find things we want to buy with it, so too "it is only in a manner of speaking [ῥήματι . . . λέγοντες] that we say we 'love' what is loved for the sake of something else; it looks as though what is really loved [φίλον . . . τῷ ὄντι] is that very thing in which all of these so-called loves terminate [ἐκεῖνο αὐτό . . . , εἰς ὃ πᾶσαι αὗται αἱ λεγόμεναι φιλίαι τελευτῶσιν]" (209A2-B3). To say of another person that he or she is what we *really* and truly love would be to lapse, like the miser, into moral fetishism.

[26] ". . . hence the good is loved? [ἀλλ᾽ ἄρα τὸ ἀγαθόν ἐστιν φίλον;]"

and "the good for any given person" Socrates understands to mean: what makes that person happy.[27] For something more definite we must go to the dialogues of Plato's middle period. Only there do we find the new theory of love which we can call distinctively Plato's.

III

The ideal society of the *Republic* is a political community held together by bonds of fraternal love.[28] The Allegory of the Metals which epitomizes

---

(220B7)—a surprisingly casual and elliptical answer: it does not *say* that the good is the πρῶτον φίλον, though this is doubtless what is meant. Socrates must think the proposition that the good is the πρῶτον φίλον so truistic that it does not even call for a formal statement, let alone defense, in the present context. His attitude is perhaps understandable, given his standing conviction that the good is the only (real) object of desire (*Grg.* 467C5-468C7, which concludes, "for we desire those things which are good, . . . while those which are neither good nor evil we do not desire, nor yet those which are evil"; cf. *Meno* 77C1-E4), and his present contention that "desire is the reason (αἰτία) for love, and we love that which we desire and when we desire it" (221D2-4).

[27] This is regarded as axiomatic in the Socratic dialogues, though never formally spelled out. It shows up, e.g., in the *Meno* (77C ff.), where the thesis that no one can desire evil things knowing that they are evil is proved by arguing that "no one desires to be wretched and miserable" (78A4-5), or in the *Euthydemus* (278E2-282D: the protrepsis to philosophy), where it is argued that wisdom is the greatest of all goods because it alone enables us to use any other good in such a way as to make us happy (εὐδαιμονεῖν, εὖ πράττειν), the presupposition of the argument being that anything will be good for any person if, and only if, it makes that person happy.

[28] Though one would hardly guess this from much that has been written about Plato's social theory. Not a word about political *philia* in Plato in T. A. Sinclair, *Greek Political Theory* (London, 1951); in the Index under *philia* there are references to Protagoras and five other authors, but none to Plato. Sheldon Wolin, in his acute critique of Plato's political philosophy, *Politics and Vision* (Boston, 1960), duly reports (47) the doctrine of the *Politicus* that "the end of the royal art was . . . a community bound together in 'a true fellowship by mutual concord and by ties of friendship' " (311B9-C1); but nine pages later he says that "it required the Christian notion of *agape* before there could be an idea of love as a force fusing together a community." He evidently has no inkling of the fact that Plato expects *philia* to be just such a force. The same is true of the study of Plato's contribution to social theory, *Enter Plato* (New York, 1964), by the sociologist, Alvin W. Gouldner. He says that while Plato "speaks well of friendship" (244), he "removes love from the Pantheon of virtues . . . strip[s] it of moral relevance" (246). One wonders

its ethos pictures all citizens as children of the same mother, the Earth (= the polis). They are told: "You are all brothers in the *polis* . . . , all akin. . . ."[29] They are expected to have the same solicitude for the welfare of the polis which men ordinarily feel for that of their own family. Those appointed to govern must excel not only in intelligence and all-around ability but also in their concern for the welfare of the polis, which is said to be a function of their love for it: "One is most concerned for what one loves" (κήδοιτο δέ γ' ἄν τις μάλιστα τούτου ὃ τυγχάνει φιλῶν, 412D). Radical institutional innovations are to insure that this affection will be wholehearted, undistracted by economic self-interest, on the one hand, by special attachments to kith and kin, on the other. The whole of the ruling class now becomes a single communal family, where no one is an "outsider"[30] and everyone is "a brother or sister or son or daughter" or other kin "to everyone he meets."[31] The maxim of this extended family is that "φίλοι have all things in common, so far as possible".[32] The last four words explain why the same institutions are not laid down for the producers in spite of the fact that, as the Allegory of the Metals so clearly implies, all of the members of the polis are expected to be φίλοι: if the communistic property and family arrangements do not apply to them, this must be due only to the fact that Plato does not think these institutions would be practicable in their case, however desirable ideally for all.[33] But there can be no doubt of his confidence that they too

---

how so imaginative a student of Plato's social theory could say such things in view, e.g., of the fact that in the *Laws* the three goals that are to guide all legislation are that the state should be intelligent, free, and "ἑαυτῇ φίλη" (693B-E, 701D; cf. also 628A-C, 697C, 698C, 699C, and especially 743C and 759B). Part of the trouble seems to be that he gets Plato *via* the Jowett translation, where φίλη is turned into "harmonious" or "at unity with itself" and φιλία into "friendship." Yet even the Jowett translation might have given Gouldner reason to doubt that "friendship" is what Plato means here. Thus in 698C one should be able to tell just from the context that Jowett's "spirit of friendship" is a feeble understatement of what is being talked about: the embattled comradeship, the fraternal solidarity, that flared up among the Athenians at the time of the Persian invasion.

[29] ἐστὲ μὲν γὰρ δὴ πάντες οἱ ἐν τῇ πόλει ἀδελφοί . . . ἅτε οὖν συγγενεῖς ὄντες πάντες . . . (415A2-8). And cf. 414E5-6, καὶ ὑπὲρ τῶν ἄλλων πολιτῶν ὡς ἀδελφῶν ὄντων ⟨δεῖ⟩ . . . διανοεῖσθαι.

[30] A. Bloom's happy rendering of ἀλλότριος (antonym of οἰκεῖος).

[31] 463BC.

[32] 424A; cf. 449C.

[33] Cf. *Laws* 739C-740B, where thoroughgoing communism in both property and family is proclaimed as the ideal (it represents "the best polis and laws,

will feel love for their motherland and for their rulers, who are their "saviors and helpers" (463B) and think of them as "φίλοι and sustainers" (547C). In a postscript which gives in a nutshell the rationale of the beneficent subjection of the producers to the philosophers we are told that those who are "naturally weak in the principle of the best" (i.e., of reason) ought to be governed by those who are strong in this principle "so that we may all be alike and φίλοι so far as possible, all governed by by the same principle."[34] Subjection[35] to another's will is justified on the assumption that it may not only coexist with, but also promote, φιλία.

Since we are given no formal definition of φιλία and φίλος in the *Republic*, let us try out what we heard from Socrates in the *Lysis*. "You will be loved," Socrates had told Lysis there, "if and only if you are useful." Does this fit the *Republic?* It fits perfectly. The institutions we find here appear designed from start to finish to make it possible for people to have each others' affection if, and only if, each "does his own,"[36] i.e., performs to the best of his ability that complex of activities through which he is best fitted by nature and nurture to make his greatest possible contribution to his polis. In doing this he would fulfill the Platonic norm of δικαιοσύνη: he would discharge all of his obligations, and earn all of his rights. For our present purpose the latter is the important point. Whatever a man can rightly claim from others in the *Republic* is tied to the performance of his job. He can claim no benefit for himself except insofar as it would enable him to be a better producer.[37] This principle, upheld in the name of δικαιοσύνη, dovetails into a conception of φιλία according to which one

---

the most excellent constitution"), but private allotments and private families are accepted since the pure ideal would be "beyond the capacity of people with the birth, rearing and training we assume" (740A).

[34] 590C-D. Cornford, for once, misses the sense by a mile when he translates ὅμοιοι here by "equal" (as I did too in *SPT*, [292], in 1941: I have corrected to "alike" in the reprint): the word could, of course, mean equal in certain contexts; but equality between subject and ruler is the last thing Plato would tolerate, let alone commend; and that "alike" is the sense here follows directly from its use in C8, ὑπὸ ὁμοίου ἄρχηται to which τῷ αὐτῷ κυβερνώμενοι in D8 alludes.

[35] Which Plato accents strongly by using the word δοῦλος, without meaning, of course, that the producers in the *Republic* are to be the slaves of the philosophers (cf. below, *SPT*, [292] and n. 25).

[36] Cf. *JHR*, Sections II and III.

[37] Thus the Guardians are denied individual property-rights because they would be "more excellent craftsmen at their own job" (421C1-2) without, than with, such rights. Cf. *JHR*, III.2.

is loved so far, and only so far, as he produces good. And here the question
we raised a moment ago in the *Lysis*—"produces good for whom?"—
answers itself: Good for the whole community, which plays no favorites,
distributing the social product to its producers with scrupulous impar-
tiality, taking from each according to his ability and giving to each according to the needs of his job.

This moral philosophy Sir Karl Popper has called "collectivist or
political utilitarianism." "Plato," he writes, "recognizes only one ultimate
standard [of justice], the interest of the state. . . . *Morality is nothing but
political hygiene* [my italics]."[38] But for Plato, as for Socrates before him,
the supreme goal of all human endeavor is the improvement of the soul—
and that means its *moral* improvement.[39] So the interest of the state would
count for nothing unless it were strictly subordinate to this end.[40] The
excellence of a state, its very legitimacy, would be judged by that standard:

> The sum and substance of our agreement comes to this: By what
> means can the members of our community come to be good men,
> having the goodness of soul that is proper to men? . . . This is
> the end to whose attainment all serious effort must be directed
> throughout life. Nothing which could hamper this should be given
> preference. In the end one should rather overturn the state, or else
> flee from it into exile, rather than consent to submit to the servile
> yoke of baser men—one should endure any fate rather than suffer the
> state to change to a polity which breeds baser human beings.
> (770C-E)[41]

[38] *The Open Society and Its Enemies*, Vol. I of the Fourth edition (Princeton,
1963), 107 (and cf. 119). There have been many replies to this indictment.
But it is not easy to rebut its thesis without endorsing antitheses which are
still further from the truth. Thus R. B. Levinson (*In Defense of Plato* [Cambridge,
Mass., 1953], 517) caps his critique (much of it pertinent) by calling on us to
"recognize Plato's altruistic concern for the welfare of the individual"; we
are to see in "every Platonic dialogue . . . a monument erected to his belief
that individual men are important."

[39] *Lg.* 707D: ". . . unlike the majority of mankind, we do not regard mere
safety and survival as matters of greatest value, but rather that men may become and be as virtuous as possible as long as they do survive."

And 705E-706A: "For I lay it down that only that law is rightly enacted
which aims, like an archer, at this and this alone: how beauty [τὸ καλόν] should
come about in consequence of it, passing over every other consideration, be
it wealth or anything else devoid of beauty and virtue."

[40] *Lg.* 630 C: ". . . every legislator worth his salt will legislate with no
other end in view than to secure the greatest virtue [of the citizens]."

[41] And see the preamble to the laws in the opening paragraphs of *Lg.* V,

To be true to what Plato says so explicitly here and assumes throughout the *Republic*, one would have to say not that morality is political hygiene but that politics is moral hygiene. Yet even so what Popper says is not entirely without foundation. One feels intuitively that something is amiss in Plato's ultramoralistic polity. But just what? The present analysis suggests an alternative diagnosis:

Consider what would happen in this utopia if someone through no fault of his own were to cease being a public asset. One of the philosophers, let us say, becomes permanently disabled and can no longer do his job or any other work that would come anywhere near the expected level of productive excellence. And to plug a possible hole in the hypothesis, let us preclude any higher spin-offs from the misfortune. It is not the case, for instance, that the man's character has been so purified during his illness that those who now come to visit him leave his bedside morally braced and elevated: that would be tantamount to shifting him to another job, the propagation of virtue. Our hypothesis is that neither in this nor in any other way can this man recoup his place as a producer. What may he then claim, now that he may no longer ground his claims on the needs of his job, but only on the value of his individual existence? As I read the *Republic*, the answer is: Nothing. In Book III Asclepius is pictured as follows:

> He would rid them of their disorders by drugs or by the knife and tell them to go on living as usual, so as not to impair their civic usefulness [ἵνα μὴ τὰ πολιτικὰ βλάπτοι]. But where the body was diseased through and through he would not try, by diet and by finely graduated evacuations and infusions, to prolong a miserable existence. . . . Treatment, he thought, would be wasted on a man who could not live in his ordinary round of duties and was thus useless to himself and to the polis. (407DE; translation after Cornford)

What are we to say? That this "political Asclepius" (497E) is not the divinity we know from other sources, the culture-hero of a vocation pledged to "love of mankind" (φιλανθρωπία)?[42] This would be true. But it would miss the point that Plato could say exactly what he did and still credit his reconditioned Asclepius with φιλανθρωπία. If men are to

---

where the rationale of the legislation is explained. (Here and in the preceding notes I have drawn on the *Laws* where much that is implicit in the tightly constructed argument of the *Republic* is spelled out at length.)

[42] Hippocrates, *Precepts* (παραγγελίαι), 6: "for if there is φιλανθρωπίη, there is bound to be φιλοτεχνίη."

be loved for their productiveness and for no other reason, why should there be breach of love in the refusal of medical treatment to the unproductive?

For another sidelight on what is morally disquieting about φιλία in the *Republic*, consider what would happen to the individual's freedom in that utopia. We know how highly this was prized in Plato's Athens. We know the current estimate of the positive side of freedom: guaranteed participation in the process by which political decisions were reached. "There is no better way to define the proper sense of 'citizen,' " says Aristotle "than in terms of having a share in judgment and office."[43] He holds that to deny a man such a share would be to treat him as though he were no better than an alien or a slave.[44] And we know how highly the negative side of freedom—the right to protected privacy—was esteemed. In Thucydides Pericles boasts that daily life in Athens is free from censorious constraint,[45] and Nicias, calling on his commanders to do their utmost for Athens in her hour of supreme peril,

> reminded them that their fatherland was the freest in the world and that in it everyone had the right to live his daily life without orders from anyone.[46]

[43] *Pol.* 1275A22-23, πολίτης δ' ἁπλῶς οὐδενὶ τῶν ἄλλων ὁρίζεται μᾶλλον ἢ τῷ μετέχειν κρίσεως καὶ ἀρχῆς. By κρίσις Aristotle must mean here effective judgment in political and legislative, no less than judicial, decisions (cf. *Thuc.* 2,40,2, ἤτοι κρίνομέν γε ἢ ἐνθυμούμεθα, where the latter "must here be used of those who originate proposals," the former of those who judge [i.e., vote for or against] them[A. W. Gomme, *ad. loc.*]; also κριταί, 3,37,4, and κρῖναι in 6,39,1). Aristotle goes on to explain (23-31) that under ἀρχή he includes that of the juror and of the ecclesiast, no less than that of the magistrate and of a member of the Council. Cf. 1275B 18-20 (much the same in 1278A 35-36, where "μετέχ[ειν] τῶν τιμῶν" = "sharing in ἀρχή" here).

[44] *Pol.* 1275A7-8.

[45] ἐλευθέρως δε [1] τά τε πρὸς τὸ κοινὸν πολιτεύομεν καὶ [2] ἐς τὴν πρὸς ἀλλήλους τῶν καθ' ἡμέραν ἐπιτηδευμάτων ὑποψίαν, οὐ δι' ὀργῆς τὸν πέλας, εἰ καθ' ἡδονήν τι δρᾷ, ἔχοντες, οὐδὲ ἀζημίους μέν, λυπηρὰς δὲ τῇ ὄψει ἀχθηδόνας προστιθέμενοι. ἀνεπαχθῶς δὲ τὰ ἴδια προσομιλοῦντες . . . (2,37, 2-3). The sense of ὑποψίαν in this context I take to be "censorious watchfulness" (*LSJ s.v.*, II). λυπηρὰς τῇ ὄψει ἀχθηδόνας refers directly to "dirty looks" at those who choose a different style of life for themselves (Croiset, "regards chargés de blâme"), indirectly to all those informal, extra-legal, pressures by which their life could be made miserable. ἀνεπαχθῶς τὰ ἴδια προσομιλοῦντες reinforces the notion of private life free from oppressive intolerance. For the recognition of [1] and [2] as distinct, though complementary, aspects of freedom, cf. Aristotle's account of liberty as the "postulate" (ὑπόθεσις) of democracy: "one [kind] of freedom is to rule and be ruled in turn. . . . The other mark of democracy is to live as one wishes [τὸ ζῆν ὡς βούλεταί τις]" (*Pol.* 1317 B2-12).

[46] *Thuc.* 7, 69, 2. Cf. Plato's account of the democratic ethos in *Rep.* 557B:

What would be left of all this in the *Republic?* Participatory democracy vanishes without a trace. So does free speech and, what Plato realizes is at least as important, free song, free dance, free art.[47] The rulers lose all right to personal privacy. Even their sex-life belongs to the state. For the greater part of their adult years intercourse is permitted them only for purposes of eugenic breeding, with partners assigned them by state officials. The end in view is the communizing—one might almost say the homogenizing—of their value-preferences, their likes and dislikes:

> Can we say that anything would be a greater evil for a polis then what breaks it up and makes it many instead of one? Or any good greater than what binds it together and makes it one?
>
> We can not.
>
> And is not the community of pleasure and of pain that binds it together—when so far as possible all the citizens are pleased or pained alike on the same occasions of gain or loss?
>
> Quite so.
>
> Whereas it is the privatization[48] of these feelings that breaks the bond—when some are intensely pained, while others are overjoyed at the very same things befalling the polis or its people?
>
> Yes indeed.[49]

---

there men are "free and the polis is full of freedom and free speech, and one has the liberty to do what he likes. And where this liberty exists it is clear that each will make his own life according to his own private design—that which pleases him." And cf. Aristotle in the preceding note.

[47] The rulers "must take the greatest care not to overlook the least infraction of the rule against innovation in gymnastic and in music counter to the established order. . . . For a new form of music is to be feared as endangering the whole [of the social order]: for nowhere are the modes of music altered without affecting the most fundamental political usages. . . . Here, in music, our guardians it seems must build their guard-house" (424B-C). Conceding that Homer is "the first and most poetic of the tragic poets," we must banish him from our state: "if you allow the honied Muse in song or verse, pleasure and pain will be king in your polis instead of law and consensus about the highest good" (607A).

[48] No such word exists in English, as probably there was none in Greek when Plato wrote ἰδίωσις here (no other occurrence is listed in *LSJ*). Shorey and Robin translate "individualization," which is close enough. Cornford resorts to periphrasis: "when such feelings are no longer universal"; so does Lee: "When feelings differ between individuals."

[49] 462A9-C1. And cf. *Laws* 739C-D: the implementation of the maxim, κοινὰ τὰ τῶν φίλων would require ideally "driving out by every means what is called 'private' [ἴδιον] out of life, and contriving, if it were possible, that even

Plato's community is to approach the unity of affective experience in a single person: When a man hurts his finger, we don't say that his finger feels the pain, but that *he* "feels the pain in his finger"; so too in "the best ordered polis . . . , when any citizen is affected for good or ill, this kind of polis will feel the affection as its own—all will share the pleasure [συνησθήσεται] or pain [συλλυπήσεται]" (462D-E).

Now that persons who love each other should respond sympathetically to each others' mishaps and triumphs, that each should rejoice when his fellows have cause for joy and grieve when they have cause to grieve, is only what we would expect. So from the fact that A and B are φίλοι we may expect that A will be pleased at B's pleasure and pained at B's pain. But to say this is not to say that each will be himself pleased or pained at those (and only those) things which please or pain the other.[50] Let A admire and B dislike the mixolydian mode and Sappho's lyrics. Then some things in their world which thrill A will chill B. Would it follow that they cannot be friends or lovers? Why should it? Why should not personal affection imply tolerance, even tender regard, for such differences? So it would, if it did mean wishing another's good for his own sake. For then A

---

things which nature made private should somehow become common—thus eyes and ears and hands would be expected to see and hear and act in common, and men would be as united as they could possibly be in what they praise and blame, rejoicing and grieving at the same things."

[50] The notion that friends are those who share each others' pleasures and pains is accepted by Aristotle, but only with the proviso which expresses what he himself considers definitive of φιλία: "Your φίλος is he who shares your pleasures at what is good [τὸν συνηδόμενον τοῖς ἀγαθοῖς] and grief at what is painful [συναλγοῦντα τοῖς λυπηροῖς] *for your sake, not for the sake of something else*" (*Rhet*. 1381A4-6).

The all-important phrase I have italicized is not present, in *N.E.* 1166A6-8: "And some [define the φίλος] as one who consorts with another and shares his preferences [τὸν συνδιάγοντα καὶ ταὐτὰ αἱρούμενον], or as one who shares the pains and pleasures of the one he loves [τὸν συναλγοῦντα καὶ συνηδόμενον τῷ φίλῳ]." But note that there is no indication here that this formula would be acceptable to Aristotle as a *definition* of φιλία. The evidence of the *Rhet.* shows that it would not: of the two formulae in 1166A2-10 only the first (A2-5, quoted in n.2, above) would be acceptable to Aristotle, since only this one states the condition which Aristotle uses to define φίλος in *Rhet.* 1380B35-1381A1 (quoted in n. 1, above), a context which leaves no doubt that Aristotle is speaking *in propria persona* (cf. ὁρισάμενοι λέγωμεν here with οἱ δὲ [τιθέασι] in *N.E.* 1166A6). That this remains the crucial condition of "perfect" φιλία in the *N.E.* is clear e.g. at 1156B9-10, "οἱ δὲ βουλόμενοι τἀγαθὰ τοῖς φίλοις ἐκείνων ἕνεκα μάλιστα φίλοι."

would have good reason for wishing that B should have what B himself deems material to the fulfillment of his own unique personality—pleased at the thought of B's having it, though A himself would only be pained if it were forced on him. To work out a *modus vivendi* in which such differences are respected might well involve practical difficulties. It would call for reciprocal adjustments and concessions. But these would be felt as implementations of mutal love, not as denials of it. This possibility does not occur to Plato. He takes it for granted that diversity of valuational response—"privatization" of feelings—would be a disruption of the love-bond,[51] a sign of mutual indifference or hostility. So the constraint on personal freedom at its deepest level—the freedom to feel whatever it be one wants to feel, whose suppression would justify that of so many other kinds of freedom—becomes not only compatible with what Plato understands by φιλία, but its indispensable ideal condition. He could not have reached this result if he had thought of love as wishing another person's good for just that person's sake, looking upon the loved one's individual being as something precious in and of itself.

IV

If—to recall the diction of the *Lysis*—we may not accord to any person we love the status of πρῶτον φίλον, whom, or what, may we "really" and "truly" love? The sections of the *Republic* I have so far discussed give no more of an answer than does the passage about the πρῶτον φίλον in the *Lysis*. Only when we come to the treatise on metaphysics and epistemology, which starts with the introduction of the Theory of Ideas in the latter part of Book V, do we get at long last what we have been looking for.[52] We get it when Plato starts talking of the philosophers as lovers of the Ideas[53] He uses for this purpose not only φιλεῖν (479E, with ἀσπάζεσθαι), but also ἐρᾶν which is so much stronger.[54] From just these data in the

---

[51] As breaking up (διασπᾷ) the community, making it "many" rather than "one" (462AB); the same implication in *Laws* 739C-D, where the citation in n. 49 goes on to speak of laws which maximize identity of pleasure and pain among the citizens as "making the polis one so far as possible" (739D3-4).

[52] 474C ff. Cf. below, *MP*, pp. 43 ff.

[53] 501D: the philosophers are the "lovers [ἐρασταί] of being and truth," i.e., of the Ideas; 490B: the philosopher's ἔρως for the Idea will lead him to a union with it which will give birth "to intelligence and truth" (a passage which states in miniature the experience of the vision of the Idea of Beauty and union with it in *Smp.* 210E-212A).

[54] Cf. above, n. 4 (i).

Republic we could have inferred that now the πρῶτον φίλον is the Idea. But we have also the *Symposium* and the *Phaedrus*, either of which would confirm this inference to the hilt. I shall be content to work with the former, and there only with the metaphysical core of the dialogue—the part in which the priestess-prophetess, Diotima, instructs Socrates in "the things of love."[55] She begins with things Socrates says he knows already:

> We love only what is beautiful.
>
> In loving it we desire to possess it in perpetuity.
>
> We desire to possess it because we think it good and expect that its possession would make us happy.[56]

[55] ἡ δὴ καὶ ἐμὲ τὰ ἐρωτικὰ ἐδίδαξεν, 201D5. τὰ ἐρωτικά is used repeatedly throughout the discourse to refer to its theme.

[56] 204D-205A; 205E-206A11; 207A2. Nygren (*op. cit.*, 180, n. 1) cites this passage to prove the "egocentric" and "acquisitive" nature of Platonic eros, taking no account of the fact that what Diotima has said so far is not meant to be the whole story: as yet she has not stated, has scarcely hinted at, that distinctive feature of Platonic eros which she proceeds forthwith to explain as "birth in beauty" (to be discussed directly in the text above). For a corrective see R. A. Markus (1955, 219-30); Markus (225 ff.) calls attention to "the radical change of perspective" when "the new picture" of love "as a begetting or procreating" is introduced. However, Markus goes a bit too far in the other direction when he remarks that while this new conception of love "is at first grafted onto the original metaphor of desire-and-fulfilment, it very soon achieves independence" (*loc. cit.*). Diotima never cuts loose from the original description of eros as desire for one's perpetual possession of the good (ἔστιν ἄρα συλλήβδην ὁ ἔρως τοῦ τὸ ἀγαθὸν αὑτῷ εἶναι ἀεί, 206A11-12); she brings in "birth in beauty" to fill out, not to amend, that description (see next note), even asserting (206E8–207A2) that "birth in beauty" *follows* (and "necessarily"!) from that agreed-upon description. She claims that only through the immortalizing effect of "birth in beauty" can one fulfill the desire to possess the good in perpetuity; how seriously she takes this implication shows up in her treatment of the Alcestis story: Alcestis' readiness to give her life for that of Admetus, which Phaedrus had explained as due to the intensity of her love for her husband (ὑπερεβάλετο τῇ φιλίᾳ διὰ τὸν ἔρωτα, 179C1), Diotima explains as due rather to her desire to win immortal fame for herself (208C-D). (A further point that should not escape notice is the force of the possessive pronoun in the [above cited] phrase in 206A11-12 and in the parallel phrase [to be cited in the next note] in 207A2. This is brought out well in Suzy Groden's translation of the two phrases: "love is for the good to always belong to oneself," "love is for the good to be eternally one's own." It gets lost in the usual translations. Thus, to render the first phrase "love is of the eternal possession of the good" [so Jowett, and similar renderings in Hamilton, Robin, Apelt & Capelle], fails to make it clear that what the lover desires is *his* possession of the good.)

Then she goes on to ask (206B1-3):

> This being the aim of love,[57] in what way and by what activity is it
> to be pursued if the eagerness and intensity of the pursuit is to be
> (properly) called "love"?

Socrates has no idea of what she is driving at.[58] She tells him: "Birth in
beauty" (τόκος ἐν τῷ καλῷ). She explains:

> We are all pregnant[59] in body and in spirit, and when we reach ma-
> turity our nature longs to give birth. But this we can do only in the
> presence of beauty, never in that of ugliness.[60] There is something
> divine about this. In pregnancy and in birth the mortal becomes
> immortal. (206C)

Beauty stirs us so deeply, Plato is saying, because we have the power to
create and only the beauty we love can release that power. He puts this,
to begin with, into his interpretation of physical, heterosexual, love. Being

[57] Following Bury (against Burnet, Robin, and others) I accept Bast's
emendation (favored by Hermann and Schanz among others) of τοῦτο of the
codices to τούτου, since the sense makes it clear that the reference of the
pronoun in διωκόντων αὐτὸ is not ἔρως itself, but its aim (love is the pursuing—
not the object of the pursuit, which is the eternal possession of the good);
and cf. 207A2, εἴπερ τοῦ ἀγαθοῦ ἑαυτῷ εἶναι ἀεὶ ἔρως ἐστίν, where the object
of ἐστίν is quite explicitly the aim of ἔρως, not ἔρως itself.

[58] He replies, "If I could [tell you the answer], Diotima, I should not be
marvelling at your wisdom and coming to you to learn of this very matter."
This suggests that Plato is now introducing a doctrine which cannot be
credited to the historical Socrates (cf. his use of a similar device in *Meno* 81A:
Socrates learns of the doctrine of transmigration from "priests and priestesses.")
I see no justification for the view (F. M. Cornford, "The Doctrine of Eros in
Plato's *Symposium*," in *The Unwritten Philosophy* [Cambridge, 1950], 75) that
"the limit reached by the philosophy" of Socrates is indicated no earlier than
in 209E4. If Plato had wanted to imply such a thing why should he have
represented Socrates as stumped already at 206B?

[59] πάντες κυοῦσιν ἄνθρωποι. For this striking image of male pregnancy   *
there is no known precedent in Greek literature. The nearest thing to it is in
Apollo's argument in the *Eumenides* (661 ff.) that the father is the true pro-
genitor (τοκεύς), the mother serving only as "nurse of the new-sown pregnancy
[τροφὸς · · · κύματος νεοσπόρου]"—a kind of human incubator.

[60] Excising ἡ γὰρ ἀνδρὸς καὶ γυναικὸς συνουσία as a gloss: cf. Bury *ad loc.*
I find the defense of the text in S. Rosen, *Plato's Symposium* (New Haven,
1968), 247, n. 125, incomprehensible: "it has the obvious function of serving
as transition from homosexual to heterosexual generation"—how so, when
there has been absolutely no reference to homosexual *generation* at all?

himself an invert, with little appreciation of passionate love between the sexes for purposes other than procreation,[61] all he sees in feminine beauty is the lure to paternity. He accepts this as an authentic, if lowgrade, form of creativity. Then, turning to other ranges of experience, he holds that what we love in each of them is always some variety of beauty which releases in us the corresponding power of "birth in beauty." Living in a culture which accepts the pederast[62] and does not constrain him, as ours did Proust, to falsify the imaginative transcript of his personal experience, transvesting Alfred into Albertine, Plato discovers a new form of pederastic love,[63] fully sensual in its resonance,[64] but denying itself consummation,[65] trans-

---

[61] At least in the middle dialogues. There is a passage in the *Laws* (839AB) which suggests a better appreciation of conjugal love: one of his reasons there for prohibiting every other form of sexual gratification is that the restriction would make men fonder of their own wives (γυναιξί τε ἑαυτῶν οἰκείους εἶναι καὶ φίλους). Cf. G. Grube, *Plato's Thought* (London, 1935), 118–19.

[62] On this see Dover, 1966, 31–42, and Appendix II, below.

[63] I say "new" because the doctrine σώφρων ἔρως (in which, it has been claimed, "Euripides anticipates Plato," [Helen North, 1966, 73 ff. *et passim*], is a doctrine of self-control, *not* of abstinence. The Uranian Aphrodite of Pausanias' speech in the *Symposium* is not meant to rule out intercourse, but to restrict it to a context in which intellectual and spiritual values prevail. Cf. Dover: "But both good and bad [eros in Pausanias' speech] aim at the physical submission of the boy. . . . [T]he difference . . . lies in the whole context of the ultimate physical act, not in the presence or absence of the act itself" (34).

[64] See Appendix II, below.

[65] This is not said in the *Symposium* (cf. Grube, *op. cit.*, 103–4) but it is suggested in the rebuff to Alcibiades' all-out attempt at seduction in 219B-D. It is unambiguously clear in *Phdr.* 250E and 255E–256E, as well as in *R.* 403BC. The latter is not contradicted by μηδενὶ ἐξεῖναι ἀπαρνηθῆναι ὃν ἂν βούληται φιλεῖν as a prize for military prowess in 468BC. The assumption that here Plato is "allowing sexual license, a completely free pick of sexual partners" to valorous athletes (Gouldner, 335) is based on a misreading of the text: φιλεῖν does not mean "intercourse" in this context (or in any other in Greek prose, to my knowledge)—for that Plato would have used συγγίγνεσθαι (as in 329C2, 329C4, 360C1, 459D8, 560B5); φιλεῖν and ἅπτεσθαι are specifically allowed to chaste lovers in 403BC, where intercourse is clearly ruled out, as also in *Phdr.* 255E, where ἅπτεσθαι, φιλεῖν, and even συγκατακεῖσθαι are proper and will stop short of intercourse in the case of the "victorious" lovers (256AB). (It should be noted that this interpretation of 468BC is entirely consistent with "opportunity of more frequent intercourse with women" (460B) as an incentive to military prowess: this has to do not with φιλεῖν but with eugenic breeding [ὡς πλεῖστοι τῶν παίδων ἐκ τῶν τοιούτων σπείρωνται].)

muting physical excitement into imaginative and intellectual energy. At
the next level, higher in value and still more energizing, he puts the love
of mind for mind, expecting it to prove so much more intense than skin-
love that mere physical beauty will now strike the lover as a "small,"
contemptible, thing.[66] Still higher in ordered succession come the beauty
of poetry, of political constitutions, of science, and of philosophy. Ascend-
ing relentlessly, the lover will come to see at last "a marvellous sort of
Beauty" (210E)—the Platonic Idea of Beauty. "And all our previous
labors," says Diotima, "were for this."[67] All previously encountered objects—bodies, minds, institutions, works of the imagination or of science—
were loved as a means of moving closer step by step to this "marvellous
sort of Beauty."

Here we find ourselves in the thick of Plato's ontology, so let us stop
to get our bearings. For every generic character which spatio-temporal
objects may have in common, Plato posits an ideal entity in which particular things "participate" so long as they have that character. We are
thus offered a tripartite ontology:

1. the transcendent, paradigmatic Form: say, the Form of Justice;
2. the things in our experience which may have or lack the corresponding character—the persons, laws, practices, states, which
   may or may not be just;
3. the character of those things—the justice they instantiate if they
   are just.[68]

That (1) is radically distinct (or, as Aristotle was to put it, "exists sepa-
rately")[69] from (3) I take to be the crux of this ontology. But what exactly does this "separation" mean? Plato never made this fully clear.
Had he done so, he would surely have seen how treacherous is one of the
ways in which he tends to represent it in his middle dialogues, thinking
of the Form as differing from its empirical instances not only categorially
—as incorporeal, eternal, intelligibles would differ from corporeal, tem-

[66] τὸ περὶ τὸ σῶμα κάλλος σμικρόν τι ἡγήσεται εἶναι, 210C (a remarkable
thing to say, considering the extreme susceptibility to physical beauty revealed in a passage like *Phdr.* 250C-E); and cf. κατεφρόνησεν καὶ κατεγέλασεν
τῆς ἐμῆς ὥρας in *Symp.* 219C4.

[67] 210E; cf. also 210A1 and 211C2.

[68] Cf. *RC*, pp. 76 ff., below.

[69] Cf. *Metaph.* 1039A25 ff., and the references in Bonitz, *Index Aristotelicus*,
860A35–38.

poral, sensibles—but also as would an ideal exemplar from imperfect "resemblances" of it.[70] This kind of language, if meant literally, would burden the Platonic Form with the logical difficulties of "self-predication"[71]—an assumption which could not be generalized without contradiction, for then, e.g., the Form, Plurality, would have to be plural, and the Form, Motion, would have to be moving, contrary to the stipulation that each Form is unitary and immutable. Did Plato ever walk into this trap? The question has been hotly debated, and this essay is not the place to pursue the controversy. All I need say here is this: If Plato's ontology had been fashioned for narrowly logical semantic, and epistemological purposes, he would have had no use whatever for exemplarism and we would have to read the language which suggests it as pure metaphor, freeing it from any self-predicative commitment. Suppose that just this had been Plato's intention. What would have been the consequence? A more coherent ontology, certainly—but a less fruitful one for other uses to which Plato put his Ideas, for his theory of love most of all. If Plato had seen in the Idea of Beauty just the character, not the paradigmatic instance of the character, then it would not have been for him the absolutely[72] and divinely[73] beautiful object of Diotima's discourse; it would not even have been beautiful—no more beautiful than ugly, as the character, Whiteness, being an abstract universal, a purely logical entity, is itself neither white nor of any other color. How then could it have been love object par excellence in a theory which so strictly conditions love on beauty? What inspired that theory was a paradigm-form so splendidly and shamelessly self-exemplifying that its own beauty outshines that of everything else.

I cannot here formulate, let alone try to answer, the many questions that spring to mind when one ponders this theory that has done so much to mold the European imagination from Plotinus to Dante and from Petrarch to Baudelaire. A proper study of it would have to take account of

[70] For sensible instances "resembling" their Form "defectively" see *Phdo.* 74E1-4, ἐνδεῖ δε καὶ οὐ δύναται τοιοῦτον εἶναι οἶον ἐκεῖνο, ἀλλ' ἔστιν φαυλότερον . . . προσεοικέναι μέν, ἐνδεεστέρως δὲ ἔχειν. Cf. also: we cannot expect the just man πανταχῇ τοιοῦτον εἶναι οἶον ἡ δικαιοσύνη (*R.* 472B); we must believe that the visible movements of the heavens τῶν ἀληθινῶν πολὺ ἐνδεῖν (*R.* 529D) and that the physical bed is not the "real" Bed, ἀλλά τι τοιοῦτον οἶον τὸ ὂν and ἀμυδρόν τι πρὸς ἀλήθειαν (*R.* 597A).

[71] The assumption that the Form corresponding to a given character has that character; cf. below, *UVP*, n. 97.

[72] *Symp.* 211A1-5.

[73] *Symp.* 211E3 αὐτὸ τὸ θεῖον καλόν.

at least three things about its creator: He was a homosexual,[74] a mystic, and a moralist. So to reach a balanced understanding of Platonic love— of the true original, not of that caricature confused with it by the illiterate and not infrequently by literati—one would need to pursue at the very least three complementary investigations:

First, a clinical study of the effect which Plato's inversion would be likely to have on one who saw anal intercourse as "contrary to nature,"[75] a degradation not only of man's humanity, but even of his animality: even to brutes, Plato believes, "nature" ordains heterosexual coupling.[76]

---

[74] The evidence tells strongly against classifying Plato as a bisexual (as, e.g., in R. B. Levinson, *op. cit.,* 118, n. 109, "Plato . . . like others of the bisexually inclined Athenians"). In every passage I can recall which depicts or alludes to the power of sexual desire the context is homosexual. For some examples see D. F. Ast (1835), *s.v.* παιδικά (to which *R.* 474D-E and 485C should be added); also *Symp.* 211D, and *Phdr.* 250D ff. And cf. Appendix II, below.

[75] *Phdr.* 251A1, *L.* 636-7. And see next note.

[76] *Lg.* 636B4-6, καὶ δὴ καὶ παλαιὸν νόμιμον δοκεῖ τὸ ἐπιτήδευμα τὰς κατὰ φύσιν περὶ τὰ ἀφροδίσια ἡδονὰς οὐ μόνον ἀνθρώπων, ἀλλὰ καὶ θηρίων, διεφθαρκέναι (England's text, defended by him *ad loc.*): "And then again this ancient usage is thought to have corrupted the pleasure of sex which is natural not only for men but even for brutes." *Lg.* 836B8-C6, "If one were to follow nature in enacting the usage [observed] before Laius, stating that it was right to refrain from the same intercourse with men and boys as with women, calling to witness the nature of wild beasts and pointing out that male has no [such] contact with male, since it is contrary to nature. . . ." (I agree with de Vries [1969,153] that Dover's explanation of "contrary to nature" here by "against the rules" will not do: something far stronger is intended.) The same indictment of παρὰ φύσιν ἡδονή occurs in *Phdr.* 250E-251A, where the sight of the beautiful boy incites the depraved lover to homosexual intercourse. The point of this passage has been blunted by mistranslation. Thus Hackforth takes τετράποδος νόμον βαίνειν ἐπιχειρεῖ καὶ παιδοσπορεῖν to mean "essays to go after the fashion of a four-footed beast, and to beget offspring of the flesh" (the same misconstruction of the sense in every translator and commentator I have consulted); hence Plato is thought to be making here "a contemputous reference to heterosexual love" (Hackforth, 1952, 98), which would be sharply at variance with the whole notion of "birth in beauty" in the *Smp.* But βαίνειν here is "to mount" (cf. de Vries [1969] *ad loc.:* he refers to LSJ, *s.v.* A, II, 1). As for παιδοσπορεῖν, this means only "to sow generative seed" (what is "contrary to nature" is precisely that this "sowing" cannot generate: cf. *Lg.* 841D4-5, σπείρειν . . . ἄγονα ἀρρένων παρὰ φύσιν); and "the way of the four-footed brute" alludes to the posture in anal intercourse (so portrayed in pottery: see, e.g., Jean Marcadé [1962], plates 136 and 147). The context is purely homosexual, and the passage was so read in antiquity: Plut. *Amat.* 751D-E, leaves no doubt on this point.

This thought would poison for him sensual gratification with anticipatory torment and retrospective guilt. It would tend to distort his overall view of sexual fulfillment, while leaving him with raw sensitiveness to male beauty and heightening his capacity for substitute forms of erotic response.

Second, a study which would connect his theory of love with his religious mysticism, exploring the implications of the momentous fact that while Plato retains traditional deities and sets high above them in the *Timaeus* a creator-god of his own devising, none of these personal divinities stirs either awe or love in his heart, while the severely impersonal Ideas evoke both, but especially love, so much so that he speaks repeatedly of communion with them as an act of blissful and fertile conjugal union.[77]

Third, a study of the place of love in the pattern of inter-personal relations recommended in his moral philosophy.

Realizing what folly it would have been to spread myself in a single essay all over these three areas, I chose to concentrate on the third. That is why I started off with Aristotle, and then approached the *Symposium via* the *Lysis* and the *Republic*. My reason may be now apparent: What needs to be stressed most of all in this area is that Plato's theory is not, and is not meant to be, about personal love for persons—i.e., about the kind of love we can have only for persons and cannot have for things or abstractions. What it is really about is love for place-holders of the predicates "useful" and "beautiful"—of the former when it is only φιλία, of the latter, when it is ἔρως. In this theory persons evoke ἔρως if they have beautiful bodies, minds, or dispositions. But so do quite impersonal objects—social or political programs, literary compositions, scientific theories, philosophical systems and, best of all, the Idea of Beauty itself. As objects of Platonic love all these are not only as good as persons, but distinctly better. Plato signifies their superiority by placing them in the higher reaches of that escalated figure that marks the lover's progress, relegating love of persons to its lower levels. Even those two personal attachments which seem to have meant more to him than did any others in his whole life—his love for Socrates in his youth and, later on, for Dion of Syracuse[78]—would be less than halfway up to the summit in that diagram.

[77] For the references see note 53 above *sub fin.;* and cf. *MP*, pp. 50–51, below.
[78] On the latter see P. Shorey, *What Plato Said* (Chicago, 1933), 45. I see no good reason to doubt the authenticity of the epigram on Dion's death *ap.* Diogenes Laertius, 3, 30 (accepted by Shorey, *loc. cit.*, and by U. v. Wilamowitz-Möllendorff [1948, 509]; defended by C. M. Bowra, *A.J.P.* 59 [1936] 393–404) whose terminal line is ὦ ἐμὸν ἐκμήνας θυμὸν ἔρωτι Δίων (cf. ἐκμήνας here with the definition of love as μανία in the *Phdr.* 265A–266A *et passim;* cf. note 80 below).

This is what we must keep in view, if we are to reach a fair assessment of Plato's conception of love, acknowledging its durable achievement no less than its residual failure.

V

Let me speak first of the achievement. Plato is the first Western man to realize how intense and passionate may be our attachment to objects as abstract as social reform, poetry, art, the sciences, and philospohy—an attachment that has more in common with erotic fixation than one would have suspected on a pre-Freudian view of man. So far as we know no earlier Greek had sensed this fact, though language had pointed the way to it by sanctioning as a matter of course the use of ἐρᾶν, no less than φιλεῖν, for something as impersonal as love of country.[79] It is left to Plato to generalize this kind of ἔρως and to see that it may reach a mad[80] obsessive intensity which is commonly thought peculiar to sexual love. He discerns, as the link between such disparate involvements, the sense of beauty. He understands how decisive a role in the motivation of the most abstruse inquiry may be played by such things as the elegance of a deduction, the neatness of an argument, or the delight which floods the mind when a powerful generality brings sudden luminous order to a mass of jumbled data. He sees that the aesthetic quality of such purely intellectual objects is akin to the power of physical beauty to excite and to enchant even when it holds out no prospect of possession. And, instead of under-

---

[79] Cf. Aristophanes, *Birds* 1316, κατέχουσι δ' ἔρωτες ἐμᾶς πόλεως. *Thuc.* 2, 43, 1, ἐραστὰς γιγνομένους αὐτῆς [*sc.* τῆς πόλεως], with Gomme's comment *ad loc.*

[80] Had I been able to work more intensively on the *Phdr.* in this essay I would have taken a crack at the extraordinary fact that here ἔρως is not only described, but *defined*, as μανία by our ultra-rationalist, Plato, and is associated as μανία in the closest terms with philosophy no less than with the mystic cults (which had been done also, though only in passing, in *Smp.* 218B, τῆς φιλοσόφου μανίας τε καὶ βακχείας [of Socrates]). This convergence of μανία and νοῦς in love does not seem to intrigue commentators. Few of them notice the paradox at all or, if they do, they seem bent on explaining it away (thus J. Pieper [1964, 49 ff.] gives μανία in the *Phdr.* a theological twist which hardly does justice to its psychological meaning; and even *qua* theology it is too onesided: Pieper objects to "madness" as the sense of μανία because that "suggests ties with the orgiastic Dionysian rites.") But even the above citation from the *Smp.* (not to refer to further evidence, which exists in abundance) would show that those "orgiastic Dionysian rites" could not have been entirely uncongenial to Plato.

taking, as did Freud, to explain the attractiveness of beauty in all of its diverse manifestations as due to the excitation of lust, open or disguised, Plato invokes another drive, the hunger to create, and argues that this is what we all seek to appease in every activity propelled by beauty. That Plato's explanation is onesided does not damn it. So is Freud's. Where comprehensive insight is denied us even partial glimpses of the truth are precious.

But, second, to return to Plato's view of that kind of love whose immediate object is a man or a woman, we can get out of it a subordinate thesis which has not only psychological but also moral validity. When he speaks of ἔρως for a person for the sake of the Idea, we can give a good sense to this at first sight puzzling notion, a sense in which it is true. It is a fact that much erotic attachment, perhaps most of it, is not directed to an individual in the proper sense of the word—to the integral and irreplaceable existent that bears that person's name—but to a complex of qualities, answering to the lover's sense of beauty, which he locates for a time truly or falsely in that person. I say "truly or falsely" to call attention to a feature of Platonic love which has never been noticed, to my knowledge, in the rich literature on this subject. This feature can best be appreciated by contrast with romantic love—at any rate, with that brand of it whose textbook example is Rousseau.

"There is no real love without enthusiasm," he writes in the *Émile*, "and no enthusiasm without an object of perfection, real or chimerical, but always existing in the imagination."[81] So if we do want "real love," we must buy it with illusion. We must transfigure imaginatively the necessarily imperfect persons in whom we vest our love. We see in the *Confessions* that this is the recipe Rousseau followed himself in what he calls there "the first and only love of my life, whose consequences were to make it unforgettable for the rest of my life and terrible in my recollection."[82]

---

[81] *Œuvres Complètes*, vol. IV of the Pléiade Edition (Paris, 1969), 743. He goes on, a little later: "Not all is illusion in love, I admit. But what is real consists of the sentiments with which it animates us for the true beauty it makes us love. This beauty is not in the object we love, it is the work of our errors. Well, what difference does that make? Would we be less willing to sacrifice all those base sentiments to this imaginary model?" For more statements, some of them quite remarkable, to the same effect elsewhere in Rousseau see M. Eigeldinger, *Jean Jacques Rousseau et la realité de l'imaginaire* (Neuchatel, 1962), Chapter 4, "L'Amour et le pays des chimères."

[82] *Œuvres Complètes*, vol. I of the Pléiade Edition (Paris, 1959), 439. The references in the next five notes are to this volume.

What excited that high-temperature passion was scarcely the plain[83] and unremarkable young woman, Madame d'Houdetot. She served him only as a mannequin to wear his fantasies. A mood of frustration and self-pity had settled on him in his middle forties and had thrown him back, so he tells us, "into the land of chimeras":[84]

> Finding nothing in existence worthy of my delirium, I nourished
> it in an ideal world which my creative imagination soon peopled
> with beings after my own heart. . . . Forgetting completely the
> human race, I made for myself societies of perfect creatures, as
> heavenly in their virtues as in their beauties.[85]

Presently Madame d'Houdetot moves into his private landscape. He had been "intoxicated with a love without an object." She provided one. "Before long I had no eye for anyone but Madame d'Houdetot, but reclothed with all the perfections with which I had come to adorn the idol of my heart."[86]

It would be a blunder to call this affair "Platonic love," which it in fact was in the vulgar sense of the term—technically there was no infidelity[87]—and which it also approached as love for an ideal object. But no Platonist could have confused the idol of *his* heart with a Madame d'Houdetot. Even in the heat of passion the Platonic Idea does not lend itself to this kind of mistake. We see in the *Phaedrus* what keeps Plato's head clear even when his senses are enflamed.[88] It is the ontology of the

---

[83] "Mad° la Comtesse de Houdetot . . . n'étoit point belle. Son visage étoit marqué de la petite vérole, son teint manquoit de finesse," etc., 439. Compare Zulietta, 318–20.

[84] 427. Erotic fantasy had been a habit of his since adolescence, 41.

[85] *Loc. cit.*

[86] 440.

[87] I.e., no genital intercourse. That there was physical contact of other sorts in abundance is stated openly enough in the *Confessions* (443–45; and see also the passages from the Correspondence in H. Guillemin's study, *Un Homme, Deux Ombres* [Geneva, 1943], Chapter IV, "Fausse Route"). But there is plenty of this in Platonic love too: cf. note 65 above. Rousseau says that "though at times carried away by my senses I sought to make her unfaithful, I never really desired this" (444); the lover depicted in *Phdr.* 254A ff. would not be human or truthful if he did not say the same *mutatis mutandis*.

[88] Not that the lover in the *Phaedrus* is less combustible: the exaltation of the erotic object depicted here outruns anything in the *Confessions* or, to stick to Plato's own culture, anything in the whole of Greek prose and almost the whole of surviving Greek verse as well; it is matched only in Sappho (with

paradigm-form. That harshly dualistic transcendentalism, which enraged Aristotle by its "separation" of Forms from things and which nowadays drives analytical philosophers to despair when they try to make logical sense out of it, proves a sterling asset in this area. It sustains a kind of idealism less addicted to the pathetic fallacy than are most other kinds. It makes for a more truthful vision of that part of the world which we are all most tempted to idealize and so to falsify—the part we love. And it makes for a gain of another, no less important, kind: Freedom from the tyranny which even the unidealized love-object can exercise over a lover. Swann did not long idealize Odette.[89] But his love for her made a tortured, degraded, slave out of him while it lasted, and disabled his spirit for the rest of his life. If there is any place at all in Plato's diagram for a creature like Odette, it would be at just one level short of the bottom. At the next higher level Swann would have been once again free and whole.

But a sterling asset may be bought at a heavy cost. Plato's theory floods with the most brilliant light a narrow sector of its theme, and there points the way to authentic spiritual achievement. Beyond those limits the vision fails. Plato is scarcely aware of kindness, tenderness, compassion, concern for the freedom, respect for the integrity of the beloved, as essential ingredients of the highest type of interpersonal love. Not that Platonic eros is as "egocentric" and "acquisitive" as Nygren has claimed;[90] it is only too patently Ideocentric and creative. But while it gives no more quarter to self-indulgence than would Pauline *agape* or Kantian good will, neither does it repudiate the spiritualized egocentricism of Socratic *philia*.[91] That first description of the aim of eros in Diotima's speech—

whom Plato openly invites comparison, 235C3: cf. Fortenbaugh, 1966, 108): "[when he encounters the youth], first there comes upon him a shuddering and a measure of that awe which the [transcendental] vision had once inspired, then reverence as at the sight of a god: did he not fear being taken for a madman he would offer sacrifice to his boy-love as to a holy image and a god . . ." (251A2-7; the translation mainly after Hackforth's).

Even so, the lover is in no danger of confusing the boy with the Idea or of decking him out with pseudo-attributes. In particular, there is no magnification of his moral or intellectual virtues, which are apparently not out of the ordinary, and the lover is not required to make believe that they are. His physical beauty is itself the "divine" (θεοειδές, 251A2) thing in him, and this suffices.

[89] Seeing her first as "bonne, naïve, éprise d'idéal," almost incapable of untruth (239), he soon discovers that she is cruel, sly, devious, deceitful, mercenary. Yet he remains as helplessly in love as before.

[90] Cf. note 56 above.

[91] Cf. Section II above and note that in the last analysis Socrates has just one

"that one should possess beauty for ever"—is never amended in the sequel in any way which would make egoistic eros a contradiction or even an anomaly.[92] It is not said or implied or so much as hinted at that "birth in beauty" should be motivated by love of persons—that the ultimate purpose of the creative act should be to enrich the lives of persons who are themselves worthy of love for their own sake. The preceding analysis shows that Diotima's failure to say or to suggest anything of the kind is no accidental oversight, but an integral feature of the structure of Plato's theory.

As a theory of the love of persons, this is its crux: What we are to love in persons is the "image"[93] of the Idea in them.[94] We are to love the persons so far, and only insofar, as they are good and beautiful. Now since all too few human beings are masterworks of excellence, and not even the best of those we have the chance to love are wholly free of streaks of the ugly, the mean, the commonplace, the ridiculous, if our love for them is to be only for their virtue and beauty, the individual, in the uniqueness and integrity of his or her individuality, will never be the object of our love. This seems to me the cardinal flaw in Plato's theory. It does not provide for love of whole persons, but only for love of that abstract version of persons which consists of the complex of their best qualities. This is the reason why personal affection ranks so low in Plato's *scala amoris*. When loved as congeries of valuable qualities, persons cannot compete with abstractions of universal significance, like schemes of social reform or scientific and philosophical truths, still less with the Idea of

---

reason for moral conduct: the perfection of his soul. In the *Crito*, his final reason for refraining from an unjust act (breaking jail) is that to commit injustice would corrupt his soul (47C–48D). Cf. the argument against Polus and Callicles in the *Grg.*: against Polus he argues that one should abstain from wrong-doing because this would make one's own soul evil; also that when one has done wrong, one should welcome punishment which purges the evil in the soul, because the man with unpurged evil has suffered the greatest possible harm and is most wretched of men (477A–478E). Similarly he argues against Callicles that "wrong-doing is the greatest of evils to the wrong-doer" (509B) because it ruins his soul and, with one's soul ruined, one would be better off dead than alive (511E–512B). Plato never repudiates this motivation for moral conduct. He supports it to the hilt in the great argument that "justice pays" in the *Republic*.

[92] Cf. note 56 above.

[93] This is most explicit in the *Phaedrus* (250E1 ff.), but also clear enough, by implication, in the *Symposium* also. This is all love for a person could be, given the status of persons in Plato's ontology.

[94] Section IV above, the terminal paragraph.

Beauty in its sublime transcendence, "pure, clear, unmixed, not full of human flesh and color and other mortal nonsense" (*Smp.* 211E1-3). The high climactic moment of fulfilment—the peak achievement for which all lesser loves are to be "used as steps"[95]—is the one farthest removed from affection for concrete human beings.

Since persons in their concreteness are thinking, feeling, wishing, hoping, fearing beings, to think of love for them as love for objectifications of excellence is to fail to make the thought of them as *subjects* central to what is felt for them in love. The very exaltation of the beloved in the erotic idyl in the *Phaedrus* views him from an external point of view. Depicting him as an adorable cult-object, Plato seems barely conscious of the fact that this "holy image"[96] is himself a valuing subject, a center of private experience and individual preference, whose predilections and choice of ends are no reflex of the lover's[97] and might well cross his at some points even while returning his love. Transposing this from erotics to politics we see the reason for the tragedy of the *Republic;* we see why its effort to foster civic love obliterates civil liberty. The fashioner of this utopia has evidently failed to see that what love for our fellows requires of us is, above all, imaginative sympathy and concern for what they them-selves think, feel, and want. He has, therefore, missed that dimension of love in which tolerance, trust, forgiveness, tenderness, respect have validity. Apart from these imperatives the notion of loving persons as "ends in themselves"[98] would make no sense. No wonder that we hear of nothing remotely like it from Plato. Had such a thought occurred to him, his theory could have seen in it only conceptual error and moral confusion. On the terms of that theory, to make flesh-and-blood men and women terminal objects of our affection would be folly or worse, idolatry, diversion to images of what is due only to their divine original. We are a prey to this error, Plato would say, because of our carnal condition, burdened with incompleteness which fellow-creatures have power to complete;[99] were we free of mortal deficiency we would have no reason

[95] ὥσπερ ἐπαναβασμοῖς χρώμενον, 211C3—an image for the idea that every other love is a means to the attainment of this one (an idea expressed no less than three times in two Stephanus pages, 210A–212B: cf. n. 67 above).

[96] 251A6.

[97] Which is what the boy's love turns out to be (255A ff.); he wants what his lover wants "only more feebly" (255E2-3).

[98] Cf. n. 24 above.

[99] This is the point of Aristophanes' myth in the *Symposium*, as has often been noticed, and it is picked up and emphasized in another way in Diotima's speech (cf. n. 20 above).

to love anyone or anything except the Idea: seen face to face, it would absorb all our love. Here we see the polar opposite of the ideal which has molded the image of the deity in the Hebraic and Christian traditions: that of a Being whose perfection empowers it to love the imperfect; of a Father who cares for each of his children as they are, does not proportion affection to merit, gives it no more to the righteous than to the perverse and deformed. Not even Aristotle had any inkling of such a notion[100]— indeed, he less than Plato, whose God is impelled by love for Beauty to create and thereby to share his own goodness with his creatures,[101] while Aristotle's Prime Mover remains eternally complete in the stillness of his own perfection. Discerning the possibility of a kind of love which wishes for another's existence, preservation, and good for that other's sake, Aristotle thought only men could have it and only few men for few. To universalize that kind of love, to extend it to the slave, to impute it to the deity, would have struck him as quite absurd.

Though so much of what I have said here has been critical of Plato, this was only incidental to the effort to understand him. And since he is a philosopher whose separate ventures must be seen in the context of his synoptic vision, let me point out in closing how Plato's speculation structures love in the same way as it does knowledge in epistemology, the world-order in cosmology, the interrelations of particular and universal, time and eternity, the world of sense and the world of thought in ontology. In each of these areas the factors of the analytic pattern are the same: the transcendent Form at one extreme, the temporal individual at the other, and, in between, the individuals' immanent characters, projections of

[100] Aristotle's conception of "perfect φιλία" does not repudiate—does not even notice—what I have called above "the cardinal flaw" in Platonic love. His intuition takes him as far as seeing that (a) *disinterested affection for the person* we love—the active desire to promote that person's good "for that person's sake, not for ours"—must be built into love at its best, but not as far as sorting this out from (b) *appreciation of the excellences instantiated by that person*; (b), of course, need not be disinterested and *could* be egoistic. The limits of Aristotle's understanding of love show up in his failure to notice the ambiguity in "loving a person for himself" (φιλεῖν τινα δι' ἐκεῖνον—a phrase which may be used to express either (a) or (b): thus in *Rhet.* 1361B37 and 1381A5-6 δι' ἐκεῖνον is used to express exactly the same thing which is conveyed by ἐκείνου ἕνεκα in 1380B36. But there are passages in which it is clearly used to express *only* (b): so, e.g., in *N.E.* 1157B3 οἱ δ'ἀγαθοὶ δι' αὑτοὺς φίλοι· ᾗ γὰρ ἀγαθοί: here "A and B are good men and A loves B for B's self" implies "A loves B because B is a good man and in so far as he is a good man."

[101] *Ti.* 29E–30B.

eternity on the flickering screen of becoming. And everywhere Plato gives the Form preeminence. In epistemology it is *the* object of knowledge; sensible particulars can only be objects of that low-grade cognitive achievement, opinion. In cosmology only the Forms represent completely lucid order; physical individuals, enmeshed in brute necessity, are only quasi-orderly, as they are only quasi-intelligible. In ontology there are grades of reality and only Forms have the highest grade. So too in the theory of love the respective roles of Form and temporal individual are sustained: the individual cannot be as lovable as the Idea; the Idea, and it alone, is to be loved for its own sake; the individual only so far as in him and by him ideal perfection is copied fugitively in the flux.

APPENDIX I

Is the Lysis *a Vehicle of Platonic Doctrine?*

THE reader should be warned that my negative answer to this question, while widely shared, is by no means universal: there have been, and there still are, distinguished scholars who reject it. For valuable bibliographical references to the controversy see D. N. Levin (1970). While I cannot argue out the question here, I can at least point out the frailty of the evidence on which the Platonic ontology of the middle dialogues has been read into the *Lysis*. This boils down to two items:

(1) The star item has been the use of the verb πάρειμι, with its participles, and its substantival derivative, παρουσία, in 217D-E. Shorey glosses:

> A subtle digression on the meaning of *presence* either illustrates the unity of Plato's thought or indicates that the *Lysis* is "late". A distinction is made between the superficial presence of a coat of paint, for example, and the indwelling presence that really alters the nature of the thing. (1938, 117)

And Taylor:

> The only object of these remarks is to warn us against supposing that when Socrates speaks of the "presence" of what is evil to what is "neither good nor bad," he is using the term in the sense in which it is employed when we explain the possession of a predicate by a thing by saying that the corresponding form is "present" to the thing. In this sense παρουσία, "presence" of the form, is an equivalent for μέθεξις, the "participation" of a thing in the form, as we see from the free use of both expressions in the *Phaedo* [the reference is to 100D, "where Socrates says that we may call the relation of form

to sensible thing παρουσία or κοινωνία or 'whatever you please' "].
It is assumed that the technical language of the theory of Forms is so
familiar a thing that Socrates needs to warn the lads not to be misled
by it. . . . (1937, 70–71)

But is Plato really using "the technical language of the theory of forms"
when he speaks of the "presence" of a quality in a thing? How so, when
the latter is as old as Homer (*Od.* 17, 347, αἰδὼς οὐκ ἀγαθὴ κεχρημένῳ
ἀνδρὶ παρεῖναι, where "shame is present in a man" is used for "the man
feels shame") and is common enough in subsequent prose and poetry
(Aeschylus, *Pers.* 391, φόβος βαρβάροις παρῆν, "terror was present in the
barbarians" for "they were terrified"; Democritus B 235, τὸ ἐπιθυμεῖν ἀεὶ
τῶν αὐτῶν πάρεστι, "desire is always present for the same things" for
"men always desire the same things")? (Taylor makes the same mistake
in his discussion of the *Gorgias*, where he takes Socrates' talk of things
"participating" [μετέχειν] in good or evil,

> using the very word (μετέχει) which appears in connexion with the
> theory of Forms as technical for the relation between the "par-
> ticular thing" and the "universal" we predicate of it (*ibid.*, 112, n. 1),

as "a grave difficulty" for those who suppose that the theory is a Platonic
invention, expounded for the first time in the *Phaedo*.) For μετέχειν in a
given property as a common expression for *having* that property see
below, *AS*, n. 2). Once we take into account the fact that there is nothing
out of the way in the use of πάρειμι in *Lysis* 217D–E—that any Greek
could have used the term to make the common sense point that there is
all the difference in the world between having one's (black) hair painted
white, on one hand, and having it turn white, on the other—it should be
clear that it is arguing in a circle to take πάρειμι and παρουσία here as
evidence of familiarity with the theory of Forms. (Cf. E. R. Dodds [1959]
on *Grg.* 497E1-3: "the use of the plural ἀγαθῶν, here and at 498D2, is
sufficient to show that the Theory of Forms is not presupposed. We find
a similar non-technical use of παρεῖναι at *Chrm.* 158E7, εἴ σοι πάρεστιν
σωφροσύνη, ἔχεις τι περὶ αὐτῆς δοξάζειν, and elsewhere.")

(2) The other item in the *Lysis* which has been offered as evidence of
Platonic ontology is the doctrine of the πρῶτον φίλον in 218D–220E:
the πρῶτον φίλον has been taken for the Platonic Form of Beauty or
Goodness. But there is not one word or phrase in the *Lysis* to name a
transcendent Form of this (or of any other) kind. At no point does the discussion shift from particular, empirical, goods ordered in the means-end

nexus to an over-arching, eternal, absolute Beauty-in-itself. The use of εἴδωλον in 219D3 surely does *not* serve this purpose, though it has sometimes been so taken (K. Glaser [1934, 56–57]: "Das Wort εἴδωλον [219D] beweist allein schon, dass *mit dem* πρῶτον φίλον *das* εἶδος *gemeint ist*" [His emphasis].) εἴδωλον is, of course, used repeatedly in the middle dialogues of the temporal participants in the transcendent Forms, contrasting them with the latter as their "images." But it need not be so used—no artist would make a strait-jacket out of a metaphor. It is not so used even in contexts where we would most expect it if the use of εἴδωλον in the *Lysis* were to be the link which connects its πρῶτον φίλον with the transcendent Form of Beauty in the *Symposium:* the εἴδωλα of virtue in *Symp.* 212A are not temporal, empirical, virtues in contrast with the Idea of Virtue, but inferior, *ersatz*, virtues; the "true" virtues which are the offspring of the philosopher's intercourse with the Idea of Beauty are *also* temporal, empirical, virtues, only better, "real", i.e., genuine ones. The exact purpose for which the metaphor is used in this passage should be clear enough from my remarks in n. 17 above: it is the vehicle of a moral, not a metaphysical, contrast. Glaser blurs this point, saying that for Plato "ein Eidolon von *allen*, auch *ethischen* Objekten angenommen werden muss" (*loc. cit.*, n. 12, his emphasis). But this misses the point. If the mere use of *Eidolon* is to be taken as evidence, and conclusive evidence, that a metaphysical doctrine is being propounded, then what has to be shown is that its use here has metaphysical import—which is just what is yet to be shown by Glaser or anyone else.

APPENDIX II

===

Sex in Platonic Love

ACCORDING to the *Concise Oxford Dictionary of Current Usage* (1954), Platonic love is "purely spiritual love for one of the opposite sex."[1] If we are to concede that this is what the term has come to mean today— we need not dispute the dictionary's authority—we should at least be careful to notice how far it has strayed away from what it meant for Plato. The first deviation—the notion that interpersonal eros is "purely spiritual love"—passes unnoticed in the scholarly literature; so far from calling attention to it, some recent studies have actually endorsed it. Thus Gould (1963, 119) writes:

> If they [the amorous couple in the *Phaedrus*] are truly lovers of wisdom, the only intercourse which will appeal to them is rational exploration together, to be companions in the adventures of the life of the mind.

And Irving Singer (1966, 80):

> In the *Phaedrus* . . . the harmony of black and white finally yields to a purely spiritual bond from which all sexuality has been exorcised.

Such statements seem to have gone unchallenged, and it may not be amiss to point out that they are out of line with the clear implications of Plato's text.

Consider what happens in the passage these statements have in view: when the man first chances on the beautiful youth the "erotic vision" provokes libidinous impulse in "the whole" of his psyche: all of it—

---

[1] Much the same, though in more guarded terms, in Webster's.

charioteer and white horse, no less than the black—is "enflamed," is "filled with the ticklings and pricklings of desire" (253E5–254A1).[2] The white horse (and *a fortiori* the driver) is "held back by shame from leaping on the beloved" (254A2-3): the impulse is checked, not dissipated. Unchecked in the black horse, "terrible and lawless deeds" would have ensued on the spot, were it not that the driver,

> falling back like a racer at the barrier, with a still more violent jerk breaks the bit from the shameless horse's teeth, bespattering its railing tongue and jaws with blood, throws it down on its legs and haunches, and punishes it. (254E)

This happens "many times" (254E6) before the lecherous horse gives in.

Now would it be reasonable to think that Plato expects this liaison to start with such raw, all-but-overpowering, lust, and then become totally desexualized as it matures? If so, why does he tell us (255E) that the boy, when he comes to return the lover's passion, "wants to see, touch, kiss, and share his couch," a desire which "ere long, as one might guess, leads to the act," so that we now find the pair "sleeping together"? Are we to suppose that such a thorough job of mortifying the flesh has intervened that kissing, embracing, and sleeping together now leaves the couple physically undisturbed—that a Masters and Johnson record of their intimacies would register no sign of genital excitement? What comes next in Plato's story is not favorable to the hypothesis: the black horse in the boy's soul "swells with desire" (σπαργῶν, 256A2) when he embraces and kisses; he "would not refuse to do his part in gratifying the lover's entreaties" (256A4-5) were it not that white horse and driver resist. So physical desire is still there in the boy, and *a fortiori* in the lover. It takes "Olympic wrestling" (256B4-5) to keep it in check.

To put my thesis positively: that form of passionate experience invented by Plato, which should count as the original, and always primary, sense

---

[2] 253E5–254A1, . . . τὸ ἐρωτικὸν ὄμμα πᾶσαν αἰσθήσει διαθερμῆναν τὴν ψυχήν, γαργαλισμοῦ τε καὶ πόθου κέντρων ὑποπλησθῇ. I have followed Stallbaum's emendation, διαθερμῆναν for διαθερμήνας of the MS. Spurned by later editors, it seems to me justified by the sense: the MS. reading would make "the charioteer" the subject of the participle, and Plato could scarcely have put reason in the position of "heating up the whole soul by means of sensation," while he would find it very natural to speak of the stimulus, τὸ ἐρωτικὸν ὄμμα, as having just this effect. However, my argument in no way depends on the acceptance of this emendation; the quoted parts of the translation I give above will do in either case.

of "Platonic love," is a peculiar mix of sensuality, sentiment, and intellect—
a companionship bonded by erotic attraction no less than by intellectual
give-and-take. Body-to-body endearment is one of its normal features,
though always subject to the constraint that terminal gratification will be
denied. And this interdict is itself only an ideal requirement; sternly
mandatory for philosophers, it is applied more leniently to others. In
lovers of the "ambitious and less philosophic" way of life (256B-C) Plato
expects lapses: "When drunk or in some other careless hour, the insolent
horses in their souls may catch them off their guard . . . and they may
then choose and do what the vulgar take for bliss." If this happens infrequently and against their best resolves, Plato's eschatology will not damn
them—which means, among other things, that they still qualify as Platonic
lovers:

> Those who have once got started on the heavenward journey no law
> would send to the dark pathways under the earth. But they shall walk
> together in a life of shining happiness and, when the time comes,
> they shall grow wings together because of their love. (256D)

Now let me take up the other point where the dictionary parts company
with Plato on "Platonic love": "love for one of the opposite sex." Here
scholars have gone to the other extreme, suggesting that for heterosexual
love Platonic eros has no place at all. Some of the finest studies have
implied as much. J. A. Symonds, the Victorian invert, whose monograph
cracked open Greek homosexuality for Englishmen of his generation,
saw Platonic love as "veiled sodomy" (1901, 54). Kenneth J. Dover, in his
admirable monograph—as precise and sophisticated a piece of scholarship on its theme as has ever appeared in any language—says that "Plato
exploited exclusively homosexual emotion for his philosophical theory
of eros" (1966, 39). I submit that this goes too far. Admittedly it fits
everything in the *Phaedrus* and also *most* of what Plato put into the *pièce
de resistance* of the *Symposium*, the speech of Diotima: boy-love forms the
base of that escalated figure along which the lover rises to ever higher
forms of love; he starts with the love of "beautiful bodies," and if one
reads attentively one will see that, sure enough, these bodies are male.[3]
However, when Diotima undertakes to state the most general condition

---

[3] The καλὰ σώματα in 210A are male: cf. γεννᾶν λόγους καλούς here with
the "fine words about virtue" induced by erotic passion at 209B, where boy-
love is clearly in view; note παιδαρίου κάλλος in 210D2 and ὀρθῶς παιδεραστεῖν
in 211B5-6.

which the pursuit of Beauty has to meet to qualify as eros, her phrase, "birth in beauty,"[4] is all too patently a generalization of procreative—hence necessarily *heterosexual*—love. Let me dwell on this formula, for it is surely the most profound thing in the dialogue. Just before she had got Socrates to agree that eros is desire to possess the good, believing that it would bring its possessor happiness. One might have expected her to construe this along commonplace, hedonistic, lines—that what we want in love is pleasure and that beauty lures by promising pleasure. That is where she surprises us. For the picture of man as pleasure-chaser she substitutes an image of man as creator, producer, new-maker: ever "pregnant,"[5] carrying a burden for which he craves release, he thrills to Beauty because only in its presence can he find the longed-for deliverance.

This understanding of love has plainly a heterosexual paradigm. In the drive to reproductive coupling Plato recognizes the archetypal expression of eros, its most elemental and universal form. And he does not understate the emotional force of the drive:

> Don't you see how all living creatures, birds and brutes, in their desire of procreation are in agony when they take the infection of love, which begins with the desire of intercourse and then passes to the care of offspring, on whose behalf the weakest are ready to battle the strongest to the last and die for them, and will suffer the torments of hunger, or make any other sacrifice, to tend their young? (207B-C)

What is it then that prompted Symonds' and Dover's remarks and led that erudite philistine, John Jay Chapman, to stigmatize the *Symposium* as

> The *vade mecum* of those who accept and continue the practice it celebrates . . . a sort of lurid devotional book—the sulphurous breviary of the pederast? (1934, 133)

At most this: conjugal love, however intense, would still remain in Plato's scheme a spiritual dead end[6]—an impulse fully spent in reaching its immediate goal, generating no surplus energy to fuel flights into the empyrean. Suppose the man in the *Phaedrus*, long before meeting that boy, had loved a beautiful girl with whom he had reared in harmonious domesticity a brood of splendid children. There is not one word in Plato

---

[4] *Smp.* 206B ff.

[5] Plato gets hold of this image in 206C (quoted above, first paragraph of Section IV), and keeps returning to it all through the sequel.

[6] Cf. the concluding lines in Dover (1966, 40).

to suggest that this relation could have been at any point for the man, or for the girl, the start of a *vita nuova*—the take-off for the ascent diagrammed in the escalated figure. Platonic—as also, later, courtly, and still later, romantic—love is meant to be a life-transforming miracle, a secular analogue to religious conversion, a magical change of perspective that opens up new, enchanted, horizons. For Plato, for whom the spirit comes to life in words, the first decisive sign of the mutation would be a sudden loosening of the tongue, a new-found flair for intellectual talk. When do we hear of this? When the man who is "pregnant in soul" encounters a "noble and well- born " soul housed in a beautiful body, he then "embraces the two in one, and in this man's company he straightway finds facility of speech about virtue and about what a good man ought to be and practice."[7] This is what starts him off on the ascent whose terminus is the face-to-face encounter with the Idea of Beauty. There, at the peak, the homosexual imagery is dropped. Communion with the Idea is consummated in conjugal intercourse which "will bring forth not images of beauty but realities" (212A). What started as a pederastic idyl ends up in transcendental marriage.

[7] *Smp.* 209A-C; cf. 210C1-3.

2

A Metaphysical Paradox*

(1965; MP)

THE paradox of which I wish to speak is the one Plato presents in its most arresting form in Book Ten of the *Republic:* the Form of a bed is the "real" bed;[1] the physical bed, the one made by the carpenter, is not "perfectly real,"[2] is "a shadowy sort of thing by comparison with reality."[3]

Western philosophy offers no better example, to my knowledge, of a pure metaphysical paradox. In any case it is the one I have lived with the longest. I was still an undergraduate when it first got under my skin—that is to say, my meta-philosophical skin, for I cannot pretend that I was tempted then or at any time thereafter to doubt that the bedmaker's bed was as real as anything could possibly be. What astounded, indeed worried, me was that someone else—not a crackpot, but a great philosopher—should have not only felt that temptation but yielded to it and in such a way as to claim for his conclusion demonstrative truth. I wondered how this could have happened. As the years passed that question was

* Presidential address delivered before the Sixty-Second Annual Meeting of the Eastern Division of the American Philosophical Association in New York City, December 27-29, 1965, published in the Association's *Proceedings* 39 (1966), pp. 5-19. (The original pagination is interpolated, in square brackets, in the text.)

[1] τὸ ὄν, 597A4; "that which bed *is*" (ὃ ἔστι κλίνη) 597A2.

[2] τελέως ὄν, 597A2.

[3] Cornford's translation of ἀμυδρόν τι, . . . πρὸς ἀλήθειαν, 597A10. Shorey has "dim adumbration" for ἀμυδρόν τι.

replaced by another: Just what did happen? For, as I came to see, if that second one could be properly answered, the first would answer itself. This is what I hope to show you in this address.

On the textual data I shall be very brief. That passage in Book Ten harks back to a discussion in Book Five (475E ff.) where Plato expounds, doubtless for the first time in his published works, what has since come to be called the notion of *grades* or *degrees* [5] of reality. These rubrics, of course, are not in his text, and I shall use them as mere names for what we do find there: the deliberate use in the comparative form of *to be* or *to be real* and their derivatives, asserting or implying that being or reality pertains in higher degree to the Ideas or Forms than to their sensible "namesakes." This may be done directly, as in the *Republic*, where Plato uses with great gusto expressions like "more real" and "less real."[4] But the same thing can—and is—done by the use of that striking expression, "the really real," for which there is no known precedent in earlier Greek prose. In so scrupulous a stylist we could have guessed that the apparent redundancy—which in one place (*Phaedrus* 247C) becomes even a triplication, "the really real reality"—is not inflated rhetoric, but is meant to put on "real" an added intensive force, matching that of the explicit comparatives in the *Republic*. And we do not need to guess. For already in that dialogue "really real"[5] is used as a variant for "perfectly real" in contrast to the "dimmer" reality of sensible things. Plato can also convey the same thing by just saying "real" or "being" with a special emphasis, as though italicizing. This too is clear in the *Republic*, for example, where it is said that the physical bed is not "the real" one (597A4-5). Applying these data to the dialogues we can plot the course of the grades of reality doctrine in Plato's works, finding that it extends as far out as the *Timaeus*,[6] and also the *Philebus*,[7] a dialogue which all scholars acknowledge as one of Plato's latest compositions. So the doctrine staked out in the *Republic* remained one of his permanent convictions, weathering the storm of perplexity and self-criticism recorded in the *Parmenides*.

What, then, does it mean? One may say that something is, or is not, real to express either of two quite different things. Consider:

1. Unicorns are not real.
2. These flowers are not real.

[4] 515D, 585B-E.
[5] κλίνης . . . ὄντως οὔσης, of the Form, Bed, 597D2.
[6] 27E-28A; 52C5-6.
[7] 58A2; 59D4.

In *1* the real is the existent in contrast to the fictitious, the imaginary. This can scarcely be its sense in *2*. In saying of *these* flowers—the ones I am pointing to—that they are not real, I presuppose their existence. This proves that neither would I have asserted their existence if I had [6] said that they are real. All I would then have said is that they *are* flowers, adding "real" or "really" to distinguish them not from figments of the imagination or of hallucinated perception but only from other objects which are also "real" enough in the first, existential, sense of the word but which are not *real flowers*, because they do not have those crucial properties things must have if they are to bear out, on investigation, the assertion that they *are* flowers, though they do have some of the *bona fide* properties of such objects—same size, shape, color—and are therefore liable to be mistaken for them.

This non-existential sense of *real* has always been in common use and is recognized as such in the Oxford English Dictionary, immediately after the existential: "that which is actually and truly such as its name implies; possessing the essential qualities denoted by its name; hence *genuine*." But modern philosophers have ignored it all too often. Kant's classical pronouncement on the hundred real thalers makes no allusion to a hundred counterfeit ones. G. E. Moore, so eager to learn philosophy from language, missed this sense of *real* in his celebrated essay, "The Conception of Reality" (1917).[8] And this has been fairly typical of the recent trend. With a few distinguished exceptions,[9] English-speaking philosophers of the twentieth century allowed the nonexistential sense of "real" to remain a sleeping dog in their discussions. It was after the Second World War, in Austin's Oxford lectures, that this sleeping dog woke up to let out some

[8] His polemic against Bradley in this essay (*Philosophical Studies* [London 1922]) is premised on the assumption that his adversary could not consistently assert the existence of something while denying its reality, unless he gave some esoteric sense ("some highly unusual and special sense," p. 208) to "real." That there might be a perfectly common and natural sense in which one could say of some existent that *it* is not real does not seem to have occurred to Moore in this essay.

[9] Chiefly among neo-Hegelians, as in Bradley who presupposes and often asserts the existence of the items—finite individuals, time, space, etc.—whose unreality he seeks to prove, and in Royce, whose discussion of "popular ways of expressing reality" identifies clearly the use of *real* to mean *genuine, true, what you can depend on* (1899, 54). Among the critics of the idealists the most valuable contribution to the nonexistential sense of *real* is made by C. I. Lewis who insists that it is "systematically ambiguous" (1929, 11), so that a real *F* may be an unreal *G*.

very frisky philosophical barks. In Lecture VII of *Sense* [7] *and Sensibilia*[10] this other sense of "real" came at least into its own. But what has all this to do with Plato?

If we were to come to him obsessed with the existential sense of "real" it would be a small miracle if we managed to avoid falling into the assumption that when he says that some things are "more real" than others he must mean that they *exist* more than others. This assumption has in fact been made by the overwhelming majority of modern interpreters, philologists and philosophers alike,[11] and continues to turn up in the latest studies, even those by analytically oriented philosophers, as in the philosophical commentary on the *Republic* by R. C. Cross and A. D. Woozley,[12] who start off their exposition of Plato's grades of reality doctrine by saying point-blank: "in what follows the expressions 'exists,' 'is real,' occur as synonyms" (p. 145). Now if this were true almost everything I want to say in elucidation of Plato' paradox would be off the track. I must, therefore, take time off to show why it cannot be true. I asserted as much in the paper I contributed to R. Bambrough's symposium, *New Essays on Plato and Aristotle* (London and New York, 1965). Here I must argue. I do so with due respect for scholars, some of them in this very audience, who think otherwise. If one disagrees with esteemed colleagues on a fundamental point, the least one can do is to give reasons.

The only one adduced by Cross and Woozley for saying that "exists" and "is real" are synonymous for Plato is that "[he] does not make this distinction" (*loc. cit.*). They mean, of course, that there is no statement or discussion or analysis of the distinction in the *Republic*. They could go farther and say that there is no such thing in any of Plato's writings, and they would still be right: I agree with G. E. L. Owen[13] against John Ackrill[14]

[10] Reconstructed from the Manuscript Notes by G. J. Warnock (Oxford, 1962).

[11] An honorable exception was pointed out to me by Professor Howard DeLong after the delivery of this address: R. G. Collingwood in *The Idea of Nature* (Oxford, 1945), pp. 55 ff.—a penetrating, if brief, interpretation of the Platonic theory, which seems to have been completely overlooked in the subsequent literature: no account is taken of it in N. R. Murphy (1951), W. D. Ross (1951), or in any other scholarly treatment of the topic thereafter to my knowledge.

[12] *Plato's Republic* (London, 1964).

[13] His view, adumbrated in his essay in the Bambrough symposium (1965, 71, note 1), is now expounded and defended in his contribution to *Plato*, I : *Metaphysics and Epistemology. A Collection of Critical Essays*, edited by G. Vlastos (New York, 1970).

[14] 1957, 271-87.

and others that the method of analysis [8] by paraphrase in the *Sophist*
which isolated perfectly the "is" of identity from its other uses was not
pushed far enough to sort out in the same way the "is" of existence from
that of predication. But what does that prove? Noam Chomsky has forcefully reminded us of that linguistic knowledge which consists in being
able to use rules of language even in the absence of any awareness of
them, to say nothing of any ability to state them.[15] This kind of knowledge
of the difference between the "is" in *Troy is famous* and *Troy is* (lame English,
but good Greek) even a Greek child would have had. The only question
then is whether Plato did or did not observe the difference—in the sense
of "observe" in which one observes a rule by following it—even if he
never stated or discussed it. This question admits of a conclusive answer.

Scattered throughout his prose, quite often in untechnical, even unphilosophical contexts, we come across expressions like these: "the really
good and noble man"; "the real sophist"; "a really divine place"; "he
had really stopped talking."[16] If we were to suppose that Plato was using
"real" as a synonym of "existing", what would we do with "really"?
"Existingly"? The fact that this is odd, indeed impossible, English would
not be of itself a good reason for holding that Plato could not have used
its Greek equivalent. Would anyone seriously suggest that Plato by un-
canny foresight coupled with exquisite consideration for posterity had
decided to use only such Greek as could be literally translated into impeccable English? The objection to "existingly" for Plato's "really" in the
examples is that, even if we did have the word, "existingly" would simply
not fit these contexts. That "really good and noble man" Plato is talking
about would be really good and noble even if he did not exist. If you
think this too subtle for Plato, consider his statement in the *Politicus*
(293E) which contrasts "the only correct constitution" with others which
"are not genuine, nor really real." Here it is certain that "really real"
cannot mean "existingly existing," since it cannot even mean "existing":
the constitutions which are said *not* to be really real are precisely the existing
ones—those which, to Plato's disgust, clutter up the political map of
Greece. In such a sentence as this Plato evidences knowing the non-
synonymy of "existing" and "real"—evidences it as conclusively as would
one who remarked, "she did not wear her cape when she sailed around the
cape," of knowing the difference between the tailor's cape and the geog-
rapher's. [9]

---

[15] *Aspects of the Theory of Syntax* (Cambridge, Mass., 1965), 8 *et passim*.
[16] *Republic* 396B; *Sophist*. 268D; *Phaedrus* 238C; *Prt*. 328D.

Now anyone who has such knowledge of the difference in "real" as between *unicorns are not real* and *these flowers are not real* would know in the same Chomskyan way that while the second "real" often admits of degrees the first one never does. If you are inquiring whether goatstags are or are not real, your language—Greek or English, it would be all the same in this respect—would not hand you a third possibility, that they might half-exist. To get any such alternative you would have to invent it; and the invention would be uphill work; it would go against linguistic gravity, as it were. Not so in the case of the non-existential use of "real." It is easy to miss this because in the case of this example, and in that of many others I could add to it (diamonds, teeth, ducks, etc.), the possibilities are also restricted to either "real" or "not real." But here it is nature, not language, that imposes the restriction. It is because the world is what it is that goatstags, diamonds, *et cetera*, are subject to that brutally exhaustive disjunction. There are other things whose nature is more accommodating. If twenty-four carat gold is indisputably "real" gold, and copper is as indisputably not, we can easily interpolate specimens by forming alloys. If the example seems farfetched, think of the ones I cited from Plato a moment ago. Take that "really good and noble man." Between him and the cunning villain who simulates his sterling qualities there are all sorts of cases of ambiguous or speckled virtue where, knowing the facts, we would still find it hard to decide whether a man is or is not good and noble, and might wind up saying, "he is and he isn't." And this is generally true wherever the qualifying predicate—the F in "a real F" or "really F"—is instantiable more or less adequately, as happens so conspicuously in those Fs which are of special interest to Plato: value-predicates, *good, beautiful, just, pious,* and so forth. In all these cases language, instead of repelling the intermediate between the real and the not real, has a built-in provision for it, and a typical symptom of it is our ability to say, for example, "he is not really educated," without implying that he is *not* educated.

If we now look at Plato's behavior—his linguistic behavior—in that passage in the *Republic* (end of Book Five) where he unveils the grades of reality doctrine, we will see that it bears all the earmarks of an extension of the sense of "real" I have just been discussing. The thesis that sensibles "are and are not"—which, on first hearing, sounds ominously as though it meant "exist and do not exist"—turns out, the moment Plato starts arguing for it,[17] to be an ellipsis for "are and are not [10] F," the first

[17] 479A5 ff.; note especially 479B9-10.

three values of F in his argument being *beautiful, just, pious,* that is to say, predicates of that very kind in which our experience so often gives us cause to fall in with the *"F and not F"* verdict on the status of actual cases. To get the same result from the existential "real" which, as his language-sense informs him, rules out as monstrosity a *tertium quid* between existence and non-existence, he would have had to fight his native language all the way, and some sign of the combat would have shown up in the text. Moreover, in that case the thesis would have been unwelcome to him. Plato does not believe that while the Form does exist, its sensible instances do and do not. In the *Timaeus* (52A) he declares "that there are first, the unchanging Form . . . ; second, its namesake and like, sensible, generated, ever changing, . . . ; third, Space. . . ." In full view of the greater reality of the Form, and the lesser reality of the other two members of the trio, Plato says that all three *exist,* and says it again without qualification a few lines later (52D2-4). Where the "is" is clearly existential, it is applied distributively to each, and conjunctively to all, grades of reality. So when the sensible instance is said to be less real than its Form, this is not said to ambiguate its existence, but on the contrary to disambiguate the sort of existence it has. By the same token the Form is said to be "really real" not to assert, but to categorize, its existence—to tell us what kind of existence *it* has.

So this is why I must reject the view that when Plato says "more real" he means "more existent." What then is there left for him to mean? More than I could hope to explore exhaustively in this address. Here I shall be content to bring out what is, at any rate, a part of what he means[18] —the part that can be plotted by tracking down the answer to the following question: What could his Forms or Ideas have in common with real gold, real coffee, real courage, real beauty, in contrast to debased gold, adulterated coffee, feeble or feigned courage, coarse, brittle, or superficial beauty? Two things, I suggest: In the first place, in all of these examples, the real F would be the *cognitively reliable F.* Thus, if you want to investigate the nature of gold, coffee, courage, beauty, you must look to the genuine article; the other kind will trick you sooner or later, for along with some F-properties, it has also, perhaps cunningly concealed, some not-F properties, and if you were to [11] take the latter for the former your mistake would be disastrous. In the second place, the real F would be the *reliably*

---

[18] A wholly distinct, though related, part of the meaning, expressed by Plato's phrase "being in itself" in contrast to "being in another" (cf. *Symposium,* 211A8-B1; *Republic,* 516B4-5; *Phaedrus,* 247E1; *Timaeus,* 52C-D1), will fall outside the present investigation.

valuable one, the kind of thing that brings fully and durably the satisfaction an *F*-thing can be counted on to yield, instead of a spurious or, at best, an inferior satisfaction, falling far short of the one you are after, or would be, if you had known the real *F*. Plato, I submit, has both of these things in mind when he speaks of his Form as "really real."

The first answers strictly to their epistemological function. On this I can be very brief, for I have expounded it at length and argued for it in the paper to which I referred above, and there would be no point in repeating myself here.[19] Here then is the gist of it: The key to it is Plato's conviction that the Forms are the objects of knowledge *par excellence*. They are incomparably the most rewarding to the mind of all the things to which it can turn in its search for truth, for their natures are logically perspicuous, or can be made so with adequate training in dialectic, and all their properties follow from their natures in conjunction with the natures of other similarly luminous and stable objects. Their physical instances are, by contrast, intellectually opaque and shifty. They do not display their intelligible structure on their sensible surface. And when we try to dig it out of them by inference and extrapolation we cannot be sure that the cluster of properties any one of them happens to have here and now it will still have later on or that other things, to all appearance similar, will have the same set of properties now or later. A thing which is *F* at one time, or in one way, or in one relation, or from one point of view, will be all too often not-*F* at another time, in another way, *et cetera*. So, generalizing with that reckless audacity characteristic of Greek philosophy at its best as at its worst, Plato infers that this is true of all sensible *F*s. All of them will always be so infected, hence none of them could ever be a *real F*, and if we take any of them to be such, we will be sure to be deceived. The Form, conversely, will never deceive, for it is by hypothesis invariantly and wholly the special *F* it is its nature to be. It is, therefore, the real *F*, the genuine one, which can be trusted absolutely in our pursuit of knowledge.

But the Forms have another function to which I barely alluded in the published paper. This I must now try to make clear. We get an inkling of it when we see the philosopher introduced in the *Republic* (474C ff.) not just as a Formknower, but as a Formlover, in dramatic contrast to sightlovers, soundlovers, and the like. And so he remains throughout the rest of the *Republic*. At first one is not sure how much [12] to make of this. Could it not be that he is expected to love the Forms simply as objects of knowledge? Certainly, some ardent inquirers do grow fond of their peculiar

[19] See *DR*, pp. 56 ff., below.

subject-matter—some biologists of their rats and hamsters, some physicists of their particles, subparticles, and antiparticles. But merely to make these similes explicit is to see at once how flat they fall by comparison with the depth of feeling Plato has for the Ideas. Where is the difference? Is it just that the kind of knowledge he expects them to yield is in so many cases knowledge of value? This is indeed true, but still not enough. Aesthetic theory, for example, so far as it succeeds in being knowledge, would be for Plato knowledge of the Form of beauty. If we could come to know this Idea, as Plato thinks we can, we would be assured of a remarkable science of aesthetics—deductively articulated, demonstrative in its certainty, unrestrictedly general in its scope. One would expect Plato to be elated at the prospect of such an accomplishment and to crow over it whenever he had the chance to speak of the philosopher as a student of the Idea of Beauty. Why doesn't he then in the *Republic*, the *Symposium*, or the *Phaedrus*? It is because this aspect of the Idea, important as it is, is overshadowed in these dialogues by another. Beauty is here above all the lure for love, the Idea of Beauty being itself the most alluring thing there is, the one most worth loving. A beautiful body, a beautiful mind, a beautiful work of artistic creation, political contrivance, or scientific insight—each of these will satisfy for a time, and some of them will satisfy continuingly, but none will satisfy completely. They are cursed by their particularity. In the very act of giving one kind of beauty, they deny another. And so this Platonic lover, whose appetite for beauty is not only voracious but omnivorous, finds always a residue of frustration in their presence. There is an overtone of restlessness in his enjoyment of them which makes him keep moving from one to another. Only when he reaches that "wonderful sort of Beauty" that waits for him at the peak of his ascent in the *Symposium* (210E) is his restlessness stilled. Here at last he has found "real" Beauty.

The experience of which and from which Plato speaks here and in kindred passages which depict the vision of the elite Forms—Beauty, Goodness, Justice, Temperance, Holiness, Knowledge—has had little attention in English-speaking philosophical commentaries in recent years. With rare exceptions, their authors seem as embarrassed by these passages as was my mother by certain indelicate lines in the Old Testament stories she read us, skipping when she reached those lines, or rushing through them in a thin, dry voice. For serious efforts to see what can be made of this part of Plato's work we would have to go back [13] to older books like Santayana's *Platonism and the Spiritual Life*, Cornford's early work, *From Religion to Philosophy*, or still earlier, Walter Pater's *Plato and Platonism*.

But in these works sound insights are marred by license of interpretation, or inaccurate scholarship, or sentimentality, or all three. The job has to be done all over again and from the bottom up, as it surely must if we are to understand Plato. Needless to say, I am not volunteering to do it now. The best I can do here is to refer you to certain of Plato's own statements which would be fundamental data for such an inquiry regardless of what conclusions were drawn from it. What I shall make of their significance will have to speak for itself, since I shall be unable to argue for it.

For the felicity of this experience Plato makes one of the most astounding claims that any philosopher has ever made for anything. He does this in Book Nine of the *Republic* (582A ff.) when winding up his great argument that the good man at fortune's worst will still be happier than the bad one at fortune's best. He implies that as a source of happiness this experience will excel all others, will indeed outdo all others put together. A man who had but this and what would come to him directly from it, even if he had nothing else besides, would still be happier than another who, lacking this, had everything else his heart could wish for. What sort of experience could it be that so floods Plato's soul with bliss? An aesthetic experience it would have to be, for one thing, if it sates his thirst for Beauty. It must be also intellectual, since it marks a climactic point in the pursuit of knowledge. At the same time it is a profoundly moral or, more exactly, moralizing experience. It is the sort of experience that makes men moral. In one passage in the *Republic* the philosopher is pictured as gazing daily at the Forms, which are "orderly and ever constant, neither wronging, nor being wronged by, one another, but abide in harmony and the rule of reason" and, as he does so, finds that his character takes on the impress of theirs. "Or do you think," asks Socrates, "it would be possible not to imitate that with which one consorts in love?" "Impossible," says Glaucon, and Socrates concludes that "the philosopher, consorting with the divine and harmonious, will himself become as harmonious and divine as any man may" (500C2-D1). You notice that Plato passes here within a single sentence and without any transitional marker from the moral to the religious dimension. And this he does time and time again. The religion to which he alludes in such contexts is not that blend of high-order patriotic entertainment and white magic which makes up so much of the public cult of the city-state, but that radically different kind of piety, intense, fervent, and other-worldly, [14] fostered by the mystic rites, Bacchic or Eleusinian, the only kind that touched Plato personally and moved him deeply. He sees vision of Form as an analogue of this kind of piety. In one of his most elevated passages he speaks of vision of Form as "celebration of perfect mysteries" (*Phaedrus* 249C). He does this even in low-temperature discourse, as in the *Phaedo* (69CD), where he remarks that the true *Bakchos*—the mystic initiate at the moment at which he feels god-possessed, one with his god—is he "who has philosophized rightly." In this sublimated rite Plato puts Form in place of God. Not only does he call the Forms "divine," but distinctly implies that they are more divine than the gods. If the latter seems preposterous, we need only recall those attributes of divinity—eternity, perfection not flawed by passion or risked in action—of which the gods of cult and myth were more caricatures than exemplars. It is, therefore, understandable that one who exalted these attributes above all others should have found in the Forms of his philosophy, and only there, entities fully worthy of his adoration and felt his vision of them as a sacred communion. Thus in one and the same experience Plato finds happiness, beauty, knowledge, moral sustenance and regeneration, and a mytical sense of kinship with eternal perfection. The Forms then are for him not only guideposts to their best instances in common experience, but are themselves the focal points of a most uncommon experience which he discovered for himself and found incomparably more satisfying than any other. The Forms are "more real" than their instances in that sense as well.

With this account before us, let us take stock of its results. It has taken the grades of reality theory as an implied analogy or, more precisely, as a bundle of implied analogies, telling us that if we think of things which are "real" because they are genuine, true, pure, in contrast with those which are not, we will have a clue to the relation of the Platonic Form to its mundane instances. Now there are many ways in which things can have, or fail to have, this kind of "reality." I offered you a range of examples: real gold, real courage, and the like. These could be easily extended to include, for instance, the real Socrates in contrast to a young admirer who parrots his dialectic and even apes his grimaces, or to the real crown, work of a master silversmith, copied by lesser craftsmen, who cannot create, and only imitate. That Plato himself should not have fastened the analogy to any one example or set of examples is significant. He doubtless needs the freedom of maneuver this ellipsis permits him. Mindful of this proviso, we may nevertheless seize on a single example to bring out the most important of the considerations I have put before you—two major ways in which [15] we may still think of the "real" once we have laid aside the existential sense of this term which, I have argued, is irrelevant to Plato's grades of reality theory, since in this theory to be real in any given degree is to *exist with just that degree of reality*. Suppose Plato had said:

The Form, F, is to sensible Fs as is real gold to gold alloyed with baser metals. My major contention has been that this ostensibly single analogy is in fact two quite different ones, either of which pure gold would ex-emplify, depending on whether we think of gold as something to *know* or something to *covet:*

First analogy: Just as one who sought to investigate the nature of gold should remember that the essential properties of this metal are those of pure gold, *so* if we want to know the nature of anything, we must con-centrate our study on its Form.

Second analogy: Just as one who bought gold at the bullion price, anxious to increase his assets, should insist on gold of standard purity, *so* if what we are after is the most valuable experience that life can offer, we must seek vision of Form.

These two analogies are the vehicles of two entirely distinct, though not unrelated, doctrines, generating two different paradoxes:

The first analogy is the vehicle of a purely epistemological doctrine— one we could have had even if Plato had not been an all-around meta-physician, but only an epistemologist, and his single philosophical dis-covery had been limited to the availability of *a priori* knowledge. If in the flush of that one discovery he had but gone on to do what we know he did in his middle dialogues—restrict knowledge to the *a priori*—he would have generated epistemological paradoxes galore, all of which he could have stated *via* the grades of reality doctrine. In modern philosophy, more plausible and at times quite fashionable theories of knowledge have armed their exponents with paradoxes which Plato could have repeated verbatim: I do not *know* this is my hand, or that I even have a hand; I do not *know* this is a table, that is a bed. The paradox becomes perhaps more vivid, but is no more startling in its implications, if locked into Platonic grades of reality language: The real bed, object of knowledge, is not the car-penter's product, object of mere opinion. It is the Form, *Bed.*

The other analogy is the vehicle of a still more hazardous philosophical venture, the construction of a metaphysical system, one of those very rare ones in secular Western philosophy which are grounded in mystical experience. I use this last term advisedly, for I refuse to think of mysticism as something confined to sporadic states of ecstatic awareness. The methodological propriety of that assumption is dubious [16] for mystical consciousness at focal intensity admits of many varieties, ranging, for example, from that qualityless, undifferentiated, unity achieved in Oriental and Western mysticism by emptying consciousness of every possible content, to Proust's total recall of a past sensation, where consciousness of vivid particularity, so far from being reduced to zero, seems heightened to the *n*th degree. In this respect Platonic vision of Form differs as much from Plotinian union with a One which transcends form or even being, as from Proustian resurrection of a fragment of one's perceptual past in the immediate present. Its closest affinities are with Spinoza's *amor intellectualis Dei*, where also beatitude is achieved in a miraculous junction of love, knowledge, moral resolve, and spiritual exaltation. But even this parallel is far from perfect. Plato's mystical experience at dead center, carefully examined, will reveal at least as many differences from Spinoza's as similarities with it. To find what Plato shares more fully with him, though no more with him than with other mystics, we should look for it in the foreground and aftermath of ecstatic consciousness. The foreground is a disillusionment with those things whose "lesser reality" every mystic would acknowledge with Plato, convinced that he can never find in them ultimate security and fulfilment. If he places such trust in things which can be seen and touched, the mystic feels, he becomes their slave, exposing himself to the torment of unsatisfied desire and of those vicissitudes or "fluctuations of the mind," as Spinoza called them, states of suspense and anxiety bordering at times on terror. He also becomes their dupe. For when he does succeed in reaching the very ones that most enthralled him, he finds the fascination they produced in absence answers to nothing in their presence; the reality he had counted on has eluded him, and what he has finally possessed is shadow, smoke, vanity, and vexation of spirit. Now whatever it be that happens inside the mystical state, we are left in no doubt as to what comes out of it. A man who has felt bound, incarcerated, buffeted, fooled, exiled, in the world of sense—the metaphors are Plato's, but many other mystics have used the same or equivalent ones— finds a liberation and peace which he expresses typically, as Walter Stace has reminded us,[20] in terms of the contrast of time with eternity. Here time without eternity represents the state of bondage; eternity, the blessedness of release; time under the aspect of eternity, regeneration. In vision of Form Plato discovers—one might almost say, invents—his own personal bridge from [17] the first to the third *via* the second. How natural then for him to say that the eternal things, the Forms, are the "really real" ones. In seeing them a creature of time touches eternity, and the contact makes it possible for him to master time, to live in it as though not of it. If he had been a poet—or, more exactly, if he had been only a poet—he would

[20] *Time and Eternity* (Princeton, 1952). I must also record my debt to the extremely suggestive discussion of "reality" in chapter 7 of this book.

have made of this a lyrical or epic theme. Being a metaphysician he uses it rather as the clue for a redescription of reality, tracing out a pattern, absolutely new in Greek thought, where eternity is incorporeal Form, and the corporeal world has meaning and value so far as it copies, or can be made to copy, Form, and where time itself is redeemed as the image of eternity.[21] This re-structuring of what there is on the scaffolding of what is more and less real is one of Plato's great achievements, perhaps his greatest.

To be great an achievement need not be flawless. I have no wish to disguise the flaws in Plato's. All of them can be traced to defective analysis: *ontological* analysis, which would have explained the difference between the sense of "real" that fits the comparatives of his theory from the existential one which does not; *semantic* analysis, which would have noted that in the required sense—that of "real" in "a real F"—"real" is syncategorematic and, therefore, relativized to the predicate which completes its sense; *logical* analysis, which would have spotted an error that has had much, perhaps too much, attention in recent controversy under the none too happy rubric of "self-predication"; *methodological* analysis, which would have sorted out clearly within the grades of reality theory its epistemological from its metaphysical content and—what is still more important —propounded the latter as a personal vision for which demonstrative certainty cannot be claimed.

If Plato had understood his own theory better in these and other ways, he might have saved his readers some unprofitable misinterpretations and spared himself some quite gratuitous errors. For instance, he could have shown us that his Forms are not meant to be "more real" in every possible way. Thus, would he not have been the first to agree that, if what we want is a good night's sleep, the ordinary, bedroom variety, bed is considerably more real? Again, the ends of his epistemology are not advanced by the assumption that in general the Form for F is itself F. The Form, *Circle*, would not be a more reliable object of knowledge if it were circular, nor the Form, *Beauty*, if it were beautiful. Only when Forms assume their other role, as objects of value, and [18] of the kind of value Plato claimed for them, would the self-characterization of Forms like Beauty have any point whatever. The Form, *Beauty*, would indeed have to be exceedingly beautiful to hold its place at the terminus of the lover's quest, and the Forms, *Justice* and *Temperance*, would have to be just and temperate if they are to have moral attributes that rub off on their con-

[21] *Timaeus*, 37D ff.

templators. But not even here would the fault be irreparable. Plato could have reclaimed a metaphorical sense for these literally senseless predications.

The gravest flaw in the theory, one which could not be mended without altering radically Plato's conception of metaphysics and of morality and politics as well, issues from his imperfect understanding of that very experience which meant more to him than any other—vision of Form. For if he had understood it as deeply as he felt it, how could he have thought of it as certifying cognitive and even political infallibility? What troubled me about Plato's metaphysical paradox when I first came across it was his confidence that he could prove it. Now that, understanding his paradox better, I admire it all the more, I think that I was right to be troubled. The mystic is the last person in the world who can afford to be an authoritarian. [19]

3

Degrees of Reality
in Plato*

(1965; DR)

FROM the Greek "is"(ἐστί) we get directly the participle ὄν, the noun, οὐσία, and the adverb, ὄντως. From the English "is" all we can get directly is the participle, *being*, but no noun or adverb. We can't say "beingness" or "beingly," and have to shift to "reality" and "really." But when we do this we lose a verb from the same stem: we can't say, "Socrates reals a man" or "Socrates reals wise," unless we want to start one of those overstrenuous linguistic games, like Hegelese or Heideggerese. If we want to talk English, we will have to break up the consanguineous Greek quartet into two etymologically unrelated groups, picking our verbs from the first, our noun and adverb (and also the exceptionally useful adjective, "real") from the second. This is no great hardship. But it makes less than obvious what leaps to the eye in the Greek: that "real" and "reality" are simply the adjectival and nominal forms of "to be," and that "is" in turn represents the verbal form of "real" and "reality."

Plato does not speak of "grades" or "degrees" of reality. He says such things as these: The Form is "completely" real,[1] or "purely" real,[2] or

---

* First published in *New Essays in Plato and Aristotle*, edited by R. Bambrough (1965), pp. 1–19. The original pagination appears here in square brackets.

[1] παντελῶς ὄν R. 477A.

[2] τοῦ εἰλικρινῶς ὄντος, R. 477A, 478D, 479D. Cf. the allied use of εἰλικρινές (followed by καθαρόν, ἄμεικτον) in *Symp.* 211E. Here it is used as a modifier not of ὄν, but of a specific Form, αὐτὸ τὸ καλόν in order to contrast that Form with its instances. And cf. p. 62, n. 19 below.

"perfectly" real,[3] or "really" real,[4] it is "more [1] real"[5] than its sensible instances, which are said to "fall between the purely real and the wholly unreal" (477A), because their state is such that "they both are and are not" (477A–478D). I want to ask three questions: First, what is the sense of "real" and "reality" in these statements? Second, why does Plato think the Forms are "more real" in this sense than are their sensible instances?[6] Third, what are the philosophical merits and demerits of this doctrine?

I

"True" is a fairly common meaning of "real" in spoken and written Greek. Thus Plato will say, "to speak (or, think) the real" for "to speak (or, think) the truth."[7] Moreover, in Greek, as in English, the predicate, "true," applying primarily to propositions, may also apply, derivatively, to things described by propositions—to objects, persons, stuffs, states, processes, dispositions, and the like.[8] In either language one can speak of "a true friend," "true gold," "true courage," and so forth. In all such cases "real" [2] can be substituted for "true" with little change of sense. We speak of "a real friend," "real gold," and the like. When we do this we think of things or persons as having those very properties in virtue of which they can be truly so described: e.g., of Jones as sympathetic, responsive, considerate, loyal, and whatever else we expect of a man whom we would call "a friend" when weighing our words, using them strictly and with a full

[3] τελέως ὄν, R. 597A.

[4] κλίνης ὄντως οὔσης: the Form, Bed, R. 597D. Cf. τὸ ὂν ὄντως (Phil. 59D) and οὐσία ὄντως οὖσα (Phdr. 247C) of the Forms. The world of becoming is ὄντως οὐδέποτε ὄν,   Ti. 28A.

[5] μᾶλλον ὄντα R. 515D. This is said of the figurines in the Cave which are to their shadows on the wall as are the Forms to their sensible instances. In R. 585D the soul, nourished ("filled") by the Forms, is said to be τὸ τῶν μᾶλλον ὄντων πληρούμενον.

[6] I regret that limitations of space make it impossible for me to deal with other recent discussions, some of which would not even agree with my way of posing the question: Hardie (1936, 27 ff.); Moreau (1939, Chap. 7); Field (1949, Chaps 2 and 3); Murphy (1951, Chap. 6 and 197 ff. in Chap. 9); Bröcker (1951, 415 ff.); Gosling (1960, 116 ff.); Allen (1961, 325 ff) But my greatest debt is to Professor G. E. L. Owen, whose views on this topic I came to know from one of his unpublished MSS, and from discussion with him in Oxford in 1960.

[7] E.g., R. 389C; the expressions τὰ ὄντα λέγειν, τἀληθῆ λέγειν, are used synonymously. Cf. Tht. 179C, 199A.

[8] For the Greek see LSJ, s.v. ἀληθής, II; ἀληθινός, I (2).

view of the facts. Grammar itself would make this obvious if we had in English, as in Greek, a copula which is a verbal cognate of "real." For we would then be saying that Jones is a "real" friend because he "reals" (= is) *sympathetic, responsive*, etc.; i.e., because he has those attributes in virtue of which sentences applying these predicates to him are true and would be found to be true if put to the test. This implicit reference to reliable truth is all that saves "real" from redundancy when used in this sense. There would be no point in saying that Jones is a "real" friend, as distinct from just saying that he is a friend, unless we were tacitly contrasting him with people who talk and act like friends, and for a time pass for friends, but then turn out to be fakes, i.e., unless we were expressing the conviction that Jones has "proved" a friend, or would "prove" one under trial.[9]

What of "more real"? We would have no use for this expression if the logic of all predicates were like that of "diamond," which divides all possible candidates for the description into just two classes, those which are ("real") diamonds, and those which are not, with no intermediate category in between: the finest imitation diamond in the Fifth Avenue jewelry shop is no more of a real diamond than is the cheapest fake in Woolworth's. But in a wide variety of predicates we do want to recognize intermediate cases between the "real" and "not real" thing of that kind. A man may not be all one expects from a *friend* or from a *scientist* or a *poet*, yet measure up so much better to these descriptions than would any number of others that we would have no hesitation in saying that he is more of a real friend,[10] or scientist, or poet, [3] than they Or, to take a very different case: We see a painting, executed only partly by Rubens, the rest of the work done by pupils in his studio. Is this a "real" Rubens? It is, and it is not. It is more of one, certainly, than is an outright fake. But it is much less of one than would be a Rubens whose every brush-stroke came from the master's hand. The latter—the "real Rubens"—is what we would use as our authoritative source of knowledge of what "a Rubens" is.

When we try out this sense of "real" and "more real" in Plato we find uses that approach it closely. A fine example is his first use of "more real": μᾶλλον ὄντα[11] in *Republic* 515D. The passage is in the Allegory of the Cave.

[9] *X* "proving *himself*" an *F*, when what is "proved" is a set of propositions asserting him to be an *F*, parallels the linguistic maneuver which allows us to say that he is a "true" *F*, when what we mean is that the relevant propositions are true.

[10] "A more real friend" would not be possible English. I cannot think of any unstrained example of "*x* is a more real *F* than is *y*" in common speech.

[11] The first occurrence of μᾶλλον with a participle of the verb *to be* in surviving Greek philosophical prose.

The man who had lived facing away from the light has just turned around to catch with dazzled eyes his first uncertain glimpse of the figures on the parapet that cast the shadows he had been taking for the "real" things his whole life long:

> What do you suppose would be his answer if we were to tell him that he had seen nothing but trash heretofore, but that now, because he is[12] somewhat closer to reality and has turned towards more real things, he sees more correctly? And if we were to point to each of these passing objects [the figures] and make him answer the question, "What is it?", don't you suppose he would be puzzled and count the things he had been seeing heretofore more true (ἀληθέστερα) than the ones pointed out to him now? (515D)

Suppose it were the statuette of a horse that he is looking at just now. In the most obvious sense of "real" this is no more of a "real horse" than are its silhouettes: no more than they is it a horse one needs to feed, can ride to town, and the like. But this sense of "real" has been screened out in the Allegory. Chained to his place, immobilized totally (he cannot even move his head), he has been drained of every mundane interest. The only thing left for him to be is *homo cognoscens*. The things he calls "horses" he scans with pure intellectual curiosity, intent on one thing only: to find out what he can, just by looking, in answer to the "What is it?"[13] [4] question. It is for just this purpose that he is now "somewhat closer to reality and has turned towards more real things": looking at the figure of a horse before him "he sees more correctly" what a horse *is*.[14] The man who made it, let us suppose, was a fine craftsman, like one of those who cut the frieze of the Parthenon; his art-work is a boon to the mind as much as to the eye, a storehouse of anatomically true information about the structure of a horse's body.[15] It

---

[12] The copula, not in the text, "is easily supplied" (Adam *ad loc.*).

[13] The question which continues to epitomize the quest for knowledge in the *Phaedo* (75D, 78D) and the *Republic* (490B, 532A-B, 533B) as it did in the earlier Socratic dialogues.

[14] The logical connection between the "more real" and that which enables one to "see more correctly" is built into the construction of Plato's sentence. The full sense I take to be: because the figure is more of a real *F* than the shadow, one sees more correctly the nature of *F* when looking at ("turned towards") the figure.

[15] All this only as an aid to the exposition. Without blowing up the Allegory in this way we could still count on a figure that yields *some* knowledge in excess of what can be got out of its shadows. So much even a third-rate artist would put into his horse.

will be a revelation to our prisoner once he gets used to the light and learns how to read three-dimensional signs. Thus this "horse" is "more real" than its shadows in the very same sense in which it is "more true" and "more clear":[16] it yields a better disclosure of what a horse is. Even so, it is not nearly as adequate for this purpose as the horse he will encounter when he climbs out of the Cave into the world above—the model from which the craftsman got his knowledge of horses, the most authoritative source the visible world can offer of true answers to the question, "What is a horse?" This is what symbolizes in the Allegory "the *F* itself,"[17] the Form.

This is the sense in which the Form of the Bed in *R.* X (597A, D) is the "really real" or "perfectly real" Bed. This we would know even if we had not been given earlier the Cave to tell us how to take these startling expressions. Plato explains himself all over again here, saying that the bed-maker's product is "something dark [ἀμυδρόν τι] by comparison with the truth [πρὸς ἀλήθειαν; i.e., by comparison with the 'true' Bed]"—"dark" to the mind when [5] it seeks light on the question, "What are those properties which make up the essence of *Bed?*"[18] The same point is made by another tale, the one compressed into the word "pure" as applied to the Forms already in the *Phaedo*,[19] then used again in the *Symposium*, and

[16] For "true" see, in addition to ἀληθέστερα at 511D6 (paralleling μᾶλλον ὄντα at D3), τὸ ἀληθές at 515C2, and the analogous use of ἀληθῶν at 516A3. Σαφέστερα at 515E4 parallels ἀληθέστερα just before; both are carry-overs from the Line: the "truer" the objects, the "clearer" their apprehension, 509D-510A and 511E.

[17] Cf. αὐτὰ τὰ ζῶα, αὐτὰ ἄστρα, αὐτὸν τὸν ἥλιον, 532A3-5, where the intensive pronoun is a forceful reminder of one of the standard expressions for the Forms which had been used not long before our passage (507B, αὐτὸ καλόν, αὐτὸ ἀγαθόν).

[18] The Form *per contra* is σαφές (cf. n. 16 above), the opposite of ἀμυδρόν (cf. *Soph.* 250E). The lucidity of the Form—its cognitive visibility, as it were—was already brought out in the Simile of the Sun: the intelligible world is the one "where truth and reality shine forth [καταλάμπει]," while the sensible world is "mixed with darkness" (508D). The same imagery in the Cave, especially at 518C: the release from the Cave is a "turning from darkness to the light" and reaches, at its height, "the brightest of realities [τοῦ ὄντος τὸ φανότατον]," the Form of the Good.

[19] When freed from the body we shall come to know "all of them [*sc.* the Forms] in their purity (αὐτῶν πᾶν τὸ εἰλικρινές), which is, I take it, the truth [τὸ ἀληθές]," 67B; cf. 66A. Καθαρόν is also used to the same effect (*Phdo* 67B; *Smp.* 211E; *R.* 585B; *Phlb.* 59C); so too ἄμεικτον (*Smp.* 211E, *Phlb.* 59C) and μονοειδές (*Phdo* 78D, *Smp.* 211B, E).

occurring three times in adverbial form in *R.* V as a variant for the "perfectly" or "completely" real.[20] As is clear in this latter passage—the first and also the fullest exposition of degrees of reality—the intended contrast is between the Form, *F*, and instances of it which are reckoned less "pure" *F*'s than it, because they are not exclusively *F*, but are *F* and not-*F*:[21] their *F* nature is adulterated by contrary characters, so that we could only get a confused[22] and uncertain idea of what it is to be *F*, one that would be subject to constant fluctuations[23] as we encountered [6] instances of *F* that turned out to be different in one or more respects from those on which we based our previous conception of it.

Here, then, is one sense of "real": that which is cognitively dependable, undeceiving. And since this will give me more than enough to explore in this paper, I shall be content to work with this alone, and shall accordingly speak of it for convenience as "the" sense of "real" for Plato. But I am not suggesting that this is the only sense of "real" for him.[24] On the contrary, I am certain that he crosses this sense with a very different one which becomes most prominent when he thinks of the "really real" things, the

[20] See p. 59, n. 3, above.

[21] The warrant for expanding the "is and is not" of 477A–479D into "is and is not *F*" is 479C3–4 taken in conjunction with 479B9–10: "Then *is* each of the many, rather than *is not*, whatever one asserts that it is (*sc.* big or small, heavy or light, etc.)?" This shows what has to be supplied when the "is and is not" formula is used without this supplement (e.g., immediately after, at C4; or, by the same token, in the earlier occurrences of the formula, 477A, 478DE).

[22] Cf. *Phlb.* 53AB: the "truest" white is the "purest" (τὸ μάλιστ' εἰλικρινές), the one least adulterated by admixture (ἀκρατέστατον) with any other color. Cf. also *R.* 523C ff.: the reason why sight and the other senses are defective in their disclosures (ἐνδεῶς δηλοῦσιν 523E) of such things as largeness, smallness, thickness, thinness, softness, hardness, etc. (523E) is that, in their sensible presentations, each of these is "confused" with its opposite: for "clearness" (σαφήνεια) in their apprehension we must resort to νόησις which is able to see them "not confused but distinguished" (οὐ συγκεχυμένα ἀλλὰ διωρισμένα) or "separated out" (κεχωρισμένον), 524C.

[23] κυλινδεῖται, 479D4; ἐν πολλοῖς καὶ παντοίως ἴσχουσιν πλανώμενοι, 484B6.

[24] This disclaimer has important consequences for the interpretation of "the" degrees-of-reality theory offered in sections II and III below. The fact is that Plato has in effect *two* (overlapping) theories, the second being a construct on the second sense of "real" which I shall mention directly. This second theory I *ignore completely* in this paper. I could not even begin to explain it properly within my space-budget.

Forms, as objects of mystical experience.[25] This calls for a separate investigation, whose results I cannot anticipate here, except to say that in this other sense of "real" the word functions as a value-predicate,[26] but one that transcends the usual specifications of value, moral, aesthetic, and religious; it connotes more than goodness, beauty, or holiness, or even than all three of them in conjunction. I will do nothing to placate those readers who will be outraged at the suggestion that Plato should use "real" in his degrees-of-reality doctrine in two senses as different as these. All I can say to them is that I am only reporting the facts as I see them; and that the facts of Plato's usage compel me to recognize the occurrence of the word in this other sense which differs demonstrably from that of "cognitively reliable." For example: while all Forms are "real" in the cognitive sense, not all could be "real" in the evaluative sense: not the Forms, Injustice, Ugliness, [7] Evil, for instance.[27] These are mentioned as *bona fide* Forms on a level with Justice, Beauty, and Goodness. Cognitively they must be on a par with the rest, members in good standing of that highest realm of intelligible Being which is made up of all, and only, Forms. Yet obviously it is not of such Forms as these that Plato thinks when he speaks of the vision of Form as "the most blessed of all mystic initiations,"[28] and of the Forms themselves as "unblemished, whole, tremorless, blessed apparitions" (*Phdr.* 250C), divine, and more so than traditional gods.[29] Plato's thought at this point is not wholly free from an incoherence[30] which we could only smooth out of the record by misrepresenting our data. But this is not the place to pursue this theme. I mention it only to warn the reader of complications I am wilfully ignoring in order to concentrate on the questions that bear more directly on the cognitive sense of "real" to which I am devoting this paper.

[25] As, e.g., at *R.* 490B, 500C; *Phdr.* 247C ff.

[26] So far as things fail to be real they are "trash" (cf. φλυαρίας, *R.* 515D) unworthy of "serious concern" (σπουδάζειν), *R.* 599AB. For the connection between worthlessness and not-being note the common use of οὐδενία (literally "nothingness") to *mean* worthlessness (twice in untechnical contexts in Plato: *Phdr.* 235A, τῆς ἐμῆς οὐδενίας; *Tht.* 176C, οὐδενία τε καὶ ἀνανδρία.) (For this use of "being" by the mystics, cf. Meister Eckhart: "a stone, to the extent that it has being, would be better than even God and the Godhead without being," R. B. Blakeney, *Meister Eckhart, a Modern Translation*, New York, 1941, p. 172).

[27] Cited without hesitations or apologies at *R.* 475E, 476.

[28] *Phdr.* 250BC. Cf. *Phdo* 69CD.

[29] By implication at *Phdr.* 249C6 (Burnet's text).

[30] Though mitigated by the fact that the bad Forms would still be good from one point of view: they would satisfy the cognitive interest.

What of that other sense of ἐστί and its derivatives—the one we convey by "exists" in English?[31] As we commonly use the word "existence,"[32] degrees of it (as distinct from degrees of perfection of things in existence) make no sense whatever; the idea of one [8] individual existing more, or less, than another would be a rank absurdity. It would take strong, un-ambiguous evidence to establish that Plato had any such thought in mind when he spoke of some things as being more, or less, real than others. And there is no such evidence. Would anyone seriously suggest that Plato wants to undermine our faith in the existence of the beds we sleep on, buy and sell, etc., when he compares their "being" unfavorably with that of their Form in R. X?[33] His contention that they are not "really real" surely *presupposes* their existence. Similarly the sight-lovers in R. V are not told

[31] I cannot go here into the difficult question of whether or not Plato ever formally distinguished the existential from the predicative uses of "is." But it may be worth pointing out that in contexts where his need to express existence in our common use of the term (see next note) is most urgent he tends to eke out "to be" with locatives: "it makes no difference whether it [the Ideal State] exists *somewhere* or will exist [εἴτε που ἔστιν εἴτε ἔσται]," R. 592B; we should not fear that the soul may be dissipated at death, "vanishing into thin air and existing *nowhere*" (καὶ οὐδὲν ἔτι οὐδαμοῦ ἔστι, *Phdo* 84B, Hackforth's translation); *Sph.* 264D, διὰ τὸ μηδαμῶς μηδέποτε μηδαμοῦ ψεῦδος εἶναι.

[32] I.e., applying it to individuals: God, crocodiles, unicorns, etc. I say this to exclude the (much rarer) cases where we apply "existence" to general terms—"justice," "opportunity," "clear thinking," and so forth—to signify not their abstract, "platonic," existence, but their concrete instantiation; in *this* use of "existence" provision for degrees of it is normal: if I were to list the countries in which "justice exists" I might well be expected to admit that it exists in higher degree in some than in others. But this is only another way of referring to degrees of perfection: "F exists in higher degree at *a* than at *b*" = "F is more completely realised at *a* than at *b*"; so we would be back to degrees of reality in the sense discussed above.

[33] Cf. N. R. Murphy, (1951, 128): "Book X is able to treat the beds made by carpenters as 'incompletely real' without casting any slur on the physical existence of what the carpenter put together." But Murphy's next step is to deny altogether the applicability of degrees of reality to the physical world. He would explain Plato's clear-cut statements to the contrary as follows: "The general rule on which he is working seems clear enough. Whenever we speak of an unreality it is not with reference to false things but to false thoughts. 'Unreal' applies only to the objects of false thinking or unfounded suggestion of some kind. It is predicable of what would be real if a false thought were true," *ibid.*, p. 129. But nothing can be more certain than that Plato considers the physical world itself less real than the Forms, and thinks he can *thereby* account for our incapacity to reach adequately true thoughts of it (R. 477-9; *Ti* 28-9).

that the faces, bodies, spectacles, etc.,[34] they love to see do not exist or only half exist (whatever that might mean): they are mistaken about the reality of the beauty—not of the existence—of the things of sense. The dream-metaphor both here (476CD) and elsewhere (*Ti* 52BC) should not be misunderstood: It could not be implying or alluding to degrees of existence, even if its point were that sensible things are mental images; for Plato would then be telling us not that they half exist, but that they do not exist and are only illusions of mortal mind. But Plato, of course, is no Parmenides: the sensible world is the *object*, not the creature, of *doxa*. He uses the dream-metaphor to liken the state of mind of the philosophically unenlightened to that of the dreamer in only one respect: both are systematically deceived in taking things which are not really (or truly) *F* for the real (and true) *F*.[35] Their mistake is not to take half existents for full existents, but deceitful resemblances of *F* for the real *F*. [9]

II

I may now tackle my next question: *Why* does Plato think the Forms cognitively "more real" than their sensible instances? His own answer to this question in *Republic* V is as direct and emphatic as it is cryptic: because, he says, the sensibles are always, the Forms never, *F* and not-*F*.[36] All he then does to explain this claim is to go down the line with a number of substitutions for *F*—beautiful, just, pious, double, large, heavy—and simply *assert* that each of the "many beautifuls" is also not beautiful, and so forth. But why this should be so, he does not say. He must be assuming that the point he is making is so familiar to his audience that it calls for no special exposition or argument at this time. In such circumstances all we can do is to thumb his works for some passage which speaks more informatively on this point. The best one by far for this purpose is *Smp*. 211A: That "wonderful sort of Beauty" the lover will see at the height of his ascent, will not be

    (1) beautiful in one respect, ugly in another,[37] nor yet

    (2) beautiful at one time, but not at another, nor yet

[34] For the interpretation of πολλὰ τὰ καλά in this passage see below, n. 41.
[35] This is explicit at *R.* 476CD, implicit at *Ti* 52BC.
[36] 479A–D. Cf. n. 21, above.
[37] For the sense of the τῇ ("there," "on that spot," "in that way") see LSJ, *s.v.* ὁ, A. VIII. 1.

(3) beautiful in relation to some things, ugly in relation to others, nor

(4) beautiful here, ugly elsewhere, being beautiful for some, ugly for others.

Here, laid out for our inspection, are four grounds on one or more of which the "*F* and not-*F*" formula can be clamped on any sensible instance of Beauty:

(1) It may be beautiful in one of its features, ugly in another, as a vase might have an exquisite shape, but garish colors.[38]

(2) It may be beautiful at one time, not at a later one,[39] as a flower, lovely in the bud, might be coarse and shapeless at full bloom.

(3) It may be beautiful by comparison with one thing, ugly by [10] comparison with another, as the beautiful girl in the *Hippias Major* is said to be ugly by comparison with a goddess.[40]

(4) It may be beautiful in one spatial location, ugly in another, as a painting meant to be seen from a certain distance might appear beautiful if properly placed, ugly if crowded into a small room.[41]

---

[38] And/or beautiful in one of its parts, ugly in another (say, flower and leaves respectively).

[39] The point to which Plato alludes when he says that the sensibles are scarcely ever, the Forms invariably, "in the same state": e.g. *Phdo* 78D–79E, 80B; *R.* 479A, 484B, 530B; *Phlb.* 59C. Cf. *Cra.* 439D; *Ti* 49E.

[40] 289D: on this account she is "no more beautiful than ugly," 289C; cf. *R.* 479B9–10. On the same ground the finger will appear both large and small, thick and thin, soft and hard, at *R.* 523E.

[41] I have expounded the "*x* is *F* and not-*F*" formula for the cases in which the *x* would be an individual. This is what Plato usually has in view when thinking of sensible instantiations of Forms, as, e.g., in the girl and finger examples above, and frequently elsewhere: the visibles in the Line are "the living creatures about us, and all things that grow naturally, and all man-made objects," *R.* 510A; the ἕκαστα τὰ πολλά are illustrated by tables and beds in *R.* 596A6–7; the "many beautifuls" by "men, horses, garments" in *Phdo* 78D, and instances of beauty, in contrast to the Form, by "a beautiful face" in *Cra.* 439D; the many similars by "you and me" in *Prm.* 129A. But (*a*) actions or, more generally, occurrences, and (*b*) usages or institutions would also count for Plato as sensible instances of Forms. Thus he is obviously thinking of (*a*) when he cites "sounds" (along with "colours and shapes and everything fashioned from such things") at *R.* 476B (cf. 480A), and of both (*a*) and (*b*) when he speaks at 479A (cf. also 479E) of the many δίκαια and ὅσια, each of which will also appear as the contrary of just or pious. The above four grounds on which an individual can be *F* and not-*F* would apply

A host of questions raised by each of these four grounds must be suppressed to concentrate on just one: Why should Plato think that a thing judged F and not-F on any of these grounds "less real" than the corresponding Form? I find the best clue to the answer in a passage in the *Phaedo* (102BC): After telling us that Simmias is both F and not-F (tall and short) on the third of the above grounds (he is taller than Socrates and shorter than Phaedo), Plato remarks that

> of course, you will admit that the truth of the matter is not expressed by the words, "Simmias is taller than Socrates." For surely it is not in Simmias' nature that he should be taller than Socrates because he [*11*] is Simmias [τῷ Σιμμίαν εἶναι],[42] but rather because of the height he happens to have.

Here

    (S1) Simmias is taller than Socrates

is a true proposition. Why then does it not "express the truth of the matter?" What sort of "truth" is it that S1, though true, does not succeed in expressing? The kind we would reach if we turned instead, for example, to one of the propositions that come into the discussion a little later (104A):

    (S2) Three is odd.

Now S2 differs from S1 in that radical way whose vast importance for the theory of knowledge Plato was the first to recognize in the history of Western thought. One way of putting this would be to say that S2 takes us out of the domain of contingent truth, which is all we can get out of S1, into that of logical necessity. This particular phraseology would not, of course, be Plato's. But he would be telling us much the same thing in his

---

just as well to actions and usages, provided only we take account of the fact that the criterion of identity would be suitably different: the *same* action or usage would be one which answers to the same description, even if performed by different individuals. Thus it is on the assumption that "burying one's ancestors" would be the same action whether performed by Tantalus, Dardanus, Zethos, or Pelops (*Hp Maj.* 293B) that it is shown to be τοῖς μὲν . . . καλόν, τοῖς δ' οὐ καλόν, 293C. For a different interpretation of "the many" Fs of *R.* V see Murphy (1951, 106 ff.) and Gosling, (1960, 116 ff.).

[42] For the significance of this construction see the passages compared with τῷ μελίττας εἶναι by E. S. Thompson (*Plato's Meno*, London, 1901), *ad Meno* 72B.

own language if he said that while S1 and S2 are both true, S1 can only be a true belief, while S2 constitutes knowledge—"knowledge" in his own ultra-strong sense of the word, which he first broached in the *Meno* (98A) when he said that a true belief becomes knowledge when it has been "bound" or "tied" by "calculation of the reason,"[43] implying that the required "binding" or "tying" is that which connects statement with statement by logical inference or term with term by logical analysis. When a belief gets this kind of "binding" it is no longer *fallible* in the importantly relevant sense, i.e., capable of being proved false by refinements and extensions of the very process which gave us reason to think it true in the first place. It has now become "infallible," or "unshakable."[44] This is strong language, but it is Plato's. It conveys the sense of complete security he gets from statements which come up to his standards for knowledge— those whose truth-claims owe nothing to sensory observation and everything to logical inference and analysis. [12]

Now since Plato habitually thinks of knowledge as a relation between the mind and its objects, he would naturally transpose what I have said for him from properties of statements expressing knowledge to properties of objects known. These are, of course, the Forms. So to have the requisite internal binding, a statement of the form "*F* is *H*" would have to be about the Forms, *F* and *H*, and be true because these characters are logically or essentially connected. The reason why *F* is *H* would then be discernible in the very "nature" of *F*, in its "what it *is*,"[45] its "isness" as Shorey once jokingly converted the Greek into impossibly literal English; or, in possible English, its *reality*. Here, Plato would assure us, we would have found our way to something completely reliable, and hence completely "real" in the sense I have explained. For whatever statements about *F* follow from the logical analysis of this character (and/or the analysis of characters to which *F* is logically related) would be *necessary* statements, hence, in Plato's language, "infallible" ones—statements which could never go wrong. Contrariwise, any statements we make about a sensible instance of *F* would be fallible precisely because the sensible instance does not admit of such

---

[43] Αἰτία in αἰτίας λογισμῷ should not be translated "cause" (the Jowett rendering, reappearing in the most recent commentary, *Plato's Meno*, R. S. Bluck, Cambridge, 1961, *ad loc.*), but as "the because" or "the reason" (the latter in W. K. C. Guthrie's translation, *Plato's Protagoras and Meno*, London, 1956.) Αἰτία, as used by Plato and Aristotle, *need* not connote causal agency.

[44] ἀναμάρτητον, *R.* 477E; ἀμεταπτώτους, *Ti* 29B.

[45] The ὃ ἔστιν (or οὐσία) which answers the τί ἔστιν question of note 13, above.

necessary connection with its predicates. When a particular, a, is F, you can't say that a is F because of *being a*: It is not because of his *being* Simmias that Simmias is taller than Socrates; there is no such thing as *being a* (*being Simmias*, unlike *being tall*, or *being human*, is not a character).[46] Hence there is nothing to which the character F can be tied in such a way that it would follow "infallibly" that a is F. So the "a is F" predication will be loose and shaky, and you should not be surprised to find the contrary of F, or of any other character you may ascribe to a, also turning up in one or more of three ways answering to the first, second, and fourth of the four grounds enumerated above:

(1) Since a will then have various features—say, its color, smell, taste, texture, weight, shape—belonging to it by empirical conjunction, not by logical connection, a may very well be F in respect of one of them, not-F in respect of one or more [*13*] others.[47] Then a will be F and not-F on the first ground: in different respects.

(2) Since a is a temporal thing, and there is no logical connection between every property it has at time 1 and every property it has at time 2, it may happen that a is F at time 1 and not-F at time 2. So a will be F and not-F on the second ground: at different times.

(4) Since a is a spatial object, and there is no logical connection between the characters it has, or appears to have, in different places, or as seen by observers from different places, a may be F and not-F, or may appear to be F and not-F on the fourth of the above grounds: at different locations, and as observed from different positions.[48]

Now if Plato were dictating this account, he would have certainly wanted us to include the third of the above grounds: the one represented in the *Hippias Major* by the girl who is supposed to be beautiful and not beautiful, because she is more beautiful than other girls but less beautiful than a goddess; in the *Phaedo* by Simmias, supposed to be tall and not tall, because he is taller than Socrates but less tall than Phaedo,[49] in the *Theaetetus* (154C–155B), by the six dice, which are supposed to be both numerous and not numerous, because they are more numerous than four dice and

---

[46] Cf. R. G. Turnbull, "Aristotle's Debt to the 'Natural Philosophy' of the *Phaedo*," *Philosophical Quarterly* 8 (1958), pp. 131 ff., at pp. 132, 140, 141.

[47] Or even F and not-F in respect of the same character—e.g., one part of it hot, another cold. Cf. n. 38, above.

[48] Cf. *Prt.* 356C; *R.* 602C; *Phlb.* 41E–42A.

[49] 102B4-6: ὅταν Σιμμίαν Σωκράτους φῇς μείζω εἶναι, Φαίδωνος δὲ ἐλάττω, λέγεις τοτ' εἶναι ἐν τῷ Σιμμίᾳ, ἀμφότερα, καὶ μέγεθος καὶ σμικρότητα.

less numerous than twelve. It should be evident from these examples that
here Plato suffers from a certain confusion. From

(P) x is more F than y, and less F than z,

he infers

(Q) x is F and not-F.

And Q does *not*, of course, follow from P. For just suppose that Simmias
were 6 feet 5 inches tall, and Phaedo 6 feet 6 inches. Simmias, then, would
still be shorter than Phaedo. But would anyone want to call him "short"
on that account? It is clear from just this that there is something wrong
with Plato's inference; or, more precisely, something misleading about it.
It would be far worse, viciously wrong, if Q were meant to express a self-
contradiction. But I think it is clear that Plato does not mean anything [14]
so extreme.[50] This we can tell from his own statement of the principle of
non-contradiction at R. 436E:

> The same thing can never act or be acted upon in contrary ways, or
> have contrary properties [literally: "or be opposites"], at the same
> time, in the same respect, and in relation to the same thing.[51]

To run afoul of this principle Simmias would have to be tall and short
in relation *to the same person*, which he obviously is not. We should, therefore, not take Q at face value, but read it only as an ellipsis for

(R) x is F in relation to y, and not-F in relation to z.

Put in this way, there is obviously no contradiction at all.[52] Then our only
remaining objection is to the use of statements of the form of (Q) as
ellipses for statements of the form of (R). That the language (English or
Greek) will not always allow "x is F," as an ellipsis for "x is F in relation
to y" should be sufficiently clear from the example I have just used. Anyone who knew that Simmias was 6 feet 5 inches, but still declared that he
was short, and then explained, when challenged, that he only meant that
Simmias was short by comparison with Phaedo, would be thought a liar,

[50] Cf. Adam's note on R. 479A.
[51] He appeals to this principle in R. 505C: "if you identify *good* with *pleasure*
(συμβαίνει . . . ὁμολογεῖν ἀγαθὰ εἶναι καὶ κακὰ ταὐτά).
[52] Cf. W. D. Ross, *Plato's Theory of Ideas*, Oxford, 1951, p. 38; G. E. L. Owen,
"A Proof in the Περὶ Ἰδεῶν," *Journal of Hellenic Studies* 67, (1957), Part One,
pp. 103 ff., at pp. 108–9.

unless he could be let off as a practical joker. So, too, would one who, knowing that Helen is the most beautiful woman that ever lived, said with a straight face that she is ugly on no better grounds than that she is ugly by comparison with Aphrodite.

Let us then offer Plato a little advice as to how he might improve the intelligibility of his theory: "Rest your case for the applicability of the *F* and not-*F* formula to sensible particulars," we might tell him, "on the three grounds you gave us a moment ago, and drop this one. For if you stick to those others, no one could misunderstand you to mean that sensible particulars are logical monstrosities, systematically violating the principle of non-contradiction. Nothing of this sort would be suggested by the fact that a particular is *F* in one respect, not-*F* in another; or *F* at one time, not-*F* at another; or *F* at one place, not-*F* at another. That you did not think of particulars as violating the principle of non-contradiction seems clear to us from the fact that when you [15] declare the principle inviolate at *R.* 436E, your own example is a sensible particular, a spinning top. And this must have been no less clear to your own contemporaries; none of them got the impression that you thought sensible things self-contra-dictory—a doctrine that would have startled them fully as much as it would us, and earned you a leading place among the stultifiers of human reason in Book Γ of the *Metaphysics*. That being the case, you had better make it clear that you would not offer "Simmias is tall and not tall," "Six dice are numerous and not numerous," etc., as examples of what you mean by the *F* and not-*F* predicament in which sensibles are involved. You do not need this form of argument, since the other three grounds suffice to make the case for your contention that the *F* and not-*F* formula applies to sensibles, but never to Forms. For this contention the "Simmias is tall and not-tall" type of argument is worse than useless: it is self-defeating. For in this respect particulars *cannot* be systematically differentiated from Forms; some Forms could also be said to be *F* and not-*F* on exactly the same ground.[53] For the number (i.e., the Form), *Six*, is greater than *Four* and smaller than *Twelve*; and the kind (i.e., the Form), *Quadruped*, is greater than *Horse*,[54] but smaller than *Animal*. So on that reckoning the Forms,

---

[53] Cf. the difficulty pointed out by Professor Demos: Allen *op. cit.*, p. 333, n. 13.

[54] Where *B*, not co-extensive with *A*, is logically included by *A*, Plato speaks of *A*'s "containing" (περιέχειν) *B*, and of *B* as a "part" (μέρος, μόριον) of *A*. *A* would then be "greater" than *B* as a whole is greater than any of its parts. Plato accordingly speaks of "great" or "small" kinds, or parts of kinds, in the *Politicus* (e.g., 262A, 265A), and of "greatest" (μέγιστα) kinds in the *Sph.*

Six, and *Quadruped*, would each be great and not great. This type of argument then had better be dropped. Or, if you must keep it, modify it so as to make it apply only in the case of *causally effective* relations. There you can find all the cases you want for x being F in one relation, not-F in another—e.g., Simmias, normally dry, not dry when immersed in water. This would bring out perfectly your contention by showing that Simmias, unlike the Forms he instantiates, is susceptible of genuinely contrary predications in suitably different (causal) relations to other things."

I submit that Plato would have good reason to accept this advice, and that we have good reason for offering it to him. For its effect would be to free his theory from an incidental blemish and make it appear to best advantage. In this way we would insure that our criticism [16] would not be wasted on superficial errors, but on the enduringly important and interesting aspects of the theory. To this I now turn, but with the utmost brevity, for a thorough discussion of the relevant issues is quite impossible within the space at my disposal.

III

In the interpretation I have offered of Plato's theory, the grounds on which sensible particulars are judged to be less real than their respective Forms coincide very largely (and, if my proposed emendation were accepted, would coincide completely) with those categorial features which disqualify them for serving as objects of a certain kind of knowledge: knowledge which, Plato says, has "infallibility," or, in less inflated, more exact, terms for what he means, logical certainty. Nothing can qualify as a cognoscendum for this purpose if it is concrete, temporal, spatial, and caught in chains of physical causation—if it is cluttered up with contingent characters. All of its properties must stick to it with logical glue, so that they can never get unstuck with changes in time, spatial location, or causal environment. It must be eternally invariant and as logically transparent as geometrical concepts come to be when all of their properties have been exhibited as the necessary consequences of their formal inter-connections. Thus it must possess those very features which are the defining characteristics of the Platonic Form. In recognizing only one kind of knowledge—knowledge of objects having these, and only these, features—Plato had no choice but to say that only the Forms were completely, or purely, or perfectly "real" in the sense I have been investigating in this paper: cognitively reliable. Thus the degrees-of-reality doctrine is, in this respect, a lucid consequence of Plato's epistemology. Recognizing only one kind of knowledge, Plato had no choice but to recognize only one kind of full or complete reality.

To put the matter in this way shows, I think, a fruitful direction our criticism of Plato may take. Instead of merely protesting his downgrading of the reality of the sensible world, we can show on what conditions Plato himself would have had cause to upgrade it: i.e., if he could have seen that this sensible world, such unpromising material for logical analysis, is the best possible material for that very different cognitive venture which, when successful, [17] results in *empirical* knowledge. If we want this sort of knowledge, its only possible subject-matter would consist of those very things we observe by the senses, or hypothesize to explain what we so observe, and whose properties we record in empirically confirmable or disconfirmable propositions. For this purpose the Platonic Forms are grotesquely unsuitable, and would have to be judged vastly less "real" than physical objects, stuffs or processes—mere ghostly replicas of them. We would thus be offering Plato not so much a refutation of his theory as an extension of it, though admittedly one whose results he would find disconcerting. For if he were to accept this offer he would then have to rule, with equally good reason, that Forms are both "more" and "less" real than their sensible instances, since they would now turn out to be more dependable than they for one purpose, less so for another. And if we could persuade him to come so far, we might then try to talk him into a further step, suggesting to him that "more real" and "less real" are themselves rather misleading expressions in this context. Would it not be better to drop these comparatives, and say outright that only the Forms are "real" as judged by the criteria of the kind of knowledge which aspires to logical certainty, while only sensibles are "real" as judged by the very different criteria of empirically testable knowledge?

No one, I trust, will object that if Plato were to assent to such a proposal he would no longer be the Plato of the dialogues, the "real" Plato of historical research. This should be only too obvious. My reason for playing with these wild counterfactuals was not to rewrite, but to illuminate, the philosophy Plato left us. By looking at it from this perspective we have a better chance to understand one of its major achievements: its exploration—the first of its kind in Western philosophy, and a largely, if not wholly, successful one—of the categorial differences between things like Beauty, Justice, Triangularity, and the like, and those individuals, states, events, processes of which such general terms can be predicated. Plato showed that all, and only, the first had to be non-sensible, incorporeal, incomposite, timeless, spaceless, incapable of causal agency, structured eternally by logical chains of entailment and bars of incompatibility. In getting results such as these, while working with the crudest of tools against formidable obstacles of ingrained linguistic habits, Plato must be rated one of the great explorers in the world of thought. To see that he [18] got these results from a *degrees*-of-reality theory, while all he needed was a *kinds*-of-reality theory, will help us to recognize the ways, good and bad, in which his theory served him. Certainly a kinds-of-reality theory would have served him much better as an instrument of categorial inquiry. One has a better chance to see and state correctly the differences between particulars and universals, if one expects in advance that both will be equally "real" in their different ways. For then one will not be tempted to misconstrue universals as a higher grade of particulars, or think of sensible particulars as inferior "imitations" or "copies" of Ideal Forms. Plato did not wholly resist this temptation, and it was then that the most serious of his logical mishaps befell him.[55] To that extent the degrees of reality theory was not an unmixed asset. But to operate with mixed assets seems to be unavoidable in the highly speculative business of metapihyscs.[56] [19]

[55] Cf. R. Robinson (1953, 260–62); Vlastos, "The Third Man Argument in the *Parmenides*," *Philos. Review* 63 (1954), pp. 319 ff.; A. Wedberg, *Plato's Philosophy of Mathematics* (1955, 36–38).

[56] I am much indebted to Professor B. A. O. Williams for useful criticism of an earlier draft which led me to make some improvements.

4

Reasons and Causes
in the *Phaedo**

(1969; RC)

THERE is a passage in this dialogue which has led many scholars—the great majority of those who have translated or discussed it in detail—to think that Plato's Forms are meant to be causes. This is the methodological and metaphysical preamble (95E-105C) to the final argument for the immortality of the soul. The importance of this passage could hardly be exaggerated: as much is to be learned from it about Plato's metaphysics, epistemology, and philosophy of science as from any other text of equal length in his corpus. But it is also one of the most perplexing. Scholars who have not confessed its difficulty have evidenced it just the same in the wild diversity of the interpretations they have put on it. According to Eduard Zeller, Plato teaches here that the Ideas are meant to be formal,

* An earlier version of this paper was delivered at Michigan State University as an Arnold Isenberg lecture; other drafts have been read elsewhere. The paper was originally printed in the *Philosophical Review* (78[1969], 291–325); the original pagination is supplied here in square brackets. It was reprinted (with some corrections) in *Plato I: Metaphysics and Epistemology*, edited by G. Vlastos (1971). It is reprinted here (by permission of the editors of the *Philosophical Review*) with some corrections and new material in some notes. I acknowledge with gratitude diverse criticisms which have helped me improve the paper and most particularly those given me by Professors Terry Penner and Richard Sorabji, whose detailed and penetrating queries have prompted revisions which have clarified and strengthened the argument, though they may not have fully met their objections.

efficient, and final causes all rolled into one.[1] Paul Shorey, at the other extreme, maintained that when Plato speaks of the Ideas as *aitiai* he is offering "only a tautological logic . . . a consistent and systematic substitution of the logical reason for all other forms of cause."[2] [*291*] More recently commentators have not hesitated to take their own perplexed reading of this text as evidence of unclear thinking in its writer. Mr. I. M. Crombie tells us there is "a nest of confusions" here, arising from Plato's "jumbl[ing] mathematical and non-mathematical topics together, and fail [ing] into the bargain to distinguish different senses of such notions as 'through' and 'in virtue of.' " He says "it would be a useful elementary exercise to make a list of such confusions in this passage."[3]

The interpretation I shall offer here is closer to Shorey's than to Zeller's, and owes no small debt to Crombie's discussion of our passage.[4] But if my analysis is even approximately correct it will show that neither is Shorey's view acceptable *in toto*, and that the "confusions" of which Crombie speaks are not in our text but in misunderstandings of it which he shares with many distinguished scholars. Not that Plato's thought here will turn out to be entirely clear or wholly true. But for all its blemishes, both substantive and expository, it will appear, I trust, to be worthy of a philosopher who was not only a pioneer of unsurpassed audacity but also, when full allowance is made for the difficulties which confronted him, a remarkably sane and clear-headed thinker.

[1] "In dieser ganzen Auseinandersetzung [with the physicists in our passage] wird nun zwischen der begrifflichen, der wirkenden und der Endursache nicht bloss nicht unterschieden, sondern alle drei werden deutlich genug für Ein und dasselbe erklärt," Ed. Zeller (1922, 687, n.1). I shall not criticize this statement directly, but my reasons for rejecting it will become clear as I proceed. I shall follow the same policy with respect to other views with which I cannot agree. Limitations of space will prevent me from engaging in controversy except in so far as I find this essential for the elucidation and support of the interpretations I propose.

[2] *What Plato Said* (1933, 179). Zeller's contrary interpretation Shorey had already rejected in Shorey (1888, 395ff., at p. 406), and still earlier in his Munich dissertation: see his citation from the latter in (1924, pp. 1ff., at p. 7, note 2).

[3] (1963, 169). I shall refer to this work throughout this essay solely by the author's name.

[4] As well as to many other authors, the following most of all: Burnet (1911); Taylor (1937); Cornford (1939, 74–80); Moreau (1939, 378ff ff.); Murphy (1951, 145–48). To each of these works I shall refer throughout this essay solely by the author's name.

I. ON THE MEANING OF αἰτία

Since so much will turn on the meaning of the word *aitia*,[5] I must begin
by calling attention to the fact that its range of significance [*292*] is far
wider than that of the word "cause" as used nowadays both in ordinary
speech and philosophical discussions. I can best do so by recalling some
of the things that count as straightforward *aitiai* in Aristotle, whose
metaphysical preconceptions did not blunt his sensitiveness to the values
of the words he used:

1. Why did the Persians invade Attica? Because the Athenians had
raided Sardis.

2. Why is this statue so heavy? Because it is made of bronze.

3. Why is he taking after-dinner walks? Because of his health.

4. Why is the angle at the semicircle a right angle? Because it is equal
to the half of two right angles.[6]

[5] Liddell and Scott, *Greek-English Lexicon*, lists the following senses for
aitia: I. *responsibility*; II. *cause*; II. *occasion, motive*; IV. *head, category* under which
a thing comes; V. *case in dispute*. In this paper I shall be concerned exclusively
with sense II, which the dictionary renders by "cause"—mistakenly so, in my
opinion, since, I shall argue, this sense has a much wider signification than
that of the English word as commonly used nowadays (the sense in which we
speak of a blow as the "cause" of the shattering of a vase or of air-pollution as
the "cause" of pulmonary irritation), or as employed by philosophers (see,
e.g., article, "Causation," by R. Taylor in the *Encyclopedia of Philosophy*, edited
by P. Edwards, New York, 1967; C. G. Hempel on causal explanation in
(1965, 347 ff); E. Nagel on causal laws in *Structure of Science* (1961, 73 ff.)

[6] Examples *1*, *3*, and *4* are from the discussion of *aitiai* in the *Posterior
Analytics*, II, 11; examples 2 and 3 from the chapter on the four *aitiai* in *Phys.*
II,3. I have recast the phrasing for obvious reasons, and given a different twist
to *2* (Aristotle does not refer to the weight of the statue, and does not think
in this connection of bronze specifically as a natural kind, but only as formable
matter; but he would not hesitate to recognize the kind of explanation illustrated in *2* as a *bona fide aitia*). I disregard problems of Aristotelian exegesis
raised by the fact that not all of the four *aitiai* in the *Post. Anal.* are obvious
duplicates of the four in the *Physics*. For my purposes it is sufficient to note
the prominence of *4* in the *Post. Anal.*, which leaves no doubt that Aristotle
would recognize it as a star example of a certain kind of *aitia*, even though he
finds it hard to squeeze it into the metaphysical mould which dictates the
classification in the *Physics* (and also in the corresponding passage in *Metaphysics*, V, 2).

I have deliberately avoided the word *aitia* in formulating these examples, so as to bring out the fact that to say that X is the *aitia* of Y comes to precisely the same thing as saying that Y happened, or happens, or is the case, *because* of X. In proof of this, if proof it needs, I need only refer to the fact that Aristotle speaks of his four [293] *aitiai* as "all the ways of stating τὸ διὰ τί [the *because*]:"[7] Aristotle's so-called four "causes" are his four "*because*s."

Now not every *because* refers to a cause, though some do, as does the first example: the Athenian raid on Sardis would be a fair example of a temporal antecedent which is the (supposed) sufficient condition of the occurrence of an event, the Persian invasion of Athens. Alternatively, a *because* may refer us to an *aitia* which, while not itself a cause, has definite causal implications. This is brought out well enough in the second example. We could hardly speak of bronze as the "cause" of the weight of a bronze statue: bronze scarcely causes itself to be heavy. What we have here is a natural kind, that is to say, a cluster of properties regularly conjoined, among which is its characteristic specific gravity. These properties have a network of connections with causal laws by means of which we are able to make relevant causal predictions, such as that a bronze statue will outweigh several wooden ones of the same dimensions.

Now consider 3: Here it would be not just awkward but positively absurd to speak of the *aitia* as the "cause".[8] The health for which the ailing man submits to his peripatetic chores does not now exist and may never come to exist, since his walks may not avail to restore it and he might even die on one of them of a heart attack; how then could this non-existent (and perhaps never-to-be-existent) thing cause his walks or anything else? To turn the answer to our *why*-question into a statement of a cause we

---

[7] καὶ πάντως ἀποδοτέον τὸ διὰ τί followed by a listing of the four *aitiai*, *Ph.* 198B5 ff. This is one of the many passages in which τὸ διὰ τί or τὸ διότι = τὸ αἴτιον in Aristotle (for some of them see H. Bonitz, *Index Aristotelicus*, 177A50 ff.).

[8] In spite of statements one finds occasionally in the literature that Aristotle "identified" *aitia* 3 with *aitia* 1 (the "final" with the "efficient" *aitia*)—some of them deriving plausibility from loose expressions in Aristotle himself (e.g., *Ph.* 198A24-27, "The last three [the formal, the efficient, and the final] often coalesce [ἔρχεται εἰς τὸ ἕν, translated "coincide" by R. P. Hardie and R. K. Gaye in the Oxford translation of the *Physics*]; for the 'what it is' and the 'for what' are one, while the first source of motion [τὸ ὅθεν ἡ κίνησις πρῶτον] is the same with these in species. . . .")—he makes it abundantly clear that he does *not* ascribe causal agency to the "final" *aitia*: *GC* 324A15, "health is not active [or "productive," ποιητικόν] except metaphorically."

would have to take a detour in full view of the intensional context and make the cause not the health the man expects from his walks but his expectation of getting it from them, backed up by a strong desire to improve his health (stronger than for any of the displaced alternatives). Some philosophers nowadays would deny us even this maneuver, holding that it makes no sense to speak of the cause of an action. Into this controversy I do not propose to enter.[9] I need [294] not in this inquiry, where all that matters is that if we were talking Greek, then, regardless of our philosophical persuasions, we would not have the slightest hesitation in saying that the man's health *is* the *aitia* of his walks, while in English the most we could do to work the man's health into a causal account of his exertions would be to say that the cause of these actions is the end-in-view and his desire to attain it.

I have left last the mathematical example, the most striking one for my purposes, for here the gap between *aitia* and *cause* is unbridgeable by any ancillary device that will stand up under examination. We are given P, "the angle at the semicircle is the half of two right angles," and Q, "the angle at the semicircle is a right angle," where P is the penultimate formula in the string of formulae which make up the currently acceptable proof of Q in the geometry of the time.[10] This leads Aristotle to take P as the *aitia* of Q, construing the entailment of Q by P, already proved a valid consequence of the axiom-set of the science, as an adequate ground of the truth of Q. Since this entailment is for Aristotle a relation whose relata are abstract items, he would not dream of saying that one of these propositions *causes* the other. Yet that is the way he is made to talk by G. R. G. Mure in the Oxford translation of the *Posterior Analytics*, by W. D. Ross in his *Commentary*, and by countless textbooks, where he is represented as saying that the premises of demonstrative inference are the "causes" of its conclusions.[11] Such statements have been defended at times by the claim that Aristotle thinks the premises *causae cognoscendi*.[12] But if *causa* in this time-hallowed phrase means no more than "reason" or

[9] The best defense of the causal account known to me is in Davidson (1963, 685 ff.) Cf. also M. White (1965, Chapter V).

[10] See Heath (1949, 72).

[11] αἰτίων τοῦ συμπεράσματος (71B22), "related to them as effect to cause," Mure in the Oxford translation; "causative of the conclusion," H. Tredennick in the Loeb translation. I have protested elsewhere this venerable mistranslation (1965, 143 ff., note 15). The present paper is an extended version of the protest.

[12] Leibniz speaks of them as causes "de notre jugement" (*Nouveaux Essais*, IV, 17, 3).

"principle" the defense is otiose, since reasons and principles have no causal efficacy; while if it does mean *cause*, the claim is [295] false, and may be collapsed by the simple reflection that it is not, in general, true that knowing a given proposition is a sufficient condition of knowing all of the propositions which it entails:[13] thus one may know the axioms of a system and be ignorant of a whole raft of theorems which a cleverer mathematician would be able to deduce from the same axioms. Aristotle, so far as I know, never made this particular blunder. But even if he had made it, we would still have no good warrant for reading it into the many passages in which he speaks of an entailing premise as the *aitia* of an entailed conclusion, since all such statements make perfect sense if understood to express the simple fact that the premise states a sufficient reason for the conclusion.

This brief discussion has shown, I trust, how much more general in signification is the Greek *aitia* than is the current meaning of the word "cause" in English speech. Greek usage would entitle us as a matter of course to speak of something as another's *aitia*, regardless of whether we are referring, as in 1 above, to a straightforward cause, or, as in 2, to a law-like conjunction of properties or factors such that the instantiation of some of them is a sufficient condition of the concurrent instantiation of others, or, as in 3, to the end-in-view of a purposeful agent whose desire to attain it by a certain action we take to be the sufficient condition of his performing the action, or finally, as in 4, to one proposition as entailing, or implying, another, so that our assurance of the truth of the former warrants equal assurance of the truth of the latter. Here then is the linguistic base from which the whole of the discussion that is to follow will start: The mere fact that Plato speaks of the Forms as *aitiai* in our passage is not of itself the slightest evidence—not even *prima facie* evidence—that he wants them to be causes. There are plenty of other things he may want to express by saying, and with the greatest emphasis, that they are *aitiai*. What he does mean can only be decided from the context. Let us proceed to this. [296]

II. THE "SAFE" BUT "IGNORANT" AITIA

Our passage falls into two divisions. Division One (95E to 99C) recounts the youthful infatuation of the Platonic Socrates[14] with the physical

[13] Cf. E. Nagel (1954, 287 ff.)

[14] Let me say here once for all that in my opinion the "Socrates" of this whole passage cannot be identified *in toto* with the historical figure, though it

philosophers and the disappointment in which it ended when he found that all they could offer was material *aitiai* and mechanical causes, while he had become convinced that only teleology could provide the "true" (98E) or "real" (99B) *aitiai* of natural phenomena. There is no talk of the Forms as *aitiai*—no mention of them at all—throughout the whole of this Division, though the way is prepared for them, by the laying-out of a series of perplexities whose solution would elude Socrates until he had hit upon the Theory of Forms. This part of Division One I shall discuss at some length in due course. The rest of it I shall ignore. Though its historical importance is incalculable—this is one of the great turning-points in European natural philosophy, the conscious abandonment of the line of thought which had led, in the systems of Leucippus and Democritus, to the first rigorously mechanistic conception of the order of nature—its message is familiar and, superficially at least, quite clear. I shall, therefore, bypass it in this paper to concentrate on the far more hazardous task of figuring out what is going on in Division Two (99C–105C), where Socrates, frustrated in his search for teleology, falls back on a second-best method of inquiry of his own.[15] [297]

---

may well be that some elements of the account in Division One would fit his intellectual biography, as suggested, e.g., by Hackforth (1955, 127–31, to which I shall refer hereafter solely by the author's name). I shall be using "Socrates" to mean the figure whom Plato makes his mouthpiece in this account, except in a few cases where the context will make it clear that I am referring to the historical Socrates.

[15] "Well, I for my part should be delighted to learn from anyone about this sort of *aitia* [that of "the good and the fitting," 99C5]. But since I have been denied this *aitia* [ἐπειδὴ δὲ ταύτης ἐστερήθην] and have failed to either find it myself or learn it from another, would you like me to show you the second journey which I have been pursuing in the search for *aitia*?" (99C-D2). Note that the reference of ταύτης in C8 (the subject of ἐστερήθην and also, with the implied change of case, of the infinitives εὑρεῖν, μαθεῖν) is to τοιαύτης αἰτίας in C7; what Socrates has failed to discover by his own labors or from those of others and is prepared to do without for the present is the teleological *aitia* itself. This leaves no room for understanding him to mean (as has been done over and over again in the literature) that his "second best journey" is (a) an alternative method of searching for *teleological aitiai* rather than (b) an alternative method of searching for *aitiai*. The text offers no direct support for (a), since nothing is said of different methods of looking for teleological *aitiai* (the natural philosophers were condemned for failing to look for such *aitiai*, not for looking for them by the wrong method). There would be indirect support for (a) if we could assume that the earlier references to teleological *aitiai* as the "true" or "real" *aitiai* (τὰς ὡς ἀληθῶς αἰτίας, 98E1; τὸ αἴτιον τῷ ὄντι,

This new method and its distinctive *aitiai* are put forward as the logical pendants of a philosophical "hypothesis,"[16] that of the Theory of Forms or Ideas, which is tersely formulated as follows in the more complete of the two statements in our passage:[17]

each of the Forms exists and it is in virtue of participating in them that other things are named after them [*sc.* for Forms]. (102A10-B2)[18]

The formula has in view three sets of items and the relation of "participation":[19]

(1) Forms, that is to say, those of the full-blown theory of Plato's middle period, presented in this dialogue for the first time. The very same terms which he had used to designate the definienda of Socrates' moral inquiries in the earlier dialogues, *eidos, idea*, he now applies to entities endowed with the following [298] set of categorial properties:

99B3) mean that these are for Plato not only *the preferred* (most fundamental, most illuminating) *explanations of natural phenomena* (which, of course, they are throughout the Platonic corpus), but *the only admissible aitiai of anything whatever*. But there is no case for such an assumption; thus Plato would not hesitate to say with Aristotle that the premise of a deductive argument constitutes the *aitia* of its conclusion, without implying the semantic absurdity that the premise is the *teleological aitia* of the conclusion. For the interpretation I have defended here see N. R. Murphy, 145–56; Shorey (1933, 534), and the references given there.

[16] 100B; 102A10-B2.

[17] The first one, in 100B, fails to mention "participation": ὑποθέμενος εἶναί τι καλὸν αὐτὸ καθ' αὑτὸ καὶ ἀγαθὸν καὶ μέγα καὶ τἆλλα πάντα.

[18] This formula is practically identical with the one in *Prm.* 130E5-6. For "named after them [αὐτῶν τούτων τὴν ἐπωνυμίαν ἴσχειν]" cf. note 29 below.

[19] For this trichotomy see Hackforth's notes and commentary on 102A-105B; R. G. Turnbull (1955, 131 ff.); D. Keyt (1963, 167 ff.). I am particularly indebted to Turnbull's discussion, my sole objection to his interpretation being to his taking βούλεται in 74D9, ὀρέγεται in 75A1 and B7, and προθυμεῖται in 75B7 to mean that *F* particulars are literally "striving" (6 ff.) to instantiate more perfectly whatever characters they happen to have. To materialize Plato's metaphors in this way is not required by anything said or implied in this or any other passage and, if admitted, would saddle Plato with absurdities: we would have to understand him to be saying that any two sticks that happen to have approximately equal length are *striving* to attain perfect equality! Turnbull's account of Plato's ontology would be all the better without this "difficulty" (8), which disappears entirely once we recognize that Plato (who, as Turnbull notes, restricts striving to animate agents) never animates things like sticks, stones, fire, and snow, or shows the least interest in doing so.

they are immutable,[20] incorporeal,[21] divine;[22] they cannot be known by means of sense-experience,[23] but only by "recollection."[24]

(2) The individual persons and objects of ordinary experience, designated by proper names and definite descriptions.

(3) The immanent characters of these individuals, designated by adjectives, abstract nouns, and common nouns. The very same words *also* name Forms. This becomes strikingly clear on those rare occasions on which Plato explicitly juxtaposes the Form with the cognate character to bring out the fact that, though closely connected, they are ontologically distinct. He does so twice in our passage, contrasting "Greatness itself" with "greatness in us" (102D),[25] and again "the Opposite itself . . . in the nature of things" (τὸ ἐν τῇ φύσει) with "the opposite itself . . . in us" (τὸ ἐν ἡμῖν),[26] and both with "the [299] opposite thing" (τὸ ἐναντίον

[20] ἀεὶ κατὰ ταὐτὰ καὶ ὡσαύτως ἔχει, 78C6: ὡσαύτως κατὰ ταὐτὰ ἔχει καὶ οὐδέποτε οὐδαμῇ οὐδαμῶς ἀλλοίωσιν οὐδεμίαν ἐνδέχεται, 78D6-7; ἀεὶ κατὰ ταὐτὰ ἔχον, 79A9-10; τὸ . . . ἀεὶ ὂν καὶ ἀθάνατον καὶ ὡσαύτως ἔχον, 79D2; τῷ μὲν θείῳ καὶ ἀθανάτῳ . . . καὶ ἀεὶ ὡσαύτως κατὰ ταὐτὰ ἔχοντι ἑαυτῷ, 80B1-3.

[21] 79B. Though they are not called ἀσώματα here, this is clearly implied.

[22] 80B1 (cited in n. 20 above) and 84A9, τὸ ἀληθὲς καὶ τὸ θεῖον.

[23] 65A9-66A8.

[24] 72E3 ff. With but a single exception, not one of these properties had even been ascribed by Socrates to the universals whose definitions he sought in the early dialogues. The exception (to which Professor John Malcolm (1958, 189-95, at 192) has called attention occurs in the *Hippias Major*, where Socrates speaks of Beauty as being "always beautiful" (ἀεὶ καλόν, 292E2 and 4; cf. 294D); but his point in saying this in this earlier dialogue is logical, not metaphysical: it is not to assert that Beauty is an eternally beautiful object, but to disqualify an absurdly parochial *definiens* of beauty ("to be rich, healthy," etc., 291D-E) since it patently fails to hold of all instances of the *definiendum* and thus fails to capture "that which is beautiful always and for everyone" (292E2).

[25] I capitalize Form-naming words to distinguish them from the same words used to name characters. Denied this, or any other, inscriptional device, Plato had to use identical linguistic tokens to refer to two distinct entities, distinguishing their reference by context only.

[26] This shows that Plato does not reserve the emphatic use of the relative pronoun ("Justice *itself*," etc.) for references to the Forms, though this is his usual practice in his middle period. He may use it upon occasion, as he does here, to refer to a character; he had so used it in the earlier dialogues to refer to the Socratic universal, as W. D. Ross points out (1951, p. 17 and note 1). Commenting on *Phaedo* 103B 5, W. J. Verdenius (1958, pp. 193 ff at p. 232) says that here "τὸ ἐν ἡμῖν ἐναντίον is part of αὐτὸ τὸ ἐναντίον"; taking the latter phrase to designate the Platonic Form, he infers that Plato's Forms are both "immanent" and "transcendent." This would be unobjectionable, if it were

πρᾶγμα), i.e., the individual that has one of two opposite characters (103B).[27]

It will be convenient to use the following symbols in schematic reference to these items:

the English capitals, F, G, as character-variables;

their phonetic cognates in the Greek alphabet, Φ, Γ, as Form-variables;

a, b, c, as stand-ins for names of individuals, and x as a variable whose values are names of individuals.

What the theory asserts then is the following: for any character, F,[28] of any individual, x, there exists a homonymous[29] Form, Φ, [300] and x is

---

meant to bring out the fact that Plato's theory in the middle dialogues provides both for immanent characters and transcendent Forms. But Verdenius appears to mean more than this; he seems to deny Plato the ontological distinction between τὸ ἐν ἡμῖν ἐναντίον and τὸ ἐν τῇ φύσει. On this see the next note.

[27] Cf. also the contrast between "Similarity itself" and "the similarity which we possess" in *Prm.* 130B. This text brings out explicitly, what is implicit in the *Phaedo* texts above, that the word designating a class-(3) item has a referent which is ontologically distinct from the referent of the same word when used of a class-(1) item. It is, therefore, a mistake to deny the ontological distinctness of class-(3) and class-(1) items, as did Shorey in commenting on *Phaedo* 103B: "there are really only two things: the idea, and the particular affected by the 'presence' of or 'participation' in the idea. . . . [The text] does not justify the duplication of the idea, which [a] is a device employed here only, and [b] with full consciousness, for the purpose of the argument" (1903, note 283; my reference marks). But [a] is false, overlooking 102D and *Prm.* 130B. And [b] is *ignoratio elenchi*: the fact that the "duplication" here does serve the purposes of the immediate argument in no way implies that it is void of ontological significance.

[28] In 1954 I had pointed out that in analyzing the regress arguments in the *Prm.* one ought to distinguish systematically between the adjective, *large*, and the Form, Largeness: the temptation to conflate these is even stronger in Greek where the adjective can be turned into a substantive by the mere addition of the definite article (and in certain contexts even without this increment). To mark the distinction I had used "F-ness" as a Form-variable, and I continue to do so in the sequel to that paper (*TMA II*) in this volume. In the present essay (and again in *FRA* below) I turn to the Greek alphabet only for reasons of typographical economy. Were it not for this, I would still prefer to write "F-ness" for the Form-variable corresponding to the character-variable "F": the recurrence of "F" in both symbols brings out more forcefully the linguistic link between "Largeness" and "large" and the ontological bond between the entities they denote.

[29] Where x is characterized by F Plato speaks of x as "named" after Φ, its

F (i.e., *x* has the character, *F*) if, and only if, *x* participates in Φ. "Participation" here designates that one-way relation of ontological dependence between temporal things and eternal Forms which is so fundamental a tenet of this philosophy. For Plato nothing could exist in space and time with a definite character, *F*, if there did not exist a corresponding Φ, while the converse would not be true at all: the existence of a specific Form, say, of a *chiliagon*, would of itself not offer the slightest assurance of its physical instantiation; not only the Form of the Ideal City (*R.* 592AB), but infinitely many other Forms as well exist which have been uninstantiated since time began and may so remain for ever in Plato's universe. So much of his intention is clear enough. But if we probe further, pressing him to tell us just what it is that happens when a particular *F* achieves the required "participation" in a Φ, Plato has no definite answer for us, and he is well aware of this fact. He makes no effort to conceal from the reader that he has yet to reach a clear-cut conception of what "participation" involves, speaking of the relation of Beauty to beautiful things as "presence [παρουσία] or association [κοινωνία] or whatever be the right word for it" (100D5-6).[30] Here is something Plato has not yet cleared up to his satisfaction, though he doubtless expects he will, remaining quite certain for the present that some such relation exists and that, were it not for this, the fact that things have characters would be unintelligible.[31] [301]

"namesake" (cf. *Phaedo* 78E, *Prm.* 133D, *Sph.* 234B7, *Ti.* 52A), interpreting the predicative statement, "*x* is *F*" as "naming" *x* "*F*": cf. the formula in *R.* 596A, "we are accustomed to posit a single Form for each plurality to which we apply the same name"; cf. also *Sph.* 251A-B, "when we speak of a man we give him many additional names: we attribute to him colors and shapes. . . . And so with everything else: we take any given thing as one and yet speak of it as many and by many names" (Cornford's translation).

[30] The above translation proceeds on the assumption that Wyttenbach's emendation of προσγενομένη in the MS. to προσαγορευομένη (which appears to have confirmation in a papyrus: cf. Hackforth's note *ad loc.*) is correct. If we stick to the MS. reading (cf. R. S. Bluck [1955] *ad loc.*) or accept Cornford's emendation (p. 77, note 1) to προσγενομένου, the last clause in the above citation would read, "in whatever manner it may come about" or "whatever the relationship may be." The difference will not be great in either case, and will not affect at all the important thing in the citation, *sc.* the avowal of uncertainty in εἴτε ὅπῃ δὴ καὶ ὅπως. For Plato's use of εἴτε ὅπῃ (augmented in the third example by εἴτε ὅπως) to avow uncertainty, see *Prm.* 133D, τὰ παρ' ἡμῖν ὁμοιώματα εἴτε ὅπῃ δή τις αὐτὰ τίθεται, *Ti.* 48C, εἴτε ἀρχὴ εἴτε ἀρχὰς εἴτε ὅπῃ δοκεῖ περὶ τὸ νῦν, and *Laws* 899B, εἴτε ἐν σώμασι ἐνοῦσαι . . . εἴτε ὅπῃ τε καὶ ὅπως.

[31] Though the expectation was never adequately fulfilled, Plato retained the

Armed with this "hypothesis," Socrates feels empowered to give two complementary answers to the question, "Why is x F?"[32] Let us begin with the first, which he calls the "safe" but "simple-minded" and "ignorant" (100DE; 105C) *aitia*. This is just that x is F because it participates in Φ.[33] What could he mean by that? Two interpretations have been advanced which I take to be mistaken.

On one of them, the Form would be a teleological *aitia*.[34] I fail to see how this could be squared with the following feature of our passage: Socrates makes it abundantly clear that he is still, at the time of speaking,

---

confidence that somehow or other things must "participate" in the Forms. In the *Parmenides*, at the end of the second regress argument, Parmenides does not conclude that the notion of participation has been invalidated, but only that "we must look for some other way [i.e., a way other than similitude] by which they participate" (133A5-6). From Aristotle's extremely harsh remarks on "participation" (*Metaph.* 991A20-22, "for to say that they [the Forms] are patterns and the other things 'participate' in them is to use empty words and poetical metaphors," 992A28, "for 'participating,' as we have just remarked, says nothing" (τὸ γὰρ μετέχειν . . . οὐθέν ἐστιν), it seems fairly clear that this remained for contemporaries one of the most obscure parts of Plato's ontology

[32] Also, "Why does x come to be F?," which is the implied question 101C2-7: "you would loudly protest that you do not know how else each thing comes to be [F] except by coming to participate [μετασχόν] in the peculiar essence [τῆς ἰδίας οὐσίας] of that [Form] in which it comes to participate [ἑκάστου οὗ ἂν μετάσχῃ] and so here you have no *aitia* of their coming to be two except their coming to participate [μετάσχεσιν] in the Dyad—in this all things must come to participate [μετασχεῖν], if they are going to be two—and in the Unit if they are going to be one . . ." (101C2-7). For the translation of μετασχόν, μετάσχῃ, μετάσχεσιν, μετασχεῖν, cf. Cornford *ad Parm.* 129A3 (p. 69, note 1): "As in the *Phaedo*, μεταλαμβάνειν, (μετάσχεσις, *Phaedo* 101D, μετάληψις, *Prm.* 131A . . .) means *beginning* to partake when the thing becomes like (γίγνεσθαι), whereas μετέχειν is used of *having* a share and corresponds to *being* like (εἶναι);" however, "beginning to partake" should be corrected to "coming to partake" for obvious reasons (Cornford does not even use it in his own translation!).

[33] Which may be abbreviated to "x if F because of Φ" but only after the context has made it clear that this is a contraction of the correct formula: thus τῷ καλῷ πάντα τὰ καλὰ καλά in 100D7-8 is used only after *participating* in Beauty (not Beauty as such) had been said to be the *aitia* in 100B4-6 and again in 100D4-6.

[34] See, e.g., Taylor, p. 203 and note 2; Bluck, p. 199; Crombie, pp. 159 ff. The "confusions" which Crombie finds in the passage arise in part from his assumption that "it is apparently taken for granted that wherever this [i.e., a formal *aitia*] is achieved something like a teleological explanation will be forthcoming" (p. 159; "apparently taken for granted" seems to concede that nothing of the kind is said, or distinctly implied, in the text).

"deprived" of the teleological *aitia* he had been looking for.[35] But it is no less clear that the alternative line of investigation he is about to explain—the "second journey"—is not something that has popped into his head at just that moment; it is a method of inquiry on which *he has been already engaged.*[36] This method takes its starting-point from the hypothesis of the Forms. Hence, if Socrates had thought of the Forms as teleological *aitiai*, [302] he would not have said that he is still "deprived" of teleological *aitiai.* He would have said that he does have them, though only on the basis of a hypothesis. On this ground the suggested interpretation must be rejected not only as unsupported by the text—there is no mention of teleology after this point in our passage—but as contrary to the un-ambiguous implications of our text. It is, therefore, unnecessary to inquire how Plato could have assigned, without grave confusion, to his Forms—entities whose most conspicuous feature is their absolute immuta-bility—the teleological function which, both in this dialogue and in the *Timaeus*, pertains exclusively to mind or soul.[37]

A second interpretation deserves a little—if only little—more con-sideration. This is that the Form is meant to take the place of Aristotle's "efficient cause." So Aristotle himself expounds our passage, imputing to "Socrates in the *Phaedo*" the view that the Forms are "a sufficient *aitia* of generation"—a view which he proceeds to demolish by retorting (a) that eternal forms could hardly have intermittent efficacy and (b) that the causes of the events we "see" are not Forms, but individual agents—we see the doctor, not "Health itself," causing the patient's recovery.[38] It is hard to believe that so patent a misreading of Plato's doctrine[39] could

[35] Cf. note 15 above.

[36] Note the preterites: πεπραγμάτευμαι in 99D1 and 100B4, ὥρμησα in 100A3.

[37] The sole pattern of teleological explanation envisaged in the *Phaedo* is that exemplified in the purposeful agency of a mind (the cosmic *nous* of Anaxagoras, 97C1 ff.; the mind of Socrates, 98C2 ff.). In the *Timaeus* those features of the cosmos which admit of teleological explanation are exclusively those which are imputed directly to the activity of divine souls: the Demiurge (46C-E *et passim*) and "his offspring" (69C ff.). And cf. n. 45 below.

[38] *De Generatione et Corruptione* (which I abbreviate to *GC* hereafter) 335B9-24. The same interpretation and parallel criticisms in the *Metaphysics*: "In the *Phaedo* it is stated that the Forms are *aitiai* both of being and of becoming. But though the Forms exist, their participants do not come into being if there is no mover, while many other things come into being—e.g., a house, a ring—of which we [Platonists] say no Forms exist" (991B3-7).

[39] The only text that could have suggested to Aristotle that the Forms are *aitiai* of generation is 101C2-7 (cited in n. 32 above). And there the *aitia* of a thing's coming to be *F* is not (i) the Form but (ii) *the thing's coming to participate*

have been taken seriously by modern scholars. Yet Hackforth quotes it as paralleling his own claim that the Ideas are meant to be causes of "qualities of concrete things," though not of concrete things themselves:[40] "Beauty itself is not the cause of a beautiful thing, but of a thing's being beautiful" (p. 144). What sense could be made of this Hackforth does not seem to have considered. Had he done so, I doubt that he would have ever committed his interpretation to print. For since all Forms are absolutely free of spatio-temporal limitations, then if one of them were supposed to be acting on a particular spatio-temporal object, a, with a determinate property, P, we would have to suppose that it is also acting on all other objects in the universe, including those which do *not* have the property, P, and, further, that all other Forms, including Forms corresponding to properties contrary to P, are simultaneously acting on a. How then could the given Form have that specific causal effect on a which would account for its being P rather than not-P, without having the same effect on all other objects, including those which are not-P? And how could it have any determinate

---

in that Form: Socrates cites not the Dyad, but τὴν τῆς δυάδος μετάσχεσιν as the *aitia* τοῦ δύο γενέσθαι; only if Plato had said that the Dyad as such is the *aitia* of, say, a birth of twins, could he have been open to the interpretation that he is counting on the Form to do the job of the "generator" or "mover" or "maker." Contrariwise, there are many passages in the dialogues where Plato not only allows, but argues passionately, for soul as the *aitia* of generation, change, and movement (e.g., the great argument in Laws X, whose demonstrand is that soul is "first αἴτιον of generation and of perishing" (891E); cf. *Phl.* 26E ff. and *Sph.* 266B). Aristotle must also have been familiar with the doctrine of the *Timaeus* (57E-58C) that material heterogeneity (ἀνωμαλότης) or unevenness (ἀνισότης) is a physical cause of movement (cf. *Ph.* 201B20). Cf. H. Cherniss (1944, 383 ff.).

[40] He quotes with approval *GC* 335B7-24, his only reservation being that he does not think it is entirely clear whether Aristotle is saying that the Forms are supposed to be *aitiai* of the generation of substances, which Hackforth would reject, or of the generation of the attributes of substances, which he would endorse: "It is only the latter that Socrates does in fact seek to account for by participation in Forms [observe Hackforth's unawareness of the difference between (i) and (ii) explained in n. 39 above: he speaks here as though Plato were being charged by Aristotle with making (ii), instead of (i), the cause of the attributes of things]. . . . Aristotle's instances, health and science . . . suggest that he is reporting correctly. . . . In any case, . . . there is no dispute about what his [Aristotle's] criticism is: namely that the Form cannot play the part of 'efficient' or 'moving' causes. It is indeed on the weakest point in the theory that he lays his finger. . . . It is not easy to see how Plato could have answered the point about intermittent operation of the Forms in terms of the *Phaedo* doctrine" (145).

effect on *a* at all, if all those other Forms are simultaneously acting on *a* with contrary effect? The only way to avoid the absurd consequences of the supposition would be to credit Forms with the power to act selectively on different objects in the universe, directing their causal influence to some of them, withholding it from others. And how could Plato have so particularized his Forms as causal agents in the world of space and time without fouling up the most fundamental of his metaphysical principles?[41] Only the most direct and explicit evidence could persuade us that he [304] blundered so grossly. And there is no such evidence. All we have to go on is the fact that he uses the same language of the relation of the Form to a thing which he would have also used if he were speaking of the relation of a cause to its effect: Φ is that "because of which [δι' ὅτι; 100D1] *x* is *F*;[42] it is that which "makes" (ποιεῖ; 100D5) *x* to be *F*; it is the *aitia* of *x*'s being *F* (e.g., 100C6–7; 101C4–5). Is there no other way of construing these statements that will make better sense?

Consider the following exchange: "Why is this figure a square?"— "*Because* it has four equal sides *and* four equal angles. If it had just the four equal sides that would not *make* it a square; it could have been, for all that, a rhombus."[43] Here it is clear that the "because" which answers

---

[41] See Cherniss (1944, 452 and n. 397) on the proposition that "the ideas themselves are never made productive agents" in Plato's philosophy. In view of this interpretation, which Cherniss maintains forcefully and consistently throughout this work, he might have done better to avoid speaking of the Ideas as "causes" of their "approximations" in the sensible world (218) or "of the particular's being" (373) or "of that which in particulars is similar whenever and wherever it occurs" (375). He makes it quite clear, of course, that by saying that the Ideas are "causes" he does *not* mean that they have causal efficacy; what remains unclear is just what *is* meant, when this is not, to justify the use of the term "cause" in this connection.

[42] The "because" can also be expressed by the "instrumental" dative: τῷ καλῷ, 100D7, E2; μεγέθει, 100E5, etc.

[43] Compare: "Those characteristics that are indispensable to an act's being just are the characteristics which make the act a just act", Susan Stebbing (1933, 429). "To teach what makes a member of any class a good member of the class . . . ," R. M. Hare (1952, 102). We find similar uses of "makes" with transparently logical import in Plato's earlier dialogues: Charmides is asked to consider "what sort of man temperance makes you by being present in you" (ὁποῖόν τινα σὲ ποιεῖ ἡ σωφροσύνη παροῦσα) and to answer accordingly the question, "What is temperance?" (*Chrm.* 160D6-7). Hippias agrees that "that which is fitting for each thing is what makes [ποιεῖ] each thing beautiful," where "fitting" is being considered as a possible *definiens* of "beautiful" (*Hpp. Ma.* 290D). Cf. W. D. Ross (1951, 16) on Socrates' request

our "Why?" is not meant to explain the occurrence of a square-shaped chalkmark on our blackboard. The occurrence is presupposed and no interest is taken in its cause. Our question is not "What made that chalkmark?" nor yet "What made that chalkmark square?", but rather "What *makes* it square?", which could only mean in this context: Why do we classify it as a square, rather than as a figure of some other shape? Our question is answered when we are shown that the chalkmark *happens to have*—not, how or why *it happened to get*—the shape that meets the logical conditions for being square. The *aitia* we are given is a logical one.

At first sight this may seem suspiciously deflationary of what is said in our text. When Socrates maintains with such dogged emphasis that a beautiful thing "is beautiful for no other reason [*305*] than because it participates in Beauty" (100C5-6), he is certainly putting forward a thesis which could not be reduced with any plausibility to the logical truth that a particular thing instantiates a concept if, and only if, it satisfies the definition. But such a reduction is the last thing I would wish to suggest. To do so I would have to argue that for Plato logic is a metaphysically noncommittal business; and who would want to say such a thing on his behalf? What is his Theory of Forms if not the claim that logical statements presuppose metaphysical ones and would be mumbo-jumbo without them? For Plato the definition of a concept is "the account of the essence" (λόγος τῆς οὐσίας) of its Form, Φ.[44] The reason why we can

---

to Hippias, "Teach me what the beautiful itself is" (*Hp. Ma.* 286D8). Ross comments:

> The question conceals a certain ambiguity, of which Plato was perhaps not aware. It might mean 'what is that very characteristic which the word "beautiful" stands for?', or it might mean 'what is the characteristic or set of characteristics, other than beauty, which a thing must have in order to be beautiful?' But the phrase 'the beautiful *itself*' points to the first interpretation; and a hint in favour of this may be seen in a passage of the Charmides (175B3), in which Socrates is asking the parallel question about self-control. He there says 'we have failed to discover what that is to which the imposer of names gave the name of self-control'. It is not, then, the connexion between beauty and its conditions that Socrates wants to know, but the nature of the very characteristic for which the word 'beauty' stands.

[44] "That reality itself [αὐτὴ ἡ οὐσία], of whose essence we give the account [ἧς λόγον δίδομεν τοῦ εἶναι] when we ask and answer our questions, is it ever invariably the same or does it vary? Equality itself, Beauty itself, each 'what is' in itself, the reality [αὐτὸ ἕκαστον ὃ ἔστιν, τὸ ὄν], does it ever admit the least alteration?" (*Phaedo* 78D1-5). Burnet rightly remarks *ad loc.* in his Commentary

speak significantly and truly of things being square or beautiful, he would
insist, is that there exists an incorporeal, immutable, intelligible object,
named "Squareness" or "Beauty," in which corporeal, mutable, sensible
objects occasionally "participate" and, when they do, are rightly called
"square" or "beautiful." So what I have called the "logical" *aitia* is at the
same time a metaphysical one for Plato; the logical function of Squareness,
Beauty, etc., he is convinced, could not be discharged aside from their
metaphysical status. But once that is granted, it is the logical function
of the metaphysical entity that does the *explanatory* work of the "safe"
aitia. When I want to know what makes this figure a square rather than a
pentagon, what answers my question is not the *existence* as such of the Form,
Square [306]—countless other Forms also exist which do not help to
answer my question—but the logical content of its definition: this is what
marks off the Form, Square, from all these other Forms and, isomorphically,
marks off every square in our world from instances of all the other figures.
And the fact that this logical function is performed by a celestial Form,
rather than·by a nominalistic *flatus vocis*, in no way alters the strictly non-
causal import of the formula, "F in virtue of satisfying the definition."
In and of itself, Plato's Squareness has no more causal efficacy than has
the nominalist's; it has no power to spawn earthly squares; if it did, so
would the Form, Myriagon, and each of the countless others that have
had no mundane progeny and never will.[45]

---

that "we must take λόγον τοῦ εἶναι together as equivalent to λόγον τῆς οὐσίας
or 'definition' (comparing *Rep.* 534B3, διαλεκτικὸν καλεῖς τὸν λόγον ἑκάστου
λαμβάνοντα τῆς οὐσίας) and as governing the genitive ῆς." Cf. also *Rep.* 532A7-
B1, and also *Laws* 895DE, where the distinction is drawn between the name,
the οὐσία it names, and the λόγος of this οὐσία. It is a mistake to suppose that
there is any Form of which there is no λόγος. The view that in *Smp.* 211A it
is said or implied that of the Form of Beauty "there is no *logos* nor knowledge"
(R. C. Cross 1954, 433 ff., at p. 443) is not warranted by the text, which only
says that Beauty "will not appear" (οὐδὲ φαντασθήσεται) *as logos* or knowledge
(since it will appear as that *of* which we have *logos* and knowledge).

[45] Note that when Plato says in the *Timaeus* that the Ideal Model may be
"likened" to the "father" of generation, the Receptacle to the "mother," and
the things that compose our world to the "offspring," 50D2-4, he makes it
very clear that he assigns no causal function to the Ideas in respect of either
of the two kinds of causality (teleological and mechanical) which he recognizes
in that dialogue (46C7 ff.). The metaphorical remarks in *R.* 506E, 507A, and
508B about the sun as the "offspring" of the Idea of the Good must be inter-
preted in the light of what Plato means when he says in the *Timaeus* that the
whole of the natural universe, not just the sun, is the "offspring" of the Ideas
generally, not just of the Idea of the Good. In the *Timaeus* the metaphor is

This interpretation of the "*F* in virtue of Φ" formula frees Plato from so much embarrassment and is so consonant with everything else we know of his metaphysical views that it would have a strong claim on us even without further confirmation.[46] In point of fact we do get confirmation for it from two distinct data in our passage. [*307*]

---

employed in the context of a cosmological scheme which enables us to control the intended meaning in a way which is altogether denied us by the allusive and unexplicated use of the metaphor in Book VI of the *Republic*. When the "father" metaphor is used in the *Timaeus* in a context which makes it clear that the metaphor does express (teleological) causal agency, it is applied not to the Forms, but to the Demiurge (28C3-4) in contradistinction to the Forms.

[46] A number of commentators entertain and, to all appearances, endorse a substantially identical interpretation, only to shy away from it a page or two later, or even a line or two later. To recount these vagaries in detail would require a special monograph (a rather tedious one). A single illustration must suffice. Cornford (1939) begins on p. 77 with an impeccable gloss on 100C4-6: "the fact that this rose is beautiful is the same thing as the fact that this rose partakes of Beauty. We learn nothing about any *cause* which would bring that fact into existence." But see what happens when he proceeds (immediately) to 100D1-8, where Plato, having spoken three lines earlier of Beauty as (a) the reason why (διότι) *x* is beautiful, goes on to speak of it also as (b) what makes (ποιεῖ) *x* beautiful and to say also (c) that *x* is beautiful *because of* Beauty (τῷ καλῷ: instrumental dative; cf. note 42, above), Cornford becomes greatly exercised over the use of "makes" and wonders: "Does it [the "makes"] mean that the thing's beauty simply *consists in* the presence either of the Form itself or of the character like that of the Form, as we say that the presence of a gay colour 'makes' the thing gay? Or does it mean that the Form, existing independently, *causes* the thing to be (or to become) beautiful by somehow imparting its own character to the thing? This is precisely the dilemma on which Socrates refuses to pronounce. The language might be expressly designed to leave it unresolved." (The italics are Conford's.) Now (b), "makes," could not have causal import unless (c), "because of," did, since the latter is used to say the same thing in 100D7 as was said by the use of "makes" at D4-5; and this in turn is the same thing as was expressed by the use of (a), δι' ὅτι in D1, the very expression used at C5, where Cornford was certain that it had no causal import; how then could he be left uncertain as to the import of "makes" at 100D5? Moreover, any uncertainty on this score could have been resolved by noting that the "makes" is used in Socratic dialogues (cf. note 43) where Cornford would not think of reading causal import into it. That Cornford himself cannot be taking very seriously the "dilemma" on which Socrates supposedly "refuses to pronounce" in 100D1-8, appears on p. 79, where he talks as though the supposed "dilemma" has been firmly resolved in favor of its non-causal horn. He speaks of "Simmias comes to partake of Tallness" as the Platonic analysis of "Simmias becomes tall": "This is a description of the same event in other words. Nothing is said as to any 'cause' in our sense, which would make such an event take place as its effect." But he backslides

In the first place, it makes good sense of the fact that this formula is proposed as the "safe" but "ignorant" or "simple-minded"[47] *aitia*. This is what it would obviously be for anyone who has already accepted the metaphysical "hypothesis" on which this *aitia* is so explicitly pegged.[48] On this hypothesis, for all x, x is F if, and only if, x participates in Φ. From this it follows with the "safety" of analytic inference that a, or b, or c, or any other x, is F *[308]* in virtue of participating in Φ. For just the same reason this *aitia* is "ignorant" i.e., uninformative.[49] Not only does it not profess to give us the slightest help in finding out the cause of any specific happening in the world; it does not even aid us in discovering its correct description: only if we already know that something is F (i.e., if

---

again on p. 80 in glossing 103D (where, e.g., snow perishes at the approach of heat): "Socrates seems to be unaware that the only efficient cause of change he actually describes is a physical cause of precisely the kind which, in the account of his youthful experiences, he had rejected as unsatisfying." If "coming to partake of Tallness" has no causal import, then Socrates would not have the slightest reason for being "unaware" of the existence of physical causes of becoming tall; why then should he be "unaware" of such causes in the case of a thing ceasing to be snow (i.e., melting) and becoming hot when it comes to partake of Heat?

[47] It is safe: 100D8, E1; 101D1-3; 105B7-C1. It is "simple, artless, and perhaps simple-minded (or stupid, εὐήθως)" 100D3-4; "ignorant," 105C.

[48] Plato, of course, would not apply the same description to the "hypothesis," i.e., to the Theory of Ideas. Obviously he would not think of *this* as "simple-minded," nor yet as having the kind of "safety" he is now talking about, since he presents it as a "hypothesis" and refrains from claiming that he has proved it conclusively in this dialogue (which, of course, does not imply that he does not think it susceptible of conclusive proof: in the exchange with Simmias at 107A8-B9 Socrates concedes that the Theory calls for further investigation, but makes no avowl of uncertainty, as was suggested by Jowett's influential but gratuitous rendering of καθ' ὅσον δυνατὸν μάλιστ' ἀνθρώπῳ by "with a sort of hesitating confidence in human reason" now happily corrected to "as far as humanly possible" in the Fourth Revised edition, Oxford, 1953 . The "safety" of the present *aitia* is due to its being so immediate a consequence of the "hypothesis" that once you accepted the latter *you would risk nothing further* in maintaining this *aitia*.

[49] This is no doubt what Shorey had in mind when he spoke of the "tautological logic" of the theory that the Ideas are *aitiai* (cf. the citation in the opening paragraph of this paper and the references in n. 3). Unhappily he failed to note that this could only be said of the "safe" *aitia*, and not at all of the "cleverer" one (to be discussed in the next section of this paper) which is conspicuously non-tautological in form, this being the very reason why it is called the "clever" *aitia*. Even in the case of the "safe" *aitia* a certain qualification is necessary (cf. n. 78 below) of which Shorey took no notice.

we have already so described it) can we proceed on the strength of this
aitia to say that it is *F* in virtue of Φ, showing that our description matches
the definition and thereby clinching the propriety of calling it "*F*" rather
than "*G*" or something else.

Second, the interpretation I have offered makes good sense of another
thing in our passage to which I have yet to make reference: the fact that
the formula, "*F* in virtue of participating in Φ," is expected to resolve
the puzzles about *aitia* which were displayed in Division One of our
passage.[50] The first four of these (96D8-E4) [309] are peculiarly mystifying
to the modern reader.[51] He is likely to find them not so much puzzles as
meta-puzzles: What perplexes him is what there is in any of them that
Plato could have thought perplexing. The first pair (98D8-E1) look almost
like a spoof. Socrates is supposed to have believed in his benighted youth
that if one man overtops another by a head, he does so *because of* a head,

[50] They are stated in 96D8-97B3, and resolved in 100E5 ff. I do not lump
96C2-D6 with the puzzles: the belief that a man grows by the intake of food and
drink involves no absurdity which needs to be cleared up by the machinery
of the "safe" *aitia*: when the clearing up is done in 100E5 ff. there is no mention
of or allusion to the belief that we grow by taking in food and drink; note also
that there is no censure or any other adverse reflection on the belief reported
in 96C7-D5, while, on the contrary, a seal of retrospective approval is given
it in the concluding words, οὕτως τότε ᾤμην· οὐ δοκῶ σοι μετρίως; The point
of 96C2-D6 is surely to illustrate *another way* in which an infatuation with the
methodology of the natural philosophers could do a tyro far more harm than
good: it could lead him to "unlearn" (96C6) familiar truths, persuading him
that he knew only those causes which he could formulate in the categories of
an elaborate physical system and hence to spurn explanations of the usual
kind which are cast in homely, everyday language, yet are far more worthy of
credence than the windy theorizings which the *physiologoi* would have put in
their place. (There is no foundation for Burnet's suggestion *ad locum* [appar-
ently swallowed by Hackforth, p. 131] that "Socrates means that his former
beliefs were upset by the question of Anaxagoras [fr. 10], 'for how could hair
come from that which is not hair and flesh from that which is not flesh?' ".
Anaxagoras' highly speculative answer to this question, if true, would not
"upset," but only *account for* the belief in 96C8-D5 that a man can increase his
bulk by eating and drinking, "when flesh was added to flesh, bone to bone,"
etc.)

[51] For many years I could not make head or tail of these puzzles, and used
to take them as symptomatic of some kind of muddle in Plato's thinking,
though without sharing Crombie's confidence that it was the kind of muddle
that a tyro in philosophy could diagnose. It was only when I reached the
interpretation of the "safe" *aitia* which I present in this paper and saw what
kind of solution it would provide to these puzzles that I began to see what
gave rise to their perplexities in the first place.

and that the same is true of horses: if one horse is taller than another by a head, the *aitia* of its superior height is—the head![52] The next pair (E1-4), on the contrary, look like commonplaces: Socrates thought at that time that 10 things are more than 8 *because* there are 2 more of them in the 10 (than in the 8); and that, given two objects, 2 and 1 yards long respectively, the first will be the longer *because* it exceeds the second by half its own length. One wonders how anyone, no matter how young and callow, could have been expected to swallow the absurdities in the first pair, or blamed for countenancing the platitudes in the second.

Light dawns in the following paragraph, where we come upon a fifth and a sixth puzzle: Why does 1, added to 1, make 2? (96E6-97A5). Why does 1, divided by 2, make 2 (halves)? (97A5-B3). Here the mode of presentation changes:[53] Instead of recounting, [*310*] poker-faced, mistakes incurred in his distant youth when he had been "utterly blinded" (96C5) by his obsessive attachment to mechanistic aetiology, Socrates now refers to similar errors from his present, entirely different, philosophical perspective, and gives us broad hints as to why he can no longer stomach[54] the answers his previous "method" of thinking had made compelling. Thus, the old answer to the question in the fifth puzzle would have been: the addition of one unit to the other is what makes 2 of them.[55] This, he now says, he no longer accepts, and for the following reason:

> For I would be astounded if, when each of them was apart from the other [ὅτε μὲν ἑκάτερον αὐτῶν χωρὶς ἀλλήλων ἦν], each was one and they were not then two, but when they approached each other [ἐπλησίασαν ἀλλήλοις] *this* became the *aitia* of their becoming two: the conjunction [ἡ σύνοδος] involved in their being put close to each other [τοῦ πλησίον ἀλλήλων τεθῆναι]. (97A2-5)[55A]

---

[52] On the face of it, this is a low-grade pun: the dative, τῇ κεφαλῇ, could be used to mean both "by a head" and "because of a head."

[53] The change in tone and perspective is marked by Cebes' question, immediately after the previous puzzles had been laid out: "And how do you think of these things *now*?" (96E5). Thereafter Socrates' verbs change from the past tense in D8-E4 to the present.

[54] "I do not accept," 96E7; "I would be [literally, "am"] astounded if," 97A2; etc., winding up at B7 with "I will have no truck with this [method of thinking [which gives rise to the puzzles]" (τοῦτον δὲ οὐδαμῇ προσίεμαι).

[55] 96E8-97A1. To simplify the exposition I abbreviate this puzzle which in the text (Burnet's, with his expansion) presents the result of adding A to B as a disjunction: either B becomes two, or A becomes two, or A and B taken together become two. The last of the three disjuncts suffices for my purposes above.

[55A] And cf. 97B2, συνήγετο πλησίον ἀλλήλων καὶ προσετίθετο ἕτερον ἑτέρῳ.

Here at last we see the gaffe Socrates had been perpetrating in that period which antedated his discovery of the "safe" *aitia*. He had been confusing the arithmetical operation of addition with a physical process—that of taking things which were "apart" to begin with and putting them "close to each other."[56] And he had been supposing that this material process was the [*311*] *aitia* of the logico-mathematical truth that the same items which count as units, if taken disjointly, will count as a pair, if taken conjointly. Looking back at this boner from his present philosophical perspective, Socrates says he would be "astounded" if such a thing were true: he would suffer that peculiar sense of intellectual outrage we all feel when asked to believe a proposition which is not just materially false but logically absurd. For obviously the things being talked about are two by hypothesis, and they would still be two regardless of whether they were jammed up together in a cupboard or situated in different galaxies a million light-years apart. How absurd then to offer their propinquity as the reason why they are two![57] So the puzzle can now be solved or, more exactly, dissolved, Plato's solvent being the "*F* in virtue of Φ" formula.[58]

[56] The literal meaning of the verb used for addition, προστίθημι Α τῷ Β, is literally "put A next to B." This dead metaphor comes alive in the passage, Socrates shifting back and forth from this verb to variant expressions which refer unmistakably to putting objects close to one another, while he denotes the inverse operation not by the usual terms for arithmetical subtraction (ἀφαίρεσις) or division (διαίρεσις), but by words which have strong physical evocations: "splitting" (σχίσις, A7: cf. διασχίσει; A6), "leading apart" (ἀπάγεται, B3), and "separating" (χωρίζεται, B3).

[57] This is reinforced by a further objection: If we were to take twoness as the effect of conjunction we would be faced with the (supposed) paradox that the opposite process of disjunction causes the same effect. Socrates is going on the assumption that if a given process causes a certain effect, the opposite process could not also cause the same effect. There is a fallacy here, but apparently not an obvious one, for I have seen no notice of it in the literature: Even if we were to concede the truth of the assumption, the conclusion would follow only if it were true that the disjunction and conjunction *of the same items* produced the same effect. But the latter would *not* be true in the two cases Socrates is discussing: he gets twoness in the first case by conjoining units A and B; he gets it in the second by disjoining not the same units, but parts inside each of them. However, this fallacy does not invalidate the fundamental insight I expound above; this can dispense entirely with this additional support, which, as it happens, is unsound.

[58] This becomes clear in Division Two of our passage where (100E5-B7) all of the puzzles are resolved seriatim by applying to each the "*F* in virtue of Φ" formula. This fundamental point, which should be made the pivot of the interpretation of the puzzles, is not even mentioned by Hackforth (p. 131): he gives no indication that the puzzle laid out in 96E6 ff. is stuffed with hints

If things are one in virtue of participating in Unity, [312] two in virtue of participating in the Dyad, then it will be clear that the "Why?" in "Why do 1 and 1 make 2?" cannot be a physical "Why?" and that its answering "because" must be extracted not from accounts of what happens to objects when they are moved about, but from "accounts of the essence"[59] of the numbers, One and Two.[60]

---

of the correct solution and that in Plato's opinion the "*F* in virtue of Φ" formula provides the correct solution. So it is hardly surprising that Hackforth should labor under the misapprehension that Plato is himself taken in by "unreal problems" (cf. the citation from Hackforth and my comment in the concluding paragraph of this Section). Crombie too thinks that Plato wallows in the very confusions which the "safe" *aitia* is meant to clear up. Thus he says that "phrases like 'the putting of one alongside one is not the cause of the occurrence of 2' [101B9-C1] are used without any clear indication whether the question is: [a] 'Why are there two things here?' (to which an answer in terms of putting one thing alongside another would be appropriate); or whether the question is: [b] 'How does the number 2 arise?' " (p. 169; I have interpolated the reference-marks). Crombie, most surprisingly, fails to take into account the fact that for Plato the number, Two, a Form, could no more "arise" than perish and, hence, could not "arise" from the putting together of two physical objects. Conversely, the fact that if we did put together two physical objects "here," we would get "two things here," would be as obvious to Plato as to anyone else. Hence Plato could have denounced "because of putting one [object] alongside another" *only* if he thought this an answer to [b]; for he would have seen it as a trivially true answer to [a]. How then could he have failed to distinguish [a] from [b]?

[59] Cf. the citation in notes 44 and 32 above, noting the force of τῆς ἰδίας οὐσίας in the latter. In the *Republic* Plato says that it is the philosopher's job to ask "what is the essence of the One itself" (τί ποτέ ἐστιν αὐτὸ τὸ ἕν, 524E6) (and by the same token of *Two* and other numbers). When one had done this one would see that the "accounts of the essence" of One and of Two allow for the participation of the same objects, taken singly, in One, taken jointly, in Two. Cf. *Hip. Maj.* 301D8-9 where much is made of the fact that *Two* can only be instantiated by a pair of individuals, each of whom is *one*; the same point is made in *Tht.* 185B2, ὅτι ἀμφοτέρω δύο, ἑκάτερον δὲ ἕν.

[60] A substantially similar interpretation will be found in Moreau (1939), my only objections to it being (a) that he has to make Plato a neo-Kantian idealist to bring it off ("La cause de la production du 2, c'est à dire d'un objet de représentation double, ce n'est donc pas le rapprochement ou la séparation dans l'espace, mais dans l'esprit. . . . Toutes les difficultés de cette sorte sont donc levées par l'idéalisme mathématique, qui fait de l'unité un act intellectuel indivisible et du nombre une pure relation," p. 382) and (b) that he does not realize how inappropriate "cause" (cf. the start of the citation) becomes when it is clear that (i) this *aitia* is not a physical one and (ii) Plato is not proposing that a psychological cause be substituted for the physical one. In spite of these

All four of the puzzles in 96D8-E4 will yield to the same treatment on the hypothesis[61] that all of them crop up because in this [*313*] benighted phase of his philosophical evolution Socrates[62] was confusing physical *aitiai* with logical ones: he was assuming that a material factor, like a head, or the material presence of two units, or the material projection of a part of one thing beyond another could account for the respective statements, all of which are true *a priori*, and could only be accounted for by referring to the meaning of the terms they use. Thus, take the most interesting of the puzzles: Why are 10 things more than 8 things? Reflecting on this in Part Two, now that he is well out of that particular fly-bottle, Socrates declares:

---

objections, I must record my heavy debt to Moreau. I have derived greater help from his discussion of the puzzles in the *Phaedo* than from any other single source.

[61] I say "hypothesis," for certainly there is nothing whatever in the wording of these six lines which states or directly implies that their puzzles arise because physical factors are being confused with logical ones. For this hypothesis I claim no more than indirect verification from the context. We start at 96A8 with the tale of young Socrates' addiction to a methodology which restricts the quest for *aitiai* to physical causes. We are then given a sequence of 6 puzzles, all of them illustrative of the same perverse line of thought (cf. Cebes' question in 96E6, which concerns the first four, but is answered by the presentation and discussion of the last two; and note that the same solution is offered for all six in 100E8-101C9). The last two puzzles are discussed *in extenso* (12 lines for these 2 as against 6 lines for the first 4); and these, as I argued above, turn out to be cases of confusion of physical with logical *aitiai*. It is, therefore, reasonable to assume that the first four are also cases of the same confusion and that this would have come out into the open if they had been discussed, instead of merely mentioned, in the text.

[62] It should be noticed that Plato does not say that *the natural philosophers* had made this confusion, but only that Socrates did so when *he* came under the spell of their teaching. Plato does not hesitate to attack his predecessors sharply for their obnoxious doctrines (see, e.g., *Phl.* 28D-29A; *Ti.* 48B; *Laws* 888E-890A and 967A-D). So it is unlikely that he would have hesitated to lambaste them in this passage if such absurdities as those in 96D8 ff. had figured in their writings. And the fact is that no surviving fragment of their original works indulges in this kind of thing. In the light of these considerations we had best refrain from ascribing such logical solecisms to the physical philosophers and mathematicians of the time (as is sometimes done in the literature: e.g., Crombie, pp. 160–61), and understand Plato to mean in our passage no more than he actually says and directly implies, i.e., that since they had failed to clarify the concept of *aitia* and to sort out its categorially different import for categorially different subject-matter, they had left their readers defenseless against such confusions as those recounted in our passage.

So you would be afraid to say [i.e., you would *not* say] that the 10
things are more than the 8 in virtue of 2 things, and that it is because
of *this* that they exceed, instead of saying that they exceed in virtue
of numerousness and because of numerousness. (101B4-6)

What Socrates is telling us, put into modern language, is that the reason
why the group of 10 is more numerous than the group of 8 is simply that
it satisfies the logico-metaphysical[63] conditions [*314*] of (greater) numerousness. If this were to strike us as uninformative, Plato would agree (this
is an "ignorant" *aitia*), but insist that it is not useless on that account, for
it would save us from misdirecting our search for *aitiai* to irrelevant
factors, such as—in his own formulation of this puzzle—the presence
in one group of two units which are not in the other. This would be the
reddest of red herrings, unless it were logically related to the relative
numerousness of the two groups, e.g., by showing that the first has as
many units as does the second *and* more units besides—not necessarily
these two units, nor necessarily *two* units: *any* number of units in the first
group over and above those in it which match, unit for unit, the ones
in the second group would fulfill the logical requirements of greater numerousness, and thus enable us to say precisely why there are more in the
first than there are in the second.[64] If the "safe" and "ignorant" *aitia*

---

[63] I say "logico-metaphysical" rather than just "logical," in deference to the
point I made earlier, that for Plato the logical relation of a term to the concept
under which it falls is at the same time the metaphysical relation of a sensible
to an eternal Form. To say that something is the case "in virtue of numerousness
and because of numerousness" (the same thing said twice over again for emphasis, first by the instrumental dative, πλήθει, and then by an accusative with
a preposition, διὰ τὸ πλῆθος) is expansible into "in virtue of participating in
the Form, Numerousness."

[64] In this discussion I have deliberately gone beyond what we get in the
text, in order to bring out the further implications of Plato's basic insight. If
he had had at his disposal techniques of analysis such as are available nowadays
to beginners, he could have offered a general formula to cover all four of the
puzzles in 96D8-E4, laying down the contextual definition, "where A, B, C are
(positive) magnitudes or cardinals, A is greater than B if, and only if, there
exists a C such that A = B + C", and then showing that this definition is
satisfied in all four cases: In puzzles *1* and *2*, A = the height of the first (man
or horse); B = the height of the second; C = the length of a head. In puzzle
3 (the one discussed in the text above), A = 10 units; B = 8 units; C = 2
units. In puzzle *4*, A = 2 yards; B = 1 yard; C = A/2 yards (= 1 yard). Had
Plato been able to clean up the problem in this way, he would have spared his
readers two blemishes in his present account which help explain why his sound

did this kind of work [315] for Plato one can see why he could find it so enlightening while ascribing to it no causal agency.

It is sad then to see him charged by serious scholars with having made the very error which, if I am right, he was the first to spot. Thus Hackforth takes him to task for posing a pseudo-problem in asking for the *aitia* of 10 being more than 8:

> The question whether the addition of 2 is the cause of 10 being greater than 8 is meaningless, because there is no more a cause of 10 being greater than 8 than there is of Thursday coming after Wednesday. (p. 131)

---

insight may be so easily missed:

(a) he says "numerousness" (πλήθει, πλῆθος) in 101B6, instead of "*greater numerousness*," and "magnitude" (μεγέθει) in 101B7, instead of "*greater magnitude*," thereby failing to bring out that both are special cases of the "greater than" relation, and that the absolute numerousness or bigness of the things he is talking about is irrelevant to the reasoning;

(b) he gives spurious reasons for rejecting "a head" (i.e., the presence of a physical magnitude the length of a head) as the cause of A's being bigger than B in the first of the two puzzles, saying (101A5-B2) that this would lead to a two-fold contradiction:

> (i) the same cause would produce contrary effects (the presence in A of a magnitude equaling a head would result in A being *bigger*, B *smaller*) and
> (ii) a cause with a given character would produce an effect of a contrary character (the head, a *small* magnitude, would make A *big*).

The appearance of contradiction arises only because the supposed effect of the alleged cause has been misstated in both cases:

In (i) the supposed effect, correctly stated, is (*P*), "A is bigger *than B*" and (*Q*), "B is smaller *than A*"—not (*P'*), "A is *bigger*," and (*Q'*), "B is *smaller*" (sc., than each would otherwise be). *P* and *Q*, so far from being contraries (as are *P'* and *Q'*), are logically equivalent propositions.

In (ii) the supposed effect, correctly stated, is not (*P''*), "A is big," but only *P* above; and *P''*, of course, does *not* follow from *P*: there is no reason why a man or a horse has to be a big man or horse in order to be bigger than another man or horse (for other examples of this fallacy in Plato see *DR*, pp. 71-72, above. I submit that here, as in the case of the fallacy I pointed out in note 57 above, Plato's residual confusions and fallacies (which are entirely understandable in a thinker who lacked the rudiments of the logic of relations) do not cancel the validity of the fundamental insight expressed in the "*F* in virtue of participating in Φ" formula. To see the traps into which Plato falls is to admire all the more the tenacity with which, in spite of these mishaps, he pursued the truth he saw.

Certainly there is no *cause* here, and who should know this better than does Plato, who gives us, as one showpiece of cockeyed thinking about *aitia*, the puzzle generated by assuming that there is a (physical) cause for the truth that $1 + 1 = 2$? But though there are no causes for such truths, there are most certainly reasons for them, and it was a mark of genius to see that where one type of *aitia*, with its peculiar methodological commitments (those of physical inquiry), is inapplicable, another type of *aitia*, with its entirely different (logico-mathematical) methodology, *is* applicable, and to make his metaphysical theory the vehicle of this insight. [316]

III. THE "CLEVER" AITIA

We can now consider Socrates' second answer to the "Why is x F?" question. Instead of mentioning just the one Form, Φ, he now refers us also to another, Γ, so related to Φ, that whatever is "named after" (i.e., characterized by)[65] Γ, will also be "named after" Φ (103E2-104B4). The first example given of the Γ-Φ relation is the pair, Three-Odd: whatever is a trio will also be odd-numbered. From this and other examples it is clear that he has in view a transitive, non-symmetrical[66] relation. He has no technical name for it and is content to use a metaphor: he speaks of Γ "bringing on" Φ.[67] I shall speak of it as "entailment," extending this term beyond its normal use as a propositional connective and allowing it to

[65] Cf. note 29 above.

[66] Plato's relation has to cover both cases such as those of the Three-Odd, Snow-Cold couplings, where the relation is clearly antisymmetric, and also others in which, for all we know to the contrary, Plato perhaps thought of the relation as symmetrical, as in the case of the Fire-Hot coupling. What is certain (from examples like Three-Odd, Two-Even, etc.) is that Plato thinks of participating in Γ as a sufficient, but not also a necessary, condition of participating in Φ.

[67] Having started off at 103E2 ff. using still more cumbersome language to express the Γ-Φ relation (which I have abbreviated above to "whatever is 'named' by Γ will also be 'named' by Φ"), he shifts casually to ἐπιφέρειν at 104E10 and uses it frequently thereafter (I surmise: simply because it is shorter), varying it with the expression discussed in the preceding note, where the Γ-Φ relation is indicated *via* the isomorphic *G-F* relation: if *G* comes to be present in *x*, then *x* will be *F*. As Shorey points out (1924, 11 and note 3; for more examples see Bonitz, *Index Aristotelicus*) the terms ἐπιφέρειν and συνεπιφέρειν as well as some of the other terms used here by Plato to express relations between Forms are also used by Aristotle to express entailment relations between general terms.

connect concepts,[67A] as we sometimes do in informal contexts.[68] The formula then for this *aitia* could be put as follows: "x *is* F *because it participates in* Γ *and* Γ *entails* Φ"; or, more elaborately: "x *is* F *because, being* G, *it must participate in* Γ; *and since* Γ *entails* Φ, x *must also participate in* Φ, *and hence* x *must be* [317] F." Plato does not spell out any such formula as this. But an examination of his text will show, I believe, that this is what the sketchier phrasings there imply. For what he understands by them we must rely on his examples. There is a flock of them. First, he gives additional arithmetical cases of Γ-Φ linkages: Five-Odd, Two-Even, Four-Even, Ten-Even.[69] Then, without any apparent shifting of gears, still talking about precisely the same relation, explaining precisely the same *aitia*, he brings in physical, biological, and other examples of Form Γ, entailing Form Φ: Fire-Heat, Snow-Cold, Fever-Sickness, Soul-Life.[70] Does this answer to the "Why is *x* F?" question give us more reason than did the preceding to think that his Forms are meant to be causes?

Let me press one of his examples, where Fever is the *aitia* of a sickness. We may assume the following background: A man displays the cluster of symptoms which would have justified us in classifying him as sick before diagnosing his particular ailment:[71] he suffers from weakness, loss of appetite, pain, and other psychological registers of physical distress. We examine him and see he is very hot.[72] We infer that he is sick *because of*

[67A] Aristotle finds it as natural to say that one attribute "follows" (ἕπεται) another (e.g. *APr.* 43B11) as that one proposition follows (i.e., is entailed by) another.

[68] If we were to convert Plato's talk about Forms into set-theoretical language, taking Φ, Γ, etc., to name sets, the "bringing-on" relation would denote the *inclusion* of the "bringer-on" in the "brought-on" *not* the membership of the former in the latter: Plato clearly has no interest in saying that the Form, Fever, is sick, or that the Form, Fire, is hot.

[69] 104A4-B2; 105A6-7; 105G9 ff.

[70] He had already introduced the Forms, Hot, Cold, Snow, Fire, to illustrate the relation of incompatibility between Forms (103C10 ff.)—a relation which I leave out of my discussion in this paper to avoid burdening still further its already overburdened exposition.

[71] These symptoms must be sufficient to warrant the classification "sick," but not sufficient to warrant the narrower one, "feverish," else we would lose the "cleverness" of the present *aitia*: we would be back in the formally tautologous, "safe" and "ignorant" *aitia*. And cf. the next note.

[72] This is how we must understand "fever" here (taking *pyretos* in its literal sense, "burning heat, fiery heat," Liddell & Scott, *Greek-English Lexicon, s.v.,* I—i.e., as that "excess of heat" in the body which Plato takes to be a *cause* of a variety of ailments in all of which the patient is feverish: *Ti* 86A2-3) if Fever-

this.[73] Socrates steps in at this point to tell us we are entitled to make this inference only because the man participates in the two Forms, Fever, Sickness, [318] the first of which entails the second. When this is abbreviated to "the Form, Fever, is what makes him sick," it has an alarming ring. It sounds as though the Form were a ghostly stand-in for bacteria. But we need only recall the foregoing argument which, I trust, cleared the Form of imputation of causal agency in the case of the "safe" *aitia*, to assure ourselves that the same clearance can be given it in the case of the present *aitia* as well. If Φ is not expected to be a cause when it is said to "make" *x* to be *F*, then by the same token Γ cannot be expected to be a cause when *it* is said to "make" *x* to be *F*.[74]

May we then conclude that here too the "makes" in the Platonic formula has a strictly logico-metaphysical force—that no greater causal significance is to be read into "the Form, Fever, makes the man sick" than into "the Form, Sickness, is what makes him sick"? Such had been Shorey's claim when he maintained against Zeller that in the whole of this passage Plato is concerned with logic, not physics, adumbrating a theory of syllogistic inference, not of causal explanation.[75] This is an attractive interpretation; one could wish it were true. And nothing would have stood in the way of our taking it as true if Plato had given only logical and mathematical examples of the Γ-Φ relation. If we had only Three-Odd, Two-Even, and the like among the examples, then certainly the Γ-Φ coupling could be strictly non-causal. That Jones's family must be odd-numbered because it happens to be a threesome is indeed austerely irrelevant to the causal order of the world. Not so when we are told that Jones is sick because he has a fever, that a burning log is hot because it is on fire, that the white stuff on the ground is cold because it is snow. To be sure, none of the entailments holding between the relevant Forms is being credited with

---

Sickness is to parallel the Fire-Heat, Snow-Cold couplings, as it is surely meant to do: if "fever" were understood here to *mean* a species of sickness in the first place, the coupling would not constitute an example of the "clever," i.e., informative, *aitia*.

[73] A very substantial inference: if valid, it empowers to infer that he is sick just from knowing that he suffers from "excess of heat," as of course we could not if we were not justified in moving from "he is sick *and* suffers from excess of heat" to "he is sick *because* he suffers from excess of heat" in the first place.

[74] Cf. my critique in note 46 above of the last of the citations from Cornford in that note.

[75] (1924, 7-8). And this is the less extreme of Shorey's claims: cf. the stronger one (which I cited in my opening paragraph and to which I alluded in note 49 above) that Plato is offering "only a tautological logic." And cf. note 78 below.

causal agency. But they are certainly expected *to have causal implications*. That the occurrence of fever is the cause of the occurrence of sickness would be a textbook example of a [*319*] cause in Greek medicine.[76] And since the Γ-Φ entailment is being offered as the justification of the causal inference, how could it be empty of causal significance? The same would be true of the Fire-Heat and Snow-Cold couplings.[77] Fire and snow, like bronze in the second example in Section I above (p. 79), are natural kinds, and the regularity of the concomitance of the characteristic properties in each of them signifies a multitude of causal interconnections with other kinds of matter in the universe. Thus when Socrates maintains that the Form, Snow, is the *aitia* of cold, he is asserting neither the metaphysical absurdity that the Form, Snow, chills selected regions of the universe, nor the semantic absurdity that snow causes itself to be chilly; but what he does assert is nevertheless tied firmly to the causal structure of the world, e.g., to the fact that if we raise the temperature beyond a certain point snow must change to water. This "must" is a causal one. And since in Plato's theory it is grounded in relations of entailment between Forms, it would have to be a fantastically strong "must": it would have to express a *physical* law that has *logical* necessity. Since Plato claims that the snow of our experience is cold because the Form, Snow, entails the Form, Cold, and since all Forms—those of physical stuffs and processes, no less than those of logic and mathematics—are eternal and sustain only immutable relations to each other, he is implying that the laws of nature, could we but know them, would have the same necessity as do the truths of arithmetic and logic.[78] [*320*]

   A theory such as this is not likely to get a sympathetic hearing from

---

[76] Cf. note 72 above.

[77] I ignore the Life-Soul coupling, which raises other problems that cannot be discussed in this paper.

[78] We could have reached the same conclusion in Section I above, if Plato had used examples like Snow and Fire in illustrating the "safe" *aitia*, instead of sticking to logico-mathematical ones (Numerousness, Greatness, One, Two) and to that tantalizing abstraction, Beauty. To simplify the exposition I played his game, using "square" as my own example. Had I shifted to, say, "*x* is bronze because it participates in the Form, Bronze," it would have become apparent that even the "safe" *aitia*, though expressed in a tautological formula, has far-reaching substantive implications for the causal order of the universe: for as I remarked above, the regular concomitance of the properties which make up that natural kind has causal implications; to say that the relevant causal laws are instantiated in *x* because *x* participates in a Platonic Form, Bronze, is to credit those laws with absolute immutability and to imply that they may be known *a priori*.

philosophers nowadays. Most of us have been brought up to think that the laws of nature are in the last analysis radical contingencies—*de facto* uniformities which we must either exhibit as special cases of still more general *de facto* uniformities or else accept as things for which no further reason can be given. Coming upon Plato's reduction of physical to logical necessity in the *Phaedo*, we may then be tempted to think of it as not only false but unreasonable, wrongheaded, indeed lightheaded, a kind of whimsy. We would do well then to reflect that in the modern period too a substantially similar view has been propounded by philosophers—by Leibniz, for example, who held that all synthetic and contingent truths must represent necessary, analytic truths, imperfectly comprehended by finite minds; that the neoHegelians, from F. H. Bradley to Professor Brand Blanshard, find in Hume's alternative to Leibniz a dissolution of causality into casuality and insist that "being causally connected involve[s] being connected by a relation of logical *necessity*";[79] and finally that, to speak from the other, far more populous side of the fence, while it is generally admitted that causal laws must support counter-factuals, the problems of explaining counter-factuals on a regularity-theory of the laws of nature is a troublesome one, and its solution is still under debate.

There had been no Hume in Plato's past. The physical philosophers had proceeded on the faith that, as Leucippus had expressed it, "nothing happens at random, but everything by reason and by necessity."[80] But when they looked critically at this axiom, [321] as Democritus, the last in the succession, was the first to do, all they could find in nature on which to base their faith in rational necessity was *de facto* regularity. He taught, we are informed, that natural explanation reduces to the principle that "things always are or happen thus" and that "there is no sense in looking for a reason for that which always happens."[81] We cannot tell from surviving fragments or reports what conclusions he drew from this remarkable reflection. But regardless of what Democritus may

[79] (1939, 515; the italics are Blanshard's). Cf. A. C. Ewing (1934, 171): there is an "intrinsic" or "inherent" bond between cause and effect of which, he says, he can only think of "cause and effect as connected by a relation of logical entailment;" and again "The cause logically entails the effect in such a way that it would be in principle possible, with sufficient insight, to see what kind of effect must follow from examination of the cause alone without having learnt by previous experience what were the effects of similar causes" (quoted from Ewing by E. Nagel (1961, 53).

[80] H. Diels and W. Kranz, *Die Fragmente der Vorsokratiker*[5], (Berlin, 1934–37), Frag. B 1.

[81] *Ph.* 252A32-B1 (= frag. A65 in Diels and Kranz).

have made of it, we can see with what force Plato could have retorted: "If you must have rational necessity in nature, you cannot get it from regularities which are matters of brute fact. The only kind of rational necessity known to me is that I find in mathematics[82] and dialetic. Do you know of any others? If so, explain yourself. Until you do, I will continue to believe that nature could exhibit rational necessity only if its laws mirrored the inter-relations of the Forms we explore in logico-mathematical reasoning."

To say this is not, of course, to suggest that Plato's view is unobjectionable. Its most glaring fault is its methodological sterility for natural science. What knowledge of the laws of nature could one hope to secure *a priori* by following out lines of entailment from terms like *fire, snow,* and *fever*? The entailments in our passage are depressing commonplaces. But even so, it is not clear that they would warrant the certitude with which they would be credited on this view. How could we know that the Form, Fire, really entails the Form, Heat? It would be no use telling us that we would know this if we had "recollected" the two concepts correctly. For how could we be sure of that? What guarantee would we have that what we learned about fire from our sense-experience, sadly limited by the parochial contingencies of our time and place, would not have led us astray? If there were [322] stuffs which burn with a cool flame elsewhere in the universe, and we had known of them, our notion of fire would have been different, and then we would not have thought of claiming that the eternal Fire is eternally linked to Heat. It is impossible to tell from our passage to what extent Plato was assailed at this time by such doubts. Here, as elsewhere, he has a way of keeping the spotlight of his discourse on just those areas where he is most confident of the answers, content to leave much else in obscurity. This artful chiaroscuro makes life difficult for anyone who tries to expound his thought systematically. Time and again we come across gaps in his thought, not knowing how he would expect us to fill them. This way of writing philosophy is not to be excused, and I have no desire to excuse it. But this much at least can be said for Plato: his silences are themselves suggestive not of confusion

[82] Plato's criticism of contemporary mathematicians in *R.* 510C-511D does not imply (or even suggest) lack of confidence in the absolute certitude of mathematics, whose subject-matter is eternal (527B7-8) and, therefore, "draws" or "leads" the soul away from the flux to eternal being (524E-525B). (It should be noted that Plato does *not* impute to the mathematicians the absurd assumption that their subject-matter consists of visible figures; he says explicitly [510D6-7] that they are *not* reasoning about these.)

but of a canny, self-critical, awareness of the limitations of his theory. The problems he persistently declines to discuss in the middle dialogues are those whose solution eludes him.

This is conspicuously true in the present case. If Plato had really thought we could syllogize our way into the secrets of the natural universe, his confidence in such a fantasy would have been pathetic. But the fact is that he offers us no such pseudo-science of nature in this dialogue.[83] His ideas on geography and astronomy he presents only in the framework of a myth.[84] If not already in this dialogue, then soon after he must have drawn the only conclusion open to a sensible and honest man who had to live with Plato's metaphysical theory: that there can be strictly speaking, no such thing as *knowledge* of nature—only educated guesses, verisimilitudes, plausibilities. Such a conclusion is clearly implied in the *Republic*. When he drops empirical sciences like physics, biology, and medicine from the curriculum of higher studies, there is no suggestion that their subject-matter will be reclaimed at a higher level by dialetic. Forms like Fire, Snow, and Fever never darken the pages of Book [323] VII of the *Republic*. His point of view remains the same in this respect when he comes to deal directly and at length with empirical topics, as he does in the *Timaeus*. There the Forms of Fire, Water, and the like are accorded a curious and revealing treatment. Their existence is formally proved,[85] and they are placed ceremoniously on their metaphysical pedestals, only to be left there, and quietly ignored in the rest of the treatise where the workings of nature are explored. The plethora of ingenious explanations of natural phenomena displayed in the sequel is spun out of the theory of the geometrical configuration of matter.[86]

---

[83] He appears to be disclaiming it by emphasizing Socrates' ignorance of natural causes (99C6-9; 100D3; 101C9-D1).

[84] Including some important scientific doctrines, such as the sphericity of the earth, its stability "at the center of the heavens" (108E4-109A6), and the implied repudiation of the ancient notion of an absolute "up" and "down" (112C1-2).

[85] 51B7-52A4.

[86] Whose geometrical configurations are never identified with the Forms of those elements. Thus Plato is not proposing to identify the geometrical figure of the tetrahedron with the Form, Fire. The only connection he postulates is that the "body" of Fire (i.e., the physical instantiation of the Form, Fire) consists of particles that have tetrahedral shape, i.e., that the Form, Fire, is instantiated by matter whose constituent particles are severally instantiations of the Form, Tetrahedron. This leaves the two Forms, Fire and Tetrahedron, perfectly distinct, with a purely contingent connection, as is indicated by the fact that Plato speaks of it as a reasonable "hypothesis" for whose correctness

We are not told that fire causes water to evaporate, melts metals, cuts up food-stuffs into digestible and assimilable particles because the Forms of Fire, Water, etc., entail the Forms of the corresponding processes. The *aitiai* of physical, chemical, and biological phenomena are not deduced from "accounts of the essence" of the Forms, but are derived synthetically from the structure of the atom. And what is claimed for them is not certainty, but verisimilitude,[87] the atomic theory itself being presented as no more than a plausible hypothesis, having no more than aesthetic elegance[88] and the saving of the phenomena to recommend it.

I implied at the start of this paper that our passage in the *Phaedo*, rightly understood, is not unworthy of Plato's philosophical stature. The reader can now see why I made this claim and may assess its merits for himself. If my interpretation is correct, Plato has not only distinguished here mechanical from teleological causes—this part of his contribution I have not attempted to discuss—but has also come within sight of the still more radical distinction between both of these and the logical *aitia* of classification and entailment. Had he availed himself, as Aristotle was to do, of the expository device of philosophical lexicography, this achievement would have been more perspicuous and also, no doubt, more complete, for in making his thought more explicit he would have attained greater lucidity himself. However, we should not be put [324] off by the fact that at no point does he say in the style of his great pupil and critic, "*aitia* has many different senses." There are other ways of exhibiting distinctions, and one way of doing so is to use them. This, I have argued, is what Plato does in our passage, most successfully of all in the part which has been least understood in the scholarly literature, where he uses the "safe" *aitia* to explode pseudo-problems which arise when the categorial

---

no more than probability can be claimed: ὑποτιθέμεθα κατὰ τὸν μετ' ἀνάγκης εἰκότα λόγον πορευόμενοι (53D; and cf. Cornford's gloss [1937, 212, n. 3]; ἔστω δὴ κατὰ τὸν ὀρθὸν λόγον καὶ κατὰ τὸν εἰκότα τὸ μὲν τῆς πυραμίδος στερεὸν γεγονὸς εἶδος πυρὸς στοιχεῖον καὶ σπέρμα [56B3-5]; and cf. what is said about the assignment of the cubical figure to earth: γῇ μὲν τοῦτο ἀπονέμοντες τὸν εἰκότα λόγον διασῴζομεν [56A1]).

[87] That the cosmology as a whole is only a "probable story" (εἰκότα μῦθον, 29D) which makes no claim to demonstrative certainty is emphasized at the start (29B-D; cf. Vlastos [1939], Section I); the same point is made repeatedly of the account of the stereometric structure of matter (53D4-6, quoted in part in the preceding note; 54A5-B2; 56A1-B6, quoted in part in the preceding note; and the concluding remark, 56C8-D1, ἐκ δὴ πάντων ὧνπερ τὰ γένη προειρήκαμεν ὧδ' ἂν κατὰ τὸ εἰκὸς μάλιστ' ἂν ἔχοι).

[88] 53D7-E8.

difference between logical and physical *aitiai* is ignored.[89] If it were then suggested that Plato cannot be after all so clear on this point, else he would not have used indiscriminately arithmetical, physical, and medical concepts when illustrating the "clever" *aitia*, I trust the answer is now apparent from what I have said in the concluding part of the paper. There is no confusion here, but the expression of his firm conviction that all intelligible necessity, physical no less than mathematical, must be grounded on logical necessity, since it represents the inter-relations of eternal Forms, be these articulated in discourse or imaged in the physical world. This conviction could easily have set him started in pursuit of a will-of-the-wisp, a physical science which deduces the laws of nature *a priori*. It is a mark of good sense, no less than of clear thinking, that in his subsequent writings he claimed the certitude of logical necessity only for propositions of mathematics and dialetic, and was content with a physical theory which, he conceded, was no more than a beautiful guess. [*325*]

[89] I.e., in 96C6-97B3, where he discusses the last two of the six puzzles; and, if my hypothesis concerning the point of the first four is accepted, in 96D8-E4 as well.

5

Justice and Happiness
in the *Republic**

(1969; JHR)

I shall use "justice" and "just" merely as counters for δικαιοσύνη and δίκαιος, whose sense is so much broader: they could be used to cover all social conduct which is morally right. I shall use "justice pays" as a handy capsule for what Socrates undertakes to prove in response to Glaucon's challenge (358B ff.): justice is good in and of itself, not merely for its

* A draft of this paper appeared under the title, "The Argument in the *Republic* that 'Justice Pays,' " (65[1968], 665–74) along with the other principal papers presented at the annual meeting of the Eastern Division of the American Philosophical Association in 1968. That draft was discussed both in my Princeton Plato seminar in the fall of 1968 and at the symposium of the meeting of the A.P.A. at which it was read. For valuable criticisms, which have led me to correct some mistakes in that draft and to improve on it in a subsequent paper, "Justice and Psychic Harmony in the *Republic*" (*Journal of Philosophy* 66[1969], 505–21; substantially identical with Sections III to VI.1 of the present version), I am indebted to Professors Richard Kraut and Andrew Robison, who were then graduate students at Princeton; to Professors Stanley Rosen and John Cooper, fellow symposiasts at the meeting, particularly to the latter, who made a number of cogent criticisms, and to Professor A. D. Woozley, who followed up with written comments an objection he made at the meeting. In spite of the revisions, the present version still retains the form of presentation forced on me by the stringent space limit imposed on the original draft: it is still abrupt in argument, short in exposition, and sparing in its references to the secondary literature (which I allow myself only when I find it strictly necessary in order to explain or justify a variant interpretation). I particularly regret that, because of these restrictions, I have been unable to

consequences; and it is so great a good that no good securable by injustice could be greater. Here "good" is an ellipsis for "good for oneself,"[1] i.e., contributes to one's own well-being or happiness, εὐδαιμονία.[2] So the thesis is that one has more to gain in happiness from being a just man than from any good one could obtain at the price of becoming unjust. Now performing a single just act, or some odd assortment of just acts, is by no means equivalent to being a just man or, in Plato's phrase, "having justice in the soul."[3] So in "justice pays" *justice* is a property not of actions as

---

discuss in detail my differences with positions taken on the same topic in the following recent papers:

R. Demos, "A Fallacy in Plato's Republic?" *Philos. Rev.* 73 (1964), 395–98.

R. Weingartner, "Vulgar Justice and Platonic Justice," *Philos. and Phenomenological Research* 25 (1964/65), 248–52.

J. Schiller, "Just Man and Just Acts in Plato's *Republic*," *Jrnl of Hist. of Philos.* 6 (1968), 1–14.

I am indebted to each of these (cf. notes 35 and 46 below), and also to the following: Mr. Jerry Neu, who read a paper on this topic to my Plato seminar in 1966; Professor Richard Kraut, who did the same (and more thereafter in his thesis); Professor David Wiggins, with whom I had a most helpful discussion while still writing this paper; Mr. Thomas Russman, for the help acknowledged in n. 58 below.

[1] *Not* for "morally good" (morally praiseworthy), for which Plato would have used καλόν. For Plato "justice is [morally] good in and of itself because it makes the just man happy" would be *false*, while "justice is good in and of itself [for the just man] because it makes the just man happy" would be true, and analytically so: to say that *X* makes me happy would be for Plato part of what it means to say that *X* is good for me in and of itself.

[2] Following the general practice I shall use "happiness" for εὐδαιμονία, but with the caveat that the strongly hedonistic connotations of the English term (under the influence of 19th-century utilitarianism) should not be read into εὐδαιμονία. For a Greek moralist the question, "Is εὐδαιμονία pleasure, or is it something else?" is always a significant one (cf. the *Philebus*; and Aristotle, *Nic. Eth.* 1098B22 ff.; and the contrast between the "happier" and "more pleasurable life" in note 6 below).

[3] Or "present" (ἐνόν) in the soul (358B5-6; 441C7). Same implication in "having" (ἔχον) justice (367B4 and E3; 435C1) or "possessing" (κτᾶσθαι) it (455B3; 591B5-6). So too in the use of ἕξις of 435B7, 443E6, and 591B4. For the moral virtues as dispositional properties see also 518D-E, where they are said to be like the virtues of the body in that οὐκ ἐνοῦσαι πρότερον ὕστερον ἐμποιεῖσθαι ἔθεσιν καὶ ἀσκήσεσιν. That Plato is not thinking of just acts as such, but of a condition of soul which expresses itself in such acts, is rightly stressed in J. D. Mabbott, "Is Plato's *Republic* Utilitarian?", *Mind* 46 (1937), 468–74, at 474, and in Schiller, *op. cit.*, 6 ff.

such, but of agents;[4] it stands for the active disposition to behave justly towards one's fellows.[5]

I

The argument to be examined here is the one in Book IV, supplemented by the studies in moral psychopathology in VIII and IX (to 580D) and by the terminal reflections in IX (588B ff.)[6] Correctly analyzed, this argument will be seen to consist of two sub-arguments whose theses are logically distinct:

Thesis I: There is a condition of soul—"psychic harmony," I shall call it—which is in and of itself a greater good to one who has it

[4] That Plato should at times state the thesis in terms of "acting justly (δίκαια πράττειν) pays" (so, e.g., in 588B7 and E4), instead of "being a just man pays" is no objection, since "acting justly" can be used to refer to the form of action characteristic of the just man and is so used when articulating the thesis: clearly so in 588B-E; and cf. 445A1-2, where "acting justly" is used in apposition to "being a just man" (πότερον αὖ λυσιτελεῖ δίκαιά τε πράττειν καὶ καλὰ ἐπιτηδεύειν καὶ εἶναι δίκαιον).

[5] That *any* just act, or arbitrarily selected set of just acts, will "pay" would be patently false (except perhaps for an egoistic utilitarian who might so define "just act" as to make it true); and that Plato would think it false is distinctly implied in the *Republic*, e.g., in the portrait of the "oligarchic" man (553E ff.): though unjust (he defrauds orphans), this man has a fine reputation for justice in his business (εὐδοκιμεῖ δοκῶν δίκαιος εἶναι, 554C12); so there would be stretches of his life during which he performs only just acts, and if just acts *per se* made one happy he would have stretches of happiness; but as Plato pictures him he is never happy: he is "torn in two by internal conflict," harbors "drone-like" and "criminal" desires only "held down under stress of fear, which makes him tremble for the safety of his whole fortune" (554B-D, Cornford).

[6] Ignoring the further argument (580-588E) that the just life is not only happier, but more pleasurable as well (note the terms in which the conclusion is formulated: εἰ τοσοῦτον ἡδονῇ νικᾷ ὁ ἀγαθός τε καὶ δίκαιος . . . , ἀμηχάνῳ δὴ ὅσῳ πλείονι νικήσει εὐσχημοσύνη τε βίου τε καὶ κάλλει καὶ ἀρετῇ (588A7-10); the same point is made in *Lg.* 734D: the temperate life is "happier" εὐδαιμονέστερος—because it is "both more pleasurable and ὑπερέχειν . . . κάλλει καὶ ὀρθότητι καὶ ἀρετῇ καὶ εὐδοξίᾳ"; it is argued that the just man's pleasures are preferable and "more real," while four other types of life, increasingly unjust, yield increasingly inferior and unreal pleasures. Additional, and puzzling, questions arise here, which I cannot tackle in this paper. The argument I shall discuss is a self-contained one, and is presented as such in Book IV: it is supposed to demonstrate that "justice pays" (and does so to Glaucon's satisfaction (445A-B) without making even anticipatory reference to 580D-588E).

than would be any he could secure at the cost of the contrary condition of soul.

Thesis II: One has psychic harmony iff [7] one has a firm and stable disposition to act justly towards others. [8]

Plato's argument for Thesis I is that this is the condition of the human soul when it enjoys health, [9] beauty, [10] and maintains the ontologically correct hierarchic, [11] internal order. This part of his story I shall not discuss; there is no need to do so, since my interpretation here would differ little from that generally held. I proceed at once to Thesis II, for here my interpretation breaks with accepted opinion and has to be expounded and defended in detail.

II

1. Late in Book IV we come across the following definition:

> . . . in the case of each one of us, whosoever is such that each of the three [psychic elements] in him *does its own* [τὰ αὑτοῦ . . . πράττη], he is a just man. . . . (441D2-E2D12-E2)

---

[7] The customary abbreviation of "if, and only if."

[8] Plato unfortunately does not distinguish these two theses as clearly and does not present them in the proper order: instead of first telling us what a precious thing psychic harmony is and *then* going on to demonstrate its connection with the disposition to act justly, he does the opposite, reserving the praise of psychic harmony for the conclusion of his argument in Book IV (444C-E).

[9] 444C-D; 591B-C (by implication: justice is the condition in which the soul "returns to its nature at its best"—Paul Shorey's translation (Plato: the *Republic*, 2 volumes, London, 1930 and 1935) of εἰς τὴν βελτίστην ἕξιν καθισταμένη—which is for it what "health and strength" are to the body); 609B-610E (injustice destroys the soul as disease the body; justice makes one "alive" [ζωτικόν], 610E). And cf. *Grg.* 504B-D, 512A-B.

[10] Κάλλος (444E1); εὐσχημοσύνη (588A9). The same implications in the very notion of psychic *harmony* and its description in terms of musical consonance and concord (443D-E). Cf. *Grg.* 503D ff., where the notion that the just and σώφρων soul is the one that has the beautiful order (κόσμος) of a work of art, where all the parts are fitted together in a harmonious composition, first comes into Plato's work (this being its first recorded expression in Greek thought: cf. Helen North, *Sōphrosynē*, Ithaca, N.Y., 1966, 162–63, and W. Jaeger, *Paideia*, II [English translation, Oxford, 1947], 146).

[11] The "natural" and "fitting" order in which the part which is rational, "divine," and "superior by nature," rules the parts which are irrational, corporeal, and "inferior by nature": 444B1-5, 444D3-11; 590C3-D6 (with which cf. 577D3-5 and 589C5-D3; 591B1-7; cf. *Phaedo* 79E-80A and *Laws* 726-728B). Cf. M. B. Foster, "On Plato's Conception of Justice in the *Republic*", *Philos. Quart.* 1 (1950–51), 206–17; and Vlastos, *SPT*, nn. 25 and 26, below.

The italicized phrase, translated in this baldly literal way, makes awkward English.[12] But this is not an unmixed evil. It will serve as a constant reminder that what we get in the original is an idiomatic, formulaic, expression which is expected to suggest, rather than state in full, what is in Plato's mind.[13] If he wanted to be more explicit he would have filled out "its own" with ἔργον ("work" or "function"), a term introduced in Book I, and explained as follows: the ἔργον of anything (of a tool, like a pruning-knife, or of a bodily organ, like an eye or an ear) is that activity which can be "performed either exclusively by that thing or else more excellently [κάλλιστα] by it than by anything else" (353A)—i.e., the activity in which that thing gets its best chance to realize the excellence (ἀρετή) proper to its own specific nature[14] and to contribute to the excellence of other things associated with it.[15] The things the definition has in view are the components of the soul disclosed in the tripartite analysis of the soul: λογιστικόν, θυμός, ἐπιθυμητικόν—the reasoning, spirited, and appetitive parts of the soul. (Cf. VI.2.i, below). One is a *just* man, the definition tells us, if each of these three parts functions optimally, and there results that state of inner peace, amity, and concord, which I have called "psychic harmony" (I above; cf. VI.2.ii, below).

2. Two things about this definition are most perplexing:

(i) It presents no discernible link with ordinary usage. What people commonly understood by δικαιοσύνη we know from a wide variety of sources, including Aristotle's splendid analysis in the opening paragraphs

[12] It goes over well enough into German as "das Seinige tun" (so in O. Apelt's translation [Leipzig, 1916]). So far as I know L. Versenyi (*Socratic Humanism* [New Haven, 1963], 94 ff.) is the only writer to conserve in English the unaugmented Greek phrase. The usual practice is to render it by "doing one's own business" (Paul Shorey, *Plato: The Republic*, Vol. I [London, 1930]) or "minding one's own business" (Cornford [*The Republic of Plato*, Oxford, 1945], following A. D. Lindsay [*The Republic of Plato*, London, 1935] and Allan Bloom, *The Republic of Plato* [New York, 1968]). L. Robin (*Platon, Oeuvres complètes*, Vol. I [Paris, 1950]) translates "faire la tâche qui est la nôtre."

[13] The Greek phrase, τὰ αὑτοῦ πράττειν, is elliptical, and could mean different things in different contexts. In *Charm.* 161B it is cited as a definition of σωφροσύνη; it is again associated with σωφροσύνη in the *Timaeus* (72A). Only in the *Republic* is it cited as a definiens of δικαιοσύνη, and here only with grave qualifications (cf. III.1 below).

[14] Cf. H. S. Thayer, "Plato: The Theory and Language of Function," *Philos. Quart.* 14 (1964), 303–18, Section 1.

[15] It is a standing assumption in Plato that if x and y are associated, y is bound to benefit if x does its own ἔργον and realizes its own goodness: "To injure is not the ἔργον of the good, but of his opposite. . . . Then neither is to injure the ἔργον of the just man, but of his opposite. . . ." (335D).

of Book V of the *Nicomachean Ethics*. The word could carry a sense broad enough to cover all virtuous conduct towards others, though for the most part it was used in a more specific sense to mean refraining from πλεο-νεξία,[16] i.e., from gaining some advantage for oneself by grabbing what belongs to another—his property, his wife, his office, and the like—or by denying him what is (morally or legally) due him—fulfillment of promises made to him, repayment of monies owed to him, respect for his good name and reputation, and so forth. What holds these two senses together is that δικαιοσύνη is the pre-eminently *social* virtue:[17] it stands for right dealings between persons. And this is precisely what is missing in the Platonic definition, which purports to define a man's justice in terms of the order which prevails within his psyche.[18] This is odd, and altogether without parallel in the Platonic corpus. Though Plato sometimes redefines Greek words, his formulae manage to keep good contact with the usual meaning—contact enough to enable one to tell instantly from the formula

[16] I despair of an adequate English translation. Its occurrence in 359C5 is rendered by "self-advantage" in Shorey, by "la convoitise" in Robin, by "Habgier" in Apelt; Cornford's "self-interest" is intolerably loose: only when self-interest is sought at the expense of others and in contravention of ἰσότης (equity, fairness) would the Greeks speak of πλεονεξία. W. D. Ross and M. Ostwald translate πλεονέκτης in *Nic. Eth.* V.1 and 2 by "grasping," J. A. K. Thompson by "covetous." In Glaucon's great speech πλεονεξία is illustrated by the Gyges story and by "going to the market-place to take whatever he pleases, entering houses and having intercourse with anyone he pleases, either putting to death or freeing from bonds any one he pleases . . ." (360B-C). Aristotle explains it (*loc. cit.*) as immoral action whose motive is "the pleasure arising from gain" (δι' ἡδονὴν τὴν ἀπὸ κέρδους, 1130B4); though the gain of which he speaks is mainly pecuniary, it is clear from this and other contexts that any advantage gained at the expense of ἰσότης would count: πλεονεξία "is concerned with honour or money or safety, or that which includes all these, if we had a single name for it" (1120B2-3); he speaks of πλεονεκτεῖν δόξης ἢ τοῦ ἁπλῶς καλοῦ (1136B22) and even χάριτος ἢ τιμωρίας (1137A1): "greed" or "covetousness" would seem to fit best in most of these contexts, though neither of these would be exactly right.

[17] As Aristotle insists (*Nic. Eth.* 1129B26-1130B5) it is "virtue in relation to another" (ἀρετὴ πρὸς ἕτερον). (But cf. n. 55 below.)

[18] Cf. E. Barker's complaint that Plato's "representation of justice in the individual (as a relation of the parts of the soul which issues in harmony. . . .) . . . hardly accords with the *social* quality inherent in the term" (*Greek Political Theory*, 3rd Edition [London, 1947], 212, n. 1), and R. Demos (1964, 396): "What is odd about Plato's Platonic justice is its seemingly striking departure from ordinary usage. Customarily, justice indicates the relation of a given person to other persons; it is a virtue which operates in social contexts. But Platonic justice is a personal virtue, defined purely in terms of the agent."

what is the word it purports to define. Not so here. If a contemporary had been told that there is an enviable state of soul, characterized by proper functioning of every one of its parts, only by accident could he have guessed that this is supposed to be the moral attribute of *justice*.

(ii) Stranger still it is that Plato should want to offer such a definition in just this context. For what is his mouthpiece, Socrates, trying to accomplish? To convince Glaucon that "justice pays." And by "justice" Glaucon, like everyone else, understands observance of the constraints of morality and law in one's social conduct.[19] How could Socrates have expected to prove to Glaucon that it pays "to keep hands off from what belongs to others" (360B6) by proving to him that it pays to have a well-ordered, harmonious, soul, choosing to call *this* "justice"? Unless we are to suppose that on this occasion Plato lapsed into flagrantly illogical and thoroughly uncharacteristic conduct, we must assume that he will be undertaking to *prove* that, appearances to the contrary notwithstanding, having that kind of soul is what "being a just man" means. I submit that Plato has an explicit argument to prove this.[20] But before proceeding to it we must consider his account of the "justice" of the polis.

III

1. Long before that definition of the "just" soul had been presented, another definition of "justice" had been stated which did not make the remotest allusion to the inner structure of the soul:

> What we laid down at the start as a general requirement when we were founding the polis,[21] this, or some form of it, is justice. We did

[19] If there were any doubt of this, another look at his speech would resolve it. Cf. the citation from 360B-C in n. 16 above.

[20] 441C ff., to be analyzed and criticized below (V.2 and 3). It is almost incredible, but true, that those very commentators who saw quite clearly the discrepancy between Plato's redefinition of justice in psychological terms and the common signification of the word failed to take notice of the argument by which Plato undertakes to *demonstrate* his definition. Neither Barker nor Demos pays the slightest attention to what happens in 441C ff. From their comments one would get the impression that Plato just *assumed* that this is what a person's "justice" means.

[21] Here and hereafter I shall use "polis" instead of "state" or "city" since neither answers precisely to the sense which "polis" carries in many of its uses. That the ideal polis which is described in the *Republic* is meant to have all the attributes of a state (including supreme control over the use of physical coercion in a given territorial area and maintenance of a legal order in that area) is clear.

lay down, and often stated, if you recall,[22] that every single person
ought to engage in that social function [literally: that function which
concerns the polis] for which his own nature is best fitted.—We did
say this.—And indeed that to do one's own and not to be meddle-
some is justice, this we have often heard from many others and have
often said ourselves.—We have said it.—This then, my friend, if
taken in a certain way, appears to be justice: to do one's own.
(433A-B)

The defining formula is imprecise, and is meant to be: that is the force of
the qualifying phrases, "this, or some form of it, is justice"; "this . . . if
taken in a certain way, is justice."[23] Plato refers to the very start of the
investigation of the nature of justice in Book II (368D ff.), where he had
presented the division of labor and production for the market as the
generative principle of a polis (369A ff.). He understands this principle to
mean that a polis arises when, and only when, men come to direct their
individual energies with a view to the needs of others no less than their
own,[24] each of them pursuing a line of work which will best mesh with
that of others to their joint benefit. Plato then proceeds to generalize this
principle, so that it will apply not only to economic activity but to all of
the forms of associated living which go on within the polis.[25] And he gives

---

But though these are sufficient conditions for the existence of a polis they are
apparently not necessary for Plato, else he would not have called the primitive
community in 369 ff. which clearly antecedes the existence of a state (no
provision for governmental functions) a "polis."

[22] The back reference is to such passages as 370A-C; 374A-D; 395B-C; 397E.

[23] It cannot be emphasized too strongly that if "doing one's own" meant
only the "one man, one trade" principle, Plato would never have thought of
using it as a definiens of "justice"; hence the qualification "this, or some form
of it" at the start of the citation, warning the reader that the principle of
functional specialization in the division of labor has to be further qualified
before it can be taken in all seriousness as the essence of justice. When endorsed without this qualification (*Laws* 846D-847A) the principle is *not* taken
as a defining formula of justice.

[24] The basis of the polis is human interdependence (369B5-C4); if each
man were self-sufficient, each able to meet his individual needs by "himself
doing his own for himself" (αὐτὸν δι' αὐτὸν τὰ αὑτοῦ πράττειν), there would
be no polis.

[25] The first generalization is at 374B ff.: the principle is invoked to justify
a professional soldiery at this point; a subclass of these "guardians" is then
selected (412C ff.) for the still higher task of government. In a broader sense
the principle is expected to hold even of the activities of children and slaves
(433D).

it a normative twist, making of it an imperative addressed to every person in a polis: Keep to that line of social conduct by which, given your natural endowments and acquired skills, you can contribute maximally to the happiness and excellence of your polis.[26] He seizes on the catch-phrase, "to do one's own," as a convenient stand-in for this maxim.

2. Though not many of Plato's contemporaries would have agreed with this definition of δικαιοσύνη, I submit that none would have failed to see that it has good links with common usage, since on this definition, as on any other, justice would involve refraining from πλεονεξία. That Plato is counting on instant agreement on this point shows up best in the second of the three arguments by which Socrates seeks to persuade Glaucon that this is a good definition of "justice". Pointing to judicial justice as bearing out his definition, he asks:

> Will they [the guardians] not aim at this above all when judging lawsuits: that no one shall have what belongs to others or be deprived of one's own [μήτ᾽ ἔχωσι τἀλλότρια μήτε τῶν αὑτῶν στέρωνται]?—At nothing but this.—Because that is just?—Yes.—So in this way too it would have to be admitted that *the having and the doing of what belongs to one* and is one's own [ἡ τοῦ οἰκείου τε καὶ ἑαυτοῦ ἕξις τε καὶ πρᾶξις] is justice? (433E6-434A1)

The phrase I have italicized strikes at the very core of δικαιοσύνη in its most specific sense (cf. II.2.i above).[27] For since πλεονεξία is "having

---

[26] I get this by putting together the following: 374B9-C2 (we assigned to each person that one ἔργον for which "he is fitted by nature," done best only when practiced on a full-time basis); 412D9-E2 (for guardians select those who "will be most eager to do whatever they think is for the best interest of the polis"); 420D4-5 (as in a work of art, what we do for a part will depend on whether or not we can thereby maximize the excellence of the whole); 421B3-C6 (greatest possible happiness not for any one class, but for the whole polis; hence "the auxiliaries and the guardians are to be compelled and persuaded to do what will make them the most excellent craftsmen of their own ἔργον, and similarly all others"); 465E4-466A6 (back reference to 420B-421C, reaffirming its principle); 519E1-520A4 (another back reference to the same, adding that "the law" requires of the citizens "to contribute to one another that by which each is able to benefit the community. . . .").

[27] Cf. the definition in Aristotle, *Rh.* 1366B9-11: "justice is the virtue because of which all have their own [τὰ αὑτῶν . . . ἔχουσι] and in conformity with the law; injustice that by which they have what belongs to others [τὰ ἀλλότρια] and contrary to the law." Aristotle adds the reference to the law to make explicit the special ethico-juridical sense (cf. note 28, below) in which the

more," i.e. more than what is rightfully one's own ("what belongs to one"),
to "have what belongs to others" would be to perpetrate πλεονεξία, and
* to "be deprived of one's own" would be to suffer it.[28] In this argument
Plato proceeds on the assumption that having all, and only, what "belongs
to one" is biconditionally related to "doing one's own." If this is not
obvious at first sight, let me rephrase the argument, abbreviating to make
the essential point more perspicuous:

> That each shall have one's own is what judges should aim for.
>
> What judges should aim for is justice.
>
> *Therefore*, that each shall have one's own and that each shall do one's
> is justice.

The premise speaks only of each "having one's own" and says nothing
of each "doing one's own." How then did the latter get into the conclusion? And get there it must, since the whole point of this argument is

---

expressions "one's own" and "another's" are used in contexts in which they
are associated with justice. Ulpian adds "jus" to "suum" to make the same
point in his famous definition, "justice is the constant and unremitting will
to render to everyone his own right [*jus suum cuique tribuere*]." As the Aristotelian definition shows, the scope of τὰ αὑτοῦ and τὰ ἀλλότρια in such contexts
is broad enough to cover everything to which persons would be morally or
legally entitled. Professor H. L. A. Hart ("Are There Natural Rights?" *Philos.
Rev.* 64, 1955, 175–91, at 176, n. 4) gives no evidence for his opinion that
these and the roughly equivalent expression, "what is due to one" (τὰ ὀφει-
λόμενα, cf. the popular definition of justice ascribed to Simonides in 331E,
335E), "are confined to property or debts": why so, if a man could claim so
much more as "his own" and his "due"?

[28] One could hardly overstress the normative load carried in the above argument, as in the Aristotelian definition cited in the preceding note and in
innumerable other contexts in Greek prose, by expressions like "one's own"
(τὰ αὑτοῦ) and "that of others" (τὰ ἀλλότρια, which I translated "what
belongs to others" in its occurrence in 433E7 and in the Aristotelian definition).
Cf. also the use of the latter in 360B6, ἀπέχεσθαι τῶν ἀλλοτρίων καὶ μὴ ἅπτεσθαι
(which I translated "to keep hands off from what belongs to others" in II.2.ii
above), and the import of the fact that σφετερίζω (literally, "to make mine
what is theirs") comes to mean commonly "to *mis*appropriate, to usurp." If
one misses this special accent that is put on the "one's own" in the "doing
one's own" and "having one's own" formulae in the above argument, it will
seem, as it does to Sir Karl Popper, "nothing but a crude juggle with the meaning of the term 'one's own,' " and "about as sound as the argument: 'It is just
to keep and practice what is one's own. This plan of stealing your money is my
own. Thus it is just for me to keep my plan, and put it into practice, i.e. steal
your money" (1963, 97).

to defend that phrase as a definiens of "justice." So unless we are to suppose
that Plato's powers of reasoning have failed completely at this juncture,
we must assume that the above argument is elliptical, carrying a suppressed premise,

Each shall have one's own iff each does his own. . . . (S)

Intercalating the missing steps—(S), and a further, obviously implied
step, (T) below—to get the complete argument, this is what Plato is
maintaining:

That each shall have one's own is what judges should aim for.
What judges should aim for is justice.
[*Therefore*, that each shall have one's own is justice. . . . (T)
But each shall have one's own iff each does one's own.] . . . (S)
Therefore, that each shall have one's own and that each shall do one's
own is justice

That Plato should thus rely on (S) as an unstated premise in this argument
shows how confident he feels that the link between "doing one's own"
and the common conception of justice would be fully apparent to his
readers: he is counting on them to understand his definition to imply that
in any community in which everyone lived up to the maxim, "do your
own," there would be no πλεονεξία.

3. But what is rightfully "mine" and "another's"? For the answer the
ordinary Greek (i.e., any contemporary Greek who did not have a special
theory of justice) would refer to (a) the standard precepts of morality—do
not steal or betray your comrades or forswear your oaths or default on
agreements; care for your parents, honor the gods, and the like (cf. 442E-
443A), and (b) the laws of the state.[29] For Plato (b) would be no final
point of reference: law counts for nothing in the *Republic* unless it is just.
As for (2), the trouble with all these precepts is that they are full of gaps.[30]
Plato's definiens for "justice" would fill these gaps. Thus consider how he

[29] For (ii) cf. the Aristotelian definition of δικαιοσύνη in n. 27 above.
[30] A point made with great emphasis in the argument with Polemarchus in
Book I, 331C, and alluded to again in Book V, 479D ("the many conventional
notions of the many [τὰ τῶν πολλῶν πολλὰ νόμιμα] concerning the beautiful
and the rest [i.e., the just, the pious, 479A]" are said to "tumble about between
being and not being purely [*sc.* just, pious]," presumably because there are so
many cases in which a thing reckoned "just" or "pious" by one of the traditional precepts will have to be reckoned "unjust" or "impious" by another).

122   MORALS, POLITICS, METAPHYSICS

tackles the question of whether or not the rulers of his state should have
private property. Common morality supplies no answer. It does say that
depriving unlawfully another of his property ("stealing") is unjust. Who,
if anyone, should own property it does not say. Plato here applies his own
criterion of "doing one's own": his guardians would be "more excellent
craftsmen of their own work" (421C1-2) without, than with, private
property. This settles the matter: real estate and chattels are not to be
"theirs."[31] In the last analysis all questions of what does, or does not,
"belong to one" would be adjudicated in this manner.

4. Two more things which call for special mention:

(i) The "doing" in the "doing one's own" formula involves not only
on-the-job conduct, but the whole of one's life, *including one's private life*.
Platonic morality leaves no room for a conception of private life in which
one has the right to do what one pleases without thought to social service.
For Plato all conduct is subject to regulation by the rulers of the state,
whose task it is to embody the vision of the Good "into the dispositions of
men, *both private* and public" [καὶ ἰδίᾳ καὶ δημοσίᾳ] (500D). By the same
token, everyone, philosopher, soldier, or tradesman, must consider in each
of his actions: Will this make of me a better craftsman at my work?[32]

(ii) The definition is meant to absorb, not invalidate, common morality.
When the ordinary duties prescribed by the latter are condescendingly
called φορτικά ("common" or "vulgar"),[33] this is done only with an eye
to more onerous obligations,[34] more flexible in form only because they

---

[31] There is no explicit appeal to the definition of "justice" at this point (as
indeed there could not be, since the definition is still to come). But see how
the justification of another practice which would entail a sacrifice of happiness
for the philosophers as a class is handled in 519D-520A: "we shall be doing no
injustice to the philosophers who arise among us, when we compel them to
concern themselves with the other citizens and to guard them [i.e., to take
part in the day-to-day administration of the state]"; it is just, because required
by the duty of maximizing one's service to the polis inherent in the "doing
one's own" principle.

[32] More on this in IV.2 below.

[33] 442E-443A. The things itemized here would be included among the καλὰ
νόμιμα, 589C7 (clearly equivalent to the δίκαια, 589B8), whose purpose is said
to be to subjugate the "beastly" to the "divine" parts of man's nature, i.e., to
serve the very highest ends of Platonic justice: cf. note 11 above.

[34] Cf. 538C-D: Men "with even a particle of decency" (Cornford for μήθ'
ὁτιοῦν μετρίους) would resist the flattering solicitations of pleasure which tempt
them to act contrary to those "convictions about what is just and honourable
in which we have been nurtured from our childhood years." Much more could
be expected from men conforming to the highest standards of justice.

are so much more stringent in their substance. Thus Plato's philosopher-rulers must avoid "the lie in the soul" (382A-C; 485C). This is a more exacting demand than just to refrain from telling lies, and will require them to tell some lies (414B ff.) in the course of "doing their own."

IV

1. The two definitions of "justice" in Book IV I shall call respectively the "psychological" (II, above) and the "social" (III, above) definitions. They occur in separate passages: the psychological one in 441C-443B, where the virtues of the individual are defined, the social one in the preceding (427E-434C) discussion of the virtues of the *polis*. At the end of that discussion it had been made clear that "doing one's own" was not meant to constitute a definition of the justice of an individual person:[35] Socrates tells Glaucon (434D-E) they must now look beyond the polis to the individual and find out if "there too" (i.e., the disposition to do one's own) is justice. He would not have said this if he had understood "doing one's own" as a definiens of the justice of the individual. However, though this formula is not meant to serve as a *definition* of the justice of the individual, it is still meant to be a true *description* of it: it is not hard to show that for Plato every just person must have the disposition named by the "doing one's own" formula. For he declares that "the same [moral] characters and dispositions which exist in the polis exist in each one of us: they could not, surely, have come to it from any other source" (435E; cf. 544D-E). So he holds as a fundamental principle (one which "it is most necessary to admit," *loc. cit.*) that

> P(I) *A moral attribute is predicable of a given polis only when, and exactly because,*[36] *it is predicable of the appropriate set of members of that polis.*

[35] As I had erroneously maintained in the first of the two papers cited in n. 1 above, against strong objections from A. Robison and R. Kraut in my seminar and subsequently from Professors Cooper and Woozley as well as others at the A.P.A. meeting; their criticisms helped me to see that I had been misled by the deceptively elliptical form in which the definition is stated in 433A-B. On the face of it, the definiendum is "justice" and the definiens "doing one's own." In fact, the definiendum is "[the] justice [of a polis]" and the definiens "[the] doing of their own [by individuals and classes in a polis]" (only individuals in 433A-D, only classes in 434C and 435B; but see n. 38 below).

[36] To say no more than "only when" would not do justice to Plato's insistence that a given character "comes to" (ἀφῖκται) and "arises in" (ἐγγεγονέναι) the polis "from the individuals" (ἐκ τῶν ἰδιωτῶν) (*loc. cit.*). It is the fact that the (appropriate set of) individuals who make up a polis are F that makes the polis F, not the other way round.

It follows directly from P(I) that if a polis is just, it is such only in so far as its people are generally just persons: only *their* justice could make it just. And it follows tautologously from the social definition of justice that what makes the polis just is the disposition of these same persons "to do their own."[37] Thus from the social definition and Plato's adherence to P(I) we get unavoidably a specification of the justice of the individual persons who compose a polis: each of them is just iff each "does his own."[38]

2. How much of a person's conduct would this specification cover? Clearly, all of it which affects the justice of the polis; hence, to begin with, everything persons are called upon to do in the line of public duty. Since their vocational activities *are* construed as public duties in this ultra-professional society, all on-the-job conduct would obviously count. What then of their private life? Would this be exempt? I have already implied (III.4.i) that it would not: for Plato vocational excellence is unthinkable without personal virtue. Thus his rulers, who "are to be consummate craftsmen of the liberty of the polis, must practice nothing which does not conduce to this."[39] To attain perfection in their work they must have morally exemplary dispositions. Their manifold technical qualifications— that they are to be clever legislators, shrewd economic planners, efficient bureaucrats, expert eugenic breeders—are taken for granted. All of the emphasis falls on their philosophic wisdom, on the one hand, and on their virtue, on the other. The latter is under constant surveillance: up to the age of fifty they are being "tested to see if they will stand firm against all seductions" (540A)—moral perfection is built directly into their job. And there are further indications in the text that the justice specified in the "do your own" formula extends over the whole of a person's conduct, public and private, in the polis:

[37] The declaration in 434C7-10 and 435B4-7 (still operative in 441D8-10) that it is the "doing one's own" by each of the three classes that constitutes the justice of each class and makes the polis just is no objection. By analogy with P(I), as by ordinary common sense, the "doing one's own" disposition and the character, "justice," could be ascribed to social classes only if, and because, they were ascribable to their members in the first place.

[38] To my knowledge, this simple deduction has never been drawn in the scholarly literature. Had it been drawn, it would surely have been noticed that this description of the individual's justice, so patently different from that provided by the psychological definition, is in urgent need of being tied by logical argument to the latter; then the significance of the argument in 441C ff. (V.2, below), as providing just this tie, could hardly have been missed.

[39] Whence it is inferred that, from childhood up, they must never "imitate" characters of low moral quality in dramatic productions, 395B-C.

(i) The formula is applied even to slaves[40] who, not being citizens, could hardly be thought of as having civic duties; also to children, who as yet have no civic duties (433D2-3).

(ii) Things people do in private contexts—the play of children, the respect shown the old by the young, the clothes and shoes people wear, even haircuts—have the gravest consequences for the whole of society (424A ff.); thus if children play "lawless" games, the "laws and the constitution" will be affected and eventually "everything, private and public, will be overturned" (424D-E).

(iii) If the scope of the "doing one's own" formula were not broad enough to cover refraining from all kinds of πλεονεξία, public or private, the biconditional, "each shall have his own iff each does his own,"[41] would fail.

So I can see no escape from the conclusion that everything in one's social conduct within the polis—all of one's dealings with other persons in the context of the only form of social life considered in the *Republic*—would come directly or indirectly within the scope of justice as specified by the "doing one's own" formula.

3. Why is it then that Plato does not accept the formula as an alternative definition of the justice of the individual, coordinate with, and complementary to, the psychological definition? The answer can only be guessed at. I, for one, would find the clue in the terms in which Plato contrasts the "doing of one's own" by a person with the "doing of their own" by the parts of his soul in 443C: he calls the first "a kind of image" of justice, and goes on to add:

> The truth of the matter was, it seems, that justice was that sort of thing [τοιοῦτόν τι], but not in regard to one's external action, but in regard to the internal action which concerns truly one's own self[42] and what is one's very own. (443C9-D1)

---

[40] Some scholars have sought to explain away this reference, suggesting that at this point Plato may be no longer thinking of the ideal state but of the contemporary world. I have argued against this suggestion in the terminal paragraph of *SER*, below. However, the force of the above remark would not be blunted even if that suggestion were correct.

[41] Proposition (S) in III.2, above.

[42] Cf. Adam *ad. loc.*: "ὡς ἀληθῶς should be construed with περὶ ἑαυτόν. The soul is the true self, as Socrates continually maintained." (Cf. next note). In a querulous note to the same passage Shorey explains τὸ δέ γε ἀληθές as "the reality of justice as distinguished from the εἴδωλον, which in this case is merely the *economic* division of labour," and adds: "Adam errs in thinking that the

What a man does is, for Plato, only an "image" of what he is; his "external" conduct is only a manifestation of his "inner" life which is the life of the "real" man, the soul.[43] Hence when he asks himself in what it is that a man's justice "truly" consists he feels constrained to look to what goes on inside a man, in a man's soul; and since he thinks of a definition of F as a statement of what F "really is," he could only count the psychological formula as the true definition of an individual's justice.

V

1. After fully conceding this privileged status of the psychological formula for the definition of the individual's justice, however, we are left with the undeniable fact that each of Plato's definitions of "justice" lays down conditions which every person in a polis will meet iff he is just. From the social definition we learn what a just person's "external" activity will be like: he will obey the "do your own" maxim in his dealings with others in the polis. From the psychological definition we learn what a just person's "inner" life will be like: each of the elements of his soul will be "doing its own" and psychic harmony will result. These two specifications are entirely distinct—so much so that if both were correct and we knew[44] only the former, we would be able to determine that a man satisfies it without our knowing, or even suspecting, that he satisfies the latter also, and *vice versa*. How then do we know that the two must always be satisfied

---

real justice is justice in the soul, and the εἴδωλον is justice in the state. In the state too the division of labour may be taken in the lower or in the higher sense." But the contrast here is between (a) justice περὶ τὴν ἔξω πρᾶξιν τῶν αὑτοῦ and (b) justice περὶ τὴν ἐντὸς [πρᾶξιν τῶν αὑτοῦ], and it is said that "in truth" (τὸ δέ γε ἀληθές) justice has to do with (b) rather than (a). So the contrast is plainly *not*, as Shorey would have it, between a "lower" and a "higher" sense of justice within both (a) and (b). But Shorey is right to this extent: in drawing the contrast between (a) and (b) Plato chooses to present (a) in its most rudimentary, economic, terms, to which he refers as ἀρχήν τε καὶ τύπον τινα τῆς δικαιοσύνης (443C1). However, the contrast in C9-D1 leaves no doubt that even if (a) were taken in its fullest and "highest" sense, Plato would still compare it unfavorably with (b), maintaining that only here man's "real" justice is manifested.

[43] In Plato's metaphysics this is the "really real" man (τὸν ὄντα ἡμῶν ἕκαστον ὄντως); the body is only a "similitude" or "image" of the soul (*Laws* 959B).

[44] I.e., those of us who are not Platonists. On Plato's assumptions to *know* either specification one would have to know the Form of justice, and this would disclose both specifications.

together? This is what Plato has to show us, else the whole of Socrates' argument against Glaucon would come to naught (cf. II.2.ii, above): to show Glaucon that it pays to have the "justice" of a harmonious psyche would do nothing to show him that "justice pays" unless it were proved that whoever has this "inner" disposition *will* have too the "outer" disposition to deal justly with his fellows. Plato is not blind to this. The demonstrand of his argument in 441C-E reads:

> . . . in the case of each one of us, whosoever is such that the three kinds [of elements] in him does its own, he is a just man *and a man who does his own*. (441D-E)[45]

I have italicized the terminal phrase: this is what makes it clear that the new definition which is advanced here is meant to connect with the earlier definition of "justice" in 433A ff., and so connect with it that anyone who instantiates the new one *will* meet the specification of the individual's justice which is implied by the social definition. This is what Plato thinks his argument in 441C-E has established. Has it? Let us run through it.[46]

2. First the isomorphic structure of state and soul, a carry-over from the preceding discussion,[47] is acknowledged:

> (A) We have agreed with good reason that the same three kinds [of elements] exist in the polis, on the one hand, in the soul of each of us, on the other. (441C5-7)

Socrates then asks,

> (B) Must it not follow at once that the individual will be wise in the way [ὡς] and through that element [ᾧ] by which the polis is wise? (C9-10)

From what is this supposed to follow? From a premise laid down back in 435A5-7: "If two things, one greater, the other smaller, are called the

---

[45] Cited, without the terminal phrase, in II.1, above. Cited in full as (G) below.

[46] The account of the argument in 441C ff. I give in the following paragraph is meant to supersede completely the one in the earlier draft (paper cited in n. 1 above, 668–69). This employed unforgivably strong-armed methods in restructuring Plato's argument and moreover failed to take explicit account of the role of the premise laid down earlier (435A5-7) on which, as I have since come to see, the reasoning directly depends, as was emphasized by Professor Cooper in his contribution to the symposium.

[47] 435D-441C: the tripartite analysis of the soul, interlarded between the social and the psychological definitions of "justice."

same, will they be similar or dissimilar in the respect in which they are called the same?" This is a fundamental Platonic principle.[48] Let me restate it a little more formally:

P(II) *If the same predicate is predicable of any two things, then, however they may differ in other ways, they must be exactly alike*[49] *in the respect in which it is predicable of each.*

Given P(II) and (A), (B) would indeed follow: If "wise" is predicated of a polis[50] in virtue of the fact that one of its elements has a certain character, then it must be predicated of a person in virtue of the fact that an analogous element in him has the *identical* character: were this not so, polis and person would not be "exactly alike" in the respect in which "wise" is predicable of each. Socrates proceeds:

(C) And after the same manner in which
the individual was brave, and in virtue of that [element], after that manner and in virtue of that [element], the polis will be brave . . . ?
(D1-2)

Here from the same premises the same inference (*mutatis mutandis*)[51] is drawn for "brave" as for "wise" at (B). Thereupon Socrates generalizes:[52]

---

[48] Taken over uncritically from Socrates, whose search for definitions is guided by the explicit assumption that all of the things correctly called "*F*" have an identical character, *F*, and that each of them is so called only because each has this self-identical character: *Euthyphro* 5D1-5, 6D9-E6; *Meno* 72A ff.

[49] That "exactly alike" is what Plato does mean is clear from the inference he draws from the cited statement: "Hence the just man *will not differ in any way* [οὐδὲν διοίσει] from the just polis in respect of the very character of justice, but will be like it" (435B1-2). Cf. Socrates' insistence that any two things which are called "*F*" "will not differ" in respect of being *F*: *Meno* 72B5, C2-3 (ᾧ οὐδὲν διαφέρουσιν ἀλλὰ ταὐτόν εἰσιν ἅπασαι); E6-73A3.

[50] I am putting (B) into the formal mode to bring it into line with P(II); the difference between the formal and the material mode is systematically ignored in Plato and would, in any case, make no difference to the reasoning in this argument.

[51] Except for the fact that while in (B) the reasoning moved from polis to person, in (C) it reverses, moving from person to polis; but this difference is irrelevant to the reasoning, for the similarity relation is symmetrical.

[52] That Socrates should not deal with the case of temperance, after that of wisdom and courage, before drawing the generalization may cause surprise. But this is easily explicable from expository considerations: In the present argument Socrates draws out the implications of P(II) for wisdom and courage, without taking the time to state the definiens of either and to identify the

(D) . . . and polis and person will possess
in the same way anything which pertains to virtue [i.e., any moral
quality whatsoever]? (D2-3)[53]

He applies this at once to the case of justice:

(E) And we shall say, o Glaucon, that a man is just in the same
way[54] in which the polis is just. (D5-6)

Confident that all has gone well so far, Socrates proceeds to get the conclusion he wants in two more steps:

(F) And surely we have not forgotten that it (the polis) was just
in virtue of each of the three kinds [of elements] in it doing its own?
(D8-10)

(G) Therefore, let us bear in mind that also in the case of each one
of us, whoever is such that each of the three kinds [of elements] in
him does its own, he is a just man and a man who does his own.
(D5-E2)

3. The simplest way to diagnose the error in this argument is to call attention to an equivocation whose precise role in it does not seem to have ever

---

elements in polis and person that have each of these virtues. These omissions
are repaired in the sequel (441E-442D) which parallels the present argument,
adding information omitted in this one. In that sequel the case of temperance
is treated as fully as that of wisdom and courage. Moreover, the essential
identity of temperance in polis and person had been anticipated (430D-432A)
in the earlier section on the virtues of the state, where the nature of temperance
had been explained at considerable length. To have reaffirmed that identity in
441C-E would have involved more repetition than Plato cares to allow himself
in an argument whose premises are kept as trim as possible so that the weight
of the composition may fall on its concluding portion, (E), (F), and (G) below.

[53] This is a proposition of such extreme plausibility that even Aristotle
subscribes to it, asserting it as a self-evident truth: "The courage, justice, and
wisdom of a polis have the same meaning and form [τὴν αὐτὴν ἔχει δύναμιν καὶ
μορφήν] as those [virtues] by whose possession each individual man is called
'just' and 'wise' and 'temperate,' " *Pol.* 1323B33-36. This is in Book VII of the
Politics, one of his earlier political writings, possibly composed before he had
developed his doctrine of "focal meaning" (cf. note 61 below). But there is
no indication that Aristotle ever rejected or modified the proposition he asserts
here in the light of his new semantic doctrine.

[54] τῷ αὐτῷ τρόπῳ. For the use of the same locution to express the same
thought—that when "*F*" is correctly predicated of *a* and *b*, *a* is *F* "in the same
way" as is *b*, i.e., has the identical character—see *Meno* 73C1-2: πάντες ἄρ'
ἄνθρωποι τῷ αὐτῷ τρόπῳ ἀγαθοί εἰσιν.

been spotted in the literature: In its primary signification "just" is a relational predicate; to speak of a person as having this property is to think of the way in which he habitually relates himself to persons[55] or groups in his conduct. This is all too plainly true on the popular notion of justice (II.2.i, above), both in its generalized sense of "virtuous conduct towards another" and the narrower one of refraining from *pleonexia*. It would be no less true on the conception of the individual's justice which is implied by Plato's social definition: "to do one's own" is an obligation one has *to* one's polis and *to* the other persons with whom one has to deal. But it so happens that among the derivative uses of "just" there is one in which it functions as a one-place group-predicate, predicable of groups as such, on condition that their members, or sub-groups composed of their members, are just in the primary sense, i.e., behave justly to one another. Using "just₁" for the primary, "just₂" for this secondary sense, let us apply the distinction to the conclusion of Plato's argument,

(G) . . . in the case of each one of us, whosoever is such that each of the three kinds [of elements] in him does its own, he is

[a] a just man and

[b] a man who does his own.

Let us start with the occurrence of "just" in [a]. Which of the two senses will fit? Clearly only the "just₂" sense: this is all that Plato has established. For this sense is clearly the one in which "just" was used immediately before at (F): to say that the polis is just "in virtue of each of its three elements doing its own" is to use "just" as a one-term predicate applicable to the polis in virtue of the fact that each of its three classes is just₁ ("does its own," thereby satisfying the "social" definition of "justice": III.2, above).[56] And since (G) is inferred from (F) in conjunction with (E),

[55] Not necessarily to persons other than himself: the relation may be reflexive. Aristotle's formula for justice in its most general sense, "virtue towards another," misses this point, but only because of the (purely technical) failure to notice that a relation need not be aliorelative. In the *Nicomachean Ethics* the question, "Can a man treat himself unjustly?" remains a significant one which Aristotle feels called upon to debate (*N.E.* V, 11). He decides it in the negative by arguing that an affirmative answer is precluded by the psychological impossibility of *voluntary* reflexive injustice (not by the conceptual impossibility of reflexive injustice).

[56] Note the complete absence in this context of any reference to the polis being just₁. The absence of such a reference is no accident, given Plato's commitment to "*x* does its own" as the definiens of "*x* is just₁." The use of the "doing one's own" formula to elucidate the notion of a polis which is just

"just man" in [a] has to mean "just₂ man": if "just₂" is the way in which the polis is just, then, if the individual is to be "just *in the way in which the polis is just*," he too has to be just₂.[57] So if Plato had twigged to the just₁/just₂ ambiguity, he would have seen that all he has proved by his elaborate argument from (A) to (G) is that when the components of a man's soul "do their own" the man is just₂. And he would then have seen that the further conclusion, [b], that this man is also just₁ ("a man who does his own") is totally unwarranted: the argument has done nothing to establish that a man who satisfies the condition for being just₂ has *ipso facto* satisfied the condition for being just₁ as well.[58]

VI

If my diagnosis of Plato's error in the argument in 441C-E is correct, his mistake is neither inexplicable nor irreparable.

1. *Not inexplicable*: He is misled by two things.

First, by his P(II). Like Socrates, he takes this for an axiomatic truth. Seeing that this holds in the standard cases—if we are to call two specimens "bees" (Socrates' example in the *Meno*)[59] they must indeed be "exactly

---

in its external relations would have been only an embarrassment to Plato: the central notion in this formula—making the best contribution one's nature allows one to make to and in one's community (III.1, above)—is inapplicable to a state in its foreign relations the notion of a community of poleis is not mooted in the *Republic*.

[57] If anyone is made uncomfortable by the fact that "in the same way" could mean any number of different things in this context, he might be reminded that as Plato uses that slippery expression, to find a man who is "exactly like" a just₂ polis we would have to find a just₂ man, i.e., one whose psychic components "do their own" inside him as the social components of the state "do their own" inside it; a just₁ man would be "exactly like" (in the relevant respect) a just₁, not a just₂, polis.

[58] In the earlier version of this essay (in *Plato*, II, edited by G. Vlastos, 1971, pp. 86–87, and in the corresponding section of "Justice and Psychic Harmony in the *Republic*," *Journal of Philosophy* 66 [1969], pp. 517–18) I had maintained that the fatal equivocation skews the argument at a still earlier point, *sc.* in (E) above, "just" being used there to mean "just₁" in its first occurrence, and "just₂" in its second. Several critics had objected, and Thomas Russman, a graduate student of philosophy at Princeton, convinced me that this contention is quite unnecessary since the flaw in the argument is completely accounted for by the equivocation in (G).

[59] 72B-C: the example which he thinks shows that any two persons are exactly alike in respect of being virtuous.

alike" in respect of being bees, though they may differ in a hundred other ways—he infers that it is true in all cases, making no provision for those in which the predicate applies to some things in a primary sense, and to others in derivative senses, materially different from the primary one, though formally so related to it as to be definable by reference to it. Had Plato seen (to turn now to an example in Aristotle)[60] how absurd it would be to expect that a man, a complexion, a habitat, and a diet must be "exactly alike" in the respect in which the predicate "healthy" applies to each,[61] he could scarcely have failed to see how little his P(II) would cover the case of a predicate like "just."

Second, he is misled by the false analogy on which he relies in generalizing from the cases of "wise" in (B) and "brave" in (C) to *all* moral predicates in (D), including "just." Not that (D) is true without qualification even in the case of the former: "wise" and "brave" hardly apply to polis and person in the same way in all respects. However, each does apply to both alike in the way which is vital for Plato's argument: when predicated of persons or of poleis, they do function as *one-place predicates* in both cases. And this is precisely what is false in the case of "just" which, as we have seen, is a one-place predicate only in its secondary sense, while in its primary sense it must be a relational predicate, since justice is the social virtue par excellence. Plato has often been criticized for his use of the polis-soul analogy. I trust it will now be clear that this is not, of itself, the source of his error. The analogy is, of course, loose; but it is not the less illuminating on that account. By representing that deceptively simple thing, the soul, as the analogue of the polis, the simile makes us see the

---

[60] *Met.* 1002A34-B1 and 1060B36-1061A7; *Top.* 106B33-37. The linguistic phenomenon Aristotle illustrates by "healthy" and by "medical" in these contexts is not precisely the same as that exemplified in the difference between "just₁" and "just₂": the derivative senses of "healthy" and "medical" to which he refers do not differ from the primary one as a one-place term, predicable of groups, would differ from a two-place term, predicable of individuals (this specific difference is not noticed by Aristotle, to my knowledge). But the two phenomena are so closely related—in both cases we have a logically primary sense, and one or more derivative senses definable in terms of the primary one—that if Plato had anticipated Aristotle's investigations of "focal meaning" (G. E. L. Owen's [1960, 169] felicitous rubric for what Aristotle calls πρὸς ἓν καὶ μίαν τινα φύσιν λεγόμενα) he would have seen that his P(II) cries out for qualification and then he could scarcely have made the error in (E).

[61] If they were "exactly alike" a healthy complexion would have, like a healthy man, a well-functioning heart and liver, and so would a healthy climate and healthy food.

soul as the complex of forces which it is—forces which may war among themselves in ways as destructive of the soul's own well-being as was the class-war of that of the city-state. That a man, no less than a polis, can, and should be, just$_2$ is a memorable insight, which need not have caused logical error, and would not, if the difference between this new sense in which a man might be called "just" and the usual one had been kept straight.[62]

2. And the mistake is *not irreparable*. Plato has all the materials required to construct an alternative argument to do the job which his present one failed to do: to prove that *a man is just$_2$ iff he is just$_1$*. This thesis has the full support of (a) his moral epistemology and (b) his moral psychology: to reject it one would have to fault basic Platonic doctrines in the area of (a) or of (b) or of both. I submit that this is how Plato would have argued had he realized the utter inadequacy of the argument in V.2 above. Part (a) of this argument would seek to convince us that if reason is "doing its own" it will be making correct moral judgments. This I shall not try to report. Part (b) would proceed as follows:

(i) The ultimate sources of wrongdoing—of injustice—are sensuality, cupidity, and vanity, the first two being by far the most prolific: they make up that monstrous beast of physical appetite[63] which is ever ready to grow new heads in every direction, absorbing a commensurate quantum of psychic energy[64] with each new head it is allowed to grow.[65] The practical reason would be impotent to induce us to act justly at any given moment if all it did was to declare what justice requires of us. Long before that moment it must have shaped the development of the beast and also that of the leonine θυμός, with its insatiable hunger for prestige; it must have prevented

[62] One could still object to the form in which Plato casts the new insight, taking upon himself to say that the word "just" should now be used in a drastically different way (we are to "deem and name 'just' that action which preserves and promotes this disposition," *sc.* the psychic harmony which results when all three components of the soul are "doing their own work," 443E6-7). Such linguistic innovations are dubious business, and I have no wish to defend Plato on this score. But I would still insist that even so no logical error would have been incurred if the linguistic legislation had been grounded a clear understanding of the just$_1$-just$_2$ distinction.

[63] "Physical" (which I add here for emphasis only) should always be understood as preceding "appetite" when used to name the "third" part of the soul (rather than as a general term for "desire": cf. 580D-E).

[64] Cf. the hydraulic metaphor for the allocation of psychic energy in 485D and Cornford's gloss in *The Unwritten Philosophy* (Cambridge, 1950), 73.

[65] For this and what follows see especially 588B ff.

from starting, or decapitated at their start, all appetites but a handful of "necessary" ones; and it must have so tamed the θυμός as to make of it a faithful ally against the beast.

(ii) Where there is justice₂, and therewith psychic harmony, control over the lion and the beast (or what is left of it) has been secured at so deep a level that reason's dominance no longer calls for the exercise of repressive force. All three are reconciled to their respective roles and so to one another. The subordinates concur willingly, even affectionately, in reason's hegemony;[66] they are slaves so attached to their master that they feel servitude as friendship.[67] In such a state of soul how could reason's orders fail to be carried out? And since reason orders only what is just, how could a soul so integrated within itself engage in unjust conduct?

(iii) Suppose, conversely, that one's state of soul has been that of injustice. If one's reason has not been doing its job, concupiscence would have waxed unchecked and would now be making its huge, insistent, demands, and the lion too would be roaring after prey of its own, each of them asking for more than one could procure for them by just means—what could there be then to stop one from resorting to unjust ones? Nothing, ever, in the case of the "tyrannical" man, with blood-curdling consequences. The not-quite-so-bad, "democratic," man achieves a *modus vivendi* among his motley appetites, good and bad, so that all get their turn; when the bad ones are on top moral scruples would be of no avail.[68] As for the "oligarchic" man, all that restrains him from injustice is his obsessive greed; so he is just when justice is good business, but when he can grab with impunity (e.g., from orphans), he grabs. None of these men, nor any others who lack psychic harmony, could have that active disposition to abstain scrupulously from πλεονεξία which is entailed by justice₁ (III above).[69]

---

[66] Note the emphases on φιλία within the psychic elements (589A3, and B5)and of the man becoming "φίλος to himself" (443D5); also the singling out of the repressive control of desire (554D1) as a sign of inner division and conflict.

[67] Take 444B1-5 with 590C8-D6.

[68] This is not said in 559D ff., but it is implied by the general theory taken in conjunction with the fact that the "democratic" man must be more unjust than the "oligarchic" one, being further down the slope of moral decline.

[69] The above argument for the thesis that a man is just₂ iff he is just₁ may be summarized as a *reductio ad absurdum* of the denial of this thesis:

(i) Assume that someone is just₂, but not just₁. If he is not just₁, then he either (a) is, or (b) is not, cognizant of what he ought to be doing in

VII

In a most valuable paper[70] Professor David Sachs has pressed two questions: Has Plato shown (a) that anyone whose justice meets Platonic standards will also meet the common ones? Has he shown (b) that if the latter standards are met, so will be the former? Sachs has argued that Plato merely assumes (a), failing to argue for it; and that he does not even assume (b). The foregoing analysis prompts different replies to Sachs' questions: If by the "Platonically just" man we are to mean with Sachs (152) the man who satisfies the psychological definition (cf. IV.1, above) then Plato *has* argued for (a). He has an explicit argument (V.2, above), and also an implicit one (VI.2, above), to prove that one who satisfies the psychological definition will satisfy the social specification of individual justice too, i.e., that he will be a man who "does his own," and hence (III.2, above) will so govern his conduct that those whom it affects will "have their own," which will certainly involve compliance with the precepts of common morality (cf. III.4.ii, above) so far as they give unambiguous determinations (cf. III.3, above) and are not overridden by the sovereign "do your own" imperative. In the case of (b) everything turns on what we are to mean by the correlative to "Platonically just"— "commonly just," I shall call it. Who is to count as the "commonly just" man? Not, surely, the sort of man who follows common justice only when material advantage so requires (like the "oligarchic" man above). Such equivocal virtue Plato denounces in the *Phaedo* (68E-69C) as a "delusive façade" (σκιαγραφία), a "slavish" thing, "with no health or truth in it"

---

order to be just₁. If (b), his reason is not making correct moral judgments, hence not doing its job, contrary to the assumption that he is just₂ (which entails that all three parts of his soul are "doing their own"). If (a), the dictates of his reason are failing of execution because of insubordination in the lower parts, hence they are not "doing their own," contrary to the assumption.

(ii) Assume that someone is just₁, but not just₂. If not just₂, one or more parts of his soul are failing to do their job: if the failure is in reason, he will not be making correct moral judgments, and hence he cannot be just₁, contrary to the assumption; if the failure is in one or both of the lower parts, their insubordination will frustrate the execution of the judgments of his reason, in which case he will not be acting morally and will not be just₁, contrary to the assumption.

[70] "A Fallacy in Plato's *Republic*," *Philos. Review* 72 (1963), 141–58.

(69B7-8); he who has it masters appetite only so far as appetite masters him.[71] Since the last thing in the world Plato would want to prove is that such pseudo-virtue brings happiness, it is no blemish in his argument that he should not make the grotesque assumption that the man who is commonly just in *this* sense is platonically just. So by the "commonly just man" we could only mean one whose devotion to the precepts of common morality is so sincere and deep that he would stand by them under severe temptation, when fancy prizes can be had by dexterous grabbing. To qualify for this sort of common justice, Plato would argue, you must have psychic harmony, for if you don't, how could you be counted on for more than fair-weather virtue? How could anyone with Gyges' ring act differently from Gyges if the condition of his soul is the usual mess?

VIII

1. It might be objected that Plato could not have used the argument I have laid out for him in VI.2, above, for it would expose him to an awkward question: justice is mandatory for *everyone*; how then could it be conditioned on so rare and difficult[72] an attainment as psychic harmony? I agree that the question is pertinent and that its implications are disturbing. I deny that Plato would have thought them so. He would have, if he had believed that only philosophers could achieve psychic harmony. For in that case, on the argument I have given him, the lower classes in his utopia could not have been just men, with fatal consequences for the justice of his ideally just state. But it is false that Plato thought psychic harmony was only for philosophers.[73] To be sure, only they could have that vision

---

[71] This is a variant of a phrase used about σωφροσύνη in 69A2; but σωφροσύνη and justice are often used quasi-synonymously by Plato: see C. W. R. Larson, "The Platonic Synonyms, δικαιοσύνη and σωφροσύνη," *American Journal of Philology* 72 (1951), 395-414—an excellent study, in spite of the overstatement in its thesis.

[72] If one balks at "rare and difficult" one might re-read 443D-E.

[73] For reason to "do its own work" it does not, of course, need to be *philosophical* reason. The special term Plato uses in the tripartite analysis (and only there) as a name for the intellectual part of the soul, τὸ λογιστικόν ("calculative"), should of itself make it clear that he is not making the absurd assumption that only theoretical, reflective, intelligence (διάνοια, νοῦς) is involved. One does not need to be a philosopher to run through practical syllogisms whose major premises are true beliefs. True belief is quite sufficient for virtue in the *Republic:* cf. the definition of courage here (429B-430B) in terms of δόξα, with the one in the Socratic dialogues in terms of ἐπιστήμη

of the Ideas whose moral effect was so energizing.[74] But the special love
for justice, temperance, etc., kindled in the philosopher by his unique
intellectual experience is anticipated at the level of sense, emotion,
imagination, and right belief by the effect of a massive psychological
conditioning which begins in earliest infancy. That this is directed at all
the citizens, not only the philosophers-to-be, is certain: it is explicitly
designed to inculcate σωφροσύνη,[75] a virtue required of all three classes.[76]
So all are subjected to what Plato calls "musical" παιδεία:[77] a process
which not only employs music itself and the other arts, but manipulates
everything in the social environment (down to games and haircuts) to
stock the growing mind with the right beliefs and, what is more, the right
emotive charges,[78] so that what one comes to call "just" one will feel
irresistibly attractive and its contrary disgustingly ugly.[79] Thus the internal

---

(*Laches* 194E-195), σοφία (*Prt.* 360D). Cf. R. G. Hoerber, "More on Justice in
the *Republic*," *Phronesis* 5 (1960), pp. 32–34 at p. 33; R. W. Hall, "Plato's Just
Man," *New Scholasticism* 43 (1968), 202–25 at 217 ff. And cf. notes 79 and 80
below.

[74] Cf. *MP*, pp. 52, above.

[75] 389D ff.; 399B-C; 402C; 410A.

[76] Cf. J. B. Skemp, "Comment on Communal and Individual Justice in the
Republic," *Phronesis* 5 (1960), 35-38 at 36.

[77] Which would be quite consistent with differential education for other
purposes (as is clearly implied in 466E ff., and probably also in 415C2 as well).

[78] Right belief lacking the requisite support from "musical" paideia will
not do: it is denounced as "slavish and brutish" (430B); cf. *Laws* 689A-B: the
"divergence of pain and pleasure from rational belief is the greatest ignorance."
Conversely, right belief with παιδεία is sufficient for moral virtue even without
philosophic wisdom: clearly so in the case of the courage of the auxiliaries in
429C-430B (their courage is *not* "slavish and brutish"), and also, by implication, in the case of the σωφροσύνη of the producers in 431D-432B: neither
would their virtue be "slavish and brutish," since it is produced by musical
paideia. And cf. the next note.

[79] This marks a radical difference between (a) the virtue denounced so
scathingly in *Phaedo* 68-69 and *R.* 430B, on the one hand, and (b) that of the
non-philosophers of the ideal state. The people in (a) act bravely, temperately,
or justly only when, and because, they believe that some ulterior non-moral
end of theirs can be the better advanced in this way; that is why Plato speaks
of them in wilful paradox as "brave because of cowardice" and "temperate
because of intemperance" (*Phaedo* 68D-69A): they have no independent love
of courage or temperance, they do not find these qualities of character desirable
and admirable in and of themselves. In (b), on the contrary, we have people
whose emotional and imaginative natures have been so molded from earliest
childhood by "musical" παιδεία that they have come to love virtue and hate

controls will be secured and a condition of soul induced which is emphatically called "harmony" in anticipation of the later use of this metaphor in the definition of temperance and justice₂.[80]

2. So this is what is left of the above objection: if Plato thought psychic harmony a necessary condition of a morally just disposition, he must have thought the latter attainable only by the people of his ideal state and, in the present world, by Platonic philosophers and their moral dependents (and, on a lower plane, by some of the citizens of the best timocracies);[81] and this would cut out the vast majority of our fellow-men, all of whom are expected to act justly. But why should this consequence bother Plato? He thinks the masses, if they lack the requisite παιδεία, capable of nothing better than a degenerate morality, that "delusive façade" of virtue:[82] they cannot be expected to do the just thing because they find justice beautiful, but only because they see in it the safest path to gratification. "But if that is what Plato thinks," it may be retorted, "is he not conceding that for the majority justice must be good only for its consequences, not in and of itself—the very thing Glaucon challenged Socrates to refute?" The answer

---

vice regardless of other considerations: to engage in an action they felt to be cowardly or intemperate would be in itself a direct source of unhappiness to them. Hence there can be no warrant for conflating (a) with (b) as is done by Helen North, who says that (a) is in fact "the level of virtue with which all but the philosophers" must be content in the *Republic* (*op. cit.* 166, n. 3), and had been done earlier (though in more guarded fashion) by R. D. Archer-Hind (*Plato's Phaedo* [Cambridge, 1896], Appendix on "Δημοτικὴ καὶ Πολιτικὴ Ἀρετή," 149–55), who represents (a) as a form of (inferior) δημοτικὴ ἀρετή (civic virtue): Plato could hardly have reckoned (a) *civic* virtue, since he brands it as "slavish" both in the *Republic* (430B) and the *Phaedo* (69B7); moreover the *Phaedo* passage shows clearly that he thought of (a) as *bogus* virtue ("delusive façade . . . no truth in it," 69B), while there is nothing bogus about the civic virtues of the lower classes in the *Republic*.

[80] 400D-401D; and, retrospectively, 522A.

[81] A conspicuous feature of Sparta and Crete was their ἀγωγή, a process which from birth onward subjected the individual to authoritarian institutional controls designed to inculcate virtue. Though Plato shudders at the neglect of "music" in these cultures, and at the brute mindlessness of the result, he thinks that the firmly controlled environment does provide, what was so sadly lacking elsewhere, that discipline over appetite which is the *sine qua non* of justice₂. For this reason his discussion of timocracy in 544C ff. is vastly more favorable to it than to the next three states, and allows that some of its citizens (non-philosophers, of course) may be good men; so, e.g., the timocratic father of the oligarchic man (549C).

[82] VII above; notes 78 and 79 above.

is clearly "Yes," and Plato could say so without inconsistency. Before getting to the proof that justice *is* good in and of itself, his Socrates embarked on a long search to find out what justice is.[83] His proof is clearly meant to hold for *that*—not for the fake the masses now call "justice": this, Plato would himself insist, *is* good only for its consequences. Could we think of him as conceding, let alone trying to prove, that this poor shadow of the real thing could be counted on to make us happy, regardless of the circumstances?

[83] With which Glaucon and Adeimantus concur; indeed the very form in which the question came to be formulated by Adeimantus (366E5-6, 367A6-8, 367E3) distinctly implies that the "praise" of justice will have to be predicated on this disclosure of its "power" (and, therefore, of its "essence").

[84] In his paper, "The State-Soul Analogy in Plato's Argument that Justice Pays" (*Journal of the Hist. of Philosophy* 12 [1974], 285-93), Leon Galis argues, on the strength of 470A-471C, that Plato is "alive to the notion of a kind of 'community' of Greek states" (289); he thinks that 352A (taken in conjunction with 351B) shows that Plato, holding that a state will be externally just if it is internally just, is in a position to argue by analogy that the same would be true of the individual person. This is a brilliant suggestion. Certainly Plato *might have so argued* for the conclusion at (G) (p. 130 above), thereby avoiding completely the fallacy with which I charge (130-31 above) his present argument at 441C-E (paraphrased at pp. 127-29 above). But to produce such an argument Plato would have had (at the very least) to amend the one in his text by adding a new premise

(Ga) A state is just to other states in virtue of each of its three kinds of elements doing its own,

and deriving from it a new conclusion,

(Gb) Therefore, a person is just to other persons in virtue of each of the three elements in his soul doing its own.

Clearly, (Ga) and (Gb) are drastically different from (G) or from anything else we get in the *Republic*.

An alternative defense against the above fallacy is offered Plato by J.R.S. Wilson ("The Argument of *Rep.* IV," *Philos. Quart.* 26 [1976], 111ff.) The argument is highly original and suggestive, but I find its textual grounding even more precarious than that of Galis. Its ingenious reasoning is too complicated for brief comment.

6

Does Slavery Exist
in Plato's *Republic?**

(1968; *SER*)

THE answer has long been in dispute. It still is. I shall review succinctly the relevant evidence. Probed dispassionately, it does not leave the issue in doubt.

Whenever the design of his ideal state entails drastic institutional changes from the *status quo*—as it does in the case of property, family, education, politics, war—Plato argues for the innovations. Slavery is firmly entrenched in the *status quo*.[1] If he had wanted [291] to abolish it, he would have argued —which he does not. So far from justifying such a measure, he does not even say he has decided on it. So unless we are to assume that he is concealing his opinion on this subject, which no one would seriously propose, we must start with the presumption that he has made no such decision.

Is there anything in the evidence to undercut this presumption? Nothing worthy of the name of evidence. Thus, when Professor John Wild reasons from what he calls "the introduction of slavery" in 547C (when the utopia degenerates into a timocracy) to its former non-existence,[2] his premise has no support from the text: nothing is said in 547C of "the introduction of slavery," but only of the enslavement of one class of *citizens* by another.[3]

---

* Originally published in *Classical Philology* 63(1968), pp. 291–95. The original pagination appears in square brackets here.

[1] Cf. M. I. Finley (1959, 145–64).

[2] (1953, 50).

[3] Cf. 547C2 with 463A. No distinction is more fundamental in Greek political thought than that between citizens and other persons in the *polis*. The enslave-

Again when he tells us that "slaves in the *Republic* would be superfluous, since *all* the necessary productive functions are performed by [free] artisans,"[4] he cites no evidence to justify the word I have italicized on which the force of the whole argument depends; there is no such evidence. When he quotes from Professor G. R. Morrow, "there is no mention of a slave class" in the *Republic*,[5] the statement is formally true: Plato does not speak of slaves as making up one of the three μέρη or εἴδη of the *polis*. But Wild does not reckon with the possibility that Plato might admit slaves in his society without thinking of them as a proper part of the *polis*,[6] and he ignores, as so many others have ignored before him, a passage in which Plato speaks of the slave as an element of the population which contributes to the excellence of the *polis*.[7]

Contrariwise, is there anything in the evidence to support the presumption that slavery must continue to exist, since nothing is said to put it out of existence? There is, though not everything that has been taken for such evidence is well taken. Professor Karl Popper refers us to *R.* 549A1–3, where it is said that the timocratic man will be rough with slaves, οὐ καταφρονῶν δούλων, ὥσπερ ὁ ἱκανῶς πεπαιδευμένος, and argues: "since only in the best city can education be found which is superior to that of timocracy, we are bound to conclude that there are slaves in Plato's best city."[8] Now Plato writes as follows of the παιδεία of the timocrats: "they have been educated not by persuasion but under compulsion, having neglected the true muse, whose companion is argument and philosophy, and have honored physical culture above music" (548BC).

---

ment of a group of citizens at a given time does not allow the slightest inference that prior to this time no non-citizens had been slaves.

[4] *Op. cit.*, pp. 50–51.

[5] (1946, 107, n. 63).

[6] Cf. n. 3 above. The Greek *polis* consists of *politai*: ἡ γὰρ πόλις πολιτῶν τι πλῆθός ἐστιν, Arist. *Pol.* 1274B41. The slave is a part not of the *polis* but of the *oikia* (*ibid.* 1252A24 ff.), he is κτήσεως μέρος τι (*ibid.* 1256A3): τῶν κτημάτων πρῶτον μὲν καὶ ἀναγκαιότατον . . . ἄνθρωπος, ps.-Arist. *Oec.* 1344A23–24. In the *Laws* Plato does not discuss the slaves when he lays down the political institutions in Book 5 and the first part of Book 6; he comes around to the slaves when he reaches the question of κτήματα in 6, 776B ff. The simplest answer to the question—which I shall not take up in this brief paper—why so little is said about slaves in the *Republic* is that κτήματα are wholly in the hands of the third class whose economic arrangements are of no interest to Plato.

[7] 433D, to be discussed below.

[8] (1963, 47).

It would be surprising if Plato thought no one could get a better education in non-timocratic contemporary states. But suppose, just for the sake of argument, that he did. Would we be bound to conclude that there are slaves in Plato's best city? Only if we knew he would consider the presence of slaves essential for the superior education it provides. And that is just what we do not know, and cannot infer from 549A. All that follows from that text is that *if* a man has ἱκανὴ παιδεία, no matter how or where acquired, he will not deal roughly with slaves, if he has slaves to deal with.[9]

Morrow has argued that since "the contrast of the heavenly and the earthly city [i.e., the ideal one of the *Republic* and the second-best one of the *Laws*] depends in part, as the *Politicus* affirms, on the presence or absence of absolute power in the organs of rule, . . . the [292] legitimacy of slavery would be even less subject to question in the heavenly than in the earthly city."[10] This argument is correct. But we could not use it to infer the existence of slavery in the *Republic*,[11] and Morrow is not suggesting that we should. If we did, we would be up against the following difficulty: the title to absolute authority over persons is conferred by philosophic wisdom.[12] This would legitimize slave ownership by philosophers. It could not also legitimize slave ownership where it would be most urgently needed: in the economic sector, which is wholly in the hands of non-philosophers.[13]

More promising material than anything we have so far considered occurs in the discussion of current usage of war in 469B5-471C3. Two remarks by Glaucon are directly relevant. The first comes very early in this passage. Socrates has just deplored the enslavement of fellow-Greeks in war (469B8-C2), and ruled that the citizens of the utopia ("the utopians," I shall call them for short) "are to own no Greek slaves themselves and counsel other Greeks to do the same" (C4-5). Glaucon agrees heartily, adding: μᾶλλόν γ᾽ ἂν οὖν οὕτω πρὸς τοὺς βαρβάρους τρέποιντο, ἑαυτῶν

---

[9] Cf. also Professor Ronald B. Levinson's discussion of what can and cannot be inferred about slavery in the *Republic* from 549A: (1953, 170, n. 76).

[10] (1939, 130).

[11] I erred in doing so when arguing against Wild in *Philosophical Review*, LVI(1947), 184 ff., at p. 187.

[12] G. R. Morrow (1939, 186 ff. at p. 200); G. Vlastos, "Slavery in Plato's Thought," *Philosophical Review* (1941), 289 ff. (= *SPT*, pp. 147 ff. below).

[13] I failed to reckon with this problem in the paper cited in the preceding note. I am indebted to Mr. Christopher Ake, a graduate student at Princeton, for calling it to my attention.

δ' ἀπέχοιντο (C6-7).[14] Now why should Glaucon think that if Greeks were to deny themselves Greek slaves they would be henceforth more likely to fight barbarians than each other? What new motive is he assuming would come into operation as a result of the prohibition? Clearly, the desire to secure slaves by military capture, which would henceforth be open to them when, and only when, they are warring with barbarians.

We could then argue as follows: If (*a*) Glaucon imputes such a motive to the utopians, we have good reason to believe (*b*) that he assumes that they own slaves and (*c*) that this assumption is correct. (*b*) would follow on the plausible assumption that Glaucon would expect the utopians to keep for their own use any slaves they bring back from their wars instead of selling them off to foreign buyers: he is hardly likely to cast the virtuous utopians in the sordid role of procuring for others merchandise whose use by themselves they would consider immoral. (*c*) is a reasonable inference from the fact that Glaucon gives every appearance of being of one mind with Socrates throughout this discussion, catching easily and accurately the drift of Socrates' thought. Thus he sees at once that Socrates' condemnation of the enslavement of fellow-Greeks in war does not imply the slightest objection to doing the same thing to barbarians—a fact which Socrates proceeds to make clear some paragraphs later (470B4-471A7). Moreover Plato could scarcely have failed to give the reader some warning if he put into Glaucon's mouth a remark premised on a misunderstanding: he has no reason to wish to mislead or confuse the reader and is too skillful a writer to do so by inadvertence. The only question then is whether (*a*) is true. It would be if "they" in Glaucon's remark—the subjects of τρέποιντο and ἀπέχοιντο—are meant to include the utopians along with other Greeks. And this seems a plausible enough assumption. For Socrates' immediately preceding comment which provoked Glaucon's remark referred both to the utopians (αὐτούς, C4) and to "the other Greeks" (C4-5). Why then should Glaucon's comment exclude the former from its scope? Nothing whatever in its wording or its thought would be more applicable to the other Greeks than it would be to them, unless we were to assume that they had already abjured slavery, which would beg the question. We may then assume (*a*), no less than (*c*) and (*b*), in which case Glaucon's remark would definitely imply that the utopians are slave owners.

[14] I take the γε as epexegetic: Glaucon is explaining why he agreed so warmly. I see no justification for weakening it to "at any rate" (P. Shorey [1930, Vol. I]; "en tout cas" (L. Robin, in the Pléiade trans.).

We could get the same implication out of a later remark by Glaucon: "For my part, he said, I agree that this is the way [οὕτω] our [293] citizens should treat their [Greek] adversaries; but barbarians they should treat as Greeks now treat one another" (471B6-8). What is the reference of οὕτω? Does it include refraining from ἀνδραποδισμός? One may argue for this on the ground that while Socrates' immediately preceding remark dealt only with devastation of lands and arson when warring on fellow-Greeks (471A9-B5), the one just before this one had referred also to enslavement: Socrates had said that Greeks should fight Greek adversaries only "to correct them with benign intent, not to punish them with enslavement or ruin" (471A6-7). If so, in recommending that "our citizens" should treat barbarians as Greeks now treat their own kind, Glaucon is assuming that they will be interested in making slaves of barbarian prisoners of war, with the same implications as before.

By such a line of argument we can get from our passage evidence that slavery is still a going concern in the utopia, providing its citizens with a practical, if inglorious, motive for fighting barbarians in preference to fellow-Greeks. But in order to build up the argument we have had to make several ancillary assumptions, and a skeptical critic could refuse to grant them. In the interpretation of Glaucon's first remark, the critic might complain that the argument for (*a*) above was particularly chancy: what Glaucon says would be perfectly intelligible if its scope had been limited to other Greek states; why then *must* we assume that he is thinking also of the utopians at just that moment? In the case of Glaucon's later remark, the critic, continuing to be difficult, but not unreasonably so, might make much more than I have done above of the fact that Socrates' topic in the immediately preceding lines is γῆν κείρειν and οἰκίας ἀνατρέπειν. Since that is sufficient to occupy Glaucon's attention here, why must he be thinking of ἀνδραποδισμός as well? I would gladly concede that these questions are well taken and that they admit of no conclusive reply. At other points too the argument I have made above is conjectural. So while the conclusion is plausible—it follows by valid inference from plausible premises—it is scarcely cogent.[15] Is there nothing stronger we can offer the skeptic?[16]

[15] Popper takes a more sanguine view of it. He says that Plato "goes on (in 471 BC) to encourage [the enslavement] of barbarians by Greeks, and especially by the citizens of his best city." How he gets this out of 471BC—where enslavement is not mentioned—he does not explain.

[16] Levinson is the only one who sees the bearings of 433D on the controversy but, as I shall argue, misjudges its evidential force.

There is indeed in 433D, and it is surprising that no earlier use appears to have been made for this purpose. It would be difficult, says Socrates here, to decide if anything would contribute more highly to the city's excellence than the disposition "in child, woman, slave, freeman, artisan, ruler, ruled, to perform as one person one's own task and not to be a busybody" (translation mainly after Shorey). Since he is referring to the disposition he calls δικαιοσύνη and uses it as his main guide in the construction of his utopia, the mention of its efficacy in slaves along with other parts of the population contributing to the city's excellence[17] leaves no reasonable doubt that he expects them to form an essential part of the society. Levinson argues that there is still a chance that "Plato in this passage has for the moment forgotten his reference to the ideal city" (*op. cit.*, p. 171). Now the lines I have quoted are the concluding portion of a ten-line period which starts at C4 and does not come to the topic of δικαιοσύνη until it has first dealt more briefly with each of the other three virtues in the Platonic quartet. So what Levinson is suggesting is that after talking about temperance (C6-7), courage (C7-8), and wisdom (D1), and doing so in terms which apply unambiguously to his utopia, Plato may have suddenly switched to a different frame of reference, so very different as to describe δικαιοσύνη in terms which not only did not, but *could not*, apply to his ideal city. I say "could not," for the whole reason for supposing a momentary forgetfulness in the middle of a period whose firmly controlled syntax betrays no abatement of alertness would be to save the hypothesis that slavery had been expunged from the *Republic* as incompatible [294] with δικαιοσύνη. To take Levinson's suggestion seriously we should also have to suppose that, after suffering this lapse when writing this sentence, Plato never noticed the blunder on rereading, and that no one else ever called it to his attention, so that it was left uncorrected. I doubt if Levinson would have himself thought his suggestion worthy of serious consideration if he had thought through its implications in this way.[18] And since there is no other ground for discounting the all

[17] I say "parts of the population," not "parts of the *polis*." Plato is taking here the broadest possible view of the instantiation of δικαιοσύνη within the confines of the utopia, including children and slaves.

[18] To support his suggestion he adduces 425A and 460A as parallel cases of "forgetfulness" in the *Republic*. These would not be true parallels, even if they were cases of "forgetfulness" at all which, in my opinion, they are not. Consider 425A: Believing, as did so many of his contemporaries, that the Athenian moral fiber deteriorated after the Persian Wars, and convinced that this was due in no small part to the corrupting effects of innovations in music (cf. *Laws* 700A-701C), Plato has high expectations of the morally improving effects

too plain reference to the slave as instantiating the characteristic virtue of
the ideal city, it must be reckoned a strong confirmation of our initial
presumption. Since this would be entitled to acceptance even without any
further support—for there is no contrary evidence—the case for the affirmative must be reckoned conclusive. [295]

---

of the controlled music and games he lays down for the young in his utopia,
and goes on to speak of the result as "restoring anything that may have
formerly gone amiss" and recovering modes of deportment and dress which
οἱ πρότερον ἀπώλλυσαν (425A5-9)—as though he were splicing the utopia into
the later history of a state such as Athens (though Athens is not mentioned
by name) which had once possessed, and then lost, purity of manners and
morals. *Pace* Shorey, who sees a "lapse" in the writing here (see his note *ad.
loc.*), I judge this to be only a rhetorical conceit, purposefully employed.
Conservatives, who would be repelled by innovations like those of the commu-
nist property arrangements for the guardians (which have been just described
and argued for in 416D3-422A3) and of the communistic family (of which a
hint is given in 423E-424A2), are being reminded that there is at least one
respect, and of the greatest moment, in which Plato's reforms will be re-
assuringly conservative, restoring those simple, manly, modest manners which
Athens once had and then lost after Marathon. Nor do I believe that Levinson is
right in saying that in 460A "Plato forgets that he has restricted himself to
laying down regulations affecting [procreation by] the guardians, and speaks
[at A5-6] as if he were dealing with the [size of] the whole city," p. 171, n. 77.
Plato would be "forgetting" only if he were implying, as is asserted without
argument by both Shorey and Cornford *ad loc.*, that the birth rate in the
guardian class would be the sole determinant of the city's state. This does not
follow strictly from the wording: he may be implying that an increase or
decrease of the size of the guardian class would bring about a corresponding
increase or decrease in the productive class and *thereby* make the *polis* "great or
small." It is most unlikely that Plato, when thinking of the size of the whole
polis, should lose sight of the largest class in it.

7

Slavery
in Plato's Thought*

(1941; *SPT*)

I. SLAVERY IN PLATO'S POLITICAL THEORY

A formal discussion of slavery is nowhere to be found in Plato. We must reconstruct his views from a few casual statements. The most important of these is a simile in the *Laws* (720), where Plato contrasts the free physician in attendance upon freemen with the slave healer of slaves. The free medical man "investigates the origin and the nature of the disease,[1] he enters into community with the patient and with his friends." He is essentially a teacher, but a teacher who also learns from the sick. He gives no autocratic orders, but educates the patient into health. Slaves, on the other hand, are incapable of such reasonable intercourse. The slave doctor's visit is hurried. He "neither gives a servant any rational account [λόγος] of his complaint, nor asks him for any; he gives an order based on empirical belief [δόξα] with the air of exact knowledge, in the insolent manner of a tyrant, then jumps off to the next ailing servant."[2] Elsewhere (*Laws* 773E), discussing the proper treatment of slaves, Plato sums up the matter in these words: "One must punish slaves justly, not spoiling them by admonition

* Read in substance at a meeting of the American Philosophical Association, December 1939. Reprinted from *Philos Rev.*, 1941, 289 ff. The original pagination is interpolated in square brackets.

[1] 720D: ἐξετάζων ἀπ' ἀρχῆς καὶ κατὰ φύσιν.

[2] *Cf.* also *Grg.* 501A, where scientific medicine is defined in similar terms, contrasting the knowledge of the natural cause (τὴν φύσιν, τὴν αἰτίαν) and the ability to give a rational account (*logos*) with τριβὴ καὶ ἐμπειρία.

as though they were freemen."³ And in another context: "Well then, should they discern this, but be unable to give any rational demonstration of it?—Impossible. The state of mind you describe is that of a slave" (*Laws* 966B).

It is clear from such passages that Plato thinks of the slave's condition as a deficiency of reason. He has *doxa*, but no *logos*. He can have true belief, but cannot know why his belief is true.⁴ He can learn by experience [ἐμπειρία] and external prescription [ἐπίταξις]. But he can neither give nor follow a rational account. He is *therefore* susceptible to persuasion.⁵ This is not [289] evidence of reason, but the reverse. *Nous* is "unmoved by persuasion" (*Tm* 51E4). The weakness of *doxa*, even of true *doxa*, is that it can be changed.⁶ Only knowledge is stable [μόνιμος], for he who knows has direct contact with the immutable Forms.⁷ This is what the slave lacks. His experience cannot yield true knowledge.⁸ In all matters of truth he is, therefore, unconditionally subject to his intellectual superiors.

³ Even Aristotle thinks that this is going too far: *Pol.* 1260B6–8.

⁴ *Ti.*: 51D-E: δόξα ἀληθὴς is ἄλογον. Only νοῦς .. ἐγγίγνεται . . . ἀεὶ μετὰ ἀληθοῦς λόγου.

⁵ Διδαχή vs. πειθώ, *Tm*, 51 E2. *Peitho* is usually translated "persuasion", and I shall follow this usage here. But "influence" or "suggestion" would be a better rendering. *Peitho* means simply changing another's mind. It puts no strings on the way this is done. "Persuasion," as ordinarily used in English, ties one down to some kind of intellectual, or, at least, rhetorical, process. You cannot persuade without some kind of argument, though it may be fallacious argument. But Plato can write διδασκάλους πεπεισμένους μισθοῖς (*Laws* 804D) without straining the word. Cf. δῶρα θεοὺς πείθει (quoted in *R.* 390E). In Greek usage *peitho* often stands for "bribe."

⁶ *Meno* 98A. Plato's educational system aspires to dye the right beliefs into the soul like fast colors into wool. But even fast colors fade. The ultimate guarantee of the stability of the state is not in the early precautions to make the guardians' good convictions proof against persuasion, oblivion, beguilement of pleasure and pressure of fear (*R.* 413BC); it is the guardians' eventual acquaintance with the unalterable Good.

⁷ E.g., *R.* 532A. "Direct" means here "through reason without the mediation of the senses."

⁸ It may be asked: What of the slave-boy in the *Meno?* Socrates confidently asserts (85E) that what the boy has done in this instance he could do "in the whole of geometry and in all other lessons." But what has he done in this instance? Socrates makes each successive point so plain that only a half-wit could miss it. Plato never suggested that slaves are stupid. He only says that they lack *logos* or *nous* and cannot apprehend the Forms. One may lack *logos* yet be a paragon of empiric acuteness (e.g., *R.* 516C; and 519A τῶν λεγομένων πονηρῶν μέν σοφῶν δέ, ὡς δριμὺ μέν βλέπει τὸ ψυχάριον . . .). At the end of the encounter the slave-boy has not discovered the Forms Square, Diagonal, etc.

Now it is an axiom of Plato's political theory that the only one fit to
rule is he who possesses *logos*.[9] The good ruler must rule for the good of
the state. He can only do this if he knows the form of the Good and then
uses the necessary "persuasion and coercion" to order the state accordingly.[10] Thus government is good for the governed,[11] but does not require
their consent.[12] [290] A democratically minded theorist like Protagoras[13]
holds that all men have a sense of "reverence and justice"; that they all
share in the "political art."[14] Plato denies this flatly: "Does it seem at all

---

Socrates gives the pieces of the puzzle and keeps prodding and correcting until
the boy has fitted them properly together. The boy then has the answer to
this particular problem, but no grasp of the underlying general truth. He knows
the true solution, but not why it is true.

Nevertheless I should not conclude that Plato thinks that this slave-boy
could not discover the Forms. This point is left undetermined. But, if the
slave-boy could master the Forms, then he ought not to be a slave. In a "true"
(i.e., Platonic) state he would be a philosopher, and *therefore* at the top, not the
bottom, of the social pyramid.

[9] E.g., *Laws* 968A: The highest magistrate "must be able to give a rational
account [*logos*] of all that admits of a rational account." Otherwise he cannot
be a "fit ruler of the whole state, but only a servant to other rulers."

[10] R. 519E: συναρμόττων τοὺς πολίτας πειθοῖ τε καὶ ἀνάγκῃ.

[11] E.g., Socrates' argument against Thrasymachus in the *Republic*, I, maintaining that government is for the benefit of the governed.

[12] *Plt.* 293A, 296B–297B. This point is all the more remarkable because it
contrasts sharply with the conception of government which underlies the *Crito*.
There Socrates thinks and acts as a responsible member of a free republic. It is
because he has himself *consented* to the laws that they are binding upon him:
παρὰ τὰς ξυνθήκας τε καὶ ὁμολογίας (52D); ξυνθήκας τὰς πρὸς ἡμᾶς παραβάς
(54C). However, it would not be impossible to find a casuistic reconciliation of
political obligation that rests upon consent with political authority that is above
consent. Plato's point, I suppose, would be that the good ruler's commands
must be obeyed, consent or no consent; though if his subjects knew the Good
as he knows it (a hypothesis which would abolish the distinction between
subject and ruler in the *Republic* and the *Politicus*), they would gladly give their
consent.

[13] It is significant that Pericles entrusted him with the framing of the constitution of Thourioi.

[14] *Prt.* 322C, D. It is suggestive to compare Protagoras' myth with the myth
of the *Politicus* and the comparable passage in *Laws* 713B ff. In the former the
setting is man's struggle for self-preservation: Prometheus' gift of fire and
Hermes' gift of "reverence and justice" put into man's hands the two weapons
that enable him to survive. Plato's aristocratic counterblast changes the setting
so as to abstract entirely from the principle of human self-reliance and self-help.
It harks back to the age of Cronos where there is no struggle with nature (πάντα

possible that a multitude in a state could ever acquire this [*sc.* political]
science?—By no means" (*Plt.* 292E, Fowler's tr.). Hence anything like
contract theory of justice strikes Plato as a pernicious error.[15] How can
men who do not know the nature of justice establish a just state by common
agreement? The only way to get justice is to recognize the fact that "some
men are by nature fitted to embrace philosophy and lead in the state,
while others are unfit to embrace it and must follow the leader" (*R.* 474C;
cf. *Laws* 690B).

It follows that the absence of self-determination, so striking in the case
of the slave, is normal in Platonic society. The fully enlightened aristocrats
are a small minority of the whole population (*e.g., Plt.* 292E). All the rest
are in some degree *douloi* in Plato's sense of the word: they lack *logos;* they
do not know the Good, and cannot know their own good or the good of
the state; [*291*] their only chance of doing the good is to obey implicitly the
commands of their superiors. Thus Plato speaks currently of subjection
to the reasonable discipline of rulers, human and divine, laws, parents,
and elders as servitude (*douleuein, douleia*).[16] This usage is not without
precedent. But Plato goes farther in this direction than any earlier writer.
It had been the proud boast of Aeschylus for his fellow-countrymen:
"They cannot be called the slaves of any man" (*Pers.* 242). It is hard to
find an instance in fifth-century literature where *douleia* is used, as Plato
uses it, in the sense of virtuous, amicable, and cheerful submission to
constituted authority, without any of the grim associations of duresse and
dishonor. Yet Plato's genial extension of the word to cover an honorable
and even fortunate estate is amply justified by the premises of his own
thought: The manual laborer, for example, is "weak by nature in the

---

αὐτόματα γίγνεσθαι τοῖς ἀνθρώποις, *Plt.* 271D; ὡς ἄφθονά τε καὶ αὐτόματα
πάντα εἶχεν, *Laws,* 713C), and where man's social life is directly under the care
of divine beings (the "divine shepherd" of the *Politicus,* the "daemons" of the
Laws). Here reverence and justice (*Laws,* 713E) are not the condition, but the
product of good government; and good government means not self-government but government of the inferior by the superior, of the mortal by the
divine.

[15] *R.* 359A, *Laws* 889D-E: that justice rests on agreement is mentioned as part
of a dangerous view, destructive of morality and religion. Yet the idea of law
as συνθήκη was so widespread that it invaded even the thought of its opponents:
e.g., Plato himself (*Crito* 52D, 54C, cited above) and Aristotle (see Bonitz, Index,
729B 53).

[16] *Laws* 698BC, 700A, 701B, 715D, 762E, 839C, 890A. For some of these
references, and for much else in this paper, I am indebted to G. R. Morrow's
"Plato and Greek Slavery", *Mind,* April, 1939.

principle of the best." Left to himself, he could not rule himself, but would be ruled by his appetites. What happier solution could there be than servitude to one who is strong in the principle of the best, "so that we may all be alike and friends so far as possible, all governed by the same principle"?[17]

When Plato speaks so innocently of the artisans of the *Republic* as the "slaves" of the philosophers, he certainly does not mean to be taken literally.[18] He neither means to degrade all artisans to the level of bondmen, nor to raise the social status of [292] the slave to that of the free laborer. There is not the slightest indication, either in the *Republic*[19] or anywhere else, that Plato means to obliterate or relax in any way that distinction. The very opposite is the case. Professor Morrow's admirable recent study has shown that Plato's law of slavery is not more but less liberal than current Attic law; and in one important respect less liberal than any known slave legislation of classical antiquity.[20] Then what is the point of speaking so freely of all sorts and conditions of political subordinates as *douloi?* The point is not practical, but theoretical. It underlines the fact that, in principle, there is no difference in Plato's political theory between the relation of a master to his slave and of a sovereign to his subjects; or, as Aristotle put this Platonic doctrine: that "mastership

[17] *R.* 590CD. (Jowett blurs the point by translating "servant" for *doulos*, much as King James' translators often render "servant" for *doulos*: e.g., Matt. 20: 27, Mark 10: 44, Gal. 4: 1, Eph. 6: 5. Lindsay's translation is more exact.) This passage has never received the attention it deserves. B. Bosanquet is the only exception I know. He sees that "this is the essential basis of Aristotle's explanation . . . of slavery," and accepts it in principle: "Plato's general account of the spiritual relation of society to inferior or immature minds, and in some degree to all minds, is unimpeachable" (*Companion to Plato's Republic, ad loc.*). I suppose that in terms of Bosanquet's political theory the philosopher would express the "real will" of the *doulos*. Hegel is more sophisticated on this point. See his stricture on Platonic philosophy: "the principle of subjective freedom does not receive its due" (*Philosophy of Right*, tr. by Dyde, par. 185, note. *Cf.* M. B. Foster, *The Political Philosophies of Plato and Hegel*, Ch. iii). But it is significant that Hegel does not criticize Plato for his denial of the *objective* freedom of the working classes. Hegel's own political theory would hardly entitle him to make this criticism.

[18] As mistaken, for example, by W. L. Newman, *The Politics of Aristotle*, I, 109–10, in a valuable reference to this passage, suggesting that this was "perhaps the source from which Aristotle derived his theory of natural slavery."

[19] On slavery in the *Republic* see *SER* above.

[20] "Plato and Greek Slavery," *Mind*, April, 1939. See pp. 194–98, and especially p. 196. For a more detailed discussion see the same author's *Plato's Law of Slavery* (University of Illinois Press, 1939).

[δεσποτεία], statesmanship [πολιτική] and kingship [βασιλική] are the same thing."[21]

In other words, Plato uses one and the same principle to interpret (and justify) political authority and the master's right to govern the slave, political obligation and the slave's duty to obey his master. His conception of all government (*archē, archein*) is of a piece with his conception of the government of slaves. Is this saying too much? One thinks of any number of important qualifications.[22] Yet substantially the statement is true. One need only refer to the *Politicus* for the explicit statement that there is no other difference between the art of slaveowner [δεσπότης 259B7] and king [βασιλικός 259C2] than the size of their respective establishments.

Whatever be the refinements of such a theory, it appears at once as a radical denial of democracy. It could no more account for the facts of democratic government in Athens, than the contract theorists could account for the fact of slavery. The [293] contract theorists generalized the government of the state by the *demos* for the *demos*. They verged on idealism at the point where they would substitute "man" for "citizen of Athens"; at that point they did not know what to do with slavery, and played with the subversive view that slavery was unnatural.[23] Plato, generalizing the government of slave by master, was forced into the opposite conclusion that democracy was unnatural. Plato idealized the institution of slavery, the contract theorists the institution of democracy.

[21] *Pol.* 1253B18; 1252A8. That this is Plato's view is clear from *Plt.* 259BC.
[22] It would be superfluous to detail these here. They are obvious to any reader of the *Republic* and the *Laws*, and I should not wish to belittle them. See especially *R.* 547C. All I am suggesting here is that Plato uses one and the same principle to interpret (and justify) authority in the case of both master and statesman and obedience in the case of both slave and subject.
[23] Contract could only be the thinnest of disguises for force, on which slavery so obviously rested (see *Pol.* 1255A5 ff.). To base slavery on agreement was to suggest the view that this agreement was unnatural and slavery invalid. How many of the contract theorists shared this view? We do not know. In the *Politics* (1253B21) Aristotle does not name his opponents who flatly maintained that slavery is conventional and contrary to nature. See *Grg.* 484AB for Callicles' view that "natural justice" may be violated by slavery. Antiphon, the sophist, undercuts the distinction between noble and low birth, between Greek and barbarian ἐπεὶ φύσει πάντα πάντες ὁμοίως πεφύκαμεν (Diels, B, 44, Fr. B, col. 2). The same principle would undercut slavery. Alcidamas, the pupil and successor of Gorgias, is said to have declared: "God left all men free; nature made no one a slave" (*Schol.* on *Rhet.* 1373B18). And a fragment of Philemon, the comic poet (ed. Meineke, Fr. 39), runs: "Though one be a slave, he has the same flesh; / By nature no one was ever born a slave."

Their conflicting idealism mirrored the real contradiction in Athenian society: a free political community that rested on a slave economy.

II. SLAVERY IN PLATO'S COSMOLOGY

Can we detect any higher overtones of the master-slave relation? Can we trace it in wholes of a different order than political society: in the human microcosm and in the physical macrocosm? One's attention is drawn in this direction by Plato's frequent references to the body as the "slave" of the soul. That this is no mere figure of speech, but is meant to convey a serious philosophical truth, is clear from three considerations. (i) It stands as a formal premise in a metaphysical argument for the immortality of the soul in the *Phaedo*.[24] (ii) It is written into the physiology of the *Timaeus*.[25] (iii) It determines leading ideas [294] in Plato's ethics.[26] Each of these matters deserves detailed discussion. But to keep this paper within reasonable limits, I proceed at once to Plato's application of the slave metaphor beyond anthropology to cosmology itself.

Let us begin with the scene in the *Phaedo* where the Platonic Socrates explains that he turned away from Ionian physics, because it did not use the right method. The right method, suggested by Anaxagoras' *nous*, but,

[24] 79E–80A. It is because "nature ordains" that soul should be ruler, the body slave, and because authority and servitude are respectively "natural" for the divine and the mortal, that soul is ὅμοιον τῷ θείῳ and body ὅμοιον τῷ θνητῷ.

[25] In the head, whose spherical form copies the shape of the universe, is placed "the divinest and holiest part" (452A), which is "lord [δεσποτοῦν] of all that is in us" (44D). The rest of the body is made to serve (ᾧ καὶ πᾶν τὸ σῶμα παρέδοσαν ὑπηρεσίαν αὐτῷ): it is a vehicle (ὄχημα) for the head, supplementing the soul's two "divine revolutions" (44D) with the "six wandering motions" (44D8; cf. 43B). The "mortal" part of the soul is housed apart "for fear of polluting the divine part" (69D); the neck was built as "an isthmus and boundary to keep the two apart" (69E).

[26] In the beginning of *Laws* v, the whole rationale of virtue is reduced to these terms: "A man's own nature consists invariably of two kinds of elements: the stronger and better are lordly [δεσπόζοντα] the weaker and worse are slaves [δοῦλα]; wherefore one must ever honour the lordly above the slavish elements in one's nature" (726). That is, honor the soul above the body and its pleasures and passions. In the *Republic* intemperance is described as insubordination of the appetites against the order of reason. It is "a meddlesomeness and interference and rebellion of one part of the soul against the whole to gain a rule to which it has no right; that part indeed whose nature is such that it ought to be slave, while the other should never be slave, but ruler" (following Lindsay's translation of 444B, except after the semicolon, where he takes τοιούτου ὄντος φύσει to refer to τῷ ὅλῳ instead of μέρους τινός). Similar expression in 442AB.

alas, not followed by this unregenerate Ionian, is defined in the following terms: "If you wish to find the cause of anything . . . , you must find out this about it: How it is best for it to exist or be acted upon or act in any other way" (97CD). Thus a scientific explanation of the shape and position of the earth must prove that it has that particular shape and position because these are "best" for it (97E).

To back this unusual view of scientific method the Platonic Socrates resorts to an analogy: What is the cause of my presence in this prison? It is not bones and sinews that keep me here, but my decision that this is for the best (99B). Physiology is not the "real" cause (τὸ αἴτιον τῷ ὄντι), but only an indispensable condition (ἐκεῖνο ἄνευ οὗ τὸ αἴτιον οὐκ ἄν ποτ' εἴη αἴτιον, 99C). Without apology this argument is transferred from the human organism to the universe at large. The reasoning takes it for granted that teleology and mechanism are related in the world-order as mind to body in man himself. But since the relation of mind to body has already been conceived as analogous to that of master to slave, it would follow that the relation of teleology to mechanism can also be so conceived: that the mechanical cause, mistakenly accepted by the Ionians as the "ruling" cause, is actually only a "slave" cause. This, of course, is so far only an inference. But if we follow the development of Plato's thought [295] in the later dialogues we shall find that this is exactly the direction in which it moves.

Physical variables, like hot and cold, dry and moist, which play such an important role in early Ionian thought, appear in the *Philebus* under the category of the measureless.[27] Lacking in order, this realm of being would be full of *hybris* and evil (26B), were measure not imposed upon it[28] by a creative agent.[29] This is *the* cause (τὸ αἴτιον, 26E): the very category that Socrates missed in the Ionians. It is the ordering *nous* of Anaxagoras now taken in good earnest and assigned to its proper place as "king of heaven and earth" (28C). The other principle is its slave: "slave to the cause [δουλεῦον αἰτίᾳ] for the purpose of generation" (27A).

In the *Timaeus* the whole account of man and the world turns on a clear-cut distinction between two kinds of causes:

(1) the "primary" cause, which is "intelligent," "divine," and productive of all that is "fair and good,"[30]

---

[27] 25D: τὸ ἄπειρον opposite of τὸ περατοειδές and of τὸ ἔμμετρον καὶ σύμμετρον (26A6, 7).

[28] Note the force of ἐπ' αὐτοῖς (30C5).

[29] τὸ δημιουργοῦν (27B), τὸ ποιοῦν (27A), ἡ τοῦ ποιοῦντος φύσις (26E).

[30] τὰς τῆς ἔμφρονος φύσεως αἰτίας πρώτας (46D), ὅσαι μετὰ νοῦ καλῶν καὶ ἀγαθῶν δημιουργοί (46E), τὰ διὰ νοῦ (47E), θεῖον νοῦν (22C).

(2) The "secondary" cause, which is "necessary," irrational, fortuitous, and disorderly.[31]

The modern reader must find something baffling about this blend of necessity with chance in the secondary cause. For us the very idea of necessity implies necessary order.[32] How conceive of necessary disorder without self-contradiction?[33] [296]

I can think of one clue: "The ideas of *douleia* and *ananke*," writes George Thomson, "are almost inseparable in Greek, the word *ananke* being constantly used to denote both the state of slavery as such, and also the torture to which the slaves were subjected."[34] No one, so far as I know, has ever thought of interpreting the *ananke* of the *Timaeus* on the pattern of slavery. Yet Plato speaks of material necessity as a "servant" (ὑπηρετοῦσιν, 46C7; ὑπηρετούσαις, 68E4) who, he also tells us, is "incapable of any *logos* or *nous* about anything" (46D4). But this, as we have seen, is the defining concept of the slave: a servant destitute of *logos*. Here, I think, is the explanation we need.

[31] ἀνάγκη (48A), ἡ τῆς ἀνάγκης φύσις (56C), τὸ ἀναγκαῖον (68E), τὰ δι' ἀνάγκης (47E); ὅσαι μονωθεῖσαι φρονήσεως τὸ τυχὸν ἄτακτον ἐξεργάζοντα' (46E). *Cf.* with this last *Phil.* 28D6, 7.

[32] In the ensuing discussion I am not speaking of Plato's concept of necessity as a whole. I am excluding from the discussion logical necessity. Like everyone else, Plato identifies this with rational order. He uses constantly ἀνάγκη, ἀναγκαῖον, etc. to mark the cogency and evidence of a deductive conclusion (e.g., *Grg.* 475A–C; *Phaedo* 91E; *Phil.* 40C; *Ti.* 53C). This kind of *ananke* is at the other extreme from the *ananke* of the secondary cause. Logical necessity is explicitly opposed to verisimilitude (*Theait.* 162E), while verisimilitude is the characteristic mood of all discourse about the material world (*Ti.* 29C; and 53D κατὰ τὸν μετ' ἀνάγκης εἰκότα λόγον). This bifurcation of *ananke* into formal order and material disorder is conserved by Aristotle. His view is tersely stated and acutely discussed by D. M. Balme in the *Class. Quarterly*, Oct., 1939: "Ananke does not govern sequences: there is no transeunt causality inherent in the material," p. 130.

[33] In *Plato's Cosmology* (162 ff.) F. M. Cornford throws some light on this problem. He points out that to Plato, as to Aristotle, chance does not mean the opposite of necessity, but the opposite of purpose. Thus a "necessary accident" means to both any unintended, but unavoidable, circumstance involved in the execution of a plan. This does explain the element of compulsion in *ananke*. But it does not explain the element of disorder.

[34] *The ORESTEIA of Aeschylus*, II, 345, (Cambridge, 1938). The association of the two words follows naturally from their obvious meaning. Aristotle defines *ananke* (in the sense of compulsion: τὴν γὰρ ἔξωθεν ἀρχήν, τὴν παρὰ τὴν ὁρμὴν ἢ ἐμποδίζουσαν ἢ κινοῦσαν, ἀνάγκην λέγομεν (*Eud. Eth.* 1224B); while the common view of *douleia*, as Aristotle reports it, is τὸ ζῆν μὴ ὡς βούλεται (*Pol.* 1317B13).

The idea of "disorderly necessity" strikes us as a flat selfcontradiction because we think of necessity in terms of a mechanical instrument, whose motions follow a strict mechanical order; that order is inherent in the instrument, and we can only use the instrument in so far as we respect its order. Plato thinks of necessity in terms of a "living instrument," whose use does not seem to depend on our understanding of its own intrinsic order, but rather on our ability to "persuade" it to follow our own purpose. In this case the order does not seem to be in the instrument but in us. This is the very image that occurs to Aristotle when he pictures the teleological order of the universe: "But it is as in a house, where the freemen are least at liberty to act at random, but all things or most things are already ordered for them, while the slaves and the beasts do little for the common good, for the most part live at random."[35] The slave does not share of his own accord the order of the common life. Left to himself he would "wander" off into disorder.[36] Order, which [297] he could not originate himself, must be imposed upon him, preferably by persuasion or, failing this, by coercion. The Demiurge, being the wisest of masters, need not resort to coercion at all: he "persuades necessity" (48A2) and makes it his "willing" slave (56C5). The notion of "persuading necessity" and the implied idea of "compelling necessity" make sense only if one keeps steadily in mind the slave metaphor. Persuading the law of gravitation does not make sense. Persuading a slave does.

To appreciate the importance of this development one must see it in historic perspective. The slave metaphor occurs at the very point where Plato turns consciously away from the cosmology of his predecessors.[37]

[35] *Met.* 1075A19. *Cf.* ὅτι ἔτυχεν and τέτακται of this passage with τὸ τυχὸν ἄτακτον of *Ti.* 46E5.

[36] But the slave's behavior is not utter disorder. It is only disorderly from the standpoint of the superior order intended by the master. At the price of inconsistency Plato is true to this feature of the slave-metaphor, maintaining that the primordial chaos had crude "traces" of the elegant order that the Demiurge was to impress upon it at creation: τὴν γενέσεως τιθήνην ὑγραινομένην καὶ πυρομένην καὶ τὰς γῆς τε καὶ ἀέρος μορφὰς δεχομένην, καὶ ὅσα ἄλλα τούτοις πάθη συνέπεται πάσχουσαν (*Ti.* 52DE). The last clause is particularly important, for it recognizes an order of causal implication *before* the chaos had been "informed with shapes and numbers" (53B). Yet Plato can only explain causal implication *through* the Forms: e.g., the necessary connection between fire and heat, snow and cold (*Phaedo* 103C ff.). This is part of a larger contradiction in Plato's thought which I have noted in "The Disorderly Motion in the *Timaios*," p. 76-7, *Class. Quarterly*, April, 1939.

[37] See W. H. Heidel, περὶ φύσεως, *Proc. Am. Acad. of Arts and Sciences*, Jan. 1910.

From the very beginnings of Ionian thought *rational* and *immanent* necessity had been an integral feature of the concept of nature. Recall, for example, the saying of Anaximander that things come into existence and perish "as it is ordained; for they make satisfaction and reparation to one another for their injustice according to the order of time."[38] To express natural necessity this early Milesian borrows words from the government of man. But that is, of course, no more than what we must still do today when we speak of the "laws" of nature. What is important is rather the absence of any suggestion of a superior agency to issue ordinances and enforce reparations. On the contrary, Anaximander excludes the intervention of a superior order in the course of nature by endowing nature itself with the attributes of divinity: it is infinite, immortal, indestructible.[39] Thinkers as opposed to one another [298] as the Ionian Heraclitus and the Italian Parmenides[40] preserve this feature of Anaximander's thought. Some verbal expressions may suggest the opposite. But a closer examination shows how firmly they adhere to the notion of autonomous nature. When Heraclitus says, for example, "The sun will not overstep his measures [μέτρα] else the Erinyes, the assistants of Justice, will find him out" Justice and the Erinyes stand for no independent entity; they simply express the inevitability of the pattern that fire follows in its unceasing transformations, "kindled in measure [μέτρα], and extinguished in measure."[41] Likewise when Parmenides writes, "strong *ananke* keeps it in the bonds of the limit,"[42] *ananke* is neither superior nor inferior to the inflexible rationality of existence, but simply identical with it.

[38] Diels, B, 1.

[39] Ibid., B, 3. (Cf. my "Equality and Justice in Early Greek Philosophy," *Class. Phil.*, 42 [1947], 156–78 at 168 ff. on Anaximander, and 174 ff. on "The Naturalization of Justice.")

[40] This connection of Parmenides with Anaximander was suggested to me by Werner Jaeger's remark: "he also calls it [sc. *ananke*] *dike* or *moira*, obviously under Anaximander's influence," *Paideia*, Eng. tr., p. 174.

[41] Diels, B, 94 and 30. Cf. also B, 80: "strife is justice." The conflict of the elements ("war") itself produces its own order. So again in B, 53: "War is father of all and king of all; some he has made gods and some men, some slaves and some free." A question might arise over B, 41: "the thought (*gnomê*) which steers (ἐκυβέρνησε) all things through all things." Is this governing thought an extraneous, superior factor? Clearly not, if one compares B, 64, "the thunderbolt that steers (οἰακίζει) the course of all things" with B, 66: "Fire in its advance will judge and convict all things" (Burnet's tr. following Diels): the "thought" is inherent in the fire; like "justice" above, simply another expression for the relentless orderliness of fire.

[42] Diels, B, 30 l. 31; cf. ll. 14 and 37.

In the atomism of Leucippus and Democritus this trend of thought comes to full maturity: "Nothing occurs at random, but everything for a reason [ἐκ λόγου] and by necessity."[43] Here is the exact opposite of Plato's doctrine: *logos* and *ananke* are coupled together; material necessity is rational and it excludes chance.[44] The inherent motion of matter which seems to Plato the source of necessary disorder is in the eyes of Democritus the very meaning of necessary order.[45] And because it is necessary, motion is coeval with matter itself. There is no need for a "first cause" to set matter in motion.[46] This was the final blow at the anthropomorphic theory of creation. Its consequences, writes Cyril Bailey, "were momentous. In the sphere of physical [299] speculation it introduced for the first time the possibility of a strictly scientific conception of the world."[47]

Why was it that Plato chose to frustrate this possibility in his cosmology?[48] It would be presumptuous to attempt to answer this question within the limits of this paper. But the answer, whatever it be, must reckon with this fact: Plato attacks Ionian physics not only on philosophical, but also on political grounds; so that both the political and the cosmological associations of slavery came into play in his polemic. The issue is the very existence of a philosophy which conceives of the government of the state and the government of the world as analogous to the government of the slave. The *locus classicus* for this attack is the tenth book of the *Laws*.

His opponents are the "modern scientists" (886D; also 888E ff.). He imputes to them not only mechanistic cosmology, but also the contract

---

[43] Ibid., 67 B, 2 (Bailey's tr.).

[44] Simpl. 330.14 τὸ δὲ καθάπερ ὁ παλαιὸς λόγος ὁ ἀναιρῶν τὴν τύχην (*Physics*, 196A, 14) πρὸς Δ. ἔοικε εἰρῆσθαι. . . . Dante's reproach, "Democrito che il mondo a caso pone" rests on a misconception. See Enriques and de Santillana, *Histoire de la Pensée Scientifique*, 111, 40, and Cyril Bailey's elegant argument in *Greek Atomists and Epicurus*, 141–43.

[45] D. L., ix, 45: τῆς αἰτίας οὔσης τῆς γενέσεως πάντων, ἣν ἀνάγκην λέγει.

[46] Plutarch, *Strom.*, 7 (*Doxographi Graeci* 581).

[47] *Op. cit.*, 122.

[48] Aristotle is often blamed for importing teleology into physics. The real culprit, of course, is Plato. Aristotle thinks as a Platonist when he repudiates the all-but-universal belief of his predecessors in natural necessity (*Phys.* 198B 12; *de part. Anim.* 639B 21). It was Plato who had led the attack on the Ionian mechanists, foisting on them his own assumption that material necessity is equivalent to chance, and thus forcing them into the absurd position of denying the *de facto* order of the universe because they will not grant the existence of teleological order. This misconception which vitiates the argument for final causes in *Phys.* ii. viii had been anticipated in the *Philebus* (28D–29E) and *Laws X*.

theory of the state.[49] The first gives rise to the second, and each to atheism. The basic error is the idea that physical bodies "are moved by the interplay of their respective forces, according as they chance to come together and somehow combine fittingly" (889B)[50]; in other words, that nature is a self-regulating system, and is not governed by the art of a divine mind. This implies that the stars are products of a natural process, not gods, but inanimate material bodies (886DE; 889B). It implies further that legislation (like every other art) is a late product of the same process, so that laws are not absolute commands, but man-made agreements (889C–890E). Instead of deriving the laws [300] from the gods, this impious view derives the gods from the laws, and variable laws at that.

To refute all this Plato maintains that the soul is the first cause of all physical motions. His elaborate argument need not be examined here. We need only note that the point of his thesis is to prove that the soul, being "older" than the body, has the right to "rule" the body.[51] And what he means by the soul's "rule" is clear from a parallel passage in the *Timaeus* (34C): soul is *despotis;* it rules the body as master rules slave. If he can prove this, Plato feels he has destroyed Ionian materialism. He can then have everything his own way: that soul or souls direct every bodily motion (896DE); that the stars have soul or souls and are divine (898D–899B); and that, in short, "all things are full of gods" (899B). Thus cosmology supports religion by establishing the existence of its gods.[52] And the link between religious cosmology and political religion is the slave metaphor.

---

[49] How easily this point may be missed is clear from A. E. Taylor's paraphrase of this passage (in the Introduction to his translation of the *Laws*, lii): "Plato's view is that atheism is the product of two historical factors, the corporealism of the early Ionian men of science . . . , and the 'sophistic' theory of the purely conventional and relative character of moral distinctions." But the text says nothing about "two historical factors." It is the same people (the σοφοὶ ἄνδρες of 888E) whose cosmology is expounded in 889B-D and whose politics is given in 889D–890A.

[50] Cf. *Sph.* 265C5-8: τῷ τῶν πολλῶν δόγματι καὶ ῥήματι χρώμενοι . . . τὴν φύσιν αὐτὰ γεννᾶν ἀπό τινος αἰτίας αὐτομάτης καὶ ἄνευ διανοίας φυούσης . . .

[51] E.g., 892A: [ψυχή] ὡς ἐν πρώτοις ἐστὶ σωμάτων, ἔμπροσθεν πάντων γενομένην, whence it is assumed by a simple conjunction (καί) that it rules every bodily change. The inference from superior age to the right to rule is made explicit in *Tm* 34C.

[52] The "gods according to the laws": 885B, 890AB, 904A. Serious confusion results when this limitation is not recognized. *Laws* x does not even attempt to prove the existence of the Demiurge, who is never mentioned among the official divinities.

III. PLATO AND ARISTOTLE

Any discussion of Plato's views on slavery invites comparison with the most famous text of antiquity on this topic: the first book of the *Politics* Aristotle's polemic is mainly directed against those who hold that slavery is contrary to nature.[53] The word "nature" is used here in at least three senses: a moral, a biological, and a cosmological one. The first states the *demonstrandum* of Aristotle's argument; the latter two decide the demonstration. *To prove*: that slavery is natural, in the sense of being good and just:[54] good for the master, to whom it provides a necessary instrument (1253B23 ff.); good also for the slave,[55] whose intellectual deficiency is supplemented by the master's superior reason.[56] This is proved first by the contention that the [*301*] difference of master and slave, commensurate with that of soul and body or of man and beast (1254B17), is a congenital one: "some things are marked out from the moment of birth to rule or to be ruled" (1254A23). This is the part of Aristotle's argument that has given greatest offense to posterity and thus attracted widest attention. Yet no less important in Aristotle's eyes is the metaphysical sanction of slavery. The difference between master and slave, he holds, is natural because it follows a pattern that pervades all nature: "because in every composite thing, where a plurality of parts, whether continuous or discrete, is combined to make a single common whole, there is always found a ruling and a subject factor, and this characteristic of living things is present in them as an outcome of the whole of nature [ἐκ τῆς ἁπάσης φύσεως]."[57]

Now let us ask: What is there in this argument that Plato too could not have said in full consistency with his own ideas about slavery? It is, of

[53] παρὰ φύσιν τὸ δεσπόζειν, 1253B20.

[54] βέλτιον καὶ δίκαιον, 1254A18.

[55] φύσει δοῦλοι οἷς βέλτιόν ἐστιν ἄρχεσθαι ταύτην τὴν ἀρχήν, 1254B19.

[56] 1252A31; cf. *Nic. Eth.* 1161A35–B1.

[57] 1254A29–32, Rackham's tr. Other passages too show that Aristotle thinks of slavery not as an isolated fact but as a special instance of a general relation which connects slavery with his whole philosophic system: e.g., *Eud. Eth.* 1249B6 ff., *Nic Eth.* 1161A32 ff.

The analogy of the master-slave to the soul-body relation enables us to connect it with the most general pattern of Aristotelian metaphysics, the relation of form to matter. Soul is the form of the body, and body the matter of the soul (*de An.* 412A16). And since ἐν τῇ ὕλῃ τὸ ἀναγκαῖον, τὸ δ' οὗ ἕνεκα ἐν τῷ λόγῳ (*Phys.* 200A14), the Aristotelian contrast of mechanism to teleology is, as in Plato, analogous to the contrast of slave to master.

course, the A B C of exegesis to distinguish between what a writer has actually said and what he could have said or ought to have said. That the Platonic dialogues give us no equivalent to the first book of the *Politics* points to a difference of temper between Plato's and Aristotle's views which must not be minimized. Nevertheless when we have made full allowance for this difference, we must still observe a fact which has escaped the notice of many modern interpreters and might modify their conclusions about Plato's moral and social philosophy: that in every one of these three points Plato would have to agree with his pupil's argument in defence of slavery:

(1) that slavery is good for the slave (as well as for the master): better to be ruled by an alien reason, than not to be ruled by reason at all (Section I of this paper);

(2) that this difference in intellectual and social status rests on a diversity of native endowment: nature is the original factor [302] in differentiating the philosopher from the producer and *a fortiori* from the slave;[58]

(3) that this difference only repeats on the human plane a pattern writ large over the cosmos: the master's benevolent reason persuading the slave's irrational force fulfils a function analogous to that of the Demiurge, persuading towards the Good the irrational *ananke* of the material universe (Section II of this paper).

IV. CONCLUSION

This study does not suggest that Plato deduced his political theory, his psychology, or his cosmology from his concept of slavery. No such deduction is to be found in his writings, and it is profitless to speculate about the unpublished adventures of his mind. What it does suggest is that his views about slavery, state, man, and the world all illustrate a single hierarchic pattern, and that the key to the pattern is in his idea of *logos* with all the implications of a dualist epistemology.[59] The slave lacks *logos*; so does the multitude in the state, the body in man, and material necessity

[58] See the use of φύσις, φύω, etc. in *R.* 370AB, 374E-376C, 428E9, 431C7, 590C3; *Plt.* 301E, 309AB, 310A; *Laws* 875C.

[59] I refer to the separation (χωρισμός) of the Forms from the particulars. Attempts to explain this away have been made by Natorp, C. Ritter, and many others. They are not convincing. See F. M. Cornford, *Plato's Theory of Knowledge*, 2 ff., and *Plato and Parmenides*, 74 ff.

in the universe. Let to itself each of these would be disorderly and vicious in the sense of that untranslatably Greek word, *hybris*. Order is imposed upon them by a benevolent superior: master, guardian, mind, demiurge. Each of these rules (ἄρχειν) in his own domain. The common title to authority is the possession of *logos*. In such an intellectual scheme slavery is "natural": in perfect harmony with one's notions about the nature of the world and of man.

There is another world-view that is the antithesis of Platonic idealism, and would be persecuted in the Platonic utopia as false, wicked, impious, subversive.[60] It is associated with Ionian physics[61] and the contract theory of the state. It is scientific in [303] temper, empirical in its theory of knowledge, democratic in its political sympathies. Plato and others of his class complained that democracy was much too lenient with slaves.[62] They never went so far as to charge what seems so evident to us today: that a consistent democratic philosophy would repudiate slavery altogether. [304]

POSTSCRIPT (1959)*

In the twenty years which have passed since I wrote this paper I have learned and unlearned things which would lead me to express myself differently on some topics. I do not mean that there are statements in this paper which I now think false. I mean only that some of them carry different shadings of emphasis than would seem to me proper now, and a few may leave a wrong impression on the reader's mind. For example, I speak of Protagoras (p. 152) as a "democratically minded theorist." This is vague enough to fall safely short of saying what I would now believe to be definitely false: that the philosophy of Protagoras provided either necessary or sufficient conditions for holding that democracy is the best form of government possible for Greeks at this time. I could not even now say that Protagoras himself thought that his philosophy provided such condi-

---

[60] *Laws* 891B; 907D ff. *Cf.* Grote's *Plato* III, 406 ff. in the 1865 edition. See also B. Farrington's *Science and Politics in the Ancient World*, London, 1939. I owe much to this stimulating essay.

[61] Is "Ionian" unnecessarily restrictive? "All the men who have ever yet handled physical investigation" constitute the fountain-head of impious unreason (*Laws* 891C) denounced by the Athenian stranger.

[62] R. 563B; "The Old Oligarch," *Ath. Pol.* 1. 10 ff.; Aristotle, *Pol.* 1313B35, 1319B28.

* This was added when the above essay was reprinted in M. I. Finley, editor, *Slavery in Classical Antiquity* (Cambridge, England, 1960).

tions. That he was held in high repute by responsible democrats, like Pericles, is certainly "significant," as I say in note 13. It may be taken as evidence of personal sympathy for democracy, but scarcely even of personal commitment to it. Any reader interested in my present assessment of the philosophy of Protagoras (though without explicit discussion of its political implications) may consult my Introduction to Plato's *Protagoras*, Liberal Arts Press, New York, 1956.

I am also uneasy about my remarks on "immanent necessity" in Heraclitus at page 157 and note 41. It is true that the fire which "governs" the world is immanent in the world, since it is a part of the world; and that the orderliness of fire is immanent in fire, since it is the product of its own "wisdom". But then the orderliness of water and earth (the other two main constituents of the Heraclitean world) is somehow imparted *to* them by fire, hence is not purely immanent in *them*; I say "somehow," for the way in which this is supposed to happen is not clear.

As for the "slave metaphor" in Plato, I do believe that it illuminates important aspects of Plato's thought which do not otherwise make sense or as good sense. But I would gladly confess that there are many, and equally important, aspects of Plato's thought which this metaphor does not illuminate. I would not wish to suggest that slavery is *the* key to Plato's philosophy. There are many locks in this marvelously complex and delicate mechanism, and I know of no one key, or set of keys, that opens all of them. Of the statements I make on this topic, the one which stands in greatest need of correction is the following, on page 156: "The notion of 'persuading necessity' and the implied idea of 'compelling necessity' make sense only if one keeps steadily in mind the slave metaphor." If this suggests, as in its context it well may, that the Demiurge *could* have "compelled" necessity had he so chosen, the suggestion would be groundless, indeed inconsistent with Plato's conception of the Demiurge. I should also disclaim the suggestion that "persuading necessity" makes sense *only* in terms of the slave metaphor.

8

ΙΣΟΝΟΜΙΑ ΠΟΛΙΤΙΚΗ*

(1964; IP)

THAT *isonomia* was so closely associated with democracy that it even served as a name for that constitution before *demokratia* came into use is scarcely a recent thesis.[1] But it was brought to the attention of scholars with renewed force shortly after the War by three able essays, published within four years of one another: "Demokratia," by A. Debrunner (1947)[2]; "Cleisthenes and the Development of the Theory of Democracy at Athens," by J. A. O. Larsen (1948)[3]; "Origins of Democracy," by V. Ehrenberg (1950).[4] But even before the third of them appeared, emphatic dissent from this thesis was voiced by a distinguished historian, the late A. W. Gomme. In a brief review of the *Festschrift* in which Larsen's paper had been published, he wrote in his characteristically lucid and forthright manner: "*Isonomia*, I still think, means a constitutional regime, whether oligarchic or democratic,

---

* Originally published in *Isonomia: Studien zur Glecheitsvorstellung im griechischen Denken*, edited by J. Mau and E. G. Schmidt (Berlin, 1964), pp. 1–35. Original page numbers appear in square brackets in this text.

[1] To go back no further than Wilamowitz (*Aristoteles und Athen II*, Berlin, 1893, p. 319): he thinks *isonomous* in the Harmodius skolion, "wofür schon Aristophanes *demokratia* gesagt haben würde," shows that the skolion can be "schwerlich viel jünger" than the tyrannicide.

[2] In *Festschrift für Tièche* (Berne, 1947), pp. 11 ff.

[3] In *Essays in Political Theory presented to G. H. Sabine* (Ithaca, 1948). (I shall refer to this essay by Larsen hereafter by the abbreviation "CD.")

[4] In *Historia* 1 (1950), pp. 515 ff. (I shall refer to this hereafter by "OD.")

the rule of order, the contrary of the irresponsible tyranny; a term that might have been used by both parties that were opposed to Hippias."[5] Gomme gave no evidence at the time to support this pronouncement; he was reserving it doubtless for the second volume of his *Historical Commentary on Thucydides.*[6] So I took no account of his opinion in a paper on "Isonomia" I published in 1953.[7] I did allude in it to the logically related view that *isonomia* meant no more than "equality before the law." This had enjoyed considerable currency at one time. But I had thought that strong, indeed conclusive, reasons against it had been [1] already given, notably by Ehrenberg in his RE article on "*Isonomia.*"[8] Referring to Ehrenberg then for this point, I felt free to devote my paper to other matters.

Rereading it now, nearly ten years later, I feel that one of the major items of unfinished business left over from it is the issue raised by Gomme's dissent. For this concerns not a detail but the fundamentals of our conception of the role of *isonomia* in the political thought of the classical period. If it means what Gomme thought it did, much of what has been written on the subject by others as well as myself is false or at least misleading. How widely his view is now shared I have no way of knowing. Nor would this be of any great consequence. In such a case numbers count for nothing. What does matter is that such a view could have been held, with such depth of conviction, by a scholar who, in addition to his great learning, had a critical intelligence of the first order. From this I can only infer that full justice has yet to be done to the other side of the controversy—that either the thesis has not been stated with the greatest attainable precision or the full weight of the evidence it commands has not yet been added to the balance. I have no confidence that I can make up for all this here. But I can at least try to bring out some things which do not seem to have been said, or said as fully as they should be. Moreover I am only too glad to have this opportunity to remedy one of the main deficiencies of "Isonomia": its treatment of the apparent counter-examples, *oligarchia isonomos* in Thucydides (3.62.3), Isocrates' application of it to Sparta (*Panath.* 178) and Plato's to

---

[5] *Class. Rev.*, 63 (1949), p. 125.

[6] Oxford 1956, pp. 109–10, 347, 379–80, 542. I shall refer to it hereafter by "*Comm. II.*" Lest my controversial differences with it give anyone a false idea of my esteem for this work and for its author, let me say once for all that I consider this one of the finest achievements of English-speaking classical scholarship in our century.

[7] *Amer. Jrnl. Philol.* 74 (1953), pp. 337–66. I shall refer to this paper hereafter by title only.

[8] Pauly-Wissowa, *Realencycl.*, Suppl. VII, cols. 293 ff., at cols. 295 ff.

the aristocratic Athens of the *Menexenus* (239A). The second and, still more, the third of these I handled in a brusque, short-winded, almost short-tempered, way, for which I now beg leave to make amends. This I shall do in Part Two: its longest section (III) I shall devote to the passage in the *Menexenus*, which presents fascinating problems all of its own. In Part One I shall deal with Herodotus and, much more briefly, with the earlier texts. [2]

PART ONE

In the Debate in Herodotus (3.80.2-82.5) the constitution "which has⁹ the fairest of all names, *isonomia*," is identified with democracy in the most positive and unmistakable way. It is that which exists where "the management of public affairs is made common"¹⁰ and "the power is given to the masses,"¹¹ where "the masses rule,"¹² and do so through the characteristic devices of the democratic *polis*: magistrates are appointed by lot¹³ and their official acts are subject to the *euthyna*¹⁴; proposals on matters of public policy are referred for decision to the assembly.¹⁵ From the omission of *demokratia* throughout the whole of the Debate we may infer that the word had not yet come into use¹⁶ when this text was written by Herodotus or

⁹ Note that the speaker is not suggesting that *he* is undertaking to give it this name, but that this is the name it already has.

¹⁰ ἐς μέσον . . . καταθεῖναι τὰ πρήγματα 3.80.2. (Here, and occasionally hereafter, I allow myself a rather free translation of the Greek, in order to make my text read more smoothly.)

¹¹ ἐς τὸ πλῆθος . . . φέρειν τὸ κράτος, 3.81.1.

¹² πλῆθος ἄρχον 3.80.6; δήμου . . . ἄρχοντος, 82.4.

¹³ πάλῳ μὲν ἀρχὰς ἄρχει, 3.80.6. One of the hallmarks of democracy: Plato, *R.* 557A, *Plt.* 289D; and cf. the reference to *Laws* 759B, at n. 73, below.

¹⁴ ὑπεύθυνον δὲ ἀρχὴν ἄρχει, 3.80.6. Cf. ἀνευθύνω, of the tyrant, 80.3.

¹⁵ βουλεύματα δὲ πάντα ἐς τὸ κοινὸν ἀναφέρει, 3.80.6. The one major democratic institution to which Otanes makes no explicit reference is the participation of the *demos* in the administration of justice. This is doubtless implied. Cf., e.g., Arist., *Pol.* 1298A 4 ff.: the sovereign power deliberates (βουλευόμενον) about judicial matters (περί θανάτου και φυγῆς καί δημεύσεως) no less than about war, alliances, etc., and the audit of magistrates.

¹⁶ Cf. CD, p. 6. The same conclusion is reached on independent (purely linguistic) grounds by A. Debrunner, *op. cit.* The earliest epigraphical occurrence of the word would be in the Athenian decree concerning Colophon (ca. 460 B. C.) IG I² 15, line 37: καὶ δεμο[κρατίαν οὐ καταλύσω], if the restoration is sound; it is retained in B. D. Meritt, H. T. Wade-Gery, and F. McGregor, *The Athenian Tribute Lists* (Princeton, 1939-53), Vol. 2, p. 69, and is apparently endorsed by M. Ostwald, "Athenian Legislation Against Tyranny," *TAPhA* 86 (1955), pp. 103 ff., at p. 113, n. 51.

his source.[17] For the Debate goes on for several paragraphs, offering repeated opportunities for the use of abstract names for each of the three constitutions under discussion. The writter makes ample use of such names for the other two: he uses *mounarchie* four times, *tyrannis* once, *oligarchie* five times. If he had *demokratia* he would surely have [3] used it at least once, instead of resorting to obvious makeshifts such as the descriptive phrase, δήμου ἄρχοντος,[18] or else the concrete δῆμος, forcing it to do double duty and stand for both the ruling power in a democracy and the constitutional form of its rule.[19] Why then did he not employ *isonomia* for

[17] I mention the possibility that Herodotus was drawing on an earlier source, (which, if true, would strengthen my argument for the early currency of *isonomia* as a name for democracy) but put no weight on it, for lack of evidence. For a survey of the literature and a judicious conclusion see K. Wüst, *Politisches Denken bei Herodot* (Diss., Munich, 1935), pp. 47 ff. Sophistic influence on Herodotus is generally admitted (especially during his residence in Athens before he joined her Panhellenic colony at Thurioi: in this connection it is extremely likely that he knew Protagoras, who took a part in drafting the legislation for the colony [Heracleides Pont. *ap.* Diogenes Laertius 9.50]). There is good reason to think that at 3.108 Herodotus is echoing a Protagorean source (cf. my "On the Pre-History in Diodorus," *AJP* 67 [1946], pp. 51 ff., at pp. 56–57). We may suspect that he is doing the same thing in this Debate, but lack the materials to prove this. Hence we had best speak of it as a conjecture (so Larsen, CD, p. 4.). T. B. L. Webster, *Political Interpretations in Greek Literature* (Manchester, 1948), p. 49, cites the Debate as a "genuine memory of Protagoras" on the ground that it represents monarchy as another form of government "beside tyranny, democracy, and oligarchy." If monarchy were so represented, the indebtedness to Protagoras would still be conjectural: we have no evidence that he invented or even expounded this idea. In any case, as Wüst points out (*op. cit.*, pp. 57 and 59), it is the *same* form of government, one-man rule, which is attacked by Otanes and Megabyzus, and defended by Darius. This is clear from the nomenclature: Otanes uses μούναρχον (80.2) and τύραννον (80.4) interchangeably, and uses the horrors of tyranny to discredit μουναρχίη at 80.3.

[18] 82.4 These genitives here do the same job which was done by ἐν ὀλιγαρχίῃ in the period which starts at 82.3.

[19] Thus in δήμῳ . . . χράσθων at 3.81.3 (where the use of δῆμος in the purely concrete sense would have required the speaker to supply something like ἄρχοντι), and in δήμου τε ἀρίστου καὶ ὀλιγαρχίης καὶ μουνάρχου at 82.1 (where all three terms stand for the constitutions, not merely for those who rule in them). Larsen (CD, p. 6, n. 6; and "The Judgment of Antiquity on Democracy," *CP* 49 [1954], pp. 1 ff., at p. 14, n. 2) has invalidated much supposed evidence for the view that δῆμος could be used to mean "democracy." I now agree with him that in δῆμον καταλύειν (or καταπαύειν) δῆμος need not refer to democracy as a form of government in sharp distinction from the people who rule under this form. He might have cited the repeated disjunc-

this purpose if, as we have just seen, it names democracy unambiguously? —Because it would not have suited the other two speakers in the Debate.[20] We can tell from their diction how sensitive to the evaluative overtones of names for constitutions are these Greek sophists who masquerade as Persian nobles. The advocate of one-man rule, Darius, speaks consistently of "monarchy" and "monarch"; "tyranny" and "tyrant" are used only by his opponents.[21] Megabyzus, defending oligarchy, avoids the word; for "Let us set up an oligarchy" he says, "Let us select the best men and give them the power."[22] So it [4] is perfectly understandable that the two detractors of popular government should have screened out *isonomia* from their speeches. If the word had half the glamor Otanes claimed for it, they would have served his cause, not theirs, by employing it.

Herodotus makes three more uses of our word in the course of the *History*. Two of them occur in his account of the Ionian revolt: Maeandrius offers to abandon the tyranny and proclaim *isonomia* to the Samians (3.142.3); Aristagoras abolishes tyranny to establish *isonomia* in Miletus and other Ionian cities (5.37.2). Here the word is used in strongest opposi-

---

tions in the recently published inscription of the decree of Eucrates (*Hesperia* 21 [1952], pp. 355–59: τὸν δῆμον τῶν ᾿Αθηναίων ἢ τὴν δημοκρατίαν τὴν ᾿Αθήνησιν καταλύσηι, lines 8–10; much the same at lines 12–14), where it is certain that δῆμον καταλύειν does not mean the same thing as δημοκρατίαν καταλύειν, else the juxtaposition of the two expressions would be a pure redundancy. On the other hand, it would be well to recognize (I) that δῆμος was used at times in the fourth century to mean purely and strictly the democratic constitution: e.g., τῶν πολιτειῶν [εἴδη] δύο, δῆμος καὶ ὀλιγαρχία, *Pol.* 1290A16; other examples in Bonitz, *Index Aristotelicus*, 176b 15 ff.; and (II) that in the earlier legal documents which speak only of κατάλυσις τοῦ δήμου (so ἐπὶ καταλύσει τοῦ δήμου in the Bouleutic Oath, *ap.* Demosth. 24. 144, which I take to be part of the original oath mentioned in Arist., *Ath. Pol.* 22.2), almost certainly because their writers did not have δημοκρατία in their vocabulary (note the three uses of this in the decree of Demophantus, *ap.* Andoc. 1.96), *demos* was used as a kind of hybrid, standing for both the ruling people and the form of their rule, and hence to that extent made to do the job which the abstract *demokratia* did more efficiently and unambiguously later on.

[20] They being the only ones who would have had the occasion to use it as their speeches have been composed: the makeshifts to which I have just referred all occur in the second and third speeches.

[21] And cf. n. 17 *sub fin.*, above.

[22] 3.81.3. He does not use ἀριστοκρατία, which would have suited him admirably (cf. J. de Romilly, "Le Classement des Constitutions jusqu'à Aristote," *REG* 72 [1959], pp. 81 ff., at p. 85), because he does not have it: the word is later than Herodotus, and is even absent from ps.-Xen., *Ath. Pol.*, where we would certainly expect it.

tion to tyranny, as also in the Harmodius *skolion* and in the fragment of Alcmaeon.[23] Does this entail support for Gomme's thesis? Why should it? Suppose we were to find that a term, X, of unknown or disputed significance, were used recurrently in strong contrast to a second, Y. Would this justify us in excluding *a priori* the possibility that in other contexts (or perhaps even in the same context) X might also be used with an implied contrast to a third, Z? Clearly not. To exclude this possibility we would need positive evidence that X covers the whole of the domain of significance opposed to that of Y, instead of covering only a part of it, albeit a most conspicuous part. In the present case, if we put tyranny on one side of a line, we would have to put democracy and oligarchy on the other,[24] dividing the field between them according to the classificatory scheme of the Debate—the standard one in popular Greek thought.[25] Then the mere fact that *isonomia* occurs in many passages in opposition to tyranny would *not* allow us to infer that it is being used in such a way as to apply disjunctively to both alteratives to tyranny, provided only they exhibit the rule of law. It might still be the case, consistently with the same data, that it is so used that its normal application would be only to the democratic alternative. Both of these possibilities would remain open in point of logic, and [5] only an inquiry into the particular uses of the word in their own context could decide between them. Let us examine the uses of *isonomia* in Herodotus for just this purpose:

[23] Notes 44 and 45, below.

[24] There is an unfortunate tendency in the literature to polarize the conflict in the Debate and in contemporary politics, making tyranny and democracy stand out as the only "real" contestants. Larsen writes that at this time "one-man rule was the chief issue in politics and political debates" (CD, p. 6) with references to Alcaeus and Solon, strangely ignoring the struggle between *gnorimoi* and *demos* before the Solonian reforms and the three-cornered conflict just after (Arist., *Ath. Pol.* 5 and 12; 13). Speaking of the Debate, Ehrenberg says, "The real conflict is, in fact, between monarchy . . . and democracy" (OD, p. 525). The same view in H. Ryffel, *Metabole Politeion*, Noctes Romanae 2 (1949), pp. 64–65. The pro-oligarchic speech is the shortest; but this is due to the fact that it begins by endorsing what Otanes had already said against monarchy (λελέχθω κἀμοὶ ταῦτα, 81.1); otherwise it would have been twice as long. Darius gives only a little less space to oligarchy than to democracy (6 and 7½ lines respectively). The strongest point for this view is that all of Otanes' speech is given over to the attack on monarchy; but this is explicable to some degree by the fact that, as first speaker, he is in the position of challenging the *status quo*, which is monarchy (cf. Darius' concluding exhortation: πατρίους νόμους μὴ λύειν, 82.5).

[25] Cf. de Romilly, *op. cit.* pp., 81–38.

The very first, the one within the Debate, is glaringly incompatible with Gomme's view, and would be decisive all by itself for the usage of Herodotus, unless its *prima facie* import were nullified or weakened by countervailing factors; but what these would be, I cannot imagine. If the word did denote either of the constitutional alternatives to tyranny, only the grossest ineptitude could have led Otanes to speak of it as the *name* of popular government; and had he made this gaffe, Megabyzus would have taken him to task for it, since he too is strongly opposed to the lawlessness ("hybris")[26] of tyranny. And that Herodotus feels nothing amiss in Otanes' use of *isonomia* is evident from the fact that he makes the same use of it himself immediately upon the close of the Debate: he calls by this name the constitution favored by Otanes (3.83.1), while later in the History (6.43.3) he calls the very same thing "democracy."[27] Hence, since Herodotus is no linguistic weather-cock, but a writer of sober and stable habits, we can approach his other two uses (at 3.142.3 and 5.37.2) with the presumption that here too the word will be used in much the same way —a presumption which only clear and positive evidence could discredit. But there is no evidence of that sort. What independent evidence exists favors it. In the first of the two passages we see *to whom* Maeandrius proclaims *isonomia*: not to *geomoroi*, hoplites, or some other select body, but to "an assembly of all the citizens.[28] We see moreover that the operative formula of the proclamation, ἰσονομίην ἡμῖν προσαγορεύω is descriptively preceded and paralleled in sense by the phrase, ἐς μέσον τὴν ἀρχὴν τιθείς—practically the same as that used at the start of the Debate to convey the substance of Otanes' proposal: ἐκέλευε ἐς μέσον . . . καταθεῖναι τὰ πρήγματα (80.2). As for the second passage, we can read it in the light of 4.137.2, where Histiaeus tells his fellow-tyrants of the Hellespont and Ionia that "each of their respective cities would prefer democratic to tyrannical government."[29] The important word here is "cities"; what Herodotus is talking about is what "each city," as distinct from some particular faction in it, would "prefer." There would certainly be oligarchic coteries in

---

[26] The connotation of this expression had been already established in the preceding speech (*hybris* at 80.2,3,4, described as lawless *phthonos* at 4, as flouting of the νόμαια πάτρια and of the constitutionally guaranteed rights of persons at 5).

[27] ὡς χρέον εἴη δημοκρατέεσθαι Πέρσας· τοὺς γὰρ τυράννους τῶν Ἰώνων καταπαύσας πάντας ὁ Μαρδόνιος δημοκρατίας κατίστα ἐς τὰς πόλιας.

[28] ἐκκλησίην συναγείρας πάντων τῶν ἀστῶν.

[29] βουλήσεσθαι γὰρ ἑκάστην τῶν πόλιων δημοκρατέεσθαι μᾶλλον ἢ τυραννεύεσθαι.

each of these cities, having varying degrees of local influence. But in Herodotus', perhaps oversimplified, view of the situation, the tide of popular sentiment is running so strongly democratic in Ionia at this time, that democracy can safely be said to be what "each city" would prefer. And this is what Mardonius is said to give them in order to win their good will for his impending [6] campaign against European Greece: τοὺς γὰρ τυράννους τῶν Ἰώνων καταπαύσας πάντας . . . δημοκρατίας κατίστα (6.43.3). Hence when Herodotus says at 5.37.2 that Aristagoras set up *isonomia* in Miletus and in other cities for the purpose of enlisting popular support for the revolt against Persia,[30] we have every reason to think that he is using the word once again with the same unique reference to democracy we have established for 3.81, 3.83, and 3.142 by distinct and independent arguments.

This result, so decisive against Gomme's view for Herodotus' use of our word, could easily be overstated in the opposite direction. With the same material before him, Ehrenberg remarked that "Herodotus used the two expressions, *demokratia* and *isonomia*, indiscriminately."[31] But a moment's reflection will show that, while true for some contexts, this would not be true for all: in οὔνομα πάντων κάλλιστον ἔχει *demokratia* obviously could not be substituted for *isonomia*.[32] Larsen, surveying the same evidence, was led to say that Herodotus "practically uses the two terms as synonyms."[33] But neither would this be quite right. Two words are not synonymous (not even "practically" so) unless not only their denotations but their connotations are the same.[34] And here everyone would agree that the connotations are distinctly different. We can agree on this regardless of residual differences as to the full and precise meaning of *isonomia*.[35] For it is clear from

[30] ὡς ἂν ἑκόντες αὐτῷ οἱ Μιλήσιοι συναπισταίατο.

[31] OD, p. 530 (cf. p. 526). This is a hasty expression, of no importance to Ehrenberg's argument. I cite it merely to illustrate the unintentional overstatement I am anxious to guard against.

[32] No one would claim that δημοκρατία is a particularly *beautiful* name.

[33] CD, p. 7. Cf. Ehrenberg, OD, p. 526: "Whatever the origin and intrinsic meaning" of *isonomia*, for "Herodotus it is simply a synonym of δημοκρατία."

[34] I am going by the usual definition of synonymy in terms of sameness of connotation or sense (*Sinn*). Sameness of denotation or reference (*Bedeutung*) for two terms would be established if one of them can be truly asserted of all, and only, those things of which the other is truly asserted. Terms satisfying this condition may still differ in sense: e.g., "Corporeal" and "Sensible."

[35] I say this not to voice a doubt of the results I present in Sections II and III of "Isonomia," but in order to make the present paper so far as possible independent of those results, thus increasing the aggregate force of the two arguments for the association of *isonomia* with democracy.

the first word in its composition that whatever the compound might mean this would involve some application or specification of the notion of equality. And this is amply sufficient to mark off etymologically the meaning of *isonomia* from that of *demokratia*, which does not mention equality,[36] as *isonomia* does not mention the people's [7] rule. And there is another difference between the two words which affects profoundly their connotations. *Demokratia* is a utility word. It would be hard to imagine a simpler, more exact, and more serviceable label for the Greek form of popular government.[37] *Isonomia* belongs to a totally different sort of linguistic genre. It

[36] The form of government named by *demokratia* has, of course, a strong commitment to the principle of equality (cf. notes 109 and 110 below). But there is all the difference in the world between what is mentioned by a linguistic term and what is implied by the concept named by the term. When critics of democracy impugn its profession to be an equal government they do not assail the word. Thus pseudo-Xenophon, complaining that in democracy ὁ δῆμος πλέον ἔχει τῶν γενναίων, etc., *Ath. Pol.* 1.1, does not suggest for a moment that *demokratia* is a misnomer. Aristotle, holding more moderately that democracy need not be "equal" government, does not say that when οὐ καθιστᾶσι κοινὴν πολιτείαν οὐδ᾽ ἴσην, *Pol.* 1296A30, the democrats belie the name of their constitution, but its "law," i.e. the constitutional principle of the "first" (and best) kind of democracy, ἡ λεγομένη μάλιστα κατὰ τὸ ἴσον: ἴσον γὰρ φησιν ὁ νόμος ὁ τῆς τοιαύτης δημοκρατίας that neither rich nor poor should be the masters, but ὁμοίους ἀμφοτέρους, 1291B30-34.

[37] The ambiguity in δῆμος (*plebs* or *populus*) is all to the good. Opponents of democracy can take it in the first sense (cf. ps-Xen. in the preceding note), while thoughtful democrats can invoke the second: so Athenagoras in Thuc. 6.39.1, ἐγὼ δέ φημι . . . δῆμον ξύμπαν ὠνομάσθαι. This ambiguity might even have been a reason for the shift to the concrete demos from the abstract quantifiers in the progression, μοναρχία, ὀλιγαρχία, δημοκρατία: *demos* would cover both of the theoretical possibilities, "many" and "all," left over from "one" and "a few" in the first two terms of the series; both possibilities apply in democratic government, since *all* share in basic rights and the *majority* ("many") decide.—The assumption that *demos* can have only the first sense has been read into the analysis of Thuc. 2.37.1 most recently by I. Th. Kakridis, in his notable monograph, *Der Thukydideische Epitaphios*, Zetemata 26 (Munich, 1961), p. 25 (hereafter I shall refer to this by "Kakridis"). He thinks that in μέτεστι πᾶσι τὸ ἴσον democracy "outstrips" its name, which would have committed it rather to τὸ ἴσον for the πλείονες only. He cites δῆμον ξύμπαν from Thuc. above only to dismiss it as idiosyncratic (because of ἐγὼ φημί), failing to consider (I) the long-standing use of *demos* with just this sense (cf. Callinus, frag. 1, δήμῳ at v. 16 = λαῷ σύμπαντι at v. 18; Plato, *Plt.* 298C, συλλέξαι δ᾽ ἐκκλησίαν ἡμῶν αὐτῶν, ἢ σύμπαντα τον δῆμον ἢ τοὺς πλουσίους μόνον, and (II) that the normal sense of *demos* in constitutional contexts is precisely τὸ ξύμπαν: in ἔδοξε τῷ δήμῳ, *demos* can only mean *populus*, all of it, not just the majority which passes a decree, concludes a treaty, etc., since the action of this majority is an act of

is more of a banner than a label. We saw how grandly it plays this role in the Debate, and can see it again in Thucydides, where πλήθους ἰσονομία πολιτική is the democrats' ὄνομα εὐπρεπές[38] doing for them the job [8] which that fulsomely moralistic expression, ἀριστοκρατία σώφρων, does for the oligarchs. From Plato's satirical attentions to it in the *Republic*,[39] we can infer that it is still flying high on the democratic masthead in the second decade of the fourth century. And it is still respectable, if a bit faded, in the later works of Isocrates around the middle of the century.[40]

the *polis*: the state decrees, makes an alliance, goes to war, etc. Even πλῆθος, when used in lieu of δῆμος in legal contexts, has precisely the same all-inclusive sense: so, e.g., in I. G. I² 10 (Tod, *GHI* I, 29), Athenian decree relative to Erythrae: οὐκ [ἀποσ]τήσομαι 'Αθηναίων τοῦ π[λ]ήθους = "against the Athenian people," line 22. And cf. Gomme's rebuttal, *CQ* 41 (1948), p. 10, and *Comm.* II, p. 109. Kakridis' remark of "*demokratia . . .* ihr Name beweist, daß die Gleichheit aller Bürger nicht zu ihrem Programm gehört," *l. c.*, should be revised to "ihr Name beweist nicht, daß die Gleichheit aller Bürger zu ihrem Programm gehört."

[38] 3.82.8. I take πλήθους here to be equivalent to δῆμος (cf. preceding note, *sub fin.*), and πολιτική to be used in contrast to arbitrary and lawless government: cf. its use in contrast to δυναστευτικῆ (here, ὀλιγαρχίᾳ) in Arist., *Pol.* 1298A33-39; it is already charged with the sense carried increasingly by πολιτεία, so that Aristotle finally comes to use πολιτεία as a name for his "polity" (implying that a similar use of the word for moderate, law-regulated constitutions has fairly wide currency: Bonitz, *Index Aristotelicus* 613A57 ff. for references) and Attic rhetoricians feel empowered to use it for "rule of law": so, e.g., Isocr. 4.125 and Ep. 7.11; Demosth. 1.5 and 15.20 (in contrast to "monarchies" in the first two, "tyranny" in the third, "oligarchy" in the fourth). Note the redundancy we would get in ἰσονομία πολιτική on Gomme's view of the sense of the former. Gomme does not seem to notice this in commenting on Thuc. 3.82.8, perhaps because he glosses πολιτική (very loosely, it seems to me) by "such as befits free citizens," *Comm.* II, p. 379.

[39] ἰσονομικοῦ at 561C will be discussed in Part Two (III) below. ἰσονομία καὶ ἐλευθερία in the relations of men to women, 563B, occurs in that panorama of equality and liberty gone wild which is designed to convince us that democracy has produced its own moral *reductio ad absurdum*. Either use would be hopelessly pedantic if *isonomia* did not have a high place in the current democratic credo. Note how impossible it would be to square these uses with the notion that *isonomia* stands for the rule of law as such. And cf. n. 67, below.

[40] *Areop.* 20 (dated 355 B. C. by J. F. Dobson in the *Oxford Classical Dictionary*, 1949), ὥσθ' ἡγεῖσθαι τὴν μὲν ἀκολασίαν δημοκρατίαν, τὴν δὲ παρανομίαν ἐλευθερίαν, τὴν δὲ παρρησίαν ἰσονομίαν . . . For παρρησία in the derogatory sense, as a characteristic of democracy, see, e.g., Plato, *R.* 557B, καὶ ἐλευθερίας ἡ πόλις μεστὴ καὶ παρρησίας, and Adam's references *ad loc.*, and those of Dodds on *Grg.* 461E2. The other use of ἰσονομία is *Panath.* 178 (dated by Dobson 342-49); to be discussed in Part Two, Section II, below.

In all these uses it is clear that the word designates in the first instance not a specific constitution but a standard by which constitutions can be evaluated.[41] If it should then serve as a name for democracy, this would be a purely derivative use, made possible by the feeling that this constitution measures up so uniquely to the norm expressed by *isonomia* that it can be singled out from all others (and, hence, named) by the mere mention of the norm. This is what happens in Herodotus.[42] And since we have no reason to think his usage idiosyncratic, we [9] may infer that the same thing would be happening quite generally before the specialized *demokratia* was brought into use.

What are we to say then of the view which long enjoyed Ehrenberg's influential support[43] that *isonomia* had been *also* an aristocratic idea, meaning "equality of noblemen," as contrasted with the extreme inequality of tyranny, and that this is what it meant to those who composed the two

[41] Strikingly so as οὔνομα κάλλιστον in the Debate, ὄνομα εὐπρεπές in Thuc. 3.82.8, and pretext for παρρησία in the citation from Isocrates in the previous note. Its moral connotations are most explicit in Thuc. 6.38.5, where Athenagoras explains the appeal he is making to the restless young men, ἀλλὰ δὴ μὴ μετὰ πολλῶν ἰσονομεῖσθαι [βούλεσθε]; by adding, καὶ πῶς δίκαιον τοὺς αὐτοὺς μὴ τῶν αὐτῶν ἀξιοῦσθαι; As I shall be arguing at Section III below, Plato attacks *isonomia* in the *Republic* precisely because he regards it as expressing a (perverse) moral norm.

[42] The same is true of his uses of ἰσηγορίη and ἰσοκρατίας: obviously so in the use of the former at 5.78 (ἰσηγορίη . . . χρῆμα σπουδαῖον; for a similar use of the word to denote democracy see Demosth. 15.18, τοῖς μετ' ἰσηγορίας ζῆν ᾑρημένοις); and so too, though less obviously, in the use of the latter in Socles plea to the Spartans "not to reinstate tyrannies in cities, ἰσοκρατίας καταλύοντες," 5.92.A. It would be wrong to infer here that ἰσοκρατίας denotes oligarchy in preference to (or even on a par with) democracy from the fact that the speaker is a representative of oligarchic Corinth addressing Spartans. In spite of the rhetorical plurals, the reference is to Cleisthenean Athens, which Herodotus knows as *demokratia* (6.131.1). And Socles appeals to the Spartans *qua* haters of tyranny, not *qua* lovers of *isokratia;* he reinforces his plea by reciting the evils of tyranny, not the merits of *isokratia.*

[43] "Eunomia" in *Charisteria Alois Rzach* (Reichenberg, 1930); revised and transl. into English in *Aspects of the Ancient World* (Oxford, 1946), pp. 70 ff., at pp. 89–90; cols. 293 ff. of his R. E. article (cited above, n. 8); OD, pp. 330–32. A similar view (but barely documented) in B. Keil, *Griechische Staatsaltertümer* in Gercke-Norden, *Einleitung in die Altertumswissenschaft*, III (Leipzig, 1912), pp. 336–37. The same view with explicit indebtedness to Ehrenberg: Larsen, CD, p. 13; and with indebtedness to Keil and Ehrenberg: G. Grossman, *Politische Schlagwörter aus der Zeit des Peloponnesischen Krieges* (Diss., Zurich, 1950). A similar view is implied in the citation from Gomme (sub fin.) in the opening paragraph of this paper.

earliest extant uses of our word: the Harmodius *skolion*[44] and Alcmaeon's fourth fragment?[45] I argued against this at length in "Isonomia" (pp. 339–47, 363–65), and see no good reason for continuing in the same vein here, especially as this view has now been abandoned by the only proponent who had put up a coherent argument for it in the past: Ehrenberg.[46] So I shall only mention the main points, as I see them: In the case of the *skolion*, aristocratic connotations for *isonomia* had been inferred from the consideration that its original constituency—the banqueting elite that sang these σκόλια—was, in all probability, aristocratic,[47] and would, therefore, be likely [10] to read into our word its own favorite preconceptions. But unfortunately for this argument, eupatrid birth cannot be taken as a reliable index of aristocratic outlook: witness the case of Solon, τῇ μὲν [φύ]σει . . . τῶν πρώτων (Arist., *Ath. Pol.* 5.3), but whose social orientation was that of a man of the center.[48] In the present case we could count on a fair number of sympathizers with Cleisthenes' New Deal within the numerous Alcmaeonid brood and their friends and allies. The "seven hundred accursed families"[49] expelled from Athens by Cleomenes at Isagoras'

[44] "Scolia anonyma," nos. 10 and 13 in Diehl, pp. 184 ff. (= frgg. 983 and 896 in D. L. Page, *Poetae Melici Graeci*, Oxford, 1962).

[45] Diels-Kranz, *Fragmente der Vorsokratiker*[6] (Berlin, 1951–52. Hereafter "*Vors.*[6]").

[46] "Das Harmodioslied" in *Festschrift Albin Lesky* (*Wien. St.* 69 [1956], pp. 57–69), pp. 67–68.

[47] It would be a safe assumption that the ratio of eupatrids to non-eupatrids in this constituency would be higher in the earlier period, hence highest in the period of the Cleisthenean reforms which, as Ehrenberg now agress, is the *terminus post quem* for Nos. 10 and 13 (the ones mentioning *isonomous*): "Das Harmodioslied" (cited at n. 46, above), p. 67. As to the *terminus ante quem*, the only firm one (but obviously much too late to be of much use) is the production of the *Acharnians*, 425 B. C. The next one for which at least plausibility can be claimed would be the last time at which tyranny was felt as a clear and present danger in fifth-century Athens. We know this happened in the three years, 488/7, 487/6, 486/5 (*Ath. Pol.* 22.3–6); and this can be narrowed still further to 488/7, bearing in mind (I) that the man ostracized then, Hipparchus Charmou, belonged to the genos of the tyrants, was ἡγεμὼν καὶ προστάτης of "the friends of the tyrants" (*l. c.* 4), and (II) that the *skolion* voices "a fighting mood directed against a present enemy" ("Isonomia," p. 343). Ehrenberg says this more strongly in "Das Harmodioslied," pp. 64–66, à propos of ξίφος φορήσω, and refers to Aristophanes' *Lys.* 631 ff., where the borrowings from our *skolion* show well its lines express the tyrant fighter's mood.

[48] Cf. "Solonian Justice," *Class. Philol.*, 41 (1946), pp. 65 ff., at p. 81.

[49] Hdt. 5.72.1; Arist., *Ath. Pol.* 20.2. We need not assume that all were eupatrids or that all the eupatrids among them were enthusiasts for *isonomia*.

behest could well be expected to furnish a eupatrid contingent capable of composing and enjoying *Harmodius* and any number of similar *skolia*. As for Alcmaeon, so long as he was confidently classed as a Pythagorean by the historians of philosophy, some sort of argument could be made for endowing him with aristocratic or, at least, anti-democratic convictions.[50] The argument collapsed at the base when the evidence for Alcmaeon's Pythagoreanism crumbled, as the histories of philosophy are now beginning to acknowledge.[51] All that remains then to connect *isonomia* with "equality of noblemen" are such things as the use of ὅμοιοι of the Spartan "peers,"[52] [*11*] and the way of life which made Thucydides call them ἰσοδίαιτοι[53] If these materials sufficed for the purpose they would enable us to import aristocratic *isonomia* into Sparta—which would still be a long

[50] See the remarks and references in "Isonomia," n. 32, on the difficult and highly speculative topic of Pythagorean politics. Where so much is conjectural, one of the few safe assumptions is that their politics would *not* be aristocratic in the most obvious of the relevant senses of the word: favoring rule by a hereditary, land-owning nobility.

[51] Cf. Raven, in G. S. Kirk and J. Raven, *The Presocratic Philosophers* (Cambridge, 1957), p. 232: "The statement [in Diog. Laert. 8.83] that he 'heard Pythagoras' doubtless means, as it usually does, no more than that he was in some sort of contact with the Pythagorean school."—If one goes through his fragments looking for ties with Pythagoras one will find much less than if one were doing this with the fragments of Empedocles (cf. in the latter's case, *Vors.*[6], B 129, speaking with admiration of Pythagoras' psychic powers), whose politics are tagged in the tradition as democratic (*demotikos*, Timaeus *ap*. Diog. Laert. 8.64). In Alcmaeon's case I did not sufficiently stress in "Isonomia" the implications of his strong interests in *experimental* medicine, which led him to undertake something unheard of at the time, dissections (of the eye: Chalcidius at *Vors.*[6], A 10; probably not the human eye, as K. Freeman says [*Companion to the Presocratic Philosophers*, Oxford, 1946, p. 137], but without support from the text; dissections of animals can be inferred from his view that "goats breathe through the ears," which Aristotle finds it necessary to deny at *Hist. Anim.* 492A14 [= *Vors.*[6], A7]). If Alcmaeon practiced medicine professionally (which there is no good reason to doubt), we would have even less reason for debiting him with an aristocratic outlook: given the low social standing of the ordinary doctor (on a level with the mechanic: Plato, *Grg.* 512D), it would be a very emancipated upper-class Greek who would go into medicine. If his social origins were humble, that would make the aristocratic outlook still more improbable.

[52] For the references see, e.g., G. Busolt and H. Swoboda, *Griechische Staatskunde*[3] *II* (Munich, 1926), p. 659, n. 4. It should be noted that all of these are fourth-century sources; the two from Thucydides do not employ the word in the relevant sense.

[53] 1.6.4. And see n. 80, below.

distance away from Harmodius and from Alcmaeon's fragment. But they
do not suffice. The fact that a military élite, ruling with an iron hand subject peoples all around it, should think of itself as a community of "peers,"
can hardly establish the supposition that it uses the term *isonomia* in defining its social credo. For this we would need some mention or, at least,
allusion to the word in our sources.[54] But while we hear frequently of
eunomia[55] in this connection, we never hear of *isonomia*, except in the single
Isocratean text to be discussed below; and this does not profess to reflect
the Spartans' view of their constitution, and their diction for it; it is the
language of an Athenian rhetorician who chooses, for the reasons we shall
see, to make democrats of the Spartans for the occasion. This leaves us
where we began: with two texts both of which are perfectly understandable
on the assumption that their writers would use our word in the same way
as did Herodotus,[56] and with no warrant for understanding them in any
other way.

Moving forward now, past Herodotus, through the Peloponnesian War,
and well into the next century, we are on much stronger ground. Here we
need not rely as much, if at all, on extrapolation from our findings in Herodotus. We have positive, independent evidence for asserting that our word
kept the same meaning until at least the middle of the fourth century: its
occurrences in Thucydides, Plato, and Isocrates, to which I referred a moment ago,[57] and a further occurrence in Thucydides (4.78.2-3), to be discussed shortly.[58] It would be a fair inference from just these texts that if
anyone were to say in this period such things as that he would prefer to
live under an ἰσόνομος πολιτεία or that this or that city enjoyed ἰσονομία
people would understand him to be referring to democracy, unless there

---

[54] Especially in long, drawn-out, adulatory accounts, like Xen., *Lac. Const.*,
or again in contexts where the "mixed constitution" view of Sparta is being
developed (e.g., Plato, *Laws* 691D ff., Arist., *Pol.* 1294B19 ff.).

[55] Cf. Ehrenberg, *Aspects of the Ancient World*, pp. 77 ff., 91 ff.

[56] Making allowance for the rapid advance of democracy in the direction of
greater equality during the first half of the fifth century, and remembering
that as people get more equality they come to expect more, so that what they
would *call* "equality" at the height of the advance will answer to a more
radical form of it than would have been previously the case.

[57] Notes 38–41, above. What changes during this period is not the sense,
but the frequency of its use: 4 in Thuc., only 3 in Plato (exclusive of the
Seventh Letter, on which see the Appendix); 2 in Isocrates. I know of none in
Aristotle or Demosthenes.

[58] It should then become clear, if it is not so already, why I do not count
this as a *prima facie* counter-example. However, anyone who wishes may do
so; the argument will be unaffected.

were special factors which [12] altered in that particular context the normal semantic value of the term. This qualification is not meant to weaken my thesis, but to guard it against specious exceptions. I can best explain what I mean by investigating those texts which have been, or might be, taken as *prima facie* evidence to the contrary. I believe I can show that, rightly understood, they even provide some confirmation of my thesis.

PART TWO

I. THUCYDIDES 3.62.3-4[59]

The Theban spokesmen say their city should not be reproached for the medism of its government during the Persian wars, for at that time Thebes "was governed neither κατ' ὀλιγαρχίαν ἰσόνομον nor as a democracy," but by a totally different type of government—a "dynasteia of a few men"— which (I) ruled arbitrarily, "in a way that comes closest to tyranny and is at the other extreme from [the rule of] law and decent order," and (II) gave the people no voice in its decisions: "they brought him [the Persian] in while controlling the people by force . . .; the city as a whole was not self-determining."[60]

Now the mere fact that ἰσόνομος is applied here to ὀλιγαρχία in no way contravenes my thesis. It would not, even if I had committed myself to the much stronger thesis that *isonomia* and *demokratia* were synonyms. The rules of language impose no formal prohibition against crossing, for special purposes, terms as opposed to one another as are "democracy" and "oli-

[59] I discussed this passage in "Isonomia," pp. 359–61, with a somewhat different purpose. I try to repeat here as little as possible. The construction of the passage remains the same (see next note) but I free the argument for it from dependence on reading οὔτε κατ' ὀλιγαρχίαν ἰσόνομον πολιτεύουσα οὔτε κατὰ δημοκρατίαν so as *not* to take ἰσόνομον as qualifying also δημοκρατίαν. However, I still think that is the right way to read the text: such a carry-over of an adjective from the first part of a disjunction to its second does not seem to me to be in Thucydides' style, and I know of no commentary support for it; those who endorse it (e.g., Larsen, CD, p. 10) would have done well to adduce some parallels.

[60] I paraphrase in such a way as to make it clear that (II), no less than (I), explains what it is about a "*dynasteia* of a few men" which frees its subjects of blame for its acts. This is the key to the correct understanding of the thought of the passage, and hence of the full sense of ἰσόνομον here. The mistaken construction of ἰσόνομον against which I proceed to argue can be traced to the assumption that the sense of ὀλιγαρχίαν ἰσόνομον, in contrast to *dynasteia*, can be made out by taking only (I) into account.

garchy" or, to take a modern example, "capitalism" and "socialism." If X and Y are terms originally designed to stand for mutually exclusive classes, there is nothing to keep us from describing, say, a newly discovered hybrid as an "X-like Y." [13] To be sure, we would not be likely to do so once a special word to cover just such a case had been devised: we speak of "mules," not of "equine asses." But there was no special name for the constitutional hybrid represented by the current form of government at Thebes. A hybrid it certainly was, according to classical conceptions. Aristotle, for instance, would have called it a "polity,"[61] the special blend he thinks makes the best of the practicable constitutions: an even mixture of democracy and oligarchy.[62] The Theban spokesmen accordingly could very well have characterized their constitution as a "democratic oligarchy," had they chosen to do so: oligarchy, since it denied the rights of active citizenship to half the Theban demos,[63] but a democratic one, since it came vastly closer to being a democracy than would many another oligarchy— perhaps closer than any oligarchy in existence at the time—in two fundamental respects: (a) the number admitted to a share in the government (all the active citizens) was relatively large, and huge by comparison to a *dynasteia*, where a mere handful monopolized the control of the state[64];

[61] It would have satisfied the following of his major requirements for a "polity": (a) property qualification for active citizenship, and so set that the active citizens will (just) outnumber the rest: *Pol.* 1279B6, 1320B27; for Thebes, see n. 63, below; (b) as much political equality as possible among the active citizens (e.g., 1295B27), who should share in the *archē* (e.g., 1272A22 ff., and cf. n. 109, below), these being general requirements of citizenship which would also hold for the polity; for Thebes see under (b) in the text; (c) rule of law (*passim*); for Thebes' reputation in this regard see, e.g., Plato, *Crito* 53B: Thebes and Megara εὐνομοῦνται.

[62] *Pol.* 1293B34, ἔστι γὰρ ἡ πολιτεία ὡς ἁπλῶς εἰπεῖν μίξις ὀλιγαρχίας καὶ δημοκρατίας.

[63] I now think that my estimate of the ratio of enfranchised to disfranchised citizens in *AJP* 73 (1952), p. 190, n. 7—same as that of other troops to lightarmed ones at Delion, according to the figures in Thuc. 4.93.3 (on which see now Gomme), i.e. 85: 100—is too low. I made no allowance for the fact that, as Gomme very reasonably suggests, even in a campaign within Boeotia, hoplite garrisons would have to be left in Boeotian cities suspected of disaffection. On this ground Gomme thinks the 7,000 figure in Thuc. represents only about two-thirds of the total hoplite muster; if so, the above ratio would have to be changed to something like 6:5. But Gomme's allowance for garrisoning within Boeotia may be too high. I am at a loss for evidence to argue the point, but suspect that the real figure was somewhere between the two ratios.

[64] I do not know how small would be the clique that ruled in a *dynasteia*. Aristotle calls the government of the Thirty at Athens a *dynasteia*, that of the

(b) the distribution [14] of power among the active citizens must have been strongly equalitarian, judging by the admission of each of them to one of the four rotating Boulai which formed in concert the sovereign Assembly.[65] *A fortiori* then they could call their constitution ὀλιγαρχία ἰσόνομος, if the word did mean what I have been contending. In that case they would mean that the equalitarian norm signified by *isonomia* was satisfied by their brand of oligarchy to make it qualify, like democracy, as responsible government. If so, their use would fit perfectly my thesis, and would so far confirm it.

But this is not what they could mean, according to Gomme. His gloss on κατ' ὀλιγαρχίαν ἰσόνομον is "i.e. a constitutional, law-abiding governl ment, in which all citizens have equal rights, though not equal politica- power (cf. 2.37.1 and 3.82.8 for democratic *isonomia*)." By "civil rights" he obviously does not mean anything as narrow as his first Thucydidean reference would suggest—μέτεστι δὲ κατὰ μὲν τοὺς νόμους πρὸς τὰ ἴδια διάφορα πᾶσι τὸ ἴσον—for this affirms only equality in the adjudication of claims and counter claims between private persons in matters of private law.[66] "Civil rights" is much broader: it would cover also the rights of private persons against state officials—against high-handed, insolent treatment, arbitrary arrest and imprisonment, sequestration of property without due process of law, and the like. Nevertheless, and this is the crux of the difference, it is designed to exclude from the scope of *isonomia* those rights by which equality of political power is attained or approximated, i.e., *political* rights. On this construction the meaning of our word is cut down to *equality before the law*.

---

400 an oligarchy (*Ath. Pol.* 36.1; 32.2 and 37.1). Oligarchies of "fixed number" might confine active citizenship (or else membership in the Council, making this the effective governing body) to as few as 600 or 1,000 (see the references in L. Whibley, *Greek Oligarchies* [Cambridge, 1896], pp. 134 ff). The unknown author of ps.-Herodes, *Peri Politeias*, a Thessalian whose sympathies seem to be with popular government, gives the 1:3 ratio of active citizens to the rest as the smallest in the oligarchies established by Sparta (at the end of the Peloponnesian War) and regards this a very reasonable ratio (30, 31). To the extreme oligarchs in Athens the Constitution of the 5,000 looks like "downright democracy" (Thuc. 8.92.1; cf. *AJP* 73 [1952], p. 190, n. 6, for the meaning of the figure, and below, n. 87).

[65] *Pap. Oxy.* 5, p. 173. Cf. J. A. O. Larsen, *Representative Government* (Chicago, 1955), pp. 31–34, and P. Cloché, *Thèbes de Béotie* (Namur; no date, probably 1952), pp. 71 ff.

[66] For the distinction between private and public law in Greek thought see J. W. Jones, *Law and Legal Theory of the Greeks* (Oxford, 1956), pp. 116 ff.

Now as I remarked at the very start of this paper, I had supposed that this construction of *isonomia* had been laid to rest some time ago. But since Gomme has revived it, it may not be amiss to indicate briefly why we can be certain that it is wrong.

In the first place, it will not fit other important texts. Thus the *isonomia* Plato attacks in the *Republic* (to be discussed below) could not possibly be equality before the law; had it been that, Plato would not have attacked, but praised, it.[67] What draws his ire is its prescription of the very thing the proposed sense for *isonomia* would exclude most of all: equality of access to political office. Or, to go back to the earlier evidence: in Herodotus the emphasis falls as heavily on political rights: what is at stake in the Debate [15] is not whether the masses are to enjoy equality under the law, but whether they are to rule the state. Nor could the second of the two references in Thucydides adduced by Gomme himself—πλήθους ἰσονομία πολιτική as ὄνομα εὐπρεπές of the democrats[68]—be intelligible if our word referred merely to equality under the law. For in this regard the difference between the democracies and the more respectable oligarchies, like Thebes, Megara, or Corinth, could not have been great.[69] How then could the democrats have chosen it for their distinctive slogan if it did not stand for something peculiarly their own, as much so as was the oligarchic claim to ἀριστοκρατία σώφρων?

In the second place, neither would the proposed sense fit the present passage; if ἰσόνομος had this sense it would not bring off the Thebans' argument. Their claim is that the difference between ὀλιγαρχία ἰσόνομος and δυναστεία would have made all the difference to the moral responsibility of their people for the acts of their government. But the only change in the status quo that would make people responsible for what their government does would be a change in their ability to determine what it does.

---

[67] In commenting on Thuc. 3.82.8 Gomme speaks of the claim of the oligarchs that σωφροσύνη was their special virtue, "democracies, owing to the passion for equality, tending always to lawlessness (so Plato, *R.* 8.557B–563E)." He takes no notice of the occurrence of *isonomia* and *isonomikos* in this very passage, and misses the occasion to ask himself how Plato could have possibly wished to pillory *isonomia* if it meant what Gomme thinks it did.

[68] Cf. n. 38, above.

[69] Though I am not suggesting that it would be negligible. It would be difficult for a court composed of active citizens to be completely impartial in adjudicating a suit between one of their own peers and a man of lower status. Even so, the difference between democracies and the better oligarchies at this respect would not be as glaring as in the area of political rights where deprivation of right would occur not in default of the law but because of the law.

This could not occur merely as a result of being given equality under the law. All this would give them would be greater security from injury to their persons and properties by other individuals or by officials—an enormous benefit, certainly, but doing nothing of itself to confer power to influence government policy or action; this could be achieved only by giving all, or at least some, of them greater political rights.

Ideally, if all are to be held responsible for a governmental decision, all should have a voice in it. To say this is not to propound a theorem in political philosophy, but to refer to something which must have been assumed without the slightest argument,[70] as a matter of simple common sense. Thus Pericles takes it for granted in his last speech in Thucydides when he tells his audience that they are just as responsible for the war as he: I advised it, but you concurred (ξυνέγνωτε, 2.60.4; ξυνδιέγνωτε, 64.1).[71] Had Pericles been a stickler for precision [16] he would not have said, "you shared in the decision," but "you had the right to share in it," since that is the vital point with regard to moral responsibility. If a group-decision is blameworthy, those who had the right to share in it but did not trouble themselves to exercise that right could still be blamed for it. Now since rights are meaningless unless they are protected, and their protection calls for the rule of law, the Thebans' emphasis on the latter at (I) in the above paraphrase of their argument is entirely understandable. This is indeed a necessary condition for the kind of responsibility they are talking about. But it is not a sufficient condition, and they are not implying that it is, else they would not have contended under (II) above that their people could not be blamed for something which was done when "the city as a whole was not self-determining." In putting this phrase into their plea they acknowledge that they think self-government also necessary. Democracy meets this condition most fully when it is a rule of law, since it is then self-government in its purest form: rule of the people by the people. Oligarchy, on the other hand, would not, even if it were a rule of the law but so narrowly based as to exlude all but a tiny clique from

[70] Had it become a matter of argument we would have heard of it in the philosophical literature. But corporate responsibility never becomes a theme of philosophical reflection in the classical period.

[71] So too by the Theban envoys to Athens in 395 B. C.: don't blame us for A, οὐ γὰρ ἡ πόλις ἐκείνα ἐψηφίσατο, but give us credit for not doing B, which ἅπασα ἡ πόλις ἀπεψηφίσατο, Xen. Hell. 3.5.8. I am indebted for this reference to Gomme, and also for Thuc. 8.1.1, where Thucydides proceeds on this assumption in a judgment of his own: The Athenians are furious at the orators who advised the Sicilian expedition, "as though they themselves were not the ones who voted for it."

any share in the sovereign decisions. What the speakers must do then is to designate the very special kind of oligarchy which does meet this additional condition to their own satisfaction; and how else could an oligarchy meet it except by allowing for a substantial degree of self-government, such as the Thebans might believe was achieved by their own constitution? This is what they would have to express by characterizing their own brand of oligarchy as ἰσόνομος. So even if this passage were our only clue to the meaning of the word, we would still be in a position to infer that its "equal law" pertains specially to those rights which insure access to the devices of self-government, and is thus specially bound to that form of government which is, in principle, pure self-government.

For confirmation we may turn to that other passage in which Thucydides uses *isonomia* to much the same purpose, but without the complication of grafting it adjectivally on *oligarchia*: 4.78.2-3. The Thessalian πλῆθος had been traditionally friendly to Athens. Hence if they were now enjoying *isonomia*, Brasidas would not have been allowed to pass. Here it should be obvious that Thucydides uses *isonomia* to refer to the kind of government in which the sovereign decisions are made by the πλῆθος itself; and since this happens *only* in democracy, our word here denotes democracy in a very straightforward way. Thucydides could have made exactly the same point by using *demokratia* in lieu of *isonomia*, leaving everything else unchanged in his text.[72] [17]

II. ISOCRATES, PANATHENAICUS 178

"But while they [the Spartans] established such *isonomia* and *demokratia* among themselves as men must observe if they are to be constantly like-minded,[73] they turned the *demos* into perioeci, reducing their spirits to a bondage as abject as that of household slaves." In the very act of applying

[72] It has been held (Gomme *ad loc.*, and J. S. Morrison *CQ* 36 [1942], p. 63; and cf. Larsen *CP* 55 [1960], p. 244), and with considerable plausibility, that Thucydides would not be likely to reckon the Penestae part of the πλῆθος τῶν Θεσσαλῶν. This would not affect my point in the slightest. In either case he would be applying *isonomia* (and could have applied *demokratia*) to whatever group he did identify with the πλῆθος τῶν Θεσσαλῶν.

[73] A common sentiment: Plato, *Laws* 759B, we must mix in some "democracy" (δῆμον: the key institution of democracy, appointment by lot, made to stand by synecdoche for democracy itself), "that they may be as like-minded as possible." Demosth. 20.108, "what makes the masters of the commonwealth like-minded in oligarchies [τὰς διὰ τῶν ὀλίγων πολιτείας: he is speaking of Sparta] is τὸ πάντας ἔχειν ἴσον ἀλλήλοις."

isonomia here to a notoriously non-democratic regime,[74] Isocrates assures us of its normal connection with *demokratia*. He does so by conjoining the two words—not merely juxtaposing them— in a very special way. As the second half of the citation shows, he is taking the Spartans to task, sternly, and somewhat melodramatically, for their unequal treatment of the perioeci. He calls the latter the "demos" of Lacedaemon[75] to insinuate the thought that they are not merely her subjects, but members of her body politic,[76] and are, therefore, entitled to an "equal" share of the land and of that fund of civil and political rights which makes up a constitution from the Greek point of view. They have been robbed on both counts, Isocrates charges. In regard to the land, "of which each ought to have ἴσον" (179), the Spartans, few as they were, have grabbed the most and the best. In regard to constitutional rights, they despoiled the perioeci "of everything in which freemen are entitled to share" (180), while loading on them sacrifices, such as front-line military service, which only free civic partners should be called upon to bear.[77] Such is the immediate sequel to our text (179–81). This makes clear the reason why Isocrates takes time to bring the honours of *isonomia* and *demokratia* to the Spartans: it is to give himself the chance to flash before the reader's mind the picture of an equalitarian polity, realized not far from Sparta, but at the heart of it, alive within the closed community of the very people who have pushed inequality so far in the expropriation and oppression of their own "*demos*." *Demokratia* then is connected with *isonomia* as the exemplary political application of the moral norm which [18] is expressed by the *ison* in *isonomia*; the word *ison* being used in this connection to carry the sense of "fair, just" in addition to that of "equal."[78]

---

[74] Sparta is commonly spoken of as an oligarchy: so by Demosthenes in the preceding note; by Isocrates himself at *Nic.* 24, where he is voicing the general point of view: cf. F. Ollier, *Le Mirage spartiate* (Paris, 1933), pp. 353–54. The philosophers are more given to thinking of it as a "mixed constitution": cf. de Romilly, *op. cit.*, pp. 95–97.

[75] The Spartans would resent this. On their view they alone compose the *demos* (so, e.g., in the rhetra, Plut., *Lyc.* 6).

[76] If he were making his thought explicit he might have called them φύσει πολίτας who are deprived νόμῳ of their civic rights: cf. *Paneg.* 105.

[77] Cf. Thuc. 6.39.2 (speech of Athenagoras): "But oligarchy gives the people a full share of the dangers, but of the benefits takes not only a larger share [πλεονεκτεῖ] but practically everything," Cf. Isocr., *Loch.* 20.

[78] Normal usage in the Greek, where ἴσον comes actually closer than any other single word to what is ordinarily meant by "just" or (morally) "fair" in English. This is obscured for most English readers by the canonical mistransla-

Is this reading too much into the text? Isocrates, certainly, does not *say* here that democracy is the "just and equal"[79] constitution *par* excellence. But there is another passage, where he practically does: *Areop.* 60–61. It is the only other one in his works in which he speaks again of Sparta as a democracy. Here he tells us *why*: "because both in their selection of magistrates and in their everyday life and in their other practices one can see that [the principles of] equality and uniformity [τὰς ἰσότητας καὶ τὰς ὁμοιότητας] are applied among them more strenuously than elsewhere— [principles] which are obnoxious to oligarchies, but constantly practiced by democracies" (61).[80] Just before, he had remarked that in most of his works we would find him "condemning oligarchies and injustices [πλεο- νεξίαις] praising democracies and just equalities [ἰσότητας]." Here democ- racy is to *isotes* as oligarchy is to *pleonexia*. When moral approval is poured on democracy in such bucketfuls we may suspect an ulterior motive. We

---

tion of δίκαιον/δικαιοσύνη by "just"/"justice" in contexts in which it means only "righteousness" (*Gerechtigkeit*). It *can* bear the former meaning, but only in spe- cial contexts, and much less frequently than the latter. As Aristotle explains so well early in Book V of *Nic. Eth.*, δικαιοσύνη can mean either (a) *"virtuous social conduct"* in general (ἀρετή . . . τελεία . . . πρὸς ἕτερον, 1129B26), or (b), that species of (a), ἐν μέρει ἀρετῆς δικαιοσύνην, 1130A14, which has to do with distributive and/or corrective justice. He uses ἴσον in moral contexts to *mean* (b), and ἄνισον (= πλεονεκτεῖν) to mean the contrary (1129A32 ff. *et passim*), confident that everyone would agree with him in this (1131A13, τὸ δίκαιον ἴσον, ὅπερ καὶ ἄνευ λόγου δοκεῖ πᾶσιν). For some examples of ἴσον with this sense: Soph., *Phil.* 685, ἴσος ἐν ἴσοις ἀνήρ; Eur., *Hec.* 805, οὐκ ἔστιν οὐδὲν τῶν ἐν ἀνθρώποις ἴσον; Thuc. 5.31.3, 5; 5.79.4; 6.39.1; Plato, *R.* 359C, τὴν τοῦ ἴσου τιμήν (in contrast to πλεονεξίαν); *Grg.* 483C, 484A, 508A (with same contrast).

[79] I know of no other way to put into English the double-barreled sense of τὸ ἴσον.

[80] For those in "everyday life" see Arist., *Pol.* 1294B18ff.: the common *agoge*, the *syssitia*, the uniformity of dress are cited by "many [who] undertake to assert that it is a democracy." As for the selection of magistrates, one of the features listed as democratic in Aristotle, *l. c.*, is "that of the two greatest offices, the *demos* elects to the one [the Senate] and shares in the other [the Ephorate]." Isocrates (*Panath.* 153) cites the fact that Lycurgus made "the magistracies filled by election, not by lot" as evidence that this was "a democ- racy mixed with aristocracy," distinguishing sharply "aristocracy" from "oligarchy," for he holds that any of the three recognized constitutions will be an aristocracy if the best men are appointed to its offices (132). This would be his reply to those who are cited by Arist., *l. c.*, B32, as making its elective procedure a ground for classifying Sparta as an oligarchy.

do not have far to look[81]: he does not praise "all democracies," he says, but the "good" ones, those which are "well-ordered." [19] We know what he means by this in the case of Athens: the "ancestral" democracy of Solon and Cleisthenes,[82] when magistrates were not appointed by lot, but elected,[83] and a strong Areopagus kept an eye on everything and everyone in Athens.[84] This "good" democracy of his then turns out to have much in common with the "ancestral constitution" of Theramenes[85] and of the crypto-oligarchs[86] who kept his program alive in Athens after his death. Are we to count Isocrates then a Theramenean, and discount accordingly his praise for democracy and righteous disdain for oligarchy as so much talk? I do not think so. But it is not necessary to pursue this issue here,[87]

---

[81] I pass over another: he is defending himself against the suspicion "of being an enemy of the *demos* and seeking to turn the state into an oligarchy," *Areop.* 57.

[82] *Areop.* 16: Solon its legislator, Cleisthenes its restorer. In the *Panath.* he pushes its origins back to the successors of Theseus (130), "not less than 1,000 years" before Peisistratus (148).

[83] More precisely, appointed by κλήρωσις ἐκ προκρίτων, *Areop.* 22, *Panath.* 145. But he considers election the more important of the ingredients of this mixed process, and thus tends to assimilate the whole process to election. Thus he mentions the fact that Lycurgus made the magistracies elective (*Panath.* 153, cited n. 80, above) as though it substantiated his contention that Lycurgus was "imitating" the Athenian constitution.

[84] *Areop.* 37ff.; cf. *Panath.* 154.

[85] Cf. W. Jaeger, "The Date of Isocrates' *Areopagiticus* and the Athenian Opposition," *Scripta Minora* II (Rome, 1960), pp. 267ff., at p. 298, n. 4, and also *Paideia* III, pp. 112ff. of the Engl. transl. (New York, 1944); and A. Fuks, *The Ancestral Constitution* (London, 1953), pp. 9 ff.

[86] I borrow the term from Larsen, "The Judgment of Antiquity on Democracy," *CP* 49 (1954), pp. 1 ff., at p. 7.

[87] But I cannot refrain from correcting a mistake which seems to be passing unchallenged in the literature. It is wrong to cite Isocrates as a "supporter of Theramenes' program" (Jaeger, *Paideia* III, p. 115) while ignoring one absolutely fundamental difference: the Theramenean restriction of active citizenship to those qualifying for hoplite census (Arist., *Ath. Pol.* 29.5; Thuc. 8.65.3; Xen., *Hell.* 2.3.48; for the probable numbers see the reference at n. 64, above, adding Xen. *l. c.*, 42, where the same formula is ascribed (by implication) to Therameness as is prescribed by Aristotle for his "polity" (n. 61, above). There is *nothing* of this in Isocrates, where the demos is to retain sovereign power ὥσπερ τύραννον, *Areop.* 26) "to appoint the magistrates, punish misdemeanors, and adjudicate disputes (*l. c.*; cf. *Panath.* 147).—In a valuable, richly documented, paper, "The Constitution of the Five Thousand," *Historia* 5 (1956), pp. 1 ff., G. de Ste. Croix has argued that (I) under this constitution probably no citizen lost the right of ἐκκλησιάζειν καὶ δικάζειν, and hence, (II),

where all that concerns [20] us is precisely the way he talks. What we want
to know is how this man, who is not much of a philosopher, but a master
rhetorician, uses words when adressing a Panhellenic public, and what we
can learn from this for the connection of *isonomia* and *demokratia* in the
general usage. If his criticism of the democracy of his day had taken the
line that it had abandoned, or weakened, its commitment to the principle
of equality, this would indeed have impaired the value of his testimony
as evidence for my thesis. But this is not the way he talks. He refers to the
leaders of the restored democracy as men who, unlike the Thirty, wished
to be governed "on terms of equality" with their fellow-citizens (τοῖς δὲ
πολίταις ἴσον ἔχειν).[88] Even when inveighing against the "bad" democ-

---

that this constitution was "basically democratic" (p. 2). Contra: (I) In the
absence of any positive information as to what rights were retained by those
not entered on the hoplite catalogue it is clear that if they did retain the right
of ἐκκλησιάζειν it was merely nominal, since the sovereign power had been
transferred by action of the Colonus assembly (Arist., *l. c.*; Thuc. 8.67.3) to
"the 5,000" and, *pace* Ste. Croix. pp. 9–10, there is no definite evidence that the
de jure status of "the 5,000" changed in the slightest when the 400 were over-
thrown four months later; on the contrary, the wording used by Aristotle to
describe the changes voted at Colonus, τὴν δ' ἄλλην πολιτείαν ἐπιτρέψαι
πᾶσαν to men of hoplite census, tallies with that used at 33.2 to extol the
subsequent regime of "the 5,000," καὶ ἐκ τῶν ὅπλων τῆς πολιτείας οὔσης (and cf.
Diod. 13.38.1, καὶ τὸ σύστημα τῆς πολιτείας ἐκ τῶν ὁπλιτῶν [Krüger's emendation for the senseless πολιτῶν of the ms.]). As for Ste. Croix's supposition that
"the judicial system under the 5,000 will have been substantially the democratic
one, except for the absence of pay" (p. 13), this is irreconcileable with the
cited wording in Aristotle (and Diodorus), since dicastic service would certainly be reckoned an integral part of the πολιτεία: cf. n. 109, below. Note
that the hoplite constitution is a well-known contemporary constitutional
pattern (so e. g. in Boeotia; and cf. ps.-Herod., *Peri Politeias*, 30–31, where it is
clear that it was fairly widespread) to which there are many allusions in
Aristotle (he identifies his polity with it in at least three passages, using practically the same formulae as at *Ath. Pol.* 33.2 above in referring to it in the
Politics: ἐκ τῶν ὁπλιτευόντων [sc. τὴν πολιτείαν], 1265B28; ἐκ τῶν τὰ ὅπλα
ἐχόντων μόνον, 1297B1; μετέχουσιν αὐτῆς οἱ κεκτημένοι τὰ ὅπλα, 1297B3),
without there ever being any question of voting or dicastic rights for those
below hoplite census. It would then follow that (II) this constitution was a
moderate oligarchy, like that of Thebes (whose four Boulai are undoubtedly
the model for the programmatic four Boulai of *Ath. Pol.* 30.3–4). This was
certainly the constitutional ideal of Theramenes (Xenophon, *l. c.*, where restriction of rights of active citizenship to hoplite census is presented as the
middle way between democracy and tyrannical oligarchy).

[88] *Areop.* 69. He goes on to say (70) that even the bad democracy is better
than oligarchy. Cf. *Paneg.* 105. Unless we choose to think (on what evidence

racy, he never hints that it is "unequal." Thus he leaves democracy, good and bad, in secure possession of *isonomia*, though with the implied warning that its *ison* ought to be, so far as possible, that "more useful" and "righteous" equality which proportions awards to merit.[89] [21]

III. PLATO, MENEXENUS 239A

Our word occurs here in a most unusual context: in that encomium of Athens which has been, and apparently still is, a phiological puzzle.[90] I must address myself briefly to this larger problem, begging the reader's indulgence for the detour. No shorter road to the meaning of *isonomia* in this text could hope to results of any scholarly interest.

I do not know) that in such passages as these Isocrates is lying, I fail to see how we could class him as an oligarch. E. Buchner (*Der Panegyrikos des Isokrates, Historia*, Einzelschriften 2 [Wiesbaden, 1958], p. 85) finds "das Bild eines gemäßigten Oligarchen" in *Paneg*. 76–79—on the strength of such things as the denunciation of θρασύτης, and the praise for "good and exact," but spare, legislation. Surely one could have such sentiments without approving of the disfranchisement of thousands of one's fellow-citizens. Having no evidence of the latter, how can we call him an "oligarch," even a "moderate" one, if we wish to use political terms with precision?

[89] I say only "implied" because, though Isocrates expounds clearly the doctrine of "the two equalities" (*Areop*. 21–22; cf. *Nic*. 14–15), he is too feeble a political theorist to make it the basis of a thoroughgoing critique of democracy. In the very next paragraph of the *Areop*. (23) he recommends the abolition of the lot for an entirely different reason (naively opportunistic, and so inept that only simpletons would be swayed by it); the lot might actually put oligarchs into office! In *Nic*. 14–15 he gives his king the maxim, "the most for the best," as an argument for monarchy; but if he has the full doctrine he uses it with clumsy inconsistency, for he concedes in the very same context that oligarchies and democracies τὰς ἰσότητας τοῖς μετέχουσι τῶν πολιτειῶν ζητοῦσι and *condemns* them for this, instead of saying (as he should in these circumstances) that their ἰσότητες (or some of them) are not "proportional" equalities.

[90] For recent surveys of the divergent opinions in German scholarship see N. Scholl, *Der platonische Menexenos*, Temi e Testi 5 (Rome, 1959), pp. 7 ff.; Ilse von Loewenclau, *Der platonische Menexenos*, Tübinger Beiträge zur Altertumswissenschaft 41 (Stuttgart, 1961), pp. 10 ff. In the following notes there will be references to views represented by French- and English-speaking scholars in work published prior to 1963. For an alternative interpretation of the *Menexenus* the reader should consult Charles E. Kahn, "Plato's Funeral Oration," *Class Philol.*, 58 [1963], pp. 220–34 (which reached me too late for comment, but has not led me to change the views I express here).

The clue to Plato's intentions in this dialogue I find, in common with several other students,[91] in the brief prelude. Here Socrates tells us how he responds to the encomia of Athens which formed according to custom the larger and most conspicuous part of such speeches. When I listen to them, says Socrates, they cast a spell (γοητεύουσιν, 235A) or a charm (κηλούμενος, 235B) over my mind; they give me, as an Athenian, the sense of having "become at that moment a greater, nobler, finer man" (235B); they bring me such "an access of grandeur"[92] that I feel as though transported to the Isles of the Blest, and "not until the fourth or fifth day do I come back to my senses and know where I am" (235C). The oratory which induced such delightful flights from reality[93] [22] could not have been over-scrupulous in its regard for truth.[94] We know that it was not.[95] Plato implies as much; at one point he says so outright: "they praise so magnificently, ascribing to thier subjects *real and unreal attributes*,[96] deco-

---

[91] See especially K. Oppenheimer, *Zwei attische Epitaphien* (Diss., Berlin, 1933), pp. 71–76 (Hereafter "Oppenheimer"); L. Méridier, Introduction to his edition and translation of the *Menexenus* in the Association Guillaume Budé's "Collection des Universités de France" (Third Edition, Paris, 1956), pp. 53–55 (Hereafter, "Méridier"). And cf. E. R. Dodds, *Plato's Gorgias* (Oxford, 1959), p. 24, n. 2.

[92] σεμνότερος ἐν τῷ παραχρῆμα γίγνομαι, 235B4–5; and cf. σεμνότης, *l. c.*, 8.

[93] This expression, amply warranted by the γοητεία (see next note) and Isles of the Blest metaphors, would have further support from Burnet's reading ἐξέστηκα (one MS. reading, against ἕστηκα in the other two), at 235A7. This is adopted by several scholars, including Oppenheimer, p. 74, who gives a good account of the psychological state induced by oratory, as described by Plato ironically both here and elsewhere (*Phaedrus* 234D, *Prt.* 315B), and speaks of "die Veränderung des Wirklichen" that takes place in consciousness while this state lasts, *l. c.*

[94] For the conjunction of γοητεία with deceit cf. *Rp.* 381E, ἐξαπατῶντες καὶ γοητεύοντες, and 413C, ἔοικε γὰρ . . . γοητεύειν πάντα ὅσα ἀπατᾷ. And cf. Gorgias, *Helena* 8–14 for the magical ἐπωιδαί, γοητείας, μαγείας, 10) power of persuasive speech to delude (καὶ τὴν ψυχὴν ἀπατήσας, 8; δόξης ἀπατήματα, 10).

[95] See, e.g., H. Strasburger, "Thukydides und die politische Selbstdarstellung der Athener," *Hermes* 86 (1958), pp. 17 ff.

[96] τὰ προσόντα καὶ τὰ μή. F. Wendland, "Die Tendenz des Platonischen Menexenus," *Hermes* 25 (1890), pp. 171 ff., at p. 174, refers to the characterization of encomiastic oratory by Anaximenes of Lampsacus as ἐνδόξων αὔξησις καὶ μὴ προσόντων συνοικείωσις, *Rhet. ad Alex.* 1425B37, and to Isocrates, *Busiris* 4: δεῖ τοὺς μὲν εὐλογεῖν τινας βουλομένους πλείω τῶν ὑπαρχόντων ἀγαθῶν προσόντ᾽ ἀποφαίνειν. Cf. Socrates' refusal in the *Symposium* to praise Eros in the style of Gorgias (198D) so as to ὡς μέγιστα ἀνατιθέναι τῷ πράγματι καὶ ὡς κάλλιστα, ἐάν τε ᾖ οὕτως ἔχοντα ἐάν τε μή(198D).

rating them with the most beautiful words . . ." (234C–235A). This is the kind of speech Socrates now proposes to recite. It has been taught him by Aspasia, he says, from "left-overs" of the one she composed for Pericles (236B).[97] We are to get, then, a Funeral Oration in the grand style, inviting comparison with the greatest of them, the one in Thucydides.[98] And just in case we have forgotten how foreign to Socrates' nature is this kind of performance,[99] almost his last words before beginning the speech are that he will be "playing" (236C)[100] and "dancing" (236D).

This histrionics are obvious in the longest part of the speech (239A–246A) which deals with Athenian history. Plato is anything but an exact historian. But there is no parallel in his other works for the distortions and falsifications we get here,[101] some of them involving events so well-known

---

[97] In Aischines' Socratic dialogue bearing her name, Aspasia had also been represented as Pericles' instructor in oratory (fr. 23, Dittmar) and in the style of Gorgias (fr. 24); cf. M. Pohlenz, *Aus Platos Werdezeit* (Berlin, 1913), pp. 260–61. Plato had a high opinion of Pericles as an orator and ascribed the best qualities of his oratory to the influence of Anaxagorean *meteorologia* (*Phdr.* 269E–270A).

[98] As well as with run-of-the-mill performances Plato would have heard or read, whose themes, style, etc., we may judge from those which survive from the fourth century: Lysias, *Or.* 2; Demosthenes (?), *Or.* 60; Hypereides, *Or.* 6.

[99] Oppenheimer, pp. 73–75, reminds us of *Ap.* 17A, *Lysis* 204D ff., *Smp.* 215C, *Tht.* 174D.

[100] Which gains special significance from Menexenus' earlier remark, ἀεὶ σὺ προσπαίζεις, ὦ Σώκρατες, τοὺς ῥήτορας, 235C.

[101] Obviously there can be no comparison with the tales about the imaginary Athens in the *Timaeus* and the *Critias*, nor yet with reference to the conjectural, legendary, or conventionally traditional past in the *Laws*, since these do not compete with historically ascertainable facts (for indications to this effect cf. 677A, 678A, 682E, 683D, 691D, 692B). When Plato comes to treat known historical events in the Laws he retains only one of the inaccuracies of the *Menex.*: the suppression of Plataean participation at Marathon (*Menex.* 240C; *Laws* 698D–699B). This error was so encrusted in the Athenian image of its own past that Plato may have been honestly mistaken on this point. (According to Herodotus the Athenians were saying just ten years after the event, μοῦνοι Ἑλλήνων δὴ μουνομαχήσαντες τῷ Πέρσῃ, 9.27.5. In 431 B. C. they are still saying they had been "alone at Marathon," Thuc. 1.73.4. The attempt of Wilamowitz to gloss over the misinterpretations of history in the *Menex.* ("Platon hat keine geschichtliche Studien gemacht und auch später in den Gesetzen ganz ähnlich erzählt," *Platon* I [Berlin, 1919], p. 265) was not, and could not, be supported by evidence. Thus, as Wilamowitz himself notices, *Platon* II² (Berlin, 1920), p. 133, the story of the Persian σαγηνεία of Eretria (*Menex.* 240B) is not treated "ganz ähnlich" in the *Laws* (698D, εἴτε ἀληθὲς εἴτε καὶ ὅπη ἀφίκετο [= "a euphemism for εἴτε ψευδές," E. B. England, *ad loc.*]); and while Artemision and Salamis are credited exclusively to the Athenians in

and so recent that [23] their misinterpretation could only have been wilful; and being so patent, it could not have been made with the intention to deceive.[102] Such a performance is inexplicable on any hypothesis except one: that Plato is parodying the [24] idealization of Athens in patriotic

---

the *Menex.* (241AB), they are more correctly referred to the "Hellenes" in the *Laws* (707BC). Anyhow, Plato would not have needed to "study history" to know when he was giving a violently tendentious account of it (as at 242A ff., where he blames all wars against Athens on the ζῆλος and φθόνος of other states, Athens herself being apparently blameless), or misstating recent events (see next note).

[102] Thus no one could possibly have believed that "we won not only that sea-fight [Arginusae], but the rest of the [Peloponnesian] war as well," 243D. For the treatment of Athenian history see Wendland, *op. cit., passim,* Pohlenz, *op. cit.,* pp. 274 ff. I have detected one falsification not mentioned in any other account known to me: When the King made the subjection of the Asiatic Greeks a condition of peace, "we were the only ones who would not give them up or swear [to the proposed pact]," while "the Corinthians, Argives, Boeotians and [our] other allies wanted to give them up, *they compacted and took the oath,*" 245C. Our sources give no support to the italicized statement. Xenophon (*Hell.* 4.8.13–15) says that the peace-terms offered by Sparta to Tiribazus (at the conference in Sardis, 392 B. C.) were rejected by the Athenian, *Theban,* and *Argive* delegates. Philochorus (fr. 149, Jacoby; *ap.* Didymus 7.20) mentions the Athenian rejection (this is probably the action of the Assembly: U. Wilcken, "Über Entstehung und Zweck des Königsfriedens," *Abh. Berlin Akademie,* 1941, philol.-hist. Kl. 15, p. 11, followed by H. Bengston, *Griechische Geschichte* [Munich, 1960], p. 261), but says absolutely nothing about its accept-ance by Thebes and Argos. But we know Thebes and Argos had cogent rea-sons for rejecting another clause of the proposed treaty, autonomy for non-Asiatic Greeks; this would have undermined the dominance of Thebes in the Boeotian confederacy and that of Argos over Corinth. From Andocides' *De Pace* it is clear that at this time (392/1) Argos is strongly opposed to the treaty (24 ff., 41); and while Thebes is represented as anxious to make peace with Sparta (20), the only Theban concession mentioned is the autonomy of Orchomenus (Cf. Cloché, *op. cit.,* p. 110: he takes this—very reasonably, I think—to be the *only* concession; hence no concession of autonomy for the other Boeotian cities). The Argives finally accept the offer in 386 B. C., when the Athenians also accept. The Thebans still hold back ("claimed the right to take the oath in the name of all the Boeotians," Xen. *l. c.* 5.1.32, i.e., were not conceding the autonomy of all Boeotian states), and are finally forced to give in when the Spartans mobilize against them. That Thebes and Argos had "compacted and taken the oath" at some previous time, when Athens had refused, is, therefore, flatly contrary to the evidence. What *could* be true is that Argos and Thebes were less concerned for the fate of the Asiatic Greeks than was Athens. To blow this up into the falsehood that Argos and Thebes had formally accepted the offer, when Athens formally rejected it, would be very much in the style of the encomium.

oratory.[103] The opening part of the encomium speaks of one of the fondest of Athenian conceits, their "autochthony," then goes on to tell of their "mother," Attica, and the gods' special love and solicitude for its inhabitants. Not only its theodicy, but its natural history, is incredibly Athenocentric. Would anyone have believed, for instance, that when the earth was producing wild beasts everywhere, it carefully exempted Attica?[104] So it would be strange indeed if the third paragraph of the encomium, which links the marvels of the land to the glories of its history by extolling the constitution, should shift to a different key. Unless we are to have Plato jumping out of the parody in this one paragraph, to jump back into it in the next, we must assume that he will be treating Athenian ideology in the same way, and must expect some violent transformations of well-known landmarks—though not so violent as to lose contact altogether with the familiar world.

But first we must remind ourselves of Plato's normal view of the credo of democracy in this middle period of his life, before he had found his way to a more temperate estimate of it in the *Politicus* and the *Laws*.[105]

---

[103] Of the writers I have been citing, Wendland, Pohlenz, Méridier, Oppenheimer, and Dodds would agree, and so would many others whom I have not had occasion to mention. Of contrary views I can only mention three: (I) Wilamowitz: "Platon hat die Rede ganz ernsthaft geschrieben und hat ihr doch die unbarmherzigste Kritik vorausgeschickt . . . weil sie den Beifall der Menge erschmeichelt" (*Platon*, II, p. 141), his reason for the latter being that "Er muß Wasser in den Feuertrank des Gorgias gießen, denn er will in der Heimat wirken" (*Platon*, I, p. 267). But if we are going to make a flatterer out of Plato, must we also make him such a clumsy one as to warn his readers in the prelude that he expects to gain their favor by such means? (II) Scholl, *op. cit.*, p. 59: "Sokrates beabsichtigt mit seiner Lobrede einen erzieherischen Einfluß auf seine Mitbürger auszuüben." But why should he falsify history for this purpose? (III) von Loewenclau: Plato is only concerned with the "ideales Urbild" of Athens (*op. cit.*, p. 90), its "reines Wesen" (p. 102) and "Geschichte ist für ihn nicht Selbstzweck" (p. 83). And why should Plato want to state the truth about the ideal Athens in the form of falsehoods about the actual one? On p. 90 the author seems to be arguing: The ideal Athens would not have done *X*; *ergo*, Plato feels justified in saying that the historical Athens did not do *X*, even if he knew that it did. Would not this be rather strange for Plato as for any other honest man?

[104] 237D. Von Loewenclau (*op. cit.*, pp. 59–60) thinks in all seriousness that this is "explained" if Attica here is the land of the Ideal Athens; "Athens reines, inneres Wesen" could not produce "wild" beasts, but only the "tame" animal, man!

[105] In the *Politicus* (302DE) he makes the provision for higher and lower forms of democracy which he had not made in the *Republic*, while making there provision for three grades of government under the rule of few. For democracy

He spread this out before us in Book VIII of the *Republic*. Here he depicts democracy as it [25] appears to him when he is scrutinizing it sharply and with critical detachment instead of making believe to be seeing it through a haze of patriotic euphoria. He starts by referring to democracy—fairly enough by contemporary standards[106]—as a form of government in which "they distribute on equal terms [sc. to all the citizens][107] the constitution[108] and the offices, and where most appointments to office are made by lot."[109] Now Plato knows how strong are the ties of equality with justice in the moral sense of his people,[110] and could hardly have failed to notice how easily the democrats could exploit these ties to their own advantage: they would take it for granted that the equal sharing of rights and privileges under their constitution is sanctioned by the ἴσον ἔχειν of justice.[111] Plato strikes directly at this assumption when he speaks of democracy two pages later (558C) as "distributing a kind of equality to equals and unequals

---

in the *Laws* see now G. R. Morrow, *Plato's Cretan City* (Princeton, 1960), *passim*.

[106] Except for the qualification at n. 109 (II), below, this would meet the difficult test of being unobjectionable to either advocates or critics of democracy.

[107] I ignore τοῖς λοιποῖς which goes with the omitted context.

[108] I.e., in its legally guarranteed rights and privileges.

[109] 557A. (I) For the idea of sharing *equally* in the constitution see notes 111 and 112, below. (II) For the idea of sharing in the offices (but not, of sharing equally: this cannot be documented; here Plato is exaggerating, though even so not distorting the truth: ἐξ ἴσου [κατὰ τὸ δυνατόν] would have covered the point): ps.-Xen., *Ath. Pol.*, 1.2, in a democracy "it is deemed right that all should share in the offices, both in the lot-drawing now in force and in elections"; Isocr., *Paneg.* 105, ἀπελαύνεσθαι τῶν ἀρχῶν implies τῆς πολιτείας ἀποστερεῖσθαι, and *Loch.* 20, δημοκρατουμένης τῆς πόλεως . . . τῶν . . . ἀρχῶν μετέχειν ἀξιοῖμεν . . . ; Arist., *Pol.* 1275A22 ff.: the best definition of citzenship (and the one that applies "especially to citzenship in a democracy") is τὸ μετέχειν κρίσεως καὶ ἀρχῆς (counting the δικαστής and ἐκκλησιαστής as holding ἀρχαί "unrestricted as to time"), and 1278A36, λέγεται μάλιστα πολίτης ὁ μετέχων τῶν τιμῶν with 1281A32, τιμὰς γὰρ λέγομεν εἶναι τὰς ἀρχάς. Cf. the formula for active citizenship in the Treaty between Olbia and (democratic) Miletus, ca. 330 B. C., *SIG* 286 (= Tod, *GHI* II, 195); τιμου-χιῶμ μετέχειν, line 9; ἀρχείω[μ] μετέχουσιγ καὶ δικαστηρίων, line 20. (iii) For appointments to office by lot see n. 13, above.

[110] See, e.g., the citations from Plato at n. 78, above.

[111] The facile identification of democracy with *isotes* and oligarchy with *pleonexia* by Isocrates at (II) above must have been fairly common in democratic talk. Cf. the references given by F. Busolt, *Griechische Staatskunde* I² (Munich, 1920), p. 418, n. 5, in documentation of the statement that "Die *isotes* und das *ison echien hapantas* ist für die Demokratie charakteristisch."

alike." I cannot go into the full meaning carried by this *tour de force* of epigrammatic compression. But so much should be clear: Plato is saying that "equality" (i.e., equal awards) should be given only to "equals" (i.e., to those whose claims are equal). And since the democrats would be sure to retort, "But all citizens do have equal claims,"[112] Plato also expects the reader (who, presumably, has not skipped Book IV of the *Republic*) to understand him to [26] be saying that the only relevant claims are those of merit (ἀρετή)—excellence at the job for which nature has fitted one.[113] If Plato is right (and there is nothing on which he has greater confidence of being right), then the rule of distributive justice which he takes to govern the democratic state—"equality for all, be they equal or unequal in merit"—is viciously wrong. It is bound to vitiate the pursuit of justice, for it will make men indifferent on principle (not merely for lack of principle) to differences of merit.[114] Their very commitment to equality will produce inequality.

We can see what this would mean for ἰσονομία even if Plato had not mentioned the word in this connection. But he does,[115] and one of the two uses shows that he takes it to epitomize the whole misguided ethos of democracy. He says that the man who would be "rightly called 'democratic'" (562A) is one who lives βίον ἰσονομικοῦ τινος ἀνδρός (561E). This man orders his soul as the democratic state orders its offices: he is as indifferent to excellence in choosing between enjoyments as is the lot[116] when choosing between candidates for office:

> When told that there are pleasures and pleasures—high and noble satisfactions, which should be honored and cultivated, and base ones, which should be chastized and suppressed—he shuts his mind against the word of truth; he shakes his head and says, "But they are all alike; they are all of equal value." (561C)

[112] Cf. the statement by Athenagoras in Thuc. 6.38.5, cited at n. 41, above; and Arist., *Pol.* 1301A34, οἱ μὲν [the democrats] ὡς ἴσοι ὄντες πάντων τῶν ἴσων ἀξιοῦσι μετέχειν.

[113] Cf. the definition of δικαιοσύνη at 433AB, bearing in mind that *excellent* performance is assumed in τὰ αὑτοῦ πράττειν: only occasionally does Plato feel it necessary to make this explicit, as at 374A, καλῶς ἐργάζεσθαι, and 394E, καλῶς ἐπιτηδεύοι.

[114] Hence the prominence of traits like πραότης, συγγνώμη, ἡδεῖα, ποικίλη, ἄναρχος in the moral profile of democracy (558AB)—concommitants of what Plato takes to be the disposition of this constitution to hand out precious rights and privileges *gratis*, without regard to the merit of their recipients.

[115] Cf. n. 39, above.

[116] 561B3-4.

This is what Plato thinks *isonomia* means in the life of Athens: equality denying priority to excellence, putting the worst on a level with the best. Now we know what will have to be changed before it can be given a place in the primped-up Athens of "Aspasia's" speech.

Three decades or more later, when writing the *Laws*, Plato expounded the doctrine of "the two equalities"[117] which, as we know from Isocrates, had gained currency among conservative political theorists in Athens by that time.[118] From the single reference to "geometrical equality" in the *Gorgias* we may conjecture that Plato had even then some such doctrine in mind.[119] Why then does he not put it to work for him in the *Menexenus*,[120] transmuting *isonomia* by simply identifying its *ison* with the "good" equality which proportions awards to merit and is the polar opposite of the promiscuous equality of the lot?—A sufficient reason would be that he could not assume at this time that the doctrine of "the two

[117] 756E–758A; cf. 744C.

[118] N. 89, above.

[119] 508A6. See Dodds *ad loc.* and on 507C8–508C3. But I have nowhere found a clear statement of the (reasonable) conjectures we still have to make in ascribing to Plato familiarity with the doctrine of the "two equalities" a third of a century before he wrote it out in the *Laws*: (I) Though "geometrical equality" does not recur in Plato, there can be no doubt that he would understand by it *proportional* equality. We may then conjecture that he would not have dragged it into the discussion with Callicles unless he meant to contrast it with a different kind of equality; and that this could only be the kind to which he refers in the *Laws* 757B as τὴν μέτρῳ ἴσην [*sc.* ἰσότητα] καὶ σταθμῷ καὶ ἀριθμῷ, hence that which Aristotle calls "arithmetical equality" (ἀριθμῷ [ἴσον], *Pol.* 1301B31; ἀριθμητικῇ ἰσότητι 1302A8) in opposition to proportional equality. (II) We may further conjecture that the point of referring to "geometrical equality" is to uphold ἰσότης against Callicles' open espousal of πλεονεξία (483D; cf. 508A7) *without thereby conceding* Callicles' assumption that if justice is ἰσότης, it would justify equality between the masses and their betters (τὸ ἴσον ἔχωσιν φαυλότεροι ὄντες, 483C). Thus "geometrical" would be used to break the democratic stranglehold on ἰσότης. If we are going to read all this into the text of the *Gorgias* the question would still remain why, if Plato had this in his head, he was so uncommunicative about it. In reply, we may conjecture (III) that Plato has not yet detached this doctrine from the metaphysical framework (507E6–508A4) in which he received it, and is unwilling to discuss the latter because (a) he is unsure of the extent of his agreement with it and/or (b) such a discussion is thematically precluded by the exclusively moral interests of the *Gorgias*. This would explain why he makes Socrates shut off the line of thought introduced by φασὶ δ' οἱ σοφοὶ at 507E6 with the abrupt and unSocratic remark at 508A7, γεωμετρίας γὰρ ἀμελεῖς.

[120] For the *Menexenus* as "an afterpiece to the Gorgias," see Dodds, *op. cit.*, p. 24.

equalities" would be familiar to the audience to which he was particularly addressing the *Menexenus*: readers and writers of epideictic oratory.[121] He could not use it here without having to explain it and argue for it, i.e., turning to an entirely different genre of discourse, whose dialectic would be an alien element in the texture of the Funeral Oration. What he needed then was some alternative mode of attack which he could carry out entirely within the stylistic conventions of an encomium of the constitution. He found this in "Aspasia's" other brain-child.

Scholars have often noticed the remarkable affinity between the praise of the Athenian constitution in the *Menexenus* and in these lines of the Periclean oration in Thucydides[122]: [28]

Though as to its name, because it is ordered with a view to[123] the many, not the few, our constitution is called "democracy"; and

[121] There is no clear mention of this doctrine, or allusion to it, in a work by a rhetorician prior to 372 B. C., the date of Isocrates' *Nicocles*.

[122] Thuc. 2.37.1. For the elucidation I am indebted most of all to Gomme (*ad loc.*; also *Class. Quart.* 42 (1948), pp. 10–11) and Kakridis (work cited at n. 37, above). For the similarities in thought and wording with *Menex.* 238B–239A see, e.g., von Loewenclau, *op. cit.*, pp. 69 ff. These are all the more striking in that (I) they constitute almost the only significant points at which the *thought* of the two orations converges (see their role among all points of contact itemized by T. Berndt, *De Ironia Menexeni Platonici*, Diss., Münster, 1881, pp. 3–4), while (II) differing strikingly from remarks made about the constitution in the other three extant funeral orations (n. 98, above). The crucial idea, common to the orations of Thucydides and Plato, of an aristocratic element in the Athenian constitution, does occur in Isocrates: *Panath.* 131 and 153 (cf. n. 80, above); cf. *Areop.* 21. But Isocrates refers it *exclusively* to the ancient, i.e., pre-Cleisthenean (*Panath.* 148) constitution. Our two passages are the only fourth- or fifth-century texts which assert, or imply, that the Athenian democracy of their own time is an aristocracy. Gomme's remarks, *Comm.* II, p. 109, conveying (unintentionally) a contrary impression, are misleading.

[123] Many good commentators and translators favor "administered by" (or some variant) for οἰκεῖν ἐς. I prefer to stick to the more literal rendering above (so, e.g., O. Regenbogen, "in Rücksicht auf"), precisely because this is vaguer, and therefore *allows* one to read into ἐς πλείονας οἰκεῖν the literal sense of *demokratia* (one would not be unprepared for the rule of the masses in a constitution ordered, or organized, "with a view to them"), but without making this the explicit and unambiguous sense of the assertion. I believe it is wrong to translate or gloss ἐς πλείονας οἰκεῖν as though it meant unambiguously τοὺς πλείονας ἄρχειν ἐν αὐτῇ or πλείονας εἶναι τοὺς διοικοῦντας αὐτήν. None of the supposed parallels (Classen lists 5.81.2; 8.38.3, 53.3, 89.2) is exact: in none of them is the verb οἰκεῖν. We should not forget that (I) the idea of the masses engaging in the actual business of government (as distinct from passing judg-

while as regards the law there is equal treatment for all in our private disputes; yet as regards our claims [to post of honor in the state], each is preferred to public office according to his particular repute—not so much for his class[124] as for his excellence: poverty or obscurity will not bar him if he has it in him to give the state good service. [29]

---

ment on proposals put before it: κρίνομεν, 2.40.2; cf. κριταί, 3.37.4, κρῖναι, 6.39.1) is suppressed throughout the whole of this speech, and (II) Thucydides had ways to assert it quite explicitly had he wished to do so. It is safer to assume that he said ἐς πλείονας οἰκεῖν because he did not want to say more, than that he slipped by inadvertence into a weaker expression. Finally, (III), there is the position of the word in this sentence: had he wanted to make the reader think of the full, literal sense of *demokratia* he would have been more likely to put it at, or near, the beginning.

[124] Kakridis and Gomme take ἀπὸ μέρους to mean ἐν μέρει. *Contra*: (I) There is no example for such a use of ἀπὸ μέρους. Kakridis retorts that neither are there examples of ἀπὸ μέρους with the sense of "from a class [of the civic body]." But since there are many examples of μέρος, μερίς, μοῖρα, μόριον with the needed sense (to the ones cited by Kakridis add Eur. *Suppl.* 238, 243, and Arist., *Pol.* 1289B30 ff. and 1326A21), the use of μέρος in this construction with ἀπὸ should pose no difficulty. (II) It would be contrary to the strategy of this address (which is still, for all its marvelous penetration and subtlety, an encomium first and foremost) to contradict explicitly the cherished formula that in a democracy the demos "rules in turn" (cf. Eur. *Suppl.* 406–407, δῆμος δ' ἀνάσσει διαδοχαῖσιν ἐν μέρει/ἐνιαυσίαισιν, and Arist. *Pol.* 1317B3-11, τὸ ἐν μέρει ἄρχεσθαι καὶ ἄρχειν is an ἐλευθερίας σημεῖον which τίθενται πάντες οἱ δημοτικοὶ τῆς πολιτείας ὅρον. Adhering then to the received sense of ἀπὸ μέρους here, I take the general sense of the whole period to be: "To be sure [μὲν], our constitution, being government for the people, is called "democracy"; but [δὲ, adversative, scaling down still further what Athenians would associate with this big word], while [1] on one hand [μὲν, concessive: in this respect no opposition to δημοκρατία κέκληται; *contra* Kakridis, but cf. n. 37, above], κατὰ τοὺς νόμους we have equality in litigation, yet [2] on the other hand [δὲ, strongly adversative, the real opposition to δημοκρατία κέκληται], κατὰ τὴν ἀξίωσιν each is preferred according to our esteem for him, [i.e.] [a] not so much for his class as [b] for his excellence." This analysis should disarm Gomme's objection that [a] "would not be a qualification of κατὰ μὲν τοὺς νόμους—πᾶσι τὸ ἴσον, nor of δημοκρατία κέκληται. No one would write, 'it is in name a democracy, *but* office-holding is not confined to a class,'" (*Comm.* II, p. 108). It is [2], not [a], which forms the qualification to δημοκρατία κέκληται in the preceding colon, and to πᾶσι τὸ ἴσον at [1]: [a] and [b] *taken together* are an elucidation of [2], which is composed in Thucydides' antithetical manner, [a] being brought in (in anticipation of what is to be spelled out in the next clauses) only to heighten still further the final climactic stress on ἀπ' ἀρετῆς προτιμᾶται.

These lines go far in dissociating the Athenian form of government from what Plato found most repugnant in it. They create the impression that this democracy is in fact an aristocracy of talent. How do they manage to do this? Ἀριστοκρατία is not mentioned or even, strictly speaking, implied. Ἀριστοκρατία, by Greek standards, would be a regime which restricts offices to the ἄριστοι. Pericles does not say quite so much of Athens. He says that when a man claims a post of honor, his claim[125] will be judged only by his ἀρετή. It would not follow strictly from this, if it were true, that all offices would be filled by men selected in this way. Some offices, perhaps many, might still be filled by a totally different process which does not wait for aspirants to step forward and press their individual claims but scoops out with mechanical regularity chance specimens from the general mass to the needed number. We know that something like this[126] happened in Athens at this time in the case of the vast majority of civic offices. Pericles does not deny this. He does not say the lot does not exist, or that it exists but does not matter. He just says nothing about it. He takes our mind away from it by putting κατ' ἀρετὴν προτιμᾶται at the peak of his taut, eventful period, and filling up the rest of it with features of the constitution which, though consistent with democracy, indeed necessary for it, were not distinctive of it. That this is government *for* the people, assuring equal treatment before the law and an equal, or nearly equal,[127] chance of appointment to (elective) office for aspirants of equal ability but of unequal wealth or birth—all this is so important in itself, and so well said, that only by great effort can one shake off the spell of the voice to recall what the speaker has either forgotten or, remembering, is determined to make us forget: government *by* the people, equality in the conduct of public affairs (not just in the settlement of private disputes), an equal vote in the Assembly and, through the lot, an equal, or nearly equal, chance of appointment to the Council, the lawcourts, and the vast majority of the magistracies. [30]

What drops out of Pericles' description of democracy forms the very core of Plato's, as we saw in the citation from *R.* 557A a moment ago.

[125] The sense of κατ' ἀξίωσιν here.

[126] With due allowance for (a) the fact that willingness to serve was presupposed, (b) δοκιμασία, and (c) μισθοφορία as a feature which made service possible for the poor.

[127] Thucydides uses τὸ πλέον to good advantage here: not that class counts for nothing (which would be false: cf., e.g., A. H. M. Jones, *Athenian Democracy* [Oxford, 1957], p. 49), but that talent counts for more. He then explains that poverty and obscurity are not bars—which is not to deny that they are handicaps.

Plato then is in a perfect position to sort out illusion from reality in Pericles' lines. Seeing how they produce their effect, he can repeat it himself, and with great gusto, for he is playing openly the game of patriotic make-believe. So he flaunts the word Pericles had held back, he says outright that the constitution, the same now[128] as in the past, is an aristocracy: it may be called "democracy" by some, but "it is in truth aristocracy with the approval of the masses" (238CD). The reason he gives in support of this startling assertion is comical: "Kings we have always—at one time hereditary, at another elected" (238D). Considering that the "kingship" in Athens now meant the office of ἄρχων βασιλεύς[129] and that its mode of appointment had been changed to sortition ἐκ προκρίτων a hundred years earlier and to pure sortition well before Plato's time, this could only be a joke. But it brings out the other word Pericles had suppressed: it names elective process,[130] which is what Plato evidently wants us to understand by "the approval of the masses." The commitment to elections here is not only more open, but more sweeping, than in the speech of Pericles where, as we noticed, it was said only that the best of those who claim office get it, while Plato says that only the best men are to get it: the "one standard" of this constitution is to be that "he who is judged wise or good holds power and office."[131] This brings him up against the problem which

[128] Attempts to explain Plato's plain words here (238C5-7), by making them refer to an Ideal Athens, untouched by historical change, are unconvincing. See Scholl's rebuttal, *op. cit.*, p. 30. Nor can I follow G. R. Morrow in his more moderate view that Plato could "seriously maintain that the Athenians of his day had retained enough features of that older [pre-Ephialtean] constitution to justify the claim that they were still living under it 'for the most part,' " because he felt "that the virtues that remained were more truly expressive of his Athens than the evidence of decline" (*op. cit.*, p. 89). The inference is frail, and the premise itself is doubtful. Plato does not seem very happy about "the virtues that remained" in the Athens of *Gorg.* 502D–503D, 515B–517A, 518E–519A, and of *Rep.* 426BC, 488BD, 493AC, and 560C–561A.

[129] Méridier (*ad loc.*) conjectures hopefully: "Mais βασιλῆς se rapporte peut-être ici à l'ensemble des archontes." He offers no parallel for such a use of βασιλῆς, and I know of none.

[130] Though χειροτονέω is the technical term for election (election by ψηφοφορία, also used by Plato in the *Laws* [Morrow, *op. cit.*, pp. 160 ff.], has no place in the Athenian constitution to my knowledge: cf. Arist., *Ath. Pol.* 43.1), αἱρέω is normal and far more common, and though it may have occasionally the more general sense of "appoint" (Morrow, p. 237) it could only have the sense of "elect" here (whether it be pure election or mixed, κλήρωσις ἐκ προκρίτων: n. 83, above); appointment by lot would make nonsense of "the approval of the masses."

[131] 238D. As Oppenheimer observes (p. 63), ὁ δόξας σοφὸς εἶναι here (and

remained vague and remote in the Periclean [31] speech: how can we be sure that elections will yield aristocratic results? As Aristotle was to observe, elections are indefensible when "the masses are too slavish."[132] In the present scheme a good deal more will be required of the masses who are to "have control of the state for the greater part" but must "give the offices and the power to those they think the best at any given time" (238D). Everything here depends on their good judgment, as Plato emphasizes by repeated allusions to δόξα in this passage.[133] If they cannot discriminate between the wise man and the one who is merely δήμῳ πιθανότατος,[134] if they will not choose the sincere and upright leader in preference to the flatterer, this scheme will not produce ἀριστοκρατία but only more δημοκρατία. So the intellectual and moral level of the electorate must be raised steeply above that of the present Athenian *demos*. The ὄχλος[135] must be transfigured into a junior partner of the ἄριστοι.

Plato solves this problem in the spirit of the encomium and with materials he brought into his discourse almost from the very start (237AB): the εὐγένεια which all Athenians enjoy in virtue of their Attic autochthony. Because of this, he says later on (245CD), the Athenians are "pure Hellenes,"[136] free from any admixture of barbarian blood.[137] And since

---

τοῖς ἀεὶ δόξασιν ἀρίστοις εἶναι three lines earlier) is a normal expression for elections. He compares Arist., *Ath. Pol.* 38.3, ἄλλους εἵλοντο δέκα τοὺς βελτίστους εἶναι δοκοῦντας. Cf. also Plato, *Laws* 946A, with ἡγῆται in place of δοκεῖ (nominations for election of *euthynoi*).

[132] *Pol.* 1282A16. Cf. 1281B16–22. And cf. Plato's concern for the fitness of the electorate in the *Laws*, e.g., at 751CD.

[133] εὐδοξίας, δόξασιν, δόξας, 238D; δόξει, 239A. Oppenheimer (pp. 62–63) has rightly connected the first of these with εὐδοκιμεῖ in Thuc. 2.37.1 and combated the widespread assumption (most recently: E. R. Dodds, *op. cit.* p. 24, n. 2) that the use of δόξα by Plato here is ironical. The irony in this passage has been misunderstood. The joke is on the Athenians—not because the δόξα of an electorate could never result in ἀριστοκρατία (else the joke would be also on the city of the *Laws*: cf. Morrow, *op. cit.*, pp. 229 ff.), but because the δόξα of the Athenian ὄχλος could not.

[134] Thucydides of Cleon, 3.36.6; and cf. 4.21.3. But also of Hermocrates, 6.35.2. It is not for him the term of disparagement it is for Plato in the *Gorgias* (458E, ἐν ὄχλῳ πιθανόν; four other listings of ὄχλος in *Grg.* in Ast, *Lexicon Platonicum*), where the rhetor is a flatterer, a make-up artist.

[135] Five times of the Athenian masses in the *Gorgias* (Ast, *s.v.*); and cf. *R.* 565.

[136] εἰλικρινῶς . . . Ἕλληνες, . . . αὐτοὶ Ἕλληνες, 245D.

[137] The themes εὐγένεια, αὐτόχθονες are worked hard in Funeral Orations and elsewhere in contemporary Attic literature and come into the mythical Athens of the *Timaeus* (for the references see von Loewenclau, pp. 51ff.).

he reads spiritual attributes into biological purity[138] he can infer from the racial homogeneity of its citizens, from [32] their equal "noble birth," such intellectual and moral equality as is required for the aristodemocracy. Extreme inequalities ("despotism and slavery") between fellow-citizens, he explains, are in order for other states, tyrannies and oligarchies, because their conglomerate civic bodies run the gamut of inequality of natural endowment. "But not so for us and ours. Brothers all, born of the same mother, we would not deem it right to be each others' slaves or masters. But ἰσογονία in respect of our nature obliges us to seek ἰσονομία in respect of our laws, and to defer to each other in nothing save on account of virtue or wisdom" (239A). The *isonomia* mentioned here is a far cry from that which Plato attacked in the *Republic*. Subordinated to the aristocratic principle of deference to virtue and wisdom, it no longer stands for the crazy justice of equality for unequals. But it still refers to features of this imaginary Athens which are genuinely equalitarian: equality under the law, equal chance to compete for office regardless of "weakness, poverty, or obscurity of family" (238D), an equal vote in elections. It thus gives the semblance[139] of democracy to a constitution which is "in truth an aristocracy."

What do we learn then of the denotation of *isonomia* from this use of it in the *Menexenus*?—That the word was so conspicuously attached to democracy that Plato could use it to link the nominal democracy he praises here with the actual one he denounces in the *Republic*, as he used *aristokratia* to keep the two apart. The fantasy of the *Menexenus* was a democracy only so far as it was *isonomia*; its democracy was a fantasy so far as it was *aristokratia*.

But I know of no other passage in which Athenian conceit *vis-a-vis* other Greeks climbs the heights of *Menex.* 245D: other Greek strains (referred to mythically as Πέλοπες, Κάδμοι, Δαναοί) are "barbarians by nature, Greeks by convention."

[138] Since this has sometimes been swallowed as serious Platonic doctrine (e.g., R. Harder, "Plato und Athen," *Neue Jahrbucher für Wissenschaft und Jugendbildung* 10 [1934], pp. 492, at pp. 498–99) I must refer to *Tht.* 175A: ὑπὸ ἀπαιδευσίας some people ignore the fact that *any man* has had myriads of ancestors, countless of Greeks and Barbarians among them.

[139] Convincing enough to mislead Wilamowitz: "Zunächst ist das ein Lob der Demokratie, das so wohl klingt und so geschickt gewandt ist wie die Rede des Theseus in den Hiketiden des Euripides" (*Platon* II, p. 131). He fails to notice the huge differences. Vv. 406–407 of Theseus' speech (cited at n. 124, above) suffice to identify *its* Athens as a true democracy.

APPENDIX: PLATO (?), EPISTLE 7, 326D, 336D

Throughout this paper I have avoided carefully any references to these
two texts, though these are usually counted among the important uses
of our word in the Platonic corpus. I must now explain my reason. It
is simply that I have now lost confidence in the authenticity of the *Seventh
Letter* (I never had any to lose in the case of the others). To launch an
investigation of these two texts would, therefore, lead me into questions
which would call for another paper or, better, a book. Putting aside now
the large question of authorship,[140] let me state the main difficulty raised
by these two texts. [*33*]

That a writer who purports to be Plato should choose to characterize
by *isonomos* and *isonomia* a virtuous constitution which he contrasts as
sharply with democracy as with oligarchy and tyranny (326D) presents
no difficulty whatever. Given the doctrine of "the two equalities," *isonomia could* be made the watchword of nondemocratic constitutions of a
great variety (including that of the *Laws* or of the more austerely aristocratic *Republic*) by simply giving its *ison* the sense of "geometrical equality."
The only question then is whether we can believe, consistently with our
other knowledge, that Plato ever came to the point of doing this. As should
be clear from the foregoing, the closest he ever came to this was in the
Menexenus. And this was still far enough. For he did not undertake there—
he could not in the fictive circumstances of a Funeral Oration—to show
how an entirely new sense could be read into the *ison* of *isonomia*, so as
to make of this word the means of rebuking and chastening, instead of
conciliating, democracy. A little later he wrote the *Republic*, a full-length
investigation of δικαιοσύνη to which the notion of *isotes* has the most direct
and urgent relevance; on this account, if on no other, some consideration of *isonomia* was called for. Plato chose instead to ignore the concept
of *isotes* in Book IV, and to make no mention of *isonomia* except in the
hostile, satirical mood of Book VIII. The idea of taking over *isonomia*,
to make a new thing out of it in conformity with his own moral doctrine,
was clearly not to his liking. And we can see why not. He may well have
felt that a word so long and so deeply associated with democracy could
not be wrenched from its familiar associations and forced to serve a dia-
metrically opposite purpose without causing confusion and misunderstand-

---

[140] Which would involve the weighing of many data. The unplatonic use of
isonomia is only one, and by no means the strongest, of the reasons which have
led me to reject the authenticity of the Letter.

ing in the mind of the public. Did he regret this decision in later years? If so, he had a perfect opportunity to correct it in the *Laws*. Since he speaks now with a new appreciation of political equality[141] and propounds *in extenso* the doctrine of the two equalities, we might have expected him to make his peace on these new terms now at long last with *isonomia*. He chose instead to ignore it completely, though he had ample occasion to bring it into his discussion, particularly when he discussed democracy in Book III and then again when he defended proportional equality in Book VI. From this it would seem that the word either remained uncongenial to him or else had become uninteresting to him.

Would it not be strange then if we should find that in a work written before he composed, or while composing,[142] the *Laws*, Plato had already appropriated *isonomia*, and was now using it in the most familiar way, feeling no need to give even a word of explanation to warn his public that he has taken it upon himself to endow it with a sense radically different from the one it had carried for a hundred and fifty years or more? Such conduct would have been understandable [34] in a rhetorician, whose standards of integrity in the use of words, none too high at best, can be adjusted quasi-automatically to the exigencies of policy. But it is not of Isocrates that we are speaking now, but of Plato. Is such conduct understandable in him? Those who find it so should offer us their explanation.[143] [35]

141 Cf., e.g., 694A, 695C-D.

142 "It would seem reasonable to assume that the letter was completed by the end of 354 or the beginning of 353," G. R. Morrow, *Plato's Epistles* (revised edition, New York, 1962), p. 181.

143 I am much indebted to Professor Martin Ostwald who did me the kindness of reading a draft of this manuscript, correcting several mistakes, and making a number of useful suggestions. Now that his masterly study, *Nomos and the Beginnings of the Athenian Democracy* (Oxford, 1969), has appeared, I am encouraged to note the very substantial convergence of our interpretations of ἰσονομία. This, however, does not extend to the references to this term in the Seventh Epistle; the reader would be well advised to read Ostwald's note on ἰσονομία in this Epistle (whose authenticity he accepts) and see how he proposes to resolve (181–82) the problem I pose above.

9

Socratic Knowledge and
Platonic "Pessimism"*

(1957; SKPP)

THOUGH modern scholarship has given us several first-rate studies of the development of Plato's thought, these have been mainly concerned with his metaphysics and epistemology. Strange as it may seem, a book-length study of the growth of Plato's ethical theory has not yet been written. Mr. John Gould's recently published book[1] is welcome as a step in this direction, though it is hardly a systematic treatment of the subject and tolerates surprising gaps; for example, it has no serious treatment of the relation of happiness to virtue—a theme on which Plato has more to say from the *Protagoras* to the *Laws* than on any single other topic in his ethics. But Gould's study has many virtues of its own. It is written with spirit, imagination, a good sense of style, good knowledge of the Greek language, and greater acquaintance with recent writings on ethics than is customary among classical scholars.[2] I cannot stop to illustrate these merits. All I can do here is to give (in the next paragraph) a general

---

* Originally published in the *Philosophical Review* 66 (1957), 226–38. The original pagination appears in the text here in square brackets.

[1] John Gould, *The Development of Plato's Ethics* (New York, 1955), xii, 241 pp.

[2] As for his translations, they are often fresh and vivid, but get spoiled by a tendency to make the original louder than it is. εὖ ζῆν becomes "making a proper *use* of being alive" (p. 59); ἀληθεῖς δόξας βεβαίους, "a true outlook on the world, capable of withstanding the world's strains" (p. 80), and ἀδικωτάτους μὲν ὄντας καί ἀνοσιωτάτους καί ἀκολοστάτους καί ἀμαθεστάτους, "men who are

idea of the book's contents, and then proceed forthwith to criticism and discussion.

Part I deals with the early, Socratic, dialogues and is appropriately entitled "The Personal Ideal." Part II moves dramatically to the other extreme in Plato's life and thought. Against the Socratic vision of the good life as an utterly free individual adventure, it sets the morality of the *Laws*, authoritarian, inquisitorial, conformist, custom-ridden. Part III deals with the long, eventful interval between these two extremes. Its title is "Growth of a Reality Principle," and it describes Plato's progressive abandonment of "idealist morality," indeed of two such moralities—that of his teacher and the one he himself projected in Books III to VII of the *Republic*. The disillusionment [226] begins already in the *Republic*; its last three books are "a chronicle of decline . . . [which] displays the gradual abandonment of all that Plato values" (p. 182). As for the later dialogues, "pessimism is [their] distinguishing mark," and the *Timaeus* is taken as a "prelude to this group,[3] in making explicit the source of pessimism, the ever incomplete victory of Reason over Necessity" (p. 203).

I. SOCRATIC KNOWLEDGE

From Aristotle to F. M. Cornford, Gould argues, the Socratic parodox, "virtue is knowledge,"[4] has been misunderstood to mean that "moral virtue . . . is to be achieved only . . . by an intellectual insight into the nature of right and wrong" (p. 4). To correct this mistake he directs our attention to two uses of Socrates' word for knowledge, ἐπιστήμη (and its verb, ἐπίσταμαι): (i) to mean "confidence," "subjective certainty," or "conviction," as for example in Herodotus' remark about Dorieus, "He well ἠπίστατο that because of his valor he would get the kingship"

---

marked by the height of injustice, who cause revulsion in gods and men alike, who are plunged in the most violent of passions and in the depths of ignorance" (p. 65).

[3] Gould accepts (p. 202, n. 3) G. E. L. Owen's thesis (*Classical Quarterly* n.s. III[1953], 79 ff.) that the *Timaeus* was written much earlier than has been and still is generally believed by scholars.

[4] The formula (which does not occur as such in any of Plato's Socratic dialogues; the nearest thing to it is *Prt.* 361B4) is generally used to mean that virtue exists if and only if knowledge exists and probably would be so used by Socrates. Thus in "Courage is knowledge of what is and is not fearful" (*Prt.* 360D) the first "is" expresses a biconditional (see *UVP* below).

(5.24.1), though Herodotus knows, and says so in the next sentence, that Dorieus did *not* get it. Here ἐπίσταμαι is used idiomatically in a way which English usage would never allow: "ἐπίσταται *p*," unlike "he knows *p*," does *not* presuppose "*p* is true"; (ii) to mean "skill," "practical ability," using the verb in a way which can be reproduced in English only by adding "how," as in "I know how to swim," which in Greek would be simply "I know to swim." Putting (i) and (ii) together, Gould comes up with the thesis that "the *epistēmē* which Socrates envisaged was a form of knowing how, knowing, that is, how to be moral" (p. 7) and further that "since *epistēmē* does not imply contemplation of an object, but understanding, in the sense of an ability to act, it remains a purely subjective faith" (p. 15).

Let us start with sense (ii). This is a perfectly good sense for *epistēmē* and also for its twin *sophia* (wisdom)[5], and this part of Gould's thesis [227] would be true and valuable, if it did not lead him to ignore the "know that" sense, which is at least as frequent in Attic Greek and so important for Socrates that in many contexts it is the only one that makes sense of what he is saying. Try the "know how" sense in this sentence and see what you can make of it: "To fear death is nothing but to think oneself wise while one is not; for it is to think one knows the unknown" (*Ap.* 29A).

And there is more at issue here than mere linguistics. Think of the doctrine Socrates is expounding. If "virtue is knowledge" meant that "for the achievement of *aretē* what is required is a form of ability," Socrates would be saying here that people fear death only because they do not have the ability not to fear it, and what could be more trivial than that? Or, to continue the citation from Gould, "ability, comparable in some respects to the creative or artistic ability of potters, shoemakers, and the like"; the analogy with these practical arts, if dragged in here, would imply that the reason we fear death is that we have not acquired skill in meeting it, and what could be farther from Socrates' thought? What Socrates wants us to understand is that we fear death only because we have *mistaken beliefs*: we think we know death to be a great evil, greater than disgrace; if we so much as knew our ignorance, our fear of death would leave us. There is no getting away from "intellectualism" here. And is not the whole of Socrates' method of (a) testing knowledge, (b) inculcating virtue, predicated on nothing short of an "intellectualist" view of moral knowledge? In (a) the *elenchus* tests statements, *not* actions. A man's

---

[5] *Epistēmē* and *sophia* are almost perfectly interchangeable in the Socratic dialogues; cf., e.g., *sophia* in the definition of courage at *Prt.* 360D, *epistēmē* in the generalization at 361B.

claim to knowledge (moral or any other; it is all the same for Socrates) is refuted when, having said *p*, he then says (or implies) *q* which is shown to contradict *p*, or when he offers a definition of a term in *p* which is shown to be faulty. This done, Socrates feels no need to inspect the speaker's actions or to refer to them in any way, and he never once does so in a Platonic dialogue to disprove pretended knowledge.[6] In (b), to make his fellows better men is, as we all know, Socrates' great aim in life. The daily practice of the *elenchus* would have been irrelevant to this aim unless Socrates did believe that to do the only thing which the *elenchus* could hope to accomplish—to correct false beliefs, confused ideas, and wrong ways of thinking—was of itself to produce a necessary condition of good moral conduct. [*228*]

To recognize all this does not require one in the least to underplay the very different sense of *epistēmē* which Gould emphasizes in this book. On the contrary, Gould might very well have argued that it was just because Socrates could, and did, take the "know how" sense for granted all along, and because he used it ruthlessly in certain arguments (all those premised on the analogy between virtue and the crafts), that he felt the intellectualist thesis to be so plausible. This, of course, could not have happened if Socrates had ever distinguished the two senses of "know." Gould says he is "by no means sure" (p. 7) that he did, but we can surely say more. Throughout Plato's Socratic dialogues we see a man who uses "knowledge" constantly to explain other things but never once doubles back on this term to turn on it his "What is . . . ?" question.[7] This is no

---

[6] I am not saying that he *could not* have done so with good reason (e.g., told Pericles to his face the things he says about him at *Grg.* 515D ff.), but that he *did not*, which is ample proof that he did not *need* to. That Socratic knowledge *is* expressed in action, as Gould insists (p. 20), is importantly true; that it is "expressed *only* in action" (p. 52, my italics) is palpably false.

[7] Even when he is under urgent provocation to do so, as when he inquires into the possibility of "knowledge of knowledge and unknowledge" in the *Charmides* or is bombarded by the sophisms about knowing in the *Euthydemus*. The question he does raise is quite different: "What is *this* or *that* knowledge?" (e.g., *Chrm.* 165C; *Euthd.* 282E, 288D-E, 292D), and the answer he expects is one that will distinguish areas of knowledge (by their specific object and use), not *modes* of knowing. I agree with Gould (p. 38) against A. E. Taylor (*Plato* [London, 1949], p. 53) that what is said at *Chrm.* 165E3-166A2 is far from making the distinction between practical and theoretical knowledge, and I would add that if Plato had wished to ascribe this important distinction to Socrates, he would not have put it into the mouth of Critias, whose role in this dialogue is that of a pretentious and unclear thinker. Plato himself does not get at this distinction until much later (*Plt.* 258D, E).

accident. The investigation of knowledge had been heretofore (and for that matter continued to be in Plato) a dependency of ontological or cosmological inquiry.[8] In renouncing this kind of speculation Socrates denied himself the only apparatus available in his day for handling the "What is knowledge?" question. Hence his concept of knowledge was likely to be as uncritical and dogmatic as his concept of virtue was imaginative and free-ranging, and with as high a tolerance of ambiguity and as specious a sense of clarity as one would expect from mere common sense. This, I suggest, is of some little help in explaining how it was that Socrates came to believe his own paradox. Finding it obvious that a man could [229] not be just without "knowing justice"[9] (in the "know how" sense, which made this statement a truism) and equally obvious that one could not "know justice" if one could not talk about it intelligently, Socrates could conclude with perfect confidence that the latter kind of "knowing" is what one must have to be a just man. Thus the heart of his paradox could appear to him a certain conclusion from evidently true premises.

What of the element of "subjective faith," which Gould finds in Socratic "knowledge"? Here I must insist that the linguistic argument has *not* been made out. That this sense for the verb "know" does occur in Herodotus (though with a frequency of less than 15 percent)[10] is interesting. But where else does it occur? The only other example cited by Gould or the dictionary or anyone else is (once) in Heraclitus.[11] If there are instances of it in *Attic* Greek, they must be rare, for they have not been dug up yet. And as for the substantive, *epistēmē*, no example of it with this sense has yet been offered; to my knowledge, none exists. Even if it

---

[8] To this even Protagoras and Gorgias are no exception. They are both *interested* in the old problem of being and not-being, and Protagoras has a solution for it ("man is its measure"), while Gorgias thinks there can be none (because, even if being did exist it would be unknowable). Socrates is just not interested, which explains why in the two Socratic dialogues where Protagoras and Gorgias are the protagonists their ontological doctrines are not even *mentioned*.

[9] This is strained English, but possible Greek: εἰδὼς ὀνησίπολιν δίκαν, Simonides *ap.* Plato, *Prt.* 346C; οἶσθα τὸ μὴ ἀδικεῖν, Aesch., *Eum.* 85.

[10] See J. E. Powell (Cambridge, 1938), *s.v.* ἐπίσταμαι.

[11] B57. Gould (p. 10, n. 6) seems to think *epistamenoi* in Heraclitus B19 also has this sense. But this would spoil the sense of the fragment, which is that these people (presumably, the common run of mankind) cannot hear or talk with *understanding* (cf. B1, B73, B107), not with *confidence*, of which they have altogether too much.

did exist, how little effect it would have on general usage is evident from
this bit of dialogue in the *Gorgias* (454D):

> Socrates: If someone asked, "Gorgias, is there such a thing as false
> conviction [*pistis*] as well as true?" I fancy you would say, "Yes."
> Gorgias: Of course.
> Socrates: Well then, is there false, as well as true, knowledge [*epistēmē*]?
> Gorgias: Never.[12]

Note that Gorgias' "never" has not been elicited by *argument*. All that
Socrates has to do is to set the two words, *pistis* and *epistēmē*, side by side
before him, and Gorgias feels the difference right away, with no temptation to counter with, "Don't we sometimes mean *pistis* by *epistēmē*?"

But why look for faith in Socratic knowledge in the first place? Gould
would like to resolve Socrates' other paradox, "Knowledge is [230]
virtue";[13] and who would not? Certainly Socrates' claim that knowledge
is such a "powerful and lordly" thing (*Prt.* 352B) that nothing can keep a
man who knows the good from doing it would be easier to believe if for
"knowledge" we were to read "knowledge *and* faith." But what sort of
faith would this be? Gould seems to have two candidates for this job:
(1) One is something he likens to Kierkegaard's notion of truth or faith,
quoting these lines from him as "an excellent commentary on Plato's
concept of certainty" (p. 21): "What is truth but to live for an idea?
Ultimately everything must rest upon a postulate; but the moment it is
no longer outside [a man], and he lives in it, then and only then does it
cease to be a postulate for him." So far as I can judge from the texts, this
sort of thing—a conviction whose certainty derives from a consciously
irrational commitment—never even occurred to Socrates (or to any other
Greek philosopher), and if it had, he would not have recommended it to
anybody, still less have dignified it by the name of "knowledge." (2) The
other is something Gould describes as "the practical assurance that the
possession of a technical skill alone can give" (p. 66). Here is our good
friend, "know how," in a further, confidence-building role—a somewhat
anticlimactic sense for "faith," but, I suppose, not impossible. Still, how
is this going to resolve the paradox? Suppose my truth-telling know-how

---

[12] Gould alludes to this passage at p. 25, but with no apparent awareness
that it is damaging to his contention that the term *epistēmē* retains the sense of
"purely subjective 'faith,' " (p. 15) in the Socratic dialogues, among which
he includes the *Gorgias*.

[13] Cf. n. 4 above.

to be of the finest; would this, added to my knowledge that a given lie is wicked, that wickedness corrupts my soul, and so on, make me so invulnerable to "rage, pleasure, grief, love, terror" that I shall never tell that lie under stress? When we read the *Apology* and the *Crito* we see with reverent wonder a man who had achieved this kind of invulnerability, and I would gladly agree with Gould that Socrates did not get it from purely "intellectual" knowledge and that its source is better described by "faith" (though certainly not in Kierkegaard's sense of the word)[14] than by anything else. But to say that Socrates had faith in many things, in knowledge most of all, is [231] not to say that what *he* called "knowledge" was faith or that he looked to anything but knowledge for *his* explanation of moral certainty. If in this he failed to understand himself, our task is to account for the misunderstanding or, at the least, to take account of it.

II. PLATONIC "PESSIMISM"

On Part II, a stimulating discussion of the *Laws*, I cannot comment, for I must save the remaining space for the tale of Plato's "pessimism" and "despair" in Part III. I have grave misgivings about this, and I must try to explain why.

Consider the *Timaeus*. Its "central utterance," I quite agree with Gould (p. 194), is that "intelliegence governs necessity by persuading her to direct the greater part of what happens in [this world] towards the best" (48A). What reason can there be for construing this as an expression of cosmic despondence? That Plato thinks of *anankē* as (a) inherently irrational and as (b) never completely brought under the dominance of reason is of itself quite inconclusive. For even so, if Plato thinks well of the results achieved by the Demiurge *in spite of* this aspect of *anankē*, his outlook cannot be called pessimistic. Well, how does he think of the results? In the concluding sentence of the dialogue he speaks of the created world as

[14] Kierkegaard's boundless admiration for Socrates ("the only *man* I admiringly recognize as a teacher," "Attack upon 'Christendom,'" *Kierkegaard Anthology*, ed. by R. Bretall [Princeton, 1951], p. 466) did not lead him to credit Socrates with "faith." He is quite explicit about this. The first thing he mentions in his "advocate upon Socrates" in the conclusion of his *Philosophical Fragments* (Princeton, 1936), p. 93, is that "we have here assumed a new organ: Faith." Cf. *Fear and Trembling* (New York, 1954), p. 79: Socrates did make the "movement of infinity" which "goes before faith"; but faith, which only enters the scene by "virtue of the absurd," Socrates "never reached."

"a perceptible god, greatest, most excellent, most beautiful, most perfect." Does this sound like a cry of despair? Perhaps what is worrying Gould is that, on Plato's metaphysical premises, any superlatives lavished on this world carry a tacit reservation. No matter how "fair" the world may be, it is necessarily less so than the trascendent original of which this world and everything in it can only be a "copy"; the lover of "true" Beauty will never be satisfied with anything he meets this side of eternity. But before drawing any rash conclusions one should note that, like those "reversible" figures in psychology, Plato's cosmological pattern is systematically ambiguous. One can look at this world thinking "It is *only* a copy" and feeling a kind of malaise or nostalgia, an impatience with the best it can offer; or, with equally good warrant from the metaphysical design, one can say to oneself, "But it is an excellent copy, such as only supreme intelligence joined with perfect goodness could produce" and rejoice at one's good luck to find oneself in a world as good as this. Both of these moods can be found in Plato, sometimes in the same dialogue, as for example in the *Phaedo*, whose first half breathes more *Weltflucht* than anything Plato ever wrote, while the "autobiographical" passage (96–99) is so confident of the world's goodness that it propounds a new method of natural inquiry which [232] will explain phenomena by showing "that it is best for them to be as they are" (98A, Hackforth's translation).

Gould takes no notice of this ambivalence, which marks not only the ontological scheme but also its epistemological pendant, the knowledge-opinion analogue to the model-copy, being-becoming polarities. "Once Plato accepted . . . the belief that in this world and about this world no certainty can be achieved, the way was open for the full feeling of despair; indeed, there was hardly any alternative" (p. 163). But surely there *was* an alternative: that certainty about this world is not needed for any purpose which Plato considered essential. Have not many modern philosophers renounced "the quest for certainty" about the world without noticeable gloom? Why not Plato? Gould argues that "on the premises of Book V [of the *Republic*], it is impossible that any understanding of the moral Forms should ever strengthen the validity of judgments about . . . moral phenomena" (*loc. cit.*). It has to be shown, not just asserted, that this is "impossible," if it really is. Plato's thought on this point may be reconstructed as follows. Phenomena resemble the Forms; so, if we know with certainty that Form *A* entails Form *B*, we count with good security on the A-B nexus in the phenomenal world, hence with vastly higher chances of making true predictions than the mere empiric who goes on nothing better than habitual association.[15] This thinking may be faulty; if so, it will be for the critic to explain where and why it goes wrong. But until this has been done, to say that "in that [viz., phenomenal] world Plato has already resigned his hopes of achieving an ultimately satisfying power of decision making" (*loc. cit.*) is either premature (if "already resigned" is short for the critical estimate "should have resigned") or false (if it stands for the historical assertion that Plato himself did any such thing at this or any other time).[16] [*233*]

Now there is one hope which, as we know from the *Laws*,[17] Plato did resign before his death: the one based on the belief that the office of the philosopher king was not above the capacities of human nature. Such an office would involve absolute power, "unaccountable" (*anhypeuthynos*) in the Greek sense of the word: not subject to legal control. Plato would have known from his teens the widespread Greek conviction that such power is too great for human frailty. He would have read this in Herodotus[18] and would have heard it from many other sources. Nevertheless, he dared believe that it was false, and on this belief he rested the slim prospects of the realization of his ideal society.[19] We can imagine

[15] For the state of the empiric, see *R.* 516C, D: he can predict (only) on the basis of customary conjunctions. For the state of the philosophers, see *R.* 520C (cf. 540C): knowledge of the Forms, supplemented by subsequent experience, will enable the philosophers "to see a thousand times better than those who live there always," i.e., the empirics. (Gould ignores these two passages when he says, p. 164, n. 3, it is "in doubt" whether Plato believed that knowledge of the Forms would facilitate moral problem solving in this world.) And since Plato thought of phenomena as copies or resemblances of the Forms, he could only have thought of the philosopher's advantage over the empiric in some such terms as those suggested in the above reconstruction.

[16] If "ultimately satisfying" were taken to mean "as intellectually satisfying as is knowledge of Forms" the statement would be true, but only trivially so, for Plato does not need this kind of "satisfaction" in dealing with the phenomenal world. If his philosophers could "see a thousand times better" than others, why should this not be satisfying enough?

[17] See below, n. 25.

[18] Especially at 3.80, in the "Debate on Constitutions." Cf. *American Journal of Philology*, LXIV (1953), 358 ff.

[19] "Our plan is difficult—we have admitted as much—but not impossible," *R.* 499C, Cornford's translation (cf. 502B). Though Plato does not discuss in the *Republic* the Herodotean (and general) view as such, he is well aware of the extent to which his own doctrine, with its contrary assumptions, would shock the Greek Public: this is "the greatest wave," 473C, greater even than that produced by his proposals to elevate women to the highest offices and to abolish the private family among Guardians ("first" and "second waves"

how hard he would find it to come around to the general view after all, and we would naturally like to know just when he found himself compelled to do so, and with what implications for his general outlook. Since the only dialogue Plato devoted to political philosophy between the *Republic* and the *Laws* is the *Politicus*, the inquiry may well be narrowed to the question whether the change for which we are looking is in evidence there.[20] Gould apparently thinks that it is, for he speaks of "Plato's despair of ever finding 'the man to rule [234] as a true man, with *epistēmē*' (*Plt.* 301D1-2)" (p. 214). I am convinced that this opinion is wrong; and since it is shared by scholars of the highest eminence,[21] I should like to cite the passage on which this opinion largely rests[22] and comment briefly on its import. Here is a literal translation of it:

(1) It is for this reason, we say, that tyranny, kingship, oligarchy, aristocracy, and democracy have arisen: because of men's mistrust

---

respectively, 457C). His rejection of the general Greek view is implied both by his assertions of the possibility of philosopher kings in Book VI and by the fact that he ignores the "corruption by power" theme in Books VIII and IX: it is not mentioned where we would most expect it, in the account of the start of the degeneration (545D ff.) in the description of the tyrant in IX.

[20] The political curtain raiser in the *Timaeus* and its complement in the *Critias* also are interesting. Here I note (a) that in the *Critias* the ideal state of Athens' imaginary past duplicates all the main features of the *Republic* but fails to mention the philosopher kings, while (b) the kings of Atlantis used wisely and virtuously their autocratic power only so long as "the divine nature lasted in them," 120E1 (cf. 121A7), but became corrupted as soon as "their mortal nature got the upper hand," 121B1. I take (a) as a slight, and (b) as a strong, indication that Plato had already abandoned the doctrine of the *Republic*. For the importance of (b) see below, n. 25.

[21] E.g., Lewis Campbell (1867, secs. III and IV of his Introduction to the *Politicus*); Wilamowitz-Moellendorff (1948, 459–60); A. E. Taylor (1949, 402–403); Grube (1935, 279–84); Diès (1935, sec. VI of his Introduction to the Budé *Politicus*, and his note on 301D-E); Shorey (1933, 313–14). For the contrary view, see in particular Skemp (1935, 51 ff., with much of which I agree).

[22] The other alleged evidence is in the Myth, but only on the supposition that the divine kings of the age of Cronus stand for Plato's philosopher kings, for which I can find no warrant, since the former are not philosophers and the latter are *not* likened to gods (*Plt.* 303B3-5, which has been taken to say so, e.g., by Campbell and Diès, *ad loc.*, simply says that the "correct" constitution is as different from the "incorrect" ones as god is from men, which is a very different thing from saying that its *ruler* differs from others as god from men; the "god among men" expression for the superior man is only in Aristotle, *Pol.* 1284A10-11, to which the *Politicus* passage has been carelessly assimilated).

of that one monarch, their disbelief that anyone could ever become worthy of his office, so as to be willing and able to govern with virtue and knowledge, dispensing rightly justice and piety to all, [their assumption that,] on the contrary, he would injure, kill, ruin whomsoever of us he pleases.

(2) For if such a man as the one we are talking about would arise, he would be loved and dwell [amongst us] governing happily the only exactly right constitution.

(3) But now when, as we say, no such men arise in states, as do queen bees in hives, whose unique superiority, physical and mental, would be immediately apparent, men are obliged, it seems, to come together and legislate, running after the tracks of the truest constitution.[23]

Many scholars have done just what Gould has done with (1): taken it as though it were an expression of *Plato's* "mistrust" and "disbelief."[24] [235] Only a second look at the text is needed to satisfy anybody that all Plato is stating here is that this is how "men" (i.e., the Greek public) have felt in this matter. The fact that Plato *reports* this common view (that of Herodotus and so many others) is not, as such, the slightest evidence that he agrees with it. As a matter of fact, he goes on at (2) to dissociate himself from it to the extent of saying, in effect, "This view is wrong: if such and such a man (i.e., one who has the 'kingly science') were to turn up, he *would* do the very thing these people think *no one* could do: he would hold absolute power without degenerating into a tyrant."[25]

---

[23] 301C6-E4. This is a carelessly written passage, one of Plato's worst, a poor sequel to the brilliance af 294A ff. At (1) Plato talks as though he meant the absurdity that mistrust of his (Plato's) ideal ruler accounted for the origins of existing states, all of them, including *tyranny!* At (3) he talks as though legislation by assemblies were the only present-day alternative to ideal monarchy, which is surprising, to say the least.

[24] Though only when they are arguing. The moment they shift to paraphrase they inadvertently correct their own mistake. See, e.g., Diès, *op. cit.*, pp. 13 and 40 of his introduction.

[25] Diès misses the point of (2) when he remarks *ad loc*, "Voir *Lois* 875A-D *la même opposition entre l'idéal rêvé* (εἴ ποτέ τις ἀνθρώπων φύσει ἱκανός) *et la réalité* (νῦν δὲ οὐ γάρ ἐστιν οὐδαμοῦ οὐδαμῶς)." It is not *la même opposition* at all. What is said at (2) above is that if there were a man "such as we are talking about" (i.e., one "who rules with real knowledge," 301B5), he would rule virtuously (without the restraints of law). What is said at *Laws* 875C,D is that if there were a ruler who had knowledge *and* the required "nature" (such as to withstand the corruptions of power), his rule would (be so excellent as) not (to) require the restraints of law. The two statements differ roughly as would "If *A*, then *C*"

But what of (3)? Is this not, after all, Plato's own endorsement of the common view expressed at (1)? By no means. All Plato says at (3) is (to translate him still more literally), "No such man is arising"; the tense is the present continuous, and the statement is the extremely obvious one that this sort of thing is not happening now,[26] which is vastly different from what is implied by the general view at (1), that [236] is, that this *could never* happen. The latter is just what Plato would have to assert to renounce the doctrine of the *Republic*; and the only reasonable basis for asserting it would be that this is contrary to *human* nature, which is precisely what Plato does say in the *Laws*, and not once but three times over.[27] Not only does he fail to say such a thing in the *Politicus*; he says quite positively something else whose decisive relevance for the point at issue is not noticed by Gould or, so far as I know, by anyone else: he declares that the best of the *law-abiding* constitutions is the (ordinary, unphilosophical) kingship (302E); and since here no one could doubt that Plato is talking about states that do (or can) exist, he is clearly implying that the capacity to bear absolute power without corruption is well within the bounds of

---

from "If *A* and *B*, then *C*." The vital difference is "*B*": This—a mortal nature incorruptible by autocratic power—is the very thing that has been said twice before in the *Laws* (691C, 713C) to be impossible of fulfillment; its impossibility is reasserted at 875B, and then again at 875D (with the ineffectual exception, ἀλλ' ἢ κατὰ βραχύ, i.e., with exceptions too slight to be worth talking about). Contrariwise, the *Politicus* says nothing about "*B*"; the nearest approach to it (though without the reference to *human nature*, which is so significant in all three passages in the *Laws*) is at (1) above, which is *not* stated as Plato's view.

[26] By adding the queen-bee simile Plato says in effect, "And there is a good reason why we are not getting such men: we do not have the social matrix ["hive"] to produce them." In the *Republic* he had used the queen-bee simile at 520B to express the thought that his philosophers will be the products of the right nurture and education, while earlier (489E ff.) he had stressed the fact that men with fine gifts perish in the absence of the right social environment "unless saved by some divine chance" (492A). Cf. G. Mueller (1951), 164. As Diès noticed, the queen-bee simile also occurs in Xenophon, *Cyr.* 5.1.24, where Cyrus is said to be "king by nature no less than the leader of the bees, growing up in the hive." Plato's remark may well involve a sideswipe at Xenophon's absurd idealization of Cyrus, who is no queen bee for Plato ("a good and patriotic general, but without the rudiments of a correct education," *Laws* 694C).

[27] In the passages cited at n. 25, above. The last (875B,C) is particularly significant because it says so explicitly that even a man who starts with "adequate," i.e., philosophical, knowledge and then gets "unaccountable, autocratic" power will be led to ruin by his "mortal nature."

human nature.[28] If even this poor, second-rate autocrat, this king without the kingly science, can hold such power without degenerating, how much more so the philosopher king? We can, therefore, conclude with reasonable confidence that Plato's early faith in enlightened absolutism was still intact when he wrote the *Politicus*.

Just when it crashed must be a guess. Mine would put it after Plato's final encounter with Dionysius the Younger, when he saw the ugly face of autocratic power at closer and more painful quarters than at any other time in his life.[29] But whether then or a few years earlier or later, the disillusionment came when he was more than 60—66 or 67, if my guess is right. At that age one does not go about finding a new philosophy. Whatever intellectual resources Plato could muster to meet this crisis would have to come from the ideas he had lived with all along. And if these had favored or indulged the impulse to despair, they would have reinforced the natural human response to the collapse of a hope he had cherished during the greater part of his adult life. We [237] would have then seen him turning away more than ever from the world, dropping in weariness or disgust all practical projects for making this world less stupid and less evil. Is this what happened? In the *Laws* Plato is as much in earnest about reforming the world as he had ever been, and far more patient than ever in his efforts to understand it. He turns in his old age to an empirical study of the legal institutions of Athens and other states with an attentiveness one would never have suspected in the author of the *Republic* or the *Politicus* and carries out from these researches whole cartloads of salvageable matter for his model state.[30] The *Timaeus*, which, I have no doubt, was written not long before the *Laws*, reflects a similar interest in the world. Plato still refuses on principle to call empirical inquiry "knowledge." But he pursues studies like physics and physiology

[28] Which he repudiates in the *Laws*, 690D ff. The kings of Argos and Messene degenerated, while those of Sparta did not, *because* the power of the former remained absolute, while that of the latter was "clipped" by the twofold kingship, the senate, and the ephors.

[29] Not before this (for had he already reached the views of the *Laws*, he would not have been likely to undertake the journey) nor after (for his other, and perhaps greater, shock, the assassination of Dion in 354, would not have taught him this particular lesson; Plato did not look on Dion as an autocrat corrupted by power but as a good man who was undone because he underestimated the villainy of his associates, *Ep.* VII, 351D,E).

[30] A point which has been noticed often; see, most recently, G. R. Morrow (1954, 8–9)—an essay to which I am very much indebted, as is evident in this paragraph, though I cannot accept its interpretation of the Nocturnal Council.

with such gusto, such inspired imagination, that we feel transported back to the fifth century, to the world of the "Presocratics." The eagerness to understand the world so far as it can be understood, and to improve it so far as it can be improved, is the dominant mood of his last years. Clouds of weariness move across this sky, as in his famous image of man as a "puppet of the gods,"[31] but they never darken it. There is much "acceptance of reality" here, to use one of Gould's favorite expressions, but it is not pessimistic in the main, and this largely because Plato never stops thinking of the actual world as a copy of an ideal model by a divine craftsman, and one which can always be improved by human imitators. Those who cannot bring themselves to believe that Plato could have retained the Theory of Forms after seeing and failing to solve its logical difficulties would do well to remember how many nonlogical reasons Plato had for refusing to let it go. Here we see its model-copy way of looking at the relation of the ideal to the actual as a remedy for the impulse to despair. If the world is *only* a copy, one does not expect it to be perfect and can assimilate new discoveries of its limitations without shattering disillusionment. And if it *is* a copy of perfection, man can expect enough of order and goodness in it to sustain his efforts to make it a little more perfect than he found it. [*238*]

[31] *Laws* 803B–804B.

PART II

Logic, Epistemology, Metaphysics

10

The Unity of the Virtues
in the *Protagoras**

(1971; UVP)

MY main task in this paper will be to tackle a problem in the *Protagoras* ∗
whose solution is long overdue—the one posed by the fact that in stating
and defending his doctrine of "the unity of the virtues"[1] Socrates employs

∗ Reprinted from the *Review of Metaphysics* 25 (1972), 415–58, with sub-
stantial additions and corrections in both text and notes. For useful criticism
I am indebted to colleagues at the University of Washington; to members of
my Plato seminar at Princeton (especially Terry Irwin, Edward Johnson, and
Paul Woodruff); and to others (including Charles Kahn, Glenn Morrow, and
H. S. Thayer).

[1] The Socratic doctrine is presented as one of the two options between
which Protagoras is required to choose in 329C–330B6, and then again, when
the debate resumes after a break, in 349B1-D1. The defense is presented in the
form of separate arguments for the unity of four pairs of virtues: (1) Justice
and Piety (330B6–331B8); (2) Wisdom and Temperance (332A4–333B6);
(3) Temperance and Justice (333B8–334C6); (4) Courage and Wisdom
(349D2–350C5). (I capitalize the names of the virtues and "Virtue" wherever
each of these terms functions as the proper name of an *eidos* or *idea*.) I shall
have nothing to say of the argument for (3) which is sabotaged by Protagoras
and is left incomplete. I shall have occasion to analyze the argument for (1)
and a part of the one for (2). In the case of the one for (4) I shall be able to
comment only on its terminal section; analysis of the rest of the argument will
not be germane to the matters with which I shall be concerned here (I have
offered a sketch of it in Vlastos, 1956, xxxii–xxxv). Nor will I have occasion
to work through the sequel to this argument (351B ff.), where the "Socratic
Paradox" is defended (for this see Vlastos, 1969).

formulae which seem hopelessly at odds both with common sense and with the procedural assumptions of his own dialectic. The proportions of this problem are obscured in standard discussions of our passage. Some scholars act as though they were blissfully unaware of its difficulties. The grit in the Platonic text gets washed out of their bland paraphrases of Socrates' views; one who has not worked through the original with stubborn attention to its wording would not know, after reading them, what is the problem I am talking about or even that there is a problem.[2] When the perplexities which bedevil the Socratic formulae are recognized in the scholarly literature, it is rarely with the resolution to untie the knots:[3]

[2] A. E. Taylor (1937, 247–48, 257) is a good example. The troublesome formulations (329C6–330B6 and 349B1-D1) of Socrates' views—those I shall be calling the "Unity Thesis" and the "Similarity Thesis"—are reported only in the form of questions put to Protagoras; Socrates' own stand is reduced without argument first (247) to the innocuous thesis that "The principle of goodness will be exactly the same in whatever relation of life it is displayed" and then (248) to the unproblematic formula which I shall be calling the "Biconditionality Thesis." Nothing better in Shorey (1933, 125 and 129, with notes): all three theses appear only in the form of non-committal questions. Of Shorey's references to other dialogues only the one to *Laches* 198A is at all helpful; *Laches* 199C-E would have been more to the point, though neither this nor any of the others really explains the formulae in the *Prt.* passage, whose apparent perversity Shorey ignores. One of them would have surfaced on p. 129, where Shorey represents Socrates as "proceed[ing] to identify courage, too, with wisdom," *if* Shorey were not using "identify" with deplorable looseness, as shown by his allusion to the definition of Courage by Nicias in the *Laches* (194E–195A): there Courage is not "identified" with Wisdom but with a species of it (knowledge of things to be dreaded and dared); to identify X with a species of Y is a far cry from identifying X with Y.

[3] Among the rare exceptions I might mention Gallop (1961), Savan (1964), and Crombie (1962, 233–35). I have found Gallop's detailed analysis of argument (1) particularly helpful, in spite of many disagreements (see notes 13, 31, and 84 below). Crombie comes closest to explaining the true meaning of the "Unity of the Virtues": ". . . the various virtue-expressions are so closely interrelated in meaning that in so far as any one of them can be properly predicated of a given thing, there is some sense in which all the others may be also." I dare say that if Crombie had not been content to say "there is some sense" and leave it at that, but had probed the Platonic text until he found the required sense, his results would have been much the same as mine. In that case, he would not have represented Socrates as holding that "wisdom and temperance are the same thing" (234), without indicating that the obvious sense of this sentence (that they are *the same virtue*) Socrates would have been the first to repudiate and would not have dreamed of trying to prove (as he in

one finds scholars excusing themselves from the attempt by implying, or
hinting, that Socrates could not really have meant the outrageous things
he says, and that he put them up only to test Protagoras and expose the
sophist's powerlessness to diagnose perversities in the Socratic theses and
fallacies used in their defense.[4] These scholars, I trust, would agree that
to cast Socrates in such a role—allowing him, in effect, to fight sophistry
with sophistry—is a desperate expedient.[5] There would be no need of
resorting to it if we could understand the Socratic formulae in a way
which purges them of their offensive features. I believe we can, and my
first and major task will be to show how. A spin-off of the undertaking
will be a new account of the two notorious sentences in our passage—

---

fact does not; as I trust will be made clear in this essay, none of Socrates'
arguments purport to prove that different virtues are the same virtue).

[4] Paul Friedländer (1964, 19–20, 26–28, and notes) concedes that Socrates
appears to have staked out an indefensible thesis ("an exaggerated form of
unity [of the virtues], unity as strict identity" [19]), but implies that in so doing
Socrates is indulging "a peculiarly iridescent irony, hard to grasp" (19), and
that his arguments are deliberately fallacious: the one for the unity of Piety
and Justice is an "artificially constructed piece of nonsense" (20), the one for
the unity of Wisdom and Temperance employs an inference that is a "conscious
deception on the part of Socrates—or an exercise in logic for the reader" (20).
(Shorey too [1903, n. 117] thinks the argument deliberately fallacious, designed
to "trip up" Protagoras). A more complex view is taken by R. E. Allen (1970,
82, 93–99). He says that "the *Protagoras* maintains a studied ambiguity" on
the question whether the virtues "are one in definition, or one in that they
introduce each other and cannot be detached"; "it does not choose between
the alternatives" (99). He appears to think that the point of the first alternative
is polemical: Socrates "attempts to lead Protagoras to admit that the virtues
are all names for the same thing, . . . synonyms" (94) and proceeds to defend
that thesis with arguments each of which "is fallacious, and some of them
blatantly and scandalously fallacious" (94)—all this in order to show up the
fact that Protagoras, "although he claims to teach virtue, does not know what
virtue is" (95).

[5] It is widely assumed that, for good purposes (pedagogical or polemical),
of his own, the Platonic Socrates does not scruple to profess to believe propositions he thinks false and to defend them by sophistical arguments. I reject this
assumption, holding it to be inconsistent with what we learn in the Platonic
corpus about Socrates' conception of the philosophic life and about his
personal character. I count it a merit of the interpretation I shall be defending
that it does not require us to suppose that Socrates would ever (knowingly, and
in a serious vein) assert categorically a false premise or endorse a fallacious
argument.

"Justice is just," "Piety is pious"—with implications for the vexed problem of "self-predication" in Plato.

I. THE THREE THESES

A careful reading of the initial posing of the issue to be debated with Protagoras (329C2-330B6) and of its subsequent restatement when the debate resumes after a break (349A8-C5) will show that Socrates employs three distinct formulae, only the first of which answers at all closely to the term "Unity of the Virtues" which has been commonly used in the scholarly literature as a label for the position which Socrates upholds in the debate. The other two formulae, perfectly distinguishable from the first (which I shall call the "Unity Thesis"),[6] I shall call the "Similarity" and "Biconditionality" Theses. I shall discuss the three theses seriatim. But let me emphasize from the start that they are not treated in the text as logically disjoint tenets, but as successive moments in the elucidation

* of a single doctrine. That is how Protagoras himself understands them. At no point does he try to drive a wedge between them or play off one against another.[7] He accepts them as complementary expressions of a theory which he rejects and combats as a whole.

1. The Unity Thesis

Socrates starts off by asking:

* * Is Virtue one [thing], and are Justice, Temperance and Piety parts of it? Or are all those [words] I have just mentioned names of the same [thing], which is one [thing]? (329C6-D1)

---

[6] There is some awkwardness in keeping "Unity of the Virtues" as the traditional label for the whole doctrine (this is so common in the scholarly literature that it would be confusing to drop it now) and using the "Unity Thesis" to designate the first of its three major articulations. But I have been unable to hit on a happier label for the first Thesis; "Synonymy" most certainly will *not* do, for the reason I shall explain.

[7] Which is particularly striking in view of his strenuous (and perfectly understandable) objection (331B8-E4) to the vagueness of the Similarity Thesis, while he never faults the Biconditionality Thesis on this score, rejecting it firmly and unequivocally on first hearing (contrast οὐδαμῶς, etc., in 329E5 with the more hesitant, Ἐκείνως μοι φαίνεται . . . in 329D8, in relation to the Similarity Thesis).

The options he is putting before Protagoras are

[A] Virtue is one thing, and Justice, Temperance, etc. are parts of it.
[B] "Virtue," "Justice," "Temperance," etc. are all names of the same thing.

These options are exclusive: Protagoras must choose between them. Since he is expected to choose—and does choose—[A], one is tempted to think that Socrates, as his adversary, has formulated in [B] the option *he* would take if faced with the same choice. I submit that this temptation must be resisted for two reasons: In the first place, [B] is put up as the alternative to [A], and [A] is *standard Socratic doctrine;*[8] therefore, on this   * point there can be no difference between him and Protagoras: confronting the same alternatives, he too would have picked [A]. In the second place, we can see what happens in the immediate sequel. Socrates' next question is,

Are they [the virtues] parts
[C] like the parts of a face . . . or
[D] like the parts of [a bar of] gold . . . ? (329D4-6)

Here the truth of [A]—the part-whole relation between Justice, Temper-   ** ance, etc., and Virtue—is presupposed by both options: both [C] and [D] fall squarely within [A]. So in opting for [D] Socrates remains committed to [A] no less than does Protagoras. This shows, once again, that he had not meant to endorse [B] against [A] in the first place.

It follows that we cannot take [B] as a definitive statement of the Unity Thesis which Socrates will uphold against Protagoras: if put in this ultra-strong form, Socrates would not have championed it. The formulation that does express his view comes later, when what has been at issue in the debate is formally restated as follows:

These [words], "Wisdom" and "Temperance" and "Courage" and "Justice" and "Piety"—five names—do they apply to one thing   *** (ἐπὶ ἑνὶ πράγματί ἐστιν)?[9] Or is there, for each of these names, a sep-

[8] That Virtue is a "whole" and that Justice, Temperance, etc. are its "parts" is unequivocally affirmed and strongly emphasized in the *Meno* (78D-79E): it is the doctrine on which the elenchus pivots. There is just one passage in the whole of the Platonic corpus which might lend color to the (virtually self-refuting) view that each of the virtues is not a part, but the whole, of Virtue: the argument in *La.* 197E ff. On this see the Appendix to this essay, below.

[9] In the two expressions,

(1) "names of one and the same thing," used in 329D1, and

arate[10] essence underlying each—a thing having its own individual power (πρᾶγμα ἔχον ἑαυτοῦ δύναμιν ἕκαστον)?[11]

Here we see Socrates putting the question in a form which is not associated with the denial of [A]. The question now is simply: Do all of these names apply to the same thing? Or must each apply exclusively to its own peculiar "essence"? Socrates takes the first, Protagoras the second, of these options.

This division is surprising. One would certainly have expected Socrates to join Protagoras in maintaining that each of the five names applies to a distinct "thing" or "essence". To deny this and affirm that, on the contrary, each of the five "applies to one thing" would be normally under-

---

(2) "names applying to one thing" (literally, "names on one thing"), used in 349B (twice),

I detect an importantly different nuance in meaning: Unlike (1), (2) sustains the ambiguity in the Greek use of "name" (to be discussed in II.1 below: proper name or descriptive predicate) in such a way that to assert (2) of five names could be understood to mean either

(2a) that these five names are all proper names of the same object, or
(2b) that the five names are either proper names *or* descriptive predicates of it.

The difference between (2a) and (2b) is of the utmost consequence: (2a)
* restricts one to a single nominatum; (2b) does not, leaving open the possibility that there are several nominata (five of them in 349B: the five virtues), each of them named by all five names, but not named in the same way by all (thus each of the nominata might have one of the five names as its proper name, while being named descriptively by the other four). I take the wording in (2) to be inconclusive as between readings (2a) and (2b), and opt for (2b) which has the sterling merit of saving the hypothesis that *there are five virtues*. I shall be arguing that (2b) is just what Socrates has in view and that excellent sense can thus be made of (2). (1), on the other hand, would be distinctly less hospitable to such an interpretation. To say of five names that all of them "are names of one and the same thing" comes much closer to saying that all five are proper names of the same object, thus locking one into (2a), to the exclusion of (2b). That is why, I suggest, Socrates associates himself strongly with (2) but, as I have argued above, never commits himself to (1).

[10] So Jowett and Guthrie for ἴδιος, whose literal sense is "private" (ἴδιος is the standard antonym of κοινός, "common").

[11] I cut off the last clause of the question in 349B1-6, "no one of which is such as another," because at that point it spills over into the Similarity Thesis. This is one of several points in the text where the rhetoric displays the assumption that the two theses are variant expressions of the same doctrine: Socrates passes without explanation from the one to the other within a single period here; he does the same again in B6–C5.

stood as implying that (i) the five virtues are *the same virtue* and (ii) that their names are *synonyms*.[12] This is how Socrates has often been understood today.[13] But he could hardly have wished to make either of these claims. Of their "identity" there could be no question. What Socrates says of Piety in the *Euthyphro*—that it is a single ἰδέα, which recurs self-identically "in" every pious act (5D1-2) and can be used as a "standard" (παράδειγμα) by looking to which we can tell whether a given act is or is not pious (6E3-6)—he would say, *mutatis mutandis*, of every one of the other four virtues. How then could he possibly tolerate, let alone uphold, the notion that each is *identical* with each? Could one think of him, for instance, conceding that if Euthyphro were to give him the definiens of Courage, he could use *that* as a "standard" by which to judge whether Euthyphro's prosecution of his father was, or was not, pious? As for claiming that the names of the five virtues were all synonyms, that would imply that any of those five words can be freely interchanged in any sentence (in a transparent context)[14] without changing its sense or truth. Try substituting "Courage" for "Piety" in

(1) "Piety is that *eidos* in virtue of which all pious actions are pious" (*Euthphr.* 6D),

[12] That two expressions which have the same reference may differ in sense has become since Frege a commonplace of semantic theory. But such a distinction is never mentioned in the Platonic corpus. For Plato words get their sense *through* their reference. So if two Form-naming words are said to apply to the same "thing" or "essence" (and, by implication, to the same *eidos*), there would be a strong *prima facie* implication that they are meant to be synonymous, unless there were a clear reason to the contrary (such as the one I shall be presenting in the sequel: that only one of the two will apply referringly as the proper name of the nominee, while the other only applies descriptively).

[13] For (i): Friedländer ("unity as strict identity"), quoted in n. 4, above. Gigon (1946, 139 *et passim*) represents Socrates as demonstrating "the identity of the virtues". Gallop (1961, 88–89) represents Socrates as concerned to refute Protagoras' denial of the "identity" of the virtues, and faults Socrates' argument at 330–31 because it "does not seriously purport to prove the identity of Justice and Holiness, but only their homogeneity," contrasting this argument with the one about Temperance and Wisdom, "which does, whatever its failings, purport to prove identity." And cf. the quotation from Shorey in n. 2, above, *sub fin.* For (ii) see the citation from Allen in n. 4, above, and see his remarks in 94–95: he takes (i) and (ii) to be the *prima facie* doctrine of the text, but does so with a good sense of the difficulties that result from so taking it.

[14] Free substitutability in opaque contexts—contexts introduced by expressions like "X thought (or believed, said, etc.) that . . . "—is obviously not required by the view that the five words are synonyms.

or "Justice" for "Piety" in

> (2) "Piety is that part of Justice which has to do with service to the gods." (*Euthphr.* 12E)

The substitutions would falsify (1) and make nonsense of (2).[15] Again if two words are synonyms the definiens of either would do for the other. Could one say this of words like "Courage" and "Temperance"—or even of words that were more closely related in the mind of the Greeks, "Justice" and "Piety"? Can one imagine Socrates accepting the definiens of "Piety" as that of "Justice," or vice versa? We know that he would not. Consider what happens in the *Euthyphro*. The search for the definition of Piety gets nowhere until Euthyphro is brought at long last to see that Piety is a "part" of Justice,[16] and therewith to see that in order to reach its definition he must find out which special "part" of Justice Piety happens to be. This project, which has Socrates' unmistakable approval,[17] would make no sense if the definiens of Piety were the same as that of Justice. How then could Socrates have wished to sponsor the thesis that "Justice" and "Piety" are synonyms?

2. The Similarity Thesis

The question now is whether or not each of the virtues is like each of the rest and like Virtue.[18] To say this Socrates uses a variety of expressions. I list them in the order of their appearance in the text, using *B* and *A* as stand-ins for names of virtues or for "Virtue":

[15] Note that both results would be prohibitive for Socrates. The sentence in (1) is his; the one in (2) is Euthyphro's, but it has Socrates' explicit approval ("It is evident to me that you have spoken well," 12E9). It should be obvious that there would be many other sentences, explicating, or commenting on, the intensions of individual virtues, where substitution of the name of one virtue for that of another would yield falsehood or nonsense.

[16] No progress had been made—Euthyphro's attempts had produced only "statues of Daedalus" that kept running away, 11C-D—until Socrates took the lead in the search by introducing this line of thought at 11E4 ff.

[17] This is clear from 12E3-4: if Euthyphro would tell Socrates "which part of Justice is Piety," Socrates would be able to understand "adequately" (ἱκανῶς) what Piety is.

[18] The latter point—the similarity of each of the virtues to Virtue (as the "whole" of which each of the virtues is a "part")—plays no role in the argument. But it is explicit in (1) below—the "parts of gold" analogy in 329D6-8 and 349C2-3—and had best be included in generalized statements of the other formulae as well.

(1) *B* and *A* "do not differ at all [οὐδὲν διαφέρει] . . . except in size." (329D7-8)

(2) *B* is "such as" *A* (ἔστιν τὸ ἕτερον οἷον τὸ ἕτερον). (330A8-B1)[19]

(3) The "power" (δύναμις)[20] of *B* is "such as" that of *A*. (330B1)

(4) *B* is "similar" (ὅμοιον) to *A* (349C3).

(5) *B* is "either the same thing as *A* or as similar to *A* as it could possibly be (ἤτοι ταὐτόν γ' ἔστιν δικαιότης ὁσιότητι ἢ ὅτι ὁμοι-όττατον). (331B4-5)[21]

(6) *B* is "almost the same as *A*" (σχεδόν τι ταὐτόν). (333B5-6)

---

[19] This is by far the most frequently used phrase. It recurs at 330B3-7, 330E5-6, 331A2-3, 331B6-7. It is to be distinguished from

(7) *B* is "such as to be an A-ish [thing]" (ἔστιν ὁσιότης οἷον δίκαιον εἶναι [πρᾶγμα], 331A7-8; I put in brackets the part of the quotation which is expendable: it is dropped in subsequent uses),

which is only verbally distinguishable from

(8) *B* is *A*-ish (φαίην ἂν τὴν δικαιοσύνην ὅσιον εἶναι, 331B2-3),

since (8) is used to affirm the direct and full negation of not-(7). (7) and (8) occur in the premise-set from which the proposition expressed by (1), (2), (4), and (5) is deduced (presumably also the proposition expressed by (3), though there is no further allusion to this part of the thesis in the ensuing argument) as should be clear from the text and, in any case, from the analysis of the argument to be offered below. A comment on the translation of οἷος: This is the pronoun used to introduce the answer to ποῖος: "What sort of man [ποῖος] is Achilles?—He is the sort of man [οἷος] not to forget an injury." The poets use it to introduce similes: "Such as [οἷον] a star sent by Zeus as an omen," so Athena flashed from Olympus to earth (*Il.* 4, 75): she descended "like" (i.e., with the speed of) a falling star.

[20] The "power" (δύναμις) of a particular virtue is that virtue itself, conceived as a dispositional quality manifesting itself in action. As Prauss (1966) remarks, "The '*dynamis*' of σωφροσύνη or δικαιοσύνη is nothing but σωφρονεῖν or δίκαιον εἶναι" (76). But I cannot follow him in the far-reaching consequences he spins out of this fact; I see no justification for his conclusion that "unlike 'quality,' 'attribute,' etc.," *dynamis* precludes "relationship to an underlying substance" (*loc. cit.*) In Socrates' ontology (and Plato's too, for that matter) the *dynamis* of Temperance exists only in the persons who *have* that *dynamis* and are logically related to it as is subject to attribute. To say this is not, of course, to impute to Socrates or Plato the Aristotelian ontology of "underlying substances," but only the pre-analytical notion of individuals who are distinguishable from each of their properties.

[21] And cf. Socrates' "astonishment" at the suggestion that "there is only a slight resemblance [Guthrie] between Justice and Piety" (ὥστε ὅμοιόν τι σμικρὸν ἔχειν ἀλλήλοις, 331E6).

The fumbling in the phraseology is extraordinary[22]; it suggests that Socrates is hunting for the right words and has not quite found them. Nor is the trouble merely verbal. The best he offers by way of specifying *how* or *in what respect(s)* the virtues are supposed to be similar is an analogy: they are not related to one another as are the parts of the face but as "the parts of [a bar of] gold, which do not differ from one another except in size" (329D).[23] What are we to make of this? To take the analogy at face-value we would have to take him to mean that the virtues are alike in respect of *all* their qualities—that they are qualitatively undifferentiated dispositions, which appears to be the very thing he says himself at (1). Could Socrates really mean that? If he did, his present claim would be as inept and self-defeating as would have been his other one, that all their names apply to the same thing, if that had been meant to say that they are all synonymous. To homogenize the virtues would be to wipe out those very marks which make up their distinctive physiognomies and enable us to classify particular actions as instances of this or that virtue. Socrates himself must be fully aware of those differences between individual virtues. He must be counting on them to vindicate diverse definitions for diverse virtues. Consider his definition of Courage: "knowledge of what is and is not to be feared."[24] How would he go about showing that this

---

[22] I cannot recall its like in any of Plato's Socratic dialogues. I take the *Prt.* to be an early work in which Plato has yet to achieve the mastery of logical vocabulary and technique which he exhibits not only in his latest work, like the *Sph.*, but even in dialogues of the middle period and, still earlier, in transitional dialogues like the *Meno*. As a work of dramatic art the *Prt.* is flawless. As a logical exercise it is full of blemishes: cf. below, p. 241, and the text over nn. 76–81; and the concluding paragraph of this essay. Among the evidences of logical inexpertness I count the failure to produce in the first part of the debate any reliable statement of the Unity Thesis: the debate is allowed to start with a formula—[B] in I.1 above—that looks like such a statement, but in fact is not, for the reasons given above.

[23] No explanation is offered for "differences in size [μεγέθει καὶ σμικρότητι]." I surmise that these refer to differences of genus and species: Justice may be thought of as bigger than Piety, since the latter is a "part" of Justice (*Euthphr.* 11E–12E); but this sort of difference is not mentioned in our passages in the *Protagoras* and plays no role in their reasoning. Cf. above, *DR*, n.54.

[24] Santas' (449) felicitous rendering of *La.* 194E–195A, τὴν τῶν δεινῶν καὶ θαρραλέων ἐπιστήμην, put forward there by Nicias; but that it is acceptable to Socrates (and indeed, as Nicias is made to say, that it derives from Socrates: "I have often heard you say . . . ," 194C) is made certain by the fact that Socrates himself employs it as a premise in a demonstrative argument, *Prt.* 360D. The allegation one meets frequently in the scholarly literature that no

is not also the definition of, say, Justice, or, again, of Temperance, except
by pointing to the fact that whenever we think of an action as brave we
do so because, and in so far as, we see it as endurance of danger or afflic-
tion, while if we had seen it as giving to another person what is due him
we would have thought of it as just, and if it had struck us as evidencing
the agent's power to keep his appetites under the curb of reason we would
have called it "temperate"? Note that one and the same act could very
well display all three of these features: any theory should allow calling a
particular act "brave" *and* "just" *and* "temperate";[25] but this would not
gainsay the fact that in manifesting these three virtues it is expressing
recognizably different moral dispositions, a fact which we would expect
Socrates to grant as readily as would anyone else. What sense then could
we make of his claim that Courage and Justice and Temperance are as
alike as are two bits of a gold bar?

---

acceptable definition of a virtue is ever reached in the Socratic dialogues is
false.

[25] One might be tempted to think that Socrates' own theory would require   *
that every virtuous action must display all five virtues. This would be a mistake.
For Socrates (a) never asserts such a doctrine in the Platonic dialogues, and
(b) is not committed to it by his view that having any virtue implies having
all the virtues (the "Biconditionality Thesis", to be discussed below): a
man who has five distinct dispositions which *may be* concurrently exercised
need not be exercising all five in each and every act. Moreover, (c)—and this
is the clincher—such a doctrine would have clashed with his view (to which
I alluded briefly in the preceding section) that Piety is a "part" of Justice,
i.e., what is called nowadays a "proper" part: Socrates declares that all pious
conduct would be just but that not all just conduct would be pious (12D1-2)."
This view obviously requires that there will be some just actions which are
not pious ones (e.g. paying one's bills may be a just act—giving one's creditors
their due—without being a pious one: it renders no service to the gods).
Socrates unhappily fails to make the distinction between virtuous *dispositions*
and *actions*: this is not even made by Plato in the middle dialogues, though it is
certainly required to make good sense of his thesis that "justice pays" (see
JHR above, nn. 3, 4, 5); it must await Aristotle (*N.E.*, Book II, especially at
1105A17 ff.) Socrates, therefore, fails to take explicit account of the fact that
only virtuous *dispositions* characterize persons (I shall, therefore, call these for
short "person-virtues" in contrast to "action-virtues"). But we may notice
that the doctrine that Piety is a part of Justice turns up in a context in which
Socrates is investigating Piety as an action-virtue (what he is looking for, he
tells Euthyphro, is that character which will enable him to determine whether
or not "any of your own actions or of anyone else are pious" [6D10-11]), while,
on the contrary, the biconditionality of the virtues is quite explicitly formulated
to hold of persons (cf. n. 26 below), without the slightest suggestion that it is
also expected to hold of actions.

3. The Biconditionality Thesis

Now we are in for a surprise. Instead of another paradox Socrates now gives us a proposition that is crystal-clear:

> Which of these two things is the case: That some men partake of one of these parts of virtue, others of some other part? Or is it the case that if a man has one he will of necessity have them all? (329E2-4)

The latter option, that of Socrates, is that the five virtues constitute coextensive dispositions: those who instantiate any one of them must instantiate every one of them. We can put this into symbolic form:

$$N[(x)(Cx \leftrightarrow Jx \leftrightarrow Px \leftrightarrow Tx \leftrightarrow Wx)]^{26}$$

or, what comes to the same thing,

$$N(C \equiv J \equiv P \equiv T \equiv W).^{27}$$

The only thing in this formula that may call for comment is the modal

---

[26] The formula may be read: "Necessarily, for all x, iff x is courageous then x is just, iff x is just then x is pious, iff x is pious then x is temperate, iff x is temperate then x is wise." Take the variable to range over persons, not over actions: Socrates is not saying that any action characterizable by one of the five virtues is *necessarily* characterizable by each of the other four. I italicize "necessarily" because, as I implied in the preceding section, it would be perfectly plausible to hold that a particular act *may* be characterized by all five virtues: what would cause trouble would be the radically distinct thesis that every act *must* be characterized by all five. This would be both counter-intuitive in itself and, as I explained in the preceding note, would clash with the doctrine of the *Euthyphro* that Piety is a "part" of Justice. It is only because necessary biconditionality is being asserted of person-virtues, not of action-virtues, that there is no inconsistency between the two doctrines.

[27] May be read: "Necessarily, the class of the courageous is coextensive with the class of the just, the class of the just with the class of the pious, the class of the pious with the class of the temperate, the class of the temperate with the class of the wise." In reading these formulae one should bear in mind that the notion of necessity in Plato (nowhere defined) is not burdened with the assumption that the necessary coextensiveness of the instance-classes of properties entails the identity of the properties (as, e.g., in R. Carnap, 1956, 18: "properties are identical iff predicators for them are L-equivalent", i.e., if it "can be shown by logical means alone . . . that whatever has the one property has the other and vice versa."). Thus the instance-classes of three of the five "Greatest Kinds" of the *Sph.*—Being, Self-Identity, Difference—are necessarily coextensive, but demonstrably distinct.

operator. This answers to the "of necessity" in the Socratic phrase, which is not expendable rhetoric: From what we know of Socrates' moral theory we can be certain that the claim he is now making is far stronger than mere *de facto* coextensiveness. Suppose for instance that all brave men happened to be poor and all poor men brave. We can be certain that Socrates would not want to link Courage with poverty as he links Courage with the other virtues. His theory does not provide for a conceptual link between poverty and any virtue—no definitional connection here, as there is between any two virtues, since Socrates claims that all of the moral virtues are species ("parts") of Wisdom.[28] That claim implies that it is impossible to be temperate, or brave, or just, or pious, unless one is wise to begin with. So Wisdom is a necessary condition for possessing any of the other virtues; and it is also sufficient, and in the same strong sense, for Socrates is convinced that he can prove on logical grounds that a man who is wise will have to be temperate, and brave, etc.[29] So stated, the doctrine in our passage becomes perfectly lucid in itself, and it is instantly recognizable as a cardinal Socratic tenet, integral to the theory that Wisdom is the necessary and sufficient condition of all moral virtue and, what is more, coherent with Socrates' personal conviction that to engage his fellows in intellectual argument calculated to advance their discernment of moral truth is *ipso facto* to improve them morally, to make them better men. The Biconditionality Thesis would be one way of enunciating the rationale of this conception of his role in life.[30] It would explain why he is so sure that the usual approach, the *ad hoc*, piecemeal, inculcation of different virtues, would be futile, and that to make men moral one must make them wise, for without Wisdom they can have no other virtue, and with Wisdom they are bound to have every virtue.

Here then we have three theses. All three purport to express the same Socratic doctrine. But while the first two are so puzzling that we are hard put to it to see how Socrates would want to affirm what they seem to affirm, the third is a transparently clear expression of a well-known Socratic tenet. This contrast might lead one to go in either of two directions. One

---

[28] As Aristotle put it, "Socrates thought that all the virtues were [kinds of] knowledge [φρονήσεις ᾤετο εἶναι πάσας τὰς ἀρετάς]," *E.N.* 1144B19-20.

[29] The sufficiency of Knowledge for virtuous action is demonstrated in the final argument in the dialogue, the one for the "power" of knowledge, 352A ff.

[30] Albeit an incomplete expression of this conception, for the thesis gives no indication of the special role Socrates assigns to Wisdom (as the key to the acquisition of all the other virtues) which leads him to think of himself as preeminently the seeker after Wisdom (rather than after any of the other four).

might use it to discredit the first two theses, writing them off as confused and inconsequential expressions of what Socrates was after. This is the way I took them when writing an Introduction to this dialogue fifteen years ago.[31] But there is another way whose viability did not occur to me at the time. This is to scan the third thesis for a clue to a different understanding of the first two which will make good sense of each of them. This is the way I want to go now. I want to use the unproblematic thesis to show that with its guidance a wholly acceptable sense can be worked out for each of the perplexing ones.

II. REINTERPRETING THE UNITY AND SIMILARITY THESES

1. Reinterpreting the Unity Thesis

I shall argue that if the Biconditionality Thesis is true, then the following proposition will have to be true,

L[32] Virtue, Wisdom, Temperance, Courage, Justice, Piety are interpredicable: if "B" is a stand-in for one of the foregoing sub-

---

[31] (1956, liv). Quoting the Biconditionality Thesis, I remarked, "This is what the argument is all about," and proceeded to ignore the other two formulations of the doctrine. There is a sense in which I was justified in taking this line. For one who is exclusively concerned—as I was at that juncture—with the substantive issue under debate, the Biconditionality Thesis *is* "what the argument is all about"; one can, therefore, afford to dismiss the other two Theses as unsuccessful formulations of the issue, which do nothing to clarify it and to assist one in assessing the merit of the contending views. However, the logical form of the debate has great interest of its own. From that standpoint Gallop (1962, 89, n. 2) was obviously right in protesting that remark of mine. But he went to the other extreme of taking all of Socrates' theses at face-value, and faulting the argument he was analyzing—argument (1) for the "Homogeneity" (i.e., the Similarity) Thesis—for having no formal bearing on the other two theses. He did not seem to realize that if these other theses were meant to be taken at face-value, the effect of their *assertion* would be so catastrophic as to trivialize the question of the *relevance* of the proofs offered for them: no argument offered on their behalf, however relevant, could have improved their logical fortunes.

[32] "L" for "Link," because, as will be seen, this proposition so links the three theses together as to make them in fact the three variant expressions of the same substantive doctrine which they are evidently meant to be in our passage.

stantives and "A" for one of the cognate adjectives, then B is A
(i.e., "A" is predicated of B),

provided that the surface-grammar of "B is A" is disregarded and A *is*
understood to apply not to the abstract entity named by "B" but to each of its
instances and to these *necessarily*.[33] To explain by example: Pick one of the
virtues, say, Justice. Then, given the Biconditionality Thesis, each of the
following sentences will be true,

Justice is wise;

Justice is temperate;

Justice is courageous;

Justice is pious;

Justice is just;

Justice is virtuous,

provided each is understood to assert its predicate-term not of the abstract
noun in the subject-position, "Justice," but necessarily to anyone who
is just—e.g., provided "Justice is wise" is understood to assert that whoever is just must be wise. When the sentences are read in this way the
truth of the first four will follow directly from the Biconditionality Thesis,
as I shall proceed to demonstrate (in the paragraph after the next); the
sixth will also follow from the same Thesis, as I shall explain; and the
fifth will be a tautology, as should be obvious. Those sentences will
remain true when their predicate-term is put in substantival form,

Justice is Wisdom;

Justice is Temperance;

Justice is Courage;

Justice is Piety;

Justice is Justice;

Justice is Virtue,

provided we read each of them as a convertible predication, e.g., read
"Justice is Wisdom" as the conjunction

[33] This reading of the "B is A" sentence-form, whose importance in what is
to follow I am signalling by italicizing its description, will be discussed further
in Section III, below, and then again in the opening paragraphs of *AS*, which
explores the use of this syntactical form in the *Sph*. "B is A," so read, will be
called "Pauline predication," for reasons to be explained.

(Justice is wise) & (Wisdom is just),[34]

reading both conjuncts in the same way as before.[35]

That Socrates himself would wish us to give this reading to sentences like "Justice is wise" and "Justice is Wisdom" is a question I shall face squarely later on (section III, below). For the present I shall assume that he does: everything in the present section will be conditionalized on this assumption. What is not in question is the fact that he does use sentences with this grammatical structure. Here are the main examples:

Justice is just;[36]
Justice is pious;[37]
Piety is pious;[38]
Piety is just;[36]
Virtue is noble;[39]
Wisdom is Courage;[40]
Justice is Wisdom;
Temperance is Wisdom;
Courage is Wisdom.[41]

[34] That Plato would take "Justice is Wisdom" to be convertible is shown by the way he uses "Wisdom is Courage" in 350C and "Courage is Knowledge [=Wisdom]" in 361B. If "Wisdom is Courage" were read as non-convertible in 350C (i.e., if understood to mean only "Wisdom is courageous") it would not be the contradictory of Protagoras' claim in 349D6-8, that some courageous men are unwise, which, if expressed as a relation between the two virtues, would be that "Courage is not wise"; what Socrates must assert in order to deny the refutand is precisely that "Courage is wise." Since he uses "Wisdom is Courage" to do the job, he must be taking this proposition to mean that "Courage is wise" no less than that "Wisdom is courageous." This conclusion is confirmed by what happens in 361B. There he says that what had been proved in the foregoing is that "Courage is Knowledge [=Wisdom]," while in 350C he had said that what he had proved is that "Wisdom is Courage": the shift would be perfectly explicable if he is taking "Wisdom is Courage" to be convertible.
[35] I.e., as Pauline predications (cf. n. 33, above).
[36] 330C.
[37] 331B.
[38] 330D.
[39] 349E.
[40] 350C (cf. n. 34, above).
[41] Cf. the citation from 361B1-2 in n. 34, above, For "Justice is Wisdom" see also R. 351C1-2: καὶ ἡ δικαιοσύνη σοφία.

The syntax of these sentences may seem peculiar at first blush. Admittedly it is not too frequent in either English or Greek. It is nonetheless fully in line with good usage in both languages. We say things like "Justice is impartial" and "Ignorance is bliss" without strain, with no sense of resorting to contrived or stilted grammar; the same would be true in Greek. I shall, therefore, proceed to use without apologies substitution-instances of the "B is A" sentence-form in L, reserving comment for the following section, by which time we shall have a better sense of their scope in our passage. My task now is to substantiate the claim I have made that L, with the proposed reading, follows from the Biconditionality Thesis. How so?

That thesis assures us that if a given person, N, happens to have any of the five virtues, he will "of necessity" have all five. So suppose N is just. It will follow at once (and necessarily) that N will be wise. If so, his Justice would have to be *wise* Justice.[42] It could not be impulsive, senti-mental, short-sighted, or rote-ridden Justice: it could not be flawed by any defect in rationality that would fault it when measured up against the high standard of Socratic wisdom; for were that the case, N's wisdom could not be inferred (and inferred with necessity) from the mere fact that he is just, as the Biconditionality Thesis assures us that it can. So N's Justice must be wise: if we accept the Biconditionality Thesis, this follows necessarily. And since what is true of N's Justice will also be true of M's and O's and of any other person's we happen to pick, it will follow by existential generalization that Justice is wise.[43] By the same reasoning we may deduce from the Biconditionality Thesis that Justice is not only wise, but also temperate, brave, and pious,[44] and we may then similarly deduce from the same premise that all five virtues are interpredicable, and therefore that the "B is A" sentence-form in L will be true for any two distinct virtues, regardless of whether the predicate-term is put in adjectival or substantival form. The Biconditionality Thesis will also assure us that "Justice is virtuous" and "Justice is Virtue" are true, since

[42] I.e., the sort of Justice whose instances are necessarily wise: a Pauline predication is nested in "N's Justice is wise."

[43] The same result can be reached more directly by noting that when the Pauline predications in "N's justice is wise" and "Justice is wise" are spelled out, the former sentence turns out to be only the latter's "universal instantia-tion" whose truth is assured immediately by the Biconditionality Thesis; and that the same thing would be true in any other instance we happen to pick; whence it follows by "universal generalization" that Justice is (Paulinely) wise.

[44] Pauline predications.

we learn from that thesis that anyone who is just is bound to have all the virtues and that whoever is virtuous is bound to be, among other things, just.[45] As for "Justice is just" and "Justice is Justice," no proof is needed, since all these sentences are used to express in this context is the tautology that necessarily whoever is just is just. What has been proved for Justice may be proved for each of the other virtues by the identical reasoning, and for Virtue by obvious extension of that reasoning. So *L* has been secured.

But how will *L* help us make sense of Socrates' saying that the names of all the virtues must apply to the same thing? It would not, taken just by itself. To do the job we must take into account a further fact which has long been known but has never been linked up with our passage in the *Protagoras*. This is that all through the archaic and classical periods the "name" (ὄνομα) was expected to perform two radically different linguistic functions: first, of course, that of the proper name: this is the original, and always the primary, use of ὄνομα; but secondly that of the common name, that is to say of the qualifying predicate or descriptive expression. Of this dual sense of ὄνομα many examples could be given, but one should suffice, for this gives us all the information we need to crack our present puzzle. The example comes from the *Phaedo*—written later than the *Protagoras*, to be sure, but entirely suitable for the purpose of illustrating an inherited, long-established, usage.[46]

In the passage on the clever αἰτία in that dialogue Socrates speaks of cases in which

not only the Form itself [say, *F*] is always entitled to its own name, but also something else [say, *G*] which is not identical with that Form,

[45] Since to be virtuous at all one would have to have at least one virtue, whence it would follow, given the Biconditionality Thesis, that one would have all the virtues, including Justice.

[46] There is no difficulty in documenting the antiquity of the use of "name" to designate predicative expressions, no less than referring ones. Thus it is clear in B9, 1, that Parmenides thinks of "fire" and "night" as *names* serving a predicative function, since he speaks of mortals "naming everything 'fire' and night,' " i.e., so classifying the contents of their putative universe; and that in B8, 40–41, not only "being", "not-being," "becoming" and "perishing", but even phrases like "changing place" and "interchanging bright color" count as names: he says that these have been posited as names with respect to Being (reading ὀνόμασται, for whose defense see Mourelatos [1970, 180 ff.]). The use of "naming" for "stating, specifying" is as old as Homer. Liddell and Scott, *Greek English Lexicon*, cites *Il.* 8, 449, "they named [ὀνόμαζον] glorious gifts." Cf. Mourelatos [1970, 184] on *name* as "abbreviated description."

but always has its character [*G* is always *F*] when it [*G*] exists. (103E2-5)[47]

In his example *G* and *F* are respectively *Three* and *Odd*:

Don't you think that [Three] may always be called both by its own name and by the name of the Odd, though [the Odd] is not identical with Three ?(104A5-7)

Since Three *is* odd, every trio is rightly called (hence, "named") "Odd." And since it is also rightly called "Three," it is entitled to both of these names: "Three" names Three, and "Odd" also names Three. Here "names" is evidently used in the two different senses I have specified. In " 'Three' names Three" to "name" is to *refer*. In " 'Odd' names Three" to "name" is to *describe*.[48] Plato does not identify these two functions as different senses of "name" and "naming." Elsewhere he notices the difference between the subject- and predicate-terms of a sentence like "Theaetetus sits," calling the first word an ὄνομα, the second a ῥῆμα. This is in the *Sophist* (261Dff.) where his analysis of the syntactical structure of a sentence has advanced in depth. But even there he does not go so far as to *say* that the ῥῆμα is itself an ὄνομα discharging a predicative instead of a nominative function.[49] To take note of the distinction between referring and predicative expressions he resorts to two different words, ὄνομα, ῥῆμα, instead of saying that the same word, ὄνομα, can be used in each

---

[47] We can make best sense of the phraseology by taking *G* here to refer to *G qua* immanent character, rather than *qua* transcendent Form (hence the expression "when it exists" which would be puzzling if asserted of a Form). But this does not affect the general point that a given *eidos* (immanent or transcendent) will always be entitled both to its own "name" and to the "name" of any *eidos* which is truly predicable of it.

[48] Though what it is predicated of is not, strictly speaking, the singular term Threeness, but the instances of that term: "Three is odd" should be construed as a Pauline predication (cf. n. 33, above), as in the other examples in the passage, where the point is so much clearer: thus in "Snow is cold" (cf. *Phdo* 103C-D), "cold" would not be predicated of the Form, Snow, (which would be absurd), but of its "participants" (cf. *RC*, n.68).

[49] I italicize "say" because I do think he implies as much: he introduces the ὄνομα/ῥῆμα distinction by saying that he wants to investigate the combination of names (περὶ τῶν ὀνομάτων . . . ἐπισκεψώμεθα . . . εἴτε ἀλλήλοις συναρμόττει εἴτε μή, εἴτε τὰ μὲν ἐθέλει, τὰ δὲ μή, 261D2-6), which implies that the acceptable combination—the one that produces sentences, instead of meaningless strings—will always involve both ὄνομα and ῥῆμα and still be a combination of names: this shows that ὄνομα is being used both in a broader sense, which includes ῥῆμα, and in a narrower sense which contrasts with ῥῆμα.   *

of these distinct ways. Still less then could we expect that he should be making this point in the *Phaedo*, though he does realize here that "Odd" names Three in a different way from that in which "Three" names Three: for he speaks of the latter as calling Three "by its own name"[50] in contradistinction to the former; "Odd" is not Three's "own name," while "Three" is. But he does not focus attention on this. What does catch his eye is the fact that in calling Three "Odd" no less than "Three" *we are not implying that Three and Odd are identical.* On this he is most emphatic. He makes the point six times over in the course of 21 lines of text. By the same token he might have added that "Odd" and "Three" are not synonyms: the fact that both may "name" the same thing does not imply that they are.

With this in mind let us return to the *Protagoras.* Having established that

> Justice is wise, temperate, courageous, pious, and virtuous,[51]

we may now avail ourselves of the descriptive use of "naming" to convert this sentence into

> Justice is named [descriptively] "Wisdom," "Temperance," "Courage," "Piety," and "Virtue."

Shifting to the other use of "naming," we may then convert

> Justice is just,

into

> Justice is named [referringly] "Justice."[52]

We can now see that Socrates is in a position to hold that all six of these "names" apply to the same thing. To explain himself he would have had to say that the first five of the "names" apply to Justice quite differently from the sixth: the first five only as descriptive predicates, the sixth also as a proper name. This Socrates does not say. But the fact that a man does not explain what he is doing in no way precludes his doing it. To use a

---

[50] 103E3; 104A2; 104A5-6.

[51] Pauline predications (like the one in "Three is odd" and "Snow is cold": cf. n. 48, above).

[52] Since "justice is just" is to be read as a Pauline predication in this context, the sentence may *also* be converted into

> Justice is named [descriptively] "Justice,"

for this will mean simply the tautology that all just persons are bound to be just.

rule of language without the least awareness of the rule is an all too common phenomenon of linguistic behavior.[53] So we have no reason to deny that Socrates could be using the ambiguity in "name" in the absence of any allusion to the ambiguity, exploiting it in speaking of both "Justice" and "Wisdom," "Temperance," etc. as "names" of Justice. Once we allow this, the question of Socrates' thereby *identifying* Justice with Wisdom, Temperance, etc., or of taking "Justice" and "Wisdom," "Temperance," etc. to be *synonyms*, does not arise: we do not identify the thing we are talking about with any of its attributes nor do we take the names of its convertible attributes to be synonyms.

Can we get textual confirmation for the proposed interpretation? At first sight, this looks like a hopeless undertaking, because Socrates' debating tactics are so unsystematic that not once in the course of the four arguments[54] by which he vindicates his doctrine does he so much as even *mention* the formula of the Unity Thesis. In none of those arguments does he allude to his claim that the names of all the virtues—"Wisdom," "Temperance," etc.—"apply to one thing." We see neither hide nor hair of this phraseology in the demonstrands or the conclusions of these arguments. However, we do get several closely related sentences in the sequel. The most striking of these occur at the conclusion of the dialogue, where Socrates says that he had tried to prove that

All [the virtues] are Wisdom,

which he spells out as

Justice is Wisdom;
Temperance is Wisdom;
Courage is Wisdom.[55]

---

[53] Cf. Chomsky (1965, 8): ". . . every speaker of a language has mastered and internalized a generative grammar that expresses his knowledge of his language. This is not to say that he is aware of the rules of the grammar *or even that he can become aware of them.* . . ." (If a "generative grammar" is obscure, "a set of rules of grammar" may be substituted for it.) I have italicized the most striking part of the statement. If it seems incredible on first hearing, let one reflect on this: A normal four-year-old knows how to use correctly the definite and indefinite article (say to him "*A* dog and *a* cat are fighting. Who do you think is going to win?" and you can count on his answering, "*The* dog" or "*The* cat"); but it will be years before he can be made aware of the rule of language which prescribes the behavior he exhibits.

[54] Cf. n. 1, above.

[55] Cf. the citation from 361B1-2 in n. 34, above. I am now substituting "Wisdom" for "Knowledge" which is clearly meant to express here precisely the same thing as is expressed by "Wisdom" elsewhere in our passage.

These sentences are respectively no more than translations into the material mode of

Justice is named [descriptively] "Wisdom" and *vice versa;*
Temperance is named [descriptively] "Wisdom" and *vice versa;*
Courage is named [descriptively] "Wisdom" and *vice versa.*

Similarly the grammatical converse of "Courage is Wisdom,"

"Wisdom is Courage" (350C4-5)

is a material-mode equivalent of

Wisdom is named [descriptively] "Courage" and *vice versa.*

This being the case, it yields valuable, if indirect, confirmation of the present interpretation. On its terms we can explain perfectly the otherwise puzzling fact that Socrates, after using the formulae of the Unity Thesis so fulsomely and repetitiously in the course of restating the issue of the debate in 369B1-C2,[56] should then be content to formulate the proposition he thinks he has proved in the ensuing argument as

Wisdom is Courage,

rather than, as he would have done had he stuck to the diction of the Unity Thesis, as

Wisdom is named "Courage" and Courage is named "Wisdom,"

or as

"Wisdom" and "Courage" apply to the same thing.

On the proposed interpretation the latter pair of sentences follows so directly from "Wisdom is Courage," that Socrates might well feel no need to spell out the consequence[57] in this tense, rapid, highly compressed argument.[58] The interpretation also makes good sense of the fact that he should say he has proved that "Wisdom is Courage," when what his

[56] The formulae were quoted above, at the start of I, 1.

[57] We cannot remind ourselves too often that our passage is not a leisurely investigation, like the *Philebus*, but a contest, whose tempo and tactics are determined by the exigencies of a live debate. Time and again Socrates skips over steps in his argument which he takes to be so obviously correct that Protagoras would have no interest in challenging them.

[58] We would get the same explanation for his failure to allude to the formula that the names of all the virtues apply to the same thing at the conclusion of the dialogue. If the proposed explanation of this formula is correct, Socrates

argument has in fact proved is (at most) that Wisdom and Courage are biconditionally related, which Protagoras had denied (349D5-8). He is evidently taking "Wisdom is Courage" to be so transparent a consequence of the Biconditionality Thesis that he does not feel called upon to explain the reason for the consequence.[59]

Will my interpretation of the Unity Thesis square with the conclusion of the second argument,

Would not then Temperance and Wisdom be one? (333B)

It would not, all too obviously, if "Temperance and Wisdom are one" were meant to assert that Temperance and Wisdom are identical virtues. But that this is not what is meant can be argued on two distinct grounds: first, on the highly general ground that Socrates could not have wished to prove these (or any other) virtues identical, because, as has been already explained, he could not have accepted the same *definiens* for both; secondly, on the more specific ground, which I now wish to explain, that the logical structure of the argument by which this proposition is derived shows that what the argument purports to prove is simply that *Temperance and Wisdom are necessarily coextensive* (as required by the Biconditionality Thesis)—*not* that they are identical virtues (which is required by nothing in our passage nor, for that matter, by a single statement in the whole of the Platonic corpus). The italicized proposition follows from the meaning which the crucial term "opposite" carries in the premises from which the conclusion is deduced:

1 Wisdom and Folly are opposites.[60]

2 Temperance and Folly are opposites.[61]

3 To one thing there is only one opposite.[62]

---

would see no point in dragging things out by showing that the sentences he uses at 361A1-2 are fully translatable into the phraseology of that formula, as explained in my text above.

[59] Having proved, as he thinks, a proposition about *persons*—that brave men are wise and wise men brave—he translates it forthwith into a proposition about the corresponding *virtues*. He sees the two as so closely connected that he feels no need to argue that since brave persons are wise, Courage must be wise, and since wise persons are brave, Wisdom must be brave. He would no doubt have done so in a more leisurely context.

[60] "Is not Wisdom completely opposite to this thing [i.e., to Folly, ἀφρο-σύνη]?" (332A4-5).

[61] "Hence Folly is the opposite of Temperance?" (332E4-5).

[62] "We have agreed that to one thing there is only one opposite, not many?" (332C8-9).

* What "opposite" means in this context is what is called "complement" in set theory: for class K, its complement, $\bar{K}$, is such that K and $\bar{K}$ are mutually exclusive and jointly exhaustive of their universe of discourse.[63] That this is precisely what "opposite" is being used to mean in this argument can be established by inspecting the derivation of 2—the only one of those three premises whose deduction gives us a context from which we can determine the meaning of the term. 2 is presented as the consequence of 7 and 8 below. 7 is derived as follows:

4 Those who act correctly act temperately,[64]

5 Those who do not act correctly act foolishly,[65]

(which, taken in conjunction, imply[66]

6 Those who do not act temperately act foolishly,

which implies in turn[67]

7 Those who do not act foolishly act temperately).

And

8 Those who act foolishly do not act temperately

comes from the text.[68]

---

[63] Hence $\bar{K}$ is the contradictory of K—not just a contrary of it.

[64] I get 4 from 332A6-8: "When men are acting correctly and usefully, do they then seem to you to be acting temperately, or the opposite?" (following Stallbaum's text, now generally accepted and reproduced by Burnet in the Oxford Text). I contract "correctly and usefully" to "correctly," since "usefully" is only epexegetic: it is not an independent qualification for no use of it as a separate premise is made in the sequel. I streamline the syntax to bring it into line with the next premise and get the uniformity of style one needs in a formal argument.

[65] This is straight out of the text (οἱ μὴ ὀρθῶς πράττοντες ἀφρόνως πράττουσι, 332B2-3).

[66] I get 6 from 5 in conjunction with

9 Those who do not act temperately do not act correctly,

having got 9 from 4 by contraposition. The conjunction of 5 and 9 implies 6 by the transitivity of class-inclusion.

[67] By contraposition.

[68] ". . . and in so acting [i.e., acting foolishly] are not behaving temperately" (B2-3). In Vlastos, 1956, xxix, n. 19, I overlooked the possibility of deriving 2 by the above sequence which involves valid inferences all the way and does not require us to fault the reasoning in the text, except on expository

Socrates then infers (332B3-4) that

> 10 Acting foolishly is the opposite of acting temperately,

which follows directly from 7 and 8. He then asserts (B4-6)

> 11 What is done foolishly is done by Folly and what is done temperately is done by Temperance;

establishes by *epagōgē* (B6-C2; D3-4) that

> 12 What is done oppositely is done by opposites;

and then asserts as already agreed to (direct inference from 10) that

> 13 What is done foolishly is done oppositely to what is done temperately (D4-5).

From 12 and 13 it follows that

> 14 What is done foolishly and what is done temperately is done by opposites (E1-4),

and from 11 and 14 that

> 2 Folly and Temperance are opposites (E4-5).

---

grounds, i.e., for leaving lacunae which I had to fill in with 6, 7, and 9 (not a serious blemish, since Socrates is under no obligation to fill in all the steps in his reasoning so long as the interlocutor is ready to tag along with the ones Socrates gives). The oversight led me to charge Socrates with a formal fallacy (the one with which he had been traditionally charged: sliding from "not temperately" to "in a way which is the opposite of temperately") from which he may be freed, as David Savan (1964, 23) has pointed out: I gladly accept Savan's correction on this point, though I am unable to agree with him that the derivation of 2 is thereby rehabilitated. The error in this segment of the argument (which accounts for Socrates' outrageous claim to have demonstrated that Wisdom and Temperance are coextensive) is accounted for by the material falsehood of premises 4 and 8, for which no reason has been given and which Protagoras should not have granted. *Pace* Savan (24–25) there is nothing in Protagoras' known views which would require him to deny that a man can act "correctly" (with a view to his own advantage: this sense of "acting correctly" has not been excluded) by behaving intemperately (e.g., by joining a tyrant in a drunken feast in order to keep the tyrant's favor) or, conversely, to deny that a man may act foolishly by behaving temperately (as would the man in the example if, to maintain his temperate regimen, he declined the invitation to the feast, thereby incurring the tyrant's wrath, with disastrous consequences to his own fortunes). Savan's argument (24–25) that Protagoras is really committed to 4 and 8 fails to reckon with this rather obvious line of objection.

Looking back over the argument we can see at once that what Socrates purports to prove by 7 and 8 is that those who act foolishly and those who act temperately make up mutually exclusive and jointly exhaustive classes, i.e., that these two classes are complements, and then proceeds to establish

* that the same relation must also hold between the corresponding attributes, Folly and Temperance. So the sense in which they are "opposites" in 2 is that they are attributes of persons who form complementary classes. And since "opposite" could only be used in 1 with the same sense as in 2,

** these two premises assure us that both Wisdom and Temperance are complements of Folly. Premise 3 then spells out the notion implied in the definition of "complement" above, from which it follows that if S and S' have the same complement, $\bar{S}$, then S and S' are coextensive classes. Hence Temperance and Wisdom have been shown to be attributes of persons who form coextensive classes. And as Socrates could have proceeded to argue, they do so necessarily, since Wisdom is conceptually tied to Temperance: a person must be wise to be temperate and cannot but be temperate if he is wise. This necessary coextensiveness of Temperance and Wisdom can be expressed in the formal mode by the conjunction

Temperance is named [descriptively] Wisdom and *vice versa*.

Then the question of their constituting *one and the same virtue* does not arise. The argument for their "unity," if sound, has established that they are "one and the same" in just the sense required by the Biconditionality

*** Thesis: they are attributes necessarily instantiated in *one and the same class of persons*.[69]

2. Reinterpreting the Similarity Thesis

Insisting that the virtues are *very* similar,[70] Socrates does not say *how*, *in what respects*, they are so very similar. What kind of similarity could he have had in view which would have struck him as far-reaching enough to be analogizable to that of bits of gold, yet not so unqualified as to blot

[69] If Socrates had been in a position to identify this sense of "the same," he would not have resorted to those curious locutions, as imprecise as they are emphatic—"either the same thing or as similar anything could possibly be," "almost the same" [items (5) and (6) respectively on p. 229, above]—to describe the relation of Justice to Piety in 331A and 333B; he would have said that there is a special (and very weak) sense in which they *are the same*, though not at all *the same virtue*.

[70] Cf. especially the language used in (1), (4), and in the second disjunct of (5) on p. 229, above.

out the distinctive qualities of the several virtues, reducing them to the homogenized uniformity which is the unhappy, and surely unwanted, suggestion of the analogy? Guessing one's way to an answer would be a hopeless enterprise if we did not know how closely Socrates is associating the similarity of the virtues with the biconditionality of the classes of their instances. He introduced the latter (329E2-4) immediately after he had brought up the gold-bar analogy, evidently not to present a new doctrine, but to clarify further the one he had expounded just before in the language of Similarity. And we know that Protagoras, with Socrates' tacit concurrence, thinks of the Biconditionality Thesis as *implied* by the Similarity Thesis: we see this at 349D2-8, where we hear Protagoras say that the falsehood of the former in the case of Courage shows the falsehood of the latter in the same case.[71] We may, therefore, make heuristic use of this logical relation between the two theses, asking ourselves: What sort of similarity would imply biconditionality? To this a plausible answer suggests itself: the sort that follows directly from L above, which is not only implied by the Biconditionality Thesis, as was explained, but also implies it, as should be obvious: if each virtue has the qualities of all the rest, then to have one virtue is to have all the rest as well;[72] thus to be just one will have to be also wise, temperate, etc., since Justice is wise, temperate, etc. In telling us that each of the virtues is wise and temperate and brave and pious and just, L as good as tells us of a five-point similarity between them: each is like the rest in all five of these respects.[73] This similarity could have struck Socrates as so pervasive as to prompt him to analogize it to the similarity of the parts of a gold bar: as each of its parts has all of the qualities characteristic of gold (each is yellow, ductile, malleable,

[71] "And this is how you will know that I speak the truth [in saying that "Courage is very different from all these" other virtues]: you will find many men who are unjust, most impious, most intemperate, and most ignorant, but exceptionally brave." One who assumes that the falsehood of p implies the falsehood of q is implying (by *modus tollens*) that q implies p.

[72] If the validity of the inference is not immediately perspicuous to the reader, he must be forgetting that a sentence like "Justice is wise" is a Pauline predication. Once it is made explicit that all such a sentence would mean in this context is that whoever instantiates Justice is wise, it should be obvious that to have Justice is to have Wisdom as well, and so on with each of the other virtues.

[73] And, to recall the language of (3) on p. 229, above, L tells us also that the corresponding similarity will hold between the *dynameis* of the virtues. Thus the *dynameis* of Justice and Temperance—the active dispositions to behave * justly and temperately—will both be dispositions to behave wisely, bravely, and piously as well, since each of the two virtues is wise and brave and pious.

and so forth), so each of the virtues has all of the qualities characteristic of virtue (each is wise, temperate, and so forth).[74] And if this is the point of the analogy, we purge it (and therewith the Similarity Thesis itself) of its most obnoxious feature: the suggestion that the virtues would be as destitute of individuating qualitative characteristics as are bits of a gold bar. This suggestion would now be totally irrelevant and unwanted. The virtues would be left in full possession of their distinctive dispositional physiognomies, though strikingly and massively similar, since each would be virtuous in all of the ways in which (on Socrates' theory) it is possible to be virtuous. So far, then, the proposed interpretation works well. How does it fare when checked further against the text?

In this case we have the good luck to find one of Socrates' four arguments stating its demonstrand quite explicitly in terms of the Similarity Thesis: what Socrates has undertaken to prove in argument (1) is

that Justice is such as [i.e., similar to] Piety and Piety such as Justice. (331B6)[75]

So here we can dispense with the indirect lines of reasoning that were required to show that the interpretation of the Unity Thesis agrees with the textual data. Here checking interpretation against the text will be easy. All we have to do is to see how Socrates goes about proving the similarity of Justice and Piety. If the proposed interpretation is correct, his proof should consist in showing that Justice and Piety are like each other in some or all of the respects which follow from the fact that the different

---

[74] By contrast to the parts of a face, each of which has ἰδίαν (*private*, i.e., *not common*) δύναμιν (an expression which Plato must find very apt: he uses it in 330A4, and then again in 349C5, having repeated the adjective in phrases like ἴδιος οὐσία [349A4] ἰδίῳ πράγματι [349C4]): the "power" of the eye is to see and only that—not to see *and* hear *and* smell, while the "power" of Wisdom is not only to act wisely but, given *L*, to act temperately *and* courageously *and* justly *and* piously. In working with the analogy we should keep track of a vital difference in the logical syntax of the two cases: In the case of a bit of gold the quality-ascriptions in "it is yellow, ductile, etc." are ordinary predications; in the case of a virtue, say Courage, the quality-ascriptions in "it is wise, temperate, etc." are Pauline. So we have different sorts of similarity: non-Pauline in the first case, Pauline in the second.

[75] At the conclusion of the argument Socrates says that this is what he would himself say "most of all" (μάλιστα), i.e., that this would be the formulation he would find most satisfactory. The same thing was implied at 330B3-7 and again at 330E3-331A4, where the refutand is expressed in a more general form by saying that no "part" of virtue is "such as" any other.

virtues can be (Paulinely) predicated of each other (proposition *L*). And so it does.

To prove his thesis Socrates invokes two premises:

1 Justice is just (330C4-5) and Piety is pious (330D8-9).
2 Justice is pious and Piety is just (331B2-3).

How does he come by *1* and *2*? Not by inferring them from the Biconditionality Thesis, from which I deduced *L* above: that would have been arguing in a circle, since Protagoras rejects Biconditionality *pari passu* with Similarity. Socrates finds another way to the above premises—a very easy one, as he thinks. Premise *1* he gets by arguing in effect: If Justice were not just, it would be unjust;[76] no one would want to say that Justice is unjust; so it has to be just.[77] Ditto for Piety being pious. By the same reasoning he justifies Premise *2*: Justice must be pious, for otherwise it would have to be impious,[78] and who would want to say that? For the same reason Piety must be just. The fallacy in this reasoning, the same one in both cases, need not detain us. It has long been recognized as a slide from "is not *F*" to "is the contradictory of *F*"[79]—and we know from other

---

[76] This is implied at 330C4-5, where the question is posed: Is Justice "just or unjust," thereby foisting on Protagoras the assumption that the disjunction is exhaustive. J. Adam and A. M. Adam who catch the same fallacy in 331A8-B1, where it is more explicit, and also at 330D5-6 (see their comments *ad loc.*) fail to notice that Socrates has slipped into it already here at 330C4-5: without it his derivation of the first conjunct in premise *1* above would be arbitrary and out of line with his derivation of the second conjunct in the same premise.

[77] I am blowing up the argument in this way, for the whole force of the deduction of "Justice is just" (which is not taken as self-evident, but is inferred: note the ἄρα in 330C7) depends on some such course of reasoning, though only the first step (the initial posing of what looks like an exhaustive disjunction) and the third (opting for the first disjunct) are explicit in the text; the elimination of the second disjunct is left implicit.

[78] 331A8-9.

[79] Moreau (1939, 43) contends that there is no substantial error: ". . . si cette substitution du terme contraire [ἄδικον, ἀνόσιον] au term négatif [μὴ δίκαιον, μὴ ὅσιον] ne se justifie pas *vi formae*, elle n'en est pas moins justifiée en ce qui concerne la matière de la discussion; tout objet susceptible d'estimation morale et qui est *non juste* est nécessairement injuste. . . ." This is surely wrong. The general opinion both in antiquity and at present would deny that every moral act must be either just or unjust, pious or impious, brave or cowardly, temperate or intemperate. Consider an act of spontaneous generosity to a friend, "an act susceptible of moral assessment." We would hardly call it "just" (the benefit is not conferred in consideration of his right to it—he

passages[80] that Plato could easily have imputed this to Socrates, or might even have fallen into it himself in this early phase of his career when he might still have been wobbly on points of logic which he firms up later on.[81] In any case, the premises are the only thing that concern us now, for they show exactly what sort of similarity Socrates had in view, and give us textual authority for saying that it is the sort I have hypothesized. By making these four propositions the premises of his demonstration Socrates tells us that Justice and Piety are proved to be similar virtues when shown to be similar in two crucial respects: each is both just and pious.[82] If he were interested in pursuing the matter further, he could have proceeded to establish by iteration of the reasoning that each is also wise, temperate, and courageous.[83] In that case his result would have coincided with my

---

has no such right). Must we then call it "unjust"? It is not classifiable as a brave act (no confrontation of danger). Must we then say that it is cowardly? If the agent is an atheist it could not be pious. Would it then be impious?

[80] The same fallacy is palmed off by Euthydemus on his interlocutor in *Euthd.* 276B2 ("and if they are not wise, must they not be ignorant?") without protest from anyone. But this is not good evidence of Socrates' unawareness of the fallacy, for he is not taking a hand in this exchange. Far more relevant are *Prt.* 360B2-3, "and if they [their fear and their confidence] are not noble [καλά] must they not be base [αἰσχρά]"—nothing had been done to establish that "noble" and "base" constitute the exhaustive possibilities for the fear and confidence which persons may feel; and *Smp.* 201E-202A: Diotima asks Socrates if he believes that "whatever is not beautiful [καλόν] must be ugly [αἰσχρόν]," and he replies, "Certainly!" Thereupon Diotima proceeds to instruct Socrates that there are "intermediates" between καλόν and αἰσχρόν, as e.g., "true opinion" is intermediate between "knowledge" and "ignorance." (Other Platonic passages adduced as parallels in the Adams' note on 331A are probably not examples of the fallacy; at any rate, they are not clear examples.)

[81] Such as the insight that contraries need not be contradictories, which is communicated with such didactic emphasis by Diotima in the preceding note, and is reasserted in *Sph.* 257B.

[82] Crucial in that, if the predications in "Justice and Piety are just and pious" are Pauline (as will be argued in Section III, below), the biconditionality of Justice and Piety would follow from their similarity in these two respects: if Justice is pious, then whoever is just would be pious; and if Piety is just, then whoever is pious would be just. There is no allusion to this point in the text. But biconditionality, closely connected with similarity by Socrates (329D-E), had been denied vehemently by Protagoras (329E5-6). It would be reasonable to think that Socrates is conducting the vindication of similarity along lines which would have a bearing on biconditionality as well, offering him the materials with which he could construct a corrollary proof of biconditionality under appropriate circumstances.

[83] It is reasonable to assume that Socrates would have done so in a less polemical, more systematic, context.

hypothesis of what the similarity of the virtues means for him, i.e., that each has the five-point resemblance with each which follows immediately from the fact that each is just and pious and wise and temperate and courageous.[84]

[84] Though there are many differences in detail between the above analysis of the argument and Gallop's (1961), they are not nearly as great as they may seem to be at first sight, and none is worth arguing over except two.

(1) He sees the big fallacy of the Socratic argument in the assumption that Premises *1* and *2* jointly imply the demonstrand

D Justice is such as (οἷον) Piety and Piety is such as Justice

(I retain my reference-marks, translations, etc. rather than his, to avoid burdening the discussion with complications which I consider inessential). Gallop thinks that Protagoras would have been entitled to concede Premises *1* and *2* yet deny *D*: "even if he [Protagoras] agrees that Justice and Holiness resemble each other in certain respects (viz., in both being just and holy) he need not agree that they are homogeneous" (90). I cannot follow him because I do not know what criteria of "homogeneity" he has in view. Socrates hasn't stated his, and we can agree in faulting him for that failure. However, if we are also going to charge him with a *non sequitur*, we will have to assume the burden of explaining the sense in which "homogeneous" is being used in statements like the one I have quoted from Gallop. For there is *a* sense of "homogeneous" in which the inference from Premises *1* and *2* to *D* would follow with analytic certainty: if Justice and Piety are both just and pious, then they are certainly homogeneous *in those two respects*. (If it be objected that this is a strained sense of "homogeneous," the answer would be that, after all, this is not Socrates' term: he operates with the still vaguer language of "similarity," and no one could find fault with the claim that if both Justice and Piety are just and pious then they are similar in those two respects.) The reason why Gallop finds that inference so objectionable can only be that he is invoking some strong sense of "homogeneity"—how strong he does not say. If Socrates is to be understood to mean complete homogeneity—i.e., that every quality of Justice is shared by Piety and conversely—then, of course, the inference is grotesquely fallacious. But in that case why bother with the inference? If that is what *D* is supposed to mean, it becomes virtually self-refuting.

(2) Another point (a more minor one) on which I disagree with Gallop's analysis is his claim (92) that the fallacy by which *1* and *2* are derived (a fallacy he acknowledges, insisting on it in the face of A. E. Taylor's perverse denial that it exists) is unimportant because "Socrates could have amended his argument to avoid it": *1* and *2*, thinks Gallop, could have been derived from "inoffensive" premises, such as that οἷον καλὸν εἶναι could be asserted of both Justice and of Piety. Surely this will not do. The suggested substitute premise is inoffensive enough, but only by fallacious reasoning could *1* or *2* be inferred from it. Thus from "Justice is καλόν" and "Whatever is pious is καλόν" it would not follow, except by illicit conversion of the latter premise, that "Justice is pious."

I have now done what I undertook to do in this section.[85] From the Biconditionality Thesis I have derived a proposition, *L*, which has shown the way to an interpretation of both the Unity and the Similarity Theses that rids each of their unacceptable features. All three theses turn out to be complementary expressions of the same basic claim which may be put most clearly by saying that having any virtue entails having every virtue, less clearly but still understandably, by saying that that what names each names all, and that they are all cogeners, all alike.

III. PAULINE PREDICATIONS IN THE *PROTAGORAS*

I may now tackle the task, deferred from the preceding section, of justifying the assumption that all substitution-instances of the "*B* is *A*" formula in *L* occurring in our passage are meant to be read in a special way: their predicate-term is asserted not of their abstract subject, but of the concrete instances of that abstract. As I explained above, the whole of the argument of the preceding section was conditionalized on that assumption. It is now time to ask if the assumption is warranted. In a sentence like "Justice is pious" the predicate certainly seems to be asserted of Justice and of nothing else. Why should we not take the sentence at face-value? Is there good reason to think that Socrates is saying anything other than that? There is, but it is not as obvious as it has sometimes been thought to be.

*   We know, to begin with, that Socrates thinks of "Justice" as the name of a universal and that he does *not* think of universals as persons, nor yet as ontological dependencies of persons, such as the actions, decisions, dispositions, practices, or policies of this or that person.[86] This being the case, to say of any universal that it is just or unjust, pious or impious, brave or cowardly would be sheer nonsense: these are moral predicates, and for that reason they are as impredicable of a logical entity, like a universal, as of a mathematical entity, like a number or a geometrical figure: to say that Justice is pious would be as absurd as to say that the number eight or a hexagon is pious. Could this, then, be what Socrates is doing here? On what grounds could we convict him of so gross an error? We have his sentence, "Justice is pious." But this is not unambiguous evidence, for it is not an unambiguous sentence. It is the sort of sentence

[85] Cf. the terminal paragraph of Section I, above.

[86] Note that if we were to think of Justice as the disposition of some person, we would not be thinking of it as a universal, but as a temporal instantiation of the universal in the life of that person.

which *could* be used, absurdly, to predicate "is pious" of the universal, Justice. But it could also be used, impeccably, to predicate "is pious" of the instances of that universal. To be sure, to use it in the latter way one would have to disregard its surface grammar which is the same as that of "Abraham is pious." But is there any difficulty about that? That is what we do as a matter of course in reading the examples I tossed out in Section II—"Justice is impartial," "Ignorance is bliss": our linguistic intuition assigns unhesitatingly "is impartial" to those who are just, not to the abstraction, Justice, and "is bliss" to those who are ignorant, not to the abstraction, Ignorance. Or consider the following sentence from a contemporary writer, Iris Murdoch, whom no one could charge with writing stilted or artificial English:

> The best kind of courage (that which would make a man act unselfishly in a concentration camp) is steadfast, calm, temperate, intelligent, loving. . . . [87]

What is the natural reading of that sentence—the only way that would have even occurred to any of us encountering it in its own context, with our mind on the author's thought, instead of inspecting it out of context, as a specimen of philosopical grammar? Clearly, the reading that ascribes the adjectives, "steadfast, calm," etc., not to the abstraction, "best kind of courage," but to those persons, if any, who have that kind of courage; that is clearly what we would understand Iris Murdoch to be saying: that *those who have* the best kind of courage, *they* are "steadfast, calm, temperate, intelligent, loving" in their courage. Or, finally, take St. Paul's, "Charity suffereth long and is kind." We may be certain that everyone who has ever read or heard that sentence before philosophical grammarians got hold of it has taken it, as a matter of course, to be predicating *long-suffering* and *kindness* of those who have the virtue of charity. It would have taken satanic perversity to construe the apostle to be imputing those moral properties to an abstract entity.

Now it would not be difficult to find sentences of the same form whose sense does conform to their surface grammar:

> Justice is a universal;
> Justice is definable;
> Justice is a moral property.

In all of them the obviously correct construction is the one that assigns

[87] 1970, 57.

the predicate to the term in the subject position in exactly the same way
as does "Abraham is pious": "is a universal" is *not* being predicated of
the instances of Justice (we would not want to say that if Socrates is just,
he is a universal), but of Justice itself. Let us call this reading of the sentence
form "*B* is *A*" (where "*B*" names a property) "Ordinary predication."
The alternative reading, required by sentences like

> Justice is impartial;
> Courage is steadfast;
> Charity is kind,

we may call, after the Pauline paradigm, "Pauline predication."[88]

So when we look at the Socratic sentence, "Justice is pious," what we
have to decide is whether it is Ordinary or Pauline predication.[89] When
the question is put that way I doubt if anyone would hesitate in opting
for the latter. But how would we justify that choice? Would it be by arguing that to read it the other way, as an Ordinary predication, would produce
absurdity? That would be too easy. That Socrates would not want to
affirm an absurdity we may all agree. But can we be sure that he would
see that reading of it *as* an absurdity? I would find it absurd to predicate
moral properties of numbers or geometrical figures. But would a Pythagorean? Probably not.[90] Why then should Socrates' standards of what
makes sense, and what does not, be closer to mine than to a Pythagorean's?
That sort of question can only be decided by empirical evidence—that is
to say, if it is being raised and answered by historians of philosophy. And
by that I do not mean people who write books on the history of philosophy.
To do this in the way Bertrand Russell wrote much of his—half of it

*   [88] I owe the term and much else to a paper on self-predication in Plato,
presented to my seminar (fall of 1965) by Professor Sandra Peterson Wallace,
who was then a graduate student at Princeton. However, while my use of
"Pauline predication" applies it to the same set of sentences as does hers, my
description of the term (first paragraph of Section II, above) differs considerably from hers. It does so for reasons whose explanation had best await the
publication of her paper (which I have been urging on her for years).

[89] The analysis of argument (1) in II, 2, above had been conditionalized
on the hypothesis that this sentence (and the other three in Premises *1* and *2*
of this argument) are Pauline predications (cf. the opening sentence in n. 82
above). I have now reached the point where I can argue for that hypothesis.

[90] See, e.g., the passages cited by Guthrie (1962, 302–303). I say "probably"
because the evidence is second-hand and it is hard to know exactly what they
meant if, as Alexander reports (*Met.* 38, 10 ff.), they made reciprocity "the
defining property of justice and found this to exist in numbers."

out of his own head, the other half out of other histories of philosophy—
is not to qualify as a historian of philosophy. Russell, who was a clear-
headed and honest man, would undoubtedly have conceded that he did
not qualify, except briefly, in his youth, when he wrote *The Philosophy of
Leibnitz.* The crux of the matter is this: If history is an empirical discipline,
so is the history of philosophy. And no one can practice the empirical
method unless he is willing to submit even the most deeply entrenched
presumptions—his own or those of others—to the arbitrament of factual
data.

Do we have such data here? Certainly. We have the context. "Justice is
pious" does not come to us as an isolated text, like a Heraclitean fragment.
It comes in a longish, argumentative, passage, where it is joined by inferential links to dozens of other sentences. So if our question is if "Justice
is pious" is being used absurdly, as an Ordinary predication, or non-
absurdly, as a Pauline one, we may look for the answer not to our intuition
—which would only inform us how *we* would have used it, while what
we want to know is how *Socrates* used it—but to its own inferential context. How does that sentence behave there? What work is it made to do?

The foregoing discussion presents us with a clear picture of what
Socrates does with "Justice is pious" in our passage. He teams it up with
the three other sentences that make up Premises *1* and *2* of Argument
(1)—all of them substitution-instances of our "*B* is *A*" sentence-form—
to establish the similarity of Justice and Piety, this, I argued, being the
sort of similarity, which follows directly from the fact that, given those
premises, it follows that Justice is just and pious and Piety is just and
pious, and hence that the two virtues resemble each other in these two
respects. Now I noted at one point[91] that the Similarity Thesis is supposed
to imply Biconditionality. So here we have a condition which must be
satisfied by our reading of the statements that Justice is just and pious,
and that Piety is just and pious. Call it "Condition C." Let us try out both
readings on those statements, and see what happens. Read as Pauline
predications, they meet Condition C to perfection. For so read, "Justice
is just and pious" implies directly that anyone who instantiates Justice
will be just *and* pious; and exactly the same is true for the Pauline reading
of "Piety is pious and just."

Suppose, alternatively, that we read those statements as Ordinary
predications. Then all we can get out of "Justice is just and pious" is
that the universal, Justice, has those two properties. And *from the fact
that a universal has certain properties nothing follows to the effect that its in-*

[91] Above, p. 247.

stances have those properties. Thus from the fact that Justice is an abstract entity, is invariant, is incorporeal, it does not follow that each of those human beings who instantiate it is an abstract entity, is invariant, is incorporeal. So if "Justice is pious" and the other three substitution-instances of our "*B* is *A*" sentence form which make the premises of Argument (1) are read as Pauline predications, Condition *C* is satisfied: the logical connection of the Similarity Thesis with the Biconditionality Thesis, on which Socrates is counting, works like a dream. If they are read as Ordinary predications it does not work at all. This is good empirical evidence for the claim that the Pauline reading of "Justice is pious" is the right reading—the one in which Socrates meant his sentence to be understood.

Additional evidence of the same sort for the Pauline reading of sub-stitution-instances of the "*B* is *A*" sentence-form can be got out of our passage. Thus consider the conclusion of Argument (4): "Wisdom is
* Courage." I trust it is obvious by this time that the "is" here cannot mean identity. So it has to be predicative. And if the predication is convertible, as it is probably meant to be,[92] what Socrates thinks he has proved is that Wisdom and Courage are inter-predicable—that Wisdom is courageous, and Courage is wise. What kind of predication would that be? That it has to be Pauline follows from the fact that it is meant to imply the bicondi-tionality of Wisdom and Courage, that is to say, that Condition *C* has to be satisfied here as before. There can be no doubt about the fact that Socrates does expect that condition to be satisfied: he takes it for granted that his conclusion "Wisdom is Courage" has proved the contradictory of Protagoras' claim[93] that Courage and Wisdom are *not* biconditionally related. So here again we can argue as before, appealing exactly to the same reasoning, which need not be repeated: if the sentences "Courage is predicated of Wisdom" and "Wisdom is predicated of Courage" are Ordinary predications, they do nothing to sustain Socrates' confidence that his conclusion implies the biconditionality of Courage and Wisdom. If, on the other hand, they are Pauline, they sustain that conclusion fully, and so immediately that we can understand why Socrates does not trouble to spell out the fact that they do.[94]

I could proceed to show that all of the other substitution-instances of

[92] Above, n. 34.

[93] See Protagoras' statement quoted in n. 71, above. He denies bicondi-tionality between Courage and any of the other four virtues. Socrates responds by undertaking to establish the biconditionality of Courage and Wisdom.

[94] Supplementary (and logically independent) reason for reading "Courage

the "*B* is *A*" sentence-form in our passage are meant to be read as Pauline predications.[95] But this would not be to my purpose. There is one pair of sentences that interests me particularly, as I stated at the start of this essay: "Justice is just," and "Piety is pious." These came into my argument in the paragraph before the last. But I did not single them out there for special attention. I wanted to bring them up in the same way in which they are brought up in the text: as two of four sentences, all four of which must mesh to implement the inference that Justice and Piety are similar because Justice is just and pious and Piety is just and pious. By observing them in their own linguistic environment we have the best chance to see two complementary things about them, neither of which has ever been noticed in print.

We can see, first, how similar in form are the sentences in Premise 1, whose syntax has been thought so scandalous, to those in Premise 2, whose syntax, so far from scandalizing anybody, does not even seem to have caught the eye of anyone who has ever published on this topic.[96]

---

is predicated of Wisdom and Wisdom of Courage" as Pauline predications may be derived by considering the premises from which Socrates purports to have proved that "Wisdom is Courage." The immediate antecedent of this conclusion is "the wisest are also most confident, and being most confident are bravest (350C2-4)," which should probably be understood to mean that the wisest are most confident and bravest (cf. Vlastos, 1956, xxxii–xxxiii, and notes), implying that those who are wise are brave, which is precisely what we would get out of "Courage is predicated of Wisdom" if we read it as a Pauline predication. If, however, we read it as an Ordinary predication, to mean "Wisdom ε courageous," we would produce a *non sequitur*: from the premise "All who have property *F* have property *G*" it does not follow that "the property *F* has itself the property *G*"; thus if "All who are wise are persons" it would not follow that "Wisdom is a person."

[95] Thus "Virtue is noble" and "Courage is noble" have to be Pauline *
predications: to mesh in with the other premises in the argument (all of which are in extensional form) they have to be translated into "All the virtuous are noble" and "All the brave are noble." I did the latter without explanation (without so much as noticing that I was making a non-trivial syntactical transformation) in 1956, xxxii. Again, if one reflects on what has been said on the conclusion of Argument (2) in Section II,1, above—that "Wisdom and Temperance are one" could only mean that Wisdom and Temperance are necessarily coextensive classes—one will see that if it were restated in the canonical form of the Unity Theory, *sc.* that "Wisdom is 'named' [predicatively] 'Temperance' " and "Temperance is 'named' [predicatively] 'Wisdom,' " the predications could only be Pauline.

[96] It was first called to my attention in Prof. Sandra Peterson Wallace's paper (n. 88, above).

If we were going by surface grammar we would have to say that in all four sentences a property is being predicated of a property, and we would then be bound to say that the absurdity perpetrated by "Justice is just" is perpetrated no less by "Justice is pious." No one has ever turned a hair over "Justice is pious"—obviously because everyone has been reading it as a Pauline predication. Why then read "Justice is just" differently? Second, when we see the four sentences working together, we observe that their cooperation demands that their true syntax should be the same— that all four have to be Pauline predications, if they are to produce a conclusion which satisfies condition C; that is to say, if they are to empower us to infer from the premise-set the sort of similarity between Justice and Piety which implies their biconditionality. We have, therefore, the best of evidence—empirical evidence—that when Socrates asserts with such vehemence in our text that Justice is just and that Piety is pious he did not mean to assert the absurdity that Justice is a just *eidos* and Piety a pious one, but the analytic truth that the *eidos*, Justice, is such that all of its instances are just, and the *eidos*, Piety, is such that all of its instances are pious. It follows that neither sentence implies that Justice or Piety is self-predicative:[97] there is no reason to think that they were meant to

---

[97] The term "self-predication" seems to have entered Platonic exegesis *via* my 1954 paper. There "Φ is self-predicable" is used to mean "Φ ε F," where "Φ" is the name of a Form, "F," the character corresponding to that Form (as, e.g., "just" to "Justice"), and "ε" is the Peano symbol for class-membership. This use of "self-predication" had been inherited by A. E. Taylor (who had illustrated "predicated of itself" *inter alia* by "Whiteness is white" and explained it as turning on a confusion between a predication and the assertion of an identity" [1937, 355]) from Bertrand Russell (where the meaning of "predicable" in the expression "predicates which are predicable of themselves" was explicitly elucidated in terms of the Peano ε [1903, 78 ff.]). Every scholar who used "self-predication" in print in discussions of the Third Man Argument and allied topics in Plato adhered to this usage during the next decade, to my knowledge. However, in 1965, we find G. E. L. Owen stretching the term to make it cover "truistic sentences such as 'man is man' and 'a man is a man' " (1965, 134 ff.) and saying that self-predication is "implied" by Aristotelian καθ' αὑτό predication (as in *Post. An.* 83A18, where the blank in "―― ἄνθρωπος ἔστι" would be filled by ὁ ἄνθρωπος or by the proper name of a man, which would not come within miles of implying "*Man* ε man"). Since there is no patent office to license scholarly terms of art, scholars are at liberty to change the sense of a technical term in this way. But there is danger of failure in communication if that very application which a term was introduced *to exclude* is subsequently assumed to be a normal use of the identical linguistic expression. In this paper "self-predication" will be used only as defined above. (And cf. n.36 in *TMA* II).

have that implication, and there is cogent reason to think that they were not. This is a finding of some importance. Let me explain why.

IV. SELF-PREDICATION IN PLATO

If Plato had committed himself to the thesis that all Forms are self-predicative, he would have shattered irreparably the coherence of his theory. For then the Form of Plurality would have to be plural, and the Form of Motion mobile, while every Form in the system is required to be unitary and immobile. The consequence would be immediate: no long and complicated chain of reasoning would have been needed to detect it. One of those two Forms figures prominently in Platonic discussions: the Form of Motion is mentioned in the *Parmenides* (129E1, 136B5) and is one of the Five Great Kinds in the *Sophist*. If Plato had declared for unrestricted self-predication it could hardly have taken long for someone to try it out on Plurality or Motion and discover the horrendous result. To block that consequence it would have sufficed to declare for restricted self-predication. Thus in the case of Unity, Identity, Rest, self-predication would have been mandatory and innocent.[98] Have we then any good reason to believe that Plato really committed himself to unrestricted self-predication? In my paper on the Third Man in 1954 I emphasized that Plato had never *asserted* such a thing. I listed it nonetheless among the general assumptions of his Theory because, I said, it "is certainly implied by various things he said and believed" (336); my references included "Justice is just" and "Piety is pious" in the *Protagoras*.[99]

---

[98] Cf. *SPPL*, 337, below.

[99] The only other references I gave were (a) the phrase in *Phd.* 100C, "if anything else is beautiful, besides Beauty itself"; (b) Socrates' statement in *Ly.* 217D7-E1 that when a man's hairs have turned white, "they have become   *
such as that which is present in them, white through Whiteness [τότε ἐγένοντο οἱόνπερ τὸ παρόν, λευκοῦ παρουσίᾳ λευκαί.]"

My view of (a) remains unchanged, as I shall explain below: the context in the *Symposium* gives us the data which assure the self-predicative construction. Not so in the case of (b). Though the context in the *Lysis* is much too meager to provide the basis for a reasoned decision on the sense of the crucial phrase οἱόνπερ τό παρόν (i.e., οἱόνπερ λευκότης: cf. παρούσης λευκότητος in D5-6), there is a parallel in the *Republic* which does provide us with the required linguistic data:

But if we discover what sort of thing Justice *is* [οἷόν ἐστι δικαιοσύνη], will we require the just man to differ in no way from it, but to be in every way such as Justice *is* [τοιοῦτον εἶναι οἷον δικαιοσύνη ἐστίν]? Or shall we

My present paper refutes that construction of those two sentences. If my present argument is correct, so far from being "the star instance of self-predication" they had been taken to be by others beside myself,[100] they are not an instance of self-predication at all. At this point a new and exciting possibility opens up: might not the same be true in all cases where a logically illicit assertion would result from taking at face-value a Platonic text that wears the look of self-predication? The only way to answer this question would be to go through each of the texts in question, investigating each in its own context to learn from the context—not from our intuition—what in all probability it is being used to say. With all the wrangling that has gone on over self-predication during the last two decades, one would have thought that such an investigation would have been carried out long before this time. If it has, I do not know of it. We have had scattered observations, many of them valuable, and opinions by the gallon. But a systematic, exhaustive scrutiny of the linguistic data which would give us a firm basis for an answer to my question has yet to appear in print. Pending its appearance, let me venture a personal forecast on the basis of my own, still incomplete, study of the texts. This is that

---

be content if he were to approximate it most closely and have a greater share of it than do the rest? (472B7-C2)

I have underscored the two occurrences of "is," because I take it to be clearly the "is" of identity, not of predication, in both cases (every translator I have consulted has so taken it, and I cannot imagine that anyone would think that a case for translating "has" instead could be made). Now if οἷον δικαιοσύνη ἐστίν here has this sense, οἷόνπερ λευκόν or λευκότης [ἔστιν] in the *Lysis* must also have the same sense. I would thus emend my gloss on *Ly.* 217D7-E1 in my 1954 paper (*loc. cit.*), "the white hairs are 'such as' or 'of the same quality as' [οἷόνπερ] Whiteness; they have the same quality that Whiteness has," by changing the last word from "has" to "is." In neither passage does the reasoning *require* that the Form should have the quality which it is. Hence reading it into the text is gratuitous; it should be rejected on grounds of methodological economy.

[100] To the references given in Vlastos, 1954, 337, n. 33, add Ross (1951, 88), who sees in those sentences "the crudest form" in which the mistake occurs in Plato; also Hackforth (1945, 22, n. 1) who cites them to illustrate Plato's thinking of Forms as "existents in such a sense that each Form itself *has* the character that it *is*." The latter reference should help dispel the illusion that the ascription of self-predication to Plato was made only by scholars whose interests and training were primarily philosophical, rather than philological: Hackforth, then Laurence Professor of Ancient Philosophy in Cambridge, was a classicist. References subsequent to my 1954 papers would be too numerous to be worth compiling.

many of the sentences which have been taken as instances of self-predication in the past will turn out to have been Pauline predications; this group will include all the cases in which the self-predicative reading will yield blatant absurdity. But there will be some for which the self-predicative reading will survive, and these will be sentences where no obvious ineptitude will result—where the sense would be extremely plausible by ancient standards, tolerably so by modern ones. Let me offer an example of each—the sort of example which can be swiftly sketched because the implications of the contextual data are so clear.

In the *Timaeus* Plato speaks of the Form of Animal as ὃ ἔστιν ζῷον:[101] a phrase which, translated literally, *could* mean "that which *is* [i.e., really is] Animal."[102] And since he also speaks of it as "the perfect Animal" (τῷ

[101] 39E 8.

[102] As A. R. Lacey has pointed out (1959, 51), the phrase ὃ ἔστιν F *"prima facie* could have three meanings:

(i) That F which is [i.e., which really is, which is real].

(ii) That thing which F is [i.e., that thing with which F is identical].

(iii) That thing which is [an] F [or "which really is F"]."

(The augments in square brackets are mine.) That the sense could not be (iii) in some occurrences of the phrase is clear from *R.* 597A4-5, οὐκ ἄρτι μέντοι ἔλεγες ὅτι οὐ τὸ εἶδος ποιεῖ, ὃ δή φαμέν εἶναι ὃ ἔστι κλίνη ἀλλὰ κλίνην τινά; . . . Οὐκοῦν εἰ μὴ ὃ ἔστιν ποιεῖ, οὐκ ἂν τὸ ὂν ποιεῖ, ἀλλά τι τοιοῦτον οἷον τὸ ὄν, ὂν δε οὐ; Here sense (iii) is clearly precluded: ὃ ἔστι κλίνη stands unambiguously for the Form in explicit contrast to an instance of the Form, which Plato designates by "κλίνη τις." And the second half of the citation (note there especially the neuter form of the participle, τὸ ὄν) shows that in ὃ ἔστιν the verb is being used as a one-place predicate (in its "complete" sense), *not* as a *
copula (the "incomplete" sense). Hence here (and, therefore, also in the first part of the citation, from which the second is inferred) *to be* would have to be translated either *to exist* (which would make no sense, because the instance, κλίνη τις, with which ὃ ἔστι κλίνη is being contrasted, *also* exists) or else *to [really] be, to be real*. So we should translate: "Were you not saying just now that he does not make the Form, which we say Bed [really] is, but *a* bed? . . . So since he does not make that which [really] is, he does not make the real one, but something which is like the real one, but is not real." H. Cherniss (1957, 260) takes "ὃ ἔστιX" to mean "what *is identical* with X," citing several passages where he thinks it is obvious that this is the sense, without explaining why this has to be the sense. K. W. Mills (1957, 146) translates "ὃ ἔστι X" "that which X really is," but argues that (iii) is in fact implied since "that which X really is" is the nominatum of "X" and " 'to name something after (a Form)' is one of Plato's descriptions of the act of predicating an attribute of something" (cf. his continued discussion of this in 1958). He is, of course, perfectly right on the latter point, and the implication would certainly follow if

παντελεῖ ζώῳ),[103] we have all the linguistic evidence we need for thinking that he would say that the Form of ζῷον is ζῷον.[104] Could that be meant as a self-predicative statement? We can assure ourselves that the answer has to be "No" without having to bank on our intuition or to indulge our charitable inclinations towards Plato, our desire to save him from making a fool of himself. We can argue for the "No" as follows: he would have absolutely nothing to gain by so thinking of the Form of Animal—it would advance none of the stated purposes for which he postulates the existence of Forms; on the contrary, it would defeat disastrously the chief among them, which is to provide the Creator with an eternal, immutable[105] model; for Plato thinks of all living things as moving, and if the Form of Animal were (an) animal the result would be a contradiction—that which by hypothesis cannot move moves. And the contradiction would be such an obvious one that he could hardly miss it.

But we have as good contextual reasons for saying that when he refers to the Form of Beauty in the *Symposium* (211C-D) as ὃ ἔστι καλόν, he does mean to predicate "is beautiful" of the Form of Beauty.[106] There the context makes it clear that this is what he wants to say, what he has to say, to implement the theory of love he is expounding.[107] If the Form, Beauty, were not itself the eternally, absolutely, universally, and flawlessly[108] beautiful object for which the Platonic lover longs, the substantive doctrine of Platonic eros would collapse, since it is visibly made to rest on the theses that what is loved is the beautiful[109] and that Beauty

---

"is *F*" (and "is named '*F*' ") were an Ordinary predication; it would not, if it were Pauline. For an extended interpretation of the sense in which the Form of *F* is the "real" *F*, or that which is "really" *F*, for Plato see above, *MP*, pp. 47 ff. and *DR*, pp. 59 ff.; but neither paper undertakes a systematic investigation of the meaning of Plato's phrase ὃ ἔστι in its various occurrences, and there does not seem to be any in the literature. An exhaustive study of this topic would be welcome.

[103] 31B; τῷ τελέῳ ζώῳ, 39E.

[104] Cf. *R*. 597B5, τριτταί τινες κλῖναι αὗται γίγνονται: one of these three "beds" is the Form of Bed.

[105] 28E, κατὰ ταὐτὰ καὶ ὡσαύτως ἔχον. 28A, ἀεὶ κατὰ ταὐτὰ ὄν.

[106] I pointed this out at the close of *MP*, above: the self-predicative reading of "the *F* is *F*" would be only a nuisance for Plato in epistemological contexts, but would have great plausibility in other contexts where "Forms assume their other role, as objects of value, and of the kind of value Plato claimed for them."

[107] Cf. IOLP, above.

[108] *Smp*. 211A1-5.

[109] *Smp*. 204D3-5.

itself is more loveable than is any of its instances.[110] To read "Beauty is
beautiful" as a Pauline predication would be to turn it into a truism of
utter inconsequence for that redirection of desire, that mutation of sensuality, which Platonic eros prescribes, while the thesis that Beauty itself is
the supremely beautiful thing in existence is meant to epitomize the
liberating, energizing, life-transforming wisdom of that doctrine. To paraphrase self-predication out of "Beauty is beautiful" would be not to
translate but to obliterate the vision which may be glimpsed as through
an iridescent crystal in that sentence.[111]

Some readers are bound to ask at this point if so fastidious a writer
could have used the same phrase, ὅ ἐστι F, so inconsistently, making it
mean, without the slightest apology or even warning, such radically different things in different places. But there is a simple explanation of such
behavior: Plato was himself unaware of the ambiguity. That ambiguous
sentences may be used without awareness of their ambiguity is a commonplace of modern linguistics. How many of us, to borrow one of Chomsky's
simpler examples, would twig to the three-way ambiguity of "I had a

[110] *Smp.* 211D-E.

[111] In a fuller treatment of the topic I would have taken time off at this point
to venture a long-overdue response to the delightful onslaught on "the self-
predicationists" by R. E. Allen (1960, 147 ff.). The following, though hardly
adequate, may be better than nothing. The crux of the difference between
his interpretation of the sentence-form, "the Form of F is F" in Plato and the
one I have defended in this paper is this: Allen takes the "is" in "is F" to
express identity. I fail to see how this could be true, e.g., in "Beauty is beautiful." Here the "is" *must* express predication, not identity, for the reason given
above: the doctrine that Beauty is (supremely) beautiful is a clear and necessary
consequence of the doctrine that Beauty is (supremely) loveworthy and that
nothing is loveworthy unless it is beautiful; the identity, "the beautiful is the
beautiful," or "Beauty is Beauty," could not begin to capture this doctrine.
Nor could identity be the intended sense of "Justice is just" and "Piety is
pious" in the *Prt.*, for that would spoil the argument (cf. II, 2, above): if
Premise *1* asserted that Justice and Piety are self-identical, how could this
truism be spliced with Premise *2* to yield the required conclusion? From
"Justice is self-identical and pious" and "Piety is self-identical and just" we
cannot infer that Justice and Piety are similar in that each is both just and
pious (or similar in some other way which could be plausibly thought to
imply the biconditionality of the two virtues). However, in spite of my other
differences on this and other points with Allen's paper, I consider it a most
valuable contribution to the debate. It was a splendid protest against the
imputation of (unrestricted) self-predication to Plato which I was sponsoring
in my 1954 paper on the Third Man, and which had been blandly accepted
by many others beside myself and appears to be still widely accepted today.

book stolen" if we happened to use the phrase?[112] This might provoke the retort that such things happen to ordinary folk in unreflective contexts, but hardly to a writer of exquisitively sensitive prose in contexts where the detection of ambiguity would have been of the utmost moment for the success of his philosophical venture. Are we to counter with the reflection that not even genius can excape the common fate of language-users, which is to know *how* to do certain things with words without knowing *that* one is doing them? This would be much too general. It would beg the question at issue, which concerns precisely the ability of the uncommonly talented to rise above common limitations. Something more definite and concrete is needed to convince the sceptic. I am ready to produce evidence of that sort. In my study of Plato's use of the "*B* is *A*" sentence-form, in the *Sophist*,[113] I believe I have shown that he uses the important substitution-instance, "Motion is resting," with no aware-ness that its evident falsehood when read as a Pauline predication can be matched by its no less evident truth when read as an Ordinary predication.

From our passage in the *Protagoras* we may learn one more thing from which anyone tempted to credit Plato with preternatural linguistic clair-voyance should take to heart: great stylist though he was, Plato could still produce a composition whose thought is so muddy. The measure of its unclarity can be taken from the variety of interpretations that have been put on it over the years by skilled and erudite scholars. In the light of the preceding discussion one need only take a second look at Socrates' discourse to see where the main source of the unclarity lies. The speaker has failed to straighten out for himself the meaning of his three theses to the point of seeing exactly how they sustain those logical interconnections which his intuition assures him they have. If he had spelled out the sort of similarity he is imputing to the virtues as I did on his behalf above, he could hardly have resorted to phraseology so vague as to say in one place (331B) that they are "either the same thing or as similar as two things could possibly be" and in another that "they are nearly the same" (333B) and explained their similarity by the gold-bar analogy which amost forces on the reader the very thing which Socrates does *not* mean: blank homogeneity. Nor yet in the case of the Unity Thesis would he have been content to say that the names of all the virtues apply to the same thing, without offering at least that modicum of explanation we get in the pas-sage in the *Phaedo* which exorcises the linguistic absurdity that all of them are proper names of the same thing. To this extent what I have

[112] 1965, 21.
[113] *AS*, below.

offered in this paper is, and is meant to be, not a reproduction of its writer's thought, but a clarification of it. My argument has been that Plato used "Justice is just" and "Justice is pious" as Pauline predications—not that he knew he did.[114] Had he come to know this, I dare say that not only his exposition of Socrates' doctrine of the Unity of the Virtues, but the whole subsequent development of his own philosophy, would have been different.

[114] This disambiguation of the "B is A" sentence-form was not to be reached even at the high-point of Plato's logical achievement represented by the *Sophist*. It was not even reached by Aristotle; cf. *TLPA*, below.

APPENDIX

The Argument in La. 197E ff.

From

    1 Courage $=_{Df}$ knowledge of things to be dreaded and to be dared,

which is taken to imply

    2 Courage is knowledge of future goods and evils (198B2-C3),

and the further premise,

    3 The science of all goods—past, present, and future—is the same science (198D1–199A8),

the conclusion is drawn on Nicias' behalf and with his concurrence

    4 Courage is the science of all goods and evils—past, present, and future (199B9-D1).

Socrates then elicits the admission of

    5 Whoever has the science of all goods and evils has not only Courage (and Wisdom) but Temperance, Justice, and Piety as well (199D4-E1);

and from *4* and *5* he infers

    6 Courage is not a part of virtue, but the whole of virtue (199E3-4).

Since *6* contradicts flatly the previous admission (190C), that

    7 "Courage is only one of the parts of virtue" (199E6-7),

Socrates infers that "we have not discovered what Courage is" (E11).

Does Socrates really think that 6 has been validly inferred from true premises? There seems to be a consensus among the commentators that he does (joined recently by Santas [1969], 452 ff.). But I find this view untenable in the face of two of its consequences, either of which would seem sufficient to discredit it:

(a) It implies that Socrates is giving up the definition in 1. I cannot square this with the following facts:

(i) Nicias presents it (194C ff.) as derived from Socratic doctrine;
(ii) Socrates builds it into his demonstrative argument in *Prt.* 360D;
(iii) Plato retains it (with appropriate modifications) in *R.* 429C–430B.

(Santas thinks he has the option of allowing Socrates to endorse the argument from 1 to 6 without having "to give up his favorite definition of courage" in 1 (455). But he seems to ignore Socrates' own assessment of the upshot of the argument, *sc.*, that "we have not yet discovered, Nicias, what Courage is" (199E): to say this is to imply that, if the argument is valid, 1 is *not* a correct answer to the question, "What is Courage?")

(b) It implies further that Socrates is conceding the falsehood of 7. But to do so

(i) would outrage common sense (it would be tantamount to saying that Courage is not *a* virtue, but all of virtue, contrary to the common meaning of the word), and

(ii) would be out of line with the explicit recognition of the part-whole relation between each of the virtues and virtue in other Socratic and Platonic dialogues (cf. the reference to *Meno* 78D8–79E in n. 8 above, and note the reference to Justice, Temperance, and Piety as "parts" of virtue in 78D8-E1; for Plato's view cf., e.g., *Lg.* 696B6, "Is not Courage one part of virtue?")

These truly formidable difficulties can be completely avoided by supposing that Socrates is *not* underwriting the argument which leads to 6, but has laid it on only to test Nicias' understanding of the definition in 1: he wants to show that, in spite of Nicias' ability to state the definition and to defend it against obvious objections from Laches, Nicias' grasp of the implications of the definition is no better than would be that of the sophists, Damon and Prodicus (cf. 197D). If one goes back to the text with this possibility in mind, one should not find it hard to spot the place at which the argument goes wrong: this is the inference from 2 and 3 to 4; and, in the course of making it, Socrates makes it very clear that the onus

of the inference rests on *Nicias:* it is *his* "argument" (κατὰ τὸν σὸν λόγον
. . . ὡς νῦν αὖ ὁ σὸς λόγος, 199C5-D1). This language puts the burden
of the inference entirely on Nicias. Socrates would have excellent reason
for declining it himself, since it is in fact invalid: from 2 and 3 all that
follows is

> 4A Courage implies the science of all goods and evils.

For if the science of all goods and evils is the same, one cannot have
knowledge of any subclass of goods and evils, without having this science.
Hence, given 1, one cannot have Courage, which is knowledge of a sub-
class of goods and evils (those in the future), without having this science.
Thus this science is a necessary condition of Courage. But it does not
follow that Courage *is* (i.e., is identical with) that science. To show that
X is a necessary condition of Y obviously falls far short of showing that
X is identical with Y.

Once we substitute 4A for 4 the aporetic conclusion is blocked. 5 remains the good Socratic doctrine which it is (the Biconditionality Thesis).
Taking it in conjunction with 4A, instead of 4, all that now follows is

> 8 Whoever has Courage has all the other parts of virtue—not only
> Courage (and Wisdom) but Temperance, Justice, and Piety as well,

which is, of course, consistent with 7.

What Plato wants us to learn from this terminal argument in the *Laches*
is that Nicias, for all his ability to rattle off Socrates' own answer to
"What is Courage?" and to answer elementary objections to it, has *not*
"discovered what Courage is," for he has not understood the crucial
implications of the Socratic definition: those which connect it with the
doctrine of the Unity of the Virtues. If Nicias had understood those
implications, he would never have concurred with 4, since this in conjunction with 5 leads unavoidably to the unacceptable conclusion in 6.

That Plato should be at pains to discredit Nicias as a spokesman for
Socratic knowledge is only what we would expect: he could hardly have
allowed this role to a man who had been guilty of that colossal folly, the
countermanding of the order to evacuate the Athenian forces at Syracuse
because an eclipse had occurred, the soothsayers had prescribed twenty-
seven days' postponement of the evacuation, and Nicias was "rather
too much under the influence of divination and the like" (Thuc. 7, 50, 4).
Nicias had taken it upon himself to associate himself with Socrates and
his doctrine. Early in the dialogue he represents himself as a familiar of
Socrates (180C9-D3) who knows what happens when you tangle with

Socrates in an elenchus (187E6–188C1). When his turn comes to propose a definition, he takes his stand on what he has "frequently heard [Socrates] saying, that each of us is good in those things in which he is wise" (194D1-2) and then, a few lines later, propounds the very definition Socrates uses in *Prt.* 360D. His defense of that definition starts off with a pastiche of Socratic doctrine (cf. *La.* 195C7-D1 with *Grg.* 511E6–512B2) and then proceeds along lines which Socrates is moved to acknowledge "in all seriousness" as perfectly sound in spite of their clash with what is commonly said (196E). It is surely of the utmost importance for Plato to show the reader how superficial and brittle are Nicias' ties with Socrates' own understanding of morality. Plato hints at this by having Nicias bring in at the last a gaggle of linguistic distinctions (197A6-C1) which Socrates gently disowns (presumably because he finds them inconsequential—not necessarily false) by saying they are derived from Prodicus *via* Damon (197D1-5). That he should then proceed— as he does, on the present interpretation—to expose Nicias' incapacity to steer the Socratic definition through the rough waters of the terminal elenchus is precisely what we would expect at the dramatic climax of the dialogue.

11

An Ambiguity
in the *Sophist**

(1970; AS)

I. A PAULINE PREDICATION

TAKE a simple sentence in natural Greek assigning some property to some individual, say, "Σοφός ἐστι Σωκράτης," "Socrates is wise." A

---

* This is a drastically revised and greatly expanded version of two working-papers presented to my Plato seminar in the fall of 1967 and privately circulated to a few other scholars: "Pauline Predications in the *Sophist*" and "Pauline and Ordinary Predications in Form-Blending." My results were reached with the help of such previous work on the same topic as was available to me at the time. I list in chronological order those books or papers which I had then found most useful:

R. Robinson, *Plato's Earlier Dialectic*, 2nd Ed. (Oxford, 1953), 260–64.

J. L. Ackrill, "Plato and the Copula," *J.H.S.* 77 (1957), Part I, 5–6.

J. M. E. Moravcsik, "Being and Meaning in Plato's *Sophist*," *Acta Philosophica Fennica*, Fasc. XIV, 1962, 23–78.

I. M. Crombie, *An Examination of Plato's Doctrines: II, Plato on Knowledge and Reality* (London, 1963), 401–10.

The untitled paper of Sandra Peterson Wallace dealing with self-predication and allied topics, presented to my Plato seminar in the fall of 1965 (cf. *UVP*, n. 88, above).

K. Lorenz and J. Mittelstrass, "Theaetetos fliegt," *Archiv für Geschichte der Philosophie* 48 (1966), 113–51, at 130–32.

J. Malcolm, "Plato's Analysis of *To On* and *To Mē On* in the *Sophist*," *Phronesis* 12 (1967), 130–46 at 139–43.

familiar doctrine of Plato's middle period[1] correlates with each such sentence in the natural language ("NL") an ontologically revealing ("OR") sentence which purports to disclose the ontological basis of its meaning and truth. Thus

NL(Socrates is wise) ↔ OR(Socrates participates in Wisdom).[2]

In the *Sophist* Plato extends this procedure to a new set of NL sentences which share the grammatical form of "Socrates is wise" but whose subject-term names a "Form" or "Kind"[3] instead of a spatio-temporal individual or occurrence. He does this in the passage which discusses the logical interrelations of the Kinds and brings the Stranger within sight of the solution of the problem of Not-Being.[4] The most provocative and puzzling

---

Crombie's treatment of my topic is the one to which I was most indebted. While differing with him at several points, as will appear, I found much that is congenial in the general position he takes, and I benefited from several of his remarks.

For critical comments on earlier drafts of this paper which helped me correct some mistakes and avoid others I am indebted to members of my Plato seminar at Princeton, most recently to Glenn P. Kessler and Bernard Russell.

Important contributions to Platonic studies bearing on my topic came to my notice since I reached the results recorded in this paper. I list in chronological order those I found most valuable: Frede (1967); Owen (1968); Owen (1971); Hartman (forthcoming); Keyt (1971). The following are annotated translations or commentaries to which I refer in this essay: Apelt (1897); Apelt revised by Wiehl (1967); Cornford (1935); Diès (1934); Robin (1950); Taylor (1961).

[1] *Phd.* 102B (cf. *Prm.* 128E–129A; 130E–131A).

[2] I capitalize substantives here and hereafter to indicate that they are being used as names of a Platonic (or Socratic) *eidos* or *idea*. Note that this is the only feature of "Socrates participates in Wisdom" that distinguishes it from an NL sentence. The use of "participates" *per se* would not serve the purpose: "Socrates participates in wisdom" would be one way in which one could say in natural Greek that Socrates is wise (cf., e.g., *Hdt.* 9, 18, 2, εἴ τι ἀλκῆς με-τέχουσι, for "if they had any courage," i.e., if they were courageous.)

[3] As has often been noticed, the terms γένος, εἶδος, ἰδέα are used interchangeably in the *Sophist*: cf., e.g., τῶν γενῶν in 254B7 with τῶν εἰδῶν four lines later, where it is certain from the context that the sense has not shifted in the least.

[4] 250A–257A. It comes at the end of a series of controversial encounters with doctrinaire ideologies (Eleatic Monism, Materialism, Idealism). It starts by demonstrating the thesis that there are determinate combinations among Kinds (250A–252E). It proceeds to recognize the search into their combinations as dialectician's work (252E–254D) and to produce a sample of such

of the correlations offered us in this passage occurs in the following exchange (256B):

> *Stranger.* So too, if Motion itself were to participate somehow [πῃ] in Rest,[5] it would not be preposterous to call it "resting" [στάσιμον]?[6]
>
> *Theatetus.* Perfectly correct, if we are to concede that some of the Kinds combine with one another, while others do not.

Cutting out expendable verbiage,[7] transposing from the formal to the material mode of speech, and changing hypotheticals into categoricals, we derive the following correlation from the Stranger's statement:

NL(Motion is resting) ↔ OR(Motion participates in Rest).

Is the NL sentence here meant to be true or false?

It would be useless to pursue this question, until we have reckoned with the syntactical ambiguity infecting a sentence of this form,[8] which was discussed in *UVP* under the labels of "Ordinary" and "Pauline" predica-

---

work by establishing the combinations among five Great Kinds (254D–257B). This section on the "Communion of Kinds" (as it is often named in modern studies) has a definite thematic coherence which justifies keeping the whole of the present inquiry within its limits.

[5] Throughout this paper "Motion" and "Rest" (and their cognate verbs and participles) will serve simply as dummies for the Greek words κίνησις and στάσις (and their cognates). The reader will constantly bear in mind that κίνησις covers all kinds of variation, of which change in spatial position is only one, and hence that its antonym, στάσις, stands for invariance in its most general sense, applying naturally to entities like Plato's Forms, which, strictly speaking, could no more be said to "rest" than "move." Alternative English renderings of στάσις—"Immobility" (Cherniss), "inactivity" (Crombie), "stability" (in my *SPPL*, as first printed in the *Philosophical Review*) —unhappily lack the cognate verb which is frequently needed if one is to preserve in the English translation the syntactical form of Plato's Greek, as one must, since syntax is all important in this discussion. Once we reconcile ourselves, on this account, to the use of "Rest" for στάσις, we might as well accept "Motion" for κίνησις in this context: we thus get a pair of true antonyms in either case, and the violence done to the English words is symmetrical.

[6] "Stationary" (Cornford, Taylor) would, of course, do greater justice to the suffix -ιμον. But I want to keep the verbal link with my "Rest" for στάσις.

[7] Including the πῃ, to which due reference will be made in the penultimate paragraph of this section.

[8] Its incidence in Plato, ignored by earlier commentators, appears to be noticed for the first time by Robinson (1953, 260 ff.: the first edition, unchanged at this point, had appeared in 1941); it is vigorously pursued by Crombie (1963, 402 ff.). Cf. Appendix II below.

tion. To recapitulate: A Platonic sentence predicating the adjective, A, of an abstract property, B, may be read as assigning A either

- (I) to B in contradistinction to B's instances, or else
- (II) to B's instances, if any,[9] in contradistinction to B, and to them necessarily.[10]

If (I), it is being read as "Ordinary" predication ("OP"); if (II), as "Pauline" predication ("PP"). Let us symbolize these two uses of "B is A":

- (I) B is$_{OP}$ A $=_{Df}$ $B \varepsilon A$.[11]
- (II) B is$_{PP}$ A $=_{Df}$ $N\{(x)[(x \varepsilon B) \rightarrow (x \varepsilon A)]\}$.[12]

[9] The truth of a Pauline predication would not depend for Plato on the historical accident of the instantiation of its terms. Thus "Justice is wise" would be necessarily true regardless of whether or not any just men exist (cf. the remark about the just state in *R.* 592A-B). (II) states that *if* B were instantiated its instances would of necessity co-instantiate A.

[10] On the indispensability of the modal operator see the comment on the formula in *UVP*, I.3, p. 233 above.

[11] The definiens may also be written, "$A(B)$," which comes to the same thing: either formula may be read, "B is an A" or "B instantiates A." A fuller reading of the first formula would be: "B is a member of the instance-class of A."

[12] The definiens may also be written, "$N[(x)(Bx \rightarrow Ax)]$." Either formula may be read: "Necessarily, for all x, if x is a B then x is an A." It should be noted that these formulae (and also the one to follow in (IIa), which is logically equivalent to them) abstract from the separation of Forms from immanent characters in the "tripartite ontology" of *Phdo* 102B ff. (cf. RC, II). The English capitals I use here (only for typographical convenience) do the job of Form-variables for which Greek capitals were used in *RC* (and will be used again in *FRA* below). As I mentioned in *RC*, it is only on rare occasions that the full apparatus of the trichotomic Forms/characters/individuals scheme is deployed in the corpus. Most of the time Plato is content to work with the dichotomic Forms/individuals scheme. In the *Sophist* he operates exclusively with the latter , collapsing the Form-character distinction, thereby allowing himself to speak about inter-Form entailment (which he now expresses by μετέχειν, μεταλαμβάνειν, and [προσ]κοινωνεῖν with genitive construction) as though it were an extensive, part-whole, relation, using such language as A "surrounding" or "embracing" B (n. 60, below) and speaking of the Kinds as forming extensive domains which may be disjoint, conjoint, or subjoint (n. 85, below). It is, therefore, permissible to use the simplified symbolism I employ above. A more elaborate symbolism, employing a separate set of Form-variables and character-variables (as in *RC* above and *FRA* below) would be a needless complication. It is useless for the purpose of elucidating the OP/PP ambiguity and exploring its implications.

The first definiens tells us that B is itself a member of the class of things which are A. The second tells us that if anything is a member of the class of things which are B, then, necessarily, that same thing will be a member of the class of things which are A.[13] What (II) says can be expressed more shortly: that the class of things which are B is, necessarily, included in the class of things which are A. This shorter definiens will be the one I shall be using hereafter:

(IIa) B is$_{PP}$ A $=_{Df}$ $N(B \subset A)$.[14]

Now let us see what happens to the NL sentence we derived above from *Sph.* 256B2-3 when it is read in each of these alternative ways. Let us begin with the second reading. "Motion is$_{PP}$ resting" is bound to be false, since Motion and Rest are contraries (in Plato's language: "opposites"[15]); and to say of two concepts, B and C, that they are contraries is to say that whatever instantiates either of them does not instantiate the other, i.e., that their instances form mutually exclusive classes. Thus "B and C are contraries" means "$N(B \subset \bar{C})$";[16] and if the classes are non-

---

[13] Strictly speaking, *the definiens in both formulae and also in (IIa) below is a contraction.* In each of the three formulae the definiens, fully spelled out, would start off, "The relation of B to A is such that . . . ." To bear this in mind is particularly important in the case of (II) and (IIa) where the formula switches from the Form B in the definiendum to the instance-class of B in the definiens: there is no switch in subject-matter, since what the definiens is meant to specify is precisely the relation between B and A which is asserted by the definiendum. Cf. Appendix II below.

[14] May be read: "Necessarily, the instance-class of B is included in the instance-class of A." (I use "$\subset$" to denote the transitive, non-symmetrical, but not antisymmetric, relation of class-inclusion which logicians denote more often than not by "$\subseteq$.")

[15] ἐναντία is Plato's only term for "contraries". Examples of ἐναντία in the *Prt.* (332B-C) are temperance/intemperance, strength/weakness, beauty/ugliness, good/evil; in the *Phdo*, large/small (103A), odd/even (104D), hot/cold (103D), musical/unmusical, mortal/immortal (105D–106D). Some of these, like odd/even, are obviously contradictories, i.e., not only mutually exclusive, but also jointly exhaustive of their universe of discourse. Others are what we would call "polar" contraries, allowing for intermediate cases where neither "opposite" applies: so "large" and "small," as is made didactically explicit in the *Sph.* (257B), with "equal" (i.e., of intermediate size) in between. Cf. *UVP*, pp. 244 and 249–50 and notes. And see n. 18, below.

[16] The modality records the fact that if two terms are contraries their co-instantiation in the same individual (at the same time, in the same respect) is precluded by the very meaning of the terms in conjunction with the principle

empty[17] this entails that "$N(B \subset C)$" is false. The corresponding inference does not hold for "B is$_{OP}$ C": from the fact that B and C are contraries we cannot infer the falsehood of "$B \varepsilon C$." Thus the concepts,
Corporeal, Incorporeal, are obvious contraries; but "Corporeal ε Incorporeal"
is not false; *Corporeal*, a concept, is just as incorporeal as is any other concept. Hence to say that Motion and Rest are contraries is to imply the
falsehood of "Motion is$_{PP}$ resting"—*not* that of "Motion is$_{OP}$ resting."
So when Plato writes that Motion and Rest are "most opposed to one
another" (ἐναντιώτατα ἀλλήλοις)[18] and that it

> is to the last degree impossible that Motion should rest and that
> Rest should move (252D9-10),

there can be no doubt that we must understand him to be implying that
the PP reading (*not* the OP reading) of "Motion is resting" is false. He is
thus expecting us to construe "Motion is not resting" (abbreviating:
"M is not R") to mean

3    $-(M$ is$_{PP}$ $R)$,[19]

i.e., as

4   $N[-(M \subset R)]$,[20]

and hence to construe "Motion is resting" as

5   M is$_{PP}$ R,

---

of non-contradiction. (I use "$\bar{C}$" for the negate of C.)

[17] Only if B were empty could it be said to be included (and, in that case,
vacuously) in both C and $\bar{C}$. That M and R are non-empty is made clear, e.g., at
249C-D.

[18] 250A. By his use of the superlative form here, and by the subsequent
question in 250C12-D2, Plato may be implying that Motion and Rest are not
only contraries but contradictories (cf. n. 15, above). He never envisages, as
does Aristotle in *Physics* Zeta, conditions under which it would be false to say
that a thing is either moving or resting (cf. my "Note on Zeno's Arrow,"
Phronesis 11 [1966], 3-18, at 13-14). However, since it is not entirely clear
that Plato means that they are contradictories, and since their being contraries
will suffice to carry his reasoning, I shall refer to them throughout as contraries.

[19] I use the dash as the negation sign.

[20] The modality in 4 is warranted by the definition in (IIa) above. Textual
authority is provided by the wording in 252D, since "impossible that p"
entails and is entailed by "necessary that $-p$."

i.e., as

6 N($M \subset R$).

Consider now the alternative, "Motion is_{OP} resting," reading of Plato's sentence. That its falsehood is not implied by the fact that Motion and Rest are contraries has just been shown. This opens up the possibility that on this reading Plato's sentence might be true. And the fact is that it *has* to be true in Plato's system, since the invariance (hence "rest") of the Platonic Form is built into its very essence: none of its categorial properties is more fundamental than is its absolute immutability. To be sure, some commentators have believed that Plato's ontology gets a drastic reconditioning in the later dialogues, and might therefore hold that even this feature of the earlier theory has now been dropped or modified; they might insist that its retention in the *Sophist* cannot be taken for granted. I am not suggesting that it be taken for granted. All I need to make my point stick can be established from data in the *Sophist* itself, taken in conjunction with the *Philebus*, a dialogue generally acknowledged to be of the same vintage.

In the *Philebus*, fully as much as in the *Phaedo*, the *Republic*, and the *Phaedrus*, the objects of "intelligence,"[21] whose cognition yields the "truest" knowledge,[22] constitute a domain of immutable being which is "ever invariantly in the same state"[23] and is utterly exempt from the becoming and perishing—and hence the "motion"—which characterizes "this world,"[24] the world constituted by the spatio-temporal participants in the Forms. The invariance which the *Philebus* ascribes so explicitly to the objects of "intelligence" is said in the *Sophist* to be the condition of "rest" and, to constitute, along with "rest," the condition of the exercise of "intelligence":

---

[21] νοῦς, which becomes Plato's favorite term for the highest form of intellectual activity in the *Phdr.* (247D1) and thereafter (*Phlb.* 59B7, D1; *Sph.* 249C3 and 7; *Ti.* 51D3-E5). In the middle dialogues it is used to mean *mind, reason,* i.e., the organ which exercises such activity, rather than the activity itself, for which Plato's characteristic term had been νόησις (*R.* 511D, 523A–524C, 534; but also *Ti.* 28A, 52A).

[22] ἐπιστήμη . . . τὸ ἀληθέστατον ἔχουσα (59B7-8; cf. 59D1-2).

[23] ἀεὶ κατὰ τὰ αὐτὰ ὡσαύτως ἀμεικτότατα ἔχοντα (59C3-4); κατὰ ταὐτὰ καὶ ὡσαύτως ὄντα ἀεί (61E2-3).

[24] τὸν κόσμον τόνδε (59A3) constituted by τὰ γιγνόμενα καὶ γενησόμενα καὶ γεγονότα (59A7-8).

Stranger. Do you think that what is invariantly in the same state and in the same respect[25] could exist without rest?

Theaetetus. By no means.

Stranger. And without these could intelligence be seen to exist or to have ever existed anywhere at all?

Theaetetus. It could not. (249B-C)

So if there is to be "intelligence," something or other in the universe must satisfy this condition. What could that be? The only set of entities in Plato's universe that would fit the bill are the Forms or Kinds, which are as certainly the objects of "intelligence" in the *Sophist* as they are in the *Philebus.*[26] For the practice of dialectic is represented in the *Sophist* as the highest possible exercise of the intellect;[27] and the task of dialectic

[25] κατὰ ταὐτὰ καὶ ὡσαύτως καὶ περὶ τὸ αὐτό. The underscored words recur in the phrase in *Phlb.* 59C, and also in 61E (quoted in n. 23, above) and in similar phrases used to characterize the Forms in dialogues of the middle period:

Phd. 78C, ἀεὶ κατὰ ταὐτὰ καὶ ὡσαύτως ἔχει; and cf. the other passages from the *Phd.* cited in *RC*, n. 20.

R. 479A, ἰδέαν . . . κάλλους ἀεὶ . . . κατὰ ταὐτὰ ὡσαύτως ἔχουσαν,

R. 479E, ἀεὶ κατὰ ταὐτὰ ὡσαύτως ὄντα,

and in the *Timaeus* (the Creator's eternal [ἀίδιον, 29A5] model is τὸ κατὰ ταὐτὰ καὶ ὡσαύτως ἔχον, 29A1). It might be objected that the phrase in the *Sph.* cited at the head of this note does not have the same force because it omits the adverb ἀεί, which occurs in the phrases I have just quoted from the middle dialogues. The objection has no force, because the omission is an accident of style, rather than the expression of a substantive reservation: thus the ἀεί is also missing in the citation from the *Timaeus*, though present (and emphatic) in a neighboring context (28A1, ἀεὶ κατὰ ταὐτὰ ὄν); cf. also the omission of the ἀεί in *Ti.* 52A1, where the Forms (of whose unqualified eternity there can be no doubt) are τὸ κατὰ ταὐτὰ εἶδος ἔχον, in contrast to the sensible world which is πεφορημένον ἀεί.

[26] Neither in *Phlb.* 59A-C nor in *Sph.* 249B-C are the invariant objects of "intelligence" denominated "Forms." But the identification is indubitable in either case, given Plato's continuing adherence to the assumption that the Forms are *cognita* par excellence. In the *Phlb.* we may also compare the description of the "Henads" in 15B as "ever the same and never admitting of either becoming or perishing."

[27] Dialectic is the prerogative of the "genuine and rightful philosopher" (253E), who perpetually "attaches himself by means of reasoning to the realm of being" (τῇ τοῦ ὄντος ἀεὶ διὰ λογισμῶν προσκείμενος ἰδέᾳ) which is "divine" (254AB).

is to explore the interrelations of the Kinds.[28] Therefore the Kinds must be "ever in the same state in the same way and in the same respect"; they must be characterized by "rest."[29] Hence Motion, which holds a place of honor among the "greatest Kinds," must be so characterized. Hence "Motion is$_{OP}$ resting" must be true.

It should be clear then that the question, "Is the sentence 'Motion is resting?' in 256B meant to be true or false?" would be conclusively answered if we were in a position to tell what Plato means by using this sentence in this context: true, if he is using it to mean "Motion is$_{OP}$ resting"; otherwise false. Now it so happens that the same sentence[30] occurs in an earlier part, 252D2-4, of our passage to which I have already alluded. Let me now quote the passage in full:

> *Stranger.* What then? Are we to allow to all [the Kinds] the power to combine with one another?
>
> *Theaetetus.* This [hypothesis] even I can refute.
>
> *Stranger.* How?
>
> *Theaetetus.* For if Motion and Rest supervened on one another, Motion itself would be absolutely [παντάπασιν] at rest and, conversely, Rest itself would move.
>
> *Stranger.* And this is to the last degree impossible—that Motion should rest, and that Rest should move?
>
> *Theaetetus.* Quite so. (252D2-11)

The hypothesis being considered here—that Rest "supervenes" on Motion and Motion on Rest—is simply that either Kind qualifies (or, is predicated of) the other.[31] It is agreed that, in the case of Motion, the consequence

---

[28] 253D-E.

[29] For a critique of older views that some sort of "mobility" or "motivity" is ascribed to the Forms in the *Sph.* (mainly as an inference from the "mark" of Being as "power to act and be acted upon" in 247E ff.) see Auguste Diès (1924, 286, n.1); and cf. Cherniss (1944), n. 397 and p. 607. For a critique of more recent views that Plato is allowing for some slight suspectibility to change in the Forms (because, allegedly, he concedes that being known implies being changed) see Appendix I to the present essay.

[30] I am ignoring grammatical differences which are irrelevant to the point under discussion. Accordingly, I speak of "Motion rests" and "Motion is resting (or, 'stationary')" as the same sentence.

[31] For this sense of "*A* ἐπιγίγνεται τῷ *B*" see e.g. *Phlb.* 37B, ὅτι δόξῃ . . . ἐπιγίγνεσθον ψεῦδός τε καὶ ἀληθές: "false" and "true" are applicable to (or, predicable of) opinion. There is no warrant for the rendering of κίνησίς τε αὐτὴ παντάπασιν ἵσταιτ' ἂν by "le mouvement deviendrait repos absolu." For sup-

of the hypothesis would be that "Motion itself would be absolutely at rest." From the fact that the truth of this consequence is rejected at once as "to the last degree impossible," we may conclude with confidence that in this context "Motion is resting" is being read as "Motion isPP resting." For if it had been read as "Motion isOP resting," it would have been reckoned not an obvious impossibility, but a demonstrable certainty.

However, there *is* something about the wording in 252D6-8 which may seem to tell against this conclusion: Theaetetus here speaks of "Motion itself" resting and then again of "Rest itself" moving. Why this emphatic use of the reflexive pronoun, it may be asked, unless it were to focus attention on the Kinds and makes us think of *them* in isolation from their instances? It is for just this purpose that the pronoun is used idiomatically all through the dialogues of the middle period. There "Justice itself," "Goodness itself," etc. become standard expressions for the Forms in contrast to their instances. Assuming apparently[32] that the pronoun is being used for the same purpose in the present context, Richard Robinson takes Plato to be "explicitly" denying here that the Kind, Motion, could rest;[33] what Plato is denying, says Robinson, is "that the adjective 'moving' could be characterized by the adjective 'resting' " (261). In saying this

port Diès has to go as far afield as Plotinus (he refers to *Enn.* VI, 11, 7). No support is offered by Taylor, who follows Diès ("motion itself might become absolute rest") in converting into an identity what is so clearly a predication in the Greek text. For the correct translation see Cornford (quoted in the text above); the same in Robin.

[32] I say "apparently" because he does not so argue, though it is hard to see why else he should cite the use of the phrase "Motion itself" as conclusive evidence that the reference is to the adjective "moving" in contradistinction to things characterized by the adjective. Anyhow, such an argument would be plausible, though perhaps less so if it is noticed that the idiom is not repeated exactly here: if it were, the pronoun would have preceded, instead of following the noun, and the definite article would have been probably added.

[33] Having ruled out the PP interpretation of the sentence on the ground that "as his reference to spinning tops in the *R.* [436E] shows, a substantive somehow characterized by the adjective 'moving' may at the same time be somehow characterized by the adjective 'resting' " (261). But all this shows is that Plato recognizes that a thing which is moving in one respect may be resting in another (a proposition reaffirmed in the description of revolution *in situ* in *Lg.* 893C, ἡ τῶν ἑστάναι λεγομένων κύκλων περιφορά.) And what is being envisaged in 256D is the far stronger proposition that a thing which is moving may be resting παντάπασιν ("absolutely" or "in every way," not "in some way" [πῃ]). So the truth of the PP reading of "Motion rests" is absolutely excluded, and this in full consistency with the statements about the spinning tops in the *R.* and the "resting" revolutions in the *Lg.*

he ignores[34] the implications of Plato's conviction that the adjective "moving" could not be investigated by dialectic, could not be known at all, *unless* it was characterized by the adjective "resting."[35] So if Robinson's interpretation were correct, we would have to assume that Plato had blanked out at this juncture on a doctrine which he had built into the foundation of his Theory of Ideas in his middle period and had reasserted as a condition of "intelligence" in the period in which he wrote the *Sophist* and the *Philebus*. This is not, of course, altogether impossible. But it is so improbable that, before committing ourselves to it, the least we can do is to look around for an interpretation of the use being made here of the reflexive pronoun that might excuse us from having to impute so grave a lapse to Plato in the middle of an exceptionally lucid dialectical exercise.

Once we look for this, there is no difficulty in finding it. In English, as in Greek, there are many contexts in which one would make just such a use of the pronoun in a sentence of the form, "*B* is *A*," used to mean "*B* is$_{PP}$ *A*," adding the pronoun after *B* only to emphasize the fact that being *A* follows strictly from being *B*, so that if *B* is present *A* may be counted on to be present and to the same degree, regardless of countervailing factors. Thus, to work this kind of usage into my earlier example:

> In frail humanity charity often coexists with spite; still, charity *itself* is never spiteful: *it* is long-suffering and kind.

What the "itself" contributes here is much the same as what the "in so far as" adds to the following paraphrase of the second colon, where the Pauline predication is allowed to surface:

> still, *in so far as* men are charitable, they are not spiteful, but longsuffering and kind.

[34] Perhaps deliberately, because of his scruples about "misinterpretation by inference" (see his admirable remarks on this, p. 2). But if he is to take us so far afield as the *Republic* in the effort to persuade us that "Motion is$_{PP}$ resting" need not be false for Plato, Robinson could hardly object if we allow Plato to be bearing in mind in 252D the obvious implications of premises which he had mentioned emphatically in the course of the four preceding Stephanus pages.

[35] Another thing Robinson ignored is that the reflexive pronouns occur only in Theaetetus' remark, dropping out in the Stranger's response which (with Theaetetus' ensuing assent) forms the last and definitive pronouncement in our passage on the topic under discussion. It would be unsafe to peg our reading of the "Motion itself is resting" in D6 on the presence of "itself," if the problematic proposition can be, and is, expressed as well without the "itself."

I submit that this is how the reflexive pronoun is functioning in our text. Thaetetus says "Motion *itself*" to underscore the paradox that would result from supposing that Motion, which is the "opposite" of Rest, participates in Rest: this would imply that in so far as things are moving, they would be resting[36]—an utter absurdity, a contradiction, since *qua* moving, they are in a state which is the logical contrary of resting.[37] Thus there is no difficulty in accommodating the reflexive pronoun on the PP reading of the sentence.[38]

Now I must turn to consider a different sort of objection: "You have laid out two alternative senses for 'Motion rests,' " I may be told, "and have argued that Plato is using the sentence in one of them in 252D. But where in the *Sophist* or anywhere else in the Platonic corpus, do you see an explanation, or even an allusion, to this distinction?"—I admit at once: Nowhere.—"If so," the objector continues, "what point could there be in your claim that Plato is using that sentence in one of the two senses *you* have distinguished? Is it not meaningless to suggest that a man who never himself made a certain distinction used sentences in one, and not the other, of its two senses?"—No, it is not meaningless. It is often possible to determine that a person is using an ambiguous sentence, *S*, in just one of its possible uses—say, to mean *S*(I) instead of *S*(II)—even if that person fails to meet any of the tests by which we decide whether or not a speaker is *aware of the difference between these two senses of S*. Thus we hear

[36] And necessarily so: as has been explained, the PP interpretation of "Motion is resting" in this context would imply not just "$M \subset R$" but "$N(M \subset R)$."

[37] This interpretation of the force of "itself" in D6-7 helps explain the modality in D8-9, to which I called attention above, and also the use of παντάπασιν in D6. If "Motion is resting" is understood to assert that in so far as anything is moving, so far it is resting, the contrariety of Motion and Rest reduces "Motion is resting" to a concealed contradiction; the sentence becomes false on logical grounds, hence well deserving to be termed "to the last degree impossible." Again, the use of παντάπασιν becomes understandable on the same interpretation: if (*per impossible*) Motion participated in Rest, then the very ascription of Motion to anything would entail ascription of Rest to it; on the hypothesis, to say that anything moves *in any given way* would be to imply that it rests in that very same way.

[38] For another instance in which "[The Form] *B* itself is *A*" is used to mean not, as the wording would suggest, "*B* is$_{OP}$ *A*," but rather "*B* is$_{PP}$ *A*," see *Phdo* 106D5-7: there "the Form of Soul itself . . . is immortal" does not mean "The Form of Soul is$_{OP}$ immortal" but "The Form of Soul is$_{PP}$ immortal," as Keyt has shown [1963, 172]: in his own terminology, the Form of Soul is said here to be "subordinate to"—not an instance of—*Immortal*.

N. utter "S" in a context in which, so far from spelling out S(I) and S(II) as alternative senses of S and telling us that the former is the one he means here, he does not allude even obliquely to these alternatives, does not even say or imply that there is some sort of unnamed ambiguity in S (as he would if, e.g., he had said that "there is a sense in which S is true," letting us guess, if we can, which is the one he has in mind). Even so, we might still be in a position to say confidently that S(I), not S(II), is what N. means by saying "S," if the following three conditions were satisfied:

(a) It is clear that N. is engaged in rational discourse (he is not indulging a taste for whimsy, he is not drunk, etc.).

(b) We can tell that S(I) would gibe with his other utterances and beliefs, while S(II) would not.

(c) We are satisfied that he would have no trouble seeing the truth of (b), if S(I) and S(II) were spelled out for him by someone else in language he can understand.

For example: We hear N. say, "I am one of the older employees of this firm" (founded fairly recently, say, in 1960). What does he mean? Is it (i) that he is an older man (he is 65) or (ii) that his period of employment in that firm is longer than that of most others (he was one of the first to be hired)? Or, for that matter, (i) and (ii) at once? He gives no visible sign of awareness of ambiguity. But he follows up his remark by saying, "You don't believe it? The fact is that I was born in 1907." We then know at once that (i), not (ii), is what he meant. How would we know this? Simply because the chronology he is invoking is clearly meant to establish (i), while it would be totally irrelevant to the truth of (ii), and this fact is as clear to him as to everyone else.

This should give a fair idea of the significance of my claim that when Plato says, "Motion itself would rest . . . and . . . Rest itself would move" in 252D, he is using the sentence-form, "B is A," in one, and not the other, of two senses which he himself has never explicitly distinguished but which *we* may distinguish on his behalf. My claim is meaningful because all three of the conditions I laid down above have been satisfied:

(a) He is arguing, not joking, etc.

(b) The flagrant falsehood he imputes to both of these sentences follows directly if they are read in the Pauline way, while if they were read the other way one of the two sentences, "Motion itself would rest," would be certainly true.

(c) No one could doubt that Plato would see the falsehood of "Motion is_PP resting" and the truth of "Motion is_OP resting" if the difference between the alternative readings were explained to him by a third party who might ask him if by "Motion is resting" he means (i) to ascribe Rest to the Kind, Motion, in contradistinction to its "participants" in space and time, or (ii) to the latter in contradistinction to the former, or, possibly, (iii) to both at once.

Thus if in 252D Plato is using "Motion rests" in sense (ii) and is doing so without being aware of its ambiguity, he is behaving as would N. in the above example, if he had spoken of himself as "one of the older employees" of the company, without its even occurring to him then (or perhaps ever) that the very same words could be used to refer to the entirely different fact that his term of service with the company was longer than that of most others. Naturally, we cannot infer a person's unawareness of ambiguity just from the fact that he gives no positive sign of having noticed it. But think of the circumstances in 252D: We are in the presence of a writer whom we know to be scrupulously truthful. He uses a sentence which we know to be ambiguous and moreover to be the sort of sentence which the writer would have known to be true in one of its possible uses, if that sense had occurred to him. We see him assert that the sentence is false, doing so with the greatest possible emphasis and without the least qualification—without so much as a hint that there might be a sense in which the sentence is true. I fail to see that in circumstances such as these we have any option but to conclude that Plato is using the sentence in only one of its possible senses, utterly unaware of the alternative reading.[39]

I now wish to argue that the very same thing is true in the later occurrence of the sentence, in the exchange between the Stranger and Theaetetus in 256B with which this inquiry began. Let me quote it once again, this time in Greek, for the argument will turn, in part, on a question of translation:

---

[39] A further indication that the OP/PP ambiguity did not occur to him in 252D is that he gives no sign of noticing that this ambiguity has a radically different import for the truth-values of "Motion rests," on the one hand, and "Rest moves," on the other. Read as Pauline predications both are false. Read as Ordinary predications the first is true, while the second remains false. Plato gives no indication of having noticed this disanalogy in the *Sophist*. In 252D, the only passage where he states explicitly whether he thinks the two sentences true or false, his condemnation falls impartially on both.

ΞΕ. Οὐκοῦν κἄν εἴ πῃ μετελάμβανεν αὐτὴ κίνησις στάσεως, οὐδὲν
ἂν ἄτοπον ἦν στάσιμον αὐτὴν προσαγορεύειν;

ΘΕΑΙΤ. Ὀρθότατά γε, εἴπερ τῶν γενῶν συγχωρησόμεθα τὰ μὲν
ἀλλήλοις ἐθέλειν μείγνυσθαι, τὰ δὲ μή.

Some commentators have taken Plato to be asserting in this passage that
it is *not* absurd to call Motion "resting", i.e., to be implying that "Motion
is resting" is true.[40] If that were the case, then the claim I have just made—

[40] Thus Apelt (1897) glosses:

> Diese auf den ersten Blick auffällige Behauptung erklärt sich durch das,
> was 249CD auseinander gesetzt worden war, dass nämlich jeder Begriff
> sowohl der Ruhe wie der Bewegung teilhaftig sei; dies letztere aber wird
> durch das Wörtchen πῃ angedeutet "in irgend einer Beziehung."

The "assertion" to which Apelt is referring is evidently the apodosis in the
Stranger's remark (256B7). In speaking of it as an "assertion" and a "surprising"
one Apelt is clearly taking it as a categorical statement. His reason for so taking
it is the Stranger's insistence in 249CD that the objects of intelligence are
immutable. (I shall ignore the further suggestion that the Stranger's declaration
there that both Motion and Rest are real is supposed to mean that each of
these Kinds is both moving and resting: nothing is said there which even remotely implies that whatever is real is both moving and resting; as is now
generally agreed, what is meant there is that both moving and resting things are
real). More recent commentators who accept the same reading of 256B7 for
the same reason are M. Frede (1967, 34; he takes it as "a cautious formulation"
of the proposition that "Motion . . . *qua* Form is in a sense (πῃ)—as are all
Forms—a participant in Rest") and W. Bröcker (he glosses: "So [i.e., resting]
is Motion, that is to say, this Idea is as Idea, . . . like every Idea, a resting
thing, hence something which participates in Rest" [*Platons Gespräche*, 2nd
edition (Frankfurt am Main, 1936), 466]). Now certainly *if* Plato had become
aware of the ambiguity in "Motion is resting," then (as I have urged above)
his doctrine in 249CD would commit him as firmly to the truth of the sentence
in the suggested sense as to its falsehood in the other sense. But what has to be
shown is that he *is* aware of the ambiguity when writing our present passage.
Apelt and Bröcker are just assuming the very thing that needs to be proved—
Plato's awareness of the ambiguity—and are relying on this to justify their
reading of the passage. Frede (*loc. cit.*) says "one sees no reason why Plato
should have avoided" conceding that Motion *qua* Form is resting. Of course,
there is no such reason; and if Plato had only thought of the point he undoubtedly *would have made* the concession. But did he think of it? This we can
only learn from our textual data, and there is nothing there to show that he did.
Other commentators who derive a categorical assertion from 256B6-8 are also
banking on Plato's awareness of ambiguity, albeit a different one—an ambiguity
within the "Motion is_PP resting" reading. Thus Auguste Diès took the line
which we saw Robinson following in n. 33, above: "Motion is resting" is

that Plato is still reading the sentence as "Motion is$_{PP}$ resting," totally oblivious of the alternative reading—would be decisively refuted. We would then have proof positive that by the time Plato reached this point in the dialogue he had caught on to the ambiguity and had now come to realize that there is a sense in which the truth of "Motion is resting" is as mandatory as is its falsehood on the other sense.

But will our text bear this construction? In the course of it we encounter three sentences which, transposed into categorical indicatives in the material mode, would run:

P Motion somehow participates in Rest.

Q "Motion is resting" is not absurd.

R Some of the Kinds mix, others do not.

Are *P* and *Q* asserted at any point in our passage? If so, where? Not, surely, in Theaetetus' response: No one could seriously maintain that his ὀρθό-τατά γε is meant to underwrite the categorical truth of *P* or that of *Q*, instead of the inference, "if *P*, then *Q*". The natural complement of ὀρθότατα would be λέγεις (as in καλῶς λέγεις, 251E6, and λέγεις ἀληθέστατα in 238B7) or else εἴρηκας (as in δικαιότατα εἴρηκας, 257A12). So filled out, this phrase could only be meant to voice agreement with the whole of the Stranger's statement.[41] This throws us back on the latter:

---

understood to mean that there are occurrences which (in different respects) instantiate both Motion and Rest (*Autour de Platon* [Paris, 1927], 502–504: the Platonic references are those I gave in n. 33 above). C. Ritter took Plato to be saying that Motion can be called "resting" because "die Bewegung, scharf aufgefässt gemessen und beschrieben kann" (*Neue Untersuchungen über Platon* [Munich, 1910], 62). As Cornford points out (287, n.3), these suggestions unhappily ignore Plato's earlier insistence (252D, 254D) that Motion and Rest cannot combine: had Plato been prepared to call Motion "resting" on the strength of the fact that in some, or all, cases in which Motion occurs there is concurrent instantiation of Rest, he would have had no reason for insisting that Motion and Rest "do not mix with one another." On the same ground I would dissent from Moravcsik's view that Plato's "theories required that the two [Motion, Rest] should partake of each other" (47, n.1): how so, if Motion and Rest "do not mix"? At the other extreme we find Cornford so confident that our passage means to *deny* that Motion rests that he suspects a lacuna and intercalates several lines of his own invention to produce a suitable context. The view for which I proceed to argue dissents as vigorously from Cornford's as from that of his adversaries: all Plato gives us is a hypothetical, thereby no more denying than affirming that Motion rests.

[41] The agreement being conditionalized on *R*, and for good reason: the consequential relation of *Q* to *P* would fail if all kinds mixed promiscuously.

if we cannot get the assertion of Q there, it would be useless to look for it in Theaetetus' response. And when we do concentrate on the Stranger's statement, we are faced with its conditional syntax which leaves both protasis and apodosis unasserted: the protasis is in the imperfect indicative;. the apodosis, in the same tense and mood, has the adverb ἄν. This is the typical syntax of the counter-factual, the grammarian's *suppositio irrealis*. To see how decisive this is for my thesis, it is necessary to take a broader view of what Plato is doing in this context.

In this concluding section of our passage he is undertaking to show that the apparently contradictory conjunction, "Motion is A and is not A," can be asserted without any risk of contradiction when (1) Same, (2) Different, and (3) Being, are substituted for A:

(1) So we must admit this, we must not boggle at it: Motion is the same[42] and not the Same [ταὐτόν τ' εἶναι καὶ μὴ ταὐτόν]. For when

---

What Theaetetus seems to be thinking is this: The selective mixing of Kinds is the very condition on which Q would follow from P; this condition would be violated if P were true: Motion and Rest are "opposites"; if *they* "mix" (as they would, if Motion participated in Rest), are there any two Kinds that will not? Thus R is an indirect way of casting aspersion on the truth of P, which implies that Motion and Rest do mix.

[42] As is clear from the context, here "the same" is an ellipsis for "the same *as itself*," and in (2), "different" is a contraction for "different *from the Different*". The reader cannot be reminded too strongly of Plato's habit of assimilating the logical syntax of two-place predicates to that of simple adjectives (cf. *DR*, p. 71; *RC*, note 64): reading "$F(a, b)$" as "$F(a)$ with reference to b," he feels licensed to drop the "with reference to b" whenever he feels it can be easily supplied from the context. His addiction to this practice is so strong that it even traps him into a childish fallacy on one occasion. Thus to prove

(H) Being $\neq$ the Same,

he argues in 255B8-C3 that since

(1) Motion and Rest *are*,

if we were to assume, contrary to (H), that Being = the Same, it would follow from (1) that

(2) Motion and Rest are the same,

which he takes to imply that

(3) Motion and Rest are the same thing.

The move from (2) to (3) is visibly precipitated by his blatant use in (2) of "the same" as though it were a simple one-place predicate: had he filled out the

we speak of it as being the same and not the Same, we do not assert
this in the same sense [οὐ . . . ὁμοίως εἰρήκαμεν]. (256A10-12).

(2) So in a way [πῃ] it is not [the] Different and it is different [οὐχ
ἕτερον . . . ἔστι πῃ καὶ ἕτερον] in conformity with the explanation
we gave just a moment ago. . . . (256C8-9)

(3) So we may fearlessly contend that Motion is different from
Being.—Most fearlessly.—So it is certain that Motion really is not
Being yet is [a] being [ὄντως οὐκ ὄν ἐστι καὶ ὄν]. (256D8-9)

In each of these texts Plato confronts a sentence infected by the same
ambiguity:

Motion is ταὐτόν;
Motion is ἕτερον;
Motion is ὄν.

He sees that each of these sentences may be used to express two radically
different propositions, depending on whether the sentence is used.

(a) to *predicate* the predicate-term of the subject-term, *or*

(b) to *identify* the predicate-term with the subject term.

That Plato sees this we can tell from his machinery of OR correlates.
This supplies radically different paraphrases to account for the two different uses of "is" in the sentence-form "*B* is *A*":[43]

---

ellipsis, writing "Motion is the same *as itself* and Stasis is the same *as itself*," he
would not have even been tempted to infer (3). For a similar critique see Owen
(1971, 266, Additional Note). For a gallant attempt to exonerate Plato from
fallacy in this argument see A. R. Lacey, "Plato's *Sophist* and the Forms,"
C.Q. N.S. 9 (1959), 43–52, at p. 49: He suggests that Plato's point "is that when
we say 'Rest and Motion are the same,' we *may mean* that they are the same as
each other, but when we say 'Rest and Motion are,' we do not mean they are
each other. . . . The argument is elliptical but not invalid." I have italicized
the part of this statement which is unacceptable: I see no basis for "we may
mean" in the text, where it is clear that if we assume Being = the Same, then
in saying (1) we *will be* asserting (3) (προσεροῦμεν, 255C1). I am stressing Plato's
faulty treatment of relational terms, because I have no option but to mimic it
in expounding his thought in the text above: if I corrected it, I would be
wiping out paradoxes which his OR paraphrases are designed to clear up.

[43] Thus it is clear at 256D8-9 that for ἡ κίνησις . . . ἔστι . . . ὄν (to repro-
duce the ambiguity one must swallow the redundancy and translate, "Motion
is being"), where "is" has use (a), the OR correlate would be

(a) NL(B is A) ↔ OR(B participates in A)

(b) NL(B is A) ↔ OR(B participates in the Same with reference to A).[44]

Motion participates in Being,

while if in that sentence the "is" had use (b), the OR correlate would be

Motion participates in the Same with reference to Being.

Our passage does not provide any direct instance of use (b) of the "is" in "B is A" with OR correlate "B participates in the Same with reference to A." However, it would give us just this correlate for "B is the same as B": It is clear at 256A12-B1 (and also, by implication, at 255B3-4 and 256A7-8) that "participates in the Same with reference to itself" is the OR correlate of

1 Motion is the same as itself.

Since *1* means the same as

2 Motion is Motion,

it is certain that the OR correlate could be still the same: NL sentences with the same sense could not but have the same OR correlates. If it be asked why then Plato does not express in our passage the identity "Motion = Motion" in the form of *2* but only in the form of *1*, the answer is clear from the context: only *1* fits the needs of his present argument; only by stating "Motion = Motion" in the form of *1* can he exhibit the ambiguity in the NL sentence "Motion is the same and not the Same" whose resolution is a decisive step in the argument that the Form of Not Being is the Form of the Different (see next note).

[44] Cf. Ackrill (1957, at 1–2). I accept his view that the distinction between the "is" of identity and the "is" of predication was recognized in the *Sophist*, while dissenting from his contention that Plato also succeeded there in marking off the existential "is" from the other two uses. (Cf. my remarks in *MP*, pp. 46–47 above). I am agreeing, in the main, with Owen (1971). Ackrill's argument for taking the "is" which is paraphrased by μετέχει ταὐτοῦ . . . as the "is" of identity has been controverted by Frede (1967, at 71–72), who holds that we should take it rather as expressing a broader sense of καθ' αὐτό predication, of which identity is a special case. Frede argues that

(i) κίνησις μετέχει ταὐτοῦ πρὸς ταὐτόν

could not have been meant to capture the sense of "NL(Motion = the Same)," for if it had been, then

(ii) κίνησις οὐ μετέχει ταὐτοῦ πρὸς ταὐτόν

would have been offered as the paraphrase of "NL(Motion ≠ the Same)," while what Plato in fact gives us is (when phrased in the same style)

(iii) κίνησις μετέχει θατέρου πρὸς ταὐτόν.

The objection is highly plausible but, I submit, inconclusive, for there is a perfectly good reason why *in this context* Plato should have offered (iii) instead of (ii) as the OR correlate of NL(Motion ≠ the Same). In a different context Plato would not have hesitated to form the OR correlate by using οὐ μετέχει τοῦ A instead of μετέχει θατέρου πρὸς τὸ A. He does this repeatedly in earlier contexts. Thus in 251E9, he writes

οὐκοῦν κίνησίς τε καὶ στάσις οὐδαμῆ μεθέξετον οὐσίας

instead of

οὐκοῦν κίνησίς τε καὶ στάσις μεθέξετόν πη θατέρου πρὸς οὐσίαν.

In 251D7 he writes

ἀδύνατον μεταλαμβάνειν ἀλλήλων

instead of

ἀνάγκη μεταλαμβάνειν τοῦ θατέρου πρὸς ἄλληλα.

In 255A2-3 he writes

οὐσίας μὴ προσκοινωνοῦν

instead of

προσκοινωνοῦν τοῦ θατέρου πρὸς οὐσίαν

(κοινωνεῖν with genitive has the same force as μετέχειν, μεταλαμβάνειν.) But here, in 256A-B, he has at last reached his goal: that of showing that the Form of Not-Being is the Form of the Different, which means, among other things, that all negative NL sentences are translatable into non-negative OR correlates mentioning (participation in) the Different. 256B2 is where he plays his trump card in this laborious game, *exhibiting* the translatability of a negative sentence by an affirmative one making suitable use of the Different (and following it up swiftly with two further exhibitions of the same thing in the case of "NL(Motion ≠ the Different)" and "NL(Motion ≠ Being)"), before proceeding to *generalize* the point at issue in 256D11-E2. This gives a completely satisfying explanation of the fact that (iii), not (ii), is given as the OR correlate of NL(Motion ≠ the Same). Hence there can be no *prima facie* objection to taking (i) as the OR correlate of NL(Motion = the Same): see Additional Note II to *AS* at p. 322 below. This analysis is to be preferred (as the simpler, more economical, hypothesis) to the one proposed by Frede, which would require us to import into the elucidation of 256A10-B1 the Form of the καθ' αὐτὸ λεγόμενον, mentioned in 255B12-13 (which, Frede claims, "teilweise die Funktionen des identifizierenden '. . . ist' erfült" [72]), in order to capture the sense of ἔστι in which "ταὐτὸν ἔστι κίνησις" is false. If that is what Plato had in mind, why did he not say so? Having mentioned the two Forms of the καθ' αὐτὸ

This brings him into position to see that the alarming sentence-form, "Motion is A and is not A,"[45] is perfectly harmless,[46] since here "is A"

λεγόμενον and the πρὸς ἄλλο λεγόμενον in 255C (and having done this, according to Frede [30], to disambiguate the ἔστι in "Motion ἔστι ταὐτόν, ἔστι ἕτερον, ἔστιν ὄν"), why does not Plato explain his οὐ ὁμοίως εἰρήκαμεν in 256A12 by saying that the sense in which "Motion ἔστι ταὐτόν" is true is covered by its participation in the Form of the καθ' αὑτὸ λεγόμενον, while the sense in which that sentence is false is covered by its participation in the Form of the πρὸς ἕτερον λεγόμενον? Since Plato finds it sufficient to name the Form of the Same and the Different in order to effect the necessary disambiguation, why should we have to understand him to be referring for that purpose to two *other* Forms which he does not name here or anywhere else in the whole of the *Sophist* after alluding to them (*ad hoc*, and for a very special purpose) in 255CD? (This argument has not been premised on my rejection of Frede's view of the meaning of 255C1-13, τὰ μὲν αὐτὰ καθ' αὑτά, τὰ δὲ πρὸς ἄλλα ἀεὶ λέγεσθαι, a variant of which is also favored by Owen [*op. cit.*, 256–58]. I do reject it—we have ample textual evidence in the dialogues [*Tht.* 152D2-6, 156E7–157A4, and 160B8-C2; *Phlb.* 51C6-7] and in ancient secondary sources [Aristotle reported *ap.* Diog. Laert. 3, 108–109; Hermodorus quoted *ap* Simpl. *Phys.* 248, 2–3] for taking the difference between καθ' αὑτό and πρὸς ἄλλο λεγόμενον to be that between what is called nowadays a "one-place" and a "two-place" predicate. But even if I did not, I would still find it methodologically unsound to impute to Plato any sense of ἔστι which makes ταὐτὸν ἔστι κίνησις true, other than the sense given us by Plato himself in the text: Identity, no more and no less.)

[45] A more exact schematization of the bogus contradictions in (2) and (3) above would supply parenthetical articles, so that this sentence-form would read,

Motion is A and not [the] A,

or perhaps even

Motion is [an] A and not [the] A.

I omit such augments in citations (1) and (2) above to simulate the stronger impression of contradiction which Plato's prickly phrases made on him. A second device I have used in citations (1), (2), and (3) above—capitalizing the substituend for A in just one of its two mentions—would also have been unavailable to Plato: having no capitals, he could not employ this inscriptional device to mark off the predicative from the nominative uses of the same term.

[46] Cf. G. E. R. Lloyd (1966, 144):

His analysis of the relations between the five kinds makes it plain, first of all, that a whole series of apparently contradictory statements, so far from being contradictory, as an Eleatic might well have thought, are consistent and true, secondly that the appearance of contradiction arises in these cases

is being used only in sense (a) in the first conjunct, only in sense (b) in the second; hence the affirmation in the first does not come within miles of colliding with the denial in the second: the latter does not deny that Motion participates in A, but only that Motion participates in the Same with reference to A. Having resolved the ambiguity in "Motion is A and is not A" to his satisfaction, Plato does his utmost to make his readers aware of it. He calls it forcefully to their attention in (1) by saying that "we do not assert in the same sense" (οὐ ὁμοίως εἰρήκαμεν) "is the same" and "is not the Same,"[47] and does as much, more swiftly but as effectively,

---

from the use of "is", "same", "different" and so on in unspecified senses. . . .

Agreeing entirely with Lloyd's first point, I dissent from his second: as Plato reads these sentences, the appearance of contradiction is created not by an ambiguous use of "same," "different," and "being" in

Motion is the same and not [the] Same;
Motion is different and not [the] Different;
Motion is [a] being and not Being,

but solely by the amphiboly in the connective "is." This follows from two considerations:

1. The "is" is the sole constituent common to the three ambiguous sentences which could account for the ambiguity in each. Hence the disambiguation of the "is" in "is . . . and is not . . . " which is effected by paraphrasing the "is" by μετέχει τοῦ A and the "is not" by μετέχει τοῦ θατέρου πρὸς τὸ A (given explicitly for the first of the three sentences, implicitly for the other two as well) would suffice to resolve the ambiguity throughout.

2. The names "Same," "Different," "Being," cannot vary in sense within any of the three sentences for (as becomes particularly clear in the OR correlates) the meaning is fixed unambiguously by Plato's assumption that each name refers to the identical Form within both of the apparently contradictory conjuncts. Thus in "Motion participates in *the Same* with reference to itself" and "Motion participates in the Different with reference to *the Same*" Plato's semantic theory requires that the italicized word have the same meaning in both of its occurrences because it refers to the same Form in both. The same thing does *not* happen in the occurrences of "is" in the associated NL sentences: if Plato had written the associated NL conjunction as κίνησις ἔστι ταὐτὸν καὶ οὐκ ἔστι ταὐτόν *neither* occurrence for ἔστι would *name* the Form of Being (though in each case participation in the Form of Being would be implied: cf. Frede, 47–48).

[47] The force of this ultra-explicit disclaimer seems to have been missed in

in (2) by a qualifying πη ("in a way" or "in a sense"),[48] while in (3) he contents himself with saying that "is A and is not A" may be asserted "fearlessly," satisfied that by this time its bogus contradiction has been thoroughly unmasked.

Now just suppose that Plato had noticed the OP/PP ambiguity in "Motion is resting," thereby realizing that "Motion is$_{OP}$ resting" is true. Had that occurred, he would have been able to add a fourth assertion to those in (1), (2), and (3) above:

---

some accounts of our passage. Thus G. E. M. Anscombe (*Monist* 50 [1966] 403–20) maintains that the principle

> whatever φ may be, φ-itself cannot be in any way describable by the opposite of "φ" (413),

which was upheld by Plato in the middle dialogues, is jettisoned in the *Sph.* where, according to her, Plato teaches that some Kinds

> may be both φ and not-φ (and that in particular sometimes φ itself may also be not-φ). (414)

Plato's οὐ ὁμοίως εἰρήκαμεν makes it abundantly clear that statements like "Motion is the same and not the Same" are calculated equivocations, hence radically different in import from the "φ and not-φ" predicament of sensible particulars in *R.* 479A-C, where there is no comparable equivocation (the "is" there does *not* switch from predication in "is φ" to identity in "is not φ"). As for the case in which the φ itself is "also not-φ"—that of Being—Plato qualifies the negation with a πη ("in a way") (241D7), whose force is equivalent to that of οὐ . . . ὁμοίως εἰρήκαμεν, as I proceed to argue in the text above and the accompanying note. The force of οὐ . . . ὁμοίως εἰρήκαμεν is also missed in W. and M. Kneale, *The Development of Logic* (Oxford, 1962), 20, where Plato is represented as holding that Being, Sameness, Difference can "*communicate with their own contraries.* [My emphasis]. Otherness, for example, is the same as itself, and sameness other than otherness." But Plato does *not* say that Sameness and Difference are "contraries" (ἐναντία). (This is another consequence of his assimilation of relational terms to the syntax of one-place predicates: no contradiction between "x is the same" and "x is different," as there is between "x is the same as y" and "x is different from y"). Kinds which Plato does call ἐναντία, like Motion and Rest, do *not* communicate (254D7-8). Not-Being communicates with Being only because not-Being (in its only admissible sense) is explicitly said *not* to be the ἐναντίον of Being (257B3-4).

[48] An adverb already used as an ambiguity-marker in 241D and 254CD, along with πως with the same force in 240B,C,E. Plato here anticipates Aristotle's usage, though in his case the force of πη (*Ph.* 266A1; *APr.* 49A8; *Somn.* 426–27), and of πως (*Metaph.* 1030A23) for the same purpose, was heightened by a contrasting ἁπλῶς.

(1) Motion is the same and not the Same;

(2) Motion is different and not [the] Different;

(3) Motion is [a] being and not Being;

(4) Motion is resting and not Rest.

To fill out the series in this way all he would need to do beyond what he had already done in our text would be simply to assert categorically the first conjunct in (4). Its second conjunct he had asserted, and with the greatest emphasis, at the very start of this section:

> *Stranger.* The first thing to be said about Motion is that it is in every way different from Rest. Or how should we put it?
>
> *Theaetetus.* In just that way.
>
> *Stranger.* So it is not Rest.
>
> *Theaetetus.* Not at all. (255E11-15)

It is only when it comes to asserting categorically its mate, the first conjunct in (4), that he holds back: this he propounds only hypothetically. Why so, if he had become aware of the fact that there is a sense in which "resting" is predicable of Motion with as good reason as are "same," "different," and "being?" Why, if he had seen this, should he employ the categorical mode in the case of the other seven relevant statements, and switch to the hypothetical in the case of the eighth—this being the very one whose falsehood he had declared in 252D, and had never retracted?[49]

To persuade us to overlook the hypothetical cast of Plato's syntax in 256B6-7 and allow the Stranger's statement the force of a categorical, only two considerations have been offered:[50] (a) the implication of 249CD that all objects of intelligence must be resting, and (b) the presence of πη in the protasis. I trust that it is now apparent that (a) of itself is worthless for the point at issue: We know that Plato could confront the sentence, "Motion rests," and fail utterly to connect it with the implication of 249CD. We know this because we have seen him do it in 252D. What reason then is there to think that now, in 256B, he must be making the connection which he missed in 252D? Certainly not in (b), since the πη there is itself enmeshed in the hypothetical construction. We are not being told *that* there is a sense in which Motion partakes of Rest, but that *if*

---

[49] And had implicitly reaffirmed in 254D, where the Stranger says that Motion and Rest are ἀμείκτω πρὸς ἀλλήλω ("do not mix with one another") and Theaetetus replies, καὶ σφόδρα γε ("absolutely"), which is the denial of the OR correlate of "Some moving things are resting."

[50] Cf. n. 40, above.

there were, *then* "Motion is resting" would not be absurd. So far from showing that Plato here had caught sight of an alternative sense of "is resting" in which what had been declared "to the last degree impossible" in 252D is in fact quite true, (b) rather tends to show the opposite. For had Plato noticed this new ambiguity in "is resting," it would have intrigued him at least as much as the one between predication and identity which he rides so hard in the same context;[51] he would have been at least as eager to resolve it.[52] But so far from doing this, he does not even hint that it can be done; he does not even say that there is *an* ambiguity in "Motion is resting" *via* which its truth may be reclaimed. What else can we conclude from this, but that he failed to see it here, as he had failed to see it in 252D?

This conclusion may not prove popular. Some will find it quite incredible that Plato would miss so clear and obvious an implication of his system when confronting the very sentence which, read in the proper way, would be an outright assertion of the implicate. Were it not for the textual evidence,[53] I too would have thought it impossible.

II. MORE PAULINE PREDICATIONS

1. 250A11-12

"And would you say equally of each and of both [Motion, Rest] that they *are?*" asks the Stranger here. Later, when itemizing the relations of

[51] Nor need we overlook in this context the other ambiguity with which Plato grapples in the *Sophist*: the one to which he refers in 241D and 254C (having anticipated it already in 240B9 ff.), the whole of our passage being part of the long quest for the resolution finally achieved in 258B ff. Note especially the concluding remarks in 259C7-D7, where he inveighs against those who are content to exploit ambiguities but shirk responsibility for clearing them up. Plato himself would have been open to this reproach if, having seen the ambiguity in "Motion is resting" which makes it true in one sense, false in another, he had failed to explain it or even to call it to the reader's attention.

[52] Plato would have found its resolution an even greater challenge, for it moves at a deeper level and would call for new line of attack: the method of OR correlates on which he relies to master the two other ambiguities would be powerless in this case ("Motion participates in Rest" is fully as ambiguous in this respect as is "Motion is resting"; to resolve this ambiguity Plato would have had to block out different modes of participation, answering respectively to "is$_{OP}$ *A*" and "is$_{PP}$ *A*.")

[53] That is to say, that part of the evidence which consists of texts in our passage in the *Sph.* which bear immediately on the problematic sentence. I could have broadened the argument by bringing in other material which also bears on it, though less directly. Aristotelian data offering collateral support are discussed briefly in *TLPA* below.

Motion to each of the other four "greatest" Kinds, he says that Motion "surely *is*, since it participates in Being" (256A1) and reiterates the statement shortly after (D8-9). What kind of predication are we getting here? We know that "Motion *is*" or "Motion is real"[54] would be true for Plato, regardless of whether he were using these sentences to mean

(I) (Motion is$_{OP}$ real) = (The Kind, Motion, is real)

or

(II) (Motion is$_{PP}$ real) = (The class of moving things is [necessarily] contained in the class of real things)

or

(III) Both (I) and (II) at once.

So Plato *could* have used the sentences to mean (I) on a given occasion, (II) on another, (III) on a third. How he *is* using it in a given context one has to find out, if one can, from the context. I want to argue that in 250A he is using "Motion *is*" in sense (II). Later on, in III,2, below, I shall argue that the sense may be different in 256A and D. My plea for sense (II) in 250A rests on two distinct considerations:

(i) 250A is the immediate sequel to that long encounter with the Friends of Forms in which the Stranger had undertaken to refute their lopsided, exclusively static, ontology, and vindicate the reality of Motion on a par with that of Rest. The philosopher, he had concluded, must admit that "Reality or the All is both at once—motionless and moving things"[55] (249D3-4); and it is now generally agreed that what this means is not

1 Reality consists of things which are both moving and resting (i.e., of things each of which is both moving and resting),

but rather

2 Reality consists of both moving and resting things (i.e., of things of which some are moving and some resting).

[54] Two points here: (i) "existent" for Plato's ὄν would be unduly restrictive (cf. Malcolm [1967]; and G. E. L. Owen's brilliant essay "Plato on Not-Being," in G. Vlastos, editor, *Plato*, Vol. 1 [New York, 1970], 223–67; and my *DR* and *MP*). I take "real" as the closest English equivalent. It matches Plato's ὄν in that it *can* be used to mean "existent," but is not restricted to this sense. (ii) Plato treats ". . ἔστι" and ". . . ὄν ἔστι" as identical in sense (cf. 256A1 with the same assertion in 256D8-9). I shall accordingly so treat " . . . is" and " . . . is real."

[55] ὅσα ἀκίνητα καὶ ὅσα κεκινημένα.

And 2 could be expressed as well by

  3 Both moving and resting things are real,

which is the PP reading of

  4 Motion and Rest are real.

This creates a strong antecedent presumption that 4 rather than

  5 Motion and Rest are$_{OP}$ real

is what is meant by "Motion and Rest are real" at 250A11-12. For it is hardly likely that, after working so hard to establish the truth of 2 (and hence of 3—the whole of the controversy with the Friends of Forms (248A–249D) had just this goal), the Stranger should suddenly turn off to a new line of thought in which "Motion and Rest are real" no longer has this implication.[56] To be sure this presumption would be nullified if something had happened in the interim to switch the Stranger's thinking to another track. But the Stranger as good as says that there has been no switch: he tells Theaetetus in 249E7 that what they must now proceed to "investigate more closely" concerns "the admission we have made just now,"[57] i.e., the ontological pronunciamento in 249D3-4. If further reassurance were needed, we get it two Stephanus pages later, in 251E–252A, where he considers what would follow if we could not "attach 'Being' to 'Motion' and to 'Rest,' nor anything else to anything else" (251D), i.e., if we could not affirm such sentences as "Motion is real," "Rest is real." Such a result, he says, would make a speedy end of doctrines like extreme

[56] If the sentence in 250A8-9 were meant to express a new assertion some new argument would almost certainly have been offered for it. That Motion, no less than Rest, exists has been regarded as a proposition which is in need of proof; the only proof offered for it is in the argument against the Friends of Forms which was concluded in 249D.

[57] I chop off this phrase in the interests of brevity. The full remark, with its implications, would only strengthen my point: he asks Theaetetus to face up now to the question which they had put earlier in (243DE) to "those who assert that the All is [the] Hot and [the] Cold" (243E1-2), i.e., if they assert that Hot and Cold *are*, must they not posit Being as "a third beside the two" (243E2-3)? His taking [λέγειν] θερμὸν καὶ ψυχρὸν . . . ἄμφω καὶ ἑκάτερα εἶναι ("asserting that the hot and the cold both are") in 243D8-e2 as strictly parallel to [λέγειν κίνησίν τε καὶ στάσιν] εἶναι . . . ἀμφότερα . . . καὶ ἑκάτερον ("[asserting that Motion and Rest] both are") in 250A11-12, shows that the latter is the same kind of assertion as the former (which is transparently an assertion about the existence of heat and cold in the cosmos: it epitomizes a physical theory that whatever exists is characterizable as either hot or cold.)

fluxism and Eleatic monism (252A). This shows that he is still on the same track as 249D3-4 and hence is not likely to have jumped out of it in the interim: he is still thinking here, as he was at 249D3-4, of the existence of Motion and Rest in the universe. For he does not understand the fluxers to be asserting the reality of the Idea of Motion, in contradistinction to that of moving things: these people had no doctrine of Ideas; their thesis, as Plato understands it,[58] is simply that everything in the universe is in motion; for them "[only] Motion is real" could only have meant "[only] moving things are real." Nor could Plato have thought of the Eleatics as contending that the Kind, Rest, is real,[59] rather than that the Real is at rest.

(ii) We get evidence of another sort for the same conclusion when we notice the kind of language Plato uses to refer to the logical relation instantiated in "Motion and Rest are real." He speaks of the subject-terms of this sentence as "contained" or "enclosed" by its predicate-term: ὡς ὑπ' ἐκείνου τήν τε κίνησιν καὶ στάσιν περιεχομένην ("both Motion and Rest being contained by it [Being]").[60] The use of this kind of language is highly significant. For since Platonic Forms are rigorously incorporeal entities, the "containment" of Form B by Form A is plainly metaphorical; and the only clearly cashable part of the metaphor is the implied reference to the relation of the logical extension of B to that of A, i.e., that all objects instantiating B are necessarily included among those instantiating A—the very fact symbolized by "$N(B \subset A)$"[61] To get the full import of the expression which Plato finds it so natural to use in this connection, one should remind oneself of an alternative expression which Plato would have found as natural for expressing the alternative reading

[58] *Cra.* 439B10 ff.; *Tht.* 182C ff.

[59] Not the remotest allusion to such a Kind in the fragments of Parmenides and Melissus or in any of Plato's numerous allusions to their philosophy.

[60] 250B8, with which compare 253D, καὶ πολλὰς [ἰδέας] ἑτέρας ἀλλήλων ἔξωθεν περιεχομένας ("many ideas, distinct from one another, *contained* from the outside") and also 255A10, περὶ γὰρ ἀμφότερα θάτερον ὁποτερονοῦν γιγνόμενον αὐτοῖν ("for whichever of them came to surround both of them") (to be discussed in the following sub-section). My translation of 250B8 above sticks to the punctuation of Burnet's Oxford text. Others prefer to take the following word, συλλαβών, with περιεχομένην, translating as, e.g., Lewis Campbell (1867, in note *ad loc.*), "under which (*sc.* Being), as embraced by it, you comprehended motion and rest. . . . " Regardless of punctuation, the force of περιεχομένην ("umschlossen," Apelt; "embraced," Cornford, following Diès; "included in," Taylor) would be the same.

[61] Cf. the terminal paragraph in Appendix II below.

of "*B* is *A*": It is good Greek, and Greek frequently used by Plato, to speak of *A* "being in" (or "being present in")[62] a given individual in order to say that the individual *has* property *A*.[63] Thus Plato writes "if temperance is in you" (εἴπερ ἔνεστιν [σωφροσύνη σοι], *Chrm.* 159A) for "if you are temperate"; of "knowledge being in a man" (ἐνούσης . . . ἀνθρώπῳ ἐπιστήμης, *Prt.* 352B), for "a man having knowledge"; "if smallness were in the One" (εἰ . . . ἐν τῷ ἑνὶ σμικρότης ἐγγίγνεται, *Prm.* 150A1-2), for "if the One were small."[64] And this relation is irreversible: no Greek speaker would have tolerated saying that an individual, *x*, "is in" *A* to assert that '*x* ε *A*' (e.g., saying "Socrates is in wisdom" for "Socrates is wise"). We may infer that the same would be true where the substituend for "*x*" is a Form: if Plato were assimilating the logical syntax of "Motion is real" to that of "Socrates is wise," he would have found it natural to say that Being "is in" Motion and very unnatural to say that Motion "is in" Being—hence natural to say that Motion contains Being, and unnatural to say that Being contains Motion. So when we see him turn to a metaphor that reverses that picture, portraying Being as containing both Motion and Rest,[65] instead of being contained by each of them, we can infer with good reason that he is using the sentence "Motion and Rest are real" as a Pauline predication.[66] Otherwise he

[62] ἔνειμι (or ἐγγίγνομαι) with dative construction.

[63] Examples of general usage: *Il.* 17, 156, εἰ γὰρ νῦν Τρώεσσι μένος πολυθαρσὲς ἐνείη, "if there were now dauntless courage in the Trojans" for "if the Trojans were now dauntlessly courageous"; *Hdt.* 3, 81, 2, τῷ δὲ οὐδὲ γινώσκειν ἔνι, "knowing is not in him" for "he has no knowledge." Other examples in the lexica.

[64] Many other examples in D. F. Ast, *Lexicon Platonicum, s.v.*

[65] For another example of this pattern—referring to *B* as being "in" *A*, or as "contained by" *A*, in cases where he would read "*B* is *A*" as "*B* is$_{PP}$ *A*"—see how Plato speaks of relation of the four species of Animal to the genus, Animal in the *Timaeus*: the Idea of Animal "contains" (περιλαβὸν ἔχει, 30C) the four species, each of the latter are "in" (ἐνούσας, ἔνεισιν, 39E) the former where the implied NL sentences would be, e.g., "The Land Animal is [an] Animal," read as "Land Animal is$_{PP}$ Animal."

[66] Note that the connective in the OR correlates of "Socrates is wise" and "Motion is real" orders the subject- and predicate-terms non-symmetrically in the same way in both cases:

NL(Socrates is wise) ↔ OR(Socrates participates in Wisdom)

NL(Motion is real) ↔ OR(Motion participates in Being).

We know that Plato would not say "Socrates is in Wisdom" but "Wisdom is in Socrates" for "Socrates is$_{OP}$ wise." So if he meant "Motion is$_{OP}$ real" when

would have used, at most, non-committal language, saying, e.g., that Being "supervenes" on Motion and Rest[67] or else, turning to the formal mode, as he so often does in our passage, that Being is "said (or asserted) of" Motion and Rest.

2. 255A-B

The Stranger lays down a principle and then proceeds to prove it. The Principle:

[P] Whatever we attribute[68] jointly to Motion and to Rest cannot be identical with either.[69]

The Proof:

For [it would follow that] Motion would rest and that Rest would move.

For whichever of them came to surround[70] both of them would com-

---

saying "Motion is real" in this context, he would have had no hesitation in saying "Being is in Motion." Hence the significance of the fact that to express the relation instantiated in "Motion is real" he writes an NL sentence which turns the predicate-term into container, instead of content, reversing the ordering effected by μετέχειν ("participating") in the OR correlate.

[67] Cf. *Phlb.* 37B, ὅτι δόξῃ . . . ἐπιγίγνεσθον ψεῦδός τε καὶ ἀληθές ("the true and false supervene on belief") for "belief may be true or false." Another perfectly non-commital term is ὑπάρχειν (see the examples in Ast. *s.v.*) which becomes, perhaps for just that reason, Aristotle's favorite term for the copula in *APr.* Other terms would be εἶναι or γίγνεσθαι, with the suffixes παρα- or προσ-. These would be closer to ἐνεῖναι, ἐγγίγνεσθαι, but not nearly as strong in suggesting the notion that the subject-term "contains" the predicate-term.

[68] προσείπωμεν. προσλέγειν *A* τὸ *B* (here and in 250B10) = predicating *A* of *B*.

[69] τοῦτο οὐδέτερον αὐτοῖν οἷόν τε εἶναι ("this cannot be either of them"). Inexplicably mistranslated by Robin as "celui-là ne pourrait appartenir ni à l'un ni à l'autre."

[70] Or "embrace." That this is the force of περὶ θάτερον γιγνόμενον follows from the literal sense of περί with accusative ("around," "round about") taken in conjunction with 250B8-10 (cf. note 60 above), where the identical logical relation (a general term predicated jointly of Motion and Rest) is expressed by περιεχομένην. None of the translations I have consulted catches the force of περι- in 255A11. Cornford (1935), who had translated περιεχομένην correctly in 250B (note 60, above), translates "περὶ . . . γιγνόμενον" "becomes applicable to both" (same in Diès, whom Cornford continues to follow); Apelt comes closer ("auf beide erstreckt"), but not close enough, and is moved further away from the true sense in Wiehl's revision where the translation ("in beide eingeht") now reads (as previously in Heindorf, quoted by Lewis Campbell, *ad hoc.*,

pel the other to change into the opposite of its own [i.e. the latter's] nature, since it [the latter] would have come to participate in its own opposite.

I submit that the "attributing" Plato is thinking of here is Pauline. To put this suggestion in a more formal way: what Plato understands by [P], translated into set-theoretical language (representing Motion and Rest by their initials, and using K as a Kind-variable), would *not* be

$$[P_{OP}](K)\{[(R \in K) \ \& \ (M \in K)] \rightarrow [(R \neq K) \ \& \ (M \neq K)]\},$$

but rather

$$[P_{PP}](K)\{[N(R \subset K) \ \& \ N(M \subset K)] \rightarrow [(R \neq K) \ \& \ (M \neq K)]\}.[71]$$

It can be shown that Plato would have good reason to think [P$_{OP}$] false and [P$_{PP}$] true.

(*i*) *Proof that* [P$_{OP}$] *must be false for Plato*: Since K may be any Kind, let it be R. Substituting R for K in the antecedent of [P$_{OP}$], we get

(1) $(R \in R) \ \& \ (M \in R).$

This is a true proposition for Plato.[72] Making the same substitution in the first conjunct of the consequent, we get

(2) $R \neq R,$

"in utroque inerit") as though Plato had actually used the language of inherence, instead of its very opposite. The true sense ("surrounds") seems to have been caught by Moravcsik (1962, 45) in his gloss on 254D.

[71] The basis for the modal operator in each conjunct in the antecedent is not in ἀναγκάσει in the text (which modifies the *implication* of the consequent by the antecedent, giving it the force of an entailment); it is the general consideration which I explained in my comment on the formula for the Biconditionality Thesis in *UVP*, I.3: without it "$R \subset K$" and "$M \subset K$" would be purely extensional formulae which would not capture the force of an eternal relation between Platonic Kinds.

[72] Since the formula in (1) makes it unambiguously clear that Rest is being predicated of the Kinds, Rest, Motion, *not* of their participants as such, there can be no reasonable doubt, given Plato's explicit commitment to the above doctrine, that he would declare the formula true. Note how different this case would be from that of "Motion is resting" in 256B. What makes it understandable that Plato might have missed the truth of this sentence in that context is precisely the fact that he did not confront there an expression which resolves the ambiguity as between "Motion is$_{PP}$ resting" and "Motion is$_{OP}$ resting" and was, therefore, defenseless against the inclination to go on reading the sentence in the way he had used it in the earlier part of our passage.

which is a contradiction. Substituting M for K, we may deduce by parity of reasoning that $M \neq M$. Hence if Plato had construed [P] as an ordinary predication it would have been for him a hypothetical with true antecedent and false consequent, i.e., a false proposition.

(*ii*) *Proof that* [P_{PP}] *must be true for Plato*: This can be proved true if it can be shown that to suppose the antecedent true and the consequent false leads to a contradiction. This can be easily done. To falsify the consequent, suppose its first conjunct false, i.e., that $K = R$. Substituting R for K in the antecedent, we get

(3) $N(R \subset R) \,\&\, N(M \subset R)$.

Since R and M are "opposites,"[73] i.e., contraries,[74] they are necessarily[75] mutually exclusive classes, i.e.,

(4) $N(R \subset \bar{M})$.

Conjoining the second conjunct in (3) with (4), we get

(5) $N(M \subset R) \,\&\, N(R \subset \bar{M})$,

hence[76]

(6) $N(M \subset \bar{M})$,

which is a contradiction, since M is non-empty.[77] Hence the negation of [P_{PP}] is false. Hence [P_{PP}] is true.

Thus when the "attributing" in [P] is Pauline the principle turns out to be true, and its strong intuitive appeal is vindicated demonstratively, while on the alternative reading it is demonstrably false.

Now let us look at Plato's own proof of [P]. Both its wording and its reasoning suggest that its demonstrand is not [P_{OP}], but [P_{PP}]: In speaking of K as "embracing" or "surrounding" M and R, Plato shows

[73] As Malcolm (1967, 141) points out, [P] applies to Rest and Motion because, and only because, they are "opposites".

[74] Cf. nn. 15 and 18 above.

[75] Cf. n. 16 above.

[76] Since the relation is transitive.

[77] And furthermore, since R too is non-empty, we may also negate [P_{PP}] by falsifying the second conjunct of its consequent, deriving therefrom by parity of reasoning the alternative contradiction,

(7) $N(R \subset \bar{R})$.

that he is thinking of the attribution in Pauline terms; this follows from
what has been said in II.*1*.(ii). As to the reasoning, it comes very close to
being an abbreviated, highly informal, version of the one for [P$_{PP}$] above.
In this proof, as in mine, a *reductio ad absurdum* of the negation of the
demonstrand is derived from the fact that M and R are contraries. Lacking
a device for representing an unknown by a variable, Plato cannot formulate
the demonstrand by first using K to stand for a term which includes M
and R in the antecedent and is not identical with either of them in the consequent, and only then proceeding to show that the consequent will be
false when R (or M) is substituted for K[78] in the antecedent. So he moves
immediately into the hypothesis that the pair has been "surrounded"[79]
by either of them, and refutes it by appealing to the impossibility of the
surrounding term being the "opposite" of the surrounded. Thus if R
were to "surround" M (which R is shown as doing in the second conjunct
of (3)), M "would have come to participate in its own opposite" (which
M is shown doing implicitly in the second conjunct of (3), explicitly
in (6), where R has been replaced by $\bar{M}$)—which could only have happened
if *per impossibile* M "had changed into the opposite of its own nature."

3. The Method of Division

If what I have just argued—that [P] is being read as [P$_{PP}$]—is correct,
we may infer at once that Plato would find the Pauline pattern of attribution compelling not only in the case of the isolated sentences previously
considered,

> Motion is resting,
> Motion is real,
> Rest is real,

but in a great multitude of others which he has no occasion to name in
our passage: in all the substitution-instances of the generalization of [P],
that is to say of [P] generalized to

> [Q] Given any two contrary Kinds, L and M, any Kind, K, attributed
> jointly to L and M, cannot be identical with either.

And since the notion of contrariety is so conspicuous here, we might as
well recall what I pointed out early in this essay (p. 275, above): that the

---

[78] Substitution-moves encountered in some analyses of the reasoning in the
literature have no foundation in the text.
[79] Cf. n. 70 above.

description of what Plato has to mean by speaking of contrary ("opposite") Kinds must represent the implied sentences as Pauline predications: "Kinds L and M are contraries" has to mean "L is$_{PP}$ $\bar{M}$" or "M is$_{PP}$ $\bar{L}$"—it cannot mean "L ε $\bar{M}$" or "M ε $\bar{L}$," for these formulae neither imply, nor are implied by, "L and M are contraries." This assures us at once that the use of Pauline predications in Plato's discourse about his Kinds could not be confined to the few instances in which we have so far met them in this study. *Wherever* Plato speaks of "opposite" Forms he is falling back on Pauline predications. Further assurance of the vast incidence of the Pauline mode of our "B is A" sentence-form in Plato may be derived by considering the implications of his Method of Division. For any set of Forms which are derived by dividing another Form, we get sentences in which the superordinate Form is predicated of a subordinate one: thus if A is divided into B and C, we would get "B is A," "C is A," and as many more sentences of the same sort as we pleased, so long as further sub-divisions proved feasible. All of these predications will be Pauline, for nothing else would make sense: when Living Creature (Ζῷον) is divided into its four main species in the *Timaeus*,[80] generating such sentences as

The Land-animal is [a] Living Creature,

Man is [a] Land-animal,

Man is [a] Living Creature,

Plato could hardly have wanted to say that the referent of the subject-term in each of these both is an immutable Form *and* lives, breathes, walks on land, and the like. Nor need we rely here wholly on this type of consideration. We have specific linguistic evidence which points unmistakably in the same direction:

Plato speaks of the Ideal Living Creature which serves the Demiurge as his model as "containing"[81] the four Kinds—God, Bird, Fish, Land-

[80] 30C-31A; 39E-40A. The ideal Living Creature is said to be that of which τἆλλα ζῷα καθ' ἕν καὶ κατὰ γένη are μόρια, 30C5-6: μόριον (simple variant of μέρος) is clearly used here in the purely logical sense in which, e.g., courage is μόριον ἀρετῆς ἕν, *Lg.* 696B, and any Form derived by division is a "part" of the divided one. The sense of καθ' ἕν is very likely the one suggested by F. M. Cornford (*Plato's Cosmology* [London, 1937], 40 and note 2), that of the *infima species* at which division stops. κατὰ γένη here may be compared with τὸ κατὰ γένη διαιρεῖσθαι, *Sph.* 253D; διακρίνειν κατὰ γένος, 253E; κατ' εἴδη διαιρέσεων, 264C; κατ' εἴδη δύνασθαι διατέμνειν, *Phdr.* 265E.

[81] 31A, τὸ γὰρ περιέχον πάντα ὁπόσα νοητὰ ζῷα . . , 30C; ἐν ἑαυτῷ περιλαβὸν ἔχει.

animal—which the Demiurge proceeds to create. The Pauline import of the use of this expression in *Sph*. 250B and of its linguistic cognate, περὶ . . . γιγνόμενον, in *Sph*. 255D, has been emphasized above. That it has the same import here is, if anything, clearer, since Plato now uses also the complementary expression, ἐνεῖναι, for the converse relation of the subordinate to the super-ordinate Form. He says that the four kinds "are in" the ideal Living Creature:

> ᾗπερ οὖν νοῦς ἐνούσας ἰδέας τῷ ὃ ἔστιν ζῷον, οἷαί τε ἔνεισιν καὶ ὅσαι καθορᾷ [in respect of the Forms which intelligence discerns in the real Animal, discerning of what sort and how many are in it; 39E]; τὰ γὰρ δὴ νοητὰ πάντα ἐκεῖνο ἐν ἑαυτῷ περιλαβὸν ἔχει [for it contains within itself all of the intelligible Animals; 30C].

We noticed above that Plato says that *F* "is in" *x*,[82] not the converse, to express the notion that *x* is characterized by *F*. So if he had wanted to assert so perverse a proposition as that the Form, Land-Animal, is characterizable as a living creature, he would have said that Living Creature is "in" Land-Animal, not vice-versa.

We know the vast importance which Plato attaches to the Method of Division in the *Phaedrus*[83] and thereafter. He speaks of it as the philosopher's method par excellence and pays it the most extravagant compliments, speaking of it on one occasion as "the instrument through which every discovery ever made in the sphere of the arts and the sciences has been brought to light.[84] So if he reads as Pauline predications all sentences of the form "*B* is *A*" which are generated by this method, there could be no escaping the conclusion that this is the normal pattern of inter-Form predication throughout this period[85] and that the possibility

---

[82] Note 65, above.

[83] "I am myself a lover of these collections and divisions, that I may have the power to speak and to think," says Socrates, and proceeds to identify dialectic itself with the practice of the Method (266BC)—a move never revoked or qualified in any subsequent dialogue.

[84] *Phlb*. 16C.

[85] Some confirmation for this conclusion may be found in the language used in the highly general description of the dialectician in 253D as one who

> discerns clearly *one* Form extending in every direction through many, each of which lies apart [κειμένου χωρίς] and many Forms, different from one another, embraced from without by one Form; and again *one* Form connected in a unity through many wholes, and many Forms, separated off in every way. (The translation owes much to Cornford's.)

of reading it as ordinary predication could only arise in special cases which are not reached, or reachable, by the method of Division.

III. NON-PAULINE PREDICATIONS IN THE *SOPHIST*

1. Ordinary Predications in the *Sophist*

In exploring the interrelations of the five great Kinds of our passage, the Stranger is concerned to establish that each of them is the same as itself[86] and not the same as any of the other four.[87] He thus propounds five identities and ten non-identities, each of which is expressible as an assertion or denial of a sentence of the form, "*B* is the same as *A*." These sentences *could only be meant to express Ordinary predication*. For what the Stranger is out to prove is that the Kinds he is talking about are numerically distinct entities[88] or, to put his point in the formal mode,

---

Exactly what are the logical relations (or types of relation) that Plato has in view in each of these four cases is a matter of controversy. But there can be no doubt about the fact that the Forms are being pictured as though they were areas or domains, some of them extending over others, some wholly discrete from others. What I have been calling "Pauline predication" is a very natural interpretation of the cases where one or more Forms are wholly included in another. As I have implied above (note 60) the wording of ὑπ' ἐκείνου τήν τε στάσιν καὶ τὴν κίνησιν περιεχομένην in 250B8 is so close to that of πολλὰς ὑπὸ μιᾶς ἔξωθεν περιεχομένας, in 253D7-8, that if the former is a Pauline predication so must the latter be.

[86] (Self-)Identity is asserted for Motion (τὴν κίνησιν ταὐτὸν εἶναι) in 256A10. It is implied for Motion and Rest (μετέχετον μὴν ἄμφω ταὐτοῦ) in 255B3; it is implied for all five of the "greatest Kinds" (διὰ τὸ μετέχειν πάντα [τὰ γένη] αὐτοῦ [= ταὐτοῦ]) in 256A7-8.

[87] Being ≠ Motion and Being ≠ Rest (τρίτον ἄρα τι παρὰ ταῦτα τὸ ὂν ἐν τῇ ψυχῇ τιθείς) 250B7. Being ≠ Identity (ἀδύνατον ἄρα ταὐτὸν καὶ τὸ ὂν ἐν εἶναι, 255C3). Being ≠ Difference (πάμπολυ διαφερέτην, 255D3-4). Motion ≠ Rest (κίνησιν, ὡς ἔστι παντάπασιν ἕτερον στάσεως, 255E11-12). Motion ≠ Identity and Motion ≠ Difference; Rest ≠ Identity and Rest ≠ Difference (οὔ τι μὴν κίνησίς γε καὶ στάσις οὔθ' ἕτερον οὔτε ταὐτόν ἐστι, 255A4-5). Identity ≠ Difference (implied at 255D9-E1 πέμπτον δὴ τὴν θατέρου φύσιν λεκτέον ἐν τοῖς εἴδεσιν οὖσαν).

[88] As is implied by repeated references to their number: "Shall we then posit the Same as a Fourth Kind over and above the three [Motion, Rest, Being]?" (255C); "then let us say that the nature of the Different is a fifth among the Kinds we have picked out" (255D).

that no two of their names have the same "meaning,"[89] i.e., (on Plato's semantic theory) the same referent. Since Plato treats three of these Kinds—Being, the Same, the Different—as adjectives of universal application[90] (each of them must characterize everything whatever,[91] including itself),[92] all three have necessarily the same extension.[93] Hence when he denies that any two of them are the same Kind, what he denies could scarcely be that they have the same extension.[94] In denying, e.g., that "Being is the same as Difference" all he could possibly mean to deny is that "same-as-Difference" could be predicated of the Kind, Being, itself, without the slightest reference to its extension. And since it is clear that the phrase "is the same" in "Being is the same as Difference" has the same meaning for Plato as in, say, "Being is the same as Motion," it follows that for any two of the five great Kinds to deny that "B is the same as A" means denying that "B ε same-as-A"—hence that all ten of the non-identities are Ordinary predications. And since the meaning of "same" would be unaltered regardless of whether one denied or affirmed that "B is the same as A," it follows further that the five identities of our passage are likewise Ordinary predications; thus "Motion is the same as itself" could only mean "Motion ε same-as-Motion." And since "different-from-A" is introduced in our passage[95] as a valid paraphrase of "not-the-same-as-A," it is clear that by affirming "B is different from A" Plato means the same as by denying "B is the same as A": both predications must be Ordinary.

---

[89] "Being" and "Same" μηδὲν διάφορον σημαίνετην for "they are the same" (255B11-12); "are we to think of this [the Different] and 'Being' as two names for a single Kind?" (255C9-10).

[90] Cf. note 42, above.

[91] ". . . For all things participate in it [the Same]" (256A); ". . . Being and the Different run through everything and through each other" (259A).

[92] I so argue below in *SPPL*.

[93] Cf. *UVP*, n. 27.

[94] Cf. Crombie (1963, 404), who brings up the closely related point that the criterion of identity of Kinds is "identity in meaning".

[95] Which ends at 257A12 (cf. note 4, above). Thereafter the Stranger starts a different (though related) investigation whose aim is to produce a general account of Not-being designed to cover all negations, not just negations of identity. This new account, though a brilliant enough achievement, is beset by many difficulties. To discuss these would take me far beyond the limits of the present inquiry. Fortunately there is no need of it, since I am only concerned here with the application of "different from" to the ten non-identities in our passage, where I take it to be clear that the sense is exclusively "$\neq$."

2. Ambivalent Predications in the *Sophist?*

In II.2, above, I argued that "Motion is" is used in 255A11-12 as a Pauline predication. That result, if accepted, would not preclude—would not even prejudice—the possibility that in other contexts the sentence could be used unambiguously to express an Ordinary predication or ambivalently to express both, as in my earlier example, it would be perfectly possible for N. to speak of himself on a certain occasion as one of the "older employees" to refer to his relative age, while on another occasion he might use the same expression to refer to the length of his association with the firm, and on a third to mean both at once. So we can examine with an open mind the sense in which Plato is likely to be using "Motion is" in 256A1 and again in 256D8-9. This is the terminal section of our passage, a substantially different context from 250A11-12 and those associated with it in II.2, above. In this later section the Stranger is wholly preoccupied with the Kind, Motion, his formal purpose being to demonstrate its non-identity with any of the other four Kinds. At this stage of the discussion he seems to have no interest in moving things as such, hence none in asserting that *they* are real. So it is probable that he is using the sentence simply and solely to express an Ordinary predication. But there is no way of excluding the possibility that he might be using it ambivalently: what the context shows is that he means, at the very least, to assert the reality of Motion; it does not show that he could not mean to assert, along with this, the reality of moving things.

CONCLUSION

The principal finding of this investigation has been that while Plato uses "*B* is *A*" *as* an ambiguous sentence-form, taking advantage of its ambiguity to assert it now in one, now in the other, of its alternative uses, he does so *without awareness of the ambiguity*. It might have been more modest to say "without any *apparent* awareness of it." But this would understate—and trivialize—what I believe this investigation has shown. That Plato offers no exposition of the two senses I have blocked out, no analysis of the different ways in which the sentence-form may be used, no paraphrases of each which would make it clear that to substitute one of the uses for the other would alter the meaning and, in some cases, the truth-value of an assertion—to see all this one need only run over the surface of his text. What I believe has been established is something considerably stronger: not only that Plato gives no positive evidence of being aware of the ambiguity, but rather that he gives positive evidence of being unaware of it. If the interpretation of the two crucial contexts in which the sentence, "Motion rests (or, is resting)," occurs is correct, it leaves us no escape from this conclusion. For here we have a substitution-instance of "B is A" in whose case we can be certain that if it were read to imply "$B \varepsilon A$" it would be necessarily true for Plato and that if he had read the sentence in this way he would have seen at once that he is committed to its truth. And what do we find in our passage? From the way he uses the sentence in 252D we can tell, I have argued, that he can only be reading it there to mean "$N(B \subset A)$": this is the only sense that would bear the burden of his vehement and unqualified denial of its truth—his saying that "it is to the last degree impossible" that "Motion should rest." Once stated in this ultra-emphatic way, this is not retracted or qualified in any subsequent part of our passage. And when Plato confronts the sentence later, in 256B, he uses it there only in unasserted form, in spite of the fact that by asserting its truth he could have filled out the last remaining gap in the formal pattern he is elaborating there. Only a man who failed to see that "Motion is resting" could be used with as good reason to mean that "Motion ε resting" as that "$N(\text{Motion} \subset \text{Rest})$" could have behaved in this way.

There is no need to record in detail the findings of the subsequent discussion. Suffice it to remind the reader that while the most common reading of "B is A" is the one which means "$N(B \subset A)$"—the import of the Method of Division for sentences of this type would be sufficient to establish this, though there is other evidence for it as well—still, the ambiguity of the sentence-form allows Plato to shift without the least strain to its radically different, "$B \varepsilon A$," reading, when this is the use that happens to suit his purpose, as it is in the case of the identities and non-identities of the concluding portion of our passage.

APPENDIX I

━━━

On the Interpretation
of *Sph.* 248D4-E4

ON the strength of these lines commentators[1] have been taking Plato to assert both

P When reality is known, it πάσχει,[2]

and

Q When reality πάσχει, it is altered (κινεῖται),

and hence to be stuck with the conclusion

---

[1] Moravcsik (1962, 37 ff.); Crombie (1963, 396 ff.); Owen (1966, 336 ff.); Keyt (1969, 1 ff.).

[2] I leave the verb untranslated, for I have yet to hit on an English rendering which preserves the true value of the Greek. To translate "suffers" would be only to resort to a metaphor, whose literal connotation would be grotesquely inappropriate. To render by "undergoes" in a sentence like *P* would be un-grammatical, unless we supplied an object which is not in the Greek. The least awkward and misleading translation (adopted by Keyt in his 1969, 1 ff.; I shall be resorting to it under pressure of necessity) is "being acted upon," and the trouble with that is (a) that it yields no cognate noun to answer to πάθος, πάθημα and (b) that its signification is much narrower than that of πάσχειν as a glance at the dictionary will show: After listing "*to have* something *done to one, suffer,* opp. *do*" as the primary sense, *LSJ* goes on to give as sense II, "*to have* something *happen to one, to be* or *come to be in a state* or *case,*" illustrating by a sentence like καί τι αὐτόθι γελοῖον παθεῖν (*Smp.* 174E2), "he said that something funny happened to him there," where to translate παθεῖν by "was done to him" would be quite false: the "funny thing" was Socrates' disap-

R When reality is known, it is altered.[3]

I want to argue that even if we grant, as I shall contend we should, that Plato accepts *P*, we have no good reason for holding that he endorses *Q*— hence none for holding that he endorses *R*. The crux of my argument will be the very simple and obvious textual point that Plato's mouthpiece, the Eleatic Stranger (the "ES"), employs *Q* as an unasserted premise: it is a doctrine which he ascribes to the Friends of Forms (the "FFs") in the course of explaining why they—not he—would run into self-contradiction by granting *P*, since they also hold *Q*, which, in conjunction with *P*, yields *R*, and *R* clashes with the great proposition, acknowledged as much by him as by them, that

S The object of (the highest form of)[4] knowledge is changeless.

Let me begin by pointing out that *Q* is not an analytic truth and that Plato would be no more inclined to think it so than would we. This would be true even if we give πάσχειν its narrower sense of "being acted upon":[5]

---

pearance, and the narrator does not represent it as something *done to him* by Socrates, but simply as something that *happened to him* at that spot (he "turned round, and Socrates was nowhere to be seen"). Sense II is, of course, the one exploited by the use of πάσχειν so common in philosophical prose after Plato, to mean no more than "*state, condition*" (sense III in *LSJ*) or even just *attribute* or *property*, as in *Sph.* 245A, where πάθος τοῦ ἑνός means no more than "property of unity," without the slightest implication of having this property in consequence of "being acted upon" by anything. Cf. Aristotle's formal adoption of πάθος to signify "accidental attribute" (e.g., *Metaph.* 1022B15, πάθος = ποιότης καθ᾽ ἣν ἀλλοιοῦσθαι ἐνδέχεται, with "white, black, sweet, bitter, heavy, light" as examples.)

[3] Of the two kinds of κίνησις—ἀλλοίωσις, φορά—mentioned in *Tht.* 181C ff., it is clear that the former is the only relevant one in the present context: φορά would be out of the question for Platonic Forms. So the question in *R*— whether or not what happens to be known κινεῖται—is simply whether or not whatever is known is *altered* when, and only because, it happens to be known. The same sense for κινεῖται is obviously required in *Q*.

[4] The parenthetical qualification would be redundant in Plato's middle period, where "knowledge" was equated with knowledge of Form. It is, however, necessary for the later period, as, e.g., in the *Philebus*, where Plato broadens his use of the term to admit cognition of the world of "becoming and perishing" (61E1; cf. 59A-C) as a less "pure" (57B1), less "true" (61E3-4), form of knowledge.

[5] It would be trivially true if πάσχειν were used in its broadest sense, which includes the sense of *state, condition*, or *attribute* for πάθος (cf. n. 1, above): it would be an outright absurdity to suggest that if *x* is in state *A* it is altered thereby.

What *is* analytic is

(1) If x acts on y, then y is acted upon by x,

since here the consequent does no more than translate into the passive voice what is asserted in the active voice in the antecedent. Not so in the case of

(2) If x acts on y, then y is altered by x,

or, in what comes to the same thing,

(3) If y is acted upon by x, then y is altered by x.

If one conceded the truth of (2) and (3) for every x and every y, one would be doing so by generalization from the innumerable cases in which the action of x on y produces an appreciable change in y, as, to pick a commonplace example, where a pebble runs at high speed into a block of softish clay. But let us change the physical model. Let x be a snowflake, y a block of granite, and let x run into y at the same high speed. Here the effect is a dramatic alteration of x, as it gets squashed against y, but no determinable (macroscopic) change in y: the surface of the granite block is undented, its dimensions remain the same. By favoring this sort of model, picking still more stolid y's, one may easily be led to think that a principle like "to every action there is an equal and opposite reaction" is a contingent truth that might not hold in every possible physical universe—to say nothing of its having to hold in the world of Plato's metaphysical imagination, when y is a Platonic Form, endowed with *eternal* invariance, a form of stability by comparison with which that of granite would be no better than that of smoke. Thus if we are to believe that Plato would find (3) acceptable in this very case—where x is a knowing mind, y a Form, and x's "acting" on y is simply x's knowing that Form—we would have to do so in the face of the fact that Plato *has no reason to concur* and, on the contrary, *strong reason to dissent*, for the truth of (3) in this case would have blockbusting consequences for the metaphysical foundation of his whole system: the absolute unalterability of the Ideas. How then could we possibly credit (or debit) Plato with endorsing Q for this special case—where the πάσχον is an Idea and its πάσχειν is its being known—unless Q were asserted clearly and unambiguously by his mouthpiece? And the plain fact is that no such thing happens in our passage.[6] To satisfy our-

---

[6] Nor yet in any other passage in the Platonic corpus, *pace* Diès, who says (in his note to *Sph.* 248E in the Budé translation) that in *Tht.* 156A "l'opposition du pâtir au repos était . . . nettement exprimée." I deny the relevance

selves of this we need only follow out its thought and note the terms in which the phrase, κινεῖσθαι διὰ τὸ πάσχειν—the only mention of Q— gets into the discourse of the ES.

At the start of our passage he asks if the FFs will say that either knowing or being known is either a ποίημα or a πάθος (D4-7). Of these four possibilities, two—that το γιγνώσκειν (active) should be a πάθος (passive) or that το γιγνώσκεσθαι (passive) should be a ποίημα (active)—are obviously out of the question: they can be washed out on grammatical grounds. We are left with the other two—that knowing is a ποίημα and being known a πάθος—which hang together (each entails the other). And the last—that being known is a πάθος—is of critical importance in the argument: its falsehood would deprive the Ideas of the only conceivable basis on which they might satisfy the proposed "mark" of Being ("capacity, however slight, for πάσχειν or acting," 248C5), for nowadays[7] no one would think of the Platonic Form as an "active" entity; to insure that the Form satisfies that "mark" Plato must have allowed it some sort of πάσχειν;[8] and to credit it with this capacity he need only have granted

---

of the reference: What is expounded in that passage is what Plato calls "the secret doctrine of Protagoras" and (a), unlike Diès, I do not believe that Plato (of all people) would accept that doctrine and moreover (b), even if he did accept it, there would still be no good reason for holding that Plato would think that what is said there has any positive implications for the case in which the "acting" entity is a mind and the "acted upon" is an eternal Form: what we get in *Tht.* 156A ff. is a description of the *physical* world where the things that are interacting are *sensible* entities. I may add, for whatever it may be worth, that the only passage in the Platonic corpus where an abstract entity is explicitly said to πάσχειν because it is the object of a mental act or disposition—*Euthphr.* 11A-B, where the φιλεῖσθαι of Piety by the gods is said to be a πάθος of it, something which it πάσχει, πέπονθε—there is not the slightest suggestion that the object is altered thereby.

[7] By contrast with an older line of interpretation—sponsored by, e.g., Eduard Zeller—that did picture the Ideas as moving entities ("powers"), doing so on the strength of nothing better than our present passage: the matter is settled in Zeller (1888, 261, n. 106) by the laconic remark that "suffering without motion is impossible," supported by a reference to "*Sph.* 248A ff." The vagueness of the reference is symptomatic of the looseness of Zeller's scholarship at this point: the only lines in "*Sph.* 248A ff." that could be thought at all relevant are 248E3-4, and their relevance would be secured by begging the question—by assuming, without the slightest argument, that (in spite of the preceding κατὰ τὸν λόγον τοῦτον) the proposition, τὴν οὐσίαν . . . κατὰ τοσοῦτον κινεῖσθαι διὰ τὸ πάσχειν, *is true for Plato* as well as for the FFs.

[8] Keyt raises two objections (by correspondence): (a) Doesn't Plato say of the Idea in *Smp.* 211B4-5 μηδὲ πάσχειν μηδέν? Reply: This phrase is not a

the entirely innocuous proposition that serving as an object of knowledge is a form of πάσχειν.

Theaetetus replies that FFs could not accept any of these possibilities—hence not even the last—without "contradicting what they had said earlier," i.e., contradicting their adherence to S, which had been ascribed to them by the ES with Theaetetus' emphatic concurrence (248A12-B1). But *where* is the supposed contradiction? There is no logical inconsistency between

P′ Being known is a πάθος.[9]

and

S The object of knowledge is changeless.

To get the contradiction which Theaetetus has in view we need the further premise

Q′ πάσχειν entails κινεῖσθαι,

which yields the conclusion R, which clashes with S. So

P′ is inconsistent with S

is a kind of enthymeme, a contraction for

P′ [in conjunction with Q′, entails R, which] contradicts S.

This sets the stage for the ES's response in D10-E4. I translate it, interspersing reference-marks:

---

detached assertion; it is embedded in a sentence which asserts that "when other things [i.e., sensibles] become and perish, it [the Idea] becomes neither greater nor lesser in any way μηδὲ πάσχειν μηδέν." Here Plato is not thinking of the Idea in relation to knowing minds, but only in relation to the "becoming and perishing" of its sensible participants (τῶν ἄλλων in 211B3 refers to τὰ ἄλλα πάντα καλὰ ἐκείνου μετέχοντα in B2). This tells us nothing of what he would have said had he considered that very special case in which the πάσχειν of the Idea would concern only its serving as an object of knowledge. (b) Does not Aristotle say that "those who assert the existence of the Ideas say that they are ἀπαθεῖς καὶ ἀκίνητοι (*Top.* 148A2-21)? Reply: This is explicable on the natural assumption that the frame of reference of Aristotle's remark is the same as Plato's in *Smp.* 211 B in (a) above—the Ideas are indeed ἀπαθεῖς in the face of physical change—and that Aristotle is indulging his well-known habits of careless reportage.

[9] I use "P′" here, and "Q′" below for propositions which differ respectively so slightly from P and Q above that they are logically interchangeable for the purposes of my argument.

I understand what you mean. Just this: [A] That if knowing is doing something, it follows of necessity that the known πάσχει. [B] And according to that doctrine, reality, when known by knowledge, so far as it is known, so far is it altered in virtue of πάσχειν, [C] which, we say, could not happen to the changeless (D10-E4).

What the ES does here is to make explicit the line of thought which Theaetetus must have had in view when he asserted that the FFs could not grant any of the four possibilities in D4-7, hence not even the last, P', because to do so would be to contradict their "earlier assertion," S. To do this he starts off by citing P' (as the consequent of the hypothetical in [A]). He then proceeds in [B] to conjoin P' with Q', which had not yet shown its face in the dialogue: it pops up here for the first time, making its entrance in a clause which is cast in indirect discourse, κατὰ τοσοῦτον κινεῖσθαι διὰ τὸ πάσχειν, and is qualified by the phrase κατὰ τὸν λόγον τοῦτον, "according to that doctrine," namely the doctrine of the FFs which yields the contradiction Theaetetus has said they would incur and which the ES is now explaining—the contradiction between P' and S, when P' is conjoined with Q'. The import of the indirect discourse in [B]—mentioning, without asserting—is heightened by the return to direct discourse in the terminal portion of the period, [C], which presents a proposition which we know the ES would have no qualms in asserting: that κινεῖσθαι cannot occur to the ἠρεμοῦν. If this reading of the passage is even approximately correct, it should be obvious that the crucial proposition, Q', has not been asserted *in propria persona* by the ES; it has only come into his discourse as the doctrine of the FFs which, joined to P', springs the contradiction to which Theaetetus referred in D8-9.

Now when we look at the paraphrases of our passage in the recent literature which takes *Plato* to be endorsing the πάσχειν of the Forms when they serve as objects of knowledge, we find that the fact that Q appears only in a passage which purports to explain the thought of the FFs is persistently ignored. Time and again we run into paraphrases of [A] and [B] which read as though [B] had been a straightforward exposition of Platonic doctrine. Keyt (1969, 1):

And on the hypothesis that to know is to act on something, that which is known is acted upon (248D10-E1). Further, *to be acted upon is to be changed* (248E3-4). Therefore, since being is known, *it is changed* (248E3-4). [My emphasis][10]

[10] If one were in any doubt that Keyt means to ascribe to Plato's mouthpiece endorsement of the italicized phrase, one's doubt would be resolved on the

Owen (1966, 338):

> But suppose knowing is doing something; then for a Form to be known is for something to be done to it: and if something is done to it, it is *changed*. [My emphasis][11]

---

next page of his paper: "Since being is acted upon, *Plato infers* [my emphasis] that it is changed."

[11] Owen offers an explanation of Plato's (alleged) wish to endorse the italicized phrase: Taking as an example of "something done" to the Form, Justice, the fact that "it captured Jones' attention yesterday," (The unhappy phrasing, which makes it look as though Justice is acting on Jones, instead of the converse, may be ignored: Owen puts no weight on it in his argument.) Owen writes: "For if Plato can claim, as he does in the *Timaeus*, that even (A) to have a history is to change, then (B) to say that justice captured the attention of Jones yesterday is to report a change in the Form" (339; my reference-marks). His reference to the *Ti.* is to 38A, which Owen glosses (in part), "To go on in time, and thus to collect a past and a future, is to grow older" and "to grow older is to have a history" (334, 335). It appears to me that, on the contrary, the doctrine of the *Ti.* compels the opposite conclusion: that Plato would have good reason to deny Q: (B) above would not be true and would not follow from (A) unless we were to assume that the capturing of the attention of Jones yesterday was part of the history of Justice. The assumption would be true only if the Form of Justice had a history. But nothing can have a history if it is not in time, and no Platonic Form is in time. Hence Plato would have reckoned the capturing of Jones' attention by this Form as part of the history of Jones, who has a history, and no part of the history of Justice, which has no history. And since he would have agreed that if something could change it would have a history, he would have inferred on just that account that no Form could change by being known. Owen would no doubt still contend that "justice captured the attention of Jones yesterday" is a statement in the past tense about Justice and, since it is true, the thing of which it is said, the Form, *must* have undergone change, since according to Plato statements in the past tense are true only of things which undergo change (*Ti.* 37E–38A). Owen's contention would (at most) expose an incoherence in Plato's thought, showing that Plato would have had *this* reason for admitting that Forms undergo change, though his own principles would have *also* required him to deny absolutely that any Form could undergo change. Owen would then have to argue that our passage in the *Sophist* shows that Plato, when faced with such a dilemma, chose, or would have chosen, the former horn. It is hard to see how such an argument could hope to succeed. The evidence which would be needed to bring it off is not available in our texts. The evidence, such as it is, tells far more strongly against the thesis that Plato would have tolerated change in Forms. Of his insistence on the absolute immutability of Form we have ample records. Of his supposed concession that knowledge of Form entails change in the known Form, no less than in its knower, we have no record at all.

Crombie (1963, 396):

> The Stranger argues . . . that there is reason to suppose that some-
> thing which is known thereby undergoes something, and that there-
> fore that which cannot undergo change cannot be known.

Crombie is so confident in ascribing Q' to the ES that he does not even
bother to spell out the ascription: from "something which is known thereby
undergoes something" he has the Stranger inferring that what is known
thereby undergoes change, just taking it for granted that the Stranger would
hold that anything which "undergoes *something*" thereby undergoes *change*.
Owen and Keyt, in their fuller summaries, do spell out the premise that
has dropped out in Crombie—and they do so in words which give no
indication that the premise occurs in a dependent clause hung from κατὰ
τον λόγον τοῦτον, and purports to tell what gets the FFs—not the ES—
into trouble.

Is there then a possible reading of our passage on which the ES would
be understood to endorse all the views—including Q'—which he ascribes
to the FFs to explain the contradiction they would incur by conceding
P'? Rummaging through translations, I have turned up only one that
offers us such a reading: that of Diès in the Budé. There the ES's opening
words at D10, Μανθάνω · τόδε γε, are rendered, "Je comprends; mais, ceci,
au moins, ils l'avoueront." If we concur with this translation, there would,
of course, be no difficulty in taking everything that follows for true-blue
Platonic doctrine:[12] the rhetorical force of "this much at least they will
admit" puts the ES in the position of implying that *it would be reasonable*
for the FFs to grant the views he will be pinning on them. It should take
no more than a glance at the text to satisfy oneself that there is *nothing* in
it to support the part of the Diès translation which has this implication:
the only non-tendentious expansion of τόδε γε would be φήσουσι, or
some equivalently neutral expression. To make the text say more would be
simply to read into it the very thing which is in dispute. If we ask the
text itself to decide the issue, all it offers is a statement which explains
what gets the FFs into the contradiction, without so much as a word to
imply that the ES himself, in the course of explaining *their* predicament,
associates himself with all their views, including the one which precipitates
the contradiction.

---

[12] Especially if we were to follow Diès further in translating κατὰ τὸν λόγον
τοῦτον in [B] as "par la même raison"—a most implausible translation (How
do we get "same" out of τοῦτον? And suppose we did, what would be the
reference of "same"—"same" as what?)

I anticipate an objection to the interpretation I have offered: "If Plato's spokesman," it may be said, "has no good reason for granting the truth of Q', why should it be otherwise with the FFs? What is it in their position, in contrast to Plato's, which would lead them to think 'the πάσχειν of Forms entails their κινεῖσθαι' a true counterfactual?" I freely admit that I have no answer to this question. Should this trouble me? It should, if we had been given a fuller account of their position, so that we could figure out what would or would not be reasonable for them to say on this particular point. But the fact is that all Plato has chosen to give us of their views consists of a few scraps, introduced for polemical, not expository, purposes. These scraps do not begin to enlighten us on why the FFs would have reason to adhere to Q'. We are left with huge gaps in our knowledge of their system and are not even able to assess the correctness of Plato's ascription to them of this adherence. This is unfortunate. But it does not destroy, or even diminish, the force of the argument for exonerating Plato himself from the same adherence. In his case our knowledge of his views is ample, and from it we can infer with confidence that he would have reason not to endorse Q'. This is sufficient to satisfy us that he does not mean to endorse Q' in the present context, where Q' appears only in indirect discourse purporting to explain a λόγος which is to all appearance the theory of the FFs.

APPENDIX II

———

More on Pauline Predications in Plato

Richard Robinson (1941) seems to have been the first modern commentator to get on the track of the OP/PP ambiguity in Plato. He spots it in the section on "The Communion of Forms" in the *Sph*,[1] reports that the assertion that *B* "combines with" or "participates in" *A* could only mean

(I) "the adjective *B* is characterized by the adjective *A*,"[2]

in some contexts in that passage, while in other contexts it could only mean

(II) "some or all substantives characterized by the adjective *B* are also characterized by the adjective *A*" (260).

In 1963 Crombie notices the same ambiguity in the same passage, probes many more occurrences of it there, and presents an equivalent analysis. That Kind *B* "partakes in" Kind *A*, he writes (402), may be for Plato

(I) a "pure property statement,"[3] asserting that "*B*-hood is itself *A*," or

[1] Cf. n. 4 in *AS*.

[2] In the quotations from Robinson and Crombie I am changing their lettering, making it conform to mine, to simplify the exposition. In Robinson's case I also drop the suffix in his "Xness" and "Yness" which hardly suits stand-ins for "adjectives."

[3] "Property-of-a-property statement" would have expressed more accurately what he means.

(II) a "class-inclusion statement," asserting that "*A*-hood belongs to *B*-hood distributively, so to speak" or that "any *B* thing is *A*."

My own investigation of the topic got started with the insight, which I owed initially to Sandra Wallace,[4] that this ambiguity has its source in the natural language, arising there in typical uses of the verb *to be*. This enlarged my perception of its incidence in the Platonic corpus. It directed me to theoretically important occurrences of it in passages so far removed, both chronologically and thematically, from the Communion of Kinds in the *Sph.* as are the sections on the Unity of the Virtues in the *Prt.* and on the clever *aitia* in the *Phdo*;[5] it alerted me to connect these passages with those which expound or practice the Method of Division in the *Phaedrus* and thereafter, where to "divide" is to generate sentences whose copula is Pauline.

The way is now open to a more sympathetic understanding of Plato's unawareness of the ambiguity. His total insensitiveness to it would have been more surprising if Pauline predications had turned up exclusively in technical diction of his own devising, instead of pervading common speech, appearing there not only in locutions of picturesque, quasi-poetic, cast, like our "Love is blind," but in sentences as common and as commonplace as "Man is [an] animal," "Fire is hot," "Gold is yellow." Suppose that such sentences, instead of being familiar coin in the currency of his mother-tongue, had been new-minted by him to do the work of Pauline predications. Would he not then have been far more likely to notice that the very same grammatical form is susceptible of the radically different OP reading—the very one which he would *not* have wanted those invented sentences to express?

How then, exactly, should Plato's Pauline predications be described? The formulae used by Robinson and by Crombie strike me as proper enough, provided only we add the modal operator. Without this, the phrases they use for (II) would be tantamount to a purely extensional interpretation which would go against the grain of Plato's ontology: In Plato's universe a substitution-instance of "All *B*'s are *A*'s" could be true without affording the least basis for inferring the truth of "Form *B* partakes in *A*" and of its NL correlate, "Form *B* is *A*."[6] Only if the bond between

[4] Cf. n. 88 in *UVP*.

[5] I have not pursued this aspect of the *Phaedo* passage; to do so would call for a separate study. I allude to it briefly in *RC*, n. 68, and *UVP*, n. 48.

[6] See my remarks on the formulae in *UVP*, I.3, pp. 232–33, above.

the properties named by "*B*" and "*A*" is a necessary one, would Plato feel justified in asserting that *A* is predicable not only of the *B*'s, but of the Form, the "*B* itself". So "class-inclusion statement" must be amended to "statement of necessary class-inclusion."

But would that suffice? I have encountered resistance on this point. There are some who feel that something is lost when we translate the sentence "Man is mortal" into "The relation of Man to Mortality is such that, necessarily, all men, if any, are mortal."[7] The objection seems to come to this: "Since for Plato both 'Man' and 'mortal' name Forms, he should be prepared to state how *they*, the Forms, are related to each other. This the proffered formula fails to do. All it states is how *their instance-classes* are related to each other; and surely in his ontology a Form is entirely distinct from its instance-classes." The objection is misconceived. It betokens failure to understand that the whole point of "Man is mortal" is to express a relation between the two Forms which can only be specified *via* their instance-classes: there is no other way.

To see this one must focus on the irreducibly dual role which Forms play in Plato's ontology. Though each is certainly an *individual* entity, each is nonetheless *general*: unlike ordinary, spatio-temporal, existents, these eternal entities are *instantiable*; each has a definite one-many relation to possible "namesakes".[8] Given this dual role, their names may function in radically different ways in sentences specifying inter-Form relations:

(I) In a sentence like "Man is$_{OP}$ eternal," "Man" functions as a singular term, "eternal" as a general one. Only by this distribution of semantic function does the sentence succeed in conveying its message which is that Man instantiates Eternity. To do this "Man" must pick out the Form Man as an individual member of the instance-class of Eternity. And "eternal" must then function as a term with a determinate range of generality which is broad enough to cover this instance among others. That it names the Form Eternity is de rigueur: all general terms are Form-namers for Plato— that is how, he thinks, they get their meaning. But if that were the only contribution "eternal" were making in this sentence, its predicative func-

---

[7] Cf. n. 13 in *AS*.

[8] This dual status is unaffected by the distinction between Form and immanent character in the "tripartite ontology" (cf. *RC*, II, and *AS*, n. 12): it is not as though the character took over the function of generality from the transcendent Form, leaving the latter in splendid isolation from possible "namesakes." No matter how transcendent, the Form continues to have *participants*: the one-many relation of the Φ to the class of *F*-things remains intact.

tion would be lost; to discharge it "eternal" must enter the sentence through its one-many relation to possible instances.

(II) In a sentence like "Man is$_{PP}$ mortal", both terms must enter the sentence in that same way. If both functioned only as names of individual Forms, then the only relation between these Forms the sentence could have expressed would be identity. Or, if "Man" were only singular, while "mortal" was general, we would get a sentence of type (I), expressing the absurdity that the Form Man is a mortal thing. So both must keep their general signification—their respective one-many relations to instances.[9] It is only in this capacity that their names can establish the correct Form-to-Form relation which is specified in this sentence. Only by indicating that the instance-class of Man is necessarily contained in the instance-class of Animal is it possible to express the fact that the Form Man has that particular relation to the Form Animal which I have called "entailment" in *RC*, III.[10]

Should one still find it a paradox that in Plato's ontology there should be

[9] The reader might well ask if my notation, using the same symbol, "*B*," in both (I) and (II) on p. 273 above, does not disguise this shift in semantic value from (I), where it stands for a singular term, used nominatively, to (II), where it stands for a general term, used predicatively. The alternative would have been to choose a different symbol for a Form-word functioning in each of these two capacities—e.g., the same letter in Roman script in the former case, in italics in the latter. The definiens would then have been altered to "B ε *A*," from "*B* ε *A*", in (I), while remaining italicized, like *A*, in (II) and (IIa). After much hesitation I rejected this option both in the interests of notational economy and on a substantive ground: while advertising the shift in function, from singular to general, in the subject-term, this alternative notation would have obscured the still more important fact that for Plato it is exactly the same entity whose dual role commissions it to do both jobs in his ontology: the same metaphysical entity which instantiates the predicate-term in (I) is itself instantiable, exactly like the predicate-term, in (II) and (IIa). Plato's ontology violates on principle the Fregean doctrine that no concept-naming expression may ever be used predicatively (a doctrine which is itself not free from difficulty, entailing, as Frege saw, the paradoxical conclusion that "the concept *horse* is not a concept" [Frege, 1952, 46; cf. Black, 1954, 246 ff.], since "horse" is not used predicatively in this sentence). For Plato every concept-naming word is systematically ambivalent: it always names a unique metaphysical existent, and yet its principal use is predicative, serving in this capacity not only manifestly, when it occurs in predicate position, but frequently also when its apparent function is only nominative, as, e.g., when it is the subject-term of a Pauline predication.

[10] The same is true of other inter-Form relations specified in sentences whose Form-naming words function as general terms. Thus to say that two Forms are

Form-to-Form relations which are constituted by the relations of their respective instance-classes, one may be reminded that Plato's language shows that this is pretty much his own perception of these relations. So, e.g., when he speaks in the *Sophist* and the *Timaeus* of Form *B* as "contained" or "surrounded" by Form *A* to express the thought that *B* entails *A*: the only thing he could be thus describing as "contained" or "surrounded" is *B*'s range of instantiation by that of *A*.[11] In the same vein he speaks in the *Phaedo* of the relation in "Three is odd," "Snow is cold," and the like, as the "bringing-on" (ἐπιφέρειν[12]) of the entailed Form by the entailing one: there is no way to cash this metaphor except to think of the instantiation of the entailing Form necessitating the co-instantiation of the other.

---

incompatible (or contrary, ἐναντία)—as, e.g., Snow and Hot—is to say that their instance-classes are necessarily exclusive. To say that they are compatible—as, e.g., Gold and Hot—is to say that their instance-classes may overlap.

[11] Cf. *AS*, nn. 65, 70, 85.

[12] Cf. n. 67 in *RC*.

12

The "Two-Level Paradoxes" in Aristotle

(1971; TLPA)

CONSTRUING textual evidence narrowly in Section I of AS above—using only Platonic texts which bear directly on the ambiguous sentence "Motion is resting"—I made no effort to explore additional data from which collateral lines of argument for my conclusion could be traced out. Here I want to deal briefly with one such set of data: a batch of texts in which Aristotle exploits with polemical intent what Owen has recently called "two-level paradoxes"[1]—sentences of the form, "the Idea of F is P," which are analyzed by Aristotle as true if P is predicated of "the Idea *qua* Idea," or false if predicated of it "*qua* F," as, e.g., "The Idea of Man is resting," whose ambiguity is resolved by the observation that "resting belongs to Man-himself not *qua* Man, but *qua* Idea [ἐπεί αὐτοανθρώπῳ οὐχ ὑπάρχει τὸ ἠρεμεῖν ᾗ ἄνθρωπός ἐστιν, ἀλλ' ᾗ ἰδέα]" (*Top.* 137B6-7).

As Aristotle looks upon these sentences, they become completely unproblematic once the distinction between asserting P of the Idea of F *qua* Idea, upon the one hand, and *qua* F, upon the other (the "P-distinction," I shall call it) has been applied to them. As he handles them, they appear to be pseudo-paradoxes, offering him no difficulty whatever nor any special philosophical challenge or interest on their own account. Never does he discuss them in a non-polemical context. And even in polemical contexts he does not stop to comment on their deep onto-

---

[1] In his highly instructive paper, "Dialectic and Eristic in the Treatment of Forms," 1970. I shall refer to it merely by author's name hereafter in this essay.

logical implications which call for a reasoned defense of the implied claim that the same metaphysical entity *can* be P *qua* one thing, not-P *qua* another. Not only in the *Topics*, where the dialectical interest might understandably have swamped the metaphysical one, but even in the *Metaphysics*, Aristotle's principal, almost his only, concern with the paradoxes is to use them as weapons in philosophical controversy. With just one exception,[2] their butt is the Platonic Theory of Ideas.[3] And since he is satisfied that their effect on it is lethal, it seems reasonable to infer that he does not believe that Plato had acknowledged the P-distinction or could have done so consistently with his known philosophical commitments. If this inference will stand, it will bring strong corroboration to my conclusion in Section I of *AS*. For if Aristotle had understood Plato to be asserting the categorical truth of "Motion is resting" in *Sph*. 256B, having denied it vehemently in 252D, Aristotle could scarcely have failed to see spread out before his eyes in a Platonic work a spectacular[4] specimen of the P-distinction, since this is the only basis on which he could have made sense of Plato's readiness to declare the sentence true in one context, false in another, untroubled by the apparent contradiction. So that inference—that Aristotle does not think that Plato himself had drawn, or could have drawn, the P-distinction—is important for my purposes: if it is sound, it confirms that Aristotle read *Sph*. 256B6-7 in the way I have defended against the view of many modern exegetes. It is important enough to be worth defending in the face of the position taken by Owen in his recent discussion of the two-level paradoxes in the *Topics* and the *Metaphysics*. Owen will not concede that Aristotle consistently refuses Plato acknowledgment of the P-distinction. He sees (119-21) Aristotle at times denying its recognition to the Platonists (as in *Top*. 148A14-22 and 146B36-147A11) while conceding it to them in other passages (as in

---

[2] The one in *Top*. 113A24-32, which appears to have been specially directed against Eudoxus (Alexander, *Met*. 98, 21-24; cf. Cherniss [1944, 9] and Owen, 110).

[3] Of the two-level paradoxes at *Top*. 148A15-22 he observes that "such arguments are useful against those who assert the existence of the Ideas" and later (154A15-20) he adds that they are ἐνεργότατοι, "most effective." The difficulties in *Metaph*. 990B27-34 and 1059A10-14, which are supposed to prove respectively that there are no Ideas of non-substances, and that there are no Ideas at all, arise from the exploitation of two-level paradoxes: both difficulties would be adequately resolved if the P-distinction were applied.

[4] None of Aristotle's substituends for {F, P} in the formula, "The Idea of F is P *qua* Idea, not P *qua* F" are nearly as striking as are {Motion, Rest}, which are, and are said to be, ἐναντιώτατα ἀλλήλοις (*Sph*. 250A).

Top. 137B3-13 and *Metaph.* 990B27-34). I shall argue that there is no good evidence that Aristotle *ever* concedes it to them. And I shall then proceed to ask: Why doesn't he? Would he really think of the Platonists as so recalcitrant to this distinction that even when it was explained to them they would still not accept it and use it in self-defense? If so, why?

Let us review briefly each of the two passages in which Owen sees Aristotle conceding the *P*-distinction to the Platonists; none of the others is worth talking about in this connection.[5] In the first of these (*Top.* 137B3-13) we are directed to look at Ideas through the lenses of the *P*-distinction and see if a suggested property of the Idea of *F* belongs to it *qua* Idea or *qua* *F*; we are given two examples of {*F*, *P*}: ({Man, Resting},[6] {Animal, Compound-of-soul-and-body}); we are told how to use this in debate. What is there then to warrant Owen's remark that Aristotle here is "apparently conceding the same recognition [*sc.* of the *P*-distinction] to the partisans of the Ideas" (121)? So far as I can see, nothing. Aristotle does not say, or imply, that it is Plato or his followers who maintain that "Resting belongs to Man-in-himself not *qua* Man, but *qua* Idea." He gives no indication of speaking for anyone but himself. In particular, the fact that he makes a pronouncement of what is true or false about the Man-himself is no such indication: Aristotle is perfectly capable of making such pronouncements about the theories of other philosophers without the least authority from them; he feels (and surely is) at liberty to volunteer the observation that such and such will be true of a sample Idea, simply because *he* has inferred this from known Platonic specifications for the Ideas. Aristotle does this sort of thing all the time, and there is no reason in the world why he should not be doing so here, inferring from the in-variance of all Ideas that the Idea of Man *qua* Idea will be "resting," and juxtaposing this with the proposition, which strikes him as a perfectly reasonable one, that the Idea of Man is not resting *qua* Man. So our text gives no support to the suggestion that here Aristotle is thinking of Plato, or his followers, as saying, or admitting, that the *P*-distinction makes "The Idea of Man is resting" true in one of the two senses stipulated by Aristotle, false in the other. To be sure, the passage, taken just by itself,

---

[5] Owen does not explain exactly why he thinks that in their case Aristotle did *not* concede the recognition of the *P*-distinction to the Platonists. I cannot detect any difference in their case from the ones where he believes the contrary. I can see no evidence of the concession in any of them, hence am content to discuss the two for which the concession has been claimed.

[6] The word for "Resting" is ἠρεμεῖν. I take it to carry exactly the same sense as do στάσις, ἑστάναι in our passage in the *Sph.*; cf. *AS*, n. 5.

is *consistent* with that suggestion. But it cannot count as evidence for it, since it is equally consistent with its contrary.

Now for the other passage, *Metaph.* 990B27-34, where Owen finds the strongest case for holding that Aristotle allows his Academic adversaries acknowledgement of the *P*-distinction: Having just reminded us that according to the received doctrine of the Academy (κατὰ μὲν τὴν ὑπόληψιν καθ' ἣν εἶναί φαμεν τὰς ἰδέας, 22–23) "there are Forms not only of substances but of many other things as well," Aristotle undertakes to demonstrate that, on the contrary,

> according to the necessities of the case and according to the opinions held about the Forms, if Forms are participatable, then there must necessarily be Ideas of substances only. (27–29)

The destructive import of this conclusion speaks for itself: if it could be shown that only Ideas like Man could be participated in, while Ideas like Beauty or Equality could not, the Theory of Ideas, as we know it from the dialogues, would be left in shambles. This is how I understand the argument: If a particular participates in the Form of *F* and the latter is in fact a *G* (as, in the example, the Idea of Double is eternal), then, if the Idea of *G* were participatable, the particular, in virtue of its participation in the Idea of *F*, would *accidentally* participate in the Idea of *G*.[7] The conclusion would be odd on any view (what would it mean to say that my two ears are *accidentally eternal?*) and demonstrably absurd on Aristotle's, for he holds that attributes like *perishable* and *imperishable* are necessary attributes[8]

---

[7] Note that it is the particular—the individual thing, τι, which participates in the Idea of *F*—that is supposed to participate "accidentally" in the Idea of *G*: in lines 32–33 the demonstrative pronoun in τοῦτο καὶ ἀϊδίου μετέχει, ἀλλὰ κατὰ συμβεβηκός refers to the preceding τι in εἴ τι αὐτοδιπλασίου μετέχει.

[8] My analysis of the argument follows closely that of Cherniss (1944, 306 and n.8). Owen reads the argument differently. He glosses the parenthesis, 990A31-34, as follows:

> Why does his eternity [that of Socrates: Owen has substituted "Man" for Aristotle's "Double" in expounding the argument] not follow from the premises [his participation in Man], as his being a man does? Because, says Aristotle, eternity is only an accident of man, i.e., not all or even most men are eternal (cf. *Met.* 1025A14-15, 1065A1-3): in fact only one man, the Paradigm, is so. (122)

My first objection would be to taking "accidentally eternal" to qualify the general term "man," instead of "*a* man" (cf. the preceding note). But over and beyond that, I would find it hard to square Aristotle's conceding that

(they are, respectively, categorial properties of sensible individual substances and non-sensible substances or forms), and we may be certain that he would hold the same of the attribute *eternal*.[9] Hence there can be no Idea of an attribute like Eternity, nor of any other which, like it, is non-substantial and, if participatable, would be participated in accidentally.

So far from seeing anything in this passage to substantiate the view that here "Aristotle is allowing the Academy a distinction between different-level predicates which he seems to refuse them elsewhere" (Owen, 122), I find in it indications to the very contrary: The crucial premise, the one that necessitates the conclusion that would sweep out of existence Plato's favorite Forms, is

> *1* If *x* participates in the Idea of *F*, and the Idea of *F* is *G*, and there exists a participatable Idea of *G*, then *x* participates *accidentally* in the Idea of *G*.

Now there is a well-known Platonic doctrine with which *1* may be usefully compared: that of the "clever *aitia*" in the *Phaedo*.[10] Let me rewrite it in the style of *1* so as to highlight similarities and differences:

> *2* If *x* participates in the Idea of *F*, and the Idea of *F* "brings on" (ἐπιφέρει) the idea of *G*, then *x* participates in the Idea of *G*.

---

eternity is an accident of man, i.e., that man is accidentally eternal, with his considered doctrine (the one to which I refer in the text above) that this type of attribute is non-accidental. And even apart from this, I would not wish, without explicit and unambiguous warrant from the text, to put Aristotle in the position of underwriting in all seriousness on this occasion so eccentric a doctrine as that man is accidentally eternal. Our passage provides no such warrant: Aristotle's phrase, τοῦτο καὶ ἀϊδίου μετέχει, can be read just as well as a statement of what, in his opinion, follows from the antecedent, εἴ τι αὐτοδιπλασίου μετέχει, but is not true simpliciter. That is to say, I take the proposition that eternity is an accident of man to be put forward by Aristotle only as a necessary, but plainly false, consequence of the Platonic view that Forms of non-substances are participatable. Owen appears to take it as a proposition whose truth Aristotle himself would underwrite. (I might add that my difference with Owen on this point does not affect the point for which I am arguing in this paragraph of the text above. Regardless of how we decide to read the parenthesis in 990A31-34, my argument that the *P*-distinction is not being imputed to the Platonists in this passage would go through).

[9] Since *eternal* would entail, and be entailed by, *imperishable*, if the latter attribute is a necessary one, so must the former.

[10] Cf. *RC*, p. 102 ff., above.

To sharpen up the comparison still further, let me rewrite 2 as

> 3 If x participates in the Idea of F, and the Idea of F is G,[11] and there exists a participatable Idea of G,[12] then x participates in G.

Between 1 and 3 there is no difference except for the presence of "accidentally" in the conclusion—a term of Aristotelian stamp, expressing no relevant notion in the Platonic doctrine: nothing in the *Phaedo* or elsewhere in the dialogues to suggest that Plato recognized a difference between two kinds of participation of individuals in Forms, accidental and non-accidental. But I do not want to make too much of this point, for there is something far more important for what is at issue. This concerns the permissible examples of Form-couples in the Platonic formulae. In the *Phaedo* Plato gives us such examples as {Three, Odd}, {Two, Even}, {Fire, Hot}, {Snow, Cold}. From couples such as these nothing untoward results in the conclusion, and for good reason: we get same-level predicates[13] inside each coupling. But when we return to Aristotle's example of 1 in *Metaph.* 990B27 ff., we are given a radically different sort of {F, G} couple; instead of the {Two, Even} of the *Phaedo*, Aristotle gives us {Two, Eternal}. And that is what causes all the trouble. To conclude that my ears participate in Evenness—that they are even-numbered—because they are two, is an ultra-secure inference; to conclude from the same premise that they participate in Eternity—that they are eternal—is a crazy inference, leading from a sober premise to a mad conclusion, which is not made perceptibly saner by the assurance that my ears are only *accidentally* eternal. What derails the inference is that we have switched levels in making up our {F, G} coupling: we have admitted an example of G which (in the lingo of the P-distinction) can only be predicable of the Idea of F *qua* Idea, whereas 2 and 3 are true only if our G is a term predicable of the Idea of F *qua* F. If Aristotle were giving his Academic adversaries benefit of the P-distinction, this is just the mistake he would not expect them to make themselves or allow anyone else to palm it off on them in a

---

[11] Substituting for OR(The Idea of F participates in the Idea of G) its NL correlate, "The Idea of F is G," with ample warrant from the text, e.g., at 104A-B, ". . . is odd," ". . . is even," as the NL correlates of OR(. . . participates in the Odd), OR(. . . participates in the Even). (For the sense of "OR" and "NL" see the opening paragraph of *AS* above.)

[12] Making explicit what is implicit in the second clause of 2, solely to bring 3 into line with 1.

[13] Predicable of sensible individuals (though the first two pairs are also predicable of Forms). There are no pairs such that one member is predicable exclusively of Forms.

serious argument. This much would be as clear to Aristotle as it is to us. Hence if Aristotle were allowing the Academy the P-distinction, he would not have thought them vulnerable to his argument in this passage: he would have expected them to reject it as a sadly misguided argument, resting on the arguer's failure to take account of the P-distinction. Hence so far from giving us reason to think that Aristotle was allowing the P-distinction to the Academy in this passage, it rather gives us reason to think the contrary. It is good, though of course not conclusive,[14] evidence that Aristotle is arguing here against opponents who he thinks *cannot* avail themselves of the P-distinction to break his argument.

Why then does he so think of them? Or to pose a more direct question, leaving Aristotle out of it for the moment: If the Academy did not make defensive use of the P-distinction, why didn't they? Not, surely, because they had never heard of it. This might explain Plato's behavior around the time he wrote the *Sophist:* Aristotle need not be credited with putting forward his two-level arguments until some time well after the *Sophist* had been written.[15] However, this would not explain why Aristotle thinks those arguments of his in the *Topics* and the *Metaphysics* have a continuing power to wreck the Theory of Ideas. So he could hardly have thought of the P-distinction as unfamiliar to the Platonists. He could only have thought of it as familiar and unacceptable. Why unacceptable? Cherniss never pursues this question. He has no occasion to do so, being convinced that the Aristotelian analysis of the two-level paradoxes is "a conscious dialectical trick"[16] which Aristotle did not expect to fool and, *a fortiori*, to scare any Platonist. Cherniss feels satisfied that Plato had in fact preceded Aristotle in seeing through the two-level paradoxes, and at a deeper level, thinking of F clearly and unambiguously as that which the Form of F *is*, not that which the Form *has*, so that the disambiguation of a sentence like "The Idea of Animal is a mortal compound of soul and body" would have been child's play for Plato: it would follow from Plato's conception of the Idea that "mortal" or "compound of soul and body" are (parts of) what the Ideal Animal *is*, and not at all what the Ideal Animal *has*—part of the essence of Animal, not an attribute of its

[14] It would be conclusive if Aristotle were a more scrupulous controversialist than he is unhappily known to be.

[15] Düring's opinion (1970, 202, n.4) that the *Sophist* is "the *terminus post quem* for all treatises in the Corpus" strikes me as a reasonable one. At any rate, there is no serious risk in assuming that what we get in the *Topics* had not been ventilated prior to the appearance of the *Sophist*.

[16] 1944, 3.

existence.[17] If one shared this generous view of the Platonic concept of the Idea and then assumed, plausibly enough, that Aristotle's long residence in the Academy would have made him privy to it, one would dismiss the exploitation of the two-level paradoxes in the *Topics* as mere debating ploys. But what would one do with the corresponding passages in the *Metaphysics*, where no one can doubt that they are seriously meant as a refutation of the Theory of Ideas? Is one to say here that Aristotle is talking through his hat, professing to demolish Plato's Theory by means of a conclusion derived from premises which deliberately misstate the Theory?

Owen, who understandably declines to take so low a view of Aristotle's debating tactics, offers his own explanation of Aristotle's confidence that even if the Platonists understood the *P*-distinction, they would be unable to make suitable use of it to render their theory invulnerable to his two-level arguments. To explain Owen's view it will be convenient to shift with him to the example in *Top.* 148A15ff.: let the ambiguous sentence be "The Idea of Man is mortal." Aristotle, Owen claims, would not admit that the Platonists could pull the teeth of the paradox by saying that this Idea is mortal *qua* Man, but not *qua* Idea: he would not, because he thinks of their Idea of Man as "a sample man," so that in their theory

> the Idea, like the King of Balustan, *is known to be mortal in common with his subjects* but required to be immortal *ex officio.* . . . (123)

I have underscored the sentence which strikes me as so patently false that I find it difficult to believe that Aristotle, for all his notorious highhandedness in dealing with opponents, would really have wished to foist it on the Platonists—that he would really have expected them to hold not only

---

[17] This is how I understand Cherniss's comments [1944, 1–3], taking these in conjunction with his later discussion of the Theory of Ideas, crisply epitomized in his formula that "Plato . . . believed that . . . the idea *is* that which the particular *has* as an attribute" (298). This had been the standard interpretation of the Platonic Theory prior to the second world war (cf., e.g., Cornford [1939, 90], ". . . it is not true that it [the Form of Bed in *R.* 597C] *has* the character. . . . Rather it *is* the character. . . .") for virtually all scholars publishing in the 'thirties and early 'forties on whom Theodore de Laguna's "Notes on the Theory of Ideas" (1934) had made no dent. Richard Robinson appears to be the single exception among English-speaking scholars in this period. He does not refer to de Laguna's paper in the first edition (1941) of his *Plato's Earlier Dialectic*. But he does so in his paper "Plato's Consciousness of Fallacy," Mind 51 (1942), reprinted in his *Essays in Greek Philosophy* (1969).

that the Idea of Man is *a* man, but also a *mortal* man! A Platonist would have had to be out of his mind to make such an admission for one of his Ideas, whose absolute immutability is built into its categorial design. Hence if we are to grant that Aristotle expected his Academic interlocutors to believe this contradiction and to be *thereby* prevented from employing the P-distinction in self-defense against his attacks, we would have to be shown that Aristotle at least *says* or *distinctly implies* such a thing. And the fact is that Aristotle does nothing of the kind; and Owen, of course, does not suggest that he does. It is not Aristotle who ekes out with this preposterous premise his offensive against the Platonists when deploying his two-level paradoxes against them. His arguments, as we read them in his text, never even hint at such a premise; it is only Owen who supplies it, putting it up as a hypothesis designed to explain the fact that Aristotle acts as though the Platonists will be unable to accept the P-distinction and use it in self-defense. Let us then look around to see if we can find an alternative hypothesis that could do the same job at a less prohibitive cost.

To come within sight of it we need only recall the passage in the *Symposium* (211A) where it is denied that the Form of Beauty is τῇ μὲν καλόν, τῇ δ' αἰσχρόν, "beautiful in one way [or, "in one respect"], ugly in another," and note that the Aristotelian formula establishes the P-distinction at the price of losing this very feature of the Idea, allowing it to be *P* and not-*P* but in different respects, *P* ᾗ *F*, not-*P* ᾗ ἰδέα τοῦ *F*.

So the Aristotelian formula would repel a Platonist from the start: its very language would warn him that to resolve the two-level paradoxes on its terms he would have to compromise the absoluteness of his Idea. And as he looked more deeply, he would find perfectly solid reasons for resisting the proffered formula. For what does it really mean to say that the Idea of Animal is immortal *qua* Idea, mortal *qua* Animal? To speak of the Idea "*qua* Idea" is to refer to it in and of itself, i.e., in contradistinction to one or more other things with which it might otherwise be confused. What could that be? In the Platonic tripartite ontology[18] the only relevant entities, besides (1) the transcendent Form, would be: (2) the empirical individuals that "participate" in it, and (3) the immanent characters those individuals possess in so far, and for as long, as they do "participate" in (1). So the Idea of Animal "*qua* Idea" could only be identical with (1) in rigorous isolation from both (2) and (3). So to say that the Idea of Animal "*qua* Idea" is immortal is simply to say that

---

[18] Cf. *RC*, above, pp. 83 ff.

(1)—that unique metaphysical existent, "the intelligible Animal" (*Ti.* 30C–31A)—is immortal.

What then of the other arm of the Aristotelian formula? What sense could a Platonist make of "the Idea of Animal *qua* Animal"? To what could he take it to refer? Obviously not to the class of things in (2), severally or collectively. No Platonist would be tempted to *identify* the transcendent Idea with its spatio-temporal participants, no matter how qualified and whittled down the identification might be. From his point of view it would be grotesque to refer to these as the Idea of *F qua F*. But what of (3)? This is a far more plausible candidate for the referent of this expression. Why should not the Platonist accept this, taking instantiations of the concept, past, present, and future, in all those individuals called "animals" as the referent of "the Idea of Animal *qua* Animal"? For the simple and sufficient reason that his ontology does not allow for the kind of straddling of ontological fences which the phrase would seem to imply. "If that is what we are talking about," he would say, "it is wrong and misleading to refer to it as 'the Idea *qua* Animal.' That expression would invite confusion, for there is no such thing as 'the Idea of Animal *qua* Animal': the only Idea of Animal there is, is what Aristotle is now calling 'the Idea of Animal *qua* Idea.' That configuration of characters we discern in individual animals whose possession we explain by the participation of those individuals in the Idea is something as distinct from the Idea as anything could possibly be: its scatter in the created universe has always temporal and spatial location, while the Idea is out of time and space. It is therefore a muddle to speak of '*the Idea* of Animal *qua* Animal'—the kind of muddle one would expect from Aristotle's misguided decision to reject our 'separate' Form and make do with immanent universals."

I submit that this analysis offers a tolerable explanation of the facts to be accounted for: that Aristotle uses the *P*-distinction in arguments whose effect, he thinks, proves the incoherence of the Theory of Ideas, and that he does so without any fear that those against whom his wrecking operation is directed may pick up his *P*-distinction and use it to save their theory by means of it after all. To reinforce the plausibility of this explanation, let me indulge in a wilful anachronism and suppose that instead of attacking the two-level paradoxes *via* his *P*-distinction, Aristotle had caught on to the syntactical ambiguity of the sentences that generate these paradoxes, and used *this* means of resolving them. Reduced to their simplest form, these sentences would be, like "Motion is resting" in the *Sophist*, substitution instances of the "*F* is *P*" sentence-form:

Man is imperishable

The Animal is immortal

The Double is eternal

Man is resting.

Suppose that our counterfactual Aristotle had observed that each of these may be read in the alternative ways expressible in my notation by "F is$_{OP}$ P" and "F is$_{PP}$ P,"[19] and had then proceeded to use this syntactical insight to resolve the paradoxes, pointing out, e.g., that "*Man* is imperishable" is evidently true if read to mean "*Man* ε imperishable," and as evidently false if read to imply, "N(*Man* ⊂ *Imperishableness*)." What would have been the consequence? The Platonists, on their side, would have welcomed this insight. They would have had no reason for resisting it. By adopting it they could have made their own position clearer, saying that on the first, level-switching, reading, Imperishableness is being truly asserted of the Form, Man, while the second, level-keeping, reading implies the falsehood that Imperishableness may be asserted of the participants of that Form.

This dénouement would have spoiled Aristotle's use of the two-level paradoxes as polemical devices against the Platonists. At this point a dark suspicion might cross our mind: Could it be that seeing some such alternative way of resolving those paradoxes, he nonetheless picked on the *P*-distinction, and did so for the very purpose of adding thereby one more weapon to his anti-Academic armory? We can prove that this suspicion is baseless, clearing the honesty of his intentions. We may do so by reminding ourselves that Aristotle himself betrays no awareness of the syntactical ambiguity in the paradox-generating sentences—no more so than does Plato. This shows up clearly in that protosyllogism of his in *Cat.* 1B12-15:

thus [i] man is predicated of the individual man,

and [ii] animal of man;

hence [iii] animal is also predicable of the individual man.[20]

The connective—"predicated of," the formal-mode equivalent of the converse of the copulative "is"—is grammatically the same in all three sentences, and Aristotle does not take the slightest notice of the fact that

[19] For the sense of the subscripts see *AS* above.

[20] J. L. Ackrill (1963, 76) *ad loc*: "He does not distinguish between the relation of an individual to its species and that of a species to its genus." What Aristotle is ignoring is the difference between class-membership and class-inclusion.

it is used to mean something very different in [ii], where it does the work of our "$\subset$," from what it does in [i] and [iii], where it is plainly the converse of our ε.[21] Thus, Aristotle's own insight into the syntactics of the two-level paradoxes being sadly limited, he does the next best thing, the only one apparently open to him with the conceptual techniques at his disposal: he hits on the P-distinction, and uses it with great gusto. What seems to escape him is that this is an ontologically loaded resolution, loaded with *his* ontology, whose universals are only the "common attributes" of classes of particulars, and therefore makes it perfectly proper for him to speak of what the Form of F is both *qua* Form and *qua* F. To use this formula as a weapon against the Platonists would certainly seem fair enough to him. But since, in so doing, he was implicitly reaffirming his own immanentist universal against their transcendent Forms, it is understandable that the arguments he constructed should seem as unconvincing to them as they seemed cogent to him.

[21] There are many examples of Aristotle's failure to display awareness of the difference in uses of "is", or "predicated of", when these expressions are used to do these two different kinds of work. Here are some:

> *Cat.* 3A37–B2: In the case of secondary substances, the species is predicated of the individual [e.g., "Socrates ε Man"], while the genus is predicated both of the species and of the individual [e.g., "(Socrates ε Animal) & (Man $\subset$ Animal)"]; the differentiae too are similarly predicated both of the species and of the individual [e.g., "(Socrates ε Biped) & (Man $\subset$ Biped)"].
>
> *APr.* 43A30–32: τὰ δὲ καὶ αὐτὰ ἄλλων καὶ αὐτῶν ἕτερα ⟨κατηγορεῖται⟩, οἷον ἄνθρωπος Καλλίου [Callias ε Man] καὶ ἀνθρώπου ζῷον [Man $\subset$ Animal].
>
> *APo.* 83B4-7: the series in which "animal" is predicated of man, and "man" of Callias, is not infinite.
>
> *Metaph.* 1058B32-35: τὸ γὰρ αὐτὸ ἐνδέχεται εἶναι, καὶ ἅμα, ἐὰν ᾖ τῶν καθόλου, ὥσπερ ὁ ἄνθρωπος εἴη ἂν καὶ λευκὸς καὶ μέλας [(Man $\cap$ White) & (Man $\cap$ Black)] καὶ τῶν καθ' ἕκαστον. εἴη γὰρ ἄν, μὴ ἅμα, ὁ αὐτὸς λευκὸς καὶ μέγας [(Socrates ε White at t_1) & (Socrates ε black at t_2)].

If I were offering an analysis of Aristotle's sentences I would be arguing that a modal operator should be added to render the intentend sense of "Man is animal" ($= N(Man \subset Animal)$) and of "Man is both white and black" ($= \Diamond[(Man \cap White) \& (Man \cap Black)]$).

13

Self-Predication and Self-Participation
in Plato's Later Period*

(1969; SPPL)

IS there any evidence in the Platonic corpus which would prove that Plato ever consciously rejected the assumption that the Form corresponding to a given character itself has that character ("self-predication,"[1] abbreviated to SP)? Harold Cherniss thought he had found this in Parmenides 157E6–158B2.[2] His interpretation has not been challenged in print to my knowledge, and it is highly persuasive. It has persuaded, among others, Colin Strang, who holds (contrary to Cherniss, but in common with many scholars) that Plato subscribed to SP in the middle dialogues; Strang refers to this text as clear evidence that Plato jettisoned SP in the Parmenides.[3] As I do not believe that the text warrants such a conclusion, I had best explain why.

In this text we are told that if anything has parts, each of these parts "must participate in the One [ἀνάγκη μετέχειν τοῦ ἑνός]" and as participating in the One "must clearly be other than the One: otherwise it would not participate in the One, but would *be* the One itself [οὐ γὰρ ἂν μετεῖχεν, ἀλλ᾽ ἦν ἂν αὐτὸ ἕν], whereas it is impossible for anything, except

---

* Reprinted (with a few corrections) from the *Philosophical Review* 78 (1969), pp. 74–78. The original pagination is interpolated in square brackets in this text.

[1] Cf. *UVP*, above, n. 97.

[2] At (1957, 258)—a paper which has already become a classic of scholarly controversy.

[3] (1963, 147–64)—a most acute contribution to its topic.

the One itself, to be the One" (157E5–158A6). The same point is made
again three lines later: "Now will not the participants in the One participate in it as different from [i.e., not identical with] it?"⁴ Cherniss holds that
here Plato [74]

(A) distinguished the "is" of predication ("is one" = "has unity")
from the "is" of identity ("is One" = "is identical with the One")
and

(B) assumes that whatever is *F* in the first sense cannot be *F* in the
second.

With (A) I have no quarrel. Certainly Plato shows here, as in other
passages,⁵ that he is perfectly capable of keeping these two senses of
"is" quite distinct. But what of (B)? Could Plato be really saying here
that if *x* has unity, *x* cannot be identical with the Form, One? To say such

---

⁴ The translation is mainly after that of J. Moreau in the *Pléiade* Plato. Differences from other translations do not affect anything vital to the controversy.

⁵ Cf. J. Ackrill (1957, 1–6, at 1–2). Ackrill's results have been controverted,
most recently by Frede, (1967). May I then state the crux of the point which,
so far as I can see, remains untouched by any criticism which has yet appeared
in print (For a fuller criticism of Frede see above *AS*, n. 44): Already in the
Phaedo (104A7–B4) it is clear that Plato *uses* language in a way which distinguishes the "is" of identity from the "is" of predication: "Such is the
nature of Three, Five, and of half of all the numbers, that while none of them
is [i.e., is identical with] the Odd itself, each of them is always odd [i.e.,
always has this property] [ὥστε οὐκ ὢν ὅπερ τὸ περιττὸν ἀεὶ ἕκαστος αὐτῶν ἐστι
περιττός]." In the *Sophist* Plato goes a long step further: he demonstrates that
he is *well aware* of the fact that two entirely different statements may be expressed by using the very same sentence, whose grammatical form is "*X* is F":

(1) "*X* is identical with [the] *F*."
(2) "*X* has the property of being *F*."

He demonstrates this by providing for radically different paraphrases to exhibit
the ontological structure of the two statements:

(1) *X* participates in Identity with respect to [the] *F*.
(2) *X* participates in [the] *F*.

For (1) see, e.g., 255B3, where it is clear that "both Motion and Rest participate in Identity [with respect to themselves]" would be Plato's paraphrase for
"Motion is Motion and Rest is Rest." For (2) cf. 256B6-7 ("Motion is resting"
to be paraphrased by "Motion participates in Rest.")

a thing would have a most unhappy consequence, of which no notice is taken by Cherniss or Strang: it would imply that this Form cannot have unity, and hence cannot be *one* Form, *one* number, *one* being, and so forth. Plato would surely have found this absolutely unacceptable. And there are several other Forms in whose case *SP* would be no less mandatory.[6] Four of the Great Kinds would be cases in point: Rest must itself be at rest; Being must [75] itself have being and (Self-)identity (self)-identity; Difference must be different from Being,[7] Identity, etc. The same thing would have to be true of those Forms which represent categorial properties of Forms: Immutability, Intelligibility, Incorporeality. In all these special cases Plato would have had no choice but to admit *SP* even if he had realized that he could, and should, reject it as a general principle.[8]

Is there good reason then to think that in the present text he maintains that Unity cannot have unity? I do not think so. All that is said here is that *if anything participates in the One*, it (the participant) cannot be identical with the One. It is not said that *if anything has unity*, it cannot be identical with the One. The antecedents of these two hypotheticals are clearly quite different propositions. The second would indeed be fatal to the One, if it had unity, as it surely must. The first would have no such consequence, unless we were given the additional premise that nothing can have unity unless it participates in the One. This additional premise is *not* asserted in our passage. Hence the possibility is left quite open that *if things other than the One have unity, they* must participate in the One, while the One itself can have unity without participating in itself or any other Form.

---

[6] A point all too little noticed in the extensive literature on this topic; but see J. Moravcsik (1963, 52): he says of "Existence exists" and "Unchangeability is unchanging" that, "unlike most statements involving self-predication, these make sense, and Plato was clearly committed to them."

[7] This proposition is formally proved at 255B8–E1.

[8] It may be well to note that the admission of *SP* for a given Form would not of itself cause Plato any of those difficulties which are rehearsed in the first part of the *Parmenides;* as I pointed out in the *TMA* I (326–29) the regress arguments could be broken, even admitting *SP*, by weakening the "Nonidentity" premise. And I know of no good reason why Plato should have banished all statements of the form "*F ε F*" on purely syntactical grounds. The real objection to *SP* is semantic—i.e., its assertion in cases where a Form could not fall within the range of significance of the corresponding predicate (e.g., "white" could not be predicated of the Form, *Whiteness*, since "white" could only apply to things falling under determinables such as "colored," "visible," "extended," which are excluded by the categorial properties of Forms). I stressed this point in lectures given in Oxford in 1960.

We could generalize this proposition as a restriction on the doctrine of participation, "$P(R)$," formulating it as follows:

$P(R)$ Given any character, F, if the corresponding Form is itself F, it is not F by participating in any Form. [76]

We could take everything said in our text *au pied de la lettre*, and still save Plato from the disaster of refusing unity to Unity, by simply assuming that he had now[9] decided to incorporate $P(R)$ into his theory. But should we take what he says here as seriously as all that?

There are two things to give us pause: first, that the whole of the second part of the *Parmenides* does not profess to be an exposition of philosophical truth. Parmenides tells Socrates he has to play this "laborious game" (137B2), positing thesis and antithesis to investigate the consequences of each in turn, if he wants to prepare himself, "by perfecting [his] training, for the sure discernment of truth" (136C4-5). A man who uses premises that will lead to contradictory conclusions must know that not all of these premises can be true. We may, therefore, be quite certain that Plato would claim no more than plausibility for some of the propositions in this part of the *Parmenides*. That no participant in the One can be identical with the One could be such a proposition. Nor is this the only considera-

---

[9] Anders Wedberg (1955), has claimed that a decision against self-participation had been built into Plato's theory from the start. He formulates the thesis in even stronger terms than my $P(R)$, writing it as
(4) An Idea is never one among the objects participating therein.
He calls this "one of the most characteristic postulates of Plato's theory of Ideas" (1955, 34) and claims that it is "clearly expressed" in *R.* 476C9–D3:

> What then? Take the man who, on the contrary, takes Beauty itself to exist and who is able to discern both Beauty itself and its participants, not taking it for its participants nor its participants for it—does this man seem to you to live wide awake or in a dream? [My translation, not different in any material respect from the one used by Wedberg.]

Now certainly the Idea of Beauty is here sharply distinguished from its participants. But this occurs in a context in which the latter had been *already* described in terms which marked them off as a set of *sensible* entities, hence by categorial stipulation entities necessarily distinct from Beauty as from any other Form. (They had been introduced a few lines earlier as "the beautiful sounds, colours, shapes, and all that is fashioned therefrom.") So the passage could not possibly count as an expression of Wedberg's (4): it does not tell us that if we were to confront a class of items undescribed except as "participants in the Idea of Beauty" we could be sure that the Idea of Beauty would not itself be a member of the class. The other passages to which Wedberg refers are even less conclusive for his purpose.

tion that casts doubt on Plato's willingness to commit himself to that thesis and, more generally, to $P(R)$. There is another passage, in the latter part of the same dialogue, whose clear import runs the other way: in 162A7-B1, Plato says that "Being must participate in Being in respect of being and in Not-being in respect of not being Not-being, if it [Being] is to have complete being (εἰ μέλλει τελέως εἶναι)."[10] The last clause leaves no doubt that the subject of this pronouncement is the Form, Being, for only that would be said "to be completely" in this context. The clear implication of *this* passage then is that Being can, and must, participate in Being in order to *be*. Self-participation, declared impossible for Unity in the preceding passage, is declared necessary for Being in the present passage. If we felt licensed to generalize what is said in this second passage, we would commit Plato to a principle of *un*restricted participation which would be the contrary of $P(R)$, namely,

> $P(U)$ Given any character, F, if the corresponding Form is itself F, it is F by participating in itself.[11]

From these data it looks as though Plato, when writing the *Parmenides*, would have found some plausibility both in the denial and in the affirmation of self-participation in the case of self-characterizing Forms at the highest tier of generality, like Unity and Being. He might well have seen advantages and disadvantages in either alternative. Affirming self-participation would offer an easy way to block the regress in the Third Man Argument: if F-ness participates in itself, no further Form would be required to account for F-ness and all the F-particulars being F.[12] The notion of self-participation would, however, be harshly counter-intuitive: μετέχειν, μεταλαμβάνειν are always used as aliorelatives in Greek prose. On this count, he might well have found the other option more attractive. [77]

Did Plato squarely face this issue and decide which of the two options would be the least objectionable from his point of view? I find no clear evidence that he did, while there seems to be some reason for supposing that he did not. Had he reached a decision on an issue of such importance, it is hard to believe that he would have refrained from saying so, especially

---

[10] Note clear implication here not only for Being (which would be only to be expected) but even for Not-being!

[11] Note that both $P(R)$ and $P(U)$ are so formulated as to allow SP without requiring it. Either would be as consistent with the prudence of selective SP as with the folly of generalized SP.

[12] Affirming self-participation would entail denial of the NI premise in the TMA (see below, TMA II, pp. 351).

in a passage like the one on the Great Kinds in the *Sophist*. It is a fundamental assumption in this passage that when a Kind has a given property,
F, it must participate in the corresponding Form. And since four of the
Great Kinds which are explored here are unavoidably self-predicative,
we would expect him to say, or at least to imply, that in their case self-
predication does, or does not, entail self-participation. But I can find
nothing in this passage that commits him unambiguously to either
alternative.[13]

[13] There is one passage in the *Sophist* which I have been tempted to construe
as evidence of an implicit commitment to P(U):

> And we shall say that it [*sc.* "the nature" (or Idea, Form, Kind) of the
> Different, D9] goes through them all [i.e., through Rest, Motion, Being,
> Identity]; for each of these is different from [each of] the others not [i]
> in virtue of its own nature but [ii] in virtue of participating in the Idea of
> the Different. (255E3-6)

From the strong adversative in [ii] we may infer (where kind *K* $\neq$ the Different)
that for "Kind *K* is different [for the contraction see *AS*, n.42, above]" [ii]
would be true (*K* would be different in virtue of participating in the Idea of
the Different) *because* [i] is false (*K* would not be different in virtue of its own
nature). Now consider 'the Different is different [e.g. from Being—cf. n.7
above]'. Here [i] is obviously true (the Different *is* different in virtue of its
own nature). Must [ii] be false? This certainly does not follow (from " — [i] →
[ii]" we cannot, without obvious fallacy, infer "[i] → — [ii]"). So [ii] *might* be
true, i.e., it might be the case that the Different is different "in virtue of participating in the nature of the Different"—i.e., that here self-predication implies
self-participation. And we could say not only that [ii] *might* be true, but that
it *is* true, if we could assume that the logical syntax of Form-in-Form participation in the *Sophist* is the same as is that of particular-in-Form participation in
the *Phaedo*: as I am pointing out below (*TMA, II*, n.28) in that dialogue
"in virtue of *F*-ness" is used interchangeably with (as a mere contraction for)
"in virtue of participating in *F*-ness." If we are entitled to this assumption
then the above remark in the *Sophist* can be taken to imply that the Different
is different in virtue of participating in the Different—which would give us
P(U). I would be inclined to settle for this conclusion, for all the deviousness
of the reasoning by which it is reached, if there were no countervailing considerations, as unfortunately there are: I have already referred in the text above
to the strongly aliorelative connotations of "participation," which would lend
an aura of paradox to the very notion of *self*-participation. If Plato had confronted an issue of such importance and reached a definite decision, he would
surely have expressed the outcome in some clear and unambiguous way. A
single sentence interspersed in the above quotation—e.g., "although the
Different itself is different from each of them in virtue of participating in its
own nature," inserted after "for" at the start of the second colon—would
have sufficed to make the point.

Thus from the texts at our disposal I, for one, hesitate to believe that Plato ever achieved the lucidity of explicit decision on the general issues of self-predication and self-participation. But on the specific issue raised by part (B) of the above interpretation of *Parmenides* 157E–158A I can be more positive. As I trust I have shown, *SP* would be mandatory for one class of Platonic Forms which includes Unity, and there is nothing in this text, strictly read, which implies that if a Form had unity it could not be Unity.[14] [78]

[14] I am much indebted to Professor Richard Sorabji for a number of useful criticisms which have led to material improvements. But he may not, of course, be held responsible for any of the views I have expressed here.

14

Plato's "Third Man" Argument
(*Parm.* 132A1–B2): Text and Logic*

(1969; TMA II)

MOST of the debates which have swirled around Plato's "Third Man" argument (the "TMA") in recent years[1] have been too heavily preoccupied with logical analysis to work intensively on Plato's text. For this I should perhaps accept some blame; a paper of mine, published in 1954, provoked some of these discussions, and may have abetted the shift of emphasis from text to logic.[2] Now I shall make an effort to restore the balance, and

* Originally published in the *Philosophical Quarterly* 19(1969), 289–301. Revised in the light of discussions of the topic with members of the Institute for Greek Philosophy and Science held at Colorado Springs in the summer of 1970. The original pagination is approximated in square brackets interpolated in the text.

[1] I started off Vlastos 1954, 319 ff. (to which I shall be referring as *TMA I*) with the remark that "hardly a text in Plato has been discussed as much in the last forty years." The volume of publication in the English-speaking word on the same topic in the following ten years exceeded that of all the preceding forty. I list in Appendix I below papers published since 1955 which are devoted to the TMA or make significant allusions to issues raised by it.

[2] Professor Harold Cherniss (whose own contribution to the debate, listed above, set an example of the attention which should be paid to Plato's text) referred to my 1954 paper as having "started a still-rising flood of literature, intended to clarify Plato's text but tending to whelm it with the symbols of modern logic" (1957, 257).

not merely to salve a guilty conscience: I have no other choice at this juncture, for, after a decade of controversy, the logical analysis of this elusive Platonic argument reached an impasse which only the text can arbitrate. A cardinal feature of the interpretation I submitted in 1954 was the inconsistency of the premises from which the regress was deduced.[3] This blemish was smoothed out beautifully in an alternative line of analysis first worked out by Professor Wilfrid Sellars (1955) and retained, with modifications, in a no less felicitous formalization offered later (1963) by Professor Colin Strang.[4] That this makes the TMA a vastly more attractive specimen of philosophical reasoning goes without saying. But is Plato really to get the credit for it, as Sellars so modestly insists? Since Plato's text is all we have of him now, we have to look to that for the answer.[5] This will be my business in this paper. I shall go about it by laying out, first of all, what I myself get from the text. This is the analysis I offered in 1954, revised in the light of more careful work on the passage and incorporating things I have learned on the [289] formal side from criticisms that have luckily come my way.[6] This part of the paper, Section I, will be annotated copiously, chiefly on matters dealing with textual points which I had failed to cover in previous papers. I shall then go on in Section II to consider the alternative interpretation, explaining its logical assets and its textual liabilities.

---

[3] Only explicable if the TMA is, as I have argued (1954, 328 ff.), "a record of honest perplexity"—an expression of philosophical puzzlement due to the failure to identify the tacit assumptions which entered into the premises of this and other objections marshalled in the *Parmenides* against the theory of Ideas.

[4] The blemish was also eliminated by a third line of analysis in Professor Geach's paper (1956). This operates with a still more complex logical machinery and at a still further remove from Plato's text. On this account I shall not bring it into the present discussion, though its prefatory remarks are among the most penetrating of recent comments on Plato's theory and have exerted a powerful influence.

[5] I did so in 1955 (439–41), but so cursorily that I now find what I wrote there virtually worthless.

[6] I learned the most from my first critics, Professors Sellars and Geach; but points raised in subsequent contributions helped futhrer to clarify my thinking. A still unpublished paper by my colleague, Professor Terence Penner, and discussion with him have proved particularly helpful. So too have proved criticisms from members of my Plato seminar at Princeton, especially those of (now Professors) Michael Tooley and Richard Kraut.

I. MY ANALYSIS OF THE TMA

Parmenides tells Socrates:

(P) This, I take it, is what leads you to hold that each Form[7] is one.[8]

(Q) Whenever you think[9] that a number of things[10] are

[7] I capitalize when εἶδος or ἰδέα are used, as frequently in Plato's text, to refer to the transcendent objects postulated in his philosophy. As I have emphasized above (RC, II), Plato also may use εἶδος (and also ἰδέα) to refer to the characters which particulars possess in virtue of "participating" in the corresponding Form. For this use see, e.g., n. 15 below.

[8] In 1969 I had been influenced by F. M. Cornford (1939: this book contains his translation of the Parmenides to which I refer here and hereafter) in translating ἓν ἕκαστον εἶδος οἴεσθαι εἶναι "that there exists one Form in each case." I justified the rendering by comparing the use of (εἶδος) ἓν ἕκαστον in R. 476A, and 596A, and κατ᾽ ἰδέαν μίαν ἑκάστου in R. 507B. I now see that while the same sense would be consistent with what is being said in this passage, it is not required by its wording, since here ἓν ἕκαστον εἶδος is not flanked, as it is in those passages, by a matching reference to the corresponding plurality of things sharing a common character. Therefore, Cornford's rendering now strikes me as an over-translation. To construe ἓν as predicative makes as good sense and should, therefore, be preferred as the more economical rendering of Plato's Greek. (For good arguments for the "each Form is one" rendering see now Teloh and Louzecky, 1972, 84–85, listed in the Appendix).

[9] "Judge" would be fully as appropriate for both uses of δοκεῖν in this sentence (so rendered by A. E. Taylor [1934], and by M. J. Moreau in the Pléiade translation. There is no dubitative nuance in δοκεῖν in this context, nor yet in that of οἴεσθαι at the start, ἡγῇ in A3, φανεῖται and φαίνεσθαι in A7-8 (cf. δοκεῖ in 130B3 and 130E5; and cf. φαίνεται in Phd. 100C4, used there of a doctrine of which Socrates is prepared to say "διισχυρίζομαι" 100D7-8; and cf. n. 32 below): Parmenides is not undertaking to refute a theory which only seems true to Socrates, but one for which Socrates had declared unequivocally (cf. πάνυ γε, "most assuredly," in 131A3) and has pressed on Zeno (128E6 ff.) as the basis for solving the antinomies in his treatise.

[10] Or, "a plurality of things" πολλ᾽ ἄττα. There is no word for "things" in the Greek. I add it to complete the sense—a sense which I take to be as general as that of "thing" in anything, something, etc., and it allows me to complete the sense of ἓν τὸ μέγα in (R) by writing "the one thing, Largeness." In TMA I (pp. 220 ff.) I had assumed uncritically that πολλ᾽ ἄττα here has the same reference as does the expression τὰ πολλά when used by Plato to refer to the sensible instances of a Form (cf. DR, n.41 above). However, when I came to think about it, I realized that this assumption had no warrant from the text (and I implied as much in my reply to Geach [1956, p. 84]). That Forms, no less than sensible particulars, are to count as large things is quite explicit in the text of the TMA, e.g., in 132B1, "all these [i.e., the first set of large

large[11] you perhaps[12] think there exists a certain[13] one[14] Form,[15] the same in your view of all of them;

(R) hence you believe that Largeness is one.[16] (132A1-4)

What Parmenides gets Socrates to concede at this point in the debate has to be read in the context of the theory to which repeated references

---

things, plus F-ness$_I$ plus F-ness$_{II}$] will be large [ταῦτα πάντα μεγάλα ἔσται]'' (cf. also 132A8, μεγάλα of the first set plus F-ness$_I$). This being the case, we have no mandate from the text to restrict the reference of πολλ' ἄττα μεγάλα to sensible particulars. It goes without saying that at this juncture in the argument Socrates would only *think* of sensible particulars if he were asked to form a set of large things on the spot. But Parmenides has used a form of words which does not require such a selection, though it *allows* it. He has, therefore, enunciated a more general principle which would cover sets containing items other than sensible particulars. The advantage of so understanding πολλ' ἄττα μεγάλα is that (Q) then warrants the general principle (1) which I proceed to formulate. This remedies a major deficiency of the formalization of the argument in *TMA I* for which Sellars had rightly taken me to task (1955, p. 416), and which I had remedied without explanation in 1965, p. 261: the way in which I had formalized (Q) in 1954 made it apply exclusively to large sensible particulars and failed to cover any of the subsequent sets of large things, each of which included one or more Forms.

[11] "That a number of large things exist" is equally possible for πολλ' ἄττα μεγάλα . . . εἶναι and would make no difference to the argument.

[12] The ἴσως here ("sans doute" in Moreau) is merely intended to elicit Socrates' assent, without suggesting that Parmenides thinks there is doubt on this point in Socrates' mind.

[13] The best I can do (following Cornford) to bring into English the contribution which the τις makes to the meaning of the phrase μία τις . . . ἰδέα. For a similar use of this pronoun cf. *R.* 479A1-2, ὃς αὐτὸ μὲν καλὸν καὶ ἰδέαν τινὰ αὐτοῦ κάλλους μηδεμίαν ἡγεῖται, and 596A εἶδος . . . τι ἓν ἕκαστον, as well as *Prm.* 132C, μίαν τινὰ . . . ἰδέαν, and 133B1-2, ἓν εἶδος ἕκαστον τῶν ὄντων ἀεί τι . . . θήσεις.

[14] The sense (to be defended in Section II, below) is "unique" (or, more precisely, "exactly one"). "Single" (so in Cornford) brings out this sense even better, and I formerly so translated μία here and ἕν in (P) and (R). Here I content myself with the simpler rendering "one," leaving it to subsequent comment to establish the intended sense.

[15] An attractive alternative translation (Cornford's) would render ἰδέα here as "character," taking it to refer to *large*, the property which all the objects "viewed" share (cf. the same use of ἰδέα, as well as of εἶδος, in *Phd.* 104B9 ff.), in contrast to εἶδος in (P) and to ἕν τὸ μέγα in (R), where the reference is clearly to the Platonic Form.

[16] Taking ἕν to be predicative, in line with my reading of ἕν in 132A1: what is said about ἕν τὸ μέγα here is simply the instantiation for Largeness of what was said there about "each Form."

had already been made. The first of these was made by Socrates in his initial exchange with Zeno:

> But tell me this: Don't you believe that there exists a certain Form of Similarity, itself all by itself [εἶναι αὐτὸ καθ᾽ αὑτὸ εἶδός τι ὁμοιό- τητος],[17] and again a certain other thing, its opposite, the Dissimi- lar;[18] and that in these two things you and I and those other things which we call "many" participate? And that those which, on one hand, participate in Similarity become similar in the respect and in so far as they do participate; on the other, those [which participate] in Dissimilarity [become] dissimilar; while those [which participate] in both become both [similar and dissimilar]? (128E6-129A6)

Here is an aggressive statement of the fundamental Platonic doctrine, first announced in the *Phaedo*, that possession of any character entails participation in the Form corresponding to that character:

> For it appears to me that if anything besides Beauty itself is beautiful it is beautiful for no other reason than because it participates in that Beauty. This I would affirm universally. (100C5-6)[19]

> . . . and it was admitted that each of the Forms exists,[20] and that by participating in them the other things get the names of the Forms.[21] (102B1-2)

[17] The phrase used in referring to the philosophical "hypothesis" (cf. next note 19) in *Phd*. 100B5-6, ὑποθέμενος εἶναί τι καλὸν αὐτὸ καθ᾽ αὑτὸ καὶ ἀγαθὸν καὶ μέγα καὶ τἆλλα πάντα. Plato leaves no doubt of his wish to identify the theory sponsored by Socrates and attacked by Parmenides in our dialogue with the one he had propounded in the works of his middle period, beginning with the *Phaedo*. Cf. also notes 8 and 13, above, 18, 19, and 21 below, and the ensuing citation from the *Phaedo* in the text above.

[18] Literally, "which is what the Dissimilar *is*" (ὃ ἔστιν ἀνόμοιον, "l'essence du dissemblable," Diès in the Budé translation). For the same expression in the *Phaedo* see RC, n.44. And cf. *UVP*, above, n. 102: I take the sense here to be clearly the second of those listed in that note.

[19] Though there had been copious references to the Forms in the preceding part of the *Phaedo* there had been none to participation. Nor had there been any earlier reference to the theory of Forms as a philosophical "hypothesis" (τίθημι, 100A5; ὑποθέμενος, 100B5; τῆς ὑποθέσεως, 100D2-3, taken together with 102A10-B2). The doctrine of participation is clearly a crux for Plato: it is that component of the theory of Forms which he is most eager to present as a hazardous venture in speculative metaphysics.

[20] Literally, "is something" (εἶναί τι).

[21] αὐτῶν τούτων τὴν ἐπωνυμίαν ἴσχειν. Cf. τὰς ἐπωνυμίας αὐτῶν ἴσχειν in *Prm*. 130E6 (to be cited in the text above). Here "names" is used to mean "predicates" in the absence of a technical term for the latter. Cf. *RC*, n. 29, *UVP*, n. 46.

That this will be the doctrine which will be drawing Parmenides' fire is made clear from the very moment Parmenides enters the debate. His first question to Socrates is,

> And tell me, Socrates, is this the division you have made, as you say: you separate on one side certain Forms themselves and on the other the things which participate in them? And you think that similarity itself exists separately from the similarity which we possess, and so too Unity and Plurality and all those things you heard of from Zeno just a moment ago? (130B)

A page later he asks again:

> Do you believe, as you say, that there exist certain Forms by participating in which the other things get their names; for example, similar by participating in Similarity, large [by participating] in Largeness, just and beautiful [by participating] in Justice and Beauty? (130E5-131A2)

It will be noticed that all three of the formulations of the theory which is pinned on Socrates in our dialogue prior to 132A1-4 mention participation in the Form without saying a word about its unity, while at 132A1-4 just the opposite happens:[22] here the unity of the Form is asserted three times over, while nothing is said of participation. But that the target of the polemic is the same can be established by internal evidence: That the unity of the Form is being taken for granted in the earlier formulations becomes apparent in 131A8-9 as the attack on the refutand laid out in 130E5-131A2 gets under way: Socrates is asked if he thinks that "the Form, *which is one* [ἓν ὄν], is in each of the many as a whole or in some other way" (131A8-9). There are copious references to the unity of the Form in the rest of the argument. Conversely, it is no less clear that participation is similarly assumed in 132A1 ff., since the large things are spoken of as the "participants" in Largeness in 132A11. It is, therefore, proper to

---

[22] Substantial variation in alternative statements of the same philosophical thesis is characteristic of Plato. Compare three sets of formulaic assertions of the existence of Forms:

    (i) *R.* 476A; 507B and 596A; *Prm.* 132A (cited in text above), 133B.
    (ii) *Phd.* 102B; *Prm.* 128E-129A; 130B; 130E-131A (cited above), 133D.
    (iii) *Phd.* 65D; *Prm.* 135A.

In (i) we hear of unity, but not of participation; in (ii) of participation but not of unity; in (iii) of neither.

formulate the hypothesis which is to be refuted in the TMA in the form in which Plato himself would have given it to us, if he were writing a tight philosophical argument in the modern manner, aiming for formal exactness and completeness, and disregarding rhetorical and stylistic interests, such as the desire to avoid repetitions and to highlight that aspect of the refutand which is to figure most prominently in the refutation:

> *1* If any set of things[23] share a given character[24] then there exists a unique[25] Form corresponding to that character;[26] and each of these things has that character[27] by participating in that Form.[28]

[23] Cf. n. 10, above.

[24] This spells out the idea in the phrase "a number of things are large" in (Q). Elsewhere (e.g., *R.* 596A) Plato expresses this by speaking of a number of things "to which we apply the same name" (cf. n. 21 above).

[25] Cf. n. 14, above.

[26] My formulation is meant to exclude *ab initio* the possibility that there might be one Form for one set of things having a given character and another Form for another set of things having the same character.

[27] A still fuller statement of this premise would include the information that things not only have, but *are apprehended* as having, a given character in virtue of the corresponding Form. I leave out this additional factor to simplify the analysis; for justification see my treatment of this point in Vlastos (1965), pp. 261–62, where I point out that the additional information enables us to construct an "epistemological" version of the TMA, paralleling the "ontological" one to which I restrict myself above.

[28] *1* answers to (Q) above, with the following correspondence and divergences:

> (i) *1* generalizes the scope of the principle by substituting "a given character" for Plato's example, *large*;
>
> (ii) *1* makes explicit the unrestricted generality of "a certain set of things" which is not explicit in the expression πολλ' ἄττα used by Plato in (Q);
>
> (iii) *1* flushes out the intensional operator, "you think that . . ." (what is under debate is the content of what Socrates says he believes, not his believing it);
>
> (iv) *1* adds the fundamental Platonic principle that possession of a given character is due to participation in the corresponding Form; it incorporates the assumption that this principle will hold true of anything—sensible particular or Form.

It should be noticed that the assumption incorporated in (iv) *has no explicit textual warrant in anything said so far in the debate,* but is *implicitly* conceded by Socrates in the immediate sequel when granting that given the large things and Largeness there will have to be "another Largeness in virtue of which all

So, given the commonplace that there is some set of things—say, the particulars *a*, *b*, *c*—that share some common character, *F*, i.e.,

1a a, *b*, and *c* are *F*,[29] [290]

it would follow from *1* that

1b There exists a unique Form (which we may call "*F*-ness")[30] corresponding to the character, *F*, and *a*, *b*, *c* are *F* by participating in *F*-ness.[31]

Now Parmenides goes on:

What then if you view in your mind Largeness itself and the other large things? Will not another Largeness show up, in virtue of which all these will appear Large? . . . So another Form of largeness will come into view,[32] over and above Largeness itself and its participants. (132A 6–11)

---

these will appear [and be: cf. n. 27, above] large." Here "in virtue of which" (expressed by the dative, here that of the relative pronoun, ᾧ) could only mean "by participation in which": the only way in which Plato's principles allow *x* to be *F* "in virtue of" some other entity, *y*, is by the participation of *x* in *y* (for the interchangeability of "in virtue of *y*" with "by participation in *y*" see *Phaedo* 100D7 and E2, where "in virtue of the Beautiful" (τῷ καλῷ) is just a variant of "in virtue of participating in the Beautiful" (διότι μετέχει-. . . τοῦ καλοῦ, 100C5–6) and 101A2, where "in virtue of Largeness" (μεγέθει, διὰ τὸ μέγεθος, 101A2) must be a variant for "in virtue of participating in Largeness" (as would follow by analogy with the preceding example, and also by instantiation of the formula in 102B1-2).

[29] A commonplace, calling for no special statement in the text.

[30] A stand-in for names of individual Forms, like Largeness, Similarity, etc. In the terminology employed by Sellars (1955, 416–17) "*F*-ness" is a representative name," not a "variable proper." A further notational point: "*F*-ness" may also be written as "*F*-ness₁" (cf. n. 33, below). The expressions "*F*-ness" and "*F*-ness₁" denote the very same Platonic Form.

[31] *1b* answers to (R) in Plato's text, generalized by the substitution of "*F*-ness" for "Largeness," and subjected to modification equivalent to (iii) and (iv) in n. 28, above.

[32] I must emphasize that the words I have translated "will show up" (ἀναφανεῖται) and "come into view" (ἀναφανήσεται)—correctly rendered as "make its appearance" and "present itself," respectively, by Cornford—are not used to denote psychological events: Parmenides' point is not that it would *look* to Socrates, or *seem* to him, that there was another Largeness, but that in point of logic there *has* to be one for him. There are many contexts in Greek argumentative prose in which this verb (with or without the prefix) is used without

Restated in the style of *1*, this may be written as

> *2* If *a*, *b*, *c*, and *F*-ness are *F*, then there exists a unique Form (which we may call "*F*-ness$_{II}$")[33] corresponding to *F*, but not identical with *F*-ness; and *a*, *b*, *c*, and *F*-ness are *F* by participating in *F*-ness$_{II}$.

Socrates agrees. Assuming that he does not do so absentmindedly, or just by caprice, but as a thoughtful spokesman for the theory under attack,[34] we must try to figure out what assumptions he must be making in connection with this theory which would require him to agree with *2*, in spite of the fact that his previous agreement with *1* does not, in point of logic, compel him to agree with either the antecedent or the consequent of the hypothetical expressed by *2*. As A. E. Taylor was the first to realize,[35]

---

the slightest subjective hue, so that what it means is not that something *appears to be* the case, but that it *evidently is* the case. So, e.g., Democritus (frg. 155) writes, φανεῖται τὸ τοῦ κυλίνδρου πεπονθὼς ὁ κῶνος, meaning that this will evidently follow from the premises. In *Laws* 896B Plato writes that such and such ἀνεφάνη, meaning that it has been shown or made evident. Cf. ἀναφανείη in *R.* 597C8 and the same verb in *Prm.* 132E7.

[33] I write "*F*-ness$_{II}$" by analogy with, say, "Elizabeth II" for the present Queen of Great Britain, named after a predecessor whose name in *her* lifetime was just "Elizabeth," though we may *now* call her "Elizabeth I" to distinguish her from Elizabeth II. "*F*-ness" in *1b* and "*F*-ness$_{II}$" in *2* correspond closely enough to Plato's own usage. He speaks of "Largeness itself" (αὐτὸ τὸ μέγα, 132A6; αὐτὸ τὸ μέγεθος, A10-11)—*not* of "the first Largeness"—to begin with, and then of "another Form of Largeness" (and could have just as well written "a second" instead of "another"). What was called "Largeness itself" to begin with may *also* be called "the first Form of Largeness" retrospectively; so we may write *F*-ness$_I$ for "*F*-ness" when this is convenient (as, e.g., in n. 30 above, and subsequently in Section II).

[34] That this must be Socrates' role in this argument follows from the fact that the TMA is not eristic word-play, but a serious objection to Plato's theory of Ideas, as we know from Aristotle: see the references to the TMA listed in Bonitz (1870, 771A 37-39).

[35] (1915-16 and 1934). As I pointed out in *TMA I* (note 36), the Aristotelian version of the TMA which appears in Alexander's *In Metaphysica* 84, 21 ff., actually speaks of the Form, *Man*, as "predicated both of particular men and *of the Form*." Some scholars have taken this to imply that Aristotle had identified self-predication as an assumption in the TMA. But "predication" is used by Aristotle much more broadly than we now use it in our debates over self-predication in Plato. For Aristotle every case in which the verb *to be* connects two terms in a sentence will count as a predication, including cases of

    (a) class-membership ("Socrates is [a] man");

    (b) identity ("man is man");

in agreeing with the antecedent of *2* which specifies that *F*-ness is *F*, Socrates must be assuming which I have called "self-predication."[36]

SP The Form corresponding to a given character itself has that character.

From the tacit premise, *SP*, given *1a* and *1b*, it follows that

2a *a*, *b*, *c*, and *F*-ness are *F*.

This gives us the antecedent of *2*. But even so, why should the consequent follow? If Socrates has agreed that all four items in *2a* are *F*, why should he not say that his commitment to *1* would be perfectly satisfied if these four items are *F* by participation in *F*-ness itself? Why should he find it necessary to resort for this purpose to *another* Form corresponding to *F*? He must be making a further assumption, which I have labeled "Non-Identity" (abbreviated to "*NI*").[37] Phrased in the same style as *SP* above, this may be written as

NI If anything has a given character by participating in a Form, it is not identical with that Form.

Only this further tacit premise could prompt one to infer from *2a* that if there is to be a unique Form by participation in which *a*, *b*, *c*, and *F*-ness

---

   (c) class-inclusion ("man is [an] animal");
   (d) class-equivalence ("man is [a] two-footed animal").

The claim that *SP* is a tacit premise of the TMA has in view only sense (a). (Cf. *UVP*, n. 97). No argument has been produced to date to show that in the phrase cited above from Alexander "predicated" is used in sense (a) rather than in one (or more) of the other three.

[36] I so labeled this assumption in *TMA I* under Taylor's influence, who had identified it uncritically with the closely related assumption that a character can be predicated of itself, which generated the Russellian paradox. I should have made it clear then (as I did later: 1965, p. 263) that "self-predication," if used at all, could only be used with a certain license. As Sellars had pointed out (1955, p. 414), the assumption which is being made here "would be formulated more correctly as 'The adjective corresponding to the name of any Form can correctly be predicated of that Form.'" Some such label as "Homo-characterization" would have been more exact, and I have tried at times to switch to this in lectures and seminars. "Self-exemplification," now suggested by J. E. M. Moravcsik, would be even better. But "self-predication" is now firmly entrenched in the literature, and I see no harm in its continuing use subject to the above proviso.

[37] This is the only technical contribution to the analysis of the TMA made in *TMA I* which appears to have been universally accepted.

are *F*, this must be "another" Form corresponding to *F*, i.e., a Form not identical with *F*-ness; hence, that, given *1*, *2a*, and *NI*, then

> *2b* There exists a unique Form (which we may call "*F*-ness II"), corresponding to *F*, but not identical with *F*-ness; and *a*, *b*, *c*, and *F*-ness are *F* by participating in *F*-ness$_{II}$.[38] [*291*]

As I remarked in *TMA I*, and as is obvious in itself, if Parmenides can go as far as *2b*, he will have accomplished his objective in this argument: he will have refuted *1*. If a proponent of *1* is also committed to the tacit assumptions which, taken in conjunction with *1*, warrant *2b*, his theory has been shown to conceal a contradiction: asserting the unity of the Form in *1*, it makes tacit commitments which imply the contrary of *1*, 2b.[39] To go on, as Parmenides does in our argument (132A11-B2), to imply that infinitely many more *F*-nesses may be deduced by iteration of the reasoning, is from the strictly logical point of view a pure bonus. It is added solely for its rhetorical effect, which is indeed dazzling: "If only one, then infinitely many" is so much more impressive than "If only one, then two," though the latter is as fatal to the refutand as is the former.

II. THE SELLARS-STRANG ANALYSIS

As analyzed above, the TMA suffers from a glaring defect which shows up at the point at which *NI* is used to derive the existence of *F*-ness$_{II}$. At that point one is moved to object that if this is to be the consequence of the adoption of *NI*, this assumption should never have been made at all, for it now becomes apparent that it cannot be held consistently with the previous commitments to *1* and *SP*. Parmenides manages to deduce *F*-ness$_{II}$ from *2a* by sticking with *NI* and ignoring the fact that *1* precludes the existence of any Form corresponding to *F* other than *F*-ness$_I$ itself. The resulting contradiction—the deduction of two Forms, *F*-ness$_I$ and *F*-ness$_{II}$, each of which is supposed to be the unique Form corresponding to *F*—shows clearly enough that *NI* is inconsistent with *1* and *SP*. But that *1*, *SP*, and *NI* form an inconsistent triad[40] could have been shown more directly: if, given *1*, we are to hold that

---

[38] For a formalization of the argument see *FRA* below.

[39] So, as I pointed out in 1955 (pp. 440–41), if my analysis is correct, the TMA falls into the classical form of refutation employed by Eleatic logic: "If *p* [and . . .], then not-*p*; therefore, not-*p*."

[40] Due to my defective axiomatization of Plato's argument in *TMA I*, I had inferred that *SP* and *NI* are an inconsistent pair. This they are not when

anything having a given character must participate in a unique Form corresponding to that character,

and, given *SP*, that

this Form itself has that character,

we could hardly go on to grant *NI*, i.e., that

nothing having that character by participating in a Form can be identical with that Form;

for it would then follow that that Form cannot be identical with itself.

Now there is a very simple maneuver that will get rid of this contradiction: replace *1* by another premise, *1'*, in which everything remains the same as in *1*, except for the substitution of "at least one Form" for "a unique Form," as follows:

1' If a number of things share a given character, then there exists at least one Form corresponding to that character; and each of those things has that character by participating in that Form.

As Wilfrid Sellars showed in 1955,[41] by using some such premise along with *SP* and *NI* we can derive the regress by an internally consistent argument: Given the first set, $\{a, b, c\}$, of *F* things, we infer by *1'* the existence [292] of *F*-ness$_I$. Given *SP*, we now infer the existence of a second set of *F* things, $\{a, b, c, F\text{-ness}\}$. Given *NI*, we then infer from this set the existence of *F*-ness$_{II}$, getting the regress started on its way, thereafter deriving by iteration of the reasoning as many subsequent *F*-ness as we please:

---

formulated as above. In *TMA I* I had formulated *SP* as "*F*-ness is F" and *NI* as "if *x* is F, *x* cannot be identical with *F*-ness," and derived the inconsistency by substituting "*F*-ness" for "*x*" in the latter formula to get "If *F*-ness is F, *F*-ness cannot be identical with *F*-ness." In the present formulation (see the reduction of *SP* and *NI* to symbolic form in *FRA*, below) the corresponding substitution is not allowable: Now *SP* does not empower us to substitute Φ for *x* in the antecedent of *NI* to get $(\Phi \neq \Phi)$ in the consequent: to make the substitution we would have to know that Φ *is F by participating in* Φ. This we learn only from *1*, which does tell us that if *x* is F, there is exactly one Φ such that *x* is F by participating in Φ—from which it would, of course, follow that if Φ is F, then *it* is F by participating in Φ.

[41] P. 419. My *1'*, above, answers to his (G) though the wording is somewhat different.

From the first set, $\{a, b, c\}$, we infer the existence of F-ness$_I$.

From the second set, $\{a, b, c, F\text{-ness}_I\}$, we infer the existence of F-ness$_{II}$.

From the Nth set, $\{a, b, c, F\text{-ness}_I, F\text{-ness}_{II}, \ldots F\text{-ness}_{N-1}\}$, we infer the existence of F-ness$_N$.

That this would be an incomparably better argument than the one I laid out in Section I is obvious. But would it be the one in the text, the one we are supposed to be analyzing? Since the difference between the premises of the two arguments is solely that between *1* and *1'*, let us consult the text to see if it will support *1'* as well as, or better than, *1*. And since the difference between *1* and *1'* is solely that between "a unique (i.e., just one) Form" in *1* and "at least one Form" in *1'*, all we need consider is what is said in the text on just this point. Here is the relevant part of the text (132A1-4) once again:

(P) This, I take it, is what leads you to hold that each Form is *one* [ἓν ἕκαστον εἶδος . . . εἶναι]:

(Q) Whenever you think that a number of things are large, you perhaps think there exists a certain *one* Form, the same in your view of all of them;

(R) hence you believe that Largeness is *one*.

Our question then is what we are expected to understand by "one" in this text.

Now it so happens that the word occurs also in the terminal sentence of the TMA:

(S) And so each Form will no longer be *one* Form for you, [ἓν ἕκαστον σοι τῶν εἰδῶν εἶναι] but infinitely many.

There can be no doubt that here "one" could only mean *just one*, for only this meaning would warrant the adversative form of the second clause of (S): there is obviously no conflict between *at least one* and "infinitely many." Since (S) records the collapse of the initial hypothesis, first stated in (P) above, the meaning of the phrase "one Form in each case" in (P), recurring with the same wording in (S),[42] must be the same in both sentences. So "one" must mean *just one* in (P), no less than in (S). If so,

---

[42] ἓν ἕκαστον εἶδος in (P), ἓν ἕκαστον τῶν εἰδῶν in (S): the only grammatical difference—shift in case and number in the word for "Form"—makes no difference to the sense.

it must have the same meaning in (R) as well, since the assertion in (R) that "Largeness is one" is the same as the assertion in (P) that "each Form is one" with "Largeness" in (R) merely used as an example of "Form" in (P). If so, the sense of "one" in the expression, "a certain one," in (Q) must be also the same, since (Q) is the premise from which (R) is inferred; the inference would be a transparent fallacy,[43] unless "one" in (Q) meant "just one" as we have found it to mean in (R). Thus even if we had no other data to give us the basis for answering the question if "one" in its three occurrences in 132A1-4 could [*293*] mean anything but "just one," we would still have had the means of satisfying ourselves that this is all it could mean.

But it so happens that we do have other texts, several of them, in which "one" is used by Plato in comparable contexts. We may look at these to see if they confirm, or disconfirm, the conclusion we have just reached:

R. 476A: . . . each Form is itself *one* [αὐτὸ μὲν ἓν ἕκαστον εἶναι] but Forms manifest themselves as a plurality in virtue of their associations with actions, etc.

R. 507B: . . . [we posit] *one* Form *in each case* [κατ' ἰδέαν μίαν ἑκάστου] assuming that it is *one* [ὡς μιᾶς οὔσης] . . .

R. 596A: For we are accustomed to posit a certain *one* Form *in each case* [εἶδος . . . τι ἓν ἕκαστον] for each plurality of things to which we apply the same name.

Prm. 131A8-9: Do you think that the whole Form is in each of the many, though it *is one* [ἓν ὄν]?

Prm. 132B5: In this way [i.e., on the hypothesis that Forms are only thoughts in our minds] *each* Form would be *one* [ἓν γε ἕκαστον εἴη].

Prm. 132C3-4: [On the same hypothesis] would it not be the thought of a certain single thing, . . . being a certain *one* Form?

---

[43] I.e., would have involved concluding that there is *just one* Largeness from the premise that there is *at least one* (or, on the alternative reading of "character" for "Form" in (Q), mentioned in note 15, above, drawing the same conclusion from the premise that there is *at least one* character, *large;* indeed, on this reading the question of drawing that conclusion would not even arise, for no one could think of Plato envisaging more than one *large,* so that the *at least* one reading of μία would be excluded *ab initio*). The conclusion I draw above could be reinforced by taking into account the contribution of τις to the phrase used here: I fail to see how "a certain one" Largeness (or *large*) could mean anything in this context but "a particular one," hence *a definitely unique* Largeness (or *large*). Cf. τι in εἶδος . . . τι ἓν ἕκαστον in *R.* 596A.

Prm. 133B1-2: . . . how great are the perplexities, if you are always going to distinguish and posit *a certain one* Form of things in each case [ἓν εἶδος ἕκαστον τῶν ὄντων . . . τι]?

Since the central affirmation of Plato's theory of Forms is that, for any given character which a set of things may share, there is *just one* Form—not *at least one*—there can be no reasonable doubt that in all of these texts, each of them stating, or alluding to, this central affirmation, "one" *tout court* is being used to mean *exactly one*. And if it be asked why Plato does not say "only one," if that is what he means, the answer is easy: he would have felt the "only" as a redundancy, for it would not have even occurred to him that anyone would have been at all likely to understand him to mean "at least one" in these contexts[44]—just as a monotheist would express his faith by saying that he believes in "one God," and would have no reason for saying "just one God," unless he were addressing persons who, he thought, might suspect that polytheism remained a live option for him. Thus, even if we did not have the concluding sentence of the TMA as a basis for resolving the problem whether *at least one* or *just one* is meant by "one" in *Prm.* 132A 1–4, we could have got the same decision in favor of the second reading—hence in favor of *1*, instead of *1'*—by reflecting on the fact that *Prm.* 132A 1–4 is so clearly a restatement of the central thesis of the theory of Forms that it is improbable in the last degree that Plato could have used here the same language with a different meaning.

Now no one has gone so far as to propose that "one," in any of its occurrences in 132A1-4, could definitely mean "at least one." What [294] Colin Strang has suggested[45] is that it is used here *ambiguously* to mean "at least one" *and also* "just one," thereby providing Parmenides with two premises,[46] equivalent respectively to my *1'* and my *1*, and leaving him at

[44] The only occasion on which Plato specifies "not more than one" or "one only" is in *R.* 597C, where a special line of thought prompts him to consider what would follow if, *per impossibile*, "god" had "created" more than one Form of Bed.

[45] 1963, pp. 148–50.

[46] The "just one Form" thesis Strang calls "*U*"—"The Uniqueness thesis"; the "at least one Form" he calls "weak *OM*"—"the weak One over Many thesis." The admission which Strang claims is extracted from Socrates in 132A1-4 by the use of ambiguous language is "strong *OM*"—"the strong One over Many thesis" that there exists "at least one and also only one" (p. 150) Form for any set of things having a given character. Thus, his "strong *OM*" is the conjunction of his *U* and his "weak *OM*." I prefer not to burden the exposition in the text above by bringing into it this variant nomenclature.

liberty to use only the former to derive the regress. When he has made *this* deduction by a perfectly coherent argument,[47] he then adverts to the other premise—the "just one" thesis, showing how *that* is contradicted by the result.

This is a most intriguing exegesis. But I do not think it feasible. In the first place, so far as I can see, the suggested ambiguous communication is not a possible linguistic performance. What is entirely possible is that "one X" should be used in contexts in which the hearer is left uncertain as to whether "at least one X" *or else* "just one X" is meant.[48] Thus (to adapt an example from Strang) if I were to say, "Peter and Paul are co-heirs of one man, James," then (*a*) I could be taken (as I should)[49] to mean that there is at least this one man whose co-heirs are Peter and Paul. But (*b*) I could also be thought to mean that there is just this one man whose co-heirs they are. Here (*a*) could happen without (*b*), or (*b*) could happen. What could not happen is that someone who understood me as in (*a*) should also understand me as in (*b*). For what distinguishes the sense in (*a*) from that in (*b*) is precisely that the former keeps alive the possibility that Peter and Paul are concurrently co-heirs of one or more other men as well, while in (*b*) this possibility is explicitly killed. For this reason *if the "one" in* 132A1-4 *were being used ambiguously*, Socrates could have understood it to mean "at least one" *instead of* "only one"; he could *not* have understood it to mean "at least one and also only one," as Strang proposes.[50] However—and this is my second objection—the italicized suggestion is itself inadmissible: it must be ruled out on textual grounds which my preceding discussion has made clear.

Unlike the one man with Peter and Paul as co-heirs in the example, the one Largeness in our text is known, *qua* Platonic Form, to be the sort of

---

So I retain my own in the above discussion, taking advantage of the substantial equivalence of my *1* with his *U* and of my *1'* with his weak *OM*. I also continue to use "*F*" and "*F-ness*" as before; for these Strang uses "*A*" and "*F(A)*" respectively.

[47] Since there is no inconsistency between *1'* and the conjunction of *SP* and *NI*.

[48] Where "at least one" is true on condition that "just one" is false. If the latter were true, so would the former *a fortiori*, since "just one" entails "at least one."

[49] Since in our legal system their being co-heirs of James is no impediment to their being co-heirs of others as well.

[50] I am abstracting (as does Strang) from the trivial sense in which "one" *could* be used to mean "at least one and only one": if used to mean "only one," this would *entail* "at least one."

thing which qualifies uniquely for the stated relation, and, what is more, the language used in our text to affirm its unity is known from other passages to be the very language regularly used to affirm its uniqueness and to do so without any ambiguity whatever. Since this very attribute of the Form—its uniqueness— is the target of the attack here, it is scarcely credible that a word used so unambiguously in other contexts should be used here ambiguously to express a thought consistent with its non-uniqueness. If Plato had wanted to express such a thought here he would have had ample means of doing so; what Strang takes him to be saying could have been said as unambiguously in Greek as in English.[51] Why then did not Plato say so, if this is what he means in an argument which, as Strang would agree, is surely serious philosophical reasoning, not word-play? Strang's reply (pp. 149–50) is that what would have been thus "gained in logical clarity [would have been] lost in elegance and concise-ness." But an [295] argument cast in the form, "If at least one Largeness, then more than one, hence not just one (as required by the theory)," would have had plenty of elegance. Nor could we say that there would have been loss in conciseness, unless we were to assume the very thing under dispute: that the words in our text do convey an equivalent meaning.

We may now turn to Sellars, the original sponsor of the "at least one" premise. How does he propose to get this from our text? In his Rejoinder (1967)[52] he apparently[53] concedes that "one" is not used with this sense in 132A1-4, but only with the "just one" sense. He writes (p. 57): "if any single sentence in my reconstruction of the TMA as a whole captures the meaning of the first sentence of the text," this is

(L) If a number of particulars *a*, *b*, *c* are all large, they are so in virtue of a Form, *namely* Largeness,

where, he explains, "Largeness" is the name of an individual Form, so that his (L) in fact affirms that there is *just one* Form in virtue of which large particulars are large. But he takes what is said in this proposition to

[51] For example, Plato would not have had the slightest difficulty in inter-calating the following in the appropriate style between 132A5 and A6: "You have admitted there is only one Largeness. Clearly then you think there is at least one. Now see what follows from the latter."

[52] I regret that this was not published in the earlier phase of the debate when, as I happen to know, it was written.

[53] The sentence I proceed to quote is annotated with the words, "But see pp. 59 ff." It is barely possible that some qualification is intended there whose import has escaped me.

express only a preliminary "inductive" phrase of the reasoning. He holds that Parmenides proceeds from (L) to a more general proposition, which Sellars put at the head of his formalization of the "deductive" phase of the TMA, as its first premise:

(G) If a number of entities are all large, there must be *a* Largeness, by virtue of which they are all large.

I have italicized here the "a" because it calls attention to the fact that what is said here definitely implies that there may be more than one Largeness. So his (G) is equivalent to an "at least one Largeness" thesis. Assuming (as I too did formerly)[54] that "a number of large things [πολλ' ἄττα μεγάλα]" in 132A2 refers exclusively to particulars, Sellars takes Parmenides to reason (with Socrates' implied assent) from "if a number of large particulars are large, there must be just one Largeness" in (L), to "if a number of entities (particulars or Forms) are large, there must be at least one Largeness" in (G).[55]

I would readily grant that this is a *possible* line of reasoning. What I then want to know is whether or not it is the *actual* one employed in the text. I look at the text, and see no sign of it there, no sentence or phrase answering to (G). This leaves Sellars free to hypothesize that, though Plato did not put it into the lines he gave Parmenides and Socrates, he expected both of them would have it in their minds by inferring it from (L). If this is a *bona fide* hypothesis—not a speculation to which, of course, everyone is entitled free of charge—reason must be offered for it. What could this reason be? Presumably,[56] the following: only on this hypothesis could Parmenides have been understood by Socrates to be deriving the regress by a proper argument. But what is this? Another hypothesis. This would be fully credible if we had reason to think that Plato had already understood what we have come to understand in the course of

---

[54] Cf. n. 10, above.

[55] From the fact that (G) appears as the first premise of the formal argument laid out in an apparently definitive answer to the question, "What, then, does the TMA look like when all these points have been taken into account?" (1955, p. 419), I had inferred at the time that (G) was what Sellars made of 132A1-4. In his Rejoinder he says this was an error and one which would not have been made by "anyone who followed his reasoning up to this point" (1967, p. 58). I am glad to be corrected on the former point, and will not argue over the latter.

[56] I infer this, in the absence of a direct answer to my question, from what is said in the course of his exceedingly complex discussion.

very recent discussions: that there are tacit premises in the argument with which a "just [296] one" thesis[57] will clash, while harmony will be restored as by a charm if an "at least one" thesis[58] is substituted. What reason have we to think that all this was clear to Plato? Are we going to argue: "Plato was a great philosopher. So his insight into the logic of his argument could not have been less than that of Professors Sellars and Strang"? To our contemporaries we impute insight not by senatorial courtesy but on evidence. To impute comparable insight to Plato we need comparable evidence. For this I have looked in vain.

[57] My *1*, Strang's *U*, Sellars' (L).
[58] My *1'*, Strang's weak *OM*, Sellars' (G)

APPENDIX I

——

Recent Papers on the *TMA*

I. *1955–1969*

R. E. Allen, "Participation and Predication in Plato's Middle Dialogues," *Philos. Review* 69 (1960), 147–64.

R. S. Bluck, "Forms as Standards," *Phronesis* 2 (1957), 115–27.

H. Cherniss, "The Relation of the *Timaeus* to Plato's Later Dialogues," *American Journal of Philology* 78 (1957), 225–66.

P. Geach, "The Third Man Again," *Philos. Review* 65 (1956), 72–78.

J. Moravcsik, "The 'Third Man' Argument and Plato's Theory of Forms," *Phronesis* 8 (1963), 50–62.

A. L. Peck, "Plato *versus* Parmenides," *Philos. Review* 71 (1962), 46–66.

D. A. Rees, "Plato and the Third Man," *Proc. of Aristotelian Society*, Supp. Volume 37 (1963), 165–76.

W. G. Runciman, "Plato's *Parmenides*," *Harvard Studies in Classical Philology* 64 (1959), 89–120.

T. Rosenmeyer, "Plato and Mass Words," *Trans. American Philol. Assoc.* 88 (1957), 88–102.

W. Sellars, "Vlastos and 'The Third Man,' " *Philos. Review* 64 (1955), 405–37.

———, "Vlastos and 'The Third Man': A Rejoinder," *Philosophical Perspectives* (Springfield, Ill., 1967), 55–72.

C. Strang, "Plato and the Third Man," *Proc. of Aristotelian Society*, Supp. Volume 37 (1963), 147–64.

G. Vlastos, "Addenda to the TMA: A Reply to Professor Sellars," *Philos. Review* 64 (1955), 438–48.

———, "Postscript to the TMA: A Reply to Mr. Geach," *Philos. Review* 65 (1956), 83–94.

———, "Addendum (1963)," in *Studies in Plato's Metaphysics*, ed. by R. E. Allen (London and New York, 1965), pp. 261–63.

———, " 'Self-Predication' in Plato's Later Period," *Philos. Review* 78 (1969), 74–78.

II. *1969–1972*

The following came to my notice after I had finished the present revision of *TMA II*:

S. Marc Cohen, "The Logic of the Third Man," *Philos. Review* 80 (1971), 448–75.

S. Panagiotou, "Vlastos on *Prm.* 132A1-B2: Some of his Text and Logic," *Philos. Quarterly* 21 (1971), 255–59.

K. W. Rankin, "The Duplicity of Plato's Third Man," *Mind* 78 (1969), 178–97.

———, "Is the TMA an Inconsistent Triad?" *Philos. Quarterly* 20 (1970), 378–80.

R. A. Shiner, "Self-predication and the 'Third Man' Argument," *Journal of the History of Philosophy* 8 (1970), 371–86.

T. G. Smith, "The Theory of Forms, Relations and Infinite Regress," *Dialogue* 8 (1969), 116–23.

H. Teloh and D. J. Louzecky, "Plato's Third Man Argument," *Phronesis* 17 (1972), 80–94.

APPENDIX II

The First Regress Argument
in *PRM*. 132 A1-B2*

a, b, c: stand-ins for names of sensible particulars

x: variable ranging over sensible particulars and Forms

L: stand-in for some character (say, *large*)

Λ: stand-in for the unique Form corresponding to L (hence, Largeness)

F: character-variable

Φ, Ψ: Form-variables

$\#$: a special operator to be read "in virtue of participating in"

The first premise duly generalized:

1 If any set of things share a given character, say, *large*, then there exists a unique corresponding Form, Largeness, such that each of these things is large in virtue of participating in Largeness.

1 $L(a, b, c) \rightarrow (\exists\Phi)\{[L(a, b, c) \# \Phi] \,\&\, (\Phi = \Lambda) \,\&$
$$(x)(\Psi)[(Lx \# \Psi) \rightarrow (\Psi = \Lambda)]\}^{1}$$

* This is a compact summary of the analysis expounded in the foregoing essay. The slight difference (distinction between Form-variables, Φ, Ψ, and proper name of a particular Form, Λ) is self-explanatory. As in *RC*, I use Greek capitals to symbolize Forms, their phonetic cognates in the English alphabet to symbolize characters.

[1] May be read: "If a, b, c are L, then there exists a Φ such that a, b, c are L, in virtue of Φ, and Φ is identical with Λ, and, for all x and for all Ψ, if x is L in virtue of Ψ, then Ψ is identical with L."

Now it is trivially true that

> 1a Some things are large; say, *a*, *b*, *c*, are large.
>
> 1a L(*a*, *b*, *c*)

It follows by modus ponens from *1* and *1a* that

> 1b There exists a unique Form, Largeness, corresponding to the character, *large*, and *a*, *b*, *c* are large in virtue of participating in this Form.
>
> 1b $(\exists\Phi)\{[L(a, b, c) \# \Phi] \,\&\, (\Phi = \Lambda) \,\&\, (x)(\Psi)[(Lx \# \Psi) \to (\Psi = \Lambda)]\}$

Parmenides then assumes, without resistance from Socrates, that it will follow that

> 2 If *a*, *b*, *c*, and Largeness are large, then there exists a unique corresponding Form, Largeness′, such that *a*, *b*, *c*, and Largeness are large in virtue of participating in Largeness′, and Largeness′ is not identical with Largeness.
>
> 2 $L(a, b, c, \Lambda) \to (\exists\Phi)\{[L(a, b, c, \Lambda) \# \Phi] \,\&\, (\Phi = \Lambda') \,\&\, (\Lambda \neq \Lambda')]$
> $\&\, (x)(\Psi)[(Lx \# \Psi) \to (\Psi = \Lambda')]\}$ [2]

To establish *2a*, the antecedent of *2*, we need

> SP The Form by participation in which anything has a given character itself has that character.
>
> SP $(x)(\Phi)[(Fx \# \Phi) \to F(\Phi)]$ [3]

From SP it follows that Λ, in virtue of which large things are large (*1b*) is itself large, i.e., that $L(\Lambda)$. Conjoining $L(\Lambda)$ with $L(a, b, c)$, we get

> 2a *a*, *b*, *c*, and Largeness are large.
>
> 2a L(*a*, *b*, *c*, Λ)

To establish *2b*, the consequent of *2*, we need an additional tacit premise,

> NI If anything has a given character in virtue of participating in a Form, that Form is not identical with that thing.
>
> NI $(x)(\Phi)[(Fx \# \Phi) \to (\Phi \neq x)]$ [4]

[2] May be read: "If *a*, *b*, *c*, Λ are L, then there exists a Φ such that *a*, *b*, *c*, Λ are L in virtue of Φ, and Φ is identical with Λ', and Λ is not identical with Λ', and, for all *x* and for all Ψ, if *x* is L in virtue of Ψ, then Ψ is identical with Λ'."

[3] May be read: "For all *x* and for all Φ, if *x* is F in virtue of Φ, then Φ is F."

[4] May be read: "For all *x* and for all Φ, if *x* is F in virtue of Φ, then Φ is not identical with *x*."

From NI it follows that

> 3 If *a*, *b*, *c*, and Largeness are large in virtue of participating in a
> Form, that Form is not identical with Largeness.
>
> 3 $(\Phi)\{[L(a, b, c, \Lambda) \# \Phi] \rightarrow (\Phi \neq \Lambda)\}$[5]

It then follows, given *1*, NI, and *2a*, that

> 2*b* There exists a unique Form corresponding to the character,
> *large*, such that this Form is not identical with Largeness. Call this
> Form "Largeness'."
>
> 2*b* $(\exists\Phi)\{[L(a, b, c, \Lambda) \# \Phi] \& (\Phi = \Lambda') \& (\Lambda \neq \Lambda') \&$
> $$(x)(\Psi)[(Lx \# \Psi) \rightarrow (\psi = \Lambda')]\}$$

Infinitely many more Forms, Largeness'', etc., may be deduced by iteration of the reasoning.

[5] May be read: "For all Φ, if *a*, *b*, *c*, Λ are L in virtue of Φ, then Φ is not
identical with Λ."

15

Plato's Supposed Theory of Irregular Atomic Figures*

(1967; IAF)

THOUGH no theory of irregular atomic figures is ever mentioned in Plato's text, leading authorities[1] on the *Timaeus* have maintained that we must suppose that he held it if we are to make sense of a chapter of his microphysiology, the one that deals with the mechanism of the sense of smell.[2] Let us review the main points.

Plato takes the following to be well-established empirical truths: pure air does not smell; if we inhale air through a filter we will see that it is odorless (66E5-7). Nor does any other kind of matter smell when it is in a stable state, but only when disintegrating, "liquefying or decomposing or melting or volatilizing" (66D7-8). The theory Plato thinks explains these data includes two main theses:

>   *1.* None of the four primary kinds of matter (earth, fire, air, water) has the required *symmetria*[3] to the veins which constitute the senso-

---

* Offered (1966) to Glenn Morrow, in his seventieth year, hoping he might reckon it one more victory of persuasion over necessity in the *Timaeus*. Originally printed in *Isis* 58 (1967), pp. 204–209. The pagination of the original appears here in square brackets.

[1] The three English commentaries to which I shall be referring in this paper by their authors' names only are R. D. Archer-Hind (1888); A. E. Taylor (1928); F. M. Cornford (1937).

[2] *Ti.* 66D1–67A6.

[3] I leave this crucial term untranslated to avoid prejudicing the interpretation of a part of the text which, as will appear, is largely responsible for the imputa-

rium of smell (66D2-4). These veins are "narrower" than they would have to be if odoriferous matter were earth or water, "broader" than if it were fire or air (D4-6).

2. Matter smells when it is either water changing into air ("smoke")[4] or air changing into water ("mist," ὀμίχλη, E2-4). [204]

⊙In the first of the three commentaries which British scholarship has contributed to the *Timaeus*, R. D. Archer-Hind's (1888), it was suggested that to satisfy the requirements of these two theses Plato must have postulated a special sort of matter "made up of irregular figures intermediate in size between the particles of air [octahedra] and those of water [icosahedra]."[5] In A. E. Taylor's commentary, nearly forty years later, a similar view was endorsed.[6] F. M. Cornford also adopted it shortly after, and filled it out in an attractive way:

> If on any face of the octahedron we plant a tetrahedron, we obtain three new faces instead of 1 old one: that is, we increase the number of faces by 2. We can therefore obtain irregular figures of 10, 12, 14, 16, 18 faces between the octahedron and the icosahedron. In vapour [= "smoke"] and mist we shall then have perceptible bodies composed of such irregular particles.[7]

---

tion of irregular atoms to Plato. The point will be discussed below in the penultimate paragraph. For the present I need only note that while συμμετρία could mean "proportion" in certain contexts, its primary meaning is, rather, "commensurability" (the ordinary Greek words for "proportion" in mathematical and scientific vocabulary are λόγος and ἀναλογία). The derivative sense of συμμετρία may be as broad as "suitable relation," "good fit," "correspondence."

[4] This is the most common meaning of καπνός. Cornford translates it by "vapour" (as do several other good translators: "vapeur" by Joseph Moreau in the *Pleiade* translation; "Dampf" by Otto Apelt in his translation of the *Timaeus*, Leipzig: Felix Meiner, 1919). Certainly the word can bear this sense in certain contexts. But a glance at its occurrences in Aristotle listed in Bonitz, *s.v.*, will show that our "smoke" comes far closer to its normal sense.

[5] Archer-Hind, p. 245, note. Another suggestion of Archer-Hind's was that this special kind of Platonic matter is "unformed," i.e., not bounded by elementary triangles. No one has taken this suggestion seriously—apparently not even Archer-Hind himself, for on the very next page he gives the entirely different one cited in the text above. "Unformed" matter is so out of line with Plato's stereometric theory of matter that it is scarcely worth discussing.

[6] With differences of too little interest to call for comment (Taylor, pp. 471–72).

[7] Cornford, p. 274.

This is a most ingenious conjecture. It constructs the series of intermediate irregular solids from the very figure which Plato had made the invariant element of his three intertransformable atoms: the triangular face of the tetrahedron, the octahedron, and the icosahedron. We may well believe that *if* Plato had interpolated irregular atoms between his air- and water-atoms, he would have had good reasons for choosing the Cornford series: he could thus have kept the deviation from the basic principles of his physics to the bare minimum.

Even so, there would be difficulties. One of them was noticed by Cornford: since Plato's theory provides for many[8] grades of size ("isotopes," as P. [205] Friedländer has called them)[9] in each of the four regular solids, it is hard to see how he could be faced by a problem to which the proposed theory would be an effective solution. As Cornford puts it: "It is difficult to imagine that all the irregular intermediate particles can be so different

[8] But not *infinitely* many, as Charles Mugler has argued, (1960, 20–26), basing his argument on the assumption that ἄπειρα in 57D5 must have the strong sense of "infinite," ignoring the possibility that it might have the weaker sense of "indefinitely numerous," or "exceedingly many," as, e.g., in Plato, *Philebus* 17B, φωνὴ . . . ἄπειρος πλήθει, and Theophrastus, *De sensu* 78, ἄπειρα δὲ εἶναι καὶ τὰ χρώματα καὶ τοὺς χυλοὺς κατὰ τὰς μίξεις. It must surely be taken in the latter way. This follows from the fact that the "number [of differences of size in each of the two types of elementary triangle] is the same as the varieties of kinds" (τὰν τοῖς εἴδεσι γένη, 57D2–3). Here "varieties of kinds" refers to subkinds of matter within each of the four basic kinds: cf. "many varieties of fire" (πυρός τε γένη πολλά, 58C5); varieties of air—aether, mist, "and other nameless kinds [ἕτερά τε ἀνώνυμα εἴδη (ἀέρος)] which have arisen because of the inequality of the triangles," D1-3; water is nonfusible when "it partakes of the small varieties of water" (τῶν γενῶν τοῦ ὕδατος ὅσα σμικρά, D6), i.e., when it consists of varieties of water formed from the smaller scalene triangles; etc. While Plato does assume that there are many more varieties of matter than those for which his language has names (cf. the "nameless kinds" of air above, and the "many other nameless kinds of juices," 60A2-3), he would have no good reason to hold that there are infinitely many of them, and never says, or implies, any such thing in his detailed discussion of the varieties of fire, air, etc., 58C5–61C2. If these varieties are finitely many, the number of different combinations that can arise from their mixtures must also be finite, though it could be enormously large. Cf. Epicurus: faced with a similar problem, he decides that "the variety of [atomic] shapes is not infinite simpliciter, but only inconceivably large" (οὐχ ἁπλῶς ἄπειροι ἀλλὰ μόνον ἀπερίληπτοι, *Epistle to Herodotus* 42–43), because there would be no use for infinitely many varieties of theoretical entities to explain finitely many observable qualitative differences (*ibid.*, 56); cf. my (1965, 140).

[9] *Plato* (1958, 255). It should go without saying that the term is borrowed from the vocabulary of modern science with deliberate license.

in size from any of the grades of water and of air that they fit passages which no grade of water or of air can affect."[10] But there is a second, far graver, difficulty, and it is strange that so perceptive a commentator as Cornford took no apparent notice of it. Even that minimal deviation from the first principles of Platonic physics that would be required by the Cornford series would still give a new and very surprising twist to Plato's theory of the atom. He commits himself from the start to just four kinds of primary matter, all four of them regular solids.[11] Having adhered faithfully to this commitment in every other part of his physics, Plato would have had to drop it at this one point and intercalate a new set of solids which would be, by Greek standards, as ugly in their asymmetry as the original four were flawless in their proportions. Just why should his Demiurge have made a place for these misshapen figures? Certainly not by choice, for he always favors beauty.[12] So it must have been by necessity. What necessity? Why must the transformation of water into air, or conversely, have to proceed through these curious transitional forms, octahedra with pyramidal swellings on at least one, but not all, of their faces? When the basic laws of the intertransformation of matter were laid down[13] it was evident that this involved only regular elements. There was no hint that the transformation might proceed through new intermediate polyhedra. Such a possibility would seem definitely excluded by the doctrine that the four regular elements make up all the matter in the world.[14] Are we then to suppose that though the Creator's initial plan was to have just those four, he later saw fit to revise it? Why should he? He wants to make it possible for us and other animals to smell some of the matter in the world and finds it in his wisdom that this can best be done by satisfying conditions 1 and 2 above. Has he no way of solving this problem save by providing for the creation of new, unstable, and unbeautiful atomic figures? I submit that he does.

Let "smoke" and "mist" consist simply of such mixtures of water and

[10] Cornford, 274-75.

[11] The existence of (just) these four kinds of matter is demonstrated early in the treatise (31B-C), long before Plato broaches their atomic construction. The same assumption is made (without argument) in the description of the primordial chaos (52D-53B). It is fully sustained in the account of the atomic theory (53C-56B). And cf. n. 14, below.

[12] 29A; 30A6-7.

[13] 56D, E.

[14] There is no disagreement among commentators on this point. Cornford himself has no hesitation in speaking of "the world's body [as] consisting of neither less nor more than four primary bodies . . ." (51-52).

air as would result when transformations from the one to the other occur not all at once (all atoms of one kind in a given mass changing suddenly into [206] atoms of the other kind), but progressively over a period of time. Suppose, for instance, that the change of a mass of icosahedra into a mass of octahedra were to take a whole hour, proceeding uninterruptedly throughout the hour. All through that hour the changing mass would be a mixture of icosahedra and octahedra, altering from an initial preponderance of the former to an eventual reversal of the ratio until the final replacement of all the icosahedra by octahedra. Everyone would agree that there is nothing farfetched about this solution. A similar one occurs to Cornford himself: "We might expect that smell would be caused by some compounds of the simple bodies, analogous to the complex juices [which cause taste]."[15] Closely similar, *mutatis mutandis*, is the solution Aristotle followed when, having decided (almost certainly under Plato's influence[16]) that each of the four elements is odorless in its normal state, he explained that either of the two dry elements will smell when, and only when, mixed with one of the two moist ones.[17] With such a solution open to Plato, why should we suppose that he preferred the radically different one of intermediate irregular figures? So far from there being any allusion to these in the text, there is even one statement which, strictly read, implies the contrary: "no type of figure has the proportions [συμμετρία] necessary for having an odour."[18] This would seem to tell against irregular figures as much as against regular ones.[19] The question before us then is whether the alternative I have now suggested would fit the text any better. Let us see.

This explanation has no trouble satisfying everything Plato says in ex-

[15] *Ibid.*, p. 273.
[16] We know of no one who had made this observation before Plato.
[17] *De sensu* 443A6 ff. We might note that if Aristotle had understood Plato to be turning to an entirely different line of explanation—that of irregular atomic figures—to account for the fact that matter smells under certain conditions, it is unlikely that he would have passed it over without critical comment both here and in polemical discussions of Plato's atomic theory, as in *De caelo* III, 7 and 8. And cf. below, n. 21, *sub fin.*
[18] D3-4 in Cornford's translation.
[19] To get around this objection Taylor and Cornford have supposed that when Plato says εἴδει δε οὐδενὶ συμβέβηκεν συμμετρία he means that no *regular* figure has this συμμετρία. But, clearly, this is not what the text says. Taylor (471) says "regular figure" is the "old geometrical signification" of εἶδος. This is just bluffing, and none too plausibly: thus, an obtuse scalene triangle would have surely counted as an εἶδος in Greek geometrical usage, no matter how old.

pounding thesis 2 above: It provides, all too obviously, for matter "going from water to air" (66E3-4), and being "in the intermediate stage [ἐν τῷ μεταξὺ τούτων] when . . . air [is changing] into water" (E1) and, therefore, "half-formed" (ἡμιγενές, D2), that is, in a transitional state from one atomic form to another. Would it then also satisfy condition 1? It is the string of statements that formulate this condition that seems to make the Archer-Hind-Taylor-Cornford theory not only tolerable but compelling: the reference to the *symmetria* of atomic figures to the olfactory veins, followed immediately by the remark that "the veins of smell have a structure too narrow for earth and water and too wide for fire and air" (D4-6) and then a little later "all odors are finer than water, thicker than air" (E4-5). This part of the text creates the overwhelming impression that the *symmetria* Plato is [207] talking about concerns the ratio of the size of each individual atom of odoriferous matter to that of the inner diameter of the veins, and that he is laying down the requirement that each atom must be neither too small nor too large by comparison with the latter—not so small as to "slip through the φλέβια[20] without contact nor too big to get into them at all."[21] If this impression were well-founded, certainly the alternative solution I have proposed would not have a leg to stand on. We would then have no choice but to take the one in the commentaries, resigning ourselves to the thought that Plato just happened to muff this

[20] "Little veins." This diminutive is not in the text of the chapter on smells. Taylor imports it from its use (65C7, D3) in the chapter on tastes.

[21] Taylor, 471 (quoted approvingly by Cornford, 274, n. 1). I suspect that Taylor and Cornford are transferring to Plato the theory which Theophrastus ascribes to Empedocles in *De sensibus*. The general principle of this theory is that matter is sensed when, and only when, it "fits the [sensory] passages" [ἐναρμόττειν εἰς τοὺς πόρους, 7; ἐναρμόττει τοῖς πόροις. 12). It cannot be sensed if the passages are too wide or too narrow: if the latter, it cannot get into them at all; if the former, it "will make its way through [so *LSJ* for διευτονεῖν] without touching (οὐχ ἁπτόμενα)" (7). Whatever διευτονεῖν may mean here, οὐχ ἁπτόμενα could not mean "without making any contact at all": since the passages twist and turn in the body, a stream of matter could hardly be thought to pass through them without making repeated collisions with their walls. So οὐχ ἁπτόμενα is more likely to mean "with insufficient contact," i.e., not sufficient contact to induce sensation. Anyhow, it would be well to note that Theophrastus himself does *not* report Plato's theory of smell in the same terms. His summary (85) virtually repeats *Ti.* 66E4-6 and gives the gist of 66D8-E4. But it ignores 66D3-6, perhaps because Theophrastus was not so sure himself of the precise meaning of these lines. Neither does he make any reference to their content in his criticism of Plato's theory (90), directing his remarks wholly to the information supplied in 66D8-E5.

particular problem. Fortunately, it can be shown that this reading of the text, however plausible at first sight, could not possibly express what Plato means.

Thus, Plato could not have thought of the internal diameter of the olfactory veins as smaller than the longest diameter of earth- or water-atoms. On his view, the parameters of the vein would have to be of an order of magnitude considerably greater than those of the largest atoms. For veins are large enough to be seen, while all atoms are far below the threshold of visibility.[22] So unless he had thought of the walls of the veins as enormously thick by comparison with their cavities—a grossly dysteleological possibility which he would have no good reason to countenance— he must have regarded the cavities as tubes through which not just one, but many, of the largest atoms could proceed abreast. If there were any doubt about this, it could be resolved by comparing the account in the immediately preceding chapter (66A, B) of the behavior of matter inside the gustatory veins. These cannot be narrower than the olfactory ones, since Plato refers to the gustatory veins (and only to them) by the diminutive, φλέβια.[23] His description of earth- and air-particles churning around each other inside these veins[24] under the [208] influence of acid flavors makes it quite plain that he thought of the veins as wide enough to allow atoms of all four kinds[25] not only comfortable transit but a substantial degree of lateral motion as well. We may therefore be confident that the *symmetria* of which he speaks, both in his account of tastes and in the immediately following account of odors, does not concern the ratio of the size of each individual incoming particle to the size of the channel inside the vein, but rather a certain kind of correspondence[26] between the consistency of the fluid that enters the vein and the internal diameter of the vein. The

[22] This is as true for Plato as it had been for the Ionian atomists. Atoms of all four of his kinds are singly imperceptible and become visible only in the mass (56C).

[23] Cf. n. 20, above. He also refers to them as "the narrow veins" (66A3).

[24] The liquids that enter the gustatory veins, having a συμμετρία "to the earthy and airy particles in the composition of the veins, move these [particles] and make them churn around each other [περὶ ἄλληλα ποιεῖν κυκᾶσθαι]," and form "hollow [films, or bubbles] stretched around incoming particles [κοῖλα ἀπεργάζεσθαι περιτεινόμενα τοῖς εἰσιοῦσιν]," 66A5-7.

[25] Reference to earth- and air-particles at 66A4; to water at B2. Fire-particles (which, being the smallest, are irrelevant to my argument) are not mentioned in this context, but are no doubt taken for granted (cf. 65E4, 5).

[26] Cf. n. 3, above.

fluid must not be so thick[27] as to clog the passage nor so ultra-fine[28] as to move past the walls of the vein without appreciable friction, thus failing to cause the atomic disturbance which—when communicated to the soul—is experienced as a sensation of taste or smell. The requirement for *this* kind of *symmetria* would be satisfied perfectly by the changing mixture of air and water in the solution I have offered: the compound would constitute a fluid thinner than water, the thicker of the two ingredients, though firmer than air—which itself, if unmixed with water, would not have sufficient viscosity to exert the requisite lateral pressure on the walls of the veins.[29] This is, to be sure, on the assumption that the veins have their given dimensions. If they were still narrower, even a stream with the consistency of pure air would be sufficient to stimulate them; whereas if they were wider than they happen to be, even water, unthinned by air, would pass through them and we would smell it.[30] Thus everything said in the text in detailing condition (1) above would remain true for the new solution. And since the new explanation is wholly free from the difficulties that bedevil its rival, we have no choice but to adopt it.

The blemish of odd-shaped atoms may now be removed from a theory whose object is to show that matter is as beautiful in its structure as it could possibly be and whose norms of structural beauty are set by the regular solids of Greek geometry. [209]

[27] This I take to be the sense of παχύτεραι, 66E4-5, and I have so translated the word above. Cf. 85C5–D1, where the πάχος of the blood denotes *thickness* or *density* which would render it "too sluggish for ready circulation in the veins" (Cornford's translation). For πάχος as applied to fluids with such senses as "thick," "curdled," "clotted," see *LSJ, s.v.*

[28] Cf. the reference to the substances which enter the gustatory veins as "pre-refined [προλελεπτυσμένων] by decomposition," 66A2-3. Here it is clear that it is the consistency of the fluid that is thought of as "fine." There is no reason to think that λεπτότεραι in 66E4 is being used differently from λεπτ- in προλελεπτυσμένων in 66A2. For λεπτός as applied to fluids (as in the case of thin milk, light wine, etc.) see *LSJ, s.v.*; and cf. λεπτότης of blood in 85C4-5.

[29] Thus the compound would be "between" (μεταξύ) the two ingredients in a sense additional to the one noticed above: it would have properties intermediate between those which would be displayed by each ingredient when unmixed with its opposite. For such a use of μεταξύ, applied to the mixture of qualitative opposites, cf., e.g., Aristotle, *GC* 328A28-31 and 334B10-13.

[30] That is why the statement at 66D3 that the four elements lack the *symmetria* requisite for smell is explained (on the present interpretation of D4-6) by the fact that the olfactory veins are "too narrow" for smelling earth and water and "too wide" for smelling fire and air.

16

Plato on
Knowledge and Reality*

(*1966; PKR*)

(*Review of* I. M. Crombie, *An Examination of Plato's Philosophical Doctrines*, Vol. II: *Plato on Knowledge and Reality*. [*New York, 1963*], *Pp. x, 573*.)

THE author is well versed in the methods and doctrines of present-day "analytical" philosophy. He reads Plato in Greek. He has read a number of the scholarly works about him: he names several good authors, and we can be sure that he has studied many more. But he refuses to debate them. With rare exceptions, he ignores their views. Almost without exception, he ignores their detailed arguments. This is a pity. For the author's aim is not to indulge in free philosophical meditations triggered by Platonic texts. It is to give us, in all seriousness, an examination of *Plato's* doctrines. His main reason for writing is to prove that the "conventional" or "traditional" (his terms) accounts of these doctrines are neither good philosophy nor Plato's. How then can he hope to convince us that he is right and that the scholars who have supported these accounts are wrong, without meeting and refuting their arguments? He finds (preface to Vol. I) "consolation" in the fact that they disagree among themselves. But when that happens we have all the greater need to know why he thinks either or neither side of the controversy should be favored. This is particularly urgent in cases where, in spite of many differences among themselves,

* Originally published in the *Philosophical Review* 75 (1966), 526–530. It is reprinted here without revisions. The original pagination is interpolated in square brackets in the text.

scholars have reached a consensus on some matter the author vehemently rejects. Since he claims no charismatic access to truth, must he not shoulder the responsibility of convicting of error those who, he implies, *are* in error? I trust he may still find time to do this. His many good qualities—the great energy manifest in his copiousness, the honesty and tenacity with which he tackles philosophical problems, his remarkable originality which puts a new, fresh look on many threadbare topics—would then be used to even better advantage, and would yield more solid and durable results.

What he has given us in this book—a full-length study of Plato's epistemology, cosmology, and metaphysics, such as we have not had in decades—ranges over such a variety of topics that I despair of reporting them. Fortunately this is not nearly so pressing, as he himself has since published a conveniently short account of the main points (see the first [526] nine chapters of *Plato, the Midwife's Apprentice*).[1] So the best use I can make of the brief space allotted to this review is to argue with him, however briefly, on some important issues. Let me pick then two things in that complex of doctrines he calls "Platonism" from which he seeks to dissociate his philosophical hero: (1) metaphysical rationalism; and (2) the conflation, in the theory of forms, of universals with (in the author's phrase) "perfect particulars." I submit that in both respects Plato was a "Platonist."

1. In the course of arguing (pp. 517 ff.) that Plato is not "a deductive metaphysician," the author tells us what a philosopher ought to be ("essentially is"): "a critic of theories and not a propounder of them. . . . [He] may have a view and he may try to recommend it. But he must not become a propagandist for it, for philosophy is essentially an attempt to see what is involved in accepting or rejecting some opinion. It is the attempt to impart scientific standards of clarity and reasonableness into [? to? import into?] the discussion of matters, the final arbitration of which must be an act of judgment" ((pp. 518–19). Now certainly Plato at times does all of the good things mentioned here. Unfortunately, at times he does the bad ones too, and with equal zest. Where, among the classics of secular philosophy, would we find a more passionately "propagandist" essay than *Laws* X? Where is the immortality of the soul defended from more patently *a priori* premises than in the *Phaedo*—or in *Phaedrus* 245C-E, where it is proved by definition? Where is philosophical materialism refuted in such simplicist terms as in *Sophist*. 245E-247E, and with more complacent finality? The author's comment that the materialists "are

_____

[1] (London, 1964.) I shall refer to this hereafter by the abbreviation *PMA*.

dealt with on a level more suited to their grosser intelligences" (p. 395) is puzzling. Is it on Plato's behalf, or on his own, that he is suggesting that, for example, Democritus had a "gross intelligence"? (Compare Aristotle, *GC* 315A35, 316A13, 325A1.) Of the theory of forms, we are told that it "is nowhere the object of what purports to be a deductive argument": the one given for it in *Timaeus* 51B-E "does not pretend to be conclusive" because "it rests on the admittedly controvertible fact that understanding is not the same thing as right opinion" (p. 521). But is there one word in Plato to suggest that *he* thinks the fact is "admittedly controvertible"—that is, by reasonable men, not just by sophists and smart alecks? When the question is raised in *Republic* V it is settled in one sentence: "How could any man of sense identify the infallible with the fallible?" (477E). This Plato must think sufficient, else he would not [527] have gone on to make the difference between knowledge and true opinion the foundation of the ontology and epistemology of the *Republic*. So the argument in the *Timaeus*, deductively based on the same premise, is as pure an example of "deductive metaphysics" as one could hope to find.

To be sure, this method is used in Plato only in piecemeal fashion, never with the majestic systematic completeness of the *Ethica more geometrico demonstrata*. In this respect the author is of course perfectly right, as also in his insistence that Plato's method of *discovery*—the "upward path" of the *Republic*—is not deductive. But the method of *proof*—the "downward path"—surely would be, if the author correctly interprets Plato as teaching "that we can attain to an ἀνυπόθετος ἀρχή or non-provisional starting point, from which we can proceed 'downwards' *establishing with certainly what has hitherto been hypothetical*" (p. 525)[2]. The phrase I have italicized seems to have been forgotten a few lines down the page when we are told that it is "left open to us to suppose that the 'way down' consists of little more than the setting out in logical order of that which has been discovered on the way up." Surely it would have to consist of quite a little more than that, if it is going to "establish with certainty" what has been hitherto provisional.

2. In one passage the author tells us that Plato's forms "[A] were universals or common natures. Or, to put it more precisely, [B] the concept of a universal was the concept that Plato was trying to isolate and give expression to when he wrote about forms" (p. 270). Now [B] is hardly the same thing as [A] "put more precisely." It is a very different thing. The difference is so great that, while disagreeing flatly with [A], one could

---

[2] Cf. *R.* 511C and 533B6-D1; *Cra.* 436D1-6 where διαγράμματα, often mistranslated as "diagrams" (e.g., Jowett, Meridier), means "proofs" in this context: cf. T. L. Heath, *Mathematics in Aristotle* (Osford, 1949), pp. 76, 80.

agree substantially with [B], as might Aristotle, for example, whose standing complaint against the theory is that its universals are also, impossibly,
eternal particulars. I would myself have a similar complaint (compare
Philosophical Review, LXIII [1954], 340, and LXV [1956], 90), though with
greater sympathy both for the point which the author makes so well—the
frustrating poverty of the linguistic and conceptual equipment at Plato's
command for this purpose—and also for the one he understands no better
than did Aristotle: that Plato wanted his forms to do much extralogical
work for which a bare universal would have been useless. (What the
author makes of Platonic mysticism may be gauged from his remark that
the ecstatic vision at the [528] height of the lover's ascent in the *Symposium*
"is the leap by which we abstract the common quality from its instances"
[p. 267].)

In expounding [B] he notes (for example, pp. 256 ff.) that in the "middle" dialogues Plato sometimes talks in ways that would befit only what
he calls "perfect schematized particulars." Among these are statements
which entail that forms are "self-reflexive" (p. 264; but the "self" is
redundant). But he contends that nonetheless Plato did not *think* of the
forms in this way. Can this be proved? The author thinks it can, appealing
to that fascinating little argument in *Republic* 596E–597D. Given, *per
impossibile*, two forms of bed, B₁ and B₂, a third "would show up whose
form [εἶδος] they both would have, and this one, not those two, would be
that which bed is" (597C8-9). As has been argued before (Nehrlich, *Mind*,
LXIX [1960], 88) this does indeed show that the form is expected to be a
universal. But how does it refute those who, like Aristotle (*Metaphysics*
1086A32-34 taken with *Nicomachean Ethics* 1096B3-5), think it is *also*
expected to be a perfect particular? On their view, B₁ and B₂ (both forms,
by hypothesis) would be "perfect" to begin with and *their* common form
would be no more perfect than they. How could it follow that the same
thing would be true if they had been ordinary beds?

A great effort is made to show that the "two-worlds picture" speaks
not for the philosopher, but for "the world-weary poet who often got
hold of Plato's pen" (p. 301). That the poet in Plato is at odds with the
philosopher would take some proving. But suppose he were. Would this
man, so savagely critical of other poets, be so soft on the one in his own
soul as to let him misrepresent his deepest philosophical convictions? A
detailed examination of our author's arguments will show, I think, that
they do not begin to establish this improbable thesis. I can give only
one example: the assault (pp. 295–305) on *Phaedo* 74A–75D (by far the
most important of the relevant texts) to prove that it does not assert
"imperfect embodiment." The author translates ἐνδεῖ τι ἐκείνου [τοῦ ὃ

ἔστιν ἴσον] τῷ τοιοῦτον εἶναι οἷον τὸ ἴσον, (74D6-7) by "[the sensible instances] fall short of the very thing which is equal [that is, of equality] with respect to being of the same character as the equal [that is, equality]" (pp. 296, 299; the parenthetic expansions are mine), and remarks that "what this statement [D6] says, if one looks at it long enough, is that [a] equality is of the same character as equality, and that [b] it is in that respect that physical equals.do not live up to its standard" (p. 299). He takes [b] to mean that [c] sensible instances of equality are also instances of inequality "in the way in which we should all allow that this is the case— as for example this penny is equal in size [529] to that penny and unequal to this halfpenny" (p. 301). Now [a] is plainly not what D6-7 says, no matter how long one looks at it: absolutely nothing is *said* here of equality being of the same character as itself (which, of course, Plato believes: who doesn't?), but only of the failure of sensible equals to be of the same character as it. Now what could this failure be? What would any philosopher, including our author, ordinarily mean by saying "that no two physical things are ever perfect instances of equality" (*PMA* 36)? Obviously, that [d] no two physical things have any metrically identical dimensions. This is an entirely different statement from [c], which is trivially true, while [d], *if* true, would be a significant truth about the physical universe. So we need definite and positive evidence to convince us that [c] after all is what Plato means here, in spite of the fact that this is certainly not what he *says* at D6-7 nor anywhere else in the sequel down to 75D. Such evidence could be fished out of an earlier statement (B8-9) on a novel reading of it which has found some support in Oxford in recent years, taking τῷ μὲν ἴσα φαίνεται, τῷ δ'οὔ to mean "seem equal to one [*thing*, (instead of [person] on the usual reading)], not equal to another."[3] But this cannot be the right sense,[4] and out author is wise to put no weight on "this tiresome passage" (p. 301). That leaves him with no definitive support for [c] in the whole of 74A-75D.

Our differences from the author on these and many other points will not deter us from giving this volume a leading place in our graduate seminars. Critically read, it will bring us both stimulation and instruction. [530]

[3] N. R. Murphy, *The Interpretation of Plato's Republic* (Oxford, 1951), p. 111, n. 1; G. E. L. Owen in *Journal of Hellenic Studies*, LXXVII (1957), 108, n. 33; J. L. Ackrill, *Philosophical Review*, LXVII (1958), 107.
[4] For then the ἐνίοτε in B8 would be pointless and the use of the singular would be unexplained (W. J. Veredenius, *Mnemosyne*, Series IV, 113 [1958], 210). Moreover the σοι in 74C1 would be misleading (Owen, *loc. cit.*).

17

On Plato's
Oral Doctrine*

(1963; POD)

(Review of Hans Joachim Krämer, *Arete bei Platon
und Aristoteles: Zum Wesen und zur Geschichte der
platonischen Ontologie* [Heidelberg, 1959], 600 pp.)

IF even half the claims of this extraordinary book could be made good,
it would be the most important contribution to Platonic studies of its
decade. So what it says deserves to be reported and carefully examined.
In the first section I restrict myself to the former: I set forth, as objectively
as I can, and without the slightest comment, a selected set of the theses K.
propounds and defends. This is only for those who have not yet read him.
Those who have may proceed forthwith to Section II, where exposition
ends and criticism begins.

I

Side by side with that part of his teaching which Plato committed to
writing, he expounded orally a "Sonderlehre" (21 et passim), a "Geheimlehre" (24 et passim), whose communication was governed by the
"Eliteprinzip" (403, n. 41). The whole of this esoteric teaching had περὶ
τἀγαθοῦ as its formal title: "so gut wie alles, was wir nach Lehre oder
Inhalt vom esoterischen Platon wissen," coincides with the λόγοι περὶ

---

* Originally published in *Gnomon* 41 (1963), 641–55. It is reprinted here
without revisions. The original pagination is interpolated in square brackets
in the text.

τἀγαθοῦ (408, n. 53). So far from being confined to a single lecture, as has been sometimes supposed, this teaching extended over virtually the whole of Plato's teaching career. The discourse of which we hear in the famous anecdote in Aristoxenus formed only "den ersten, einführenden Teil einer Gesprächsreihe, die Platon immer wieder—sei es periodisch, sei es von Fall zu Fall—einzelnen Adepten der Philosophie, wie Dionysios, oder auch kleineren Gruppen gegenüber *regelmäßig* zur Anwendung brachte" (406: K.'s italics). This oral teaching was "durchaus sokratisch, dem suchenden nur im dialektischen Gespräch zugänglich" (22). And its main tenets had been reached much earlier than has been generally assumed. They can be dated not only as far back as the *Republic*, but much earlier: "Das Eins als Seinsprinzip ist durch den *Protagoras* und den *Lysis* gesichert" (501); the coordinate principle of Plurality is "mit dem Nachweis des Ersten so gut wie gesichert" (505) for the same period, and it is "probable" (*loc. cit.*) that this was the Indeterminate Dyad of the Great and the Small. Thus there never was "eine schriftstellerische Periode Platons, welche die Prinzipien-lehre noch nicht voraussetzt" (502).

Trustworthy reports of the contents of this esoteric teaching we get from various sources, including the following: Aristotle (*Phys.* 209B11, *Met.* A6; and many other passages); Aristoxenus (*Harm. Elem.*, 30,16–31,34 Meibom); Hermodorus (*ap.* Simpl. *Phys.* 247, 30ff, quoting Porphyry reporting Dercyllides reporting Hermodorus); the fragments from Books 1 and 2 of Aristotle's *de Bono* in Alexander's *Commentary to the Meta-physics*, and Alexander *ap.* Simpl. *Phys.* 454,19ff; Theophrastus, *Met.* 6A24ff; 11A27ff; Sextus Empiricus, *Adv. Math.* 10, 248–80[1] and Porphyry *ap.* Simpl. *Phys.* 453,30ff. [*641*]

In addition to what we get from these secondary sources, we have most valuable, if oblique, intimations of esoteric doctrine in the dialogues them-selves. A few examples: In Plato's injunction in the *Philebus* (16D) to grasp τὸν ἀριθμὸν αὐτοῦ [sc. τοῦ πλήθους τῶν ἰδεῶν] . . . τὸν μεταξὺ τοῦ ἀπείρου καὶ τοῦ ἑνός "die Ideen-Zahlen in ihrer eigentlichen Bedeu-tung greifbar werden" (244); and a comparison of 16C with 14E, 18A, and 19A in the same dialogue shows that πέρας and ἄπειρον are the con-stituents not only of all sensibles but also of the Ideas (245). From *Prm.* 157C ff it should be clear to us that the Ideas are constituted from the

---

[1] To just this part of the essay περὶ ἀριθμοῦ in *Adv. Math.* 10, 248–309 I shall refer hereafter by the abbreviation "Sx." It is a text of such importance for K.'s book that if its reliability as a platonic source were disallowed K.'s most original contribution to the reconstruction of Plato's oral doctrine would collapse.

One and Plurality (420), provided we admit, as we should, that "die Ordnung, die hier (*Prm*. 158C) beschrieben ist, ist nichts anderes als der Ideenkosmos der 'Politeia' (500C)" (138). By comparing *Tht*. 176E with R. 506A and the *Parmenides* we discover that the Good is the One (427); by extending the comparison to include passages in the *Gorgias*, the *Symposium*, and the *Phaedrus* we may conclude that ἕν und ἄπειρον (πολλά) sind das ἀγαθὸν αὐτό und das κακὸν αὐτό und verhalten sich wie Norm und Entartung" (144).

When we bring together what we thus extract from the dialogues with what is reported in our secondary sources from Aristotle down, we discover in Plato's esoteric teaching a philosophical system of encyclopedic scope, and so impressive in content and method that it furnished Aristotle, for example, with the most important and characteristic elements of his meta-physical and moral philosophy: the concept of ἀρετή in Aristotle's ethical treatises and the principle of the mixed constitution in the *Politics* were derived from the discourses On the Good (371–72), which were also the source of "the fundamentals of the aristotelian philosophy concerning first things in metaphysics and physics" (374). This esoteric Plato "ist nicht primär Lehrer der Ideen, sondern gehört wesentlicher und umfas-sender in die Geschichte der griechischen ἀρχή-Problematik" (516). Plato's answer to this question brings him closer to Parmenides than to any other of his predecessors: Plato's "Seinsgrund" is "wesenhaft das in sich undifferenzierte, aller Individuation vorausliegende Absolute, . . . das nach Zahl, Zusammenhang, Zeit und Graduierung Eine" (536, with copious references to Parmenides' fr. 8). His great advance over Parmenides was to set over against this One the Indeterminate Dyad. If there were only the One, there would be no world—neither the world of Ideas, nor that of phenomenal existence. But given a principle of indeterminate multiplicity and variety upon which the One can exert its "one-making power" (137), we can be assured of "the concrete fulness of appearances: kosmos, organism, soul, state, the products of the fine arts and of all τέχναι" (537). For the Platonic One is not an "abstract" and "speculative" principle, but "die letzte Sublimierung, der Inbegriff der Phänomene selbst" (301–302). Take any "Seiendes," no matter what, and you will find that its unity is the ground of its "Seiendheit." For since "nichts kann ein *Ding* sein, ohne daß es zugleich *ein* Ding wäre" (473), anything that is owes its "substantielle Beharrung und Beständigkeit" (537) to its oneness. And for that very reason it owes much more: "Dauer, Identität, und Sub-sistenz sind jedoch die Charaktere der Wahrheit und des Erkennens, aber auch die Leistungsfähigkeit, Tauglichkeit und Brauchbarkeit, kurz die

Arete einer Sache setzt ihre Beständigkeit voraus" (537). Hence the ground of its "Beständigkeit" must also be the ground of its "Erkennbarkeit," on one hand, and of its goodness, its ἀρετή, on the other.

This very last point, as the title of the volume intimates, is at the center of the investigation. In previous reconstructions the axiological role of Plato's One had been either wholly excluded (as, e.g., in Stenzel's) or else accorded quite perfunctory acknowledgment (as in the case of Wilpert's: of the several scores of pages devoted to περὶ τἀγαθοῦ in *Zwei aristotelische Frühschriften über die Ideenlehre*, 1949; (hereafter, ZaF), less than two are given over to this aspect of the oral doctrine). This is the major item of unfinished business in the recovery of Plato's esoteric doctrine, and it is fully worked out in this volume. We conduct here an examination of the late dialogues, particularly of the *Philebus* and the *Politicus*, [642] which reveals "daß dort alle einzelnen Bereiche des empirischen Seienden unter einem nahezu einheitlichen Begriff von Arte stehen" (281). This is a concept of Arete as the μέτριον, ἔμμετρον, ξύμμετρον and, still more specifically, as the realization of the right mean in a subject-matter which is indeterminate (ἄπειρον) per se, susceptible of indefinite variations in the direction of the "more" or the "less" (*Phil.* 24A-4, 25C, 52C) or of "excess" and "defect" (*Polit.* 283CD). Even the word, μέσον, comes into Plato's vocabulary in this connection in the *Politicus* (284E): τὸ μέτριον καὶ τὸ πρέπον καὶ τὸν καιρὸν καὶ τὸ δέον καὶ πάνθ' ὁπόσα εἰς τὸ μέσον ἀπῳκίσθη τῶν ἐσχάτων (and cf. *Laws* 728DE, 792B). With this in mind we come to the categorial scheme of the περὶ τἀγαθοῦ reported by Sextus (with support from Alexander and the Hermodorus fragment: the references in K. 282ff). Here the Indeterminate Dyad is the ἀρχή of whatever falls under Excess/Defect and Inequality, while the One is the ἀρχή of the domain of Equality.

That Equality, as used in this scheme, is a principle of good, harmonious order is suggested by comparison with the role of τὸ ἴσον, ἰσότης in the *Philebus* (26A, 26DE) and is confirmed by the examples used in the Sextus passage (Sx): At Sx 272 the examples of ἰσότης/ἀνισότης are μονή/κίνησις,[2] κατὰ φύσιν/παρὰ φύσιν, ὑγίεια/νόσος, εὐθύτης/στρεβλότης. In other examples of Opposites, previously given in Sx (264), the good/evil contrast is even more explicit: ἀγαθόν/κακόν, δίκαιον/ἄδικον, συμφέρον/ἀσύμφορον, ὅσιον/ἀνόσιον, εὐσεβές/ἀσεβές, κινούμενον/ἠρεμοῦν. So we may infer that here too the same sort of value-charged Equality/Inequality are the

---

[2] With μονή/κίνησις here compare the emphasis on the *stability* of the good and 'measured' state in the *Philebus* (24D4-5).

ruling principles. When we are then told at *Sx* 268 that ἐπὶ μὲν τῶν ἐναντίων ὡς ἐπίπαν οὐδὲν ϑεωρεῖται μέσον (examples: disease/health, death/life, motion/rest) . . . , ἐπὶ δὲ τῶν πρός τί πως ἐχόντων ἔστι τι μέσον (examples: ἴσον as mean of greater/smaller, ἱκανόν [cf. *Phlb.* 25D, 60C,67A] as the mean of the More/Less, σύμφωνον [cf. *Phlb.* 25E, and also 26A] as the mean of ὀξύ/βαρύ), we may surmise that the doctrine which is expounded here in abbreviated, mutilated form intends to stake out *a class of pairs of Opposites in which one member of each pair* (the bad member) *is itself conceived as a Correlative and,* more precisely, *as a deviation from the right mean in the direction of either Excess or Defect.* Thus in the case of the pair consisting of κατὰ φύσιν/παρὰ φύσιν, the former stands for the due mean, the latter for departures therefrom in the direction of either the more, or the less, than the mean—e.g., of hotter or colder than the normative state, dryer or more moist, bigger or smaller, and so forth. To be sure, this is not said in Sx. But it is a reasonable "extrapolation" (K. 290), which is confirmed by a passage in the "Divisiones Aristoteleae." Here (Diog. Laert. 3, 104–105; codex Marcianus of the "Divisiones" [Mutschmann] 68) we get a tripartion of Opposites: 1. Those which are opposed as goods to evils, as, e.g., justice/injustice. 2. Those in which neither opposite is good or evil, as, e.g., heavy/light. 3. Those in which both opposites are evil, as, e.g., prodigality/avarice. The opposites in the third class are the Correlatives we are looking for; and in the codex Marcianus of the "Divisiones" [Mutschmann] 68 they are depicted quite explicitly as aberrations from the mean: ὡς κακὸν κακῷ δὲ ἐναντίον ἐστὶν ἡ ὑπερβολὴ τῇ ἐνδείᾳ καὶ τὰ καϑ' ὑπερβολὴν καὶ ἔλλειψιν λεγόμενα. "Mit der dritten Möglichkeit, der Zuordnung zweier Unwerte nach Überschuß und Mangel, tritt die gesuchte Struktur von ὑπερβολή, μεσότης und ἔλλειψις auf dem Boden der platonischen Vorträge [Über das Gute] explizit entgegen" (294). So we have found ἀρετή, conceived as a mean, at the heart of the categorial scheme of Plato's oral teaching. And since the mean is a manifestation of Equality, which is in turn a manifestation of the One, the "Seinsgrund" is revealed as the ground of value no [643] less than of being—and not only of moral value, but of all value whatsoever, for as we know from the *Philebus* and the *Politicus*, the μέτριον and ἔμμετρον are also normative for politics, medicine, music, for all the arts, even for the physical cosmos. The One is thus established as "the highest objective norm of value" (511); it is the αὐτὸ τἀκριβές of *Politicus* 284D.

But the fact that the One thus serves as the first principle of Plato's esoteric axiology, epistemology, and ontology in no way implies that it can be positively described, like other concepts: "der Seinsgrund ist vermöge seines Hinaufgehobenseins über alles Seiende nicht positiv prädizierbar, weil alle denkbaren Prädikationen, die er ja aus sich entläßt, *nach* ihm liegen und darum auf ihn nicht wirklich angewendet werden können. Das Absolute entzieht sich streng genommen als unvergleichbar jeder näheren Bestimmung ünd sprachlichen Erfassung, *sofern sie nicht negativ limitierend ist*" (466; K.'s italics). Thus Plato stands as close to Plotinus as to Parmenides: "das Eins Plotins und der Neuplatoniker erweist sich, geschichtlich betrachtet, als das Eins Platons" (516)

II

The foregoing has not offered a summary, let alone a complete summary, of this book. My only aim has been to convey some idea of its subject-matter, scope, orientation, and, above all, of its astonishing claims. To have attempted more would have been hopeless. Even a bare summary of everything of importance in this book (or, more precisely, of everything that would be important if it were true) would have required many times the space allowable for the whole of this review. I must now proceed to critical comment. But where shall I begin? Practically every thesis I have reported calls for the most detailed and painstaking scrutiny. It would take scores of pages to do this for even one of them. The best I can do in the circumstances is to fasten, almost arbitrarily, on four topics, and make a few remarks on each.

1. *The Sextus Passage* (Sx: *Adv. Math.* 10, 248–80): I have reported K.'s treatment of this passage so fully in the foregoing both because of the great current interest of this text—it has been in the center of discussions of Plato's oral doctrine in recent decades[3]—and also because what K. has done with it deserves attention on its own account. He has given us a clever piece of exegesis, an imaginative and resourceful extension of Wilpert's work. But is it true? Since K. endorses as fully as did Wilpert the evidential value of Sx for the determination of Plato's teaching, K.'s results are open to the same questions. The most searching of these were voiced by Ackrill in his review of ZaF in *Mind*[4] seven years before the publication of K.'s book. These criticisms K. does not confront. If he has [644] read that review, he gives no sign of it in this book. The only criti-

---

[3] Among the more important discussions are Ph. Merlan (1934); Wilpert (1941); de Vogel (1949); also Wilpert, ZaF (1939) and its review by W. Jaeger, *Gnomon* 23 (1951), 246–53, and by J. Ackrill, *Mind* 61 (1952), 102–13; also Merlan (1953, 174–76).

[4] Mentioned in the preceding note.

cisms of Wilpert he seems to have taken at all seriously (294, n.108; cf. 250, n.11) are Jaeger's.[5]

What has he done to meet these? Simply to jettison Wilpert's assumption that Sx derives from Aristotle's *De Bono* and put in its place the hypothesis that the material in Sx has been transmitted "durch die innerakademische, auf den Schriften anderer Platonschüler beruhende, Schultradition" (250, n.11). How much of an improvement is that? In the first place, no evidence is offered for this new hypothesis. If, as K. says (250, n.11), Wilpert's assumption was "ohne Grund," his own seems no better: it bears all the earmarks of an *ad hoc* construction, with nothing better to support it than the desire to meet Jaeger's criticisms while retaining faith in Sx. What is particularly surprising, in view of the vast evidential weight Sx is expected to carry, is the complete absence of a *Quellenkritik* of this whole text. There is no discussion, not so much as a mention, of other material in Sextus which parallels Sx.[6] There is no serious confrontation of the problem raised by the fact that everything in Sx which is taken by K. as a disclosure of Platonic philosophy is presented by Sextus as the teaching of Pythagoreans,[7] except for a single, parenthetical reference to Plato at 258, where he is not credited with this teaching, nor attached to it in any way, but is mentioned only in the teaching assigned to the Pythagoreans as the philosopher of the Ideas. What are we to make of this state of affairs if we are to believe with K. that what Sx attributes so explicitly and exclusively to the Pythagoreans was in fact the very heart of Plato's philosophy, treasured as such within the Academy, and documented there with reports of *Peri Tagathou* by the hand of the original

[5] Listed in the review of *Zaf* mentioned in n. 3, above.

[6] Cf. the references in R. G. Bury's notes to Sx in his edition and translation of Sextus Empiricus, vol. 3 (London, 1936) and in J. E. Raven (1948, 105, n.1). And see particularly the parallels in K. Janacek (1956, 100 ff, at 106); but Janacek should have started the citation from Sx at 261, ἐπισυντεθεῖσαν [τὴν μονάδα] δ᾽ ἑαυτῇ καθ᾽ ἑτερότητα ἀποτελεῖν τὴν καλουμένην ἀόριστον δυάδα to bring out the parallel with καὶ ἡ κατὰ ἐπισύνθεσιν τῆς μονάδος γινομένη ἀόριστος δυάς at *Pyrr. Hyp.* 3, 153. Three things are worth noticing in this connection: (a) This derivation of the Dyad from the One is never ascribed to Plato by Aristotle or the commentators, while (b) it is independently attested for neopythagoreanism by Alexander Polyhistor *ap.* Diog. Laert. 8, 25 and by Hippolytus, *Refut.* 6, 23; conversely (c) an entirely different view of the relation of the Dyad to the One is ascribed by Sextus to Plato: *Adv. Math.* 4, 21–22; *Adv. Phys.* 2, 302–307.

[7] οἱ περὶ τὸν Σάμιον Πυθαγόραν, 248; Pythagoras, 261; Pythagoreans, 263; Πυθαγορικῶν παῖδες, 270. Cf. also 282, where doctrine expounded in the foregoing is now said to represent the position τῶν προτέρων [Πυθαγορικῶν].

members of the Academy? We could scarcely suppose that Sextus was in direct contact with such an academic source and, in the face of its authority, took it upon himself to overrule its ascriptions to Plato and reassign them to the Pythagoreans. The best we could do in the circumstances would be to postulate, as Sextus' immediate source, some mediator who appropriated academic material in the eclectic manner of the [645] late-hellenistic neopythagorean "Fälscherliteratur" to which Jaeger refers in his review (251). This may be what K. himself is now supposing, since at one point he alludes to "einige fremde Einsprengsel im Text des Sextus, die der pythagoreischen Quelle zur Last zu legen sind." [8] But he does not seem to realize that, if this were the case, *any item in Sx which is not otherwise attested for Plato* (and not just the wording, but the doctrine) *would then be suspect*, since it might then be due, compatibly with this hypothesis, to the compiler's concurrent utilization of non-academic sources, or to his own reformulation of academic materials in a manner which distorts their original import, or even to his own invention. [9] Nor would this be the only hazard to which the material in Sx would be exposed by the hypothesis of a pythagorean (or eclectic) mediator. For suppose we were even sure that a given item in Sx, not independently attested for Plato, had passed intact through the mediator's hands and reached Sextus' page in the very words of the original academic source. Would that be sufficient reason for ascribing it to *Plato*? Certainly not, unless we were in a position to say that it was itself an accurate report of *Platonic* (not merely academic) doctrine, clearly designated as such within the Academy and properly distinguished from more or less similar views of other members of the Academy. From what we know of the prevailing habits of philosophical reportage, how good are the prospects that the item had enjoyed such treatment? Thus everything for which Sx is the sole authority for supposed Platonic teaching is doubly suspect: first, because of the possibilities within the Academy itself of confusion with non-Platonic academic doctrine or of deformation through inventive interpretation or careless reporting; second, because of the further possibilities of infiltration of alien matter or of distortion of authentic matter in passing through the hands

----

[8] 284, n. 90, in a reference to Wilpert which I take to be K.'s own opinion. I regret that in the course of a 600 page book he did not express himself more clearly on this important point.

[9] This would be ample justification for Jaeger's conclusion (loc. cit.): "insbesondere scheint es mir nicht angängig den Pythagoräer [sc. who was utilized by Sextus] zum Ausgangspunkt einer Rekonstruktion des Aufbaus der Schrift περὶ τἀγαθοῦ zu machen."

of Sextus' immediate, non-academic, source. When we take all this into
account, what confidence can we repose in Sx?

Let us consider a single example which has its own intrinsic interest, for
it concerns a major issue in the reconstruction of the esoteric Plato to
which I did not find it possible to allude in Section I: at Sx 269 we
read: . . . καὶ τούτων αὐτῶν ἐπάνω τι γένος τετάχθαι, καὶ πρῶτον
ὑπάρχειν διὰ τὸ καὶ πᾶν γένος προϋπάρχειν τῶν ὑφ' αὐτὸ τεταγμένων
εἰδῶν. ἀναιρουμένου γοῦν αὐτοῦ πάντα τὰ εἴδη συναναιρεῖται, τοῦ δὲ
εἴδους ἀναιρεθέντος οὐκέτ' ἀνασκευάζεται τὸ γένος· ἤρτηται γὰρ ἐξ ἐκείνου
τοῦτο, καὶ οὐκ ἀνάπαλιν. If we could take this text with K. as an authentic
report of Plato's oral teaching, we would be able to settle once for all a
question which affects the fundamentals of reconstructions of his doctrine,
particularly those which derive from Stenzel: given two Forms, related as
genus to species, would Plato assign ontological priority to the genus?
Cherniss has argued most forcefully (1944, 44–48, with notes) that the
answer is "No." K., who would have us answer it, "Yes," must first of all
be disabused of his misapprehension that this [646] answer can *also* get independent grounding from Aristotle, who may then be used to confirm the
testimony of Sx on this point. He writes: "Der Gebrauch von γένος und
εἴδος ist übrigens . . . , ebenso wie das Gesetz des μὴ συναναιρεῖσθαι
des γένος mit dem εἴδος, das eine ontische Hierarchie voraussetzt, für
Platon durch die 'Divisiones Aristoteleae' 64, 65, c. M. und Sextus Emp.
X 269, das letztere sinngemäß durch den frühen aristotelischen 'Protrepti-
kos' (fr. 5a Walzer) sowie ausdrücklich durch Aristoteles 'Metaph.' 1019A1 ff
(vgl. 1059B38 ff) bezeugt" (431–432).[10] But here are the relevant lines (2–4)
from *Metaph.* 1019A1 ff: . . . τὰ δὲ [λέγεται πρότερα καὶ ὕστερα] κατὰ
φύσιν καὶ οὐσίαν, ὅσα ἐνδέχεται εἶναι ἄνευ ἄλλων, ἐκεῖνα δε ἄνευ ἐκείνων μή,
ἧ διαιρέσει ἐχρῆτο Πλάτων. There is nothing here to say, "ausdrücklich"
or otherwise, that Plato applied the distinction of πρότερα/ὕστερα κατὰ
φύσιν to the genus/species distinction. That Aristotle would so apply it
we do know.[11] But that means nothing for the point at issue, which is
whether or not Aristotle is telling us that Plato did so too. For obviously
Plato could have applied it, e.g., to the distinction between Ideas and

---

[10] Cf. also 259, n. 32: "Ausdrücklich schreibt Aristoteles sie [sc. the "Denk-
form" which includes the rule of μὴ συναναιρεῖσθαι of the genus with the
species] Platon zu 'Metaphysik' 1019A1–4." Cf. also 274, and 293, n. 105.

[11] *Top.* 141B27-29: a good definer should proceed διὰ τοῦ γένους καὶ τῶν
διαφορῶν . . . , ταῦτα δὲ τῶν ἀπλῶς γνωριμοτέρων καὶ προτέρων τοῦ εἴδους
ἔστιν. συναναιρεῖ γὰρ τὸ γένος καὶ ἡ διαφορὰ τὸ εἴδος . . . ἔστι δὲ καὶ
γνωριμότερα. . . .

sensibles (for other possible applications see, e.g., Cherniss 1944, n.33), without applying it to the distinction between genus and species. Does Aristotle's text then say that Plato did the latter? It obviously does not.

Nor do we get a different result if, following K.'s instructions, we compare 1059B38 ff: ᾗ δὲ συναναιρεῖται τοῖς γένεσι τὰ εἴδη, τὰ γένη ταῖς ἀρχαῖς ἔοικε μᾶλλον. ἀρχὴ γὰρ τὸ συναναιροῦν. This is a straightforward statement of Aristotelian doctrine, without one word in it, or in its context, to imply that Aristotle is here ascribing the same doctrine to Plato. As for the other passage mentioned by K., the fragment from the Protrepticus, this too is presumably Aristotelian doctrine, and cannot be used as evidence that Aristotle shared it with Plato, since it says or implies nothing of the kind. All that remains then of the evidence K. has given us for ascribing to Plato an "ontische Hierarchie" based on the "natural" priority of genus to species is, apart from Sx above, the codex Marcianus of the Divisiones Aristoteleae (Mutschmann) 65. 66. Assuming, as is often done, that the latter reports academic views,[12] we can now ask: How much would it advance our effort to ascertain whether or not Plato held this particular view, if we conceded the hypothesis that Sx was derived not from the *de Bono*, but from an academic source mediated to Sextus by a neopythagorean compiler? So far as I can see, the answer would be: Not at all. For in the first place, we would not be able to rule out the possibility that Sextus' immediate source picked up this particular doctrine from other (e.g., peripatetic) quarters. In the [647] second place, even if it were a carry-over from an academic tradition, it would afford us no assurance that *Plato* had once held it. Thus the fact that we find it in Sx is no good reason for inferring that it is an authentic Platonic doctrine. If we do want to infer this, we will have to produce *other* evidence for it. What would that be? I know of nothing better than Alexander (*Metaph.* 55, 22–23). How good that is one may decide for oneself after taking two things into account: (a) since Alexander is talking here (55, 20 ff)

[12] Widespread academic adherence to this doctrine might also be inferred from the unspecified reference of δοκεῖ at Top. 123A15. Even if we were to grant the validity of this inference, it would settle nothing for the point at issue here, i.e. whether or not *Plato* shared this doctrine. If we have independent grounds (as I am convinced we do) for holding that both the letter and the spirit of Plato's Theory of Ideas is inimical to the conception that logical generality *entails* ontological superiority (which would mean, e.g., that Virtue is more real than Justice, Plane Figure more real than Circle, and so forth), we would expect Plato to resist the present doctrine even if it enjoyed high favor among younger colleagues whose commitment to the Ideas was different from his.

of both Plato and the Pythagoreans (ἐδόκει αὐτοῖς) he is open to the
suspicion that on this as on other points "he is running together and
probably confusing Platonic and Pythagorean doctrines" (Cherniss, 1944.
168); (b) Alexander's phrase τὰ γὰρ ἁπλούστερά τε καὶ μὴ συναναιρού-
μενα πρῶτα τῇ φύσει has no direct reference in this context to genera: the
examples—lines/planes, points/lines—are not related as genera/species.

If one were to examine in the same way everything in K.'s reconstruction
of περὶ τἀγαθοῦ which has only Sx to support it, what would be left
of K.'s discovery that the doctrine of the mean was enshrined in Plato's
esoteric ontology? Not much, in my opinion, except a tissue of ingenious
guesses. I offer this merely as an opinion, since I cannot carry out here,
item by item, the critique that would be required to prove it. But at
least I have offered the reader some reasons for treating Sx, as an independently reliable witness for Platonic doctrine, with the very greatest
reserve.

2. *The Aristotelian testimony*: K.'s treatment of this is, on the whole,
more critical than that of other recent champions of the esoteric Plato.
Thus he is apparently conceding to Cherniss[13] that the passage in the
de Anima (404B18–27) which has been lavishly used in modern reconstructions[14] "bezieht [sich] nicht direkt auf περὶ τἀγαθοῦ" (414, n.68,
cf. also 431). Since he uses "περὶ τἀγαθοῦ" to designate "die Lehrtätigkeit
Platons überhaupt" (409), and since the doctrine of the *de Anima* passage
could not possibly be squeezed out of the dialogues either, I take this to be
his way of saying that it cannot be regarded as genuine Platonic doctrine.
Are we to understand him to be passing the same verdict on the notorious
mathematical "intermediates"? Of these he says (following Wilpert, *ZaF*,
205, n.11) that "gar nicht sicher ist, ob sie in den Lehrgesprächen überhaupt behandelt waren" (278). We could have wished for a more definite
statement of his view. More is at stake here than the fate of just this [648]
doctrine. For suppose we were to conclude that Plato had *not* professed it.
What would we then make of Aristotle's emphatic ascription of it to
Plato, made upon occasion (e.g., *Metaph*. A. 6) in the same context which

[13] On the strength of Cherniss (1944, Appendix 9, 565 ff., and 1945, 14 ff.),
and before the publication of the review of Saffrey (*Gnomon* 31 [1959], 36–51),
where Cherniss has proved his case as conclusively as anything has ever been
proved by sound scholarly argument in this highly controversial area. For what
might nonetheless be reasonably said on the other side see F. Solmsen's
review of Cherniss 1945 in *Class. Weekly* 140 (1946), 164–68; for all its brevity
this is still the best critique of this book I have seen in print.

[14] E.g., Robin (1909, *passim*), and (1935, 145); Stenzel (1959, 94 ff.); Saffrey
(1955, *passim*); and Ross (1951, 209 ff., 214 ff.).

credits Plato with other doctrines whose authenticity, according to K., is beyond suspicion? Why should Aristotle string out true and false testimony in the very same passage and with no apparent change of tone? K. seems to have no inkling of the gravity of this question for one who holds, as he does, that Aristotle may be guilty of "Fehlinterpretation" or tendentious "Umformulierung [of platonic doctrine] in die eigene Terminologie," but never "der Konstruktion eines ganz neuen Sachverhalts" (420, n.79). If Plato did not really hold the doctrine of the intermediates, would not this be a clear case of outright fabrication of a substantive item in the philosophy which, according to Aristotle, Plato himself professed? And were K. clearheaded as to consequences of his own views, he would have seen that the same problem faces him in the case of the Idea-numbers. For if anything is clear in the Aristotelian testimony it is its ascription to Plato of Ideas which are *identical* with numbers. As K. himself correctly states the point: "Aristoteles stellt in A, M und N der 'Metaphysik' fest, daß Platon neben den mathematischen noch andere Zahlen angenommen habe . . . *die er mit den* εἴδη *identifizierte*" (250, with copious references; the italics are mine). But K.'s view of the Idea-numbers is that the Number of an Idea is only its "structure": "In ihrer Struktur aufgedeckt erweist sich die Idee als Zahl" (253).

His references here (notes 18, 19) are not to Aristotle, but to Sx 258 and Theophrastus, *Metaph.* 6B11 ff. And the Sextus passage he interprets after Wilpert (ZaF, 157 ff), glossing, "Es handelt sich offenbar um die Zahl der in der Definition enthaltenen Bestimmungen," 253, n.18.[15] But if that is to be our interpretation of the Idea-numbers, we will not only be *ignoring* Aristotle's testimony but, as Cherniss has pointed out in a

---

[15] For further explanation of this obscure doctrine one may consult Wilpert and, for a critique, Ackrill's review. As the latter points out, the radical flaw of this interpretation is that it foists on Plato an assumption (rightly repudiated on Plato's behalf by Cherniss) that all Ideas fit into an all-comprehensive diairetical scheme (a "Begriffspyramide," as K. likes to call it), where *One* is at the apex as the summum genus and every other Idea has its place at some subordinate level, levels being ranked in a unique enumerable serial order of descending generality. K. labors under the misapprehension that the Ideas could not be ordered at all (and would, therefore, constitute an "Ideenchaos," 429), unless they had just this order. This arbitrary assumption vitiates his controversy with Cherniss on this point and skews his reading of Plato's text: he takes (127–28) the reference to the philosopher's "descent" from the ἀνυπόθετον at *R.* 511BC and even the fact that the Ideas are said at 500C to be τεταγμένα as conclusive evidence that Plato was already committed to the "Begriffspyramide" when he wrote the *Republic*.

critique of Ross (1945, 92, n.112), we would in fact be *rejecting* it. For if we hold that the Number of an Idea-number is its "structure," we must deny that the Number is the Idea. For two Ideas could very well have the same "structure" and hence the same Number (any two Ideas of the same level of logical generality would have the same Number on this view); if that Number were identical with each of them, they would be identical with each other, and this would make shambles of the "Ideenkosmos." Ross tacitly recognized the logical incompati- [649] bility of the two views (represented by the testimony of Theophrastus and Aristotle) which he had tried to "reconcile" in his commentary to Theophrastus' *Metaphysics* (Oxford, 1929), 58–59. In his *Plato's Theory of Ideas* (1951)[16] he in fact rejected the testimony of Aristotle (under the euphemism that it should not be taken "literally"), conceding here (218) "that Plato did not identify the Ideas with numbers, but only assigned numbers to Ideas." K. does not seem to have caught up with this development. He twice refers to Ross's earlier view (253, n.19; 435) ignoring Ross's modification of this view in his later book. He reproaches Cherniss for not recognizing that the conflict between the testimony of Theophrastus and Aristotle on this point is "dadurch [sc., thanks to Ross] der Sache nach aufgehoben" (435), unaware that Ross, who is thus credited with having solved the problem in 1929 found it necessary (probably under pressure from Cherniss's criticism) to take a new position in 1951.

K. thus spared himself the necessity of explaining a grave discrepancy between what Aristotle says about Plato's esoteric doctrine and what K. himself is willing to accept as such.

3. *The Story in Aristoxenus* (*Harm. Elem.*, 30, 16–31, 14 Meibom.): As K. observes (408), there is nothing to show this happened very late in Plato's life, or that it happened only once. But neither, conversely, is there anything to show that it happened often and as the first of a *"Gesprächsreihe."*

Nothing can be inferred from the article in οἱ λόγοι περὶ μαθημάτων, etc.; when K. gets "Die bekannten Lehren" (407) out of οἱ λόγοι he pulls a rabbit from a hat. The only argument he gives us that deserves serious consideration is the one that refers us to the tense in which much of the action is described: ἐφαίνετο, ὑποκατεφρόνουν, κατεμέμφοντο, etc. These he takes to be imperfects of repetition (402). But clearly this is not conclusive, for the imperfects can be read quite differently.[17]

---

[16] And he retouched accordingly p. LXVII of the Introduction in his second edition of *Aristotle's Metaphysics* (Vol. 1, Oxford, 1958)—an edition not available to K. at the time of writing.

[17] In the primary use of the tense, to denote continued action in the past,

The question then cannot be decided by Aristoxenus' grammar,[18] but from the general sense of what he is trying to tell us. Could he really mean to say that this remarkable episode happened not only once but over and over again, successive audiences turning up in all innocence to Plato's lecture to get the same surprise each time they came? This would make so much more of a good story that were it in Aristoxenus' mind he would surely have said so more explicitly and emphatically. As the text now reads, I submit that in all probability what Aristoxenus means to say is that what was often repeated was the tale (᾽Αριστοτέλης ἀεὶ διηγεῖτο), not what happened according to the tale. From this I do not con- [650] clude that there were no Gesprächsreihen on the Good in the Academy. There may have been. Who knows.[19]

From τὴν περὶ τἀγαθοῦ ἀκρόασιν we can infer that Plato gave a speech: Aristoxenus is not likely to have referred to a dialogue as an ἀκρόασις or to the participants in a discussion as τῶν ἀκουσάντων or to have compared them to Aristotle's auditoire (cf. τοῖς μέλλουσιν ἀκροᾶσθαι παρ' αὐτοῦ at the close of the passage). From the reaction of the audience—"some sneered, some were full of reproaches"—we can infer with Cherniss (*Riddle of the Early Academy*, p. 12) that it included a substantial portion of persons "who had no preliminary experience of the sort of thing he [Plato] was likely to say." So it must have been open to the public. To avoid this consequence, so awkward for the "Geheimlehre" theory, K. (405, 406,

since the continued action need not be long (as in εὐθὺς ἀμείβετο, ταχὺ ἀπεπήδων: cf. B. S. Gildersleeve, *Syntax to Classical Greek*, 1900, 88–89) and has, in any case, so little to do "with the absolute duration of the action"(Gildersleeve, loc. cit.) that in many contexts the same action may be denoted indifferently by the aorist or the imperfect: see how Thucydides mixes aorists and imperfecst in introducing speeches: ἔλεγον τοιάδε, ἔλεξεν ὧδε, ἐπεῖπον τοιάδε, παρήνει τοιάδε (all from Book 1).

[18] As to this, the introductory phrase, Καθάπερ ᾽Αριστοτέλης ἀεὶ διηγεῖτο τοὺς πλείστους τῶν ἀκουσάντων παρὰ Πλάτωνος τὴν περὶ τἀγαθοῦ ἀκρόασιν παθεῖν, hardly favors the repetition theory.

[19] If Alexander did use the plural (as K. seems to infer [407, n.50] from Simpl., Phys. 454, 20, ᾽Αλέξανδρος αὐτὸς ἐκ τῶν περὶ τἀγαθοῦ λόγων τοῦ Πλάτωνος ὁμολογῶν λέγειν, which is used also in Ep. 7. 330B, τῶν περὶ φιλοσοφίαν λόγων) we could make nothing of it, since λόγοι could mean "statements" or "arguments" as much as "discourses"; one could very well use the plural in referring to what is said in a single discourse (the obvious use of οἱ λόγοι in the Aristoxenus passage). The plurals λόγοι, συνουσίαι in Simplicius and Philopponus doubtless have the significance K. reads into them (*loc. cit.*); but the evidential value of these late sources for the point at issue is very doubtful.

n.47) supposes that in the case of this particular ἀκρόασις Plato must have been carrying out the object mentioned by the writer of the *Seventh Letter* at 340BC: to put to the proof newcomers to philosophy, δεικνύναι . . . δεῖ τοῖς τοιούτοις ὅτι ἔστι πᾶν τὸ πρᾶγμα οἷόν τε καὶ δι' ὅσων πραγμάτων καὶ ὅσον πόνον ἔχει.[20] This makes a strained parallel with Aristoxenus' story, where Plato is not depicted as addressing philosophical neophytes, outlining for their benefit the program of philosophical studies and impressing upon them its rigors and hardships.

Anyhow, the "Geheimlehre" theory will not square with *Laws* 968E, οὕτω δὴ πάντα τὰ περὶ ταῦτα [the studies of the members of the Nocturnal Council περὶ πάντων τῶν σπουδαίων, 966B] ἀπόρρητα μὲν λεχθέντα οὐκ ἂν ὀρθῶς λέγοιτο, ἀπρόρρητα δὲ διὰ τὸ μηδὲν προρρηθέντα δηλοῦν τῶν λεγομένων. K. quotes this passage twice (28, n.27; 476, n.172). but is too distracted by the intriguing "not ἀπόρρητα but ἀπρόρρητα" contrast, to notice the explicit repudiation of *secrecy of doctrine* in the very context in which *privacy of inquiry* is stressed. The latter, doubtless normal in the Academy, no more implies a Platonic "Geheimlehre" than does the distinction between "exoteric" and more restricted discussions in Aristotle imply any secrecy about the latter.

As for the meaning of καὶ τὸ πέρας[21] ὅτι ἀγαθόν[22] ἐστιν ἕν, K. says that ἕν here is not "prädikatives Numerale, sondern Prädikatssubstantiv" (424), because (a) the unity of goodness would be "der Sache nach banal" (423), and (b) could not have surprised the audience, since it was already well-[651] known in Athens and was in any case conveyed by the fact that the lecture had been announced "unter dem Titel περὶ τἀγαθοῦ (nicht περὶ τἀγαθῶν) [sic]," *loc. cit.* But (a) there is nothing "banal" about the unity of the Good as a *Platonic Idea*. The crux of the difference in orientation between the philosopher and the φιλοθεάμων in the *Republic* is precisely that the latter πολλὰ τὰ καλὰ νομίζει, . . . καὶ οὐδαμῆ ἀνεχόμενος ἄν τις ἕν τὸ

---

[20] Quoting this sentence (406, n.47), K. glosses, "der absichtlich schockieren soll," connecting it thereby with παντελῶς . . . παράδοξόν τι ἐφαίνετο in Aristoxenus. But "schockieren" is not in the letter or spirit of the sentence or its context.

[21] For the adverbial sense see Cherniss, op. cit., 87, n. 2. It is accepted by K., as well as by W. Bröcker, "Plato über das Gute," *Lexis* 2, 1949, 47–66, at 47; R. da Rios, *Aristoxeni Elementa* (1954), 45. Still against: C. J. de Vogel, *Greek Philosophy* 1 (Leiden, 1950), 274, who translates "and that the Finite is the Good, which is identical with the One".

[22] K. favors τἀγαθόν, Macran's conjecture (without MS. authority, on account of τἀγαθοῦ ἀκρόασιν earlier). But ἀγαθόν, without the article, could carry the same sense.

καλὸν φῇ εἶναι (479A); and in the *Laws* it is still a matter of highest consequence that the Guardians should come to know περὶ ἀγαθοῦ . . .
ὅπως ἕν τε καὶ ὅπη (966A). Once this is clear, (b) answers itself: neither
a title nor comedy nor gossip could have prepared persons untrained in
philosophy for what *Plato* would mean by the one Good, even if he were
not expounding the more mysterious doctrine of the good One.

4. *Phaedrus 274B–278E*: How important K. thinks this passage can be
gauged from the fact that he prints its closing lines, 278B8-E3, at the
head of his book, right after the dedication. By reference to this alone, he
thinks, the "opponents of the esoteric Plato" could be confuted (393):
those who reject the authenticity of the *Seventh Letter* would still have been
compelled, he holds, to admit that Plato withheld the most important
truth of his philosophy from the dialogues and disclosed them only in
his oral teaching, had they not "misinterpreted" (Schleiermacher, Zeller)
or "ignored" (Cherniss) the implications of this passage in the *Phaedrus*.
Let us then see what is said in its crucial, concluding, part (278B8-E3):

(A) If a composer of speeches, poems, or political treatises

(B) (1) has composed "with knowledge of the truth (εἰδὼς ᾖ τὸ
ἀληθὲς ἔχει, (2) is able to come to their aid (ἔχων βοηθεῖν) by proceeding to a cross-examination regarding the things of which he has
written[23] (εἰς ἔλεγχον ἰὼν περὶ ὧν ἔγραψε), and (3), by his own
spoken discourse (καὶ λέγων αὐτός) is able to show up the inferiority
of [his] written [to (his) spoken] word (δυνατὸς τὰ γεγραμμένα
φαῦλα ἀποδεῖξαι)—

(C) such a man we should not designate by the name of [i.e.,
which refers to] the former [i.e., to (A)] (οὔ τι τῶνδε ἐπωνυμίαν
ἔχοντα δεῖ λέγεσθαι τὸν τοιοῦτον),

(D) but rather by a name which refers to the latter [i.e., to (B)]
with which he is gravely concerned (ἀλλ’ ἐφ’ οἷς ἐσπούδακεν
ἐκείνων)."

(C), continued: If he had nothing better (τιμιώτερα) in his head
than what he put into his poems or writings, we should call him *poet*
or *-writer* ("speechwriter" or "law-writer": λόγων συγγραφέα ἢ
νομογράφον).

---

[23] Taking περὶ ὧν ἔγραψε to mean "de quibus scripsit" (Stallbaum, followed
e.g., by Robin). The alternative, "regarding the things he has written" (i.e.,
"his [written] statements," Hackforth), is not so likely. But the sense is
not greatly affected either way.

(D), continued: If he had written with true understanding or wisdom, we should draw attention to that in his name; and since to call him σοφός would not become mortal humility, we may call him φιλόσοφος or something of the kind.

Two things should be noticed:

(I) It is not said here that all, or most, of whatever is put into writing is false.[24] The contrary is implied at (B) (1) given the strong positive connotations of βοηθεῖν[25] (sc. [652] ταῦτα, his compositions). To "come to the help" of statements is obviously to *defend* them: to vindicate them against stupid or malicious misunderstanding, to refute sophistical objections to them, to reinforce them by showing how they follow from strong premises or have illuminating implications. If all written compositions were wholly, or mainly, compacted of falsehood, they would not admit or deserve such defense; and then the ability to "come to their aid" would not be a mark of the man who "knows the truth." So Plato must be assuming that the writings of a man who can satisfy the conditions laid down in (B) *do* contain a good deal of truth. That he does make just this assumption is confirmed within (B) (2) by the ἔλεγχος our man will undertake in coming to the aid of what he has written. If the latter were largely false, to go into such an ἔλεγχος would be to invite disaster. It follows that in the next statement, (B) (3), that he has the ability τὰ γεγραμμένα φαῦλα ἀποδεῖξαι, the word φαῦλα cannot mean "false": if he were showing up his writings as false, he would not be "helping" them. All it can mean is "inferior,"[26] which makes perfect sense: from the fact that a written statement is vastly inferior to an oral argument which comes to its aid, it obviously does not follow that the written statement is wholly, or even partly, false.

(II) It is neither said, nor implied, that to live down the name of "writer" and earn the title of φιλόσοφος a man has to *change subjects*,

---

[24] The full-strength form of this thesis (with the "all"), if expressed in writing, would reenact the paradox of the Liar.

[25] Cf. its earlier uses in the passage, especially at 276C, where λόγῳ βοηθεῖν is complementary to ἱκανῶς τἀληθῆ διδάξαι. Cf. also its uses elsewhere in the dialogues, e.g., *Phaedo* 88E, (of Socrates) πρᾴως ἐβοήθει τῷ λόγῳ.

[26] So understood in every translation or commentary I have consulted: "deteriora," Stallbaum; "the inferiority of written speech," W. H. Thompson; "minderwertig," C. Ritter; "de peu que sont ses écrits," Robin; "the inferiority of his writings," Hackforth.

e.g., that if he had been writing on politics, he must now turn to a different, and more exalted, topic, like metaphysics. The contrary is distinctly implied by the wording at (B) (2) εἰς ἔλεγχον ἰὼν περὶ ὧν ἔγραψε: if he had been writing about politics, he would be expected to go into an elenchus *concerning politics*. The same thing is implied, but not so distinctly, at (B) (1): εἰ μὲν εἰδὼς ᾗ τὸ ἀληθὲς ἔχει συνέθηκε ταῦτα leaves us with the question, "with knowledge of the truth *about what?*" In this context, this question, once put, answers itself: the truth about *the subjects of his compositions.*

Consider now what K. has made of our text. I quote the greater part of his gloss on 278C4-D1, interspersing numerals in square brackets for convenient reference:

> [1] Die Begriffe ἀληθὲς (vgl. 276C9) und φαῦλα sind hier sinnge-mäß aufeinander bezogen wie nachher das Gegensatzpaar ἐκεῖνα-τάδε. [2] Alle vier Glieder betreffen den *inhaltlichen* Gegensatz zwischen Schrift und Ungeschriebenem: [3] "das Wahre" liegt ebenso wenig in der *Methode* des dialektischen Unterrichts wie die Mängel des Geschriebenen in seinem literarischen Charakter—dann bedürfte es keiner besonderen ἀπόδειξις—, und [4] der Philosoph trägt seinen Namen . . . weil er durch diejenigen Gegenstände, "mit denen es ihm eigentlich Ernst ist" und die er deshalb unge-schrieben läßt (ἐκεῖνα), all das, worin er allenfalls mit anderen Schriftstellern thematisch übereinstimmt (τάδε = Staatschriften: 276E2f), wesenhaft übertrifft. (395)

[1] This is misleading. It suggests that τὸ ἀληθὲς falls exclusively in the domain of oral utterance, which is false, as has been shown at (I) above.

[2] This is false, for the reason given at (II) above: the oral discourse of the man of understanding may have the same subject as his written dis-course, and at (B) (2) it *does* have the same subject: when a man goes into an elenchus περὶ ὧν ἔγραψε, there is *no* "inhaltlicher Gegensatz" between his writing and his talk.

[3] What is here said to be in need of no particular ἀπόδειξις, most certainly needs ἀπόδειξις. The vast methodological superiority of oral to written discourse claimed by Plato is far from self-evident. It is probably false.

[4] That the φιλόσοφος bears his name because he excels others in virtue of concerning himself with a different set of *objects* is not said in the

text. That his σπουδή is restricted to a special set of *objects* is not said in the text. That he refrains from writing [653] about a special set of *objects* is not said in the text. None of these three things is even implied by anything said in the text.

Both here and elsewhere (23,461–62, 464, n.167) K. has taken our text to distinguish two sets of "Dinge" or "Gegenstände" (or two kinds of "Inhalt") such that the former are all φαῦλα, while all of the latter are τιμιώτερα and worthy of σπουδή, the two sets forming, respectively, the appropriate topics of written and oral discourse. That this is wrong should be clear, quite apart from what has been said above in elucidation of the text, by giving a moment's thought to what would follow if it were right: that Plato considered the topics of which he wrote in the dialogues φαῦλα; that he would not count them among the things ἐφ' οἷς ἐσπούδακεν. Now two of the topics he treats extensively in the dialogues are the Ideas and the soul. Could anyone say that Plato felt anything less than veneration for the Ideas? And that he had no σπουδή for the soul? This is by no means the only case in this book where one or more Platonic texts are misread with disastrous consequences for the interpretation of Plato's thought. The reader has very likely inferred as much for himself from my report of K.'s theses in Section I. Even so, it may not be amiss to warn him that he should test for himself every case where the issue of an argument depends on what K. says the text means.

Did Plato then have no oral doctrine? It is not the reviewer's task to fill the vacuum which would be left if he succeeded in refuting the major thesis of this book. Not that I claim to have done the latter. K. has many other arguments which I have not enumerated, let alone rebutted. But since I do believe that all of them fail, and that the picture of Plato's "esotericism" they are used to build up is radically misconceived, it may be well to mention (since I can do no more) a reasonable alternative which provides an oral basis for ancient ascriptions of ἄγραφα δόγματα to Plato without crediting him with a private (and secret!) philosophy meant to supersede the one he published in the dialogues. In the first place, it is not hard to think of Plato engaging in a great deal of philosophical discussion and rating this dialectic a far more valuable activity than written composition, regarding the latter merely a provisional and fragmentary record of truth discovered and vindicated in live debate. To say this is only to suggest that Plato practiced in the Academy what he preached in the *Phaedrus*. But then, going one step farther, we may hazard the supposition that in the course of these arguments Plato explored with his associates not only the views we know in the dialogues but a great many other theories as well which he found attractive enough to merit exposition and defense in oral argument but which he did not succeed in working out fully and confidently enough to think them worthy of publication. The One and the Dyad of the Great and the Small, the mathematical intermediates, and the Idea-numbers might have been speculations of this kind. If so, we could account for the discrepancies between what Plato expounds in the dialogues and what Aristotle ascribes to him in the *Metaphysics* and the *Physics*, provided only we make allowance for Aristotle's [654] failure to take account of the distinctions, qualifications, and dubitations with which Plato hedged in these theories when arguing for them with members of his own familiar circle.

In closing I must remind the reader that I have not tried to "cover" this book in the manner usually expected in a review. I have done no more than mention some of its theses and point out a few of its mistakes. Having confined myself to the interpretation of the texts, I have not been able to examine its philosophical notions which contain, in my opinion, some very serious misapprehensions and confusions. But even if I had carried through this critique to a finish. I would still have liked to close by calling attention to those entirely admirable qualities which make this book a remarkable performance: vigor of argument, boldness of conception, breadth of vision. Had K. done no more for us than challenge us to free ourselves from σμικρολογία, he would still have placed us greatly in his debt. [655]

APPENDIX

Does Ti. 53C8-D7 give support to the Esotericist Thesis?

PROFESSOR Krämer honored me by replying to my critique. He did so in a paper, "Retraktationen zum Problem des esoterischen Platon" (*Museum Helveticum* 21 [1964], 137–67), which also controverts another critic of his book. I would have gladly responded in kind, were it not that to continue the controversy would have required me to divert time and energy earmarked for other projects. A quick rejoinder could have been polished off in no time at all. But of what use would that have been? A decent response to each of the many issues K. raises in his paper—the only sort of reply which could hope to advance the inquiry, rather than win a contest—would have required an essay longer than the original review. I would have considered this a meritorious project and gladly scrounged the time for it, had I been honestly convinced that the question of the "esoteric Plato" is one of the burning issues of present-day Platonic scholarship. I must confess that I have felt, and still do, quite the opposite. I am satisfied that the considerations I have urged in the above review are sound and, brief though they are, suffice to show that the grandiose construction, reared with such magnificent industry, in K.'s book, is a work of the imagination whose claim to sober truth is minimal, and this not for lack of erudition (on that score K. could hardly be faulted) but for want of precision in the formulation of his claims and of close attention to what can, and what cannot, be properly reckoned textual evidence for them. I, therefore, beg to be excused (at least for the present) from any further part in this debate, for I have other work to which, rightly or wrongly, I attach greater importance.

But since it might be thought churlish to offer no response at all to

K.'s earnest rebuttal, I venture to submit a sample of the counter-critique I would have offered if I had had the time and energy to produce it. I content myself with examining one of his arguments which I find not untypical of his reply. My comments on it will at least help explain why I find his paper as unconvincing as I have found his book.

He offers now a passage from the *Timaeus* which he thinks "illuminates from another side and definitively[1] secures" his interpretation of the *Phaedrus* against my criticisms in the above review. This is the passage:

τὰ δὲ τρίγωνα πάντα ἐκ δυοῖν ἄρχεται τριγώνοιν . . . ταύτην δὴ πυρὸς ἀρχὴν καὶ τῶν ἄλλων σωμάτων ὑποτιθέμεθα κατὰ τὸν μετ' ἀνάγκης εἰκότα λόγον πορευόμενοι· τὰς δ' ἔτι τούτων ἀρχὰς ἄνωθεν θεὸς οἶδεν καὶ ἀνδρῶν ὃς ἂν ἐκείνῳ φίλος ᾖ. (53C8-D1, 4–7)

He makes several remarks about it, of which the following is crucial:

Die literarische Darstellung des Timaios wird dabei ausdrücklich pejorativ als εἰκὼς λόγος (μῦθος) bezeichnet und in ihrer Geltung gegenüber der weiterreichenden innerakademischen Lehre eingeschränkt. (152)

Now the quotation from Plato raises obscure and difficult questions on which much has already been written and much more remains to be said. To deal with it fully would be impracticable short of a special monograph evaluating critically the speculations in the scholarly literature concerning what Plato may have had in view in this cryptic reference to the derivation from higher principles of the primary triangles of his physical theory. Since I cannot undertake anything of the sort now, let me stay with the single question raised in K.'s gloss in the context of his claim that the quotation from the *Timaeus* provides "definitive confirmation" of K.'s interpretation of the *Phaedrus*—the interpretation I have explained and discussed in the above review. This question is so central that an affirmative answer to it would suffice to make good K.'s claim. This is the question: Does the Platonic text say or imply that this, or any other part, of the cosmological doctrine of the *Timaeus* is εἰκὼς λόγος (μῦθος) *because* it is expounded in written form? The answer is clearly No. That the text does not *say* so is obvious: no reference to "literarische Darstellung" here. That neither does it *imply* such a thing is perhaps not immediately obvious, but becomes clear enough when we stop to ask ourselves, Does Plato ever take it upon himself to explain *why* the whole of the physical theory of the *Timaeus* is εἰκὼς λόγος (μῦθος)? Of course he does. His explanation

[1] *endgültig.*

is given in one of the most important (and most familiar) passages of the dialogue:

> This is the determination we must make concerning an image and its model: statements are akin to the subject-matter they set forth; statements concerning that which is invariant and stable and perspicuous to intelligence will themselves be invariant and unshakable . . . ; while statements concerning that which is likened to that other [i.e., to the eternal model] and is only a likeness will be only likely and will stand in due proportion to statements of the former kind: as being is to process, so is truth to belief. (29B3-C3)

We ask Plato: "*Why* is the account you are now giving us εἰκὼς λόγος (μῦθος)?" And what does he say? Is it "because it has been written down"? No, there is not the remotest allusion to the fact that the form of exposition, fictionally an oral discourse by the ἀστρονομικότατος Timaeus, is in fact Plato's σύγγραμμα after all. The answer—the complete answer: no dangling threads in the formal disquisition which starts at 29B3 and continues in a mammoth period all the way to D3, or in any of its subsequent echoes thereafter—is: "Because the thing I am here discussing is process, a similitude of Being, and may *therefore* have (at best) only verisimilitude." From this explanation it would follow that if the same subject-matter had been presented orally—disclosed by word of mouth to an Academic huddle, instead of being *literarisch dargestellt* for all the world to read—it would still be cursed with verisimilitude; and, conversely, if the topic of discussion (oral *or* written) were "the eternal model," that discourse would not need to be so disabled: it would not *necessarily* miss being 'invariant and unshakeable" by virtue of its topic.[2] Thus anyone who refers us to the *Timaeus* to find there evidence that Plato believed that statements of exact philosophical truth must be withheld from his writings and disclosed only orally inside the Academy is wasting our time.

---

[2] At the risk of laboring the obvious, let me remind the reader that there are stretches of Platonic text—e.g., the whole discussion of the mingling of the Forms in the *Sph.*—which deal exclusively with this kind of subject-matter; and that accounts of the world of becoming are the exception, not the rule, in the Platonic corpus. So far then from literary exposition being the *explanation* of the verisimilitude which Plato imputes to the physical doctrine of the *Timaeus*, even the claim that Plato assumes a *de facto correlation* between literary exposition and verisimilitude in the expounded doctrine would be most implausible: there are plenty of statements in the *Timaeus* itself (not to speak of other dialogues) whose topic is Being, of which no one—presumably not even K.—would claim that *they* are fraught with verisimilitude.

Now it could be said on K.'s behalf that in the passage I have quoted from his paper he has not really claimed that "die literarische Darstellung des Timaios wird dabei ausdrücklich pejorativ als εἰκὼς λόγος (μῦθος) bezeichnet" *because* it is *literarisch*, not *mündlich*, "dargestellt." Have I then been beating a straw man? Not at all. For as I have explained above, the whole point of adducing the above quotation from *Ti.* 53 was to show that it "illuminates" and "secures" K.'s interpretation of the doctrine of the *Phaedrus* on the difference between oral and written discourse. To bring this fact into the open I chose to make explicit the connection which is being implicitly made in the course of K.'s argument. For if in glossing the Platonic passage K. were only giving us the conjunction

(1) *Ti.* 53C-D is (a) *literarische Darstellung and* (b) its doctrine is *ausdrücklich pejorativ gezeichnet als* εἰκὼς λόγος (μῦθος),

he would be only reporting an obvious fact with which everyone could agree, regardless of whether one were an obsessive esotericist or a fanatical anti-esotericist, and he would thus have done nothing to advance the esotericist thesis: (1) would have been simply *irrelevant* for K.'s argument. It gains relevance only if we read K.'s gloss on the Platonic text not, as in the case of (1), as a collocation of logically unrelated propositions, but as a suggestion that (b) is the case *because* of (a), i.e., as claiming

(2) It is *because Ti.* 53C-D is (a) *literarische Darstellung* that (b) its doctrine is *bezeichnet als* εἰκὼς λόγος (μῦθος).

It is, therefore, perfectly proper to direct criticism, as I have done above, to (2), instead of (1), even though K.'s own statement, cited above, comes much closer to (1) than to (2) and may, with perfect truth, be described as neither saying nor implying (2).

I cannot forbear going one step farther at this juncture to point out to K. how much better off he would have been if he had done himself the thing I was compelled to do for him in order to salvage a coherent (though false) argument from his script. Suppose *he* had substituted "(b) *because of* (a)," which is what his argument requires, for the approximation to "(a) *and* (b)" which he chose to write. Since he knows as well as any of us (and much better than most) the text of the *Timaeus*, he would have seen at once the vast discrepancy between

(2) (b) because of (a),

and

(3) (b) because of (c),

where "(c)" stands for "it is an account of a likeness of Being, not of Being itself," and recognized that while (3) is affirmed in the most explicit and emphatic way in the dialogue, there is no trace of (2) there. In that case, he would have freed his exposition from an item whose relevance to his argument depends on its being taken to say what it does not say and could not have said without evident falsehood to Plato's text.

18

A Note on "Pauline Predications" in Plato*

(1974; NPP)

FOR Plato, as for us,

    (1) Fire is hot,

    (2) Snow is cold,

are impeccable sentences, well-formed and true. Admittedly, he does not assert either of them in so many words. But he distinctly implies (2) when he remarks:

οὐδέποτε χιόνα γ' οὖσαν δεξαμένην τὸ θερμόν . . . ἔτι ἔσεσθαι ὅπερ ἦν, χιόνα καὶ θερμόν (*Phaedo* 103D).

For to say this is to imply that

    (3) Snow is hot

is always false:[1] there could never have been an occasion on which snow would be hot; hence (2) would be bound to be always true. Now in the Platonic ontology the nouns, "fire," "snow" and the adjectives, "hot," "cold," get their meaning by referring to their respective Forms. Some scholars have doubted or denied that things like Fire and Snow have a place in the authorized gallery of Platonic Forms. But in the passage on "the clever *aitia*" in the *Phaedo* Plato treats Fire, Snow, Fever as εἴδη on a par with ultra-respectable Forms, like Odd and Even; and this is sufficient for my present purpose.[2]

    Proceeding on this assumption, I ask: How would Plato want us to un-

---

* Reprinted with corrections and deletions from *Phronesis* 19 (1974), 95-101. I acknowledge with thanks the journal's permission to reprint this essay.

  [1] The ἐναντία of this passage are contradictories: *hot* is to *cold*, as *odd* is to *even*.

  [2] Cf. *RC*, 76ff. above.

derstand the "is" in (1), (2), and (3)? Is he using the copula in the same way it is most commonly used in Greek (as in English) subject-predicate sentences, *sc.* to indicate that the individual named by the subject-term is a member of the class of those possessing the attribute expressed by the predicate-term? This use of "is" may be conveniently indicated, after Peano, by the letter *epsilon* (for "ἐστι"), writing "Socrates ε wise," for "Socrates is wise." It is beyond dispute that there are many true assertions about Forms in Plato's ontology that may be expressed by using "is" in just this way. For example:

Justice ε incorporeal   Justice ε intelligible
Justice ε invisible   Justice ε eternal

So when I confront sentences (1), (2), and (3) above, my question is whether or not in each of them the copula is being also used in the same way. Thus, in the case of (1), I want to know if Plato meant to assert

(1a) Fire ε hot.

Had he done so he would have propounded a piece of egregious nonsense: Heat is a property which only corporeal things could have. If we took (1a) to be what Plato meant in (1) we would be supposing that he wants to say in all seriousness that one of his incorporeal Forms has a corporeal property.

A parallel, if less blatant, absurdity would turn up if we chose our examples from the *Protagoras*. When Plato there (331B2) asserts

(4) Justice is pious,[3]

would we want to understand him to be implying

(4a) Justice ε pious?

To do so would be to suppose that Plato would want an abstract Form to have a property which only concrete individuals—persons—and, by legitimate extension, their actions, dispositions, institutions, laws, etc., could possibly have. So to apply that predicate to the abstract term "Piety" would be as absurd a move as to apply it to a number or to the multiplication sign. Moreover, consider the case of

(5) Injustice is impious

which, though not asserted in the same context in the *Protagoras*, is clearly implied. Would anyone want to say that some Socratic εἴδη are impious, cowardly, greedy, lascivious, unwise? Accordingly I infer that if (4a) were what Plato meant by (4), he would be asserting an absurdity—a more innocent-sounding one, to be sure, than that in (1a), but an absurdity nonetheless. Is this, then, what really happened?

That it *could* have happened cannot be ruled out *a priori*: Plato has no magic talisman to guarantee him immunity to aberration. So all we can reasonably

---

[3] Cf. *UVP*, pp. 252ff. above.

say in such a case is this: If we are to admit that he did make so gross an error, we must have the clearest, strongest, possible evidence to compel the admission. Is there such evidence? When I wrote my first paper on the Third Man (1954),[4] I had not faced this particular question, for it had simply not occurred to me then that sentences like (1), (2), (3), and (4) could be thought susceptible of this interpretation. However, I had faced a closely related question—the one arising over a sentence like

(6) Justice is just,

which wears its semantic perplexity on its face, since the natural interpretation of a sentence is the "self-predicative" reading,[5]

(6a) Justice ε just.

At that time (6a) seemed to me not only the most natural interpretation of (6), but the inevitable one—the only one left open by the Greek (or English) language, once we exclude the use of "is" to mean identity which I felt certain then, and still do now, could not be what Plato means.[6] The thing that simply did not occur to me at the time is that, once identity was excluded, there would still be another way of reading "is," a very natural one, which would by-pass with perfect safety the absurdity of (6a). Nor had this alternative reading occurred at that time to anyone else who had noticed in print the oddity of "Justice is just" and "Piety is pious": de Laguna (1934),[7] Richard Robinson (1942),[8] Hackforth (1945),[9] Ross (1958)[10] were to all appearances as confident as was I that the mere fact that Plato wrote (6) proved that (6a) was what he meant.

For me that confidence was shattered when I suddenly noticed in 1965[11] that the immediate textual environment of those two sentences contained two

---

[4] *Phil. Rev.* 63, 319ff.

[5] I have consistently used this term *only* in the way which is explained above, 258, n. 97.

[6] No one would want to assert the English sentence "Justice is just" if what he wants to assert is "Justice is Justice." Greek idiom is more flexible, but not to the point of licensing a good stylist to write e.g. η δικαιοσύνη αὐτὸ τοῦτο δίκαιόν ἐστιν (*Prt.* 330 C4-5) for anything but "Justice, that thing itself, is just": if we were to substitute "Justice" for "just" in our translation we would get outright mistranslation. For a non-linguistic argument against the identity-reading of the copula in Platonic sentences like "Justice is just" see above 263, n. 111.

[7] "Notes on the Theory of Ideas," *Phil. Rev.* 43, 450ff.

[8] "Plato's *Parmenides*," *Class. Philology* 37, 51ff.

[9] *Plato's Examination of Pleasure* (Cambridge), 22, n. 1.

[10] *Plato's Theory of Ideas* (Oxford, 1951), 88.

[11] When reading a paper by Professor Sandra Peterson (then a graduate student at Princeton) which she presented to my seminar in the late fall of 1965. A further debt to that paper is acknowledged in note 14, below.

others, with the same grammatical form—"Justice is pious" and "Piety is just"—whose copula no one would have the slightest inclination to read as an *epsilon*. In the case of *these* sentences the copula was evidently not meant to assign the predicate to the εἶδος named by the subject-term, but to unnamed instances of that εἶδος; thus it is evident that when Plato asserted (4) in the *Protagoras* what he meant was not the absurdity in (4a), but the radically different proposition which makes eminently good syntactical sense and which we know to be true-blue Socratic doctrine,[12] *sc.*

(4b) Justice is such that anyone who has this property is [necessarily][13] pious.

I speak of this way of reading (4) as a "Pauline predication,"[14] using this phrase as a quasi-mnemonic device. Its point is only to recall a venerable paradigm of such use of sentences whose grammatical form is identical with that of (4):

(7) Charity is kind

Consider also the following sentences:

(8) Love is blind

(9) Justice is impartial

(10) Honesty is rare

(11) Gold is yellow

(1) Fire is hot

(2) Snow is cold

Each of these sentences *may* be read along the lines of (4b)—e.g. (7) to mean that charity is such that anyone who has this virtue is a kind person, (11) to mean that any golden thing is yellow. And a Platonist *must* so read them: he has no other option; what is permissible for the rest of us is absolutely mandatory in his case, for *his* ontology denies him, on pain of absurdity, to read the copula of those sentences as a Peano *epsilon*. Thus in the case of (11) if, using "gold" as an honest-to-goodness "mass term,"[15] we (materialists, or empiricists, or ontological eclectics or agnostics) were to think of it as only a name for all the gold scattered throughout the physical universe, we would have perfect license to insist that what we mean by (11) is precisely

(11a) Gold ε yellow:

---

[12] I.e. the biconditionality of the virtues (*Prt.* 329E4) for which Socrates is arguing in this context.

[13] Why this modality is required for the Platonic interpretation of (4) is explained above, 232-33.

[14] See *UVP* 254, n. 88, above, and the starred note to that note, below.

[15] Cf. W. V. Quine, *Word and Object* (New York, 1960), 91ff.; T. G. Rosenmeyer, "Plato and Mass Words," *Trans. Amer. Philological Association* 88 (1958), 88ff. at 92ff.

for certainly that stuff out there in the world *is* yellow. But once we have abjured ontological promiscuity and taken Platonic vows, our doctrinal commitment to the notion that "gold" names Gold—an incorporeal eternal object—rules out that reading absolutely; what it requires of us is the alternative reading

> (11b) Gold is (a Form) such that any (material) instance of it is [necessarily] yellow.

Isn't that line of interpretation the one St. Paul would obviously have taken if *he* had been a Platonist? What else could he then have meant by (7) except

> (7b) Charity is such that anyone who is charitable is [necessarily] kind?

Thus to speak of (1), (2), (3), (4) as "Pauline predications" is just a way of nudging the reader to make him think of that great Pauline text which everyone *could* read, with perfect license from the language (English or Greek), to mean (7b), and which a Platonist, straitjacketted in his ontology, could *only* read in that way to keep his sanity.

Once it occurred to me that (4b), not (4a), was the right reading of (4) in Plato, it became no less evident that the right reading of (6) should be not (6a) but

> (6b) Justice is such that anyone who has this property is [necessarily] just.

in which case (6), so far from being absurdly false, is analytically true. To say this became "evident" to me is, of course, only to say that the idea carried high subjective conviction. The claim of objective validity for it could only be won by treating the intuition as a hypothesis to be tested against the relevant evidence and recommended to others only on the strength of results so obtained. This is what I have offered in *UVP* above.

The explanation of my use of this term has, I trust, disarmed any suggestion that when I read certain sentences in Plato as "Pauline predications" I understand them *only* as assertions about the instance-classes of εἴδη, involving no assertions about those εἴδη themselves. This is the last thing I would want to say; a careful reading of my text will show, I trust, that I never said or implied such a thing. However, I might well have spelled out more fully that disclaimer and emphasized it more strongly. I make it all too briefly in 274, n. 13 above, in a gloss on the two formulae I use in defining the Pauline reading of the sentence-form, "*B* is *A*" (where the substituends for "*B*" and "*A*" are Form-naming words), by means of formulae

> (II) Necessarily, for all *x*, if *x* is a *B*, then *x* is an *A*

or, equivalently,

> (IIa) Necessarily, the instance-class of *B* is included in the instance-class
>   of *A*.

I point out in that note that in both formulae

> Strictly speaking, the definiens . . . is a contraction. In each . . . the
> definiens, fully spelled out, would start off, "The relation of *B* to *A* is
> such that . . ."

This remark, to which I allude again (320 above) in the Appendix to *AS*
should make it clear that, for example, "Fire is hot," when asserted by Plato,
would indeed be meant as an assertion about the Forms, Fire, Heat, not just
about their mundane instances: it is meant to tell us that the Form, Fire, has
eternally a definite relation to the Form, Heat, though the relation can only
be specified *via* the relation of their instance-classes.[16] For all its transcendentalism, Plato's metaphysics can only fix the interrelations of a multitude
of celestial Forms by charting those of their earthly shadows. If there is irony
in this fact—the interrelations of these Forms begin to look like shadows of
their shadows—the irony is generated by Plato's metaphysics, not by the
Pauline reading of a class of Plato's sentences.

[16] Hence the use of spatial metaphors like "containing" and "embracing" to express
the inter-Form relation signified by Pauline predication (cf. above 298, n. 65; 299,
n. 70; 304, n. 85; 321-22 and n. 10).

19

What did Socrates Understand by His "What is F?" Question?[1]

(1976; SQ)

IN a vigorous and influential paper (1973) Professor Terry Penner argues for a new answer to this question.[2] He honours me by naming me an adherent of the old answer. This I continue to be, for nothing in his paper persuades me to change sides.

This is what Penner thinks Socrates wanted to know when asking "What is courage?" in the *Laches*:

> . . . that question is not a request for the meaning of a word or a request for an essence or a universal . . . , but rather a request for a psychological account (explanation) of what it is in men's psyches that makes them brave. For the "What is X?" question is often put [by Socrates] as "What is that single thing by virtue of which (with or by which) the many *F* things are *F*?"; and I will be arguing that that too is a causal

---

[1] This brief note, composed in 1976, has circulated among friends, eliciting helpful comments from several of them, particularly from Myles Burnyeat. I present it with minor revisions, as a companion piece to the next essay ("Socrates on 'The Parts of Virtue' ") and to the starred notes to *UVP*.

[2] And for much else in his splendidly imaginative and far-ranging paper, raising the fundamental issues which I address further in the companion essay and starred notes and shall address further in the work on the philosophy of S. on which I am now engaged. In the meantime I must thank Penner for the exceedingly generous terms in which he refers to views of mine expressed in earlier work (going back to the fifties and early sixties, anteceding the new developments in my thinking on S. set forth in *UVP*, which had not yet come into the public domain when Penner's paper was composed).

or explanatory question rather than an epistemological or semantical one (56-57).

This is a fair statement of what is in controversy. Though complex and far-reaching issues are involved, I content myself in this brief note with arguing for just two things which, if true, should suffice to vindicate the old answer:

(1) Against Penner I argue that S.'s examples show that what Penner calls the "semantical"[3] answer *is* the one S. wants, though I would prefer to call it the "constitutive" answer: in asking, "What is Courage?" what S. wants to know is what *constitutes* Courage.[4]

(2) In agreement with Penner, I recognize S.'s overwhelmingly practical interest in the question. But I maintain this does not prove, or even support, Penner's thesis. For S. comes to that question with a conception of the dynamics

---

[3] In adopting this term from Penner for the purposes of this note, I wish to emphasize (as no doubt he would too) that S.'s search for the meaning of words he investigates is anything but a lexicographical inquiry into contemporary Greek usage. It involves an analysis of the concepts named by those words—an analysis which may lead (and, in the case of the names of basic moral concepts, does lead) to a radical revision of the meaning which attaches to those words in unreflective current usage. It is worth noting that when this does happen the radical revision of the meaning of the word is derived by a purely dialectical exercise, at times by even less, as in the case of the inquiry into the meaning of "courage" in the *Laches*: To correct the misconception of this virtue Laches reveals in saying that the brave man is he who

keeping his place in the ranks, fights the enemy, and does not run away (190E),

all S. has to do is to parade a line of counter-examples:

those who are brave in facing perils at sea, in illness, in poverty, in politics, and also those who are brave not only in the face of pain or terror but who are also tough in fighting desire and pleasure, standing their ground or turning against the enemy (191D-E).

These examples so stretch the application of the word as to break the traditional moral dogma that had kept courage a class-bound, sex-bound, virtue. All this is accomplished not (as Penner's thesis would require) by engaging in a causal investigation of the way persons behave under stress, but simply by appealing to the interlocutor's linguistic intuitions, counting on his ability to recognize instantly new cases of courage as they are brought into his ken.

[4] It should be noted that the constitutive answer may have genuine explanatory power even when it is clearly non-causal. S.'s answer to "What is Courage?" most certainly purports to explain why we should assign this noble quality to, say, a slave, if he meets danger with "knowledge of what is and is not to be feared," while denying it to an intrepid knight upon discovering that his disregard of danger, ungrounded in Socratic knowledge of good and evil, is mere rashness. I would, therefore, object to Penner's coupling of "explanatory" with "causal" in sharp contrast to the "semantical." As my discussion will show the latter too is, and is meant to be, explanatory.

of motivation which requires only the constitutive answer to complete his explanation of "what it is in men's psyches that makes them brave."

Most of this note I shall devote to (1). The Socratic model of rational action is so simple that a long-winded answer to (2) is not necessary for my present purpose.

I.

Answers to "What is virtue?" are faulted in the *Meno* for citing various kinds of virtue (manly, womanly, and so forth [71E]) or listing particular virtues (justice, temperance, and so forth [74A]), failing to spot that "single identical character they all possess which makes them virtues [or, 'because of which they are virtues,' δι' ὃ εἰσὶν ἀρεταί, 72C]." For an example of what is needed S. directs Meno to "What is figure?" and offers two specimens of what it would take to meet head-on the "What is *F*?" question in that case: "the only thing which always accompanies color" (75B); "the limit of a solid" (76A). Both are model answers because each purports to give a formula which covers all possible kinds of figures, stating "what is the same in all" (75A). Each shows clearly that the single thing "by virtue of which" differently shaped things have figure is simply what constitutes the property, figure—not what causes things to have this property.

Penner ignores this example, presumably because of his view (43) that the *Meno* is a "transitional" dialogue and that its doctrines are not those of Socrates, but of "Socrates-Plato." That there are doctrines in the *Meno* which are foreign to the Socrates of the earlier dialogues—that knowledge is "recollection" and that true opinion *sans* knowledge may suffice as a guide to right action—is well known. But the "What is *F*?" question is logically independent of either of these doctrines, and it is structurally insulated from both of them in the composition of the dialogue: it is pursued solely in the first third of the work which does not contain a single sentence uncharacteristic of the Socrates of the earlier dialogues. Why then should we suppose that the "What is *F*?" question has changed so drastically that while it was causal in earlier dialogues, it has become strictly non-causal in the *Meno*? Penner gives no reason, and I know of none; in a longer discussion I would argue that there *is* none. But there is no need to rest my whole case on the *Meno*. The same result can be derived from other dialogues.

When Laches misses the point of Socrates' question, this is how he is put back on the right track:

> What I mean is like this (ὧδε λέγω): as if in the case of quickness [I were asking] what on earth is it that is [quickness] in running and in playing the lyre and in talking and in learning and in many other things—what is the same in nearly every [quick] action worth men-

tioning: of the arms and the legs and the mouth and the voice or the mind. Isn't that what you too would mean?—Of course.—So if someone were to ask me, "Socrates, what is that which you call 'quickness' in all of them?" I would say, it is the *dynamis* of going through much in little time (τὴν ἐν ὀλίγῳ χρόνῳ διαπραττομένην δύναμιν) whether in speech or in running or in all other cases (192A-B).

Penner reckons with this example, and thinks it fits his interpretation because, he says, quickness "is explicitly said to be a *dynamis*, a power" (40, n. 8 sub fin). His comma after *dynamis* begs a question. That quickness is said to be a *dynamis* *is* explicit; that it is said to be a power is *not*; that it is meant to be such is almost certainly false. For while *dynamis* can mean "power"—that is, of course, its primary and most frequent use—it need not. The word lends itself to a variety of extended uses, in some of which "power" is no more than a dead metaphor. So, for example, when it refers to the meaning of a word: both the verb, *dynamai*, and the noun, *dynamis*, are regularly used for this purpose in Attic Greek (including, notably, Plato's), as a glance at the dictionaries will show. In this use the causal connotation is, at most, dubious. And there is another use of *dynamis* for which not even a vestige of causal reference could be claimed. This is its use as a perfectly general term for "quality" before the special word for that purpose, *poiotēs*, had gained currency—a word which is still so unfamiliar decades after the composition of the *Laches* that when Plato uses it in the *Theaetetus*, he does so hesitantly and self-deprecatingly, apologizing for its "oddness"—ἀλλόκοτον ὄνομα, he calls it (182A). When *dynamis* is used in this way it can be abstractly non-causal. This is certain, since the word can be used to designate a purely logical property. It is so used in the *Charmides*: "And do we not say that *the greater* has this sort of *dynamis*, namely, of being [greater] in relation to something?" (168B), i.e. *greater* is a relational property and, as Socrates goes on to make clear, a special sort of relational property which has been called "aliorelative" or "nonreflexive" in modern times: where *A* is greater than *B*, then *A* ≠ *B*; or, as Socrates puts it, *A* cannot "have its own *dynamis* in relation to itself" (168E5).

This being the case, that S. should call quickness a *dynamis* does not entail that he thinks of it as a power. To be sure, neither does it entail that he does not so think of it: the context must decide. We learn something from it which tells strongly against the former option when we notice that this *dynamis* is self-identical in every variety of quick action. If Socrates had called quickness a *dynamis* because he thought of it as the power which causes a given action to be quick, he would be making the extraordinary assumption that the cause of everything done quickly by anyone anywhere is *the same*,[5] e.g. that the very

---

[5] The *F* in the 'What is *F*?' question is "that which is *the same in all*" the cases

same thing which caused a man to run quickly would also cause him to learn and to think quickly. Is it at all plausible that Socrates would be tempted to entertain such a fantastic notion which would fly in the face of the most common experience—say, that of a superlatively fast runner who is a hopeless learner and a sluggish thinker? It would be gratuitous, to say the least, to hold that Socrates is pegging his question on a premise of which there is no hint in the text and which is never mooted in Greek physical speculation even in its wildest vagaries.[6]

Conversely, there is no difficulty in making sense of his question if its import were constitutive or semantical. This is clear from the answer he gives it in the above quotation. Quaint though it may seem to the modern reader, "going through much in little time" is not a bad shot at what constitutes "quickness": it would fit nicely all contexts in which a Greek speaker would use the word to designate the property of actions he wants to mark off as "quick" from a contrasting class he reckons "slow." It would explain the

---

which are rightly classified as *F*: "Try to say once again: being what, is it *the same in all* of them?" (*La*. 191E10-11; cf. *Eu*. 5D1-5; *M*. 72C2-3, 75A4-5 and 7-8, 75E2.)

[6] It has been suggested to me that good sense could still be made of the idea that S. thought of quickness as a power which enables those who have it to do things quickly, by supposing that he would think of it as a power of a higher order of generality—"quickness(H)", let us call it—which could be exercised in some actions but not in others, depending on what additional conditions are satisfied. This power could be imputed to a person who does some things quickly without entailing that he would do all things quickly. Thus, both A who runs fast and thinks slowly, and B who runs slowly and thinks fast, would have quickness(H). The suggestion would have embarrassing consequences: since for S. quickness and slowness are logically on a par, then, by the same token, S. would also postulate the power of slowness(H) to "explain" the slowness of A's thinking and B's running. I put "explain" in quotes to indicate the objection to this interpretive epicycle. Does it not become evident at this point that any explanatory value ascribed to this causal hypothesis would be bogus? The question is not addressed to S., for there is no suggestion in the text that he harbored such a postulational mythology.

Burnyeat (1971, 225-26) who, to my knowledge, was the first to sponsor a causal interpretation of the Socratic principle that what is done *F*-ly is done "because of" the *F* ("the abstract noun [or substantivized adjective] identifies the attribute which makes the agent perform the kind of action to which the adverb applies" [226]), is well aware of its difficulty when so understood, and proceeds to amend the Socratic principle accordingly ("the principle should read, 'Whatever is done in the same way is done by the same *kind* of thing," [228]), conceding that "in this amended form [the principle] no longer has the powers [which, on the suggested interpretation] S. claimed for it" (*loc. cit.*). The advantage of the non-causal interpretation is that in its unamended form the Socratic principle has exactly the truth which S. thought it obviously had— so obviously that he consistently presented it as self-evident, calling for no argumentative support whatever.

meaning of the word to one who did not have any inkling of what it is that causes the Olympic victor to run faster and Theaetetus to think faster than do others, and who never dreamed of assuming that the cause, whatever it be, is the same, but had no difficulty in classifying the one as a quick runner, the other as a quick thinker.

The same reading of the "What is quickness?" question would also give a sensible interpretation of S.'s saying in another context that quick actions are done "with" quickness—a context which has suggested to at least one (excellent) translator that S. is thinking of quickness as their cause. This is how Guthrie[7] translates *Prt.* 332B6-C2:

> If something is done with strength, it is done strongly, and if with weakness weakly, if with speed quickly, and if with slowness slowly?
> . . . What is done in the same manner is done by the same agency, and if contrariwise by the contrary?

If S. had really thought of strength, weakness, quickness, and slowness as the "agencies" which Penner's thesis requires, and Guthrie's translation declares them to be, this passage would be a museum piece of that fatuous error which derives a cause for an event by reifying the event's description. S. would be setting up "quickness" as the causal explanation of quick actions—an explanation which explains nothing, since the description of the explanandum, transposed from adverb to abstract noun, constitutes the sole specification of the explanans. Could S. have been so bemused? We cannot exclude the possibility *a priori*. But we would need strong, unambiguous evidence to convict him of such confusion.

Nothing answering to this description has been produced to date, while, conversely, we do have unambiguous evidence to the contrary: S.'s offer of the definition of Figure in the *Meno* as a model for the answer to "What is that because of which all virtues are virtues?" admits of no other construction: that Figure might be something which causes things to be figured is so manifest an absurdity that no one could impute it to S. The same would be true in yet another case, this one from the *Hippias Major*:[8]

---

[7] W.K.C. Guthrie, *Plato: Protagoras and Meno* (Baltimore, 1956, 63). But in his *History of Greek Philosophy*, Vol. 4 (Cambridge, 1975) he rightly observes of the instrumental dative (in the case of the form of Piety as that "by which" all pious acts are pious, *Euthyphro* 6D) that "it means no more than . . . that its presence in the instances gives the objective justification for calling them pious" (118-19); and in a footnote he alludes to *Prt.* 332B-C as a parallel passage. Did he forget how he had translated it twenty years earlier? Or did he change his mind?

[8] I do not know what Penner's chronology does with this dialogue. He does not name it among those he attributes to "Socrates-Plato."

For that which we were seeking was that because of which all beautiful things are beautiful—like that because of which all big things are big, namely, the exceeding: for all big things are big because of that: even if they don't seem big, yet, if they do exceed, then of necessity they are big (294A8-B4).

One would like to believe that it would be agreed without argument that S. could not have made the mistake of regarding the Beauty of an object as that which causes the object to be beautiful. But just in case a doubt of that might cross our mind,[9] we can settle it by noting his wish that the answer to 'What is it that makes things beautiful?' should be modelled on the answer to 'What is it that makes them big?' His definiens of "the big"—"the exceeding" (i.e. having dimensions which exceed those of the things with which it is being compared)—shows unambiguously enough that "the F because of which all F things are F" is simply the property F, *not* something which causes things to have that property, and that the "because" *is* semantical: the way in which an ant's "exceeding" (the dimensions of) other ants 'makes' it a *big* ant could only be the way in which a closed rectilinear figure's three-sidedness 'makes' it triangular. And the desired answer to the question is no less explanatory for all that. It takes the paradox out of the fact that we, in all seriousness, reckon that ant a *big* ant, even though it doesn't "seem big": small though it may seem by comparison with, say, a baby elephant, yet, since it satisfies the definiens, "of necessity" it *is* big.

II.

Why should a man whose supreme goal in life is to propagate virtue be so eager to discover what a word like "courage" means? To this we might well retort: "Why shouldn't he?" Few words are so highly charged with emotive force. If we have the wrong idea of what it means to be brave or cowardly, we shall honor and scorn the wrong things; our valuations will foster conduct which is valueless or worse. Plain common sense would take anyone as far as this. S.'s doctrine of "the power of knowledge"[10]—the impossibility of acrasia—takes him vastly further. The backbone of this doctrine is the belief that all men desire the good and desire nothing else, except as a means to the good or as a part of it.[11] To get S.'s explanation of "what it is in men's psyches

[9] It should on Penner's thesis, since the case of things being beautiful because of Beauty is treated as strictly parallel to that of men being just because of Justice and wise because of Wisdom (*Hp Maj.* 275C).

[10] *Prt.* 352Aff.

[11] *Grg.* 469B-C et passim; *Meno* 77C-78A.

that makes them brave" conjoin this belief with the approved answer to "What is Courage?"—"knowledge of what is, and is not, to be feared,"[12] where "to be feared" in any given situation is always and only the option which offers the agent the lesser good. It will follow from the latter that the courageous course of action is the very one which yields more of good, less of evil, than would any cowardly alternative. It will follow from the former that one who knows this course will be bound to desire it more than he would desire any alternative to it, and will, therefore, be bound to take it.

If S. were offering only his definition of "Courage" and were leaving the matter at that, he would not be disclosing what it is, in his view, that "makes men brave"—"makes" them in the full-bodied, causal, sense. In this Penner is perfectly right, and his stress on it is a valuable contribution. What he fails to notice in his paper is how this definition hooks up with S.'s conception of the dynamics of motivation *thereby* acquiring causal significance. Without this hook-up we would be left wondering why the acquisition of knowledge of what is, and is not, to be feared should be expected to bring about not only intellectual enlightenment but invincible moral strength under stress. With it—with S.'s reliance on desire for good as a never failing dynamo in the psyche—we can understand why he should think that the true understanding of what "Courage" means is also the way to the true explanation of what makes men brave.

[12] *Prt.* 360D; *La.* 194S-195A.

20

SOCRATES ON "THE PARTS OF VIRTUE"

(1980; SPV)

IN *UVP* (225) I observe that this is "standard Socratic doctrine," assuming that this would be generally agreed. The publications of Penner, Taylor, and Irwin (see Preface and the starred note to *UVP* 221) have disabused me of this illusion. I must, therefore, support my claim in detail. I welcome the task.

I begin with the *Meno.* In my cursory reference to this dialogue in *UVP* (227, n. 8), restricted to 78D-79E, I meant only to remind the reader of the presence of this doctrine in the dialogue; so I cited only the passage where its previous exposition, made without benefit of the "parts"/"whole" terminology, is resumed under this nomenclature. Let me now go back to the point, much earlier in the dialogue, where S.'s conception of the relation of the generic term, "virtue," to each of the particular virtues is introduced. This comes at the very start of the dialogue's first elenchus. S. asks, "What do you say that virtue is?" (71D5) and Meno responds by naming several kinds of virtue (manly, womanly, and so forth). S. faults the reply (72A6ff.) *via* the bee/virtue analogy: to answer the question "What is bee?" it is no use referring to "many bees of all sorts" (πολλὰς καὶ παντοδαπάς); one must pick out that single "essence" in respect of which bees differing "in beauty, in size, or anything else of that sort" (72B5-6) "do not differ at all but are all the same" (72C2-3). S. is already implying that virtues do differ in various ways and are "the same" only in respect of "that single form [or, character: *eidos*] they all possess by virtue of which they are all virtues" (72C7-6). But the analogy is loose (it is only a "picture" [72A8]); it slurs over the fact that bees are individuals which may belong to varieties of bee while the virtues *are* varieties of virtue.

To explain the relation more precisely S. moves to a more exact analogy: "justice" is to "virtue" as is "the round" to "figure" and "white" to "color." To reinforce the distinction S. invokes the contrast between "*an F*" and "*the F*" ("*a* virtue" [ἀρετή τις, 73E1], "*a* figure" [74B8], "*a* color" [74C7] as *vs*. "virtue," "figure," "color"). And he brings out the semantic import of this syntactic contrast. He observes that by referring to a given character as "*an*" F we imply that it is not the only F—that there are other Fs besides it:

> about the round I would say that it is *a* figure, not simply figure. I would speak thus for this reason: there are other figures as well (73E3-6).

And he explains that in applying "*F*" as a (generic) "name" to each of the characters that fall under it *we are not identifying the* F *with any of them*:

> since you denominate (προσαγορεύεις)[1] these many [characters] by a single name (ἑνί τινι ὀνόματι), and you are not saying that any of them *is* [i.e. is identical with] figure, these being even[2] opposite to one another, tell me, what is that which covers (κατέχει)[3] the round no less than the straight—that [thing] which you name[4] "figure" and

---

[1] As προσαγορεύω is being used here the force of the prefix is alive: referring to something *as* "an" F, one gives it a name "in addition to" (προσ-) its own, as in τὸν Ἀγαμέμνονα προσαγορεύεις ποιμένα λαῶν, Xen. *Mem.* 3,2,1; τοὺς φιλοσόφους τοιούτους (θείους) προσαγορεύω, Plato, *Sph.* 216C1 (These examples and others in *LSJ s.v.*, 3). And cf. n. 3 below *sub fin.* The prefix does not always have this force; προσαγορεύω may be used as a simple variant for καλῶ, as in *Gorg.* 474E, *Crat.* 397D, *Prt.* 355B.

[2] S. says καὶ ἐναντία for emphasis: he is referring to the case of "opposites," where the distinctness of the Fs is especially striking, and is not implying that distinctness as such is conditioned on "oppositeness": cf. Plato's explanation in *Philb.* 12E of how figures may differ from figure: "generically (γένει) all figure is one, but of its parts (μέρη) some are absolutely opposite (ἐναντιώτατα), while others have very many differences [without being 'opposites']. . . ."

[3] For this sense of κατέχει (translated "embraces" by Guthrie, "contient" by Robin) see *LSJ s.v.*, sense II.4, *to be spread over, cover*. For the same relation in the case of characters attributed to contraries Plato in the *Sph.* uses περὶ . . . γίγνεσθαι (255A11), περιέχειν (250B8): cf. above *AS*, 297 and n. 60. In *Sph.* 250B10 the speech-act is προσλέγειν where the force of the prefix is even stronger than in προσαγορεύειν, which is used in the *Sph.* with the same nuance as in *Meno* 74D5 (cf. n. 1 above): πολλοῖς ὀνόμασι ταὐτὸν τοῦτο ἑκάστοτε προσαγορεύομεν, 251A5-6.

[4] Here "name" has its basic sense of proper name—"the original, and always the primary, use of ὄνομα," as I remark in *UVP* 238. Cf. Plato's reference to "Three"

say that the round is no more [a] figure than is the straight . . . (74D5-E2).

Only after this ground has been thoroughly covered is the "parts"/"whole" vocabulary brought in (at 78Dff.) to name the relation of the virtues to virtue, i.e. after it has been made fully clear that in S.'s view the fact that the name "virtue" applies to all the virtues no more confounds their distinctness from virtue and from each other than the distinctness of roundness from straightness is impugned by the fact that each is [a] figure.

What would the sponsors of the PTI view (see p. 427) have us do with this long passage in the *Meno* which makes it so clear that for S. all the virtues can no more be the same virtue than all figures the same figure and all colors the same color?

Penner ignores the question. Why he feels licensed to do so he does not say. I surmise that, if pressed, he would refer us to his view (43) that the *Meno*, along with the *Euthyphro* and the *Euthydemus*, expounds the views not of Socrates, but of "Socrates-Plato." But the "parts of virtue" doctrine is expounded in the first third of the work, which does not allude in any way to the new theses that learning is "recollecting" and that true opinion suffices for right action; it reads throughout like a true Socratic dialogue of search. Why should we suppose that this doctrine which forms the framework of the search is unSocratic? Moreover, in another essay ("Socrates on Virtue and Motivation," *Phronesis*, Suppl. Vol., 1973) Penner does not hesitate to use this same section of the *Meno* on a par with the *Gorgias* (see the reference to *Meno* 77B-78D in conjunction with *Grg.* 466A-468D at p. 142) as a source for Socratic doctrine in the case of S.'s thesis that no one desires evil. He does so presumably because the expression of this thesis in the *Meno* is closely paralleled by its expression in the *Gorgias*. But the use of "parts" in the *Meno* for the divisions of a generic concept is also paralleled in the *Gorgias*: in 463Aff., rhetoric, cookery, etc. are "parts" of "flattery," while gymnastics and medicine are "parts" of the art of body-care, and justice and legislation are "parts" of the art of soul-care. Why should this use of "parts," pucka Socratic in the *Gorgias*, be unSocratic in the *Meno*? Similar use of "part" is made also in the *Hippias Major* (299B): Pleasure derived through eyes and ears is that "part" of pleasure which purports to define "beauty." (I do not mention now the same use of "parts" in the *Euthyphro*, the *Protagoras*, and the *Laches*, because for one reason or another Penner would disallow them; but in my view all three would be highly relevant: for the *Euthyphro* see *UVP* 228

---

as "Three's own name" (*Phaedo* 104A6) which also takes the name "Odd," this being not its "own" but the Odd's "own" name.

and starred note to that page; for the *Laches*, the concluding paragraphs of the present essay; for the *Protagoras*, UVP 225 and double starred note to that page. Taken together with the *Meno*, the *Gorgias*, and the *Hippias Major*, they exhibit pervasive use of "parts" in Socratic dialogues to refer to the relation of subordinate to superordinate concepts.)[5]

The evidence of the *Meno* for the "parts of virtue" doctrine is also ignored, also without explanation, by Taylor. In his case I cannot even surmise what his reason might be. He makes copious use of the *Meno* as a source for other Socratic doctrines.

Irwin, the only one of the sponsors of PTI to address this issue, claims that

M. 78D-79C does not . . . show that S. recognizes parts of virtue; he simply allows Meno this view to refute him . . . (304-305).

But I see no reason to suppose that in 78D-79C S. is engaging in *ad hominem* argument. The text gives no indication that he is now shifting to a different mode of discourse from that of the clearly didactic line he had followed throughout the earlier exposition of the distinction between virtue and the virtues. However, let us suppose for the sake of argument that everything said in 78D-7 should be stricken from the record on which we are to base our judgment of S.'s own view of the relation of the virtues to one another and to virtue as a whole. Even so, the implications of what S. had explained long before this passage would be decisive for the point at issue: if S. thinks that justice is to virtue as is the round to figure and white to color, how could he hold that "all the virtues are the same virtue" (Irwin, 86)?[6]

[5] I submit that *this* is the correct description of the relation S. has in view, *not* that of species to genus, as has been usually assumed in the scholarly literature (so most recently in Allen [1970], 87ff., and frequently in earlier work as e.g. in Thompson [1901], 83, and Bluck [1961], 231). As normally conceived, species are not coinstantiable, while what S. calls "parts" may fall into any of the following categories:

(i) necessarily not coinstantiable, as in the case of "odd" and "even" (*Euthyphro* 12C-E);
(ii) necessarily coinstantiable, as in the case of the virtues, when they are conceived as "person-virtues," as they generally are in the *Protagoras*, but *not* in the *Euthyphro* (cf. UVP 230, n. 23, and starred note).
(iii) possibly coinstantiable, as in the case of the "part" of the pleasurable which consists of things giving pleasure through eyes or ears (*Hip. Maj.* 299B), since this sub-class of the pleasurable overlaps with other sub-classes of it consisting of things which give pleasure through other senses.

To be faithful to S.'s thought our analysis of the "whole"/"part" relation should exhibit it as a highly general relation of which the species/genus relation, as usually understood, is a distinct species.

[6] On the same ground I cannot accept Paul Woodruff's view [1976] that the virtues,

To the evidence in the *Meno* should be added that provided in the *Laches*. Here too at the start of the search for a definition the notion of "parts of virtue" is introduced to serve the same regulative function:[7]

> Let us not start off . . . by inquiring into the whole of virtue . . . Let us first see if we have a proper understanding of a part of it . . . So which of the parts of virtue should we pick? (190C8-D3)

In the *Meno*, where the question is "What is virtue?," the "parts"/"whole" distinction is used to direct the search to the "whole," away from one or more of its "parts." In the *Laches* it is used for the converse purpose: to restrict the search to one of the "parts." And the linguistic vehicles of the distinction are the same: cf. ὅλης ἀρετῆς as *vs.* μέρους τινος in *Laches* 190C-D with ἀρετὴ . . . τὸ ὅλον as *vs.* μόριον . . . ἀρετῆς in *Meno* 79B6-C1.[8] This notion, which S. first invoked to get the search off to the right start, he brings up again towards the end of the dialogue, at the point where its terminal argument is introduced:

> You know that we had started off by investigating courage as part of virtue. And you too gave your answer supposing it *to be a part, there being other parts as well* which, taken together, are called "virtue" . . . And do you now agree with me on these parts? For I say that temperance, justice, and the like are parts of virtue, along with courage. Wouldn't you too? . . . Well then, so far we are in agreement . . . (198A1-B2)

The genitive absolute in ὄντων δὴ καὶ ἄλλων μερῶν whose translation I have italicized in the above quotation is epexegetic: "there being other parts as well" explains the meaning of saying that courage is "a part of virtue" exactly as in *Meno* 73E3-6 (quoted on p. 419 above) "there are other figures as well" explains the meaning of saying that roundness is "*a* figure" and that the name "figure" applies to characters as distinct as is the round from the

---

though distinct, have the same definiens. He, unlike the sponsors of PTI (with whom, on other grounds, he has much in common), holds that the "parts of virtue" doctrine, as expounded and used in the *Meno* and other Socratic dialogues, is genuinely Socratic. I fail to see how he can do so *and* hold that S. thinks that the virtues are all definitionally the same. Since S. in the *Meno* invokes the relation of different figures to figure and of different colors to color as "models" (77A9, 79A10) for the relation of different virtues to virtue, he could no more allow the same definiens for different virtues than for different figures or for different colors.

[7] The function of S.'s ontological doctrines as "regulative principles of dialectic," rightly emphasized by Allen [1970, 69-79], might well have included the part/whole relation between subordinate and superordinate Socratic *eidē*.

[8] Cf. also σύμπασα ἀρετή in *La*.199E4 with σύμπασα [ἀρετή] in *Meno* 89A4.

straight. Could there be any doubt that in the *Laches* we have the same "parts of virtue" doctrine as in the *Meno*?

To maintain PTI its sponsors must deny that these references to that doctrine in the *Laches* express S.'s own view; they must explain them away as *ad hominem* assertions of propositions which he believes to be false. Neither Taylor nor Irwin say so; they simply ignore what S. says at 190C8-D3 and then again at 198A1-B2. So too does Penner in his analysis of the terminal argument in the *Laches*: he speaks of the proposition that courage is a part of virtue as a "premise S. elicits from Nicias" (61).[9] This simply misdescribes the text: what S. elicits from Nicias is not the premise, but concurrence with it. Having introduced it himself, entirely on his own initiative, earlier on in his dialogue with Laches, he re-introduces it now and re-asserts it unambiguously *in propria persona* ("For *I say* that temperance, justice . . . are parts of virtue, along with courage . . . *so far we are in agreement*"). From the hopeful start of the search for courage at 190C down to its aporetic denouement in the terminal argument of the dialogue it is S. himself who maintains, and induces his interlocutors to concur, that courage is "a part" of virtue.

[9] He is claiming that it is elicited to serve as the refutand of the terminal argument. The claim is contrary to S.'s explicit description of the upshot. What S. says has been refuted by the argument is Nicias' Socratic definition of courage ("We have not discovered, Nicias, what courage is" [199E11]), *not* the premise that courage is a part of virtue.

STARRED NOTES TO VARIOUS ESSAYS

———

* *IOLP* 21, n. 59. In his review of the first edition of this book (in *Arion* NS 2/1 [1975], 116ff.) Diskin Clay suggests that I misinterpret the sense of κυοῦσιν . . . πάντες οἱ ἄνθρωποι:

> The image of male pregnancy springs up from his translation like Zeus from the head of Athena. It is Diotima who says according to Vlastos' translation, "we are all pregnant." What she has in mind is human fecundity or ripeness . . . (124-125).

Two comments: (1) The primary sense of κύω *is* pregnancy, not just "fecundity or ripeness"; of this there can be no doubt (cf. *LSJ s.v.*) (2) The image is most certainly meant to apply to males: its force would be sadly blunted if it were restricted to females in 206C-D; anyhow, it is quite explicitly applied to males in the sequel (209A-C).

* *IOLP* 25, n. 74, "In every passage I can recall . . ." I should have been more specific. What I meant was: every passage in which Plato appears to be voicing his own sentiment (through Socrates or some other dramatic mouthpiece), instead of that of other persons, real or imaginary.

** *IOLP* 25, n. 76. Sir Kenneth Dover has objected (in private correspondence) to this criticism, and on re-reading what he had written in his paper I feel that the objection is well taken:

> What [Plato] did believe was that the act was "unnatural," in the sense "against the rules"; it was a morally ignorant exploitation of pleasure beyond what is "granted" (κατὰ φύσιν ἀποδεδόσθαι, *Lg.* 636C4), the product of an ἀκράτεια (C6) which can be aggravated by habituation and bad example. His comparison of homosexuality with incest (837E8-838E1) is particularly revealing.

As the last sentence shows, by "against the rules" Dover does mean something far stronger than is usually understood by that expression. So my criticism was misplaced.

*** *IOLP* 25, n. 76. In *Greek Homosexuality* (Oxford, 1978), 163, Dover maintains that the reference to the "four-footed beast" is heterosexual. But he ignores Plutarch's reading of the passage. Why should we assume that we are in a better position than he to catch the true import of the image? Nor does Dover seem to me to give due weight to the fact that the only passages in which it is unambiguously clear that Plato condemns sexual intercourse for being "contrary to nature" rather than for some more general reason are those in which it is homosexual (μὴ φύσει, *Lg.* 836C5; παρὰ φύσιν, *Lg.* 636C6, 841D5; in the third of these, though παιδοσπορεῖν is condemned in intercourse with both concubines and male partners, only in the case of the latter—on the usual punctuation, which Dover does not protest—is it stigmatized as "unnatural."

* JHR 120. For useful criticism and improved formulation of Plato's argument here and on p. 121 see Nicholas D. Smith, "An Argument for the Definition of Justice in Plato's *Republic* (433E6-434A1)," *Philosophical Studies* 35 (1979), 373-83.

* JHR 124, n. 37. Cf. 433D1-5: there the justice of "doing one's own" is ascribed to individuals in the most explicit way.

* JHR 136. That the lower classes would consist (predominantly) of just persons is a safe inference from the general description of the Platonic state as the "perfectly good polis," "good" in the moral sense of the term, "wise and brave and temperate and just" (427E7-11): Not one of the great moralists of the West has been so insistent upon the dependence of the moral quality of a society upon the moral character of its members. Quite apart from specific texts (435E, 445C-D, 544D-E) the whole of *R.* VIII is devoted to the exposition of the idea that the character of the polis can be no different than that which predominates among its citizens. So if there were no justice in the personal character of the producers (who compose by far the largest segment of the civic body) there could be no justice in the polis. Moreover, Plato explicitly ascribes the virtue of *sōphrosynē* to the producers no less than to their rulers:

> In which civic class would you say that temperance is present when they [the citizens] are in this condition? In the rulers or in the ruled?—In both, surely (431E4-6).

This virtue Plato's "musical paideia" is designed to inculcate in them no less than in the upper classes:

> As for the mass of men [ὡς πλήθει, as understood by James Adam *ad loc.* and translated by Cornford, Robin, Grube, Bloom], are not these the main points in temperance: to be obedient to rulers and to be themselves rulers over pleasures of drink, sex, and food? (389D-E).

Could Plato have held that the producers can, and must, be temperate, while maintaining that they need not, and cannot, be just persons?

For a forthright "Yes" to this question one should read John Cooper ("The Psychology of Justice in Plato," *American Philosophical Quarterly* 14 [1977], 151ff.), who argues that (1) Plato's definition of individual justice at 442C-443E restricts it to those who have knowledge (*epistēmē*) and, therefore, to the philosophers, and moreover (2) that Plato "has not provided any ground [in his definition of the justice of the polis at 432D-435A] . . . for attributing even a reduced form of the virtue to the individuals themselves" (153). Now, obviously, no one would disagree with him on (1). But he takes no account of the fact that the definitions of the cardinal virtues in individuals (442C-443E) have in view the ideal case—that of the philosophers. That *their* justice requires philosophical wisdom is trivially true. But does that permit us to infer that Plato means to deny even a reduced form of it to non-philosophers? If so, how could we account for the fact that in the *Laws*, where few indeed are to be philosophers, all of the citizens are expected to be just persons (see e.g. the passages cited above in *IOLP*, p. 14 and notes—to which many others could be added—bearing in mind that here, as in the *Republic*, no one who is not just would count as virtuous)? As to (2), while it is true that Plato's definition of the justice of the city does not state the conditions for the justice of individuals, he must nonetheless be counting on the latter in any society which satisfies the definition of the former: if the individuals who compose the just city are not themselves just persons, how could they be counted on to act in ways which satisfy the definition of the just city, as Plato expects them to act (433D)? On Plato's model of moral motivation, how could the mass of the population be expected to act justly every day of their lives, unless they too, no less than their rulers, have "justice in their soul"—a condition which, on Plato's view of it, can be produced in persons *sans* philosophical knowledge, else it would be denied in principle to the gentlemen-farmers of the *Laws*? (For an adumbration of what it would mean in Plato's moral psychology for a non-philosopher to be "ruled by reason" see Richard Kraut, "Reason and Justice in Plato's Republic," *Phronesis*, Suppl. Vol. I [1973], 207ff. at 216-22.)

For a more guarded view see T. Irwin (1977, 200-202 and 220, with the notes to those pages). He holds that "Plato rejects [the view that philosophical knowledge is necessary for virtue] nowhere in the *Republic*" but does not affirm it either;

> some passages might be taken to concede virtue to someone with right belief
> if we had unequivocal evidence elsewhere that Plato concedes it, but there is
> no such evidence in the *R*. His comments are obscure, and perhaps indicate
> some ambivalence; he never says what the lower classes have if they have no
> virtue, since he is not interested in the lower classes in the *R*. (330).

That last remark is, of course, the reason why Plato tells us so little on what sort of virtue may be expected of the lower classes in the *Republic*, compelling us to resort to inference. I agree with some of the things Irwin says on this point in his careful and discriminating discussion. But I must take strong exception to two things:

(1) In n. 26 (2) on p. 319 he holds that Plato's remark at 431E4-6 (quoted above, in the first paragraph of the present starred note) "implies nothing about the virtue of individuals." I find this unintelligible. I cannot understand how, on Plato's conception of temperance, virtue could be present in a class without being present in individuals who compose the class; thus, who but individuals could control impulses to "drink, sex, and food" (description of temperance in the last quotation in that paragraph)?

(2) At p. 220 Irwin argues that because

> (a) a musically educated man regards virtue as a source of honour and pleasure
> in itself, but cannot explain what it is in virtue which would justify his
> choice of those action,

it somehow follows that

(b) he does not choose virtue for its own sake [I have interpolated the reference-marks].

I cannot understand why Irwin expects us to agree that (b) follows from (a). Thus if a "musically educated" producer has learned to delight in good craftsmanship and to find sloppy work revolting, to love the orderly, disciplined way of life and hate its contrary, the fact that he cannot "justify" these preferences (in philosophically sophisticated lines of reasoning acceptable to Plato or to Irwin) would be no reason for denying that he chooses good workmanship and an orderly style of life "for their own sake." Even philosophers have preferences whose rationale they cannot explain. Why shouldn't others too?

* *UVP* 221. As I explain in the Preface, the solution I offer in this essay confronts an alternative one, along radically different lines, produced by Terry Penner (1973, 35ff.), endorsed in the main by C.C.W. Taylor (1976, 103ff.) and Terence Irwin (1977, 86ff. et passim). (In these notes, as also in *SPV* above, I refer to each of these works by the author's name and to the interpretation they jointly sponsor as the "PTI" view.) On this interpretation S. propounds two principal theses:

(1) All the virtues are the same virtue.
(2) What is named by "virtue" and by the names of each of the five virtues is a psychological state which is the "motive-force" of virtuous conduct.

What can be said in favor of these theses is stated with resourcefulness and vigor by Penner, Taylor, and Irwin. To restate it here would be redundant. So I restrict myself to criticism. In *SPV* above I set forth my objections to (1); there will be more on this score in the starred notes which are to follow. My response to (2) will be developed in a later publication. It is adumbrated, in part, in *SQ* above. I may add this further indication of the ground of my objection:

That moral virtue is for S. a psychological state I take to be a truism: What else could a state of character be? However, as Penner propounds it, this proposition is loaded with a negative entailment:

When S. asked "What is bravery?" and so forth, he did not want to know what the meaning of the word "bravery" was, nor what the essence of bravery was, nor what the universal *bravery* was. His question was not (what has become) the philosopher's question . . . ; it was not a request for a conceptual analysis . . . His question was rather the general's question, "What is bravery?"—that is, "What is it that makes brave men brave?" The general asks this question not out of interest in mapping our concepts, but out of a desire to learn something substantial about the human psyche. He wants to know what psychological state it is, the imparting of which to his men will make them brave . . . (39-40).

I would reply that S.'s question is *both* "the general's" and "the philosopher's" question. What he seeks to identify *is* the universal Courage, the "essence" (*ousia*) or "form" (*eidos*) which, when instantiated in persons, is what "makes" them brave—not in the causal, but, as I explained in *SQ* above, in the constitutive sense of "makes." What

S. seeks to understand in his question, "What is Courage?" is what *constitutes* men's courage—not what produces it; to refer to the object of his inquiry, when formulated through this question, as "the motive-force" of courageous conduct would be a mistake. As I have argued above in *SQ*, in S.'s model of the dynamics of the psyche the motive force of virtuous conduct (and of vicious conduct too: of all conduct) is always *desire* for the good. Knowledge of the good is what gives direction to this dynamic force. A Socratic virtue, like Courage, being a form of knowledge, is a guide to the good, not an additional dynamo. The power of knowledge is its ability to inform, not to engender, that desire for the good which moves us to pursue it.

As a preface to the debates in which I engage my esteemed critics in these notes I want to say how grateful I feel to each of them for the critical attention they have given my work. Though *UVP* appeared too late to elicit Penner's critical response, it luckily appeared in time to offer a massive critical target for Taylor in his admirable commentary on the *Protagoras* and then, shortly after, to elicit sustained criticism from Irwin in notes to his book which are models of terse, lucid, and good-tempered controversial argument. I could hardly have asked for more thoughtful, fair-minded, and altogether helpful critics.

* *UVP* 224, " . . . not treated in the text as logically disjoint tenets . . ." Note that when the debate is resumed in 349A6ff., S. in his recapitulation is content to refer merely to the unity and the similarity of the virtues (the first of which "spills over" into the second within the confines of a single period, as I remark in n. 11), while Protagoras responds by taking the biconditionality of the virtues, which S. has not mentioned now, as the very issue to which he is asked to say "Yes" or "No."

** *UVP* 224, ". . . of the same thing, which is one thing." For the benefit of the Greekless reader I may point out that "thing" in both of its occurrences translates nothing in the Greek. The literal translation would be: " . . . of the same, this being one."

* *UVP* 225, *"standard Socratic doctrine."* I erred in making this very large claim without adducing detailed support for it. This I now provide in *SPV* above.

** *UVP* 225, " . . . the truth of [A] . . . is presupposed by both options." The sponsors of PTI have to assume that S. either repudiates both of the analogies in 329D4-8 (so apparently Taylor 108) or else accepts the gold analogy while remaining free of the "parts of virtue" doctrine which is so conspicuous in both analogies (so apparently Penner 50 and, more clearly, Irwin 305). I submit that there is no textual warrant for either of these moves. That the parts-of-gold analogy is a very bad one (as I emphasize, *UVP* 230) is not of itself a good reason for thinking that S. is tacitly rejecting it: he does not dissociate himself from it in the text, does not apologize for it or disparage it in any way, says nothing that would indicate that he is uncommitted to it to the extent of thinking it a vivid, though crude, picture of similarity in contrast to the equally vivid and crude picture of dissimilarity in the parts-of-a-face analogy. And if we allow him to keep it, as we must, the concession carries the "parts of virtue" doctrine with it, for this is why he brings it up in the first place: to illustrate, however, clumsily, one way in which the "parts" of virtue might be related *inter se*.

In any case, nothing is to be gained for the PTI view by dissociating S. at 329D4-8 from the "parts of virtue" doctrine, since he proceeds (329E2-4) to build that doctrine into his very next question, this time in language as lucid and exact as anything one could wish. If S. believed that virtue has no "parts," why should he have planted the falsehood into this formulation of the issue, when he could easily have deleted it by simply asking if everyone who has any virtue must have every virtue? If we were coming to this passage with the presumption that the "parts of virtue" doctrine is unSocratic, we would, of course, discount the mention of "parts of virtue" in both of the questions in this text as throw-away, *ad hominem*, patter. When that presumption is itself in controversy that reason for so reading the text is ruled out. It is ruled out *a fortiori* when that presumption is falsified by evidence in numerous other Socratic dialogues (see *SPV*).

   *** *UVP* 225, "These . . . five names—do they apply to one thing?" or, more literally, "these . . . five names—are they names on one thing?" What would it mean on the present interpretation of S.'s view to say that they are? What exactly is that "one thing" which all five are supposed to name? Let me preface the answer by recalling in greater detail what I mentioned in *SPV* above: In *La.* 190C8-D3 and 199A1-9, as well as in *Meno* 74D-E (taken together with 78D7-79C3) and 89A3 and also in *Prt.* 329C-E, 349B-D and 361B (in all of which the view expressed is Socratic, as I have argued in *SPV* and ** *UVP* 225 above), it is clear that S. thinks of virtue as one "whole" composed of parts (cf. ὅλης ἀρετῆς in *La.* 190C8; [μέρη] ἃ σύμπαντα ἀρετὴ κέκληται in *La.* 198A5; ἀρετὴ . . . τὸ ὅλον in *Meno* 79C1; [ἀρετή] ἐπιστήμη ὅλον in *Prt.* 361B5-6). So the answer to that question is: 'Exactly that "one thing" which is the "whole" composed of the five "parts".'

   This answer might provoke the retort: "But that 'whole' is being thought of, quite explicitly, as composite—as a plurality of 'parts.' Is there good reason to think that S. would find it natural to refer to it as 'a unity,' as 'one thing'?" Certainly there is, since we know that Aristotle would find it so. In the analysis of the various uses of "unity" in *Met.* Delta he writes:

> Those things are also called one whose genus is one though distinguishable by opposite differentiae—these too are called one because the genus which underlies the differentiae is one: e.g. horse, man, and dog form a unity [literally, 'a certain one (thing),' ἕν τι] because all are animals . . . (1016A24-27; translation after Ross).

Thus even if the relation of the five virtues to each other were no closer than that of five species of the same biological genus, even then, we learn from Aristotle, one could still refer to the whole which they compose as ἕν τι. But in point of fact, in the case of the virtues the relation is still closer. For the species in Aristotle's example have separate instance-classes; the genus does not have the same instance-class as does any given species of it. But in the case S. has in view *the five "parts" have the same instance-class with one another and with the "whole."* Hence S. would have that much stronger reason for thinking of that "whole" as "one thing," as "one" with its five "parts." He could do so without prejudice to the definitional distinctness of the six attributes— Virtue, and each of the five virtues—which are logically conjoined to form the "whole": the definitional distinctness of those six attributes is absolutely independent of their having distinct instance-classes: the same instance-class will do for each, provided only it can be differently described (as the class of virtuous men, or of brave men, or of pious men, etc.). In principle, there would be no difficulty in producing appropriately different descriptions in each of the six cases (thus the descriptions "virtuous," "brave," "pious," would differ as would the generic description, "persons possessing knowledge of good and evil," from different determinations of it, "possessing such knowledge pertaining to fearful things" in the case of "brave" and "possessing such knowledge pertaining to our duties to the gods" [τὰ προσήκοντα . . . περὶ θεούς, *Gorg.* 507A] in the case of "pious").

I take "one" at *Prt.* 333B4, "hence would not Temperance and Wisdom be one (ἓν ἂν εἴη)?" to be used with the same sense. Here S. formulates the conclusion of the preceding argument which, on my analysis of it (*UVP* 243-46 and starred notes), purports to prove that Temperance and Wisdom have the same instance-classes. If Aristotle feels no awkwardness in saying that horse and man may be called one because they are both animals, species of *one* genus, though their instance-classes are completely separate, S. should feel none in saying that Temperance and Wisdom are one because they are both virtues, "parts" of *one* "whole," and their instance-classes are entirely the same.

* *UVP* 226, n. 9, "(2a) restricts one to a single nominatum; (2b) does not . . ." On the first claim: In all of the cases in which "name *of*" is used in the earlier dialogues (as also in the passage of the *Phaedo* I discuss in *UVP* 238-40) it is used to mean "proper name." This is clear in all occurrences of this expression in the passages in the *Meno* and the *Laches* to which I refer in the preceding starred note (and it is strikingly clear in the *Phaedo* passage: see the citations from 103E and 104A in *UVP* 238-39). *Prt.* 329D1, "or are all those [words] I have just mentioned names of the same [thing], which is one [thing]," cannot be cited as a counter-example, because (as I have argued in *UVP* 225 and the double starred note to that page) this is the option which S. *rejects*; 329D1 thus confirms my claim that "name of" is used to mean "proper name": the option which S. and Protagoras agree to set aside at this point in the dialogue is that all five names are proper names of one and the same thing.

On the second claim: In saying this I did not mean to suggest that "name *on (epi)*" is used exclusively to designate the disjunct "either proper name or descriptive predicate." I take "name on" simply as a loose, all-purpose, expression which *can* be so used in the Platonic corpus, but need not be used there to mean *only* this. If, as Irwin suggests (rightly, I believe) it is used in *Sophist* 244C1 for the same purpose for which "name of" is used in 244D6, this is no counter-example: if "name on" can be used for either of the two purposes in (2b), there is no reason why it should not be used for just one of them in appropriate contexts. Nor have I suggested that whenever *onoma* is being used to mean "descriptive predicate" *only* "name *on*" can be the linguistic vehicle: Plato may speak of "denominating" subordinate concepts "by the name" of the superordinate (*Meno* 74D5-6, ἑνί τινι προσαγορεύεις ὀνόματι; cf. *SPV*, n. 1); or he may say that the subordinate concept is "also" (καί, *Phaedo* 104A2, 6) or "nonetheless" (ὅμως, *Phaedo* 104A7, B3) "named" by the latter (cf. *UVP* 238-40). Plato is not the sort of writer who affects terminological fixity. My point is simply that when he speaks in the *Protagoras* of those five names as names "on" one thing this is not sufficient reason for understanding him to mean what he would have meant if he had said (and does say in the rejected option, 329D1) that all five are names *of* that one thing; "name on" allows, but is not restricted to, the non-nominative use of "naming." [See p. 445 for additional note.]

* *UVP* 227, "This is how S. is being understood today." For "today" now read 'prior to 1973.'

** *UVP* 227, "Of their identity there could be no question." Neither here nor at any other point in *UVP* do I make the effort to ascertain what S. himself would have been likely to mean if he had either asserted or denied that the five virtues are "the same." Nor has this question been raised by other parties to the debate. To raise it is to become aware that there is no unproblematic answer to it, for there is no indication that S. ever gave any thought to this topic. Neither in the early dialogues nor in the rest of the Platonic corpus is the great "What is *F*?" question posed about identity— which is as good as saying that no critical investigation is ever pursued there of the meaning or, better, meanings of this far from univocal term. The first Greek known to have attempted it is, of course, Aristotle, impelled by his conviction that each of the major terms of the philosopher's vocabulary has "many uses" (πολλαχῶς λέγεται) and that it is the ABC of philosophical reflection to try to sort them out. In *Topics* 1, 7, 103A24ff. he sorts out three uses of "numerical identity" (τὸ ἓν ἀριθμῷ ταὐτόν):

(1) The "principal and primary" use (κυριώτατα καὶ πρώτως) he reserves (a) for things whose (proper) names are synonyms (example: ἱμάτιον λωπίῳ) or (b) for attributes which are "the same in definition" (example: "man" and "biped pedestrian animal"). Call these respectively "identity(1a)" and "identity(1b)."
(2) As a "secondary" use he recognizes the relation of an attribute to any of its *propria* (i.e. to attributes which do not constitute its essence but nonetheless belong to it alone and are interpredicable with it: *Top.* 102A18-19). His example: "capable of receiving knowledge" as *proprium* of "man." This relation I shall call "identity(2)."
(3) He mentions also a very weak use, "accidental identity."

We may begin by eliminating the third of these uses: All parties to the dispute would agree that whatever may have been the bond between the five virtues which S. had in view, it was not, at any rate, an accidental one. So if we accept Aristotle's analysis of contemporary usage—and I know of no reason why we should not—we are left with the following options: identity(1a), identity(1b), identity(2). The first of these—synonymy—we may eliminate at once: all parties to the dispute would repudiate it. So the choice falls between identity(1b), definitional identity, and identity(2), interentailment. Since the upholders of PTI reject the latter, I assume that they are clearly for the former option. (They do not address the point directly; but I assume that they would all agree with Taylor that S. "sees nothing objectionable in the thesis that the different virtues have the same *logos*" [107].)

If we opt for identity(1b) it becomes inexplicable that (*pace* Taylor's translation of the *Protagoras*: see starred note to *UVP* 256 below) S. shrinks from asserting identity in an unqualified way. Thus in the case of the relation of Justice to Piety he says that they are "either the same thing or extremely similar" (331B4-5) and "almost the same thing" (333B5-6). Why so, if he does believe that Justice and Piety are the same in definition? If two attributes have the same *logos*, the same essence, why should they be "almost" the same? If, on the other hand, we opt for identity (2) the difficulty vanishes: In the light of what Aristotle tells us we can see that [i] s. *could* have said that the virtues are "the same" to assert no more than identity(2) and yet [ii] might have felt some need to qualify the assertion, lest he be misunderstood to be using "the same" in its "principal and primary" sense which, on this hypothesis, he does *not* mean. Here [ii] calls for no further comment, but in support of [i] we may remind ourselves that there is an occasion in the early dialogues where S. slips into saying that two things—here happiness and virtue—are the same (*Crito* 48B7-8: living "well" [i.e. happily] and living "honourably and justly" are "the same"), and there it would be uncontroversial that definitional identity is not what he means: he never asserts or implies that "happiness" and "virtue" are the same in definition, and when he does present a formal argument for the bond of virtue to happiness, all he purports to have proved is that virtue is the necessary and sufficient condition of virtue (*Gorg.* 507B8-C6), i.e. that the two attributes are interentailing.

I submit that these considerations warrant the following conclusion: While S. has never subjected the concept of identity to critical analysis and hence has no abstract description of the concept to guide his uses of it and give him the protection he needs from falling into confused phrases and faulty inferences, this should not keep us from using the distinction between identity(1b) and identity(2) to understand statements of his whose meaning *is* clear. In *Prt.* 329E2-4 it is clear that all he asserts of the relation of the virtues to each other is identity(2). In his references to the various virtues as "parts" of Virtue it is equally clear that he is implicitly denying that their relation is identity(1b). Between the clear assertion and the clear denial there is an area of unclarity which leaves him prey to the muddled thinking which surfaces in the phrases "either the same thing or extremely similar" and "almost the same."

In the absence of such an advance in insight we could not expect from him an explicit commitment to ,that negation which would be the critical move in distinguishing biconditionality from identity(1b), i.e. the denial that any two virtues could be the same in definition. He could assume that they could not—as he clearly does in the *Meno*, else he could not have analogized the distinctness of the virtues to that of shapes and colors (cf. n. 6 to *SPV*). So if S. were to be confronted with identity(1b) and identity(2) as clear options between which he should choose, he would certainly have preferred the latter, since the former was blocked for him by the parts-of-virtue doctrine, while the latter was unobstructed by anything he believed. But the fact is that he never did confront those alternatives, so far as we can see from what is actually said in our text. What we see there, when we examine it closely, is the following:

(1) A flawlessly clear and firm statement of biconditionality, unglossed in any way which would suggest that the general relation instantiated here has been perceived as such.

(2) A vague, infirm, statement of "similarity" (as I observe in *UVP* 250, the "fumbling" in the phraseology is extraordinary).

(3) An assertion of the "unity" of the virtues which (as I have argued in *** *UVP* 225) would not strain the use of the term "one" (as we know from Aristotle) even if "one" were being used to mean no more than that the virtues are distinct determinations of a generic concept, and still less if, as is the case, not only does each fall under that concept but each is necessarily coinstantiable with each. But the assertion is not accompanied by any sort of explanation that this is *why* they are said to be "one," still less by any argument to prove that this is a logical implicate of their biconditionality.

This being the case we have good reason to dissociate his view from identity(1b), and therewith from the undefined "identity" ascribed to him by the advocates of PTI (what else but identity(1b) *could* they mean?), and to associate it with identity(2), doing so with a constant awareness of the residual unclarity of his thought which shows through the cracks when he says that Piety and Justice are "either the same or extremely similar" (331B) and are "nearly the same" (333B)—an unclarity which will dog his steps, threatening to trip him up sooner or later. If I were revising, instead of annotating, *UVP*, I would wash out of the text "Of identity there could be no question" and more to the same effect in what precedes and follows, replacing it by the above far more reserved description of what I now take to be the truth.

*** *UVP* 227. There is a flaw in the argument I am making here, as critics have shown (Taylor 105-106; Irwin 304): the argument is question-begging. That S. could have used the definiens of Courage as a standard for determining the piety of Euthyphro's conduct is *per se* wildly implausible; but if the upholders of PTI will stomach the implausibility, they cannot be refuted by an argument which assumes, as mine implicitly does, that Courage and Piety *are* different virtues for S. The outrage to common sense will not bother the critics. Irwin retorts that S. would not hesitate to "outrage common sense for the sake of a better theory" (*loc. cit.*). Thus my argument cannot be premised on the evident truth that the distinctness of Courage from Piety would be axiomatic for S.'s contemporaries. What needs to be established is that it would also be axiomatic *for him*. This is what I should have undertaken to show at this point, adducing the evidence I now review in *SPV*.

(While fully concurring with the truth of Irwin's reply, I demur at his use of *Laches* 191C-D to support it. Laches' common sense is *not* outraged by the radical extension of the concept of courage required to cover the wide spectrum of cases to which S. refers him. He shows no surprise, offers no resistance; cf. *SQ*, n. 3. And his concurrence is enthusiastic [καὶ σφόδρα γε, 191E3]. His reason welcomes the novelty, is not affronted by it. For Socratic outrage to common sense Irwin would have done better to cite S.'s doctrine of the impossibility of acrasia.)

**** *UVP* 227, n. 12. That the distinction between sense and reference is never mentioned in the Platonic corpus, though true, does nothing to advance my argument, as both Taylor (106) and Irwin (304) have pointed out. The next sentence should have read, "For Plato *Form-naming* words get their sense through their reference," for as is clear from the immediate sequel this is all I had in mind. The restriction to Form-naming words is vital to my claim. When thus restricted it cannot be faulted by Irwin's counter-examples of non-synonymous proper names of *concrete individuals* in the Platonic corpus ("Astyanax" and "Skamandrius" for Hector's son in *Crat.* 391D-393B; "Eōos" and "Hesperus" in Plato's epigram on *Astēr*.) My claim is that since for S. any (non-equivocal) abstract word "*F*" ("virtue," "courage," etc.) names (referringly) a unique character ("a single Form," *Euthyphro* 5D3-4, *Meno* 72C7) *F*, and derives its sense *from* that character, no two such words can name (referringly) the same character if they differ in sense. To show that for S. a concrete individual, who instantiates multiple characters, may have multiple non-synonymous names (one for each of his characters), would not touch my claim. The only one of Irwin's counter-examples which *is* relevant is the case of "pleasant" and "good" in the hedonist theory in the *Prt.* and the *Philebus*; and this boomerangs. In the *Prt.* passage (355B-C, E) S. treats these as inter-substitutable in his argument, and speaks of them as such, mentioning no restriction on their inter-substitutability. Surely this is sterling evidence that he does think that for this theory they would be synonymous. Irwin gives no evidence to the contrary; he merely offers us his opinion that if Plato did make this claim, the claim would be "implausible and unnecessary."

* *UVP* 228, "This project, which has S.'s unmistakeable approval . . ." Woodruff

(1976, n. 8) tries to explain away S.'s approval of the project, saying that it is meant
to show "that the genus-differentia strategy is hopeless." He gives no textual evidence
to support this opinion which casts S. in the role of tricking Euthyphro into a blind
alley. Irwin (301, n. 57) says that S. is not really approving because he remarks at
12E9 that his interlocutor only "seems" to have spoken well. The use of "seems"
proves nothing: urbane understatement is characteristically Socratic. Irwin ignores S.'s
preceding remark (12E3-4) which I quote in n. 17: nothing there could be construed
as dubitative. What is more important, he ignores what has gone before it in the text:
having introduced on his own initiative the "part"/"whole" relation of Piety to Justice,
S. explains it elaborately by two different examples (12A9-D10), asks Euthyphro to
"teach" him which part of Justice *is* Piety (12E1-2), and says that if so instructed
"we will have learned adequately what is reverent and pious, and what is not." Taylor
takes a different line—a far sounder one methodologically, it seems to me—in dealing
with this passage. Instead of expunging the difficulty, he confronts it, and explains
it as due to the fact that S.'s doctrine is "imprecise" and "takes no account of the ways
in which these ways of behaving well [which arise from the knowledge of what is good
and bad] are *different*, e.g. in that they presuppose different, though possibly overlapping areas of activity for their exercise." (107) I agree completely with the quoted
statement. But I fail to see how it meets the difficulty the passage in the *Euthyphro*
creates for the PTI view. That the Socratic doctrine in the *Prt.* is "imprecise" everyone
would agree. But in Taylor's view it is precise enough to entail a doctrine of identity,
over and above biconditionality—identity in its strongest sense, allowing that the
different virtues *have the same definition*. If S. does believe this, how could he bring to
his search for the definition of Piety the presumption that it is as different from that
of Justice as is that of *odd* from *number* in his example?

* *UVP* 229, n. 20, "The 'power' (*dynamis*) of a particular virtue is that virtue itself
conceived as a dispositional quality manifesting itself in action." And cf. the phrasing
I use in n. 73: ". . . the *dynameis* of Justice and Temperance [are] the active dispositions
to behave justly and temperately . . ." Taylor (110) misunderstands me [to mean that
justice, etc. are in S.'s view mere "tendencies" to perform acts which are just, etc. and
fall short of being what Taylor describes as "permanent states of the person which
enable him to perform" such acts (*loc. cit.*). I most certainly believe that Socratic virtues
are such "permanent states of character" and have said nothing to the contrary in *UVP*
or elsewhere: the above citations, and other statements to the same effect in *UVP*,
neither state nor imply that dispositions are "tendencies." (Irwin's interpretation of
my view is free from this error.) Taylor is apparently unaware of the fact (to which
Irwin calls attention [295]) that in contemporary philosophical usage "disposition"
need not mean what he and Penner call "tendencies" (cf. W. V. Quine, *Word and
Object* [Cambridge, Mass., New York, and London, 1960], p. 223: "Dispositions
. . . are conceived as built-in, enduring structural traits"). However, Taylor is quite
right in thinking that by "dispositions" I do *not* mean "motive-forces," which I believe
to be a misdescription of what S. understands by moral dispositions: see my remarks
in * *UVP* 221 above.

* *UVP* 230, " . . . his definition of Courage . . ." *Can* we be sure that this is what
S. puts forward as a *definition*, instead of just a true statement about Courage? I believe
that we can, but not for the reason I give in n. 24. Paul Woodruff (1976, 110ff.)
rightly objected that the mere fact that a proposition about Courage is accepted by

S. as true does not suffice to show that he would consider it an acceptable answer to the question, 'What is Courage?' i.e. a correct definition of that virtue. In "F is G," where G is an attribute universally and exclusively true of F, it would not follow that it would constitute a correct definiens of "F": clearly not, if G were a *pathos* of F, instead of its *ousia* (*Euthyphro* 11A-B; and cf. *** *UVP* 227, above). The objection is well taken and does not seem to have been answered so far in the scholarly literature. But it is not unanswerable:

We know that G would be no mere *pathos* of F, but its very *ousia*, if it were "that because of which" each of the "many" Fs is F: by comparing 6D9-11 with 11A7-8 in the *Euthyphro* we can see that to ask "What is that because of which all the Fs are F?" and "What is the *ousia* of F?" is to ask the same question calling for the same answer. (We can get the same information from the *Meno* by comparing 72B1-2 with 72C6-8.) It follows that to state "that because of which all the Fs and F" *is* to state the definiens of F. Therefore, since in *Prt.* 360C1-7 the formula "ignorance of what is and is not to be feared" is put forward as a statement of "that because of which cowards are cowardly," the formula must be a statement of the definiens of "cowardice." That the corresponding formula about courage in 360D4-5 is likewise a Socratic definition of it follows by obvious analogy: it is derivable by identical reasoning from a set of premises identical *mutatis mutandis* with those from which the counterpart formula about cowardice was derived at 360C5-6.

** *UVP* 230, n. 23, " . . . but this sort of difference is not mentioned in our passage in the *Protagoras* . . ." For good reason: in that passage Justice and Courage, considered only as "person-virtues" (cf. *UVP*, n. 25), are necessarily coinstantiable, and therefore do not sustain the genus-species relation to any virtue or to virtue: see *SPV*, n. 5.

*** *UVP* 230, n. 24, "Santas' felicitous rendering" of the Greek phrase is "knowledge of what is to be dreaded or dared." It was my intention to use it in the text above but, to my regret, I was diverted from it somehow or other, and fell back on the more usual rendering.

* *UVP* 231, n. 25, " . . . 'person-virtues' . . . 'action-virtues' . . ." I find it inexcusable that here (and in previous notes in *UVP*) I failed to refer to Crombie's anticipation of this analytic point: cf. the parallel distinction he draws (1962, 209) between what he calls "person-abstract" and "thing-abstract." I was well acquainted with his book (I referred to it earlier in *UVP* [n. 2]) and must have absorbed so completely this distinction from it that when later on I faced the problem of the apparently grave discrepancy between the *Euthyphro* and the *Protagoras* on this point I turned spontaneously to the required distinction without recalling its source. (A minor feature of his view, which I do not share, is that "it is natural" to use the abstract noun for person-abstracts, the articular adjective in the neuter for thing-abstracts; cf. Irwin 295, n. 10; for strictly parallel use of abstract noun and articular neuter to refer to person-virtues, see the Protagorean phrase at *Prt.* 325A1, δι-καιοσύνη καὶ σωφροσύνη καὶ τὸ δίκαιον εἶναι.

Pace Irwin (*loc. cit.*), that "common to all pious *actions* is some reference to *person* piety" is no objection to the analytic point which Crombie and I are making, and it is no defense of PTI: For S. all pious actions are indeed only actions of pious persons (no truism: it could be significantly denied, and would be e.g. by Aristotle: "if the acts that are in accordance with the virtues have themselves a certain character [if they are just, temperate, etc.] it does not follow that they are done justly or temperately [only just, temperate persons could have the just, temperate dispositions required to do just and temperate acts justly and temperately]" (*N. E.* 1105A28-30; translation by Ross). We must, therefore, agree with Irwin that the piety of an action could not be correctly identified without reference to that knowledge of good and evil (pertaining to our duties to the gods: cf. the second paragraph of *** *UVP* 225, above) which directs the agent's performance of it. But while all pious actions are for S. actions of pious persons, not all actions of pious persons are pious actions (thus, as I explained in *UVP* n. 25, some of their actions might be just without being pious); and the Piety of pious persons is not identical with the Justice of those same persons (the two virtues they possess would answer to different descriptions: cf. the penultimate paragraph of *** *UVP* 225).

Let me emphasize that the distinction between "action-virtues" and "person-virtues" is an artifact of analysis. It is *our* distinction—ours in the sense that we are the ones to notice and give an explicit account of it. It is *his* only in the sense that he observes it, thereby avoiding the glaring inconsistency he would otherwise incur if he denied in the *Euthyphro* what he affirmed in the *Protagoras*, namely that Piety and Justice were necessarily coinstantiable. If S. had recognized the distinction we are mapping on his statements in the two dialogues he would have grasped the entailments warranted by that distinction and this would have saved him from the trap into which he falls in his argument in *Prt.* 332A-333B (on which see the last three paragraphs of * *UVP* 246 below).

* *UVP* 239, n. 46, " . . . *onoma* used both in a broader sense, which includes *rhēma*, and in a narrower sense which contrasts with *rhēma*." Similarly dual use of *onoma* for both the predicative and the nominative function in the *Meno* and the *Laches*: cf. the starred note to * *UVP* 226, n. 9, above.

* *UVP* 243, " . . . that *Temperance and Wisdom are necessarily coextensive* . . ." What I mean, of course, is that they are attributes whose *instance-classes* are coextensive.

* *UVP* 244, "What 'opposite' means in this context . . ." A correction paralleling the one in the preceding starred note is called for here. The definition should be rephrased to read: "What 'opposite attributes' means in this context is 'attributes' whose instance-classes form what are called 'complements' in set theory."

* *UVP* 246. For "the same relation" read "the corresponding relation."

** *UVP* 246, " . . . that both Wisdom and Temperance are complements of Folly." What I mean is that both Wisdom and Temperance have instance-classes which are the complement of the instance-class of Folly.

*** *UVP* 246: In my analysis of S.'s reasoning in this argument I have made two claims:

(A) If instead of assuming dogmatically that by "one" in the conclusion, "Temperance and Wisdom would be one," S. means "one and the same virtue," we take it upon ourselves to learn from the reasoning what that word is used to mean in the statement of what the reasoning purports to have proved, we shall have good reason to hold that it means no more than is required by the Biconditionality Thesis, i.e. that the instance-classes of these attributes are (necessarily) the same (which over-fulfills the condition for one of the senses of "one" recognized by Aristotle, as I have shown above, *** *UVP* 225).

(B) S.'s argument is logically valid (see n. 65).

This second claim I have now been given good reason to renounce. Taylor, whose analysis of this Socratic argument is the most detailed and, all things considered, the most instructive that has yet been offered, charges (128-29) that there is equivocation on "opposites" in

1 Wisdom and Folly are opposites,

and

3 To one thing there is only one "opposite."

He is charging that "opposites" is used in *1* to mean "contradictories" (terms whose instance-classes would be set-theoretical complements), but in *3* to mean only "polar opposites," i.e. "qualities at either end of a continuous scale," which allows for intermediate cases that are not cases of either "opposite" (if he broadened his description of "polar opposites," as he well might, he could have usefully illustrated S.'s uses of such terms by referring to *Gorg.* 467D: "intermediate" cases between the extremes, "good" and "bad," which are said to be "neither good nor bad," are clearly recognized there). If S. is using "opposites" at *3* to mean "polar opposites," then, certainly, he is switching to a sense of the term sharply different from the one I defined for him: "polar opposites" are clearly *not* attributes whose instance-classes form set-theoretical complements.

Is S. using "opposites" in that other sense in *3*? I know of no clear case in Plato's earlier dialogues where S. uses the term "opposites" in just that way (cf. *UVP* 249-50 and notes 80 and 81). Neither of the examples given by Taylor (*Prt.* 346D1-3 and 351D6-7) are called "opposites" in their text. Nor are they in the example I offered Taylor above: "good" and "bad" are not called "opposites" at *Gorg.* 467E-469A. However, Taylor could very well argue that since "good" and "bad" *are* called "opposites" in our present passage (*Prt.* 332C5-6), where there is no reference to "intermediates," and those same attributes are said to have "intermediates" at *Gorg.* 467E-468A, and moreover since *kalon* and *aischron* are called "opposites" at *Prt.* 332C3 and 4, and are said to have "intermediates" at *Prt.* 346D3, the conjunction of those two pairs of statements suffices to show that S., to maintain consistency, would have to mean "polar opposites," not contradictories, at *3*, and hence may be justly charged with an equivocation which ruins the validity of his argument.

Its validity may be further impugned on a different, though parallel, ground: the reasoning assumes that the sense of "opposites" which holds for person-attributes, conformably with S.'s theory of their necessary biconditionality, will also hold for action-attributes, which are *not* covered by that theory. For as Alan Code has pointed out to me (in written comment, quoted with his permission), in the sense of "opposite" in which Wisdom and Folly are "opposites" in premise *1*,

> acting temperately is not the opposite of acting intemperately. For if it were, then the class of temperate actions would be the complement of the class of intemperate actions, and thus every action would be either temperate or intemperate. But there are some actions which are neither.

In the case of person-attributes the disjunction "temperate"/"intemperate" is exhaustive. The biconditionality of those attributes precludes the possibility that someone who is not a temperate person might still be a pious or brave or just person: the instance-class of "person-temperate" coincides with that of "person-pious" etc. Not so in the case of action-attributes ("*A*-attributes" for short). S. cannot hold that any action which is not *A*-virtuous must be *A*-vicious. For since he holds (*Euthyphro* 11Eff.)

that *A*-Piety is a "part" of *A*-Justice, he must hold that there are instances of *A*-Justice which are not instances of *A*-Piety—actions which are just actions, but not pious actions, like paying one's bills in n. 25, without being impious actions either (for these, on S.'s view [cf. * *UVP* 221, n. 25], could only be done by impious persons who, given biconditionality in *P*-attributes, would have to be unjust persons, who could not perform just actions). Thus, to maintain consistency, S. cannot use "opposites" in *3*, which has to cover *A*-attributes no less than *P*-attributes, in the same sense as in *1*, whose "opposites" have complementary instance-classes, which is not true in the case of *A*-attributes. We have this further reason, then, for agreeing with Taylor that there is equivocation on "opposites" as between premises *1* and *3*.

So I must certainly renounce claim *B* above, that S.'s argument is logically valid. What follows from this for my claim *A*? Taylor appears to think that if *B* is false, so too must *A*. Given the flaw in the argument, he writes, "it cannot be maintained that Plato's intention in this argument is clearly to establish the Biconditionality Thesis only" (130). I beg to differ. The flaw in S.'s argument shows that S. failed to prove what I claim he aimed to prove. It does not show that he did not aim to prove it. And this is all that matters in my controversy with the partisans of PTI. If they are right, S.'s aim in this argument should be to prove identity(1b). Their case is not advanced if what he tried, and failed, to prove is identity(2). (A minor anomaly in Taylor's handling of this argument is his view [128-29] that the argument, if it were valid, would establish identity(1a), i.e. synonymy. On Taylor's view, but not on mine (cf. *** *UVP* 227, n. 12, above), identity(1b) and synonymy are entirely distinct theses and S. holds identity(1b) without holding the synonymy thesis. Why then is S. constructing an argument which, if valid, would prove the synonymy thesis?)

* *UVP* 247, n. 75, the *dynameis* of Justice and Temperance . . . will both be dispositions to behave wisely, bravely, and piously as well . . ." For "be" read "entail" so that it will be clearer that I do *not* mean "be identical with."

* *UVP* 249, "Premise *1* he gets by arguing in effect: If Justice were not just, it would be unjust . . ." Benson Mates ("Identity and Predication in Plato," *Phronesis* 24 [1979], 211-29, at n. 26) finds it "puzzling" that I should claim that "Justice is just" here is being inferred, instead of being taken as self-evident. If S. did expect to secure concurrence simply on the ground of the self-evidence of that thesis, why does he move at Protagoras with the disjunction.

Justice itself, that very thing, is it just or unjust? (330C4-5)?
Why does he not simply ask, "Justice itself, that very thing, is it not just?" And why does he repeat the maneuver in the case of Piety at 330D5-6?

** *UVP* 249, "The fallacy in the reasoning . . . a slide from 'is not *F*' to 'is the contradictory of *F*' . . ." I would now deny that this crude fallacy—or any fallacy—is being committed here. What happens in *Gorg.* 467E-468A shows conclusively that in the case of "good"/"evil" S. recognizes "intermediates" which are "neither good nor evil." I take no account of this passage in *UVP* here or in the supporting footnote 80, where I cite two other passages as "good evidence of S.'s unawareness of the fallacy [of assuming that contraries must be contradictories]": *Prt.* 360B2-3, and *Smp.* 201E-202A (the latter being of special interest: S. treats the disjunctions *kalon/aischron*, wise/ignorant as exhaustive, and has to be talked out of this stand by Diotima). What I had not yet understood was the point now expounded in the penultimate paragraph of *** *UVP* 246: because the theory of the biconditionality of the virtues is meant to hold only for *P*-virtues and *P*-vices, contraries behave very differently for S. in their case from the way they do in that of other attributes where contraries are not contradictories, as they have to be in the case of those *P*-attributes. This explains why S. believes that the contraries in our present passage, as also in *Prt.* 360B2-3 and *Smp.* 201E-202B (all cases of *P*-attributes) are treated as contradictories, while those in *Gorg.* 467E-468A are *not*: the contraries of the latter passage are, quite explicitly, attributes of actions and of physical objects. The new thing S. learns from Diotima in *Smp.* 202A is that even in the case of *P*-attributes contraries need not be contradictories (which is Plato's way of saying that at this point he is breaking with his old teacher). I would suggest that *Prt.* 346D, cited by Taylor (113), is not a counter-example to my proposal: the contraries which are used as an example there, "white"/ "black" (in the plural) range over both *P*-attributes and others; the inference S. draws from that example does concern persons, but in doing so he is expounding the thought of Simonides which need not be his own too.

In reaching this new outlook on *Prt.* 330C5ff. I have been influenced by Taylor's gloss on that text:

> Since 346D1-3 shows Plato aware of the distinction [between contraries and contradictories] we should not take him to be confusing the notions of contrary and contradictory as such, but rather to be treating these particular pairs as pairs of contradictories (113).

I have adopted this suggestion, but developed it differently. The justification Taylor gives for it is not connected closely enough to the texture of the Socratic theory of the virtues and is defeated by the counter-examples he sets up, which are not relevant to S.'s primary concerns.

* *UVP* 250, n. 80. The translation of the Greek phrase should be corrected, for the sake of accuracy, to "and if not wise, must you not have been ignorant?"

* *UVP* 251, n. 54, part (2). Here I have misunderstood Gallop. His claim is not that premises *1* and *2* could have been derived "from inoffensive premises," but that they are logically dispensable altogether: Protagoras could have dropped them and still got the result he wants, *sc.* "that Justice and Holiness have qualities in common, and are hence homogeneous."

* *UVP* 252, "We know . . . that S. thinks of 'Justice' as the name of a universal . . ." By "universal" I understand nothing more than the abstract character which S. takes to be named by the abstract expression (abstract noun in feminine form ["Piety"] or substantivized articular neuter adjective ["the pious"]), believing it to recur self-identically in all of the cases of which the corresponding adjective ("pious") or adverb ("piously") is true (*Laches* 191E-192B; *Euthyphro* 5D, 6D-E; *Meno* 72B-C), which he calls *eidos, idea, ousia*, and seeks to define. "Universal" is the term Aristotle created for an entity satisfying this description: "I call 'universal' that whose nature it is *to be predicated of* a number of things" [*De Int.* 17A38] or "*to belong to* a number of things" [*Metaph.* 1038B11-12]. That S. takes the names of the virtues to name this very entity seems clear in Plato's text. To recognize this does not of itself give one the slightest reason for disagreeing with the proponents of PTI that the names of the virtues name "states of character" or "psychological states," provided there is no confusion as to whether the nominee is (a) the abstract character itself or (b) its instantiation in a given person as that person's psychological state. I cannot be sure that this necessary discrimination is being observed in expositions of PTI. Taylor at one point (108) implies very clearly that the names of the virtues in Socratic inquiry designate (a), not (b): " . . . the discussion [concerning the virtues] is in any case concerned with states of character *considered in the abstract*, not with *particular instances* . . ." (my italics). At another he speaks of justice as possibly "seen [by S.] as a force in a man causing him to act justly" (119). Here he cannot mean to impute to S. the absurdity that a "state of character considered in the abstract" could cause a particular person to act justly. So he must mean (b), not (a), at this point, whereas he means (a), not (b), at the preceding. If he were clear on this, why should he object to viewing the Socratic *eidos* as a universal? He apparently does object, though I cannot be sure what is the extent and locus of his objection.

Penner (with whom Taylor associates himself, though just how closely he is doing so he does not make clear) objects emphatically:

> When S. asked "What is bravery?" and so forth, he did not want to know what . . . the essence of bravery was, nor what the universal *bravery* was (39).

Why should we believe that S. did not want to know what that essence, or universal, was? Because "Courage" names a state of character, a psychological state, which (according to Penner and Taylor is a "motive-force" which causes persons to act bravely). The reasoning seems to be: S. did not want to know (a) *because* he wanted to know (b). But (b) is what S. expects to come to know *by* discovering (a). What impels him to seek to know (a) is his practical interest in knowing and fostering (b). He wants Laches to tell him what is that "which is the same in all those [cases] of bravery" (*Laches* 191E) so that he may be in a position to help persons develop that psychological state, that state of character, which instantiates bravery (*Laches* 189E-190A). How then does the fact that bravery is a psychological state show that S. does not want to know "what the universal *bravery* was"?

* *UVP* 254, n. 88, ". . . . the publication of her paper . . ." It appeared in 1973 (I list it in the bibliography). She defines "Pauline predication" as follows:

> I call "Pauline predications" sentences which (a) attach to some subject expression which Plato would say named a form a predicate which someone might reasonably allege as inappropriate to the named form as "just" is alleged inappropriate to justice and which (b) we naturally take to be true (458).

Condition (b) is, surely, unduly restrictive: If "Justice is just" is to be reckoned a Pauline predication, should not "Justice is unjust" be so reckoned too? The negation would not affect that feature of the form of the sentence to which she aims to call attention at (a). This part of her definition could easily be corrected. But I would not know what to do with (a), whose stipulated reliance on what "someone might reasonably allege as inappropriate" does not seem to me precise and general enough to be workable. However, if she had placed her use of the term into the public domain prior to the publication of my paper (1972), I would certainly have respected her right to it and would have found another name for what I have been using "Pauline predication" to mean, namely,

> any sentence in subject-predicate form whose subject-term names an abstract property and whose predicate-term is predicated not of that property, but of its instances, if any.

I believe that this simpler and more general concept, however named, will prove more serviceable and will be more widely adopted for that reason (as e.g. by Mates in the paper cited at * *UVP* 249 above).

* *UVP* 256, " . . . the 'is' here [in 'Wisdom is Courage'] cannot mean identity." Taylor's transcript of this proposition in his analysis of S.'s reasoning in this argument (349E-350C), as distinct from his animadversions on it, is fully in line with my claim: he reports S.'s conclusion as "All and only the courageous are wise," i.e. as a convertible Pauline predication. But his translation goes another way. This part of Plato's sentence in 350C4-5 he translates " . . . wisdom would be the same as courage," thereby adding a word which is not in the Greek: the word *the same*. The addition would be acceptable as an interpretation of the sense, *if* by "the same" Taylor had given the reader to understand that identity(2) is meant. But since Taylor emphatically rejects this sense, the effect (inadvertent, no doubt) of adding "the same" is to convey the impression that identity(1b) is being asserted in the text. On the same ground, I would query his translation of the conclusion of S.'s second argument against Protagoras (332A-335B5) as "So good sense [Taylor's translation of *sōphrosynē*] and wisdom would seem to be one and the same": the last three words correspond to nothing in the Greek text. Earlier on (** *UVP* 227) I stated categorically that in none of our texts does S. go so far as to say that the five virtues, or any two of them, "are the same." Since this is plainly true, we would best serve the Greekless reader by refraining from putting it into our translation when it is not in Plato's text. (For "identity(1b)" and "identity(2)" see ** *UVP* 227 above.)

* *UVP* 257, n. 95, " . . . 'Virtue is noble' and 'Courage is noble' have to be Pauline predications to mesh in with the other premises . . ." Taylor (155) remarks that this is "possible" but "unlikely." His opinion that it is "unlikely" does not prevent him from so transcribing, in the language of the first-order predicate calculus, all sentences of this form in this argument. To justify the opinion he appeals to a parallel argument in the *Laches* (192C-D), claiming that "it is clear that in that argument the predications are non-Pauline." I disagree emphatically: there is as good reason for taking every one of them to be Pauline as for those which he regards as "possibly" Pauline in the present argument.

* *UVP* 258, n. 97. A novel definition of "self-predication" is proposed by Alexander Nehamas in "Self-Predication and Plato's Theory of Forms" (*Amer. Philos. Quart.* 16 [1979], 93-100). He suggests that we should understand "The F itself is F" (where the substituend for "the F" would be an abstract noun, say, *Piety*, and for "F" the cognate adjective, *pious*) to mean

[A] The F itself . . . is what it is to be F.

The proposal is, on the face of it, extremely attractive. If it were viable it would exorcise the paradoxes which self-predications like "Beauty is beautiful" generate in Plato's ontology. Unhappily the remedy is too drastic: the cure will work only if we are prepared to understand self-predications as identities, which Nehamas himself would find unacceptable: he rejects (96, n. 14) the Cherniss-Allen view that "Beauty is beautiful" should be construed to mean "Beauty is Beauty." He does not realize that his own proposal would have the same result. See my discussion of the point in "On a Proposed Redefinition of 'Self-Predication' in Plato," *Phronesis* 26 (1981), 76-79.

* *UVP* 259, n. 99 (b): the interpretation of *Lysis* 217D7-E2. A better parallel— clearer in its import for the point at issue, and chronologically closer to the *Lysis*—

is *Chrm.* 169-E1-5. I translate ultraliterally keeping the word order also the same, so far as possible:

> If someone has knowledge which knows itself, he would himself be *such as is that which he has*: just as when speed someone has, [he would be] speedy, when beauty, beautiful, when knowledge, knowing; so too when knowledge which knows itself someone has, knowing himself he will himself then be.

(First let me get out of the way a red herring with which a literalist might confuse us: "knowledge which knows itself" in the last colon could only be a makeshift to which Plato resorts in the absence of an expression like "self-knowledge" in current Greek idiom: it is entirely clear from the context that what S. has in view is knowledge in which the known includes the knowing, not the absurd notion of knowledge in which knowledge is the knower.)

Our question is pin-pointed on the "is" in the underscored phrase: In which of the following ways, both of them consistent with the grammar, should we read it:

(a) as the "is" of predication (as in "snow is white": snow *has* the quality "white,"

or

(b) as the "is" of identity (as in "white is white": "white" *is* the quality "white")?

Going the (a) way we get:

> the man who has speed will be such as the quality (τοιοῦτος . . . οἱόνπερ) speed *has*.

Going the way of (b) we get:

> the man who has speed will be such as the quality (τοιοῦτος . . . οἱόνπερ) speed *is*.

(a) winds up in the absurdity of an (abstract) quality having the (physical) quality which no abstraction could have: it commits us to saying that men, rockets, etc. are speedy *and* so is speed; speedy men are "such as speed" because they are speedy *and it* is speedy.

(b) winds up in the tautology that speed is speed, which is all S. needs in this connection, since the point he is making is that if (1) *x* has a given quality named by an abstract noun or noun-phrase (Speed, Beauty, Knowledge, Knowledge which knows itself), then (2) the adjective or participle cognate to that name will be applicable to *x* (speedy, beautiful, knowing, knowing himself)—a principle which is not supported by the further (absurd) principle that (1) entails (2) *because* the quality has the quality. No such support is needed, because to say of an individual, *x*, that *x* is "such as" *F* (or "like" *F*: οἷος may be translated either way) is not the same thing as saying of *x* that it is "such as" (or "like") some other individual, *y*. When we say that *x* is such as *y* we are comparing *x* and *y* in respect of some unnamed quality (or set of qualities) which each has, while when we say that *x* is such as *F* we are naming the quality which *x* has, and the question of *comparing x* with *F* in respect of *F* does not arise. (It should not be forgotten in this connection that to say of *x* that it is "such as" [οἷον] F is felt in Greek as virtually a way of saying that x is F. A good example of this quasi-periphrastic use of οἷον in the *Protagoras* occurs in 331A7-B1 [on which cf. UVP 229, n. 19]: saying of Piety that it is ἄδικον in A9 parallels syntactically saying of Justice that it is οἷον μὴ ὅσιον, and is equivalent in sense to saying that Piety is οἷον μὴ δίκαιον: οἷον F, used four times in A8-9, becomes finally tiresome and is then replaced by plain F because the οἷον is not felt to be essential to the sense. (One may observe a similar use of "like" in current American colloquial English: "like cheap, eh?" for "isn't it cheap?")

Now let us look at the *Lysis* passage. Here are its last two lines:

> Well then, this is what I ask now: if something [some quality] is present in something, will that which has it be such as (τοιοῦτον . . . οἷον) that [quality] (*is*) which is present in it?

I have supplied parenthetically the (understood) "is" which raises here the same question as the "is" in the previous passage. In my 1954 paper I took it for granted there is just one way to read S.'s question here:

(a) If, say, Whiteness, is the quality which is present in a thing, will that thing be such as the quality which Whiteness *has*?

It did not occur to me that it could be read, consistently with the same grammatical data, as

(b) If Whiteness is present in a thing, will that thing be such as the quality which Whiteness *is*.

Since here, as in the *Charmides* passage, the grammar allows us reading (b), it would be (as I observe in the note) "gratuitous" to take S. to be saying (a) which, apart from being absurd, is totally immaterial to what he is arguing for.

* UVP 261, n. 103. I use "complete" here to mean the grammatically complete use of *esti* (and its participles) to form the full predicate-term of a Greek sentence, regardless of whether or not *esti* so used translates into "exists" *or* into "is real," the latter being, of course, a grammatically *in*complete use of "is" in an English sentence.

* UVP 266, *Appendix.* With the help of Alan Code (in privately submitted comment) and D. Devereux ("Courage and Wisdom in Plato's *Laches*," *Journal of the Hist. of Philosophy* 15 [1977], 119ff. at 138-40), I realized that my attempt to salvage a logically valid argument from what is offered in *Laches* 197Eff. was a failure. I then proceeded to develop an alternative analysis of the argument in that passage. For this new analysis I shall argue in detail in a future publication. I submit it here in outline, so that the reader may see just where the differences from the one in *UVP* 266 will lie:

(Premise) *1* Courage =df= knowledge of things which are fearful (δεινά) and confidence-sustaining (θαρραλέα) (194E11-195A1, 196D1-2, 199A10-B1).

(Premise) *2* Courage is a part of virtue (198A1-9; also 190C8-D5).

(Premise) *3*(A) Fearful things =df= expected future evils (198B5-9).

(B) Confidence-sustaining things =df= expected future goods (198B6-7).

(Conclusion from *1* & *3*):

    4 Courage = knowledge of expected future evils and goods (198C2-4; 199B3-4).

(Premise) 5 Knowledge of expected future goods and evils = knowledge of past or present goods and evils = knowledge of all goods and evils, past, present or future (198D1-199A8; 199B6-7).

(Conclusion from *4* & *5*):

    6 Courage = knowledge of all goods and evils, past, present or future (199B9-C1; cf. 199C5-D1).

(Premise) 7 Virtue = knowledge of all goods and evils, past, present or future (199D4-S1).

(Conclusion from *6* & *7*):

    8 Courage = virtue entire (199E4).

(Conclusion from *8*):

    9 Courage is not a part of virtue (199E3).

(Conclusion from *9*):

    10 The definition of "courage" in *1* is not correct.

On this analysis, as on the one in the Appendix, the refutand is the Socratic definition of Courage in premise *1*, and *not*, as most of the recent commentators have maintained (Santas 1971, 202ff.; Penner 1973, 60-63; Woodruff 1976, 110-14; Irwin, 302), premise *2*. Why the text compels this interpretation I have tried to show in the terminal paragraph of *SPV*. With *1* as the refutand, the mechanics of the demonstration are as follows: the negation of *2* is deduced from the premise-set [*1, 3, 5, 7*]. Since *2* is a truism (as I explain in *SPV*, it asserts no more than that Courage is not the only virtue there is), this result shows that at least one member of the premise-set is false. Since no suspicion is cast on *3, 5,* or *7*, the stigma of falsehood falls unambiguously on *1*.

What is the point of the argument? Since *1* is certainly Socratic, the point must be Socratic self-criticism. He constructs an argument which shows him that something has gone wrong somewhere, but he can't tell exactly what and where. Can we tell? I believe so. The root of the problem is in the strict identity in *1*. Since this is a *Socratic definition* what it asserts is identity in its strongest possible form—too strong for S.'s present purposes. If S. had asserted in premise *1* not definitional identity, but necessary interentailment (not identity(1b) but identity(2): cf. ** *UVP* 227, above) he could have avoided the trouble: the contradiction at *9* would be forestalled if for *1* we were to substitute

    1* Necessarily, one has courage iff one has knowledge of fearful and confidence-sustaining things.

For then all we could derive from *1** and *3* would be

    4* Necessarily, one has courage iff one has knowledge of expected future evils and goods,

which, conjoined to *5*, would yield only

    6* Necessarily, one has courage iff one has knowledge of all goods and evils, past, present or future, and then, even if we were to leave unchanged the next premise,

7 Virtue = knowledge of all goods and evils, past, present or future,

we could still not derive the lethal

8 Courage = virtue,

but only the innocuous

8* Necessarily, one has courage iff one has virtue entire,
which, unlike 8, is perfectly consistent with

2 Courage is a part of virtue.

Looking back at what I said in the Appendix to *UVP*, I can now see *my* mistake:
I charitably gave S. the benefit of supposing that he asserted no more than interentailment at 4, which would indeed block the path to the contradiction. What I failed
to see is that at 4 and thereafter S. was falling into a ditch he had dug himself by his
initial commitment to identity(1b) at *1*.

But I don't want to suggest that it was just a mistake in logic—a failure to straighten
out his concept of identity and realize that identity(2), not identity(1b), would do as
the connective between "courage" and "knowledge of things which are fearful and
confidence-sustaining." That was symptomatic of a deeper, substantive, error, which
has often been called his "intellectualism": his failure to give their due weight to extra-
cognitive, emotional, factors, like fear and confidence (or, more precisely, to see the
extra-cognitive components *of* those emotional factors) in his understanding of the
dynamics of the psyche. This is a matter of great importance in forming a just estimate
of S.'s moral psychology. I hope to discuss it at length in a future publication.

UVP 226, n. 9, [This omitted note should precede the note for * *UVP* 226, n. 9
on p. 430.—G.V.] ". . . the ambiguity in the Greek use of 'name' . . . : proper
name or descriptive predicate. . . ." To illustrate I did not need to go so far afield
as the passage in the *Phaedo* which I discuss later on in *UVP* (238-240). There are
perfectly good examples of this dual use of *onoma* in earlier dialogues: In the *Meno*
"what on earth is that whose name is 'figure'?" (74E11) "name" is used to mean
proper name ("figure" is the name *of* figure, and of absolutely nothing else); in the
preceding remark, "you denominate each of these many [figures] by this single name
[*sc.* 'figure']" (74D5-6), the word is used to mean common name or qualifying predicate: you denominate the round "figure" without implying that it is the proper name
of the round. The same use in *Laches* 198A7-9, "But I call [*sc.* 'virtue'] temperance
and justice, etc., in addition to courage," while in the immediately preceding statement, ". . . there being other parts as well, which taken together are called 'Virtue' "
(198A4-5), "Virtue" is the proper name of the whole constituted of all of these parts:
cf. the preceding starred note. For unambiguous examples of "naming" or "calling"
to refer to the proper name see *Laches* 192A9-B2 and B5-8; 198C6-7.

BIBLIOGRAPHY

Ackrill, John. Review of P. Wilpert's *Zwei aristotelisch Frühschriften* in *Mind*, 61 (1952), 102–13.

"Plato and the Copula: *Sophist* 251–259," *Journal of Hellenic Studies*, 77 (1957, Part I), 1–6.

Aristotle's CATEGORIES and DE INTERPRETATIONE, translated with notes and glossary (Oxford, 1963).

Adam, J., *The REPUBLIC of Plato*, 2 vols. (Cambridge, 1902).

Adam, J., and Adam, A. M. *Plato's Protagoras* (Cambridge, 1893).

Allen, R. E. "Participation and Predication in Plato's Middle Dialogues," *Philos. Review*, 69 (1960), 147–64.

"The Argument from Opposites in *Republic* V," *Rev. of Metaphysics*, 15 (1961), 325 ff.

Plato's EUTHYPHRO and the Earlier Theory of Forms (London and New York, 1970).

Apelt, O. *Platonis "Timaios" et "Kritias,"* translated with notes (Leipzig, 1919).

Platonis "Sophista," translated with notes (Leipzig, 1897). Revised edition by Reiner Wiehl (Hamburg, 1967).

Platon, "der Staat," with notes; new edition, with introduction by P. Wilpert, edited by K. Bormann (Hamburg, 1961).

Platonis "Symposium," translated with notes (Leipzig, 1926). Revised edition by Annemarie Capelle (Hamburg, 1960).

Archer-Hind, R. D. *The TIMAEUS of Plato* (London, 1888).

Plato's PHAEDO (Cambridge, 1896).

Ast, D. Friedrich. *Lexicon Platonicum* (first edition, 1835; reprinted, Berlin Hermann Barsdorf, 1908).

Austin, J. L. *Sense and Sensibilia*, reconstituted from the Manuscript Notes by G. J. Warnock (Oxford, 1962).

Bailey, Cyril. *Greek Atomists and Epicurus* (Oxford, 1928).

Bambrough, R., ed. *New Essays on Plato and Aristotle* (London and New York, 1965).

Barker, E. *Greek Political Theory*, 3rd Edition (London, 1947).

Bengston, H. *Griechische Geschichte* (Munich, 1960).

Berndt, T. *De Ironia Menexeni Platonici* (Diss., Munster, 1881).

Blakeney, R. B. *Meister Eckhart, a Modern Translation* (New York, 1941).

Black, Max. *Problems of Analysis* (Ithaca, N.Y., 1954).

Blanshard, Brand. *The Nature of Thought*, II (London, 1939).

Bloom, A. *The REPUBLIC of Plato*, translated with notes and an interpretive essay (New York, 1968).

Bluck, R. S. *Plato's PHAEDO* (London, 1955).

"Forms as Standards," *Phronesis* 2 (1957), 115–27.

Bonitz, H. *Index Aristotelicus* (vol. 5 of the Prussian Academy edition of Aristotle), (*Berlin*, 1870).

Bosanquet, B. *Companion to Plato's Republic* (New York, 1895).

Bowra, C. M. *American Journal of Philology*, 59 (1936).

Brentlinger, John A., ed. *The SYMPOSIUM of Plato*, translated by Suzy Q. Groden, drawings by Leonard Baskin (University of Massachusetts Press, 1970).

Bretall, R. ed. *Kierkegaard Anthology* (Princeton, 1936).

Bröcker, W. "Plato über das Gute," *Lexis* 2 (1949), 47–66.

"Platons ontologischer Komparativ," *Hermes* 87 (1959), 415 ff.

Buchner, E. *Der PANEGYRIKOS des Isocrates, Historia*, Einzelschriften 2 (Wiesbaden, 1958).

Burnet, J. *Plato's PHAEDO* (Oxford, 1911).

Bury, R. G. Notes to edition and translation of the works of *Sextus Empiricus*, Vol. 3 (London, 1936).

Busolt, F. *Griechische Staatskunde* I (Munich, 1920).

and H. Swoboda. *Griechische Staatskunde* II (Munich, 1926).

Campbell, Lewis. *The SOPHISTES and POLITICUS of Plato* (Oxford, 1867).

Carnap, R. *Meaning and Necessity*, enlarged edition (Chicago, 1956).

Chapman, John Jay. *Lucian, Plato, and Greek Morals* (Boston, 1934).

Cherniss, H. *Aristotle's Criticism of Plato and the Early Academy*, (Baltimore, 1944).

Riddle of the Early Academy, (Berkeley, 1945).

"The Relation of the TIMAEUS to Plato's Later Dialogues," *American Journal of Philology* 78 (1957), 225–66.

Chomsky, Noam. *Aspects of the Theory of Syntax* (Cambridge, Mass., 1965).

Cloché, P. *Thèbes de Beotia* (Namur; no date, probably 1952).

Collingwood, R. G. *The Idea of Nature* (Oxford, 1945).

Cornford, F. M. *From Religion to Philosophy* (London, 1912).

Plato and Parmenides (London, 1939).

The REPUBLIC of Plato, translated with introduction and notes (New York, Oxford University Press, 1945).

"The Doctrine of Eros in Plato's *Symposium*," in *The Unwritten Philosophy*, ed. W. K. C. Guthrie, (Cambridge, 1950).

Plato's Cosmology (New York, 1952).

Plato's Theory of Knowledge (London, 1957).

Croiset, Alfred. *Plato's Hippias Major, Charmides, Laches,* and *Lysis* with Introduction and Notes in the Budé translation of Plato (4th ed., 1956, Paris).

de Ste. Croix, G. "The Constitution of Five Thousand," *Historia*, 5 (1956).

Crombie, I. M. *Examination of Plato's Doctrines,* Vol. I: *Plato on Man and Society* (1962), Vol. II: *Plato on Knowledge and Reality* (1963) (London).

Plato, the Midwife's Apprentice (London, 1964).

Cross, R. C. "*Logos* and Forms in Plato," *Mind* 63 (1954), 433 ff.

Cross, R. C., and A. D. Woozley. *Plato's REPUBLIC* (London, 1964).

Davidson, D. "Actions, Reasons, and Causes," *Journal of Philosophy*, 40 (1963).

Debrunner, A. "Demokratia," in *Festschrift für E. Tièche* (Berne, 1947).

De Lacy, P. H. "Problem of Causation in Plato's Philosophy," *Class. Phil.* 34 (1939).

De Laguna, Th. "Notes on the Theory of Ideas," *Philos Rev.*, 43 (1934), 443–70.

Demos, R. "A Fallacy in Plato's REPUBLIC," *Philos. Rev.*, 73 (1964).

de Vogel, C. J. "Problems concerning later Platonism (I)," *Mnemosyne*, 4, 2 (1949), 197–216.

Greek Philosophy I (Leiden, 1950).

De Vries, G. J. *A Commentary on the PHAEDRUS of Plato* (Amsterdam, 1969).

Diels, H., and W. Krauz. *Die Fragmente der Vorsokratiker* (Berlin, 1934-37).

Diès, A. Plato's *Politicus* (2nd ed., 1941), *Theaetetus* (1923), *Sophist* (1925) with Introduction and Notes in the Budé translation of Plato (Paris).

Dodds, E. R. *Plato's GORGIAS* (Oxford, 1959).

Dover, K. J. "Eros and Nomos," *Bulletin of the Institute of Classical Studies*, No. 11 (1966), 31–42.

Ehrenberg, V. "Isonomia," August Pauly and Georg Wissowa, eds., *Real-Encyclopädie der classischen Altertumswissenschaft* (Stuttgart, 1894 ff.), Supplementary Volume VII.

"Eunomia," in *Charisteria Alois Rzach* (Reichenberg, 1930), revised and translated into English in *Aspects of the Ancient World* (Oxford, 1946).

"Origins of Democracy," *Historia*, 1 (1950).

"Das Harmodioslied," in *Festschift Albin Lesky* (*Wien. St.* 69, 1956).

Eigeldinger, M. *Jean Jacques Rousseau et la réalité de l'imaginaire,* (Neuchâtel, 1962).

Enriques, F., and G. de Santillana. *Histoire de la Pensée Scientifique* (Paris, 1936–39.)

Ewing, A. C. *Idealism* (London, 1934).

Farrington, B. *Science and Politics in the Ancient World* (London, 1939).

Field, G. C. *The Philosophy of Plato* (Oxford, 1949).

Finley, M. I. "Was Greek Civilisation Based on Slave Labour?" *Historia*, 7 (1959), 145–64.

Fortenbaugh, W. "Plato *Phaedrus* 235C3," *Classical Philology* 61 (1966), 108–09.

Foster, M. B. "On Plato's Conception of Justice in the *Republic*," *Philos. Quart.*, 1 (1950–51), 206–17.

Frede, Michael. *Prädikation und Existenzaussage* (Gottingen, 1967; Heft 18 in series *Hypomnemata*, ed. by A. Dihle, H. Erbse, Chr. Habicht, G. Patzig, and B. Snell).

Frege, G. *The Philosophical Writings*. P. Geach and M. Black, edd. English translations by Geach, Black, and others (Oxford, 1952).

Freeman, K. *Companion to the Presocratic Philosophers* (Oxford, 1946).

Friedländer, P. *Plato*, Vol. I (New York, 1958).

Fuks, A. *The Ancestral Constitution* (London, 1953).

Gallop, D. "Justice and Holiness in *Prot.* 330–331," *Phronesis* 6(1961), 86–93.

Gauthier, R. A., and J. Y. Jolif. *L'Ethique à Nicomaque*, Tome II, Commentaire, Deuxième Partie, Livres VI-X, Deuxième Edition (Louvain, 1970).

Geach, P. "The Third Man Again," *Philos. Review*, 65 (1956), 72–82.

Gigon, O. "Studien zu Platons *Protagoras*," in *Phyllobolia fur Peter von der Muhl* (Basel, 1946), 91–152.

Gildersleeve, B. S. *Syntax to Classical Greek* (1900).

Glaser, K. "Gang und Ergebnis des Platonischen Lysis," *Wiener Studien*, 53 (1935), 47–67.

Gomme, A. W. *Historical Commentary on Thucydides, Book I* (Oxford, 1956).

Gosling, J., "*Rep. V*: τὰ πολλὰ καλά, etc.," *Phronesis* 5 (1960), 116 ff.

Gould, John. *The Development of Plato's Ethics* (New York, 1955).

Gould, Thomas. *Platonic Love* (London, 1963).

Gouldner, Alvin W. *Enter Plato: Classical Greece and the Origins of Social Theory* (New York, 1965).

Groden, Suzy Q., translation and introduction. *The Poems of Sappho* (Indianapolis, 1966).

Grossman, G. *Politische Schlagworter aus der Zeit des Peloponnesischen Krieges* (Diss., Zurich, 1950).

Grube, G. M. A. *Plato's Thought* (New York, 1964).

Guillemin, H. *Un Homme, Deux Ombres* (Geneva, 1943).

Gulley, N. *The Philosophy of Socrates* (London, 1968).

Guthrie, W. K. C., translation of *Plato's Protagoras and Meno* (London, 1956).

Hackforth, R. *Plato's Examination of Pleasure* (England, 1945).

   Plato's PHAEDRUS (Cambridge, 1952).

   Plato's PHAEDO (Cambridge, 1955).

Hall, R. W. "Plato's Just Man," *New Scholasticism*, 43 (1968), 202–25.

Hamilton, W., translation, *Plato, the SYMPOSIUM* (Baltimore, 1951).

Harder, R. "Platon und Athen," *Neue Jahrbucher fur Wissenschaft und Jugendbildung*, 10 (1934).

Hardie, W. F. R. *A Study in Plato* (Oxford, 1936).

Hare, R. M. *The Language of Morals* (Oxford, 1952).

Hart, H. L. A. "Are there Natural Rights?" *Philos. Rev.*, 64 (1955), 175–91.

Hartman, Edward. "Predication and Immortality in the *Phaedo*," forthcoming in *Archiv für die Geschichte der Philosophie*.

Heath, T. L. *Mathematics in Aristotle* (Oxford, 1949).

Heidel, W. H. περὶ φύσεως, *Proc. Am. Acad. of Arts and Sciences*, Jan., 1910.

Hempel, C. G. *Aspects of Scientific Explanation* (New York, 1965).

Hoerber, R. G. "More on Justice in the *Republic*," *Phronesis*, 5 (1960), 32–34.

Jaeger, W. *Paideia*, II, III (English translation, Oxford, 1947).

"The Date of Isocrates' *Areopagiticus* and the Athenian Opposition," *Scripta Minova* II (Rome, 1960).

Janacek, K. "Sextus Empiricus an der Arbeit," *Philologus*, 100 (1956), 100 ff.

Jones, A. H. M. *Athenian Democracy* (Oxford, 1957).

Jones, J. W. *Law and Legal Theory of the Greeks* (Oxford, 1956).

Kahn, Charles. "Plato's Funeral Oration," *Class. Philology* 58 (1963).

Kakridis, I. Th. *Der Thukydideische Epitaphios, Zetemata* 26, (Munich, 1961).

Keil, B. *Griechische Staatsaltertumer*, in Gercke-Norden, *Einleitung in die Altertumswissebschaft*, III (Leipzig, 1912).

Keyt, D. "The Fallacies in *Phaedo* 102A-107B," *Phronesis*, 8 (1963).

"Plato's Paradox that the Immutable is Unknowable," *Philos. Quarterly* 19 (1969), 1–14.

"The Mad Craftsman of the *Timaeus*," *Philos. Review* 80 (1971), 230–35.

Kirk, G. S., and J. Raven. *The Presocratic Philosophers* (Cambridge, 1957).

Krämer, H. T. *Arete bei Platon und Aristoteles* (Heidelberg, 1959).

"Retraktationen zum Problem des esoterischen Platon," *Mus. Hel.* 21 (1964), 137–67.

Lacey, A. R. "Plato's *Sophist* and the Forms," *Class. Quarterly*, N.S. 9 (1959), 43–52.

Larsen, J. A. O. "Cleisthenes and the Development of the Theory of Democracy at Athens," in *Essays in Political Theory Presented to G. H. Sabine* (Ithaca, 1948).

"The Judgment of Antiquity on Democracy," *Class. Philology* 49 (1954).

Representative Government (Chicago, 1955).

Larson, C. W. R. "The Platonic Synonyms, δικαιοσύνη and σωφροσύνη," *American Journal of Philology*, 72 (1951), 395–414.

Lee, H. D. P. Plato: *The REPUBLIC*, translated with introduction (Baltimore, 1955).

Levin, D. N. "Some Observations Concerning Plato's *Lysis*," in *Essays in Greek Philosophy*, edited by J. P. Anton and G. L. Kustas, (Albany, 1971).

Levinson, R. B. *In Defense of Plato* (Cambridge, Mass., 1953).

Lewis, C. I. *Mind and the World-Order* (New York, 1929).

Lindsay, A. D. *The REPUBLIC of Plato* (London, 1935).

von Loewenclau, Ilse. *Der platonische MENEXENOS*, Tübinger Beiträge zur Altertumswissenschaft 41 (Stuttgart, 1961).

Lorentz, K., and J. Mittelstrass. "Theaitetos fliiegt," *Archiv für Geschichte der Philosophie*, 48 (1966), 113–51.

Mabbott, J. D. "Is Plato's *Republic* Utilitarian?" *Mind*, 46 (1937), 468–74.

Malcolm, J. "On the Place of the Hippias Major in the Development of Plato's Thought," *Archiv für Geschichte Philosophie* 50 [1958], 189–95.

"Plato's Analysis of *To On* and *To Mē On* in the *Sophist*," *Phronesis* 12 1967), 139–43.

Markus, R. A. "The Dialectic of Eros in Plato's *Symposium*," *Downside Review*,

73, 1955 (reprinted in *Plato*, Vol. II, ed. by Gregory Vlastos, New York, 1971, 132–43).

Mercadé, Jean. *Eros Kalos* (Geneva, 1962).

Méridier, L. Introduction to and translation of Plato's *Menexenus*, in the Budé translation (Third Edition, Paris, 1956).

Meritt, B. D., H. T. Wade-Gery, and F. McGregor. *The Athenian Tribute Lists* (Princeton, 1939–53).

Merlan, Ph. "Beiträge zur Geschichte des antiken Platonismus (I)," *Philologus*, 89, 1934, 35–53.

   From Platonism to Neoplatonism (1953), pp. 174–76.

Mills, K. W. "Plato, *Phaedo* 74B-C, Part I," *Phronesis* 2 [1957], 128–47; Part II, *ibid.*, 3 [1958], 40–58.

Moore, G. E. "The Conception of Reality," in *Philosophical Studies* (London, 1922).

Moravcsik, Julius M. E. "Being and Meaning in the 'Sophist,' " *Acta Philosophica Fennica*, Fasc. XIV, 1962 (Helsinki).

   "The 'Third Man' Argument and Plato's Theory of Forms," *Phronesis* 8 (1963), pp. 50–62.

Moreau, J. *La Construction de l'Idéalisme Platonicien* (Paris, 1939).

Morrow, G. R. *Plato's Law of Slavery* (Urbana, Ill., 1939).

   "Plato and Greek Slavery," *Mind*, XLVIII (1939).

   "The Demiurge in Politics," *Proc. of the American Philosophical Association*, XXVII (1954).

   Plato's Cretan City (Princeton, 1960).

   Plato's Epistles (revised edition, New York, 1962).

Mourelatos, Alexander P. D. *The Route of Parmenides* (New Haven, Conn., 1970).

Mueller, G. *Studien zu den Platonischen Nomoi* (*Zetemata*, Heft 3: Munich, 1951).

Mugler, Charles. *La Physique de Platon* (Paris, 1960), pp. 22–26.

Murdoch, Iris. *The Sovereignty of Good* (London, 1970).

Murphy, N. R. *The Interpretation of Plato's Republic* (Oxford, 1951).

Nagel, E. *Sovereign Reason* (New York, 1954).

   The Structure of Science (New York, 1961).

Newman, W. L. *The Politics of Aristotle*, I (Oxford, 1887).

North, Helen. *Sophrosyne* (Ithaca, 1966).

Nygren, Anders. *Eros and Agape* (English translation by P. S. Watson, Harper Torchbook edition, New York, 1969).

Ollier, F. *Le Mirage Spartiate* (Paris, 1933).

Oppenheimer, K. *Zwei attische Epitaphien* (Diss., Berlin, 1933).

Ostwald, M. "Athenian Legislation Against Tyranny," *Transactions of Amer. Philological Association*, 86 (1955), 103–28.

   Nomos and the Beginnings of the Athenian Democracy (Oxford, 1969).

Owen, G. E. L. "The Place of the *Timaeus* in Plato's dialogues," *Class. Quarterly*, N. S. 3 (1953), 79–95.

"A Proof in the περὶ Ἰδεῶν," *Journal of Hellenic Studies*, 57 (1957, Part 1), 103–11.

"Logic and Metaphysics in Some Earlier Works of Aristotle," in *Aristotle and Plato in the Mid-Fourth Century*, ed. by I. During and G. E. L. Owen, (Goteborg, Almquist & Wicksell, 1960), pp. 163–90.

"Aristotle on the Snares of Ontology," in *New Essays on Plato and Aristotle* (London and New York, 1965).

"Dialectic and Eristic in the Treatment of the Forms," in *Aristotle on Dialectic:* the TOPICS," Proceedings of the Third Symposium Aristotelicum, edited by G. E. L. Owen (Oxford, Clarendon Press, 1970), 103–25.

Page, D. L. *Poetae Melici Graeci* (Oxford, 1962).

Pater, Walter. *Plato and Platonism.*

Peck, A. L. "Plato *versus* Parmenides," *Philos. Review* 71 (1962), pp. 46–66.

Pieper, J. *Enthusiasm and Divine Madness*, English translation by Richard and Clara Winston (New York, 1964).

Pohlenz, M. *Aus Platos Werdezeit* (Berlin, 1913).

Popper, Karl. *The Open Society and Its Enemies*, Vol. I (Fourth Edition, Princeton, 1963).

Powell, J. E. *Lexicon to Herodotus* (Cambridge, 1938).

Prauss, G. *Platon und der logische Eleatismus* (Berlin, 1966).

Raven, J. E. *Pythagoreans and Eleatics* (Cambridge, 1948), p. 105, n. 1.

Rees, D. A. "Plato and the Third Man," *Proc. of Aristotelian Society*, Supp. Volume 37 (1963), pp. 165–76.

du Rios, R. *Aristoxeni Elementa* (1954).

Robin, L. *La Théorie Platonicienne des Idées et des Nombres* (Paris, 1909).

    Platon (Paris, 1935).

    Platon, Oeuvres Complètes, Tomes I, II: the Pléiade translation (with the collaboration of J. Moreau).

Robinson, Richard. *Plato's Earlier Dialectic*, 2nd edition (Oxford, 1953).

    "Plato's Consciousness of Fallacy," *Mind* 51 (1942), reprinted in his *Essays in Greek Philosophy* (Oxford, 1969).

de Romilly, J. "Le Classement des Constitutions jusqu'à Aristotle," *Révue des Études Grecques* 72 (1959), 81 ff.

Rosen, S. *Plato's Symposium* (New Haven, 1968).

Rosenmeyer, T. "Plato and Mass Words," *Trans. American Phil. Assoc.* 88 (1957), pp. 88–102.

Ross, W. D. *Plato's Theory of Ideas* (Oxford, 1951).

Royce, J. *The World and the Individual, First Series* (New York, 1899).

Runciman, W. G., "*Plato's Parmenides*," *Harvard Studies in Classical Philology* 64 (1959), pp. 89–120.

    Plato's Later Epistemology (Cambridge, 1962).

Russell, Bertrand. *The Principles of Mathematics* (Cambridge, England, 1903).

Ryffel, H. *Metabolē Politeion, Noctes Romanae* 2 (Berne, 1949).

Sachs, David. "A Fallacy in Plato's *Republic*," *Philos. Review*, 72 (1963), 141–58.

Saffrey, H. D. *Le* περὶ φιλοσοφίας *d'Aristote et la Théorie Platonicienne des Idées Nombres* (Leiden, 1955).

Santayana, George. *Platonism and the Spiritual Life* (New York, 1927).

Savan, David. "Self-predication in *Protagoras* 330-31," *Phronesis* 9 (1964) 130-35.

"Socrates' Logic and the Unity of Wisdom and Temperance," in R. B. J. Butler, ed., *Analytical Philosophy*, Vol. II (Oxford, 1965), 20-26.

Schiller, J. "Just Man and Just Acts in Plato's *Republic*," *Journal of History of Philosophy* 6 (1968), 1-14.

Scholl, N. *Der platonische MENEXENOS, Temi e Testi,* 5 (Rome, 1959).

Sellars, W. "Vlastos and 'The Third Man,'" *Philos. Review* 64 (1955), pp. 405-37.

"Vlastos and 'The Third Man': A Rejoinder," *Philosophical Perspectives* (Springfield, Ill., 1967), pp. 55-72.

Shorey, P. "The Interpretation of the TIMAEUS," *American Journal of Philology*, 9 (1888), 395-418.

The Unity of Plato's Thought (Chicago, 1903).

"The Origin of the Syllogism," *Classical Philology*, 19 (1924), 1-19.

Translation, *Plato: The Republic*, 2 volumes (London, 1930 and 1935).

What Plato Said (Chicago, 1933).

Sinclair, T. A. *Greek Political Theory* (London, 1951).

Singer, Irving. *The Nature of Love, Plato to Luther* (New York, 1966).

Skemp, J. B. *Plato's STATESMAN;* translation, with introductory essays and footnotes (London, 1952).

"Comment on Communal and Individual Justice in the *Republic*," *Phronesis*, 5 (1960), 35-38.

Stace, Walter. *Time and Eternity* (Princeton, 1952).

Stebbing, Susan. *A Modern Introduction to Logic*, Second Edition (London, 1933).

Stenzel, J. *Zahl und Gestalt* (Darmstaat, 1959), pp. 94 ff.

Strang, C. "*Plato and the third Man*," *Proc. of Aristotelian Society*, Supp. Volume 37 (1963), pp. 147-64.

Strasburger, H. "Thukydides und die politische Selbstdarstellung der Athener," *Hermes*, 86 (1958), 17 ff.

Symonds, J. A. A Problem in *Greek Ethics, Being an Inquiry into the Phenomenon of Sexual Inversion Addressed Especially to Medical Psychologists and Jurists* (printed for private circulation, London, 1901).

Taylor, A. E. "Parmenides, Zeno, and Socrates," *Proc. Arist. Soc.* 16 (1915-16), reprinted in *Philosophical Studies* (London, 1934).

A Commentary on Plato's TIMAEUS (Oxford, 1928).

Plato's PARMENIDES (Oxford, 1934).

Plato, the Man and his Work, Fourth (revised) Edition (London, 1937).

Plato (London, 1949).

Plato: the Sophist and the Statesman, ed. by R. Klibansky and Elizabeth Anscombe (London, 1961).

Thayer, H. S. "Plato: The Theory and Language of Function," *Philos. Quart.*, 14 (1964), 303-18.

Thompson, E. S. *Plato's Meno* (London, 1901).

Thomson, George. *The ORESTEIA of Aeschylus* (Cambridge, 1938).

Turnbull, R. G. "Aristotle's Debt to the 'Natural Philosophy' of the *Phaedo*," *Philosophical Quarterly*, 8 (1955).

Verdenius, W. "Notes on the *Phaedo*," *Mnemosyne*, S. IV, II (1958).

Versenyi, L. *Socratic Humanism* (New Haven, 1963).

Vlastos, G. (works other than those included in this volume):

"The Disorderly Motion in the *TIMAEUS*," *Class. Quart.*, 33 (1939), 71–83.

"On the Pre-History in Diodorus," *Amer. Jrnl. of Philology* 67 (1946), 51–59.

"The Physical Theory of Anaxagoras," *Philosophical Review*, LVI (1947), 184 ff, p. 137.

"Isonomia," *Amer. Jrnl. of Philology* 74 (1953), 337–66.

"The Third Man Argument in the *PARMENIDES*," *Philos. Rev.* 63 (1954), 319–49.

Plato's *PROTAGORAS* in translation, edited with an Introduction (New York, 1956).

"Justice and Equality," in *Social Justice*, edited by R. Brandt (Englewood Cliffs, N.J., 1962). A slightly corrected version of the first two sections of this essay has appeared in *Human Rights*, edited by A. I. Melden (Belmont, Calif., 1970).

"Minimal Parts in Epicurean Atomism," *Isis* 56 (1965), 121–47.

"Socrates on Arasia," *Phoenix* 23 (1969), 71–88.

Watson, P. S. translation, *Eros and Agape* (New York, 1969).

Webster, T. B. L. *Political Interpretations in Greek Literature* (Manchester, 1948).

Wedberg, Anders. *Plato's Philosophy of Mathematics* (Stockholm, 1955).

Weingartner, R. "Vulgar Justice and Platonic Justice," *Philos. and Phenomenological Research* 25 (1964/65), 248–52.

Wendland, P. "Die Tendenz des Platonischen Menexenus," *Hermes*, 25 (1890), 171 ff.

Whibley, L. *Greek Oligarchies* (Cambridge, 1896).

White, M. *Foundations of Historical Knowledge* (New York, 1965).

Wilamowitz, U. V. *Aristoteles and Athen* II (Berlin, 1893).

Platon, I, II (Berlin, 1919 and 1920).

Wilamowitz-Moellendorff, U. V. *Platon* (re-issue of the Third Edition, Berlin and Frankfort, 1948).

Wilcken, U. "Über Entstehung und Zweck des Königsfriedens," *Abh. Berlin Akademie*, 1941, philol.-hist. Kl. 15.

Wild, John. *Plato's Enemies and the Theory of Natural Law* (Chicago, 1953).

Wilpert, P. "Neue Fragmente aus περὶ τἀγαθοῦ," *Hermes* 1941, 225–60.

Zwei aristotelische Frühschriften über die Ideenlehre (Regensburg, 1949).

Wolin, Sheldon. *Politics and Vision* (Boston, 1960).

Wust, K. *Politisches Denken bei Herodot* (Diss., Munich, 1935).

Zeller, E. *Philosophie der Griechen*, Fifth Edition (Leipzig, 1922). English translation by Sarah F. Alleyne and Alfred Goodwin, New Edition, London, 1888).

INDEX
OF GREEK WORDS

=====

(This index to the 1973 edition was prepared by Bonnie Vernier. The references—to text or notes—are given only by page number. This index is to the first edition. It has not been feasible to include citations for corrections and new material—Publisher's Note.)

INDEX
OF NAMES

———

(This index to the 1973 edition has been prepared by Bonnie Vernier. This index is to the first edition. It has not been feasible to include citations for corrections and new material—Publisher's Note.)

INDEX

OF PASSAGES

(This index to the 1973 edition has been prepared by Edward Johnson. This index is to the first edition. It has not been feasible to include citations for corrections and new material—Publisher's Note.)

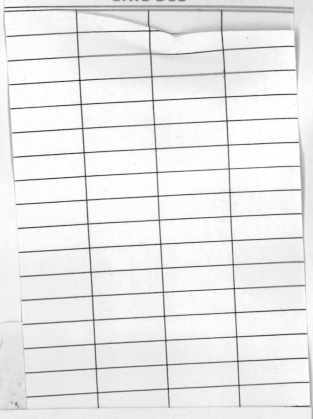